FRENCH, ITALIAN & GERMAN

Avalon Travel
a member of the
Perseus Books Group
1700 Fourth Street
Berkeley, CA 94710, USA

Printed in Canada by Friesens.
Fifth edition. Fifth printing May 2013.

For the latest on Rick's lectures, guidebooks, tours, and public television series, contact Europe Through the Back Door, P.O. Box 2009, Edmonds, WA 98020, tel. 425/771-8303, fax 425/771-0833, www.ricksteves.com, rick@ricksteves.com.

ISBN-10: 1-59880-187-2
ISBN-13: 978-1-59880-187-3

Europe Through the Back Door Managing Editor: Risa Laib
Europe Through the Back Door Editors: Cameron Hewitt, Jill Hodges, Gretchen Strauch
Avalon Travel Editor: Jamie Andrade
French Translation: Scott Bernhard, Paul Desloover, Sabine Leteinturier, Steve Smith
Italian Translation: Simona Bondavalli, Giulia Fiorini, Manfredo Guerzoni, Alessandra Panieri
German Translation: Julia Klimek, Martin Minich
Phonetics: Risa Laib, Cameron Hewitt
Production: Darren Alessi
Cover Design: Kimberly Glyder Design
Maps & Graphics: David C. Hoerlein, Zoey Platt
Photography: Rick Steves, Dominic Bonuccelli, Julie Coen, Paul Orcutt
Front Cover Photo: Paris © Ray & Sheila Atkins/Atkins Images/DRR.net

Distributed to the book trade by
Publishers Group West, Berkeley, California

Although the author and publisher have made every effort to provide accurate, up-to-date information, they accept no responsibility for loss, injury, bad crêpes, or inconvenience sustained by any person using this book.

Rick Steves' [illegible]

Country Guides

Rick Steves' Best of Europe
Rick Steves' Croatia & Slovenia
Rick Steves' Eastern Europe
Rick Steves' England
Rick Steves' France
Rick Steves' Germany
Rick Steves' Great Britain
Rick Steves' Ireland
Rick Steves' Italy
Rick Steves' Mediterranean Cruise Ports
Rick Steves' Northern European Cruise Ports
Rick Steves' Portugal
Rick Steves' Scandinavia
Rick Steves' Spain
Rick Steves' Switzerland

City and Regional Guides

Rick Steves' Amsterdam, Bruges & Brussels
Rick Steves' Greece: Athens & the Peloponnese
Rick Steves' Barcelona
Rick Steves' Budapest
Rick Steves' Florence & Tuscany
Rick Steves' Istanbul
Rick Steves' London
Rick Steves' Paris
Rick Steves' Prague & the Czech Republic
Rick Steves' Provence & the French Riviera
Rick Steves' Rome
Rick Steves' Venice
Rick Steves' Vienna, Salzburg & Tirol

Rick Steves' Phrase Books

French
French/Italian/German
German
Italian
Portuguese
Spanish

Other Books

Rick Steves' Europe Through the Back Door
Rick Steves' Europe 101: History and Art for the Traveler
Rick Steves' European Christmas
Rick Steves' Postcards from Europe

(Avalon Travel)

CONTENTS

Illustrations

Maps

Hi, I'm Rick Steves.

I'm the only monolingual speaker I know who's had the nerve to design a series of European phrase books. But that's one of the things that makes them better. You see, after 30 summers of travel through Europe, I've learned first-hand (1) what's essential for communication in Europe, and (2) what's not. I've assembled the most important words and phrases in a logical, no-frills format, and I've worked with native Europeans and seasoned travelers to give you the simplest, clearest translations possible.

This three-in-one edition is a lean and mean version of my individual French, Italian, and German phrase books. If you're lingering in a country, my individual phrase books are far better at helping you connect with the locals, but if you're on a whirlwind trip, this handy three-in-one book gives you all the essential phrases.

This book is more than just a pocket translator. The words and phrases have been carefully selected to make you a happier, more effective budget traveler. The key to getting more out of every travel dollar is to get closer to the local people, and to rely less on entertainment, restaurants, and hotels that cater only to foreign tourists. This book will not only help you order a meal at a locals-only European restaurant—it will help you talk with the family that runs the place. Long after your memories of the museums have faded, you'll still treasure the personal encounters you had with your new European friends.

A good phrase book should help you enjoy your European experience—not just survive it—so I've added a healthy dose of humor. A few phrases are just for fun and aren't meant to be used at all. Most of the phrases are for real and should be used with "please." I know you can tell the difference.

To get the most out of this book, take the time to internalize and put into practice the pronunciation tips. I've spelled out the pronunciations as if you were reading English. Don't worry too much about memorizing grammatical rules, like which gender a particular noun is—forget about sex and communicate!

This book has three nifty menu decoders to help you figure out what's cooking. You'll also find tongue twisters, telephone tips, and handy tear-out "cheat sheets." Tear out the sheets and keep them handy, so you can easily memorize key phrases during otherwise idle moments. As you prepare for your trip, you may want to have a look at my annually-updated ***Rick Steves' Best of Europe*** guidebook or my individual country guides for France, Italy, Germany, and Switzerland.

My goal is to help you become a more confident, extroverted traveler. If this phrase book helps make that happen, or if you have suggestions for making it better, I'd love to hear from you. I personally read and value all feedback. My address is Europe Through the Back Door, P.O. Box 2009, Edmonds, WA 98020, tel. 425/771-8303, fax 425/771-0833, rick@ricksteves.com.

Happy travels, and good luck as you hurdle the language barrier!

Rick Steves

FRENCH

GETTING STARTED

Challenging, Romantic French

...is spoken throughout Europe and thought to be one of the most beautiful languages in the world. Half of Belgium speaks French, and French rivals English as the handiest second language in Spain, Portugal, and Italy. Even your US passport is translated into French. You're probably already familiar with this poetic language. Consider: ***bonjour, c'est la vie, bon appétit, merci, au revoir,*** and ***bon voyage!*** The most important phrase is ***s'il vous plaît*** (please), pronounced see voo play. Use it liberally. The French will notice and love it.

As with any language, the key to communicating is to go for it with a mixture of bravado and humility. Try
to sound like Maurice Chevalier or Inspector Clouseau.

French pronunciation differs from English in some key ways:

Ç sounds like S in sun.
CH sounds like SH in shine.
G usually sounds like G in get.
But G followed by E or I sounds like S in treasure.
GN sounds like NI in onion.
H is always silent.
J sounds like S in treasure.
R sounds like an R being swallowed.
I sounds like EE in seed.
È and **Ê** sound like E in let.

É and EZ sound like AY in play.
ER, at the end of a word, sounds like AY in play.
Ô sounds like O in note.

In a Romance language, sex is unavoidable. A man is ***content*** (happy), a woman is ***contente.*** In this book, when you see a pair of words like "***content / contente,***" use the second word when talking about a female.

French has four accents. The cedilla makes ***Ç*** sound like "s" (***façade***). The circumflex makes ***Ê*** sound like "eh" (***crêpe***), but has no effect on ***Â, Î, Ô,*** or ***Û.*** The grave accent stifles ***È*** into "eh" (***crème***), but doesn't change the stubborn ***À*** (***à la carte***). The acute accent opens ***É*** into "ay" (***café***).

French is tricky because the spelling and pronunciation seem to have little to do with each other. ***Qu'est-ce que c'est?*** (What is that?) is pronounced: kehs kuh say.

The final letters of many French words are silent, so ***Paris*** sounds like pah-ree. The French tend to stress every syllable evenly: pah-ree. In contrast, Americans say **Par**-is, emphasizing the first syllable.

In French, if a word that ends in a consonant is followed by a word that starts with a vowel, the consonant is frequently linked with the vowel. ***Mes amis*** (my friends) is pronounced: may-zah-mee. Some words are linked with an apostrophe. ***Ce est*** (It is) becomes ***C'est,*** as in ***C'est la vie*** (That's life). ***Le*** and ***la*** (the masculine and feminine "the") are intimately connected to words starting with a vowel. ***La orange*** becomes ***l'orange.***

French has a few sounds that are unusual in English: the French ***u*** and the nasal vowels. To say the French ***u,*** round your lips to say "oh," but say "ee." Vowels combined with either ***n*** or ***m*** are often nasal vowels. As you nasalize a vowel, let the sound come through your nose as well as your mouth. The vowel is the important thing. The ***n*** or ***m,*** represented in this book by n̲ for nasal, is not pronounced.

There are a total of four nasal sounds, all contained in the phrase ***un bon vin blanc*** (a good white wine).

Nasal vowels:	**Phonetics:**	**To make the sound:**
un	uhn	nasalize the U in lung.
bon	bohn	nasalize the O in bone.
vin	van	nasalize the A in sack.
blanc	blahn	nasalize the A in want.

If you practice saying ***un bon vin blanc***, you'll learn how to say the nasal vowels . . . and order a fine wine.

Here's a guide to the rest of the phonetics in this section:

ah	like A in father.
ay	like AY in play.
eh	like E in let.
ee	like EE in seed.
ehr, air	sounds like "air" (in ***merci*** and ***extraordinaire***).
ew	pucker your lips and say "ee."
g	like G in go.
ī	like I in light.
or	like OR in core.
oh	like O in note.
oo	like OO in too.
s	like S in sun.
uh	like U in but.
ur	like UR in purr.
zh	like S in treasure.

FRENCH BASICS

In 1944, American GIs helped liberate Paris using only these phrases.

Meeting and Greeting

Good day.	*Bonjour.*	bohn-zhoor
Good morning.	*Bonjour.*	bohn-zhoor
Good evening.	*Bonsoir.*	bohn-swar
Good night.	*Bonne nuit.*	buhn nwee
Hi / Bye. (informal)	*Salut.*	sah-lew
Welcome!	*Bienvenue!*	bee-an-vuh-new
Mr.	*Monsieur*	muhs-yur
Mrs.	*Madame*	mah-dahm
Miss	*Mademoiselle*	mahd-mwah-zehl
How are you?	*Comment allez-vous?*	koh-mahnt ah-lay-voo
Very well, thank you.	*Très bien, merci.*	treh bee-an mehr-see
And you?	*Et vous?*	ay voo
My name is___.	*Je m'appelle___.*	zhuh mah-pehl
What's your name?	*Quel est votre nom?*	kehl ay voh-truh nohn
Pleased to meet you.	*Enchanté.*	ahn-shahn-tay
Where are you from?	*D'où êtes-vous?*	doo eht voo
I am / We are...	*Je suis / Nous sommes...*	zhuh swee / noo suhm
Are you...?	*Êtes-vous...?*	eht-vooz
...on vacation	*...en vacances*	ahn vah-kahns
...on business	*...en voyage d'affaires*	ahn voy-yahzh dah-fair

See you later.	*À bientôt.*	ah bee-an-toh
So long! (informal)	*Salut!*	sah-lew
Goodbye.	*Au revoir.*	oh reh-vwar
Good luck!	*Bonne chance!*	buhn shahns
Have a good trip!	*Bon voyage!*	bohn voy-yahzh

The greeting "***Bonjour***" (Good day) turns to "***Bonsoir***" (Good evening) at sundown.

Essentials

Good day.	*Bonjour.*	bohn-zhoor
Do you speak English?	*Parlez-vous anglais?*	par-lay-voo ahn-glay
Yes. / No.	*Oui. / Non.*	wee / nohn
I don't speak French.	*Je ne parle pas français.*	zhuh nuh parl pah frahn-say
I'm sorry.	*Désolé.*	day-zoh-lay
Please.	*S'il vous plaît.*	see voo play
Thank you.	*Merci.*	mehr-see
Thank you very much.	*Merci beaucoup.*	mehr-see boh-koo
No problem.	*Pas de problème.*	pah duh proh-blehm
Good. / Very good. / Excellent.	*Bien. / Très bien. / Excellent.*	bee-an / treh bee-an / ehk-sehl-ahn
You are very kind.	*Vous êtes très gentil.*	vooz eht treh zhahn-tee
Excuse me. (to pass)	*Pardon.*	par-dohn
Excuse me. (to get attention)	*Excusez-moi.*	ehk-skew-zay-mwah
It doesn't matter.	*Ça m'est égal.*	sah meht ay-gal
You're welcome.	*Je vous en prie.*	zhuh vooz ahn pree
Sure.	*Bien sûr.*	bee-an suhr
O.K.	*D'accord.*	dah-kor
Let's go.	*Allons-y.*	ahl-lohn-zee
Goodbye.	*Au revoir.*	oh reh-vwar

Where?

Where is...?	*Où est...?*	oo ay
...the tourist information office	*...l'office du tourisme*	loh-fees dew too-reez-muh
...a cash machine	*...un distributeur automatique*	uhn dee-stree-bew-tur oh-toh-mah-teek
...the train station	*...la gare*	lah gar
...the bus station	*...la gare routière*	lah gar root-yehr
Where are the toilets?	*Où sont les toilettes?*	oo sohn lay twah-leht
men / women	*hommes / dames*	ohm / dahm

You'll find some French words are similar to English if you're looking for a ***banque, pharmacie, hôtel,*** or ***restaurant.***

How Much?

How much is it, please?	*Combien, s'il vous plaît?*	kohn-bee-an see voo play
Write it?	*Ecrivez?*	ay-kree-vay
Is it free?	*C'est gratuit?*	say grah-twee
Included?	*Inclus?*	an-klew
Do you have...?	*Avez-vous...?*	ah-vay-voo
Where can I buy...?	*Où puis-je acheter...?*	oo pwee-zhuh ah-shuh-tay
I would like...	*Je voudrais...*	zhuh voo-dray
We would like...	*Nous voudrions...*	noo voo-dree-ohn
...this.	*...ceci.*	suh-see
...just a little.	*...un petit peu.*	uhn puh-tee puh
...more.	*...plus.*	plew
...a ticket.	*...un billet.*	uhn bee-yay
...a room.	*...une chambre.*	ewn shahn-bruh
...the bill.	*...l'addition.*	lah-dee-see-ohn

How Many?

one	*un*	uhn
two	*deux*	duh
three	*trois*	twah

four	*quatre*	kah-truh
five	*cinq*	sank
six	*six*	sees
seven	*sept*	seht
eight	*huit*	weet
nine	*neuf*	nuhf
ten	*dix*	dees

You'll find more to count on in the "Numbers" section (page 15).

When?

At what time?	*À quelle heure?*	ah kehl ur
open / closed	*ouvert / fermé*	oo-vehr / fehr-may
Just a moment.	*Un moment.*	uhn moh-mahn
Now.	*Maintenant.*	man-tuh-nahn
Soon.	*Bientôt.*	bee-an-toh
Later.	*Plus tard.*	plew tar
Today.	*Aujourd'hui.*	oh-zhoor-dwee
Tomorrow.	*Demain.*	duh-man

Be creative! You can combine these phrases to say: "Two, please," or "No, thank you," or "Open tomorrow?" or "Please, where can I buy a ticket?" Please is a magic word in any language, but especially in French. The French love to hear it. If you want to buy something and you don't know the word for it, just point and say, "***S'il vous plaît***" (Please). If you know the word for what you want, such as the bill, simply say, "***L'addition, s'il vous plaît***" (The bill, please).

Struggling

Do you speak English?	*Parlez-vous anglais?*	par-lay-voo ahn-glay
A teeny weeny bit?	*Un tout petit peu?*	uhn too puh-tee puh
Please speak English.	*Parlez anglais, s'il vous plaît.*	par-lay ahn-glay see voo play
You speak English well.	*Vous parlez bien anglais.*	voo par-lay bee-an ahn-glay
I don't speak French.	*Je ne parle pas français.*	zhuh nuh parl pah frahn-say

We don't speak French.	*Nous ne parlons pas français.*	noo nuh par-lon pah frahn-say
I speak a little French.	*Je parle un petit peu français.*	zhuh parl uhn puh-tee puh frahn-say
Sorry, I speak only English.	*Désolé, je ne parle qu'anglais.*	day-zoh-lay zhuh nuh parl kahn-glay
Sorry, we speak only English.	*Désolé, nous ne parlons qu'anglais.*	day-zoh-lay noo nuh par-lon kahn-glay
Does somebody nearby speak English?	*Quelqu'un près d'ici parle anglais?*	kehl-kuhn preh dee-see parl ahn-glay
Who speaks English?	*Qui parle anglais?*	kee parl ahn-glay
What does this mean?	*Qu'est-ce-que ça veut dire?*	kehs-kuh sah vuh deer
How do you say this in French / English?	*Comment dit-on en français / anglais?*	koh-mahn dee-tohn ahn frahn-say / ahn-glay
Repeat?	*Répétez?*	ray-pay-tay
Speak slowly, please.	*Parlez lentement, s'il vous plaît.*	par-lay lahn-tuh-mahn see voo play
Slower.	*Plus lentement.*	plew lahn-tuh-mahn
I understand.	*Je comprends.*	zhuh kohn-prahn
I don't understand.	*Je ne comprends pas.*	zhuh nuh kohn-prahn pah
Do you understand?	*Vous comprenez?*	voo kohn-preh-nay
Write it?	*Ecrivez?*	ay-kree-vay

A French person who is asked, "Do you speak English?" assumes you mean, "Do you speak English fluently?" and will likely answer no. But if you just keep on struggling in French, you'll bring out the English in most any French person.

Handy Questions

How much?	*Combien?*	kohn-bee-an
How many?	*Combien?*	kohn-bee-an
How long is the trip?	*Combien de temps dure le voyage?*	kohn-bee-an duh tahn dewr luh voy-yahzh
How many minutes?	*Combien de minutes?*	kohn-bee-an duh mee-newt

How many hours?	*Combien d'heures?*	kohn-bee-an dur
How far?	*C'est loin?*	say lwan
How?	*Comment?*	koh-mahn
Can you help me?	*Vous pouvez m'aider?*	voo poo-vay may-day
Can you help us?	*Vous pouvez nous aider?*	voo poo-vay nooz ay-day
Can I...?	*Puis-je...?*	pwee-zhuh
Can we...?	*Pouvons-nous...?*	poo-vohn-noo
...have one	*...avoir un*	ah-vwar uhn
...go in for free	*...aller gratuitement*	ah-lay grah-tweet-mahn
...borrow that for a moment / an hour	*...emprunter ça pour un moment / une heure*	ahn-pruhn-tay sah poor uhn moh-mahn / ewn ur
...use the toilet	*...utiliser les toilettes*	oo-tee-lee-zay lay twah-leht
What? (didn't hear)	*Comment?*	koh-mahn
What is this?	*Qu'est-ce que c'est?*	kehs kuh say
What is better?	*Qu'est-ce qui vaut mieux?*	kehs kee voh mee-uh
What's going on?	*Qu'est-ce qui se passe?*	kehs kee suh pahs
When?	*Quand?*	kahn
What time is it?	*Quelle heure est-il?*	kehl ur ay-teel
At what time?	*À quelle heure?*	ah kehl ur
On time? / Late?	*A l'heure? / En retard?*	ah lur / ahn ruh-tar
How long will it take?	*Ça prend combien de temps?*	sah prahn kohn-bee-an duh tahn
At what time does this open / close?	*À quelle heuere c'est ouvert / fermé?*	ah kehl ur say oo-vehr / fehr-may
Is this open daily?	*C'est ouvert tous les jours?*	say oo-vehr too lay zhoor
What day is this closed?	*C'est fermé quel jour?*	say fehr-may kehl zhoor
Do you have...?	*Avez-vous...?*	ah-vay-voo
Where is...?	*Où est...?*	oo ay
Where are...?	*Où sont...?*	oo sohn

Where can I find / buy...?	*Où puis-je trouver / acheter...?*	oo pwee-zhuh troo-vay / ah-shuh-tay
Where can we find / buy...?	*Où pouvons-nous trouver / acheter...?*	oo poo-vahn-noo troo-vay / ah-shuh-tay
Is it necessary?	*C'est nécessaire?*	say nay-suh-sair
Is it possible...?	*C'est possible...?*	say poh-see-bluh
...to enter	*...d'entrer*	dahn-tray
...to picnic here	*...de pique-niquer ici*	duh peek-neek-ay ee-see
...to sit here	*...de s'assoir ici*	duh sah-swar ee-see
...to look	*...de regarder*	duh ray-gar-day
...to take a photo	*...de prendre une photo*	duh prahn-druh ewn foh-toh
...to see a room	*...de voir une chambre*	duh vwar ewn shahn-bruh
Who?	*Qui?*	kee
Why?	*Pourquoi?*	poor-kwah
Why not?	*Pourquoi pas?*	poor-kwah pah
Yes or no?	*Oui ou non?*	wee oo nohn

To prompt a simple answer, ask, "***Oui ou non?***" (Yes or no?). To turn a word or sentence into a question, ask it in a questioning tone. "***C'est bon***" (It's good) becomes "***C'est bon?***" (Is it good?). An easy way to say, "Where is the toilet?" is to ask, "***Toilette?***"

Yin and Yang

good / bad	*bon / mauvais*	bohn / moh-vay
best / worst	*le meilleur / le pire*	luh meh-yur / luh peer
a little / lots	*un peu / beaucoup*	uhn puh / boh-koo
more / less	*plus / moins*	plew / mwan
cheap / expensive	*bon marché / cher*	bohn mar-shay / shehr
big / small	*grand / petit*	grahn / puh-tee
hot / cold	*chaud / froid*	shoh / frwah
warm / cool	*tiede / frais*	tee-ehd / fray
open / closed	*ouvert / fermé*	oo-vehr / fehr-may
entrance / exit	*entrée / sortie*	ahn-tray / sor-tee
push / pull	*pousser / tirer*	poo-say / tee-ray

arrive / depart	*arriver / partir*	ah-ree-vay / par-teer
early / late	*tôt / tard*	toh / tar
soon / later	*bientôt / plus tard*	bee-an-toh / plew tar
fast / slow	*vite / lent*	veet / lahn
here / there	*ici / là-bas*	ee-see / lah-bah
near / far	*près / loin*	preh / lwan
indoors / outdoors	*l'intérieur / dehors*	lan-tay-ree-yoor / duh-or
mine / yours	*le mien / le vôtre*	luh mee-an / luh voh-truh
this / that	*ce / cette*	suh / seht
everybody / nobody	*tout le monde / personne*	too luh mohnd / pehr-suhn
easy / difficult	*facile / difficile*	fah-seel / dee-fee-seel
left / right	*à gauche / à droite*	ah gohsh / ah dwaht
up / down	*en haut / en bas*	ahn oh / ahn bah
above / below	*au-dessus / en-dessous*	oh-duh-sew / ahn-duh-soo
young / old	*jeune / vieux*	zhuhn / vee-uh
new / old	*neuf / vieux*	nuhf / vee-uh
heavy / light	*lourd / léger*	loor / lay-zhay
dark / light	*sombre / clair*	sohn-bruh / klair
happy (m, f) / sad	*content, contente / triste*	kohn-tahn, kohn-tahnt / treest
beautiful / ugly	*beau / laid*	boh / leh
nice / mean	*gentil / méchant*	zhahn-tee / may-shahn
intelligent / stupid	*intelligent / stupide*	an-teh-lee-zhahn / stew-peed
vacant / occupied	*libre / occupé*	lee-bruh / oh-kew-pay
with / without	*avec / sans*	ah-vehk / sahn

Big Little Words

I	*je*	zhuh
you (formal)	*vous*	voo
you (informal)	*tu*	tew
we	*nous*	noo
he	*il*	eel

she	*elle*	ehl
they	*ils*	eel
and	*et*	ay
at	*à*	ah
because	*parce que*	pars kuh
but	*mais*	may
by (train, car, etc.)	*par*	par
for	*pour*	poor
from	*de*	duh
here	*ici*	ee-see
if	*si*	see
in	*en*	ahn
it (m / f)	*le / la*	luh / lah
not	*pas*	pah
now	*maintenant*	man-tuh-nahn
only	*seulement*	suhl-mahn
or	*ou*	oo
this / that	*ce / cette*	suh / seht
to	*à*	ah
very	*très*	treh

Quintessential Expressions

Bon appétit!	*bohn ah-pay-tee*	Enjoy your meal!
Ça va?	*sah vah*	How are you? (informal)
Ça va. (response to *Ça va?*)	*sah vah*	I'm fine.
Sympa. / Pas sympa.	*sahn-pah / pah sahn-pah*	Nice. / Not nice.
C'est chouette. ("That's a female owl")	*say shweht*	That's cool.
Ce n'est pas vrai!	*suh nay pah vray*	It's not true!
C'est comme ça.	*say kohm sah*	That's the way it is.
Comme ci, comme ça.	*kohm see, kohm sah*	So so.
D'accord.	*dah-kor*	O.K.

Formidable!	*for-mee-dah-bluh*	Great!
Mon Dieu!	*mohn dee-uh*	My God!
Tout de suite.	*toot sweet*	Right away.
Voilà.	*vwah-lah*	Here it is.

COUNTING

NUMBERS

0	*zéro*	zay-roh
1	*un*	uh_n_
2	*deux*	duh
3	*trois*	twah
4	*quatre*	kah-truh
5	*cinq*	sa_n_k
6	*six*	sees
7	*sept*	seht
8	*huit*	weet
9	*neuf*	nuhf
10	*dix*	dees
11	*onze*	oh_n_z
12	*douze*	dooz
13	*treize*	trehz
14	*quatorze*	kah-torz
15	*quinze*	ka_n_z
16	*seize*	sehz
17	*dix-sept*	dee-seht
18	*dix-huit*	deez-weet
19	*dix-neuf*	deez-nuhf
20	*vingt*	va_n_
21	*vingt et un*	va_nt_ ay uh_n_
22	*vingt-deux*	va_nt_-duh

23 *vingt-trois* vant-twah
30 *trente* trahnt
31 *trente et un* trahnt ay uhn
40 *quarante* kah-rahnt
41 *quarante et un* kah-rahnt ay uhn
50 *cinquante* san-kahnt
51 *cinquante et un* san-kahnt ay uhn
60 *soixante* swah-sahnt
61 *soixante et un* swah-sahnt ay uhn
70 *soixante-dix* swah-sahnt-dees
71 *soixante et onze* swah-sahnt ay ohnz
72 *soixante-douze* swah-sahnt-dooz
73 *soixante-treize* swah-sahnt-trehz
74 *soixante-quatorze* swah-sahnt-kah-torz
75 *soixante-quinze* swah-sahnt-kanz
76 *soixante-seize* swah-sahnt-sehz
77 *soixante-dix-sept* swah-sahnt-dee-seht
78 *soixante-dix-huit* swah-sahnt-deez-weet
79 *soixante-dix-neuf* swah-sahnt-deez-nuhf
80 *quatre-vingts* kah-truh-van
81 *quatre-vingt-un* kah-truh-van-uhn
82 *quatre-vingt-deux* kah-truh-van-duh
83 *quatre-vingt-trois* kah-truh-van-twah
84 *quatre-vingt-quatre* kah-truh-van-kah-truh
85 *quatre-vingt-cinq* kah-truh-van-sank
86 *quatre-vingt-six* kah-truh-van-sees
87 *quatre-vingt-sept* kah-truh-van-seht
88 *quatre-vingt-huit* kah-truh-van-weet
89 *quatre-vingt-neuf* kah-truh-van-nuhf
90 *quatre-vingt-dix* kah-truh-van-dees
91 *quatre-vingt-onze* kah-truh-van-ohnz
92 *quatre-vingt-douze* kah-truh-van-dooz
93 *quatre-vingt-treize* kah-truh-van-trehz
94 *quatre-vingt-quatorze* kah-truh-van-kah-torz
95 *quatre-vingt-quinze* kah-truh-van-kanz
96 *quatre-vingt-seize* kah-truh-van-sehz

97	*quatre-vingt-dix-sept*	kah-truh-van-dee-seht
98	*quatre-vingt-dix-huit*	kah-truh-van-deez-weet
99	*quatre-vingt-dix-neuf*	kah-truh-van-deez-nuhf
100	*cent*	sahn
101	*cent un*	sahn uhn
102	*cent deux*	sahn duh
200	*deux cents*	duh sahn
1000	*mille*	meel
2000	*deux mille*	duh meel
2001	*deux mille un*	duh meel uhn
2002	*deux mille deux*	duh meel duh
2003	*deux mille trois*	duh meel twah
2004	*deux mille quatre*	duh meel kah-truh
2005	*deux mille cinq*	duh meel sank
2006	*deux mille six*	duh meel sees
2007	*deux mille sept*	duh meel seht
2008	*deux mille huit*	duh meel weet
2009	*deux mille neuf*	duh meel nuhf
2010	*deux mille dix*	duh meel dees
million	*million*	meel-yohn
billion	*milliard*	meel-yar
number one	*numéro un*	new-may-roh uhn
first	*premier*	pruhm-yay
second	*deuxième*	duhz-yehm
third	*troisième*	twahz-yehm
once / twice	*une fois / deux fois*	ewn fwah / duh fwah
a quarter	*un quart*	uhn kar
a third	*un tiers*	uhn tee-ehr
half	*demi*	duh-mee
this much	*comme ça*	kohm sah
a dozen	*une douzaine*	ewn doo-zayn
some	*quelques*	kehl-keh
enough	*suffisament*	soo-fee-zah-mahn
a handful	*une poignée*	ewn pwahn-yay
50%	*cinquante pour cent*	san-kahnt poor sahn
100%	*cent pour cent*	sahn poor sahn

French numbering is a little quirky from the seventies through the nineties. Let's pretend momentarily that the French speak English. Instead of saying 70, 71, 72, up to 79, the French say, "sixty ten," "sixty eleven," "sixty twelve" up to "sixty nineteen." Instead of saying 80, the French say, "four twenties." The numbers 81 and 82 are literally "four twenty one" and "four twenty two." It gets stranger. The number 90 is "four twenty ten." To say 91, 92, up to 99, the French say, "four twenty eleven," "four twenty twelve" on up to "four twenty nineteen." But take heart. If little French children can learn these numbers, so can you. Besides, didn't Abe Lincoln say, "Four score and seven..."?

MONEY

Where is a cash machine?	*Oú est un distributeur automatique?*	oo ay uhn dee-stree-bew-tur oh-toh-mah-teek
My ATM card has been...	*Ma carte a été...*	mah kart ah ay-tay
...demagnetized.	*...démagnétisée.*	day-mag-neht-ee-zay
...stolen.	*...volée.*	voh-lay
...eaten by the machine.	*...avalée par la machine.*	ah-vah-lee par lah mah-sheen
My card doesn't work.	*Ma carte ne marche pas.*	mah kart neh marsh pah
Do you accept credit cards?	*Vous prenez les cartes de crédit?*	voo preh-nay lay kart duh kray-dee
Can you change dollars?	*Pouvez-vous changer les dollars?*	poo-vay-voo shahn-zhay lay doh-lar
What is your exchange rate for dollars...?	*Quel est le cours du dollar...?*	kehl ay luh koor dew doh-lar
...in traveler's checks	*...en cheques de voyage*	ahn shehk duh voy-yahzh
What is the commission?	*Quel est la commission?*	kehl ay lah koh-mee-see-ohn

Any extra fee?	*Il y a d'autre frais?*	eel yah doh-truh fray
Can you break this? (large to small bills)	*Vous pouvez casser ça?*	voo poo-vay kas-ay sah
I would like...	*Je voudrais...*	zhuh voo-dray
...small bills.	*...des petits billets.*	day puh-tee bee-yay
...large bills.	*...des gros billets.*	day groh bee-yay
...coins.	*...des pièces.*	day pee-ehs
€50	*cinquante euros*	seeng-kwayn-tah eh-oo-roo
Is this a mistake?	*C'est une erreur?*	sayt ewn er-ror
This is incorrect.	*C'est incorrect.*	say in-koh-rehkt
Did you print these today?	*Vous les avez imprimés aujourd'hui?*	voo layz ah-vay an-pree-may oh-zhoor-dwee
I'm broke / poor / rich.	*Je suis fauché / pauvre / riche.*	zhuh swee foh-shay / poh-vruh / reesh
I'm Bill Gates.	*Je suis Bill Gates.*	zhuh swee "Bill Gates"
Where is the nearest casino?	*Oú se trouve le casino le plus proche?*	oo suh troov luh kah-see-noh luh plew prohsh

France uses the euro currency. Euros (€) are divided into 100 cents. Use your common cents—cents are like pennies, and the currency has coins like nickels, dimes, and half-dollars.

Money Words

euro (€)	*euro*	eh-oo-roo
cents	*centimes*	sahn-teem
money	*argent*	ar-zhahn
cash	*liquide*	lee-keed
cash machine	*distributeur automatique*	dee-stree-bew-tur oh-toh-mah-teek
bank	*banque*	bahnk
credit card	*carte de crédit*	kart duh kray-dee
change money	*changer de l'argent*	shahn-zhay duh lar-zhahn

Key Phrases: Money

euro (€)	*euro*	eh-oo-roo
money	*argent*	ar-zhahn
cash	*liquide*	lee-keed
credit card	*carte de crédit*	kart duh kray-dee
bank	*banque*	bahnk
cash machine	*distributeur automatique*	dee-stree-bew-tur oh-toh-mah-teek
Where is a cash machine?	*Oú est un distributeur automatique?*	oo ay uhn dee-stree-bew-tur oh-toh-mah-teek
Do you accept credit cards?	*Vous prenez les cartes de crédit?*	voo preh-nay lay kart duh kray-dee

exchange	*bureau de change*	bew-roh duh shahnzh
buy / sell	*acheter / vendre*	ah-shuh-tay / vahn-druh
commission	*commission*	koh-mee-see-ohn
traveler's check	*cheque de voyage*	shehk duh voy-yahzh
cash advance	*crédit de caisse*	kray-dee duh kehs
cashier	*caisse*	kehs
bills	*billets*	bee-yay
coins	*pièces*	pee-ehs
receipt	*reçu*	ruh-sew

At French banks, you may encounter a security door that allows one person to enter at a time. Push the ***entrez*** (enter) button, then ***attendez*** (wait), and ***voilà***, the door opens. Every ***distributeur automatique*** (cash machine) is multilingual, but if you'd like to learn French under pressure, look for these three buttons: ***annuler*** (cancel), ***modifier*** (change), ***valider*** (affirm). Your PIN code is a ***code.***

Key Phrases: Time

minute	*minute*	mee-newt
hour	*heure*	ur
day	*jour*	zhoor
week	*semaine*	suh-mehn
What time is it?	*Quelle heure est-il?*	kehl ur ay-teel
It's...	*Il est...*	eel ay
...8:00.	*...huit heures.*	weet ur
...16:00.	*...seize heures.*	sehz ur
At what time does this open / close?	*À quelle heuere c'est ouvert / fermé?*	ah kehl ur say oo-vehr / fehr-may

TIME

What time is it?	*Quelle heure est-il?*	kehl ur ay-teel
It's...	*Il est...*	eel ay
...8:00 in the morning.	*...huit heures du matin.*	weet ur doo mah-tahn
...16:00.	*...seize heures.*	sehz ur
...4:00 in the afternoon.	*...quatre heures de l'après-midi.*	kah-truh ur duh lah-preh-mee-dee
...10:30 in the evening.	*...dix heures et demie du soir.*	deez ur ayd-mee dew swar
...a quarter past nine.	*...neuf heures et quart.*	nuhv ur ay kar
...a quarter to eleven.	*...onze heures moins le quart.*	ohnz ur mwan luh kar
...noon.	*...midi.*	mee-dee
...midnight.	*...minuit.*	meen-wee
...early / late.	*...tôt / tard.*	toh / tar
...on time.	*...à l'heure.*	ah lur
...sunrise.	*...l'aube.*	lohb
...sunset.	*...le coucher de soleil.*	luh koo-shay duh soh-lay
It's my bedtime.	*C'est l'heure où je me couche.*	say lur oo zhuh muh koosh

Timely Expressions

English	French	Pronunciation
I'll return / We'll return...	*Je reviens / Nous revenons...*	zhuh reh-vee-an / noo ruh-vuh-nohn
...at 11:20.	*...à onze heures vingt.*	ah ohnz ur van
I'll be / We'll be...	*Je serai / Nous serons...*	zhuh suh-ray / noo suh-rohn
...there by 18:00.	*...là avant dix huit heures.*	lah ah-vahn deez-weet ur
When is checkout time?	*À quelle heure on doit libérer la chambre?*	ah kehl ur ohn dwah lee-bay-ray lah shahn-bruh
At what time does...?	*À quelle heure...?*	ah kehl ur
...this open / close	*...c'est ouvre / ferme*	say oov-reh / fehrm
...this train / bus leave for ___	*...ce train / bus part pour ___*	seh tran / bews par poor
...the next train / bus leave for ___	*...le prochain train / bus part pour ___*	luh proh-shan tran / bews par poor
...the train / bus arrive in ___	*...le train / bus arrive à ___*	luh tran / bews ah-reev ah
I want / We want...	*Je veux / Nous voulons...*	zhuh vuh / noo voo-lohn
...to take the 16:30 train.	*...prendre le train de seize heures trente.*	prahn-druh luh tran duh sehz ur trahnt
Is the train...?	*Le train est...?*	luh tran ay
Is the bus...?	*Le bus est...?*	luh bews ay
...early / late	*...en avance / en retard*	ahn ah-vahns / ahn ruh-tar
...on time	*...à l'heure*	ah lur

In France, the 24-hour clock (military time) is used by hotels and stores, and for train, bus, and ferry schedules. Informally, the French use the 24-hour clock and "our clock" interchangeably—17:00 is also 5:00 ***de l'après-midi*** (in the afternoon).

About Time

English	French	Pronunciation
minute	*minute*	mee-newt
hour	*heure*	ur

in the morning	*dans le matin*	dahn luh mah-tan
in the afternoon	*dans l'après-midi*	dahn lah-preh-mee-dee
in the evening	*dans le soir*	dahn luh swar
at night	*la nuit*	lah nwee
every hour	*toutes les heures*	toot layz ur
every day	*tous les jours*	too lay zhoor
last	*dernier*	dehrn-yay
this (m / f)	*ce / cette*	suh / seht
next	*prochain*	proh-shan
high season	*haute saison*	oht say-zohn
low season	*basse saison*	bahs say-zohn
in the future	*dans l'avenir*	dahn lah-vahn-eer
in the past	*dans le passé*	dahn luh pah-say

The Day

day	*jour*	zhoor
today	*aujourd'hui*	oh-zhoor-dwee
yesterday	*hier*	yehr
tomorrow	*demain*	duh-man
tomorrow morning	*demain matin*	duh-man mah-tan
day after tomorrow	*après demain*	ah-preh duh-man

The Week

week	*semaine*	suh-mehn
last week	*la semaine dernière*	lah suh-mehn dehrn-yehr
this week	*cette semaine*	seht suh-mehn
next week	*la semaine d'avance*	lah suh-mehn dah-vahns
Monday	*lundi*	luhn-dee
Tuesday	*mardi*	mar-dee
Wednesday	*mercredi*	mehr-kruh-dee
Thursday	*jeudi*	zhuh-dee
Friday	*vendredi*	vahn-druh-dee
Saturday	*samedi*	sahm-dee
Sunday	*dimanche*	dee-mahnsh

The Month

month	*mois*	mwah
January	*janvier*	zhahn-vee-yay
February	*février*	fay-vree-yay
March	*mars*	mars
April	*avril*	ahv-reel
May	*mai*	may
June	*juin*	zhwan
July	*juillet*	zhwee-yay
August	*août*	oot
September	*septembre*	sehp-tahn-bruh
October	*octobre*	ohk-toh-bruh
November	*novembre*	noh-vahn-bruh
December	*décembre*	day-sahn-bruh

The Year

year	*année*	ah-nay
spring	*printemps*	pran-tahn
summer	*été*	ay-tay
fall	*automne*	oh-tuhn
winter	*hiver*	ee-vehr

Holidays and Happy Days

holiday	*jour férié*	zhoor fay-ree-ay
national holiday	*fête nationale*	feht nah-see-oh-nahl
school holiday	*vacance scolaire*	vah-kahns skoh-lair
religious holiday	*fête religieuse*	feht ruh-lee-zhuhz
Bastille Day (July 14)	*le quatorze juillet*	luh kah-torz zhwee-yay
Is it a holiday today / tomorrow?	*C'est un jour férié aujourd'hui / demain?*	say tuhn zhoor fay-ree-ay oh-zhoor-dwee / duh-man
What is the holiday?	*C'est quel jour férié?*	say kehl zhoor fay-ree-ay
Is a holiday coming up soon?	*C'est bientôt un jour férié?*	say bee-an-toh uhn zhoor fay-ree-ay
When?	*Quand?*	kahn

Merry Christmas!	*Joyeux Noël!*	zhwah-yuh noh-ehl
Happy New Year!	*Bonne année!*	buhn ah-nay
Easter	*Pâques*	pahk
Happy anniversary!	*Bon anniversaire de mariage!*	bohn ah-nee-vehr-sair duh mah-ree-yahzh
Happy birthday!	*Bon anniversaire!*	bohn ah-nee-vehr-sair

The French sing "Happy Birthday" to the same tune we do. Here are the words: ***Joyeux anniversaire, joyeux anniversaire, joyeux anniversaire*** (fill in name), ***nos voeux les plus sincères.***

Other celebrations include May 1 (Labor Day), May 8 (Liberation Day), and August 15 (Assumption of Mary). France's biggest holiday is on July 14, Bastille Day. Festivities begin on the evening of the 13th and rage throughout the country.

If a holiday falls on a Thursday, many get Friday off as well: The Friday is called ***le pont,*** or the bridge, between the holiday and the weekend. On school holidays (***vacances scolaires***), families head for the beach, jamming resorts.

TRAVELING

TRAINS

The Train Station

English	French	Pronunciation
Where is...?	*Où est... ?*	oo ay
...the train station	*...la gare*	lah gar
French State Railways	*SNCF*	S N say F
train information	*renseignements SNCF*	rahn-sehn-yuh-mahn S N say F
train	*train*	tran
high-speed train	*TGV*	tay zhay vay
fast / faster	*rapide / plus rapide*	rah-peed / plew rah-peed
arrival	*arrivée*	ah-ree-vay
departure	*départ*	day-par
delay	*retard*	ruh-tar
toilet	*toilette*	twah-leht
waiting room	*salle d'attente*	sahl dah-tahnt
lockers	*consigne automatique*	kohn-seen-yuh oh-toh-mah-teek
baggage check room	*consigne de bagages*	kohn-seen-yuh duh bah-gahzh
lost and found office	*bureau des objets trouvés*	bew-roh dayz ohb-zhay troo-vay

tourist information	*office du tourisme*	oh-fees dew too-reez-muh
platform	*quai*	kay
to the platforms	*accès aux quais*	ahk-seh oh kay
track	*voie*	vwah
train car	*voiture*	vwah-tewr
dining car	*voiture restaurant*	vwah-tewr rehs-toh-rahn
sleeper car	*voiture-lit*	vwah-tewr-lee
conductor	*conducteur*	kohn-dewk-tur

You'll encounter several types of trains in France. Along with the various local and milk-run trains, there are:

- the slow ***Regionale*** trains
- the medium-speed ***Trains Express Regionaux***
- the fast ***EuroCity*** international trains
- the super-fast trains: ***TGV*** (within France and to Switzerland), ***Thalys*** (to Belgium), and ***Artesia*** (to Italy)

Railpasses cover travel on all of these trains, but you'll be required to pay for a reservation (€3 per trip) on ***TGV*** and ***Artesia*** trains. On ***Thalys*** trains, you'll pay a Passholder Fare (about €15 second class or €30 first class), if your railpass covers all the countries on the route you'll be taking. The French railway system limits the number of TGV and international-train reservations sold to railpass holders, so plan ahead or be flexible. See www.ricksteves.com/rail for more advice on reservations, railpasses, and information about the Eurostar train that connects Paris to London.

Getting a Ticket

Where can I buy a ticket?	*Où puis-j'acheter un billet?*	oo pweezh ah-shuh-tay uhn bee-yay
A ticket to ___.	*Un billet pour ___.*	uhn bee-yay poor
Where can we buy tickets?	*Où pouvons-nous acheter les billets?*	oo poo-vohn-nooz ah-shuh-tay lay bee-yay
Two tickets to ___.	*Deux billets pour ___.*	duh bee-yay poor

TRAVELING

Is this the line for...?	*C'est la file pour...?*	say lah feel poor
...tickets	*...les billets*	lay bee-yay
...reservations	*...les réservations*	lay ray-zehr-vah-see-ohn
How much is the fare to ___?	*C'est combien pour aller à ___?*	say kohn-bee-an poor ah-lay ah
Is this ticket valid for ___?	*Ce billet est bon pour ___?*	suh bee-yay ay bohn poor
How long is this ticket valid?	*Ce billet est bon pour combien de temps?*	suh bee-yay ay bohn poor kohn-bee-an duh tahn
When is the next train?	*Le prochain train part á quelle heure?*	luh proh-shan tran par ah kehl ur
Do you have a schedule for all trains departing for ___ today / tomorrow?	*Avez-vous un horaire pour tous les trains qui partent pour ___ aujourd'hui / demain?*	ah-vay-vooz uhn oh-rair poor too lay tran kee par-tahn poor ___ oh-zhoor-dwee / duh-man
I'd like to leave...	*Je voudrais partir...*	zhuh voo-dray par-teer
We'd like to leave...	*Nous voudrions partir...*	noo voo-dree-ohn par-teer
I'd like to arrive...	*Je voudrais arriver...*	zhuh voo-dray ah-ree-vay
We'd like to arrive...	*Nous voudrions arriver...*	noo voo-dree-ohn ah-ree-vay
...by ___.	*...avant ___.*	ah-vahn
...in the morning.	*...le matin.*	luh mah-tan
...in the afternoon.	*...l'après-midi.*	lah-preh-mee-dee
...in the evening.	*...le soir.*	luh swahr
Is there a...?	*Il y a un...?*	eel yah uhn
...earlier train	*...train plus tôt*	tran plew toh
...later train	*...train plus tard*	tran plew tar
...overnight train	*...train de nuit*	tran duh nwee
...cheaper train	*...train moins cher*	tran mwahn shehr
...cheaper option	*...solution meilleure marché*	soh-lew-see-ohn may-ur mar-shay
...local train	*...TER (train express régional)*	tay ay ehr (tran ehk-sprehs ray-zhee-oh-nahl)
...express train	*...train direct*	tran dee-rehkt
What track does the train leave from?	*Le train part de quel voie?*	luh tran par duh kel vwah

On time?	*À l'heure?*	ah lur
Late?	*En retard?*	ahn ruh-tar

Reservations, Supplements, and Discounts

Is a reservation required?	*Une réservation est obligatoire?*	ewn ray-zehr-vah-see-ohn ay oh-blee-gah-twahr
I'd like to reserve...	*Je voudrais réserver...*	zhuh voo-dray ray-zehr-vay
...a seat.	*...une place.*	ewn plahs
...a berth.	*...une couchette.*	ewn koo-sheht
...a sleeper.	*...un compartiment privé.*	uhn kohn-par-tuh-mahn pree-vay
...the entire train.	*...le train entier.*	luh tran ahn-tee-ay
We'd like to reserve...	*Nous voudrions réserver...*	noo voo-dree-ohn ray-zehr-vay
...two seats.	*...deux places.*	duh plahs
...two couchettes.	*...deux couchettes.*	duh koo-sheht
...two sleepers.	*...un compartiment privé pour deux personnes.*	uhn kohn-par-tuh-mahn pree-vay poor duh pehr-suhn
Is there a supplement?	*Il y a un supplément?*	eel yah uhn sew-play-mahn
Does my railpass cover the supplement?	*Le supplément est inclus dans mon pass?*	luh sew-play-mahn ay an-klew dahn mohn pahs
Is there a discount for...?	*Il y a une réduction pour les...?*	eel yah ewn ray-dewk-see-ohn poor lay
...youth	*...jeunes*	zhuhn
...seniors	*...gens âgés*	zhahn ah-zhay
...families	*...familles*	fah-mee

Ticket Talk

ticket window	*guichet*	gee-shay
reservations window	*comptoir des réservations*	kohn-twahr day ray-zehr-vah-see-ohn

Key Phrases: Trains

English	French	Pronunciation
train station	*gare*	gar
train	*train*	tran
ticket	*billet*	bee-yay
transfer (n)	*correspondance*	kor-rehs-pohn-dahns
supplement	*supplément*	sew-play-mahn
arrival	*arrivée*	ah-ree-vay
departure	*départ*	day-par
platform	*quai*	kay
track	*voie*	vwah
train car	*voiture*	vwah-tewr
A ticket to ___.	*Un billet pour ___.*	uhn bee-yay poor
Two tickets to ___.	*Deux billets pour ___.*	duh bee-yay poor
When is the next train?	*Le prochain train part á quelle heure?*	luh proh-shan tran par ah kehl ur
Where does the train leave from?	*Il le train part d'où?*	eel luh tran par doo
Which train to ___?	*Quel train pour ___?*	kehl tran poor

English	French	Pronunciation
national	*en France*	ahn frahns
international	*internationaux*	een-tehr-nah-see-ohn-oh
ticket	*billet*	bee-yay
one way	*aller simple*	ah-lay san-pluh
round trip	*aller retour*	ah-lay-ruh-toor
first class	*première classe*	pruhm-yehr klahs
second class	*deuxième classe*	duhz-yehm klahs
non-smoking	*non fumeur*	nohn few-mur
validate	*composter*	kohn-poh-stay
schedule	*horaire*	oh-rair
departure	*départ*	day-par
direct	*direct*	dee-rehkt
transfer (n)	*correspondance*	kor-rehs-pohn-dahns
with supplement	*avec supplément*	ah-vehk sew-play-mahn
reservation	*réservation*	ray-zehr-vah-see-ohn

seat...	*place...*	plahs
...by the window	*...côté fenêtre*	koh-tay fuh-neh-truh
...on the aisle	*...côté couloir*	koh-tay kool-wahr
berth...	*couchette...*	koo-sheht
...upper	*...en haut*	ahn oh
...middle	*...milieu*	meel-yuh
...lower	*...en bas*	ahn bah
refund	*remboursement*	rahn-boor-suh-mahn
reduced fare	*tarif réduit*	tah-reef ray-dwee

Changing Trains

Is it direct?	*C'est direct?*	say dee-rehkt
Must I / Must we...?	*Je dois / Nous devons...?*	zhuh dwah / noo duh-vohn
...make a transfer	*...prendre une correspondance*	prahn-druh ewn kor-rehs-pohn-dahns
When? / Where?	*À quelle heure? / Où?*	ah kehl ur / oo
Do I change here for ___?	*Je transfère ici pour ___?*	zhuh trahns-fehr ee-see poor
Do we change here for ___?	*Nous transférons ici pour ___?*	noo trahns-fehr-ohn ee-see poor
Where do I change for ___?	*Où je transfère pour ___?*	oo zhuh trahns-fehr poor
Where do we change for ___?	*Où nous transférons pour ___?*	oo noo trahns-fehr-ohn poor
At what time?	*À quelle heure?*	ah kehl ur
From what track does the train leave?	*Le train part de quelle voie?*	luh tran par duh kehl vwah
How many minutes in ___ to change trains?	*Combien de minutes à ___ pour changer de train?*	kohn-bee-an duh mee-newt ah ___ poor shahn-zhay duh tran

On the Platform

Where is...?	*Où est...?*	oo ay
Is this...?	*C'est...?*	say

...the train to ___	*...le train pour ___*	luh tran poor
Which train to ___?	*Quel train pour ___?*	kehl tran poor
Which train car to ___?	*Quelle voiture pour ___?*	kehl vwah-tewr poor
Where is first class?	*Où est la première classe?*	oo ay lah pruhm-yehr klahs
front	*à l'avant*	ah lah-vahn
middle	*au milieu*	oh meel-yuh
back	*au fond*	oh fohn
Where can I validate my ticket?	*Où puis-je composter mon billet?*	oo pwee-zhuh kohn-poh-stay mohn bee-yay

You must ***composter*** (validate) your train ticket (and any reservation) prior to boarding. Look for the waist-high orange machines on the platform and insert your ticket and reservation separately—watch others and imitate.

On the Train

Is this seat free?	*C'est libre?*	say lee-bruh
May I...?	*Je peux...?*	zhuh puh
May we...?	*Nous pouvons...?*	noo poo-vohn
...sit here	*...s'asseoir ici*	sah-swar ee-see
...open the window	*...ouvrir la fenêtre*	oo-vreer lah fuh-neh-truh
...eat your meal	*...manger votre repas*	mahn-zhay voh-truh ruh-pah
Save my place?	*Garder ma place?*	gar-day mah plahs
Save our places?	*Garder nos places?*	gar-day noh plahs
That's my seat.	*C'est ma place.*	say mah plahs
These are our seats.	*Ce sont nos places.*	suh sohn noh plahs
Where are you going?	*Où allez-vous?*	oo ah-lay-voo
I'm going to ___.	*Je vais à ___.*	zhuh vay ah
We're going to ___.	*Nous allons à ___.*	nooz ah-lohn ah
Tell me when to get off?	*Dîtes-moi quand je descends?*	deet-mwah kahn zhuh day-sahn

Tell us when to get off?	*Dîtes-nous quand on descend?*	deet-noo kahn ohn day-sahn
Where is a (good-looking) conductor?	*Où est un (beau) conducteur?*	oo ay uhn (boh) kohn-dewk-tur
Does this train stop in ___?	*Ce train s'arrête à ___?*	suh tran sah-reht ah
When will it arrive in ___?	*Il va arriver à ___ à quelle heure?*	eel vah ah-ree-vay ah ___ ah kehl ur
When will it arrive?	*Il va arriver à quelle heure?*	eel vah ah-ree-vay ah kehl ur

Reading Train and Bus Schedules

European schedules use the 24-hour clock. It's like American time until noon. After that, subtract twelve and add P.M. So 13:00 is 1 P.M., 20:00 is 8 P.M., and 24:00 is midnight. One minute after midnight is 00:01.

French train schedules show blue (quiet), white (normal), and red (peak and holiday) times. You can save money if you get the blues (travel during off-peak hours).

à, pour	to
arrivée	arrival
de	from
départ	departure
dimanche	Sunday
en retard	late
en semaine	workdays (Monday-Saturday)
et	and
heure	hour
horaire	timetable
jour férié	holiday
jours	days
jusqu'à	until
la semaine	weekdays
par	via

pas not
samedi Saturday
sauf except
seulement only
tous every
tous les jours daily
vacances holidays
voie track
1-5 Monday-Friday
6, 7 Saturday, Sunday

Going Places

France	*la France*	lah frahns
Belgium	*la Belgique*	lah behl-zheek
English Channel	*la Manche*	lah mahnsh
Austria	*l'Autriche*	loh-treesh
Czech Republic	*la République Tcheque*	lah reh-poob-leek chehk
Great Britain	*la Grande-Bretagne*	lah grahn breh-tahn-yuh
Germany	*l'Allemagne*	lahl-mahn-yuh
Greece	*la Grèce*	lah grehs
Ireland	*l'Irlande*	leer-lahnd
Italy	*l'Italie*	lee-tah-lee
Netherlands	*les Pays-Bas*	lay peh-ee-bah
Portugal	*le Portugal*	luh por-tew-gal
Scandinavia	*la Scandinavie*	lah skahn-dee-nah-vee
Spain	*l'Espagne*	luh-spahn-yuh
Switzerland	*la Suisse*	lah swees
Turkey	*la Turquie*	lah tehr-kee
Europe	*l'Europe*	lur-rohp
EU (European Union)	*UE (l'Union Européenne)*	ew uh (lewn-yohn ur-oh-pay-ehn)
Russia	*la Russie*	lah roo-see
Africa	*l'Afrique*	laf-reek
United States	*les États-Unis*	layz ay-tah-zew-nee
Canada	*le Canada*	luh kah-nah-dah
world	*le monde*	luh mohnd

Major Transportation Lines in France

Local Places

If you're using the ***Rick Steves' France*** guidebook, you're also likely to see these place names. When French clerks at train stations and train conductors don't understand your pronunciation, write the town name on a piece of paper.

Alsace	ahl-sahs
Amboise	ahm-bwahz

Annecy	ahn-see
Antibes	ahn-teeb
Arles	arl
Arromanches	ah-roh-mahnsh
Avignon	ah-veen-yohn
Bayeux	bah-yuh
Beaune	bohn
Beynac	bay-nak
Bordeaux	bor-doh
Calais	kah-lay
Carcassonne	kar-kah-suhn
Chambord	shahn-bor
Chamonix	shah-moh-nee
Chartres	shart
Chenonceau	shuh-nohn-soh
Cherbourg	shehr-boor
Chinon	shee-nohn
Collioure	kohl-yoor
Colmar	kohl-mar
Côte d'Azur	koht dah-zewr
Dijon	dee-zhohn
Dordogne	dor-dohn-yuh
Giverny	zhee-vehr-nee
Grenoble	gruh-noh-bluh
Honfleur	ohn-floor
Le Havre	luh hah-vruh
Loire	lwar
Lyon	lee-ohn
Marseille	mar-say
Mont Blanc	mohn blahn
Mont St. Michel	mohn san mee-shehl
Nantes	nahnt
Nice	nees
Normandy	nor-mahn-dee
Paris	pah-ree
Provence	proh-vahns

Reims	rans (rhymes with France)
Rouen	roo-ahn
Roussillon	roo-see-yohn
Sarlat	sar-lah
Strasbourg	strahs-boorg
Verdun	vehr-duhn
Versailles	vehr-sī
Villefranche	veel-frahnsh

BUSES AND SUBWAYS

At the Bus or Subway Station

city bus	*bus*	bews
long-distance bus	*car*	kar
bus stop	*arrêt de bus*	ah-reh duh bews
bus station	*gare routière*	gar root-yehr
subway station	*station de Métro*	stah-see-ohn duh may-troh
subway map	*plan du Métro*	plahn dew may-troh
subway entrance	*l'entrée du Métro*	lahn-tray dew may-troh
subway stop	*arrêt de Métro*	ah-reh duh may-troh
subway exit	*sortie*	sor-tee
direct	*direct*	dee-rehkt
connection	*correspondance*	kor-rehs-pohn-dahns
batch of 10 tickets	*carnet*	kar-nay

In Paris, you'll save money by buying a ***carnet*** (batch of 10 tickets) at virtually any Métro station. The tickets, which are sharable, are valid on the buses, Métro, and RER (underground rail lines) within the city limits.

Taking Buses and Subways

How do I get to __?	*Comment je vais à __?*	koh-mahn zhuh vay ah

TRAVELING

How do we get to ___?	*Comment nous allons à ___?*	koh-mahn nooz ah-lohn ah
How much is a ticket?	*C'est combien le ticket?*	say kohn-bee-an luh tee-kay
Where can I buy a ticket?	*Où puis-je acheter un ticket?*	oo pwee-zhuh ah-shuh-tay uhn tee-kay
Where can we buy tickets?	*Où pouvons-nous acheter les tickets?*	oo poo-vohn-noo ah-shuh-tay lay tee-kay
One ticket, please.	*Un billet, s'il vous plaît.*	uhn bee-yay see voo play
Two tickets.	*Deux billets.*	duh bee-yay
Is this ticket valid (for ___)?	*Ce ticket est bon (pour ___)?*	suh tee-kay ay bohn (poor)
Is there...?	*Il y a...?*	eel yah
...a one-day pass	*...un pass à la journée*	uhn pahs ah lah zhoor-nay
...a discount if I buy more tickets	*...une réduction si j'achet plusieurs tickets*	ewn ray-dewk-see-ohn see zhah-shay plewz-yur tee-kay
Which bus to ___?	*Quel bus pour ___?*	kehl bews poor
Does it stop at ___?	*Il s'arrête à ___?*	eel sah-reht ah
Which bus stop for ___?	*Quel arrêt pour ___?*	kehl ah-reh poor
Which subway stop for ___?	*Quel arrêt de Métro pour ___?*	kehl ah-reh duh may-troh poor
Which direction for ___?	*Quelle direction pour ___?*	kehl dee-rehk-see-ohn poor
Must I / Must we...?	*Je dois / Nous devons...?*	zhuh dwah / noo duh-vohn
...transfer	*...prendre une correspondance*	prahn-druh ewn kor-rehs-pohn-dahns
When does the... leave?	*Le... part quand?*	luh... par kahn
...first / next / last	*...premier / prochain / dernier*	pruhm-yay / proh-shan / dehrn-yay
...bus / subway	*...bus / Métro*	bews / may-troh

Key Phrases: Buses and Subways

bus	*bus*	bews
subway	*Métro*	may-troh
ticket	*ticket*	tee-kay
How do I get to ___?	*Comment je vais à ___?*	koh-mahn̲ zhuh vay ah
Which stop for ___?	*Quel arrêt pour ___?*	kehl ah-reh poor
Tell me when to get off?	*Dîtes-moi quand je descends?*	deet-mwah kahn̲ zhuh day-sahn̲

What's the frequency per hour / day?	*Combien de fois par heure / jour?*	kohn̲-bee-an̲ duh fwah par ur / zhoor
Where does it leave from?	*D'où il part?*	doo eel par
What time does it leave?	*Il part à quelle heure?*	eel par ah kehl ur
I'm going to ___.	*Je vais à ___.*	zhuh vay ah
We're going to ___.	*Nous allons à ___.*	nooz ah-lohn̲ ah
Tell me when to get off?	*Dîtes-moi quand je descends?*	deet-mwah kahn̲ zhuh day-sahn̲
Tell us when to get off?	*Dîtes-nous quand on descend?*	deet-noo kahn̲ ohn̲ day-sahn̲

TAXIS

Getting a Taxi

Taxi!	*Taxi!*	tahk-see
Can you call a taxi?	*Pouvez-vous appeler un taxi?*	poo-vay-voo ah-puh-lay uhn̲ tahk-see
Where is a taxi stand?	*Où est une station de taxi?*	oo ay ewn stah-see-ohn̲ duh tahk-see
Where can I get a taxi?	*Où puis-je trouver un taxi?*	oo pwee-zhuh troo-vay uhn̲ tahk-see

Key Phrases: Taxis

Taxi!	*Taxi!*	tahk-see
Are you free?	*Vous êtes libre?*	vooz eht lee-bruh
To ___, please.	*À ___, s'il vous plaît.*	ah ___ see voo play
meter	*compteur*	kohn-tur
Stop here.	*Arrêtez-vous ici.*	ah-reh-tay-voo ee-see
Keep the change.	*Gardez la monnaie.*	gar-day lah moh-nay

Where can we get a taxi?	*Où pouvons-nous trouver un taxi?*	oo poo-vohn-noo troo-vay uhn tahk-see
Are you free?	*Vous êtes libre?*	vooz eht lee-bruh
Occupied.	*Occupé.*	oh-kew-pay
To ___, please.	*À ___, s'il vous plaît.*	ah ___ see voo play
To this address.	*À cette adresse.*	ah seht ah-drehs
Take me to ___.	*Amenez-moi à ___.*	ah-muh-nay-mwah ah
Take us to ___.	*Amenez-nous à ___.*	ah-muh-nay-nooz ah
Approximately how much will it cost to go...?	*C'est environ combien d'aller...?*	say ahn-vee-rohn kohn-bee-an dah-lay
...to ___	*...à ___*	ah
...to the airport	*...à l'aéroport*	ah lah-ay-roh-por
...to the train station	*...à la gare*	ah lah gar
...to this address	*...à cette adresse*	ah seht ah-drehs
Any extra supplement?	*Il y a un supplément?*	eel yah uhn sew-play-mahn
It's too much.	*C'est trop.*	say troh
Can you take ___ people?	*Pouvez-vous prendre ___ passagers?*	poo-vay-voo prahn-druh ___ pah-sah-zhay
Any extra fee?	*Il y a d'autres frais?*	eel yah doh-truh fray
Do you have an hourly rate?	*Avez-vous un taux par heure?*	ah-vay-vooz uhn toh par ur
How much for a one-hour city tour?	*Combien pour une visite d'une heure en ville?*	kohn-bee-an poor ewn vee-zeet dewn ur ahn veel

TRAVELING

So you'll know what to expect, ask your hotelier about typical taxi fares. Fares go up at night (7:00 P.M. to 7:00 A.M.) and on Sundays, and drivers always charge for loading baggage in the trunk. Your fare can nearly double if you're taking a short trip with lots of bags. In smaller towns, cabbies are few and customer satisfaction is important. Strike up a conversation and make a new friend.

If you're having a tough time hailing a taxi, ask for the nearest taxi stand (***station de taxi***). The simplest way to tell a cabbie where you want to go is by stating your destination followed by "please" ("***Louvre, s'il vous plaît***"). Tipping isn't expected, but it's polite to round up. So if the fare is €19, round up to €20.

In the Taxi

The meter, please.	*Le compteur, s'il vous plaît.*	luh kohn-tur see voo play
Where is the meter?	*Où est le compteur?*	oo ay luh kohn-tur
I'm in a hurry.	*Je suis pressé.*	zhuh swee preh-say
We're in a hurry.	*Nous sommes pressés.*	noo suhm preh-say
Slow down.	*Ralentissez.*	rah-lahn-tee-say
If you don't slow down, I'll throw up.	*Si vous ne ralentissez pas, je vais vomir.*	see voo nuh rah-lahn-tee-say pah zhuh vay voh-meer
Left / Right / Straight.	*À gauche / À droite / Tout droit.*	ah gohsh / ah dwaht / too dwah
I'd like to stop here for a moment.	*J'aimerais m'arrêter ici un moment.*	zhehm-uh-ray mah-reh-tay ee-see uhn moh-mahn
We'd like to stop here for a moment.	*Nous aimerions nous arrêter ici un moment.*	nooz ehm-uh-rohn nooz ah-reh-tay ee-see uhn moh-mahn
Please stop here for ___ minutes.	*S'il vous plaît arrêtez-vous ici pour ___ minutes.*	see voo play ah-reh-tay-voo ee-see poor ___ mee-newt
Can you wait?	*Pouvez-vous attendre?*	poo-vay vooz ah-tahn-druh

TRAVELING

Crazy traffic, isn't it?	*C'est fou, cette circulation, non?*	say foo seht seer-kewl-ah-see-ohn nohn
You drive like ...	*Vous conduisez comme...*	voo kohn-dwee-zay kohm
...a madman!	*...un fou!*	uhn foo
...Michael Schumacher.	*...Michel Schumacher.*	mee-shehl "Shumacher"
You drive very well.	*Vous conduisez très bien.*	voo kohn-dwee-zay treh bee-an
Where did you learn to drive?	*Où avez-vous appris à conduire?*	oo ah-vay-vooz ah-preez ah kohn-dweer
Stop here.	*Arrêtez-vous ici.*	ah-reh-tay-voo ee-see
Here is fine.	*Ici c'est bien.*	ee-see say bee-an
At this corner.	*À ce coin.*	ah say kwan
The next corner.	*Au coin prochain.*	oh kwan proh-shan
My change, please.	*La monnaie, s'il vous plaît.*	lah moh-nay see voo play
Keep the change.	*Gardez la monnaie.*	gar-day lah moh-nay
This ride is / was more fun than Disneyland.	*Ce trajet est / était plus drôle que Disneyland.*	suh trah-zhay ay / ay-tay plew drohl kuh "Disneyland"

DRIVING

Rental Wheels

car rental agency	*agence de location de voiture*	ah-zhahns duh loh-kah-see-ohn duh vwah-tewr
I'd like to rent...	*Je voudrais louer...*	zhuh voo-dray loo-ay
We'd like to rent...	*Nous voudrions louer...*	noo voo-dree-ohn loo-ay
...a car.	*...une voiture.*	ewn vwah-tewr
...a station wagon.	*...un break.*	uhn brayk
...a van.	*...un van.*	uhn vahn
...a motorcycle.	*...une motocyclette.*	ewn moh-toh-see-kleht
...a motor scooter.	*...un vélomoteur.*	uhn vay-loh-moh-tur
...the Concorde.	*...le Concorde.*	luh kohn-kord

Key Phrases: Driving

car	*voiture*	vwah-tewr
gas station	*station service*	stah-see-ohn sehr-vees
parking lot	*parking*	par-keeng
accident	*accident*	ahk-see-dahn
left / right	*à gauche / à droite*	ah gohsh / ah dwaht
straight ahead	*tout droit*	too dwah
downtown	*centre-ville*	sahn-truh-veel
How do I get to ___?	*Comment je vais à ___?*	koh-mahn zhuh vay ah
Where can I park?	*Où puis-je me garer?*	oo pwee-zhuh muh gah-ray

How much per...?	*Combien par...?*	kohn-bee-an par
...hour	*...heure*	ur
...half day	*...demie-journée*	duh-mee zhoor-nay
...day	*...jour*	zhoor
...week	*...semaine*	suh-mehn
Unlimited mileage?	*Kilométrage illimité?*	kee-loh-may-trahzh eel-lee-mee-tay
When must I bring it back?	*Je dois le ramener à quelle heure?*	zhuh dwah luh rah-muh-nay ah kehl ur
Is there...?	*Est-ce qu'il y a...?*	ehs keel yah
...a helmet	*...un casque*	uhn kahsk
...a discount	*...une réduction*	ewn ray-dewk-see-ohn
...a deposit	*...une caution*	ewn koh-see-ohn
...insurance	*...une assurance*	ewn ah-sewr-rahns

Parking

parking lot	*parking*	par-keeng
parking garage	*garage de stationement*	gah-rahzh duh stah-see-ohn-mahn
parking meter	*horodateur*	oh-roh-dah-tur

Where can I park?	*Où puis-je me garer?*	oo pwee-zhuh muh gah-ray
Is parking nearby?	*Il y a un parking près d'ici?*	eel yah uhn par-keeng preh dee-see
Can I park here?	*Je peux me garer ici?*	zhuh puh muh gah-ray ee-see
Is this a safe place to park?	*C'est prudent de se garer ici?*	say prew-dahn duh suh gah-ray ee-see
How long can I park here?	*Je peux me garer ici pour combien de temps?*	zhuh puh muh gah-ray ee-see poor kohn-bee-an duh tahn
Must I pay to park here?	*Je dois payer pour me garer ici?*	zhuh dwah pay-yay poor muh gah-ray ee-see
How much per hour / day?	*Combien heure / jour?*	kohn-bee-an par ur / zhoor

Many French cities use remote meters for curbside parking. After you park, look for a meter at the street corner and buy a ticket to place on the dash. If you're not certain you need a ticket, look at the dashboards of cars parked nearby. If they have tickets, you'll need one, too. Ask a local for help finding the ***horodateur*** (parking meter).

FINDING YOUR WAY

I am going to ___.	*Je vais à ___.*	zhuh vay ah
We are going to ___.	*Nous allons à ___.*	nooz ah-lohn ah
How do I get to ___?	*Comment je vais à ___?*	koh-mahn zhuh vay ah
How do we get to ___?	*Comment nous allons à ___?*	koh-mahn nooz ah-lohn ah
Do you have...?	*Avez-vous...?*	ah-vay-vooz
...a city map	*...un plan de la ville*	uhn plahn duh lah veel
...a road map	*...une carte routière*	ewn kart root-yehr
How many minutes...?	*Combien de minutes...?*	kohn-bee-an duh mee-newt
How many hours...?	*Combien d'heures...?*	kohn-bee-an dur

...on foot	*...à pied*	ah pee-yay
...by bicycle	*...à bicyclette*	ah bee-see-kleht
...by car	*...en voiture*	ahn vwah-tewr
How many kilometers to ___?	*Combien de kilomètres à ___?*	kohn-bee-an duh kee-loh-meh-truh ah
What's the... route to Paris?	*Quelle est la... route pour Paris?*	kehl eh lah... root poor pah-ree
...most scenic	*...plus belle*	plew behl
...fastest	*...plus directe*	plew dee-rehkt
...most interesting	*...plus intéressante*	plewz an-tay-reh-sahnt
Point it out?	*Montrez-moi?*	mohn-tray mwah
I'm lost.	*Je suis perdu.*	zhuh swee pehr-dew
We're lost.	*Nous sommes perdu.*	noo suhm pehr-dew
Where am I?	*Où suis-je?*	oo swee-zhuh
Where is...?	*Où est...?*	oo ay
The nearest...?	*Le plus proche...?*	luh plew prohsh
Where is this address?	*Où se trouve cette adresse?*	oo suh troov seht ah-drehs

TRAVELING

Route-Finding Words

city map	*plan de la ville*	plahn duh lah veel
road map	*carte routière*	kart root-yehr
downtown	*centre-ville*	sahn-truh-veel
left	*à gauche*	ah gohsh
right	*à droite*	ah dwaht
straight ahead	*tout droit*	too dwah
first	*premier*	pruhm-yay
next	*prochain*	proh-shan
intersection	*carrefour*	kar-foor
corner	*au coin*	oh kwan
block	*paté de maisons*	pah-tay duh may-zohn
roundabout	*rondpoint*	rohn-pwan
ring road	*rocade*	roh-kahd
stoplight	*feu*	fuh
square	*place*	plahs
street	*rue*	rew
bridge	*pont*	pohn

tunnel	*tunnel*	tew-nehl
highway	*grande route*	grahnd root
national highway	*route nationale*	root nah-see-oh-nahl
freeway	*autoroute*	oh-toh-root
north	*nord*	nor
south	*sud*	sewd
east	*est*	ehs
west	*ouest*	wehs

The shortest distance between any two points in France is the ***autoroute,*** but the tolls add up. You'll travel cheaper, but slower, on a ***route nationale.*** Along the ***autoroute,*** electronic signs flash messages to let you know what's ahead: ***bouchon*** (traffic jam), ***circulation*** (traffic), and ***fluide*** (no traffic).

The Police

As in any country, the flashing lights of a patrol car are a sure sign that someone's in trouble. If it's you, try this handy phrase: "***Pardon, je suis touriste***" (Sorry, I'm a tourist). Or, for the adventurous: "***Si vous n'aimez pas ma conduite, vous n'avez que descendre du trottoir.***" (If you don't like how I drive, get off the sidewalk.)

I'm late for my tour.	*Je suis en retard pour mon tour.*	zhuh swee ahn ruh-tar poor mohn toor
Can I buy your hat?	*Je peux acheter votre chapeau?*	zhuh puh ah-shuh-tay voh-truh shah-poh
What seems to be the problem?	*Quel est le problème?*	kehl ay luh proh-blehm
Sorry, I'm a tourist.	*Pardon, je suis touriste.*	par-dohn zhuh swee too-reest

Reading Road Signs

attention travaux	workers ahead
autres directions (follow when leaving a town)	other directions
céder le passage	yield
centre-ville	to the center of town

déviation	detour
entrée	entrance
péage	toll
prochaine sortie	next exit
ralentir	slow down
réservé aux piétons	pedestrians only
sans issue	dead end
sauf riverains	local access only
sens unique	one-way street
sortie	exit
stationnement interdit	no parking
stop	stop
toutes directions (follow when leaving a town)	all directions
travaux	construction
virages	curves

For an illustrated look at traffic signs, see page 512.

Other Signs You May See

à louer	for rent or for hire
à vendre	for sale
chambre libre	vacancy
chien méchant	mean dog
complet	no vacancy
dames	women
danger	danger
défense de fumer	no smoking
défense de toucher	do not touch
défense d'entrer	keep out
eau non potable	undrinkable water
entrée libre	free admission
entrée interdite	no entry
en panne	out of service
fermé pour restauration	closed for restoration
fermeture annuelle	closed for vacation

guichet	ticket window
hommes	men
hors service	out of service
interdit	forbidden
occupé	occupied
ouvert / fermé	open / closed
ouvert de ___ à ___	open from ___ to ___
poussez / tirez	push / pull
prudence	caution
solde	sale
sortie de secours	emergency exit
tirez / poussez	pull / push
toilettes	toilets
WC	toilet

SLEEPING

Places to Stay

hotel	*hôtel*	oh-tehl
small hotel	*pension*	pah<u>n</u>-see-oh<u>n</u>
small hotel with restaurant	*auberge*	ow-behrzh
castle hotel	*hôtel-château*	oh-tehl-shah-toh
room in a private home	*chambre d'hôte*	shah<u>n</u>-bruh doht
youth hostel	*auberge de jeunesse*	oh-behrzh duh zhuh-nehs
country home rental	*gîte*	zheet
vacancy	*chambre libre*	shah<u>n</u>-bruh lee-bruh
no vacancy	*complet*	koh<u>n</u>-play

Reserving a Room

I like to reserve rooms a few days in advance as I travel. But if my itinerary is set, I reserve before I leave home. To reserve from home by fax or email, use the handy form in the appendix (online at www.ricksteves.com/reservation).

Hello.	*Bonjour.*	boh<u>n</u>-zhoor
Do you speak English?	*Parlez-vous anglais?*	par-lay-voo ah<u>n</u>-glay

Key Phrases: Sleeping

I want to make / confirm a reservation.	*Je veux faire / confirmer une réservation.*	zhuh vuh fair / kohn-feer-may ewn ray-zehr-vah-see-ohn
I'd like a room (for two people), please.	*Je voudrais une chambre (pour deux personnes), s'il vous plaît.*	zhuh voo-dray ewn shahn-bruh (poor duh pehr-suhn) see voo play
...with / without / and	*...avec / sans / et*	ah-vehk / sahn / ay
...toilet	*...WC*	vay say
...shower	*...douche*	doosh
Can I see the room?	*Je peux voir la chambre?*	zhuh puh vwar lah shahn-bruh
How much is it?	*Combien?*	kohn-bee-an
Credit card O.K.?	*Carte de crédit O.K.?*	kart duh kray-dee "O.K."

Do you have a room...?	*Avez-vous une chambre...?*	ah-vay-vooz ewn shahn-bruh
...for one person	*...pour une personne*	poor ewn pehr-suhn
...for two people	*...pour deux personnes*	poor duh pehr-suhn
...for tonight	*...pour ce soir*	poor suh swar
...for two nights	*...pour deux nuits*	poor duh nwee
...for this Friday	*...pour ce vendredi*	poor suh vahn-druh-dee
...for June 21	*...pour le vingt et un juin*	poor luh vant ay uhn zhwan
Yes or no?	*Oui ou non?*	wee oo nohn
I'd like...	*Je voudrais...*	zhuh voo-dray
We'd like...	*Nous voudrions...*	noo voo-dree-ohn
...a private bathroom.	*...une salle de bains.*	ewn sahl duh ban
...your cheapest room.	*...la chambre la moins chère.*	lah shahn-bruh lah mwan shehr
...___ beds for ___ people in ___ rooms.	*...___ lits par ___ personnes dans ___ chambres.*	___ lee par ___ pehr-suhn dahn ___ shahn-bruh

How much is it?	*Combien?*	kohn-bee-an
Anything cheaper?	*Rien de moins cher?*	ree-an duh mwan shehr
I'll take it.	*Je la prends.*	zhuh lah prahn
My name is ___.	*Je m'appelle ___.*	zhuh mah-pehl
I'll stay...	*Je reste...*	zhuh rehst
We'll stay...	*Nous restons...*	noo rehs-tohn
...one night.	*...une nuit.*	ewn nwee
...___ nights.	*...___ nuits.*	___ nwee
I'll come...	*J'arrive...*	zhah-reev
We'll come...	*Nous arrivons...*	nooz ah-ree-vohn
...in the morning.	*...dans la matinée.*	dahn lah mah-tee-nay
...in the afternoon.	*...dans l'après-midi.*	dahn lah-preh-mee-dee
...in the evening.	*...dans la soirée.*	dahn lah swah-ray
...in one hour.	*...dans une heure.*	dahnz ewn ur
...before 4:00 in the afternoon.	*...avant quatre heures dans l'après-midi.*	ah-vahn kah-truh ur dahn lah-preh-mee-dee
...Friday before 6 P.M.	*...vendredi avant six heures du soir.*	vahn-druh-dee ah-vahn seez ur dew swar
Thank you.	*Merci.*	mehr-see

SLEEPING

Using a Credit Card

If you need to secure your reservation with a credit card, here's the lingo.

Is a deposit required?	*Je dois verser un accompte?*	zhuh dwah vehr-say uhn ah-kohnt
Credit card O.K.?	*Carte de crédit O.K.?*	kart duh kray-dee "O.K."
credit card	*carte de crédit*	kart duh kray-dee
debit card	*carte bancaire*	kart bahn-kair
The name on the card is ___.	*Le nom sur la carte est ___.*	luh nohn sewr lah kart ay
The credit card number is...	*Le numéro de carte de crédit est...*	luh noo-mehr-oh duh kart duh kray-dee ay
0	*zéro*	zay-roh
1	*un*	uhn
2	*deux*	duh
3	*trois*	twah

4	*quatre*	kah-truh
5	*cinq*	sank
6	*six*	sees
7	*sept*	seht
8	*huit*	weet
9	*neuf*	nuhf
The expiration date is...	*La date d'expiration est..*	lah daht dehks-pee-rah-see-ohn ay
January	*janvier*	zhahn-vee-yay
February	*février*	fay-vree-yay
March	*mars*	mars
April	*avril*	ahv-reel
May	*mai*	may
June	*juin*	zhwan
July	*juillet*	zhwee-yay
August	*août*	oot
September	*septembre*	sehp-tahn-bruh
October	*octobre*	ohk-toh-bruh
November	*novembre*	noh-vahn-bruh
December	*décembre*	day-sahn-bruh
2009	*deux mille neuf*	duh meel nuhf
2010	*deux mille dix*	duh meel dees
2011	*deux mille onze*	duh meel ohnz
2012	*deux mille douze*	duh meel dooz
2013	*deux mille treize*	duh meel trehz
2014	*deux mille quatorze*	duh meel kah-torz
2015	*deux mille quinze*	duh meel kanz
2016	*deux mille seize*	duh meel sehz
2017	*deux mille dix-sept*	duh meel dee-seht
Can I reserve with a credit card and pay in cash?	*Je peux réserver avec une carte de crédit et payer en liquide?*	zhuh puh ray-zehr-vay ah-vehk ewn kart duh kray-dee ay pay-yay ahn lee-keed
I have another card.	*J'ai une autre carte.*	zhay ewn oh-truh kart

If your ***carte de crédit*** is not approved, say, "***J'ai une autre carte***" (I have another card)—if you do.

The Alphabet

If phoning, you can use the code alphabet below to spell out your name if necessary. Unless you're giving the hotelier your name as it appears on your credit card, consider using a shorter version of your name to make things easier.

a	ah	Anatole	ahn-ah-tohl
b	bay	Berthe	behrt
c	say	Célestin	say-luh-steen
d	day	Désiré	day-zee-ray
e	uh	Emile	eh-meel
f	"f"	François	frahn-swah
g	zhay	Gaston	gah-stohn
h	ahsh	Henri	ahn-ree
i	ee	Irma	eer-mah
j	zhee	Joseph	zhoh-zuhf
k	kah	Kléber	klay-behr
l	"l"	Louis	loo-ee
m	"m"	Marcel	mar-sehl
n	"n"	Nicolas	nee-koh-lahs
o	"o"	Oscar	ohs-kar
p	pay	Pierre	pee-yehr
q	kew	Quintal	kween-tahl
r	ehr	Raoul	rah-ool
s	"s"	Suzanne	soo-zahn
t	tay	Thérèse	tay-rehs
u	ew	Ursule	oor-sool
v	vay	Victor	veek-tor
w	doo-bluh vay	William	weel-yahm
x	"x"	Xavier	zhahv-yehr
y	ee grehk	Yvonne	ee-vuhn
z	zehd	Zoé	zoh-ay

Just the Fax, Ma'am

If you're booking a room by fax...

I want to send a fax.	*J'aimerais vous envoyer un fax.*	zhehm-uh-ray vooz ahn-voy-ay uhn fahks

What is your fax number?	*Quel est votre numéro de fax?*	kehl ay voh-truh noo-mehr-oh duh fahks
Your fax number is not working.	*Votre numéro de fax ne marche pas.*	voh-truh noo-mehr-oh duh fahks nuh marsh pah
Please turn on your fax machine.	*Vous pourriez brancher votre fax, s'il vous plaît.*	voo poor-yay brahn-shay voh-truh fahks see voo play

Getting Specific

I'd like a room...	*Je voudrais une chambre...*	zhuh voo-dray ewn shahn-bruh
We'd like a room...	*Nous voudrions une chambre...*	noo voo-dree-ohn ewn shahn-bruh
...with / without / and	*...avec / sans / et*	ah-vehk / sahn / ay
...toilet	*...WC*	vay say
...shower	*...douche*	doosh
...sink and toilet	*...cabinet de toilette*	kah-bee-nay duh twah-leht
...shower and toilet	*...salle d'eau*	sahl doh
...shower down the hall	*...douche sur le palier*	doosh sewr luh pahl-yay
...bathtub and toilet	*...salle de bains*	sahl duh ban
...double bed	*...grand lit*	grahn lee
...twin beds	*...deux petits lits, lits jumeaux*	duh puh-tee lee, lee zhew-moh
...balcony	*...balcon*	bahl-kohn
...view	*...vue*	vew
...only a sink	*...lavabo seulement*	lah-vah-boh suhl-mahn
...on the ground floor	*...au rez-de-chaussée*	oh ray-duh-shoh-say
...television	*...télévision*	tay-lay-vee-zee-ohn
...telephone	*...téléphone*	tay-lay-fohn
...air conditioning	*...climatisation*	klee-mah-tee-zah-see-ohn
...kitchenette	*...kitchenette*	keet-chehn-eht
Is there an elevator?	*Il y a un ascenseur?*	eel-yah uhn ah-sahn-sur
Do you have a swimming pool?	*Vous avez une piscine?*	vooz ah-vay ewn pee-seen

I arrive Monday, depart Wednesday.	*J'arrive lundi, et pars mercredi.*	zhah-reev luhn-dee ay par mehr-kruh-dee
We arrive Monday, depart Wednesday.	*Nous arrivons lundi, et partons mercredi.*	nooz ah-ree-vohn luhn-dee ay par-tohn mehr-kruh-dee
I'm desperate.	*Je suis désespéré.*	zhuh swee day-zuh-spay-ray
We're desperate.	*Nous sommes désespérés.*	noo suhm day-zuh-spay-ray
I'll sleep anywhere.	*Je peux dormir n'importe où.*	zhuh puh dor-meer nan-port oo
We'll sleep anywhere.	*Nous pouvons dormir n'importe où.*	noo poo-vohn dor-meer nan-port oo
I have a sleeping bag.	*J'ai un sac de couchage.*	zhay uhn sahk duh koo-shahzh
We have sleeping bags.	*Nous avons les sacs de couchage.*	nooz ah-vohn lay sahk duh koo-shahzh
Will you call another hotel for me?	*Vous pourriez contacter un autre hôtel pour moi?*	voo poor-yay kohn-tahk-tay uhn oh-truh oh-tehl poor mwah

Offering some of the best budget beds in Europe, French hotels are rated from one to four stars (check the blue & white plaque by the front door). For budget travelers, one or two stars is the best value. Prices vary widely under one roof. A room with a double bed (***grand lit***) is cheaper than a room with twin beds (***deux petits lits***), and a bathroom with a shower (***salle d'eau***) is cheaper than a bathroom with a bathtub (***salle de bains***). Rooms with just a toilet and sink (***cabinet de toilette***, abbreviated *C. de T.*) are even cheaper, and a room with only a sink (***lavabo seulement***) is the cheapest.

Families

Do you have...?	*Vous avez...?*	vooz ah-vay
...a family room	*...une grande chambre, une suite*	ewn grahn shahn-bruh, ewn sweet
...a family rate	*...un tarif famille*	uhn tah-reef fah-mee-yee

...a discount for children	*...un tarif réduit pour enfants*	uhn tah-reef ray-dwee poor ahn-fahn
I have...	*J'ai...*	zhay
We have...	*Nous avons...*	nooz ah-vohn
...one child, ___ months / years old.	*...un enfant, de ___ mois / ans.*	uhn ahn-fahn duh ___ mwah / ahn
...two children, ___ and ___ years old.	*...deux enfants, de ___ et ___ ans.*	duhz ahn-fahn duh ___ ay ___ ahn
I'd like...	*Je voudrais...*	zhuh voo-dray
We'd like...	*Nous voudrions...*	noo voo-dree-ohn
...a crib.	*...un berceau.*	uhn behr-soh
...a cot.	*...un lit de camp.*	uhn lee duh kahn
...bunk beds.	*...lits superposés.*	lee sew-pehr-poh-zay
babysitting service	*service de babysitting*	sehr-vees duh "babysitting"
Is... nearby?	*Il y a... près d'ici?*	eel-yah... preh dee-see
...a park	*...un parc*	uhn park
...a playground	*...un parc avec des jeux*	uhn park ah-vehk day zhuh
...a swimming pool	*...une piscine*	ewn pee-seen

Equivalent to our word "kids," the French say ***les gamins*** or ***les gosses.*** Snot-nosed kids are ***les morveux*** and brats are ***les momes.***

Confirming, Changing, and Canceling Reservations

You can use this template for your telephone call.

My name is ___.	*Je m'appelle ___.*	zhuh mah-pehl
I have a reservation.	*J'ai une réservation.*	zhay ewn ray-zehr-vah-see-ohn
We have a reservation.	*Nous avons une réservation.*	nooz ah-vohn ewn ray-zehr-vah-see-ohn
I'd like to... my reservation.	*Je voudrais... ma réservation.*	zhuh voo-dray... mah ray-zehr-vah-see-ohn
...confirm	*...confirmer*	kohn-feer-may
...reconfirm	*...reconfirmer*	ray-kohn-feer-may

...cancel	*...annuler*	ah-noo-lay
...change	*...modifier*	moh-dee-fee-ay
The reservation is / was for...	*La réservation est / était pour...*	lah ray-zehr-vah-see-ohn ay / ay-tay poor
...one person	*...une personne*	ewn pehr-suhn
...two people	*...deux personnes*	duh pehr-suhn
...today / tomorrow	*...aujourd'hui / demain*	oh-zhoor-dwee / duh-man
...the day after tomorrow	*...après demain*	ah-preh duh-man
...August 13	*...le treize août*	luh trehz oot
...one night / two nights	*...une nuit / deux nuits*	ewn nwee / duh nwee
Did you find my / our reservation?	*Avez-vous trouvé ma / notre réservation?*	ah-vay-voo troo-vay mah / noh-truh ray-zehr-vah-see-ohn
What is your cancellation policy?	*Quel est le règlement pour annuler?*	kehl ay luh reh-gluh-mahn poor ah-noo-lay
Will I be billed for the first night if I can't make it?	*Je dois payer la première nuit si je ne peux pas venir?*	zhuh dwah pay-yay lah pruhm-yehr nwee see zhuh nuh puh pah vuh-neer
I'd like to arrive instead on ___.	*Je préfère arriver le ___.*	zhuh pray-fehr ah-ree-vay luh
We'd like to arrive instead on ___.	*Nous préférerions arriver le ___.*	noo pray-fay-ree-ohn ah-ree-vay luh
Is everything O.K.?	*Ça va marcher?*	sah vah mar-shay
Thank you. See you then.	*Merci. À bientôt.*	mehr-see. ah bee-an-toh
I'm sorry, I need to cancel.	*Je suis désolé, car je dois annuler.*	zhuh swee day-zoh-lay kar zhuh dwah ah-noo-lay

Nailing Down the Price

How much is...?	*Combien...?*	kohn-bee-an
...a room for ___ people	*...une chambre pour ___ personnes*	ewn shahn-bruh poor ___ pehr-suhn

SLEEPING

English	French	Pronunciation
...your cheapest room	*...la chambre la moins chère*	lah shahn-bruh lah mwan shehr
Is breakfast included?	*Le petit déjeuner est compris?*	luh puh-tee day-zhuh-nay ay kohn-pree
Is breakfast required?	*Le petit déjeuner est obligatoire?*	luh puh-tee day-zhuh-nay ay oh-blee-gah-twar
How much without breakfast?	*Combien sans le petit déjeuner?*	kohn-bee-an sahn luh puh-tee day-zhuh-nay
Is half-pension required?	*La demi-pension est obligatoire?*	lah duh-mee-pahn-see-ohn ay oh-blee-gah-twar
Complete price?	*Tout compris?*	too kohn-pree
Is it cheaper if I stay three nights?	*C'est moins cher si je reste trois nuits?*	say mwan shehr see zhuh rehst twah nwee
I will stay three nights.	*Je vais rester trois nuits.*	zhuh vay rehs-tay twah nwee
We will stay three nights.	*Nous allons rester trois nuits.*	nooz ah-lohn rehs-tay twah nwee
Is it cheaper if I pay in cash?	*C'est moins cher si je paie en liquide?*	say mwan shehr see zhuh pay ahn lee-keed
What is the cost per week?	*Quel est le prix à la semaine?*	kehl ay luh pree ah lah suh-mehn

Some hotels offer ***demi-pension*** (half-pension), consisting of two meals per day: breakfast and your choice of lunch or dinner. The price is often listed per person rather than per room. Hotels that offer half-pension often require it in summer. The meals are usually good, but if you want more freedom, look for hotels that don't push half-pension.

Choosing a Room

English	French	Pronunciation
Can I see the room?	*Je peux voir la chambre?*	zhuh puh vwar lah shahn-bruh
Can we see the room?	*Nous pouvons voir la chambre?*	noo poo-vohn vwar lah shahn-bruh
Show me another room?	*Montrez-moi une autre chambre?*	mohn-tray-mwah ewn oh-truh shahn-bruh
Show us another room?	*Montrez-nous une autre chambre?*	mohn-tray-nooz ewn oh-truh shahn-bruh

Do you have something...?	*Avez-vous quelque chose de...?*	ah-vay-voo kehl-kuh shohz duh
...larger / smaller	*...plus grand / moins grand*	plew grahn / mwan grahn
...better / cheaper	*...meilleur / moins cher*	meh-yur / mwan shehr
...brighter	*...plus clair*	plew klair
...in the back	*...derrière*	dehr-yehr
...quieter	*...plus tranquille*	plew trahn-keel
Sorry, it's not right for me.	*Désolé, ça ne me convient pas.*	day-zoh-lay sah nuh muh kohn-vee-ahn pah
I'll take it.	*Je la prends.*	zhuh lah prahn
We'll take it.	*Nous la prenons.*	noo lah prahn-nohn
The key, please.	*La clef, s'il vous plaît.*	lah klay see voo play

Breakfast

Breakfast is rarely included, but at least coffee refills are free.

How much is breakfast?	*Combien coûte petit déjeuner?*	kohn-bee-an koot puh-tee day-zhuh-nay
Is breakfast included?	*Le petit déjeuner compris?*	luh puh-tee day-zhuh-nay kohn-pree
When does breakfast start?	*Le petit déjeuner commence à quelle heure?*	luh puh-tee day-zhuh-nay koh-mahns ah kehl ur
When does breakfast end?	*Le petit déjeuner termine à quelle heure?*	luh puh-tee day-zhuh-nay tehr-meen ah kehl ur
Where is breakfast served?	*Le petit déjeuner est servi où?*	luh puh-tee day-zhuh-nay ay sehr-vee oo

Hotel Help

I'd like...	*Je voudrais...*	zhuh voo-dray
We'd like...	*Nous voudrions...*	noo voo-dree-ohn
...a / another...	*...un / un autre...*	uhn / uhn oh-truh
...towel.	*...serviette de bain.*	sehrv-yeht duh ban

...clean towel.	*...serviette propre.*	sehrv-yeht proh-puh
...pillow.	*...oreiller.*	oh-reh-yay
...fluffy pillow.	*...coussin.*	koo-san
...clean sheets.	*...draps propres.*	drah proh-pruh
...blanket.	*...couverture.*	koo-vehr-tewr
...glass.	*...verre.*	vehr
...sink stopper.	*...bouchon pour le lavabo.*	boo-shohn poor luh lah-vah-boh
...soap.	*...savon.*	sah-vohn
...toilet paper.	*...papier hygiénique.*	pahp-yay ee-zhay-neek
...electrical adapter.	*...adaptateur électrique.*	ah-dahp-tah-tewr ay-lehk-treek
...brighter light bulb.	*...ampoule plus forte.*	ahn-pool plew fort
...lamp.	*...lampe.*	lahmp
...chair.	*...chaise.*	shehz
...roll-away bed.	*...lit pliant.*	lee plee-ahn
...table.	*...table.*	tah-bluh
...Internet access.	*...accès internet.*	ahk-sehs an-tehr-neht
...different room.	*...autre chambre.*	oh-truh shahn-bruh
...silence.	*...le calme.*	luh kahlm
...to speak to the manager.	*...parler à la direction.*	par-lay ah lah dee-rehk-see-ohn
I've fallen and I can't get up.	*Je suis tombé et je ne peux pas me lever.*	zhuh swee tohn-bay ay zhuh nuh puh pah muh lay-vay
How can I make the room warmer / cooler?	*Comment rendre la chambre plus chaude / plus fraiche?*	koh-mahn rahn-druh lah shahn-bruh plew shohd / plew frehsh
Where can I wash / hang my laundry?	*Où puis-je faire / étendre ma lessive?*	oo pwee-zhuh fair / ay-tahn-druh mah luh-seev
Is a... nearby?	*Il y a une... près d'ici?*	eel-yah ewn... preh dee-see
...self-service laundry	*...laverie automatique*	lah-vah-ree oh-toh-mah-teek
...full service laundry	*...blanchisserie*	blahn-shee-suh-ree
I'd like / We'd like...	*Je voudrais / Nous voudrions...*	zhuh voo-dray / noo voo-dree-ohn

...to stay another night.	*...rester encore une nuit.*	rehs-tay ahn-kor ewn nwee
Where can I park?	*Je peux me garer où?*	zhuh puh muh gah-ray oo
What time do you lock up?	*Vous fermez à quelle heure?*	voo fehr-may ah kehl ur
Please wake me at 7:00.	*Réveillez-moi à sept heures, s'il vous plaît.*	ray-veh-yay-mwah ah seht ur see voo play
Where do you go for lunch / dinner / coffee?	*Vous allez où pour déjeuner / dîner / un café?*	vooz ah-lay oo poor day-zhuh-nay / dee-nay / uhn kah-fay

If you'd rather not sleep with a log-style French pillow, check in the closet to see if there's a fluffier American-style pillow, or ask for a "***coussin,***" (pron. koo-san).

Hotel Hassles

Come with me.	*Venez avec moi.*	vuh-nayz ah-vehk mwah
I have a problem in the room.	*J'ai un problème dans la chambre.*	zhay uhn proh-blehm dahn lah shahn-bruh
It smells bad.	*Elle sent mauvaise.*	ehl sahn moh-vehz
bugs	*insectes*	an-sehkt
mice	*souris*	soo-ree
cockroaches	*cafards*	kah-far
I'm covered with bug bites.	*Je suis couvert de piqures d'insectes.*	zhuh swee koo-vehr duh pee-kewr dan-sehkt
The bed is too soft / hard.	*Le lit est trop mou / dur.*	luh lee eh troh moo / dewr
I can't sleep.	*Je ne peux pas dormir.*	zhuh nuh puh pah dor-meer
The room is too...	*La chambre est trop...*	lah shahn-bruh ay troh
...hot / cold.	*...chaude / froide.*	shohd / frwahd
...noisy / dirty.	*...bruyante / sale.*	brew-yahnt / sahl
I can't open / shut...	*Je ne peux pas ouvrir / fermer...*	zhuh nuh puh pah oov-reer / fehr-may
...the door / the window.	*...la porte / la fenêtre.*	lah port / lah fuh-neh-truh
Air conditioner...	*Climatisation...*	klee-mah-tee-zah-see-ohn

Lamp...	*Lampe...*	lahmp
Lightbulb...	*Ampoule...*	ahn-pool
Electrical outlet...	*Prise...*	preez
Key...	*Clef...*	klay
Lock...	*Serrure...*	suh-roor
Window...	*Fenêtre...*	fuh-neh-truh
Faucet...	*Robinet...*	roh-bee-nay
Sink...	*Lavabo...*	lah-vah-boh
Toilet...	*Toilette...*	twah-leht
Shower...	*Douche...*	doosh
...doesn't work.	*...ne marche pas.*	nuh marsh pah
There is no hot water.	*Il n'y a pas d'eau chaude.*	eel nee yah pah doh shohd
When is the water hot?	*L'eau sera chaude à quelle heure?*	loh suh-rah shohd ah kehl ur

Checking Out

When is check-out time?	*A quelle heure on doit libérer la chambre?*	ah kehl ur ohn dwah lee-bay-ray lah shahn-bruh
I'll leave...	*Je pars...*	zhuh par
We'll leave...	*Nous partons...*	noo par-tohn
...today / tomorrow.	*...aujourd'hui / demain.*	oh-zhoor-dwee / duh-man
...very early.	*...très tôt.*	treh toh
Can I / Can we...?	*Je peux / Nous pouvons...?*	zhuh puh / noo poo-vohn
...pay now	*...régler la note maintenant*	ray-glay lah noht man-tuh-nahn
The bill, please.	*La note, s'il vous plaît.*	lah noht see voo play
Everything was great.	*C'était super.*	say-tay sew-pehr
I slept like a baby.	*J'ai dormi comme un enfant.*	zhay dor-mee kohm uhn ahn-fahn
Will you call my next hotel...?	*Pourriez-vous appeler mon prochain hotel...?*	poor-yay-vooz ah-puh-lay mohn proh-shahn oh-tehl

...for tonight	*...pour ce soir*	poor suh swar
...to make a reservation	*...pour faire une réservation*	poor fair ewn ray-zehr-vah-see-ohn
...to confirm a reservation	*...pour confirmer une réservation*	poor kohn-feer-may ewn ray-zehr-vah-see-ohn
I will pay for the call	*Je paierai l'appel.*	zhuh pay-uh-ray lah-pehl
Can I / Can we...?	*Je peux / Nous pouvons...?*	zhuh puh / noo poo-vohn
...leave baggage here until ___	*...laisser les baggages ici jusqu'à ___*	lay-say lay bah-gahzh ee-see zhews-kah

I never tip beyond the included service charges in hotels or for hotel services.

Camping

camping	*camping*	kahn-peeng
campsite	*emplacement*	ahn-plahs-mahn
tent	*tente*	tahnt
The nearest campground?	*Le camping le plus proche?*	luh kahn-peeng luh plew prohsh
Can I / Can we...?	*Je peux / Nous pouvons...?*	zhuh puh / noo poo-vohn
...camp here for one night	*...camper ici pour une nuit*	kahn-pay ee-see poor ewn nwee
Are showers included?	*Les douches sont comprises?*	lay doosh sohn kohn-preez
shower token	*jeton*	zhuh-tohn

In some French campgrounds and hostels, you need to buy a ***jeton*** (token) to activate a hot shower. To avoid a sudden cold rinse, buy two ***jetons*** before getting undressed.

EATING

RESTAURANTS

Types of Restaurants

Diners around the world recognize French food as a work of art. French cuisine is sightseeing for your tastebuds.

Styles of cooking include ***haute cuisine*** (classic, elaborately prepared, multi-course meals); ***cuisine bourgeoise*** (the finest-quality home cooking); ***cuisine des provinces*** (traditional dishes of specific regions, using the best ingredients); and ***nouvelle cuisine*** (the "new style" from the 1970s, which breaks from tradition with a focus on small portions and close attention to the texture and color of the ingredients).

Here are the types of restaurants you're likely to encounter:

Restaurant—Generally elegant, expensive eatery serving ***haute cuisine***
Brasserie—Large café with quick, simple food and drink
Bistro—Small, usually informal neighborhood restaurant offering mainly ***cuisine bourgeoise***
Auberge, Hostellerie, or ***Relais***—Country inn serving high-quality traditional food
Routier—Truck stop dishing up basic, decent food
Crêperie—Street stand or café specializing in crêpes (thin pancakes, usually served with sweet fillings such as chocolate, Nutella, jam, or butter and sugar)

Salon de thé—Tea and coffee house offering pastries, desserts, and sometimes light meals
Buffet-express or ***snack bar***—Cafeteria, usually near a train or bus station
Cabaret—Supper club featuring entertainment

Finding a Restaurant

Where's a good... restaurant nearby?	*Où se trouve un bon restaurant... près d'ici?*	oo suh troov uhn bohn rehs-toh-rahn... preh dee-see
...cheap	*...bon marché*	bohn mar-shay
...local-style	*...cuisine régionale*	kwee-zeen ray-zhee-oh-nahl
...untouristy	*...pas touristique*	pah too-ree-steek
...vegetarian	*...végétarien*	vay-zhay-tah-ree-an
...fast food	*...service rapide*	sehr-vees rah-peed
...self-service buffet	*...buffet de libre service*	boo-fay duh lee-bruh sehr-vees
...Chinese	*...chinois*	sheen-wah
with terrace	*avec terrace*	ah-vehk tehr-rahs
with a salad bar	*avec un buffet salade*	ah-vehk uhn boo-fay sah-lahd
with candles	*avec bougies*	ah-vehk boo-zhee
romantic	*romantique*	roh-mahn-teek
moderate price	*prix modéré*	pree moh-day-ray
splurge	*faire une folie*	fair ewn foh-lee
Is it better than McDonald's?	*C'est mieux que Mac Do?*	say mee-uh kuh mahk doh

Restaurants normally serve from 12:00 P.M. to 2:00 P.M., and from 7:00 P.M. until about 10:00 P.M. Cafés are generally open throughout the day. The menu is posted right on the front door or window, and "window shopping" for your meal is a fun, important part of the experience. While the slick self-service restaurants are easy to use, you'll often eat better for the same money in a good family bistro. The inside seating in all French restaurants is now non-smoking.

Getting a Table

At what time does this open / close?	*À quelle heure c'est ouvert / fermé?*	ah kehl ur say oo-vehr / fehr-may
Are you open...?	*Vous êtes ouvert...?*	vooz eht oo-vehr...
...today / tomorrow	*...aujourd'hui / demain*	oh-zhoor-dwee / duh-man
...for lunch / dinner	*...pour déjeuner / dîner*	poor day-zhuh-nay / dee-nay
Are reservations recommended?	*Les réservations sont conseillé?*	lay ray-zehr-vah-see-ohn sohn kohn-seh-yay
I'd like...	*Je voudrais...*	zhuh voo-dray
We'd like...	*Nous voudrions...*	noo voo-dree-ohn
...a table for one / two.	*...une table pour un / deux.*	ewn tah-bluh poor uhn / duh
...to reserve a table for two people...	*...réserver une table pour deux personnes...*	ray-zehr-vay ewn tah-bluh poor duh pehr-suhn
...for today / tomorrow	*...pour aujourd'hui / demain*	poor oh-zhoor-dwee / duh-man
...at 8 P.M.	*...à huit heures du soir*	ah weet ur duh swar
My name is ___.	*Je m'appelle ___.*	zhuh mah-pehl
I have a reservation for ___ people.	*J'ai une réservation pour ___ personnes.*	zhay ewn ray-zehr-vah-see-ohn poor ___ pehr-suhn
I'd like to sit...	*J'aimerais s'asseoir...*	zhehm-uh-ray sah-swar
We'd like to sit...	*Nous aimerions nous asseoir...*	nooz ehm-uh-rohn nooz ah-swar
...inside / outside.	*...à l'intérieur / dehors.*	ah lan-tay-ree-yoor / duh-or
...by the window.	*...à côté de la fenêtre.*	ah koh-tay duh lah fuh-neh-truh
...with a view.	*...avec une vue.*	ah-vehk ewn vew
...where it's quiet.	*...dans un coin tranquille.*	dahnz uhn kwan trahn-keel
Is this table free?	*Cette table est libre?*	seht tah-bluh ay lee-bruh

Can I sit here?	*Je peux s'asseoir ici?*	zhuh puh sah-swar ee-see
Can we sit here?	*Nous pouvons nous asseoir ici?*	noo poo-vohn nooz ah-swar ee-see

Better restaurants routinely take telephone reservations. Guidebooks include phone numbers and the process is simple. If you want to eat at a normal French dinnertime (later than 7:30 P.M.), it's smart to call and reserve a table. Many of my favorite restaurants are filled with Americans at 7:30 P.M. and can feel like tourist traps. But if you drop in at (or reserve ahead for) 8:30 or 9:00 P.M., when the French are eating, the restaurants feel completely local.

The Menu

menu	*carte*	kart
special of the day	*plat du jour*	plah dew zhoor
specialty of the house	*spécialité de la maison*	spay-see-ah-lee-tay duh lah may-zohn
fast service special	*formule rapide*	for-mewl rah-peed
fixed-price meal	*menu, prix fixe*	muh-new, pree feeks
breakfast	*petit déjeuner*	puh-tee day-zhuh-nay
lunch	*déjeuner*	day-zhuh-nay
dinner	*dîner*	dee-nay
appetizers	*hors-d'oeuvre*	or-duh-vruh
sandwiches	*sandwichs*	sahnd-weech
bread	*pain*	pan
salad	*salade*	sah-lahd
soup	*soupe*	soop
first course	*entrée*	ahn-tray
main course	*plat principal*	plah pran-see-pahl
meat	*viande*	vee-ahnd
poultry	*volaille*	voh-lī
fish	*poisson*	pwah-sohn
seafood	*fruits de mer*	frwee duh mehr
children's plate	*assiette d'enfant*	ahs-yeht dahn-fahn

vegetables	*légumes*	lay-gewm
cheese	*fromage*	froh-mahzh
dessert	*dessert*	duh-sehr
munchies	*amuse bouche* ("mouth amusements")	ah-mewz boosh
drink menu	*carte des consommation*	kart day kohn-soh-mah-see-ohn
beverages	*boissons*	bwah-sohn
beer	*bière*	bee-ehr
wine	*vin*	van
service included	*service compris*	sehr-vees kohn-pree
service not included	*service non compris*	sehr-vees nohn kohn-pree
hot / cold	*chaud / froid*	shoh / frwah
with / and / or / without	*avec / et / ou / sans*	ah-vehk / ay / oo / sahn

In France, a menu is a ***carte,*** and a fixed-price meal is a ***menu*** (also called ***menu touristique***). So, if you ask for a ***menu*** (instead of the ***carte***), you'll get this fixed-price meal, which includes your choice of an appetizer, entrée, and dessert for one set price. The ***menu*** is usually a good value, though most locals prefer to order à la carte (from the ***carte,*** what we would call the menu). ***Service compris (s.c.)*** means the tip is included. For a complete culinary language guide, travel with the excellent ***Marling Menu-Master*** for France.

Ordering

waiter	*Monsieur*	muhs-yur
waitress	*Mademoiselle, Madame*	mahd-mwah-zehl, mah-dahm
I'm / We're ready to order.	*Je suis / Nous sommes prêt à commander.*	zhuh swee / noo suhm preh ah koh-mahn-day
I'd like / We'd like...	*Je voudrais / Nous voudrions...*	zhuh voo-dray / noo voo-dree-ohn
...just a drink.	*...une consommation seulement.*	ewn kohn-soh-mah-see-ohn suhl-mahn

...a snack.	*...un snack.*	uhn snahk
...just a salad.	*...qu'une salade.*	kewn sah-lahd
...a half portion.	*...une demi-portion.*	ewn duh-mee-por-see-ohn
...the tourist *menu*. (fixed-price meal)	*...le menu touristique.*	luh muh-new too-ree-steek
...to see the menu.	*...voir la carte.*	vwar lah kart
...to order.	*...commander.*	koh-mahn-day
...to pay.	*...payer.*	pay-yay
...to throw up.	*...vomir.*	voh-meer
Do you have...?	*Avez-vous...?*	ah-vay-voo
...an English menu	*...une carte en anglais*	ewn kart ahn ahn-glay
...a lunch special	*...un plat du jour*	uhn plah dew zhoor
What do you recommend?	*Qu'est-ce que vous recommandez?*	kehs kuh voo ruh-koh-mahn-day
What's your favorite dish?	*Quel est votre plat favori?*	kehl eh voh-truh plah fah-voh-ree
Is it...?	*C'est...?*	say
...good	*...bon*	bohn
...expensive	*...cher*	shehr
...light	*...léger*	lay-zhay
...filling	*...copieux*	kohp-yuh
What is...?	*Qu'est-ce...?*	kehs
...that	*...que c'est*	kuh say
...local	*...que vous avez de la région*	kuh vooz ah-vay duh lah ray-zhee-ohn
...fresh	*...qu'il y a de frais*	keel yah duh fray
...cheap and filling	*...qu'il y a de bon marché et de copieux*	keel yah duh bohn mar-shay ay duh kohp-yuh
...fast (already prepared)	*...qui est déjà préparé*	kee ay day-zhah pray-pah-ray
Can we split this and have an extra plate?	*Nous pouvons partager et avoir une assiette de plus?*	noo poo-vohn par-tah-zhay ay ah-vwar ewn ahs-yeht duh plew
I've changed my mind.	*J'ai changé d'avis.*	zhay shahn-zhay dah-vee

Nothing with eyeballs.	*Rien avec des yeux.*	ree-an ah-vehk dayz yuh
Can I substitute (something) for __?	*Je peux substituer (quelque chose) pour __?*	zhuh puh soob-stee-too-ay (kehl-kuh shohz) poor
Can I / Can we get it "to go"?	*Je peux / Nous pouvons prendre ça "à emporter"?*	zhuh puh / noo poo-vohn prahn-druh sah ah ahn-por-tay
"To go"?	*"À emporter"?*	ah ahn-por-tay

Once you're seated, the table is yours for the entire lunch or dinner period. The waiter or waitress is there to serve you, but only when you're ready. To get his or her attention, simply ask, "***S'il vous plaît?***" ("Please?").

This is the sequence of a typical restaurant experience: The waiter will give you a menu (***carte***) and then ask what you'd like to drink (***Vous voulez quelque choses à boire?***), if you're ready to order (***Vous êtes prets à commander?***) or what you'd like to eat (***Qu'est ce que je vous sers?***), if everything is okay (***Tout va bien?***), if you'd like dessert (***Vous voulez un dessert?***), and if you're finished (***Vous avez terminer?***). You ask for the bill (***L'addition, s'il vous plaît***).

Tableware and Condiments

plate	*assiette*	ahs-yeht
extra plate	*une assiette de plus*	ewn ahs-yeht duh plew
napkin	*serviette*	sehrv-yeht
silverware	*couverts*	koo-vehr
knife	*couteau*	koo-toh
fork	*fourchette*	foor-sheht
spoon	*cuillère*	kwee-yehr
cup	*tasse*	tahs
glass	*verre*	vehr
carafe	*carafe*	kah-rahf
water	*l'eau*	loh
bread	*pain*	pan
butter	*beurre*	bur

Key Phrases: Restaurants

Where's a good restaurant nearby?	*Où se trouve un bon restaurant près d'ici?*	oo suh troov uhn bohn rehs-toh-rahn preh dee-see
I'd like...	*Je voudrais...*	zhuh voo-dray
We'd like...	*Nous voudrions...*	noo voo-dree-ohn
...a table for one / two.	*...une table pour un / deux.*	ewn tah-bluh poor uhn / duh
inside / outside	*a' l'intérieur / dehors*	ah lan-tay-ree-yoor / duh-or
Is this seat free?	*C'est libre?*	say lee-bruh
The menu (in English), please.	*La carte (en anglais), s'il vous plaît.*	lah kart (ahn ahn-glay) see voo play
The bill, please.	*L'addition, s'il vous plaît.*	lah-dee-see-ohn see voo play
Credit card O.K.?	*Carte de crédit O.K.?*	kart duh kray-dee "O.K."

margarine	*margarine*	mar-gah-reen
salt / pepper	*sel / poivre*	sehl / pwah-vruh
sugar	*sucre*	sew-kruh
artificial sweetener	*édulcorant*	ay-dewl-koh-rahn
honey	*miel*	mee-ehl
mustard	*moutarde*	moo-tard
ketchup	*ketchup*	"ketchup"
mayonnaise	*mayonnaise*	mah-yuh-nehz
toothpick	*cure-dent*	kewr-dahn

The Food Arrives

Is it included with the meal?	*C'est inclus avec le repas?*	say an-klew ah-vehk luh ruh-pah
I did not order this.	*Je n'ai pas commandé ça.*	zhuh nay pah koh-mahn-day sah
We did not order this.	*Nous n'avons pas commandé ça.*	noo nah-vohn pah koh-mahn-day sah

Heat this up?	*Vous pouvez réchauffer ça?*	voo poo-vay ray-shoh-fay sah
A little.	*Un peu.*	uhn puh
More. / Another.	*Plus. / Un autre.*	plew / uhn oh-truh
One more please.	*Encore un s'il vous plaît.*	ahn-kor uhn see voo play
The same.	*La même chose.*	lah mehm shohz
Enough.	*Assez.*	ah-say
Finished.	*Terminé.*	tehr-mee-nay

After bringing your meal, your server might wish you a cheery "***Bon appétit!***" (pronounced bohn ah-pay-tee).

Compliments to the Chef

Yummy!	*Miam-miam!*	myahm-myahm
Delicious!	*Délicieux!*	day-lee-see-uh
Magnificent!	*Magnifique!*	mahn-yee-feek
Very tasty!	*Très bon!*	treh bohn
I love French food / this food.	*J'aime la cuisine française / cette cuisine.*	zhehm lah kwee-zeen frahn-sehz / seht kwee-zeen
Better than my mom's cooking.	*Meilleur que la cuisine de ma mère.*	meh-yur kuh lah kwee-zeen duh mah mehr
My compliments to the chef!	*Mes compliments au chef!*	may kohn-plee-mahn oh shehf

Paying for Your Meal

The bill, please.	*L'addition, s'il vous plaît.*	lah-dee-see-ohn see voo play
Together.	*Ensemble.*	ahn-sahn-bluh
Separate checks.	*Notes séparées.*	noht say-pah-ray
Credit card O.K.?	*Carte de crédit O.K.?*	kart duh kray-dee "O.K."
This is not correct.	*Ce n'est pas exact.*	suh nay pah ehg-zahkt
Explain this?	*Expliquez ça?*	ehk-splee-kay sah

Can you explain / itemize the bill?	*Vous pouvez expliquer / détailler cette note?*	voo poo-vay ehk-splee-kay / day-tay-yay seht noht
What if I wash the dishes?	*Et si je lave la vaisselle?*	ay see zhuh lahv lah veh-sehl
Is tipping expected?	*Je dois laisser un pourboire?*	zhuh dwah lay-say uhn poor-bwar
What percent?	*Quel pourcentage?*	kehl poor-sahn-tahzh
tip	*pourboire*	poor-bwar
Keep the change.	*Gardez la monnaie.*	gar-day lah moh-nay
This is for you.	*C'est pour vous.*	say poor voo
May I have a receipt, please?	*Je peux avoir une fiche, s'il vous plaît?*	zhuh puh ah-vwar ewn feesh see voo play

In France, slow service is good service (fast service would rush the diners). Out of courtesy, your waiter will not bring your bill until you ask for it. While a service charge is included in the bill, it's polite to round up for a drink or meal well-served. This bonus tip is usually about 5 percent of the bill (e.g., if your bill is €19, leave €20). When you hand your payment plus a tip to your waiter, you can say, ***"C'est bon"*** (say bohn), meaning, "It's good." If you order your food at a counter, don't tip.

SPECIAL CONCERNS

In a Hurry

I'm / We're in a hurry.	*Je suis / Nous sommes pressé.*	zhuh swee / noo suhm preh-say
I need / We need...	*J'ai besoin / Nous avons besoin...*	zhay buh-swan / nooz ah-vohn buh-swan
...to be served quickly.	*...d'être servi vite.*	deh-truh sehr-vee veet
Is that possible?	*C'est possible?*	say poh-see-bluh
Will the food be ready soon?	*Ce sera prêt bientôt?*	suh suh-rah preh bee-an-toh

If you are in a rush, seek out a brasserie or restaurant that offers *service rapide* (fast food).

Dietary Restrictions

I'm allergic to...	*Je suis allergique à...*	zhuh sweez ah-lehr-zheek ah
I cannot eat...	*Je ne peux pas manger de...*	zhuh nuh puh pah mahn-zhay duh
He / She cannot eat...	*Il / Elle ne peut pas manger de...*	eel / ehl nuh puh pah mahn-zhay duh
...dairy products.	*...produits laitiers.*	proh-dwee lay-tee-yay
...wheat.	*...blé.*	blay
...meat / pork.	*...viande / porc.*	vee-ahnd / por
...salt / sugar.	*...sel / sucre.*	sehl / sew-kruh
...shellfish.	*...crustacés.*	krew-stah-say
...spicy foods.	*...nourriture épicée.*	noo-ree-tewr ay-pee-say
...nuts.	*...noix.*	nwah
I'm a diabetic.	*Je suis diabétique.*	zhuh swee dee-ah-bay-teek
No salt.	*Sans sel.*	sahn sehl
No sugar.	*Sans sucre.*	sahn sew-kruh
No fat.	*Sans matière grasse.*	sahn mah-tee-yehr grahs
Low cholesterol.	*Allégé.*	ah-lay-zhay
No caffeine.	*Décaféiné.*	day-kah-fay-nay
No alcohol.	*Sans alcool.*	sahnz ahl-kohl
I'm a...	*Je suis...*	zhuh swee
...vegetarian. (male)	*...végétarien.*	vay-zhay-tah-ree-an
...vegetarian. (female)	*...végétarienne.*	vay-zhay-tah-ree-ehn
...strict vegetarian.	*...strict végétarien.*	streekt vay-zhay-tah-ree-an
...carnivore.	*...carnivore.*	kar-nee-vor
...big eater.	*...gourmand.*	goor-mahn

Is any meat or animal fat used in this?	*Il y a des produits ou dérivés animaux dans ça?*	eel yah dayz proh-dwee oo day-ree-vay ah-nee-moh dahn sah

Children

Do you have...?	*Vous avez...?*	vooz ah-vay
...a children's portion	*...une assiette enfant*	ewn ahs-yeht ahn-fahn
...a half portion	*...une demi-portion*	ewn duh-mee-por-see-ohn
a high chair / a booster seat	*une chaise enfant / un réhausseur*	oon shehz ahn-fahn / uhn ray-oh-sur
plain noodles / plain rice	*pâtes natures / riz nature*	paht nah-toor / ree nah-toor
with butter	*avec beurre*	ah-vehk bur
no sauce	*pas de sauce*	pah duh sohs
sauce or dressing	*sauce à part*	sohs ah par
Nothing spicy.	*Rien d'épicé.*	ree-an day-pee-say
Not too hot.	*Pas trop chaud.*	pah troh shoh
He will / She will / They will...	*Il va / Elle va / Ils vont...*	eel vah / ehl vah / eel vohn
...share our meal.	*...partager notre repas.*	par-tah-zhay noh-truh ruh-pah
We need our food quickly, please.	*Nous avons besoin de notre repas très vite, s'il vous plaît.*	nooz ah-vohn buh-swan duh noh-truh ruh-pah tray veet see voo play
More napkins, please.	*Des serviettes, s'il vous plaît.*	day sehrv-yeht see voo play
Sorry for the mess.	*Désolé pour le désordre.*	day-zoh-lay poor luh day-zor-druh

WHAT'S COOKING?

Breakfast

breakfast	*petit déjeuner*	puh-tee day-zhuh-nay
bread	*pain*	pan
roll	*petit pain*	puh-tee pan
little loaf of bread	*baguette*	bah-geht
toast	*toast*	"toast"
butter	*beurre*	bur
jelly	*confiture*	kohn-fee-tewr
pastry	*pâtisserie*	pah-tee-suh-ree
croissant	*croissant*	kwah-sahn
cheese	*fromage*	froh-mahzh
yogurt	*yaourt*	yah-oort
cereal	*céréale*	say-ray-ahl
milk	*lait*	lay
hot chocolate	*chocolat chaud*	shoh-koh-lah shoh
fruit juice	*jus de fruit*	zhew duh frwee
orange juice (fresh)	*jus d'orange (pressé)*	zhew doh-rahnzh (preh-say)
coffee / tea	*café / thé*	kah-fay / tay
Is breakfast included?	*Le petit déjeuner est compris?*	luh puh-tee day-zhuh-nay ay kohn-pree

French hotel breakfasts are small, expensive, and often optional. They normally include coffee and a fresh ***croissant*** or ***baguette*** with butter and jelly. You can also save money by breakfasting at a ***bar*** or ***café,*** where it's acceptable to bring a ***croissant*** from the neighboring ***boulangerie*** (bakery). You can get an ***omelette*** almost any time of day at a café.

Snacks and Quick Meals

crêpe	*crêpe*	krehp
buckwheat crêpe	*galette*	gah-leht
quiche...	*quiche...*	keesh

Key Phrases: What's Cooking?

food	*nourriture*	noo-ree-tewr
breakfast	*petit déjeuner*	puh-tee day-zhuh-nay
lunch	*déjeuner*	day-zhuh-nay
dinner	*dîner*	dee-nay
bread	*pain*	pan
cheese	*fromage*	froh-mahzh
soup	*soupe*	soop
salad	*salade*	sah-lahd
meat	*viande*	vee-ahnd
fish	*poisson*	pwah-sohn
fruit	*fruit*	frwee
vegetables	*légumes*	lay-gewm
dessert	*dessert*	duh-sehr
Delicious!	*Délicieux!*	day-lee-see-uh

...with cheese	*...au fromage*	oh froh-mahzh
...with ham	*...au jambon*	oh zhahn-bohn
...with mushrooms	*...aux champignons*	oh shahn-peen-yohn
...with bacon, cheese, and onions	*...lorraine*	lor-rehn
paté	*pâté*	pah-tay
onion tart	*tarte à l'oignon*	tart ah loh-yohn
cheese tart	*tarte au fromage*	tart oh froh-mahzh

Light meals are quick and easy at ***cafés*** and ***bars*** throughout France. A ***salade, crêpe, quiche,*** or ***omelette*** is a fairly cheap way to fill up, even in Paris. Each can be made with various extras like ham, cheese, mushrooms, and so on. ***Crêpes*** come in dinner or dessert varieties.

Sandwiches

I'd like a sandwich.	*Je voudrais un sandwich.*	zhuh voo-dray uhn sahnd-weech
We'd like two sandwiches.	*Nous voudrions deux deux sandwichs.*	noo voo-dree-ohn duh duh sahnd-weech
toasted	*grillé*	gree-yay
toasted ham and cheese sandwich	*croque monsieur*	krohk muhs-yur
toasted ham, cheese, and fried egg sandwich	*croque madame*	krohk mah-dahm
cheese	*fromage*	froh-mahzh
tuna	*thon*	tohn
fish	*poisson*	pwah-sohn
chicken	*poulet*	poo-lay
turkey	*dinde, dindon*	dand, dan-dohn
ham	*jambon*	zhahn-bohn
salami	*salami*	sah-lah-mee
boiled egg	*oeuf à la coque*	uhf ah lah kohk
garnished with veggies	*crudités*	krew-dee-tay
lettuce	*laitue*	lay-too
tomato	*tomate*	toh-maht
onions	*oignons*	oh-yohn
mustard	*moutarde*	moo-tard
mayonnaise	*mayonnaise*	mah-yuh-nehz
peanut butter	*beurre de cacahuètes*	bur duh kah-kah-weet
jelly	*confiture*	kohn-fee-tewr
pork sandwich	*sandwich au porc*	sahnd-weech oh por
Does this come cold or warm?	*C'est servi froid ou chaud?*	say sehr-vee frwah oo shoh
Heated, please.	*Réchauffé, s'il vous plaît.*	ray-shoh-fay see voo play

Sandwiches, as well as small quiches, often come ready-made at ***boulangeries*** (bakeries).

If You Knead Bread

bread	*pain*	pan
thin, long loaf	*baguette*	bah-geht
sweet, soft bun	*brioche*	bree-osh
crescent roll	*croissant*	kwah-sahn
lace-like bread (Riviera)	*fougasse*	foo-gahs
dark-grain bread	*pain bisse, pain de seigle*	pan bees, pan duh seh-gluh
onion and anchovy pizza	*pissaladière*	pees-ah-lah-dee-yehr
cheese pastry	*croûte au fromage*	kroot oh froh-mahzh

Say Cheese

cheese...	*fromage...*	froh-mahzh
...mild	*...doux*	doo
...sharp	*...fort*	for
...goat	*...chèvre*	sheh-vruh
...bleu	*...bleu*	bluh
...with herbs	*...aux herbes*	ohz ehrb
...cream	*...à la crème*	ah lah krehm
...of the region	*...de la région*	duh lah ray-zhee-ohn
Swiss cheese	*gruyère, emmenthal*	grew-yehr, eh-mehn-tahl
Laughing Cow	*La vache qui rit*	lah vahsh kee ree
cheese platter	*le plâteau de fromages*	luh plah-toh duh froh-mahzh
May I taste a little?	*Je peux goûter un peu?*	zhuh puh goo-tay uhn puh

In France, the cheese course is served just before (or instead of) dessert. It not only helps with digestion, it gives you a great opportunity to sample the tasty regional cheeses.

Soups and Salads

soup (of the day)	*soupe (du jour)*	soop (dew zhoor)
broth	*bouillon*	boo-yohn

...chicken	*...de poulet*	duh poo-lay
...beef	*...de boeuf*	duh buhf
...with noodles	*...aux nouilles*	oh noo-ee
...with rice	*...au riz*	oh ree
thick vegetable soup	*potage de légumes*	poh-tahzh duh lay-gewm
Provençal vegetable soup	*soupe au pistou*	soop oh pees-too
onion soup	*soupe à l'oignon*	soop ah lohn-yohn
cream of asparagus soup	*crème d'asperges*	krehm dah-spehrzh
potato and leek soup	*vichyssoise*	vee-shee-swah
shellfish chowder	*bisque*	beesk
seafood stew	*bouillabaisse*	boo-yah-behs
meat and vegetable stew	*pot au feu*	poht oh fuh
salad...	*salade...*	sah-lahd
...green / mixed	*...verte / mixte*	vehrt / meekst
...with goat cheese	*...au chèvre chaud*	oh sheh-vruh shoh
...chef's	*...composée*	kohn-poh-zay
...seafood	*...océane*	oh-shay-ahn
...tuna	*...de thon*	duh tohn
...veggie	*...crudités*	krew-dee-tay
...with ham / cheese / egg	*...avec jambon / fromage / oeuf*	ah-vehk zhahn-bohn / froh-mahzh / uh
lettuce	*laitue*	lay-too
tomatoes	*tomates*	toh-maht
onions	*oignons*	ohn-yohn
cucumber	*concombre*	kohn-kohn-bruh
oil / vinegar	*huile / vinaigre*	weel / vee-nay-gruh
dressing on the side	*sauce à part*	sohs ah par
What is in this salad?	*Qu'est-ce qu'il ya dans cette salade?*	kehs keel yah dahn seht sah-lahd

Salads are usually served with a vinaigrette dressing and often eaten after the main course.

Seafood

seafood	*fruits de mer*	frwee duh mehr
assorted seafood	*assiette de fruits de mer*	ahs-yeht duh frwee duh mehr
fish	*poisson*	pwah-sohn
anchovies	*anchois*	ahn-shwah
clams	*palourdes*	pah-loord
cod	*cabillaud*	kah-bee-yoh
crab	*crabe*	krahb
herring	*hareng*	ah-rahn
lobster	*homard*	oh-mar
mussels	*moules*	mool
oysters	*huîtres*	wee-truh
prawns	*scampi*	skahn-pee
salmon	*saumon*	soh-mohn
salty cod	*morue*	moh-rew
sardines	*sardines*	sar-deen
scallops	*coquilles*	koh-keel
shrimp	*crevettes*	kruh-veht
squid	*calamar*	kahl-mar
trout	*truite*	trweet
tuna	*thon*	tohn
What's fresh today?	*Qu'est-ce frais aujourd'hui?*	kehs kay fray oh-joord-wee
Do you eat this part?	*Ça se mange?*	sah suh mahnzh
Just the head, please.	*Seulement la tête, s'il vous plaît.*	suhl-mahn lah teht see voo play

Poultry

poultry	*volaille*	voh-lī
chicken	*poulet*	poo-lay
duck	*canard*	kah-nar

turkey	*dinde, dindon*	dand, dan-dohn
How long has this been dead?	*Il est mort depuis longtemps?*	eel ay mor duh-pwee lohn-tahn

Meat

meat	*viande*	vee-ahnd
beef	*boeuf*	buhf
flank steak	*faux-filet*	foh-fee-lay
ribsteak	*entrecôte*	ahn-truh-koht
bunny	*lapin*	lah-pan
cutlet	*côtelette*	koh-tuh-leht
frog's legs	*cuisses de grenouilles*	kwees duh greh-noo-ee
ham	*jambon*	zhahn-bohn
lamb	*agneau*	ahn-yoh
meat stew	*ragoût*	rah-goo
mixed grill	*grillades*	gree-yahd
pork	*porc*	por

Avoiding Mis-Steaks

By American standards, the French undercook meats. In France, rare (***saignant***) is nearly raw, medium (***à point***) is rare, and well-done (***bien cuit***) is medium.

tenderloin	*médaillon*	may-dī -yohn
T-bone	*côte de boeuf*	koht duh buhf
tenderloin of T-bone	*tournedos*	toor-nah-doh
alive	*vivant*	vee-vahn
raw	*cru*	krew
very rare	*bleu*	bluh
rare	*saignant*	sayn-yahn
medium	*à point*	ah pwan
well-done	*bien cuit*	bee-an kwee
very well-done	*très bien cuit*	treh bee-an kwee

roast beef — *rosbif* — rohs-beef
sausage — *saucisse* — soh-sees
snails — *escargots* — ehs-kar-goh
steak — *onglet* — ohn-glay
veal — *veau* — voh

How Food is Prepared

assorted — *assiette, variés* — ahs-yeht, vah-ree-ay
baked — *cuit au four* — kweet oh foor
boiled — *bouilli* — boo-yee
braised — *braisé* — breh-zay
cold — *froid* — frwah
cooked — *cuit* — kwee
deep-fried — *frit* — free
fillet — *filet* — fee-lay
fresh — *frais* — fray
fried — *frit* — free
grilled, broiled — *grillé* — gree-yay
homemade — *fait à la maison* — fay ah lah may-zohn
hot — *chaud* — shoh
in cream sauce — *en crème* — ahn krehm
medium — *moyen* — moh-yahn
microwave — *four à micro-ondes* — foor ah mee-kroh-ohnd
mild — *doux* — doo
mixed — *mixte* — meekst
poached — *poché* — poh-shay
rare — *saignant* — sayn-yahn
raw — *cru* — krew
roasted — *rôti* — roh-tee
sautéed — *sauté* — soh-tay
smoked — *fumé* — few-may
sour — *aigre* — ay-gruh
spicy hot — *piquant* — pee-kahn
steamed — *à la vapeur* — ah lah vah-pur
stuffed — *farci* — far-see
sweet — *doux* — doo

topped with cheese	*gratinée*	grah-tee-nay
well-done	*bien cuit*	bee-an kwee
with rice	*avec du riz*	ah-vehk dew ree

Veggies

vegetables	*légumes*	lay-gewm
mixed vegetables	*légumes variés*	lay-gewm vah-ree-ay
with vegetables	*garni*	gar-nee
artichoke	*artichaut*	ar-tee-shoh
asparagus	*asperges*	ah-spehrzh
beans	*haricots*	ah-ree-koh
beets	*betterave*	beh-teh-rahv
broccoli	*brocoli*	broh-koh-lee
cabbage	*chou*	shoo
carrots	*carottes*	kah-roht
cauliflower	*chou-fleur*	shoo-flur
corn	*maïs*	mah-ees
cucumber	*concombre*	kohn-kohn-bruh
eggplant	*aubergine*	oh-behr-zheen
garlic	*ail*	ah-ee
green beans	*haricots verts*	ah-ree-koh vehr
leeks	*poireaux*	pwah-roh
lentils	*lentilles*	lahn-teel
mushrooms	*champignons*	shahn-peen-yohn
olives	*olives*	oh-leev
onions	*oignons*	ohn-yohn
peas	*pois*	pwah
pepper...	*poivron...*	pwah-vrohn
...green / red / yellow	*...vert / rouge / jaune*	vehr / roozh / zhohn
pickles	*cornichons*	kor-nee-shohn
potato	*pomme de terre*	pohm duh tehr
radish	*radis*	rah-dee
rice	*riz*	ree
spaghetti	*spaghetti*	"spaghetti"
spinach	*épinards*	ay-pee-nar

tomatoes	*tomates*	toh-maht
truffles	*truffes*	trewf
zucchini	*courgette*	koor-zheht

Fruits

apple	*pomme*	pohm
apricot	*abricot*	ah-bree-koh
banana	*banane*	bah-nahn
berries	*baies*	bay
cherry	*cerise*	suh-reez
date	*datte*	daht
fig	*figue*	feeg
fruit	*fruit*	frwee
grapefruit	*pamplemousse*	pahn-pluh-moos
grapes	*raisins*	ray-zan
lemon	*citron*	see-trohn
melon	*melon*	muh-lohn
orange	*orange*	oh-rahnzh
peach	*pêche*	pehsh
pear	*poire*	pwar
pineapple	*ananas*	ah-nah-nah
plum	*prune*	prewn
prune	*pruneau*	prew-noh
raspberry	*framboise*	frahn-bwahz
strawberry	*fraise*	frehz
tangerine	*mandarine*	mahn-dah-reen
watermelon	*pastèque*	pah-stehk

Nuts

almond	*amande*	ah-mahnd
chestnut	*marron, chataîgne*	mah-rohn, shah-tayn
coconut	*noix de coco*	nwah duh koh-koh
hazelnut	*noisette*	nwah-zeht
peanut	*cacahuète*	kah-kah-weet
pistachio	*pistache*	pee-stahsh
walnut	*noix*	nwah

Just Desserts

dessert	*dessert*	duh-sehr
cake	*gâteau*	gah-toh
fruit cup	*salade de fruits*	sah-lahd duh frwee
tart	*tartelette*	tar-tuh-leht
pie	*tarte*	tart
whipped cream	*crème chantilly*	krehm shahn-tee-yee
pastry	*pâtisserie*	pah-tee-suh-ree
fruit pastry	*chausson*	shoh-sohn
chocolate-filled pastry	*pain au chocolat*	pan oh shoh-koh-lah
buttery cake	*madeleine*	mah-duh-lehn
crêpes	*crêpes*	krehp
sweet crêpes	*crêpes sucrées*	krehp sew-kray
cookies	*petits gâteaux*	puh-tee gah-toh
candy	*bonbon*	bohn-bohn
low calorie	*bas en calories*	bah ahn kah-loh-ree
homemade	*fait à la maison*	fay ah lah may-zohn
We'll split one.	*Nous le partageons.*	noo luh par-tah-zhohn
Two forks / spoons, please.	*Deux fourchettes / cuillères, s'il vous plaît.*	duh foor-sheht / kwee-yehr see voo play
I shouldn't, but...	*Je ne devrais pas, mais...*	zhuh nuh duh-vray pah may
Magnificent!	*Magnifique!*	mahn-yee-feek
It's heavenly!	*C'est divin!*	say dee-van
Death by pleasure.	*C'est à mourrir de plaisir.*	say ah moo-reer duh play-zeer
Orgasmic.	*Orgasmique.*	or-gahz-meek
A moment on the lips, forever on the hips.	*Un moment sur les lèvres et pour toujours sur les hanches.*	uhn moh-mahn sewr lay lehv-ruh ay poor too-zhoor sewr lay ahnsh

Ice Cream

ice cream...	*glace...*	glahs
...scoop	*...boule*	bool

...cone	*...cornet*	kor-nay
...cup	*...bol*	bohl
...vanilla	*...vanille*	vah-nee
...chocolate	*...chocolat*	shoh-koh-lah
...strawberry	*...fraise*	frehz
sherbet	*sorbet*	sor-bay

DRINKING

Water, Milk, and Juice

mineral water...	*eau minérale...*	oh mee-nay-rahl
...carbonated	*...gazeuse*	gah-zuhz
...not carbonated	*...non gazeuse*	nohn gah-zuhz
tap water	*l'eau du robinet*	loh dew roh-bee-nay
whole milk	*lait entier*	lay ahnt-yay
skim milk	*lait écrémé*	lay ay-kray-may
fresh milk	*lait frais*	lay fray
chocolate milk	*lait au chocolat*	lay oh shoh-koh-lah
hot chocolate	*chocolat chaud*	shoh-koh-lah shoh
fruit juice	*jus de fruit*	zhew duh frwee
100% juice	*cent pour cent jus*	sahn poor sahn zhew
orange juice	*jus d'orange*	zhew doh-rahnzh
freshly squeezed	*pressé*	preh-say
apple juice	*jus de pomme*	zhew duh pohm
grapefruit juice	*jus de pamplemousse*	zhew duh pahn-pluh-moos
iced tea	*thé glacé*	tay glah-say
with / without...	*avec / sans...*	ah-vehk / sahn
...sugar	*...sucre*	sew-kruh
...ice	*...glaçons*	glah-sohn
glass / cup	*verre / tasse*	vehr / tahs
small / large	*petite / grande*	puh-teet / grahnd
bottle	*bouteille*	boo-teh-ee
Is the water safe to drink?	*L'eau est potable?*	loh ay poh-tah-bluh

To get free tap water at a restaurant, say, "***L'eau du robinet, s'il vous plaît.***" The French typically order mineral water (and wine) with their meals. The half-liter plastic water bottles with screw tops are light and sturdy—great to pack along and re-use as you travel.

Coffee and Tea

coffee...	*café...*	kah-fay
...black	*...noir*	nwar
...with milk	*...crème*	krehm
...with lots of milk	*...au lait*	oh lay
...American-style	*...américain*	ah-may-ree-kan
espresso	*express*	"express"
espresso with a touch of brandy	*café-calva*	kah-fay-kahl-vah
espresso with a touch of milk	*noisette*	nwah-zeht
instant coffee	*Nescafé*	"Nescafé"
decaffeinated / decaf	*décaféiné / déca*	day-kah-fay-nay / day-kah
sugar	*sucre*	sew-kruh
hot water	*l'eau chaude*	loh shohd
tea / lemon	*thé / citron*	tay / see-trohn
tea bag	*sachet de thé*	sah-shay duh tay
herbal tea	*tisane*	tee-zahn
lemon tea / orange tea	*thé au citron / thé à l'orange*	tay oh see-trohn / tay ah loh-rahnzh
peppermint tea / fruit tea	*thé à la menthe / thé de fruit*	tay ah lah mehnt / tay duh frwee
small / big	*petit / grand*	puh-tee / grahn
Another cup.	*Encore une tasse.*	ahn-kor ewn tahs
Is it the same price if I sit or stand?	*C'est le même prix au bar ou dans la salle?*	say luh mehm pree oh bar oo dahn lah sahl

EATING

Every ***café*** or ***bar*** has a complete price list posted. In bigger cities, prices go up when you sit down. It's cheapest to stand at the bar (***au bar*** or ***au comptoir***), more expensive to sit in the dining room (*la salle*), and most expensive to sit outside (*la terrasse*). Refills aren't free.

Wine

I would like...	*Je voudrais...*	zhuh voo-dray
We would like...	*Nous voudrions...*	noo voo-dree-oh<u>n</u>
...a glass...	*...un verre...*	uh<u>n</u> vehr
...a carafe...	*...une carafe...*	ewn kah-rahf
...a half bottle...	*...une demi-bouteille...*	ewn duh-mee-boo-teh-ee
...a bottle...	*...une bouteille...*	ewn boo-teh-ee
...a 5-liter jug...	*...un bidon de cinq litres...*	uh<u>n</u> bee-doh<u>n</u> duh sa<u>n</u>k lee-truh
...a barrel...	*...un tonneau...*	uh<u>n</u> toh-noh
...a vat...	*...un fût...*	uh<u>n</u> foewt
...of red wine...	*...de vin rouge...*	duh va<u>n</u> roozh
...of white wine...	*...de vin blanc...*	duh va<u>n</u> blah<u>n</u>
...of the region.	*...de la région.*	duh lah ray-zhee-oh<u>n</u>
...the wine list.	*...la carte des vins.*	lah kart day va<u>n</u>

In France, wine is a work of art. Each wine-growing region and vintage has its own distinct personality. I prefer drinking wine from the region I'm in. Ask for ***vin de la région***, available at reasonable prices. As you travel, look for the ***dégustation*** signs welcoming you in for a tasting. It's normally free or very cheap. To get a decent table wine in a region that doesn't produce wine (Normandy, Brittany, Paris / Ile de France), ask for ***un Côtes du Rhône.***

Wine Words

wine	*vin*	va<u>n</u>
table wine	*vin de table*	va<u>n</u> duh tah-bluh
house wine (cheapest)	*vin ordinaire*	va<u>n</u> or-dee-nair
local	*du coin*	dew kwa<u>n</u>
of the region	*de la région*	duh lah ray-zhee-oh<u>n</u>
red	*rouge*	roozh

white	*blanc*	blahn
rosé	*rosé*	roh-zay
sparkling	*mousseux*	moo-suh
sweet	*doux*	doo
semi-dry	*demi-sec*	duh-mee-sehk
dry	*sec*	sehk
very dry	*brut*	brewt
full-bodied	*robuste*	roh-boost
fruity	*fruité*	frwee-tay
light	*léger*	lay-zhay
mature	*prêt à boire*	preh ah bwar
cork	*bouchon*	boo-shohn
corkscrew	*tire-bouchon*	teer-boo-shohn
vineyard	*vignoble*	veen-yoh-bluh
harvest	*vendange*	vahn-dahnzh
What is a good vintage?	*Quelles est un bon millésime?*	kehl ay uhn bohn mee-lay-zeem
What do you recommend?	*Qu'est-ce que vous recommandez?*	kehs kuh voo ruh-koh-mahn-day

Wine Labels

The information on a French wine label can give you a lot of details about the wine. Listed below are several terms to help you identify and choose a specific wine.

AOC (appellation d'origine contrôlée)	a wine that meets nationwide laws for production of the highest-quality French wines
VDQS (vin délimité de qualité supérieure)	quality standards for specific regional wines
vin de pays	local wine (medium quality)
vin de table	table wine (quality varies)
millésime	vintage
mis en bouteilles dans nos caves	bottled in our cellars
cru	superior growth
cépage	grape variety

Beer

beer	*bière*	bee-ehr
from the tap	*pression*	preh-see-ohn
bottle	*bouteille*	boo-teh-ee
light / dark	*blonde / brune*	blohnd / brewn
local / imported	*régionale / importée*	ray-zhee-oh-nahl / an-por-tay
a small beer	*un demi*	uhn duh-mee
a large beer	*une chope*	ewn shohp
low-calorie beer (hard to find)	*biere "light"*	bee-ehr "light"
alcohol-free	*sans alcool*	sahnz ahl-kohl
hard apple cider	*cidre*	see-druh
cold	*fraîche*	fraysh
colder	*plus fraîche*	plew fraysh

Bar Talk

Would you like to to go out for a drink?	*Voulez-vous prendre un verre?*	voo-lay-vooz prahn-druh uhn vehr
I'll buy you a drink.	*Je vous offre un verre.*	zhuh voo oh-fruh uhn vehr
It's on me.	*C'est moi qui paie.*	say mwah kee pay
The next one's on me.	*Le suivant est sur moi.*	luh see-vahn tay sewr mwhah
What would you like?	*Qu'est-ce que vous prenez?*	kehs kuh voo pruh-nay
I'll have a...	*Je prends un...*	zhuh prahn uhn
I don't drink alcohol.	*Je ne bois pas d'alcool.*	zhuh nuh bwah pah dahl-kohl
alcohol-free	*sans alcool*	sahnz ahl-kohl
What is the local specialty?	*Quelle est la spécialité régionale?*	kehl ay lah spay-see-ah-lee-tay ray-zhee-oh-nahl

Key Phrases: Drinking

drink	*verre*	vehr
(mineral) water	*eau (minérale)*	oh (mee-nay-rahl)
tap water	*l'eau du robinet*	loh dew roh-bee-nay
milk	*lait*	lay
juice	*jus*	zhew
coffee	*café*	kah-fay
tea	*thé*	tay
wine	*vin*	van
beer	*bière*	bee-ehr
Cheers!	*Santé!*	sahn-tay

What is a good drink for a man / a woman?	*Quelle est une bonne boisson pour un homme / une dame?*	kehl ay ewn buhn bwah-sohn poor uhn ohm / ewn dahm
Straight.	*Sec.*	sehk
With / Without...	*Avec / Sans...*	ah-vehk / sahn
...alcohol.	*...alcool.*	ahl-kohl
...ice.	*...glaçons.*	glah-sohn
One more.	*Encore une.*	ahn-kor ewn
Cheers!	*Santé!*	sahn-tay
To your health!	*À votre santé!*	ah voh-truh sahn-tay
Long live France!	*Vive la France!*	veev lah frahns
I'm feeling...	*Je me sens...*	zhuh muh sahn
...tipsy.	*...éméché.*	ay-may-shay
...a little drunk.	*...un peu ivre.*	uhn puh ee-vruh
...wasted. (m / f)	*...ivre mort / ivre morte.*	ee-vruh mor / ee-vruh mort
I'm hung over.	*J'ai la gueule de bois.*	zhay lah guhl duh bwah

PICNICKING

At the Grocery

Is it self-service?	*C'est libre service?*	say lee-bruh sehr-vees
Ripe for today?	*Pour manger aujourd'hui?*	poor mahn-zhay oh-joord-wee
Does it need to be cooked?	*Il faut le faire cuire?*	eel foh luh fair kweer
Can I taste it?	*Je peux goûter?*	zhuh puh goo-tay
Fifty grams.	*Cinquante grammes.*	san-kahnt grahm
One hundred grams.	*Cent grammes.*	sahn grahm
More. / Less.	*Plus. / Moins.*	plew / mwan
A piece.	*Un morceau.*	uhn mor-soh
A slice.	*Une tranche.*	ewn trahnsh
Four slices.	*Quatre tranches.*	kah-truh trahnsh
Sliced.	*Tranché.*	trahn-shay
Half.	*La moitié.*	lah mwaht-yay
A few.	*Quelques.*	kehl-kuh
A handful.	*Une poignée.*	ewn pwahn-yay
A small bag.	*Un petit sachet.*	uhn puh-tee sah-shay
A bag, please.	*Un sachet, s'il vous plaît.*	uhn sah-shay see voo play
Can you make me...?	*Vous pouvez me faire...?*	voo poo-vay muh fair
Can you make us...?	*Vous pouvez nous faire...?*	voo poo-vay noo fair
...a sandwich	*...un sandwich*	uhn sahnd-weech
...two sandwiches	*...deux sandwichs*	duh sahnd-weech
To take out.	*Pour emporter.*	poor ahn-por-tay
Can I / Can we use...?	*Je peux / Nous pouvons utiliser...?*	zhuh puh / noo poo-vohn oo-tee-lee-zay
...the microwave	*...le micro-onde*	luh mee-kroh-ohnd
May I borrow a...?	*Je peux emprunter...?*	zhuh puh ahn-pruhn-tay

Do you have a...?	*Vous avez...?*	vooz ah-vay
Where can I buy / find a...?	*Où puis-je acheter / trouver un...?*	oo pwee-zhuh ah-shuh-tay / troo-vay uhn
...corkscrew	*...tire-bouchon*	teer-boo-shohn
...can opener	*...ouvre boîte*	oo-vruh bwaht
Where is a good place to picnic?	*Il y a un coin sympa pour pique-niquer?*	eel yah uhn kwan sahn-pah poor peek-nee-kay
Is there a park nearby?	*Il y a un parc près d'ici?*	eel yah uhn park preh dee-see
Is picnicking allowed here?	*On peut pique-niquer ici?*	ohn puh peek-nee-kay ee-see

Ask if there's a ***marché*** (open air market) nearby. These lively markets offer the best selection and ambience.

Tasty Picnic Words

open air market	*marché*	mar-shay
grocery store	*épicerie*	ay-pee-suh-ree
supermarket	*supermarché*	sew-pehr-mar-shay
super-duper market	*hypermarché*	ee-pehr-mar-shay
delicatessen	*charcuterie-traiteur*	shar-koo-tuh-ree-tray-tur
bakery	*boulangerie*	boo-lahn-zhuh-ree
pastry shop	*pâtisserie*	pah-tee-suh-ree
sweets shop	*confiserie*	kohn-fee-suh-ree
cheese shop	*fromagerie*	froh-mah-zhuh-ree
picnic	*pique-nique*	peek-neek
sandwich	*sandwich*	sahnd-weech
bread	*pain*	pan
roll	*petit pain*	puh-tee pan
ham	*jambon*	zhahn-bohn
sausage	*saucisse*	soh-sees

cheese	*fromage*	froh-mahzh
mustard...	*moutarde...*	moo-tard
mayonnaise...	*mayonnaise...*	mah-yuh-nehz
...in a tube	*...en tube*	ahn tewb
yogurt	*yaourt*	yah-oort
fruit	*fruit*	frwee
juice	*jus*	zhew
cold drinks	*boissons fraîches*	bwah-sohn frehsh
straw(s)	*paille(s)*	pah-yee
spoon / fork...	*cuillère / fourchette...*	kwee-yehr / foor-sheht
...made of plastic	*...en plastique*	ahn plah-steek
cup / plate...	*gobelet / assiette...*	gob-leh / ahs-yeht
...made of paper	*...en papier*	ahn pahp-yay

For convenience, you can assemble your picnic at a ***supermarché*** (supermarket)—but smaller shops or a ***marché*** (open-air market) are more fun. Get bread for your sandwich at a ***boulangerie*** and order meat and cheese by the gram at an ***épicerie.*** One hundred grams is about a quarter pound, enough for two sandwiches. To weigh and price your produce at more modern stores, put it on the scale, push the photo or number (keyed to the bin it came from), and then stick your sticker on the food. To get real juice, look for ***100%*** or ***sans sucre*** on the label.

MENU DECODER

FRENCH/ENGLISH

This handy decoder won't list every word on the menu, but it'll help you get ***riz et veau*** (rice and veal) instead of ***ris de veau*** (calf pancreas).

à l'anglaise	boiled
à la carte	side dishes
à la vapeur	steamed
à point	medium (meat)
abricot	apricot
agneau	lamb
ail	garlic
aïoli	garlic mayonnaise
alcool	alcohol
amande	almond
amuse bouche	munchies
ananas	pineapple
anchois	anchovies
artichaut	artichoke
asperges	asparagus
assiette	plate
assiette d'enfant	children's plate
au jus	in its natural juices

auberge	country inn
aubergine	eggplant
avec	with
baguette	long loaf of bread
baies	berries
banane	banana
Béarnaise	sauce of egg and wine
beignets	fritters with fruit
betterave	beets
beurre	butter
beurre blanc	sauce of butter, white wine, and shallots
beurre de cacahuètes	peanut butter
bien cuit	well-done (meat)
bière	beer
bifteck	steak
biologique	organic
bisque	shellfish chowder
bistro	small, informal restaurant
blanc	white
bleu	blue (cheese); very rare (meat)
blonde	light (beer)
boeuf	beef
boissons	beverages
bon	good
bonbon	candy
bouchée à la reine	pastry shell with creamed sweetbreads
bouillabaisse	seafood stew
bouilli	boiled
bouillon	broth
boulangerie	bakery
boule	scoop
Bourguignon	cooked in red wine
bouteille	bottle
braisé	braised
brasserie	large café with simple food
brioche	sweet, flaky roll
brocoli	broccoli

brouillés	scrambled
brune	dark (beer)
brut	very dry (wine)
cabillaud	cod
cacahuète	peanut
café	coffee
café américain	American-style coffee
café au lait	coffee with lots of milk
café crème	coffee with milk
café noir	black coffee
café-calva	espresso with a touch of brandy
calamar	squid
canard	duck
carottes	carrots
carte	menu
carte des consommation	drink menu
carte des vins	wine list
cassoulet	bean and meat stew
cerise	cherry
cervelle	brains
champignons	mushrooms
charcuterie	delicatessen
chataîgne	chestnut
chaud	hot
chausson	fruit pastry
cheval	horse
chèvre	goat
chinois	Chinese
chocolat	chocolate
chope	large beer
chorizo	pepperoni
chou	cabbage
chou-fleur	cauliflower
cidre	hard apple cider
citron	lemon
complet	whole; full
compris	included

concombre	cucumber
confiserie	sweets shop
confit	cooked in its own fat
confiture	jelly
consommé	broth
copieux	filling
coq	rooster
coquilles	scallops
cornichon	pickle
costaud	full-bodied (wine)
côte de boeuf	T-bone
côtelette	cutlet
courgette	zucchini
couvert	cover charge
crabe	crab
crème	cream
crème (velouté) d'asperges	cream of asparagus soup
crème brulée	caramelized custard
crème caramel	custard with caramel sauce
crème chantilly	whipped cream
crêpe	crêpe
crêpes froment	buckwheat crêpes
crêpes sucrées	sweet crêpes
crêpes suzette	crêpes flambéed with orange brandy sauce
crevettes	shrimp
croissant	crescent roll
croque madame	ham, cheese, and egg sandwich
croque monsieur	ham and cheese sandwich
croûte au fromage	cheese pastry
cru	raw
crudités	raw vegetables
cuisses de grenouilles	frog legs
cuit	cooked
cuit au four	baked
cure-dent	toothpick
datte	date
déjeuner	lunch

demi	half; small beer
demi-bouteille	half bottle
demi-sec	semi-dry (wine)
dinde	turkey
dîner	dinner
doux	mild, sweet (wine)
eau	water
édulcorant	artificial sweetener
emmenthal	Swiss cheese
entier	whole
entrecôte	rib steak
entrée	first course
épicée	spicy
épinards	spinach
escargots	snails
et	and
express	espresso
fait à la maison	homemade
farci	stuffed
faux-filet	flank steak
figue	fig
filet	fillet
fines herbes	chopped fresh herbs
flambée	flaming
foie	liver
forestière	with mushrooms
fort	sharp (cheese)
fougasse	lace-like bread
frais	fresh
fraise	strawberry
framboise	raspberry
frit	fried
froid	cold
fromage	cheese
fromage à la crème	cream cheese
fromage aux herbes	cheese with herbs
fromage blanc	fresh white cheese eaten with sugar

fromage bleu	bleu cheese
fromage chèvre	goat cheese
fromage de la région	cheese of the region
fromage doux	mild cheese
fromage fort	sharp cheese
fromagerie	cheese shop
froment	wheat
fruit	fruit
fruité	fruity (wine)
fruits de mer	seafood
fumé	smoked
galette	buckwheat crêpe
garni	with vegetables
gâteau	cake
gazeuse	carbonated
glace	ice cream
glaçons	ice
grand	large
gras	fat
gratinée	topped with cheese
grenouille	frog
grillades	mixed grill
grillé	grilled
gruyère	Swiss cheese
hareng	herring
haricots	beans
Hollandaise	sauce of egg and butter
homard	lobster
hors d'oeuvre	appetizers
huile	oil
huîtres	oysters
île flottante	meringues floating in cream sauce
importée	imported
jambon	ham
jardinière	with vegetables
jus	juice
kasher	kosher

La vache qui rit	Laughing Cow (brand of cheese)
lait	milk
laitue	lettuce
langue	tongue
lapin	rabbit
léger	light (not heavy)
légumes	vegetables
lentilles	lentils
light	light (low calorie)
madeleine	buttery cake
maïs	corn
maison	house
mandarine	tangerine
marron	chestnut
médaillon	tenderloin
melon	canteloupe
menu du jour	menu of the day
meunière	fried in butter
micro-onde	microwave
miel	honey
mille feuille	light pastry
millésime	vintage date (wine)
mixte	mixed
morceau	piece
mornay	white sauce with gruyère
morue	salty cod
moules	mussels
mousseux	sparkling
moutarde	mustard
Nescafé	instant coffee
noir	black
noisette	hazelnut
noix	walnut
noix de coco	coconut
Normande	cream sauce
nouvelle	new
oeufs	eggs

oeufs à la coque (mollet / dur)	boiled eggs (soft / hard)
oeufs au plat	fried eggs
oeufs brouillés	scrambled eggs
oignon	onion
olives	olives
onglet	steak
ou	or
pain	bread
pain bisse	dark-grain bread
pain complet	whole-grain bread
pain de seigle	dark bread
palourdes	clams
pamplemousse	grapefruit
pas	not
pastèque	watermelon
pâtes	pasta
pâtisserie	pastry; pastry shop
pêche	peach
petit	small
petit déjeuner	breakfast
petits gâteaux	cookies
petits pois	peas
piquant	spicy hot
pissaladière	onion and anchovy pizza
pistache	pistachio
plat du jour	special of the day
plat principal	main course
plâteau	platter
plâteau de fromages	cheese platter
poché	poached
poire	pear
poireaux	leeks
poires au vin rouge	pears poached in red wine and spices
pois	peas
poisson	fish
poivre	pepper

poivron	bell pepper
pomme	apple
pomme de terre	potato
pommes frites	French fries
porc	pork
potage	soup
potage de légumes	thick vegetable soup
poulet	chicken
pour emporter	to go
pression	draft (beer)
prix fixe	fixed price
profitterole	cream puff with ice cream
Provençale	with garlic and tomatoes
prune	plum
pruneau	prune
quenelles	meat or fish dumplings
quiche	quiche
quiche au fromage	quiche with cheese
quiche au jambon	quiche with ham
quiche aux champignons	quiche with mushrooms
quiche lorraine	quiche with bacon, cheese, and onions
radis	radish
ragoût	meat stew
raisins	grapes
ratatouille	eggplant casserole
régionale	local
rillettes	cold, minced pork
ris de veau	sweetbreads
riz	rice
robuste	full-bodied (wine)
rosbif	roast beef
rosé	rosé (wine)
rôti	roasted
rouge	red
routier	truck stop with simple food
saignant	rare (meat)
salade	salad

sans	without
saucisse	sausage
saucisse-frites	hot dog and fries
saumon	salmon
scampi	prawns
sec	dry
sel	salt
service compris	service included
service non compris	service not included
sorbet	sherbet
soufflé	soufflé (light, fluffy eggs baked with savory fillings)
soufflé au chocolat	chocolate soufflé
soupe	soup
soupe à l'oignon	onion soup
soupe au pistou	Provençal vegetable soup
spécialité	specialty
steak tartare	raw hamburger
sucre	sugar
tapenade	olive, anchovy paste
tartare	raw
tarte	pie
tarte à l'oignon	onion tart
tarte au fromage	cheese tart
tarte tatin	upside-down apple pie
tartelette	tart
tasse	cup
terrine	pâté
thé	tea
thon	tuna
tire-bouchon	corkscrew
tisane	herbal tea
tournedos	tenderloin of T-bone
tourteau fromager	goat-cheese cake
tranche	slice
tranché	sliced
très bien cuit	very well-done (meat)

tripes	tripe
truffes	truffles (earthy mushrooms)
truite	trout
vapeur	steamed
variés	assorted
veau	veal
végétarien	vegetarian
vendange	harvest (wine)
verre	glass
vert	green
viande	meat
vichyssoise	potato, leek soup
vignoble	vineyard
vin	wine
vin de table	table wine
vin ordinaire	house wine
vinaigre	vinegar
volaille	poultry
yaourt	yogurt

ACTIVITIES

SIGHTSEEING

Where?

Where is...?	*Où est...?*	oo ay
...the tourist information office	*...l'office du tourisme*	loh-fees dew too-reez-muh
...the best view	*...la meilleure vue*	lah meh-yur vew
...the main square	*...la place principale*	lah plahs pran-see-pahl
...the old town center	*...la vieille ville*	lah vee-yay-ee veel
...the museum	*...le musée*	luh mew-zay
...the castle	*...le château*	luh shah-toh
...the palace	*...le palais*	luh pah-lay
...an amusement park	*...un parc d'amusement*	uhn park dah-mooz-mahn
...the entrance / exit	*...l'entrée / la sortie*	lahn-tray / lah sor-tee
Where are...?	*Où sont...?*	oo sohn
...the toilets	*...les toilettes*	lay twah-leht
...the ruins	*...les ruines*	lay rween
Is there a festival nearby?	*Il y a un festival dans la région?*	eel yah uhn fehs-tee-vahl dahn lah ray-zhee-ohn

At the Sight

Do you have...?	*Vous avez...?*	vooz ah-vay

Key Phrases: Sightseeing

Where is...?	*Où est...?*	oo ay
How much is it?	*C'est combien?*	say kohn-bee-an
At what time does this open / close?	*À quelle heuere c'est ouvert / fermé?*	ah kehl ur say oo-vehr / fehr-may
Do you have a guided tour?	*Vous avez une visite guidée?*	vooz ah-vay ewn vee-zeet gee-day
When is the next tour in English?	*La prochaine visite en anglais est à quelle heure?*	lah proh-shehn vee-zeet ahn ahn-glay ay ah kehl ur

...information...	*...des renseignements...*	day rahn-sehn-yuh-mahn
...a guidebook...	*...un guide...*	uhn geed
...in English	*...en anglais*	ahn ahn-glay
Is it free?	*C'est gratuit?*	say grah-twee
How much is it?	*C'est combien?*	say kohn-bee-an
Is the ticket good all day?	*Le billet est valable toute la journée?*	luh bee-yay ay vah-lah-bluh toot lah zhoor-nay
Can I get back in?	*Je peux rentrer?*	zhuh puh rahn-tray
At what time does this open / close?	*À quelle heuere c'est ouvert / fermé?*	ah kehl ur say oo-vehr / fehr-may
What time is the last entry?	*La dernière entrée est à quelle heure?*	lah dehrn-yehr ahn-tray ay ah kehl ur

Please

PLEASE let me in.	*S'IL VOUS PLAÎT, laissez-moi entrer.*	see voo play lay-say-mwah ahn-tray
PLEASE let us in.	*S'IL VOUS PLAÎT, laissez-nous entrer.*	see voo play lay-say-nooz ahn-tray
I've traveled all the way from ___.	*Je suis venu de ___.*	zhuh swee vuh-new duh
We've traveled all the way from ___.	*Nous sommes venus de ___.*	noo suhm vuh-new duh

I must leave tomorrow.	*Je dois partir demain.*	zhuh dwah par-teer duh-man
We must leave tomorrow.	*Nous devons partir demain.*	noo duh-vohn par-teer duh-man
I promise I'll be fast.	*Je promets d'aller vite.*	zhuh proh-may dah-lay veet
We promise we'll be fast.	*Nous promettons d'aller vite.*	noo proh-meh-tohn dah-lay veet
It was my mother's dying wish that I see this.	*C'était le dernier souhait de ma mère que je voies ça.*	say-tay luh dehrn-yay soo-ay duh mah mehr kuh zhuh vwah sah
I've always wanted to see this.	*J'ai toujours voulu voir ça.*	zhay too-zhoor voo-lew vwar sah

Tours

Do you have...?	*Vous avez...?*	vooz ah-vay
...an audioguide	*...un guide audio*	uhn geed oh-dee-oh
...a guided tour	*...une visite guidée*	ewn vee-zeet gee-day
...a city walking tour	*...une promenade guidée de la ville*	ewn proh-muh-nahd gee-day duh lah veel
...in English	*...en anglais*	ahn ahn-glay
When is the next tour in English?	*La prochaine visite en anglais est à quelle heure?*	lah proh-shehn vee-zeet ahn ahn-glay ay ah kehl ur
Is it free?	*C'est gratuit?*	say grah-twee
How much is it?	*C'est combien?*	say kohn-bee-an
How long does it last?	*Ça dure combien de temps?*	sah door kohn-bee-an duh tahn
Can I / Can we join a tour in progress?	*Je peux / Nous pouvons joindre une visite qui a commencé?*	zhuh puh / noo poo-vohn zhwahn-druh ewn vee-zeet kee ah koh-mahn-say

Entrance Signs

adultes	the price you'll pay
dernière entrée	last admission before sight closes

exposition	special exhibit
ticket global	combination ticket with another sight
visite guidée	guided tour
vous êtes ici	you are here (on map)

Discounts

You may be eligible for a discount at tourist sights, hotels, or on buses and trains—ask.

Is there a discount for...?	*Il y a une réduction pour...?*	eel yah ewn ray-dewk-see-ohn poor
...youth	*...les jeunes*	lay juh-nehs
...students	*...les étudiants*	layz ay-tew-dee-ahn
...families	*...les familles*	lay fah-meel
...seniors	*...les gens âgés*	lay zhahn ah-zhay
...groups	*...les groupes*	lay groop
I am...	*J'ai...*	zhay
He / She is...	*Il / Elle a...*	eel / ehl ah
...___ years old.	*...___ ans.*	___ ahn
...extremely old.	*...très âgé.*	treh ah-zhay

In the Museum

Where is...?	*Où est...?*	oo ay
I'd like to see...	*Je voudrais voir...*	zhuh voo-dray vwar
We'd like to see...	*Nous voudrions voir...*	noo voo-dree-ohn vwar
Photo / Video O.K.?	*Photo / Vidéo O.K.?*	foh-toh / vee-day-oh "O.K."
No flash / tripod.	*Pas de flash / trépied.*	pah duh flahsh / tray-pee-yay
I like it.	*Ça me plaît.*	sah muh play
It's so...	*C'est si...*	say see
...beautiful.	*...beau.*	boh
...ugly.	*...laid.*	lay
...strange.	*...bizarre.*	bee-zar
...boring.	*...ennuyeux.*	ahn-new-yuh
...interesting.	*...intéressant.*	an-tay-reh-sahn

...pretentious.	*...prétentieux.*	pray-tahn-see-uh
...thought-provoking.	*...provocateur.*	proh-voh-kah-tur
...B.S.	*...con.*	kohn
I don't get it.	*Je n'y comprends rien.*	zhuhn yuh kohn-prahn ree-an
Is it upside down?	*C'est à l'envers?*	say ah lahn-vehr
Who did this?	*Qui a fait ça?*	kee ah fay sah
How old is this?	*C'est vieux?*	say vee-uh
Wow!	*Sensass!*	sahn-sahs
My feet hurt!	*J'ai mal aux pieds!*	zhay mahl oh pee-yay
I'm exhausted!	*Je suis épuisé!*	zhuh sweez ay-pwee-zay
We're exhausted!	*Nous sommes épuisé!*	noo suhmz ay-pwee-zay

France's national museums close on Tuesdays. For efficient sightseeing in Paris, buy a Museum Pass. It'll save you money and time (because you're entitled to slip right into museums, bypassing the notorious lines).

SHOPPING

Shops

Where is a...?	*Où est un...?*	oo ay uhn
antique shop	*magasin d'antiquités*	mah-gah-zan dahn-lee-kee-tay
art gallery	*gallerie d'art*	gah-luh-ree dar
bakery	*boulangerie*	boo-lahn-zhuh-ree
barber shop	*coiffeur*	kwah-fur
beauty salon	*coiffeur pour dames*	kwah-fur poor dahm
book shop	*librairie*	lee-bray-ree
camera shop	*magasin de photo*	mah-gah-zan duh foh-toh
cell phone shop	*magasin de portables*	mah-gah-zan duh por-tah-bluh
cheese shop	*fromagerie*	froh-mah-zhuh-ree
clothing boutique	*boutique, magasin de vêtements*	boo-teek, mah-gah-zan duh veht-mahn

ACTIVITIES

Key Phrases: Shopping

Where can I buy...?	*Où puis-je acheter...?*	oo pwee-zhuh ah-shuh-tay
Where is...?	*Où est...?*	oo ay
...a grocery store	*...une épicerie*	ewn ay-pee-suh-ree
...a department store	*...un grand magasin*	uhn grahn mah-gah-zan
...an Internet café	*...un café internet*	uhn kah-fay an-tehr-neht
...a launderette	*...une laverie*	ewn lah-vuh-ree
...a pharmacy	*...une pharmacie*	ewn far-mah-see
How much is it?	*C'est combien?*	say kohn-bee-an
I'm just browsing.	*Je regarde.*	zhuh ruh-gard

coffee shop	*café*	kah-fay
delicatessen	*charcuterie-traiteur*	shar-koo-tuh-ree-tray-tur
department store	*grand magasin*	grahn mah-gah-zan
flea market	*marché aux puces*	mar-shay oh pews
flower market	*marché aux fleurs*	mar-shay oh flur
grocery store	*épicerie*	ay-pee-suh-ree
hardware store	*quincaillerie*	kan-kay-yay-ree
Internet café	*café internet*	kah-fay an-tehr-neht
jewelry shop	*bijouterie*	bee-zhoo-tuh-ree
launderette	*laverie*	lah-vuh-ree
newsstand	*maison de la presse*	meh-zohn duh lah prehs
office supplies	*papeterie*	pah-pay-tuh-ree
open-air market	*marché en plein air*	mar-shay ahn plan air
optician	*opticien*	ohp-tee-see-an
pastry shop	*pâtisserie*	pah-tee-suh-ree
pharmacy	*pharmacie*	far-mah-see
photocopy shop	*magasin de photocopie*	mah-gah-zan duh foh-toh-koh-pee
shopping mall	*centre commercial*	sahn-truh koh-mehr-see-ahl

souvenir shop	*boutique de souvenirs*	boo-teek duh soo-vuh-neer
supermarket	*supermarché*	sew-pehr-mar-shay
sweets shop	*confiserie*	kohn-fee-suh-ree
toy store	*magasin de jouets*	mah-gah-zan duh zhway
travel agency	*agence de voyages*	ah-zhahns duh voy-yahzh
used bookstore...	*boutique de livres d'occasion...*	boo-teek duh lee-vruh doh-kah-zee-ohn
...with books in English	*...avec des livres en anglais*	ah-vehk day lee-vruh ahn ahn-glay
wine shop	*marchand de vin*	mar-shahn duh van

In France, most shops close for a long lunch (noon until about 2:00 P.M.), and all day on Sundays and Mondays. Grocery stores are often open on Sunday mornings.

Shop Till You Drop

opening hours	*les heures d'ouverture*	layz ur doo-vehr-tewr
sale	*solde*	sohld
I'd like...	*Je voudrais...*	zhuh voo-dray
We'd like...	*Nous voudrions...*	noo voo-dree-ohn
Where can I buy...?	*Où puis-je acheter...?*	oo pwee-zhuh ah-shuh-tay
Where can we buy...?	*Où pouvons-nous acheter...?*	oo poo-vohn-noo ah-shuh-tay
How much is it?	*C'est combien?*	say kohn-bee-an
I'm just browsing.	*Je regarde.*	zhuh ruh-gard
We're just browsing.	*Nous regardons.*	noo ruh-gar-dohn
Do you have...?	*Vous avez...?*	vooz ah-vay
...more	*...plus*	plew
...something cheaper	*...quelque chose de moins cher*	kehl-kuh shohz duh mwan shehr
Better quality, please.	*De meilleure qualité, s'il vous plaît.*	duh meh-yur kah-lee-tay see voo play

genuine / imitation	*authentique / imitation*	oh-tahn-teek / ee-mee-tah-see-ohn
Can I / Can we see more?	*Je peux / Nous pouvons en voir d'autres?*	zhuh puh / noo poo-vohn ahn vwar doh-truh
This one.	*Celui ci.*	suh-lwee see
Can I try it on?	*Je peux l'essayer?*	zhuh puh leh-say-yay
A mirror?	*Un miroir?*	uhn meer-war
Too...	*Trop...*	troh
...big.	*...grand.*	grahn
...small.	*...petit.*	puh-tee
...expensive.	*...cher.*	shehr
It's too...	*C'est trop...*	say troh
...short / long.	*...court / long.*	koor / lohn
...tight / loose.	*...serré / grand.*	suh-ray / grahn
...dark / light.	*...foncé / clair.*	fohn-say / klair
What is it made out of?	*De quoi c'est fait?*	duh kwah say fay
Is it machine washable?	*C'est lavable en machine?*	say lah-vah-bluh ahn mah-sheen
Will it shrink?	*Ça va rétrécir?*	sah vah ray-tray-seer
Will it fade in the wash?	*Ça va déteindre au lavage?*	sah vah day-tan-druh oh lah-vahzh
Credit card O.K.?	*Carte de crédit O.K.?*	kart duh kray-dee "O.K."
Can you ship this?	*Vous pouvez l'envoyer?*	voo poo-vay lahn-voy-ay
Tax-free?	*Hors taxe?*	or tahks
I'll think about it.	*Je vais y penser.*	zhuh vay zee pahn-say
What time do you close?	*Vous fermez à quelle heure?*	voo fehr-may ah kehl ur
What time do you open tomorrow?	*Vous allez ouvrir à quelle heure demain?*	vooz ah-lay oo-vreer ah kehl ur duh-man

The French definition of customer service is different from ours. At department stores, be prepared to be treated as if you're intruding on the clerk's privacy. Exchanges are possible with receipts. Refunds are difficult. Buy to keep.

Street Markets

Did you make this?	*C'est vous qui l'avez fait?*	say voo kee lah-vay fay
Is that your lowest price?	*C'est votre prix le plus bas?*	say voh-truh pree luh plew bah
Cheaper?	*Moins cher?*	mwan shehr
My last offer.	*Ma dernière offre.*	mah dehrn-yehr oh-fruh
Good price.	*C'est bon marché.*	say bohn mar-shay
I'll take it.	*Je le prends.*	zhuh luh prahn
We'll take it.	*Nous le prenons.*	noo luh prahn-nohn
I'm nearly broke.	*Je suis presque fauché.*	zhuh swee prehsk foh-shay
We're nearly broke.	*Nous sommes presque fauché.*	noo suhm prehsk foh-shay
My friend...	*Mon ami...*	mohn ah-mee
My husband...	*Mon mari...*	mohn mah-ree
My wife...	*Ma femme...*	mah fahm
...has the money.	*...a l'argent.*	ah lar-zhahn

Clothes

For...	*Pour...*	poor
...a male baby / a female baby.	*...un bébé garçon / un bébé fille.*	uhn bay-bay gar-sohn / uhn bay-bay fee
...a male child / a female child.	*...un petit garçon / une petite fille.*	uhn puh-tee gar-sohn / ewn puh-tee fee
...a male teenager / a female teenager.	*...un adolescent / une adolescente.*	uhn ah-doh-luh-sahn / ewn ah-doh-luh-sahnt
...a man.	*...un homme.*	uhn ohm
...a woman.	*...une femme.*	ewn fahm
bathrobe	*peignoir de bain*	peh-nwar duh ban
bib	*bavoir*	bah-vwar
belt	*ceinture*	san-tewr
bra	*soutien gorge*	soo-tee-an gorzh
clothing	*vêtement*	veht-mahn
dress	*robe*	rohb
flip-flops	*tongues*	tohn-guh

gloves	*gants*	gahn
hat	*chapeau*	shah-poh
jacket	*veste*	vehst
jeans	*jeans*	"jeans"
nightgown	*chemise de nuit*	shuh-meez duh nwee
nylons	*collants*	koh-lahn
pajamas	*pyjama*	pee-zhah-mah
pants	*pantalons*	pahn-tah-lohn
raincoat	*imperméable*	an-pehr-may-ah-bluh
sandals	*sandales*	sahn-dahl
scarf	*foulard*	foo-lar
shirt...	*chemise...*	shuh-meez
...long-sleeved	*...à manches longues*	ah mahnsh lohn-guh
...short-sleeved	*...à manches courtes*	ah mahnsh koort
...sleeveless	*...sans manche*	sahn mahnsh
shoelaces	*lacets*	lah-say
shoes	*chaussures*	shoh-sewr
shorts	*shorts*	short
skirt	*jupe*	zhoop
slip	*jupon*	zhoo-pohn
slippers	*chaussons*	shoh-sohn
socks	*chaussettes*	shoh-seht
sweater	*pull*	pool
swimsuit	*maillot de bain*	mī-yoh duh ban
tennis shoes	*baskettes*	bahs-keht
T-shirt	*T-shirt*	"T-shirt"
underwear	*sous vêtements*	soo veht-mahn
vest	*gilet sans manche*	gee-lay sahn mahnsh

Colors

black	*noir*	nwar
blue	*bleu*	bluh
brown	*marron*	mah-rohn
gray	*gris*	gree
green	*vert*	vehr
orange	*orange*	oh-rahnzh

pink	*rose*	rohz
purple	*violet*	vee-oh-lay
red	*rouge*	roozh
white	*blanc*	blahn
yellow	*jaune*	zhohn
dark / light	*foncé / clair*	fohn-say / klair
A shade...	*Un teint...*	uhn tan
...lighter.	*...plus clair.*	plew klair
...brighter.	*...plus coloré.*	plew koh-loh-ray
...darker.	*...plus foncé.*	plew fohn-say

Materials

brass	*cuivre jaune*	kwee-vruh zhohn
bronze	*bronze*	brohnz
ceramic	*céramique*	say-rah-meek
copper	*cuivre*	kwee-vruh
cotton	*cotton*	koh-tohn
glass	*verre*	vehr
gold	*or*	or
lace	*dentelle*	dahn-tehl
leather	*cuir*	kweer
linen	*lin*	leen
marble	*marbre*	mar-bruh
metal	*métal*	may-tahl
nylon	*nylon*	nee-lohn
paper	*papier*	pahp-yay
pewter	*laiton*	lay-tohn
plastic	*plastique*	plah-steek
polyester	*polyester*	poh-lee-ehs-tehr
porcelain	*porcelaine*	por-suh-lehn
silk	*soie*	swah
silver	*argent*	ar-zhahn
velvet	*velours*	veh-loor
wood	*bois*	bwah
wool	*laine*	lehn

Jewelry

bracelet	*bracelet*	brah-suh-lay
brooch	*broche*	brohsh
earrings	*boucles d'oreille*	boo-kluh doh-ray
jewelry	*bijoux*	bee-zhoo
necklace	*collier*	kohl-yay
ring	*bague*	bahg
Is this...?	*C'est...?*	say
...sterling silver	*...de l'argent*	duh lar-zhahn
...real gold	*...de l'or véritable*	duh lor vay-ree-tah-bluh
...stolen	*...volé*	voh-lay

SPORTS

Bicycling

bicycle / bike	*bicyclette / vélo*	bee-see-kleht / vay-loh
mountain bike	*VTT*	vay-tay-tay
I'd like to rent a bike.	*Je voudrais louer un vélo.*	zhuh voo-dray loo-ay uhn vay-loh
We'd like to rent two bikes.	*Nous voudrions louer deux vélos.*	noo voo-dree-ohn loo-ay duh vay-loh
How much per...?	*C'est combien par...?*	say kohn-bee-an par
...hour	*...heure*	ur
...half day	*...demie-journée*	duh-mee-zhoor-nay
...day	*...jour*	zhoor
Is a deposit required?	*Une caution est obligatoire?*	ewn koh-see-ohn ay oh-blee-gah-twar
deposit	*caution*	koh-see-ohn
helmet	*casque*	kahsk
lock	*antivol*	ahn-tee-vohl
air / no air	*air / pas d'air*	air / pah dair
tire	*pneu*	puh-nuh
pump	*pompe*	pohmp
map	*carte*	kart
How many gears?	*Combien vitesses?*	kohn-bee-an vee-tehs

What is a...	*Quel est un...*	kehl ay uhn...
route of about ___ kilometers?	*circuit de ___ kilometers?*	seer-kwee duh ___ kee-loh-meh-truh
...good	*...bon*	bohn
...scenic	*...panoramique, beau*	pah-noh-rah-meek, boh
...interesting	*...intéressante*	an-tay-reh-sahn
...easy	*...facile*	fah-seel
How many minutes / hours by bicycle?	*Combien de minutes / d'heures à vélo?*	kohn-bee-an duh mee-newt / dur ah vay-loh
I like hills.	*J'aime les côtes.*	zhehm lay koht
I don't like hills.	*Je n'aime pas les côtes.*	zhuh nehm pah lay koht

For more on route-finding, see "Finding Your Way," beginning on page 44 in the French Traveling chapter.

Swimming and Boating

Where can I / can we rent a...?	*Où puis-je / pouvons-nous louer...?*	oo pwee-zhuh / poo-vohn-noo loo-ay
...paddleboat	*...pédalo*	pay-dah-loh
...rowboat	*...barque*	bark
...boat	*...bâteau*	bah-toh
...sailboat	*...voilier*	vwah-lee-ay
How much per...?	*C'est combien par...?*	say kohn-bee-an par
...hour	*...heure*	ur
...half day	*...demie-journée*	duh-mee-zhoor-nay
...day	*...jour*	zhoor
beach	*plage*	plahg
nude beach (topless)	*plage naturiste (monokini)*	plahg nah-toor-eest (moh-noh-kee-nee)
Where's a good beach?	*Où est une belle plage?*	oo ay ewn behl plahg
Is it safe for swimming?	*On peut nager en sécurité?*	ohn puh nah-zhay ahn say-kew-ree-tay

flip-flops	*tongues*	tohn-guh
pool	*piscine*	pee-seen
snorkel and mask	*tuba et masque*	too-bah ay mahsk
sunglasses	*lunettes de soleil*	loo-neht duh soh-lay
sunscreen	*crème solaire*	krehm soh-lair
surfboard	*planche de surf*	plahnsh duh surf
surfer	*surfeur*	surf-ur
swimsuit	*maillot de bain*	mī-yoh duh ban
towel	*serviette*	sehrv-yeht
waterskiing	*ski nautique*	skee noh-teek
windsurfing	*planche à voile*	plahnsh ah vwahl

In France, nearly any beach is topless. For a nude beach, look for a ***naturiste plage***.

Sports Talk

sports	*sport*	spor
game	*match*	"match"
team	*équipe*	ay-keep
championship	*championnat*	shah-pee-oh-nah
soccer	*football*	foot-bahl
basketball	*basket*	bah-skeht
hockey	*hockey*	oh-kay
American football	*football américain*	foot-bahl ah-may-ree-kan
baseball	*baseball*	bahz-bahl
tennis	*tennis*	teh-nees
golf	*golf*	"golf"
skiing	*ski*	"ski"
gymnastics	*gymnastique*	zheem-nah-steek
Olympics	*Olympiques*	oh-leem-peek
medal...	*médaille*	meh-dī
...gold / silver / bronze	*d'or / d'argent / du bronze*	dor / dar-zhahn / duh brohnz
What sport / athlete / team is your favorite?	*Quel sport / jouer / équipe est votre preferé?*	kehl spor / zhoo-ay / ay-keep ay voh-truh pray-fuh-ray

Where can I see a game?	*Où puis-je voir un match?*	oo pwee-zhuh vwar uhn "match"
jogging	*jogging*	zhoh-geeng
Where's a good place to jog?	*Où puis-je faire du jogging?*	oo pwee-zhuh fair duh zhoh-geeng

ENTERTAINMENT

What's happening tonight?	*Qu'est-ce qui ce passe ce soir?*	kehs kee suh pahs suh swar
What do you recommend?	*Qu'est-ce que vous recommandez?*	kehs kuh voo ruh-koh-mahn-day
Where is it?	*C'est où?*	say oo
How to get there?	*Comment le trouver?*	koh-mahn luh troo-vay
Is it free?	*C'est gratuit?*	say grah-twee
Are there seats available?	*Il y a des places disponible?*	eel yah day plahs dee-spoh-nee-bluh
Where can I buy a ticket?	*Où puis-je acheter un billet?*	oo pwee-zhuh ah-shuh-tay uhn bee-yay
Do you have tickets for today / tonight?	*Avez-vous des billets pour aujourd'hui / ce soir?*	ah-vay-voo day bee-yay poor oh-zhoor-dwee / suh swar
When does it start?	*Ça commence à quelle heure?*	sah koh-mahns ah kehl ur
When does it end?	*Ça se termine à quelle heure?*	sah suh tehr-meen ah kehl ur
The best place to dance nearby?	*Le meilleur dancing dans le coin?*	luh meh-yur dahn-seeng dahn luh kwan
Where do people stroll?	*Les gens se balladent où?*	lay zhahn suh bah-lah-dahn oo

Entertaining Words

movie...	*film...*	feelm
...original version	*...version originale (V.O.)*	vehr-see-ohn oh-ree-zhee-nahl

...in English	*...en anglais*	ahn ahn-glay
...with subtitles	*...avec sous-titres*	ah-vehk soo-tee-truh
...dubbed	*...doublé*	doo-blay
music...	*musique...*	mew-zeek
...live	*...en directe*	ahn dee-rehkt
...classical	*...classique*	klahs-seek
...folk	*...folklorique*	fohk-loh-reek
...opera	*...d'opéra*	doh-pay-rah
...symphony	*...symphonique*	seem-foh-neek
...choir	*...de choeur*	duh koh-ur
...traditional	*...traditionnelle*	trah-dee-see-oh-nehl
rock / jazz / blues	*rock / jazz / blues*	rohk / zhahz / "blues"
male singer	*chanteur*	shahn-tur
female singer	*chanteuse*	shahn-tuhz
concert	*concert*	kohn-sehr
show	*spectacle*	spehk-tahk-luh
sound and light show	*son et lumière*	sohn ay lew-mee-ehr
dancing	*danse*	dahns
folk dancing	*danse folklorique*	dahns fohk-loh-reek
disco	*disco*	dee-skoh
bar with live music	*bar avec un groupe musical*	bar ah-vehk uhn groop mew-zee-kahl
nightclub	*boîte*	bwaht
(no) cover charge	*(pas de) admission*	(pah duh) ahd-mee-see-ohn
sold out	*complet*	kohn-play

For concerts and special events, ask at the local tourist office. Cafés, very much a part of the French social scene, are places for friends to spend the evening together. To meet new friends, the French look for ***pubs*** or ***bars américains.***

Paris has a great cinema scene, especially on the Champs-Élysées. Pick up a ***Pariscope,*** the periodical entertainment guide, and choose from hundreds of films (often discounted on Mondays). Those listed V.O. (rather than V.F.) are in their original language.

CONNECT

PHONING

I'd like to buy a...	*Je voudrais acheter une...*	zhuh voo-dray ah-shuh-tay oon
...telephone card.	*...carte téléphonique.*	kart tay-lay-foh-neek
...cheap international telephone card.	*...carte téléphonique à code internationale.*	kart tay-lay-foh-neek ah kohd an-tehr-nah-see-oh-nahl
The nearest phone?	*Le téléphone le plus proche?*	luh tay-lay-fohn luh plew prohsh
It doesn't work.	*Ça ne marche pas.*	sah nuh marsh pah
May I use your phone?	*Je peux téléphoner?*	zhuh puh tay-lay-foh-nay
Can you talk for me?	*Vous pouvez parler pour moi?*	voo poo-vay par-lay poor mwah
It's busy.	*C'est occupé.*	say oh-kew-pay
Will you try again?	*Essayez de nouveau?*	eh-say-yay duh noo-voh
Hello. (on the phone)	*Âllo.*	ah-loh
My name is ___.	*Je m'appelle ___.*	zhuh mah-pehl
Sorry, I speak only a little French.	*Désolé, je parle seulement un petit peu de français.*	day-zoh-lay zhuh parl suhl-mahn uhn puh-tee puh duh frahn-say
Speak slowly and clearly.	*Parlez lentement et clairement.*	par-lay lahn-tuh-mahn ay klair-mahn
Wait a moment.	*Un moment.*	uhn moh-mahn

In this section, you'll find phrases to reserve a hotel room (page 49) or a table at a restaurant (page 66). To spell your name on the phone, refer to the code alphabet (page 53).

Make your calls using a handy phone card (***carte téléphonique***), sold at post offices, train stations, and tobacco (***tabac***) shops. There are two kinds of phone cards: an insertable card that you slide into a phone in a phone booth, and a cheaper-per-minute international telephone card (with a scratch-off PIN code) that you can use from any phone, even your hotel room. Post offices often have easy-to-use metered phones.

At phone booths, you'll encounter these words: ***inserer votre carte*** (insert your card) and ***composer votre numéro*** (dial your number); it will also tell you how many ***unités*** are left on your card. If the number you're calling is out of service, you'll hear the dreaded recording: "***Le numéro que vous demandez n'est pas attribué.***" For more tips, see "Let's Talk Telephones" in the appendix (page 501).

Telephone Words

telephone	*téléphone*	tay-lay-fohn
telephone card	*carte téléphonique*	kart tay-lay-foh-neek
cheap international telephone card	*carte téléphonique à code internationale*	kart tay-lay-foh-neek ah kohd an-tehr-nah-see-oh-nahl
PIN code	*code*	kohd
phone booth	*cabine téléphonique*	kah-been tay-lay-foh-neek
out of service	*hors service*	or sehr-vees
post office	*Poste*	pohst
operator	*standardiste*	stahn-dar-deest
international assistance	*renseignements internationaux*	rahn-sehn-yuh-mahn an-tehr-nah-see-oh-noh
international call	*appel international*	ah-pehl an-tehr-nah-see-oh-nahl
collect call	*appel en PCV*	ah-pehl ahn pay-say-vay
credit card call	*appel avec une carte de crédit*	ah-pehl ah-vehk ewn kart duh kray-dee
toll-free	*gratuit*	grah-twee
fax	*fax*	fahks
country code	*code international*	kohd an-tehr-nah-see-oh-nahl

area code	*code régional*	kohd ray-zhee-oh-nahl
extension	*poste*	pohst
telephone book	*bottin, annuaire*	boh-tan, ahn-new-air
yellow pages	*pages jaunes*	pahzh zhohn

Cell Phones

Where is a cell phone shop?	*Où est un magasin de portables?*	oo ay uhn mah-gah-zan duh por-tah-bluh
I'd like...	*Je voudrais...*	zhuh voo-dray
We'd like...	*Nous voudrions...*	noo voo-dree-ohn
...a cell phone.	*...un portable.*	uhn por-tah-bluh
...a chip.	*...une puce.*	ewn pews
...to buy more time.	*...acheter plus de temps.*	ah-shuh-tay plew duh tahn
How do you...?	*Comment vous...?*	koh-mahn voo
...make calls	*...appelez*	ah-puh-lay
...receive calls	*...reçevez les appels*	ruh-suh-vay layz ah-pehl
Will this work outside this country?	*Ça marche en dehors de ce pays?*	sah marsh ahn duh-or duh suh peh-ee
Where can I buy more time for this phone?	*Où puis-je acheter une recharge pour ce portable?*	oo pwee-zhuh ah-shuh-tay ewn reh-sharzh poor suh por-tah-bluh

EMAIL AND THE WEB

Email

My email address is ___.	*Mon adresse email est ___.*	mohn ah-drehs ee-mayl ay
What's your email address?	*Quelle est votre adresse email?*	kehl ay voh-truh ah-drehs ee-mayl
Can I use this computer to check my email?	*Je peux utiliser cet ordinateur pour regarder mon email?*	zhuh puh oo-tee-lee-zay seht or-dee-nah-tur poor ruh-gar-day mohn ee-mayl
Where can I get get access to the Internet?	*Où est-ce que je peux accéder à l'internet?*	oo ehs kuh zhuh puh ahk-say-day ah lan-tehr-neht

Key Phrases: Email and the Web

email	*email*	ee-mayl
Internet	*internet*	an-tehr-neht
Where is the nearest Internet café?	*Où se trouve le café internet le plus prôche?*	oo suh troov luh kah-fay an-tehr-neht luh plew prohsh
I'd like to check my email.	*Je voudrais regarder mon email.*	zhuh voo-dray ruh-gar-day mohn ee-mayl

Where is an Internet café?	*Où se trouve un café internet?*	oo suh troov uhn kah-fay an-tehr-neht
How much for... minutes?	*C'est combien pour... minutes?*	say kohn-bee-an poor... mee-newt
...10	*...dix*	dees
...15	*...quinze*	kanz
...30	*...trente*	trahnt
...60	*...soixante*	swah-sahnt
Help me, please.	*Aidez-moi, s'il vous plaît.*	ay-day-mwah see voo play
How...	*Comment...*	koh-mahn
...do I start this?	*...je démarre ça?*	zhuh day-mar sah
...do I send a file?	*...j'envoie un fichier?*	zhahn-vwah uhn fee-shee-ay
...do I print out a file?	*...j'imprime le fichier?*	zhan-preem luh fee-shee-ay
...do I make this symbol?	*...je fais ce symbole?*	zhuh fay suh seem-bohl
...do I type @?	*...je tape arobase?*	zhuh tahp ah-roh-bahs
This doesn't work.	*Ça ne marche pas.*	sah nuh marsh pah

Web Words

website	*site web*	seet wehb
Internet	*internet*	an-tehr-neht

surf the Web	*surfer le web*	surf-ay luh wehb
download	*télécharge*	tay-lay-sharzh
@ sign	*signe arobase*	seen ah-roh-bahs
dot	*point*	pwan
hyphen (-)	*tiret*	tee-ray
underscore (_)	*souligne*	soo-leen
Wi-Fi	*Wi-Fi*	wee-fee

On Screen

delete	annuler	**message**	message
send	envoyer	**save**	sauver
file	fichier	**open**	ouvrir
print	imprimer		

MAILING

Where is the post office?	*Où est la Poste?*	oo ay lah pohst
Which window for...?	*Quel guichet pour...?*	kehl gee-shay poor
Is this the line for...?	*C'est la file pour...?*	say lah feel poor
...stamps	*...les timbres*	lay tan-bruh
...packages	*...les colis*	lay koh-lee
To the United States...	*Aux Etats-Unis...*	ohz ay-tah-zew-nee
...by air mail.	*...par avion.*	par ah-vee-ohn
...by surface mail.	*...par surface.*	par sewr-fahs
How much is it?	*C'est combien?*	say kohn-bee-an
How much to send a letter / postcard to ___?	*Combien pour envoyer une lettre / carte postale pour ___?*	kohn-bee-an poor ahn-voh-yay ewn leht-ruh / kart poh-stahl poor
I need stamps for ___ postcards to...	*J'ai besoin de timbres pour ___ cartes postales pour...*	zhay buh-swan duh tan-bruh poor ___ kart poh-stahl poor
...America / Canada.	*...l'Amérique / le Canada.*	lah-may-reek / luh kah-nah-dah
Pretty stamps, please.	*De jolis timbres, s'il vous plaît.*	duh zhoh-lee tan-bruh see voo play

Key Phrases: Mailing

post office	*la Poste*	lah pohst
stamp	*timbre*	tan-bruh
postcard	*carte postale*	kart poh-stahl
letter	*lettre*	leht-ruh
air mail	*par avion*	par ah-vee-ohn
Where is the post office?	*Où est la Poste?*	oo ay lah pohst
I'd like to buy stamps for ___ postcards / letters to send to America.	*Je voudrais acheter timbres pour ___ cartes postales / lettres d'envoyer pour l'Amérique.*	zhuh voo-dray ah-shuh-tay tan-bruh poor ___ kart poh-stahl / leht-ruh dahn-voh-yay poor lah-may-reek

I always choose the slowest line.	*Je choisis toujours la file la plus lente.*	zhuh shwah-see too-zhoor lah feel lah plew lahnt
How many days will it take?	*Ça va prendre combien de jours?*	sah vah prahn-druh kohn-bee-an duh zhoor

You can also buy stamps at ***tabac*** (tobacco) shops—very handy, so long as you know in advance the amount of postage you need.

Licking the Postal Code

post office	*la Poste*	lah pohst
stamp	*timbre*	tan-bruh
postcard	*carte postale*	kart poh-stahl
letter	*lettre*	leht-ruh
envelope	*enveloppe*	ahn-vuh-lohp
package	*colis*	koh-lee
box	*boîte en carton*	bwaht ahn kar-tohn
string	*ficelle*	fee-sehl
tape	*scotch*	skotch
mailbox	*boîte aux lettres*	bwaht oh leht-truh

air mail	*par avion*	par ah-vee-oh<u>n</u>
express	*par express*	par ehk-sprehs
surface (slow and cheap)	*surface (lent et pas cher)*	sewr-fahs (lah<u>n</u> ay pah shehr)
book rate	*tarif-livres*	tah-reef-lee-vruh
weight limit	*poids limite*	pwah lee-meet
registered	*enregistré*	ah<u>n</u>-ruh-zhee-stray
insured	*assuré*	ah-sew-ray
fragile	*fragile*	frah-zheel
contents	*contenu*	koh<u>n</u>-tuh-new
customs	*douane*	doo-ah<u>n</u>
to / from	*à / de*	ah / duh
address	*adresse*	ah-drehs
zip code	*code postal*	kohd poh-stahl
general delivery	*poste restante*	pohst rehs-tah<u>n</u>t

HELP!

Help!	*Au secours!*	oh suh-koor
Help me!	*À l'aide!*	ah layd
Call a doctor!	*Appelez un docteur!*	ah-puh-lay uhn dohk-tur
Call...	*Appelez...*	ah-puh-lay
...the police.	*...la police.*	lah poh-lees
...an ambulance.	*...une ambulance.*	ewn ahn-bew-lahns
...the fire department.	*...les pompiers.*	lay pohn-pee-yay
I'm lost.	*Je suis perdu.*	zhuh swee pehr-dew
We're lost.	*Nous sommes perdus.*	noo suhm pehr-dew
Thank you for your help.	*Merci pour votre aide.*	mehr-see poor voh-truh ayd
You are very kind.	*Vous êtes très gentil.*	vooz eht treh zhahn-tee

France's medical emergency phone number is 15. ***SOS médecins*** are doctors who make emergency house calls. If you need help, someone will call an ***SOS médecin*** for you.

Theft and Loss

Stop, thief!	*Arrêtez, au voleur!*	ah-reh-tay oh voh-lur
I have been / We have been robbed.	*On m'a / Nous a volé.*	ohn mah / nooz ah voh-lay
A thief took...	*Un voleur à pris...*	uhn voh-lur ah pree
Thieves took...	*Des voleurs ont pris...*	day voh-lur ohn pree

Key Phrases: Help!

accident	*accident*	ahk-see-dahn
emergency	*urgence*	ewr-zhahns
police	*police*	poh-lees
Help!	*Au secours!*	oh suh-koor
Call a doctor / the police!	*Appelez un docteur / la police!*	ah-puh-lay uhn dohk-tur / lah poh-lees
Stop, thief!	*Arrêtez, au voleur!*	ah-reh-tay oh voh-lur

I've lost...	*J'ai perdu...*	zhay pehr-dew
...my money.	*...mon argent.*	mohn ar-zhahn
...my passport.	*...mon passeport.*	mohn pah-spor
...my ticket.	*...mon billet.*	mohn bee-yay
...my baggage.	*...mes bagages.*	may bah-gahzh
...my purse.	*...mon sac.*	mohn sahk
...my wallet.	*...mon portefeuille.*	mohn por-tuh-fuh-ee
...my faith in humankind.	*...ma foi en l'humanité.*	mah fwah ahn lew-mah-nee-tay
We've lost our...	*Nous avons perdu nos...*	nooz ah-vohn pehr-dew noh
...passports.	*...passeports.*	pah-spor
...tickets.	*...billets.*	bee-yay
...bags.	*...bagages.*	bah-gahzh
I want to contact my embassy.	*Je veux contacter mon ambassade.*	zhuh vuh kohn-tahk-tay mohn ahm-bah-sahd
I need to file a police report for my insurance.	*Je veux porter plainte à la police pour mon assurance.*	zhuh vuh por-tay plant ah lah poh-lees poor mohn ah-sewr-rahns

See page 503 in the appendix for contact information on the US embassy in Paris.

Helpful Words

ambulance	*ambulance*	ahn-bew-lahns
accident	*accident*	ahk-see-dahn
injured	*blessé*	bleh-say
emergency	*urgence*	ewr-zhahns
emergency room	*aux urgences*	ohz ewr-zhahns
fire	*feu*	fuh
police	*police*	poh-lees
smoke	*fumée*	foo-may
thief	*voleur*	voh-lur
pickpocket	*pickpocket*	peek-poh-keht

Help for Women

Leave me alone.	*Laissez-moi tranquille.*	lay-say-mwah trahn-keel
I want to be alone.	*Je veux être seule.*	zhuh vuh eh-truh suhl
I'm not interested.	*Ça ne m'intéresse pas.*	sah nuh man-tay-rehs pah
I'm married.	*Je suis mariée.*	zhuh swee mah-ree-ay
I'm a lesbian.	*Je suis lesbienne.*	zhuh swee lehz-bee-ehn
I have a contagious disease.	*J'ai une maladie contagieuse.*	zhay ewn mah-lah-dee kohn-tah-zhuhz
You are bothering me.	*Vous m'embêtez.*	voo mahn-beh-tay
He is bothering me.	*Il m'embête.*	eel mahn-beht
Don't touch me.	*Ne me touchez pas.*	nuh muh too-shay pah
You're disgusting.	*Vous êtes dégoutant.*	vooz eht day-goo-tahn
Stop following me.	*Arrêtez de me suivre.*	ah-reh-tay duh muh swee-vruh
Stop it!	*Arrêtez!*	ah-reh-tay
Enough!	*Ça suffit!*	sah sew-fee
Get lost!	*Dégagez!*	day-gah-zhay
Drop dead!	*Foutez-moi la paix!*	foo-tay-mwah lah pay
I'll call the police.	*J'appelle la police.*	zhah-pehl lah poh-lees

SERVICES

Laundry

Is a... nearby?	*Il y a une... près d'ici?*	eel-yah ewn... preh dee-see
...self-service laundry	*...laverie automatique*	lah-vah-ree oh-toh-mah-teek
...full service laundry	*...blanchisserie*	blahn-shee-suh-ree
Help me, please.	*Aidez-moi, s'il vous plaît.*	ay-day-mwah see voo play
How does this work?	*Ça marche comment?*	sah marsh koh-mahn
Where is the soap?	*Où se trouve la lessive?*	oo suh troov lah luh-seev
Are these yours?	*C'est à vous?*	say ah voo
This stinks.	*Ça pue.*	sah pew
This smells like...	*Ça sent comme...*	sah sahn kohm
...spring time.	*...le printemps.*	luh pran-tahn
...a locker room.	*...un vestiare.*	ewn vehs-tee-ar
...cheese.	*...le fromage.*	luh froh-mahzh
I need change.	*J'ai besoin de monnaie.*	zhay buh-swan duh moh-nay
Same-day service?	*Lavé le même jour?*	lah-vay luh mehm zhoor
By when do I need to drop off my clothes?	*Je dois déposer mon linge quand?*	zhuh dwah day-poh-zay mohn lanzh kahn

When will my clothes be ready?	*Mon linge sera prêt quand?*	mohn lanzh suh-rah preh kahn
Dried?	*Séché?*	say-shay
Folded?	*Plié?*	plee-ay
Ironed?	*Repassé?*	ray-pah-say
Hey there, what's spinning?	*Pardon, qu'est-ce qui tourne?*	par-dohn kehs kee toorn

Clean Words

full-service laundry	*blanchisserie*	blahn-shee-suh-ree
self-service laundry	*laverie automatique*	lah-vah-ree oh-toh-mah-teek
wash / dry	*laver / sécher*	lah-vay / say-shay
washer / dryer	*machine à laver / machine à sécher*	mah-sheen ah lah-vay / mah-sheen ah say-shay
detergent	*lessive*	luh-seev
token	*jeton*	zhuh-tohn
whites	*blancs*	blahn
colors	*couleurs*	koh-lur
delicates	*délicats*	day-lee-kah
handwash	*laver à la main*	lah-vay a lah man

Haircuts

Where is a barber / hair salon?	*Où se trouve un salon de coiffure hommes / femmes?*	oo suh troov uhn sah-lohn duh kwah-fur ohm / fahm
I'd like...	*J'aimerais...*	zhehm-uh-ray
...a haircut.	*...une coupe.*	ewn koop
...a permanent.	*...une permanente.*	ewn pehr-mah-nahnt
...just a trim.	*...juste raffraîchir.*	zhoost rah-freh-sheer
Cut about this much off.	*Coupez ça à peu près.*	koo-pay sah ah puh preh
Cut my bangs here.	*Coupez ma frange ici.*	koo-pay mah frahnzh ee-see
Longer / Shorter here.	*Plus long / Plus court ici.*	plew lohn / plew koort ee-see

I'd like my hair...	*J'aimerais mes cheveux...*	zhehm-uh-ray may shuh-vuh
...short.	*...courts.*	koort
...colored.	*...colorés.*	koh-loh-ray
...shampooed.	*...lavés.*	lah-vay
...blow dried.	*...séchés.*	say-shay
It looks good.	*C'est bien.*	say bee-an

Repair

These handy lines can apply to any repair, whether it's a ripped rucksack, bad haircut, or crabby camera.

This is broken.	*C'est cassé.*	say kah-say
Can you fix it?	*Vous pouvez le réparer?*	voo poo-vay luh ray-pah-ray
Just do the essentials.	*Ne faites que le minimum.*	nuh fayt kuh luh mee-nee-muhm
How much will it cost?	*Ça coutera combien?*	sah koo-teh-rah kohn-bee-an
When will it be ready?	*Ce sera prêt quand?*	suh suh-rah preh kahn
I need it by ___.	*Il me le faut avant ___.*	eel muh luh foh ah-vahn
We need it by ___.	*Il nous le faut avant ___.*	eel noo luh foh ah-vahn
Without it, I'm...	*Sans, je suis...*	sahn zhuh swee
...lost.	*...perdu.*	pehr-dew
...toast.	*...grillé.*	gree-yay
...dead in the water.	*...une épave.* ("a shipwreck")	ewn ay-pahv

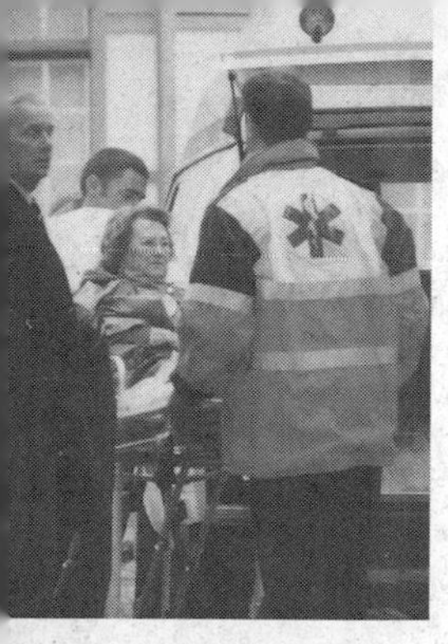

HEALTH

I am sick.	*Je suis malade.*	zhuh swee mah-lahd
I feel (very) sick.	*Je me sens (très) malade.*	zhuh muh sahn (treh) mah-lahd
My husband / My wife...	*Mon mari / Ma femme...*	mohn mah-ree / mah fahm
My son / My daughter...	*Mon fils / Ma fille...*	mohn fees / mah fee
My male friend / My female friend...	*Mon ami / Mon amie...*	mohn ah-mee / mah ah-mee
...feels (very) sick.	*...se sent (très) malade.*	suh sahn (treh) mah-lahd
It's urgent.	*C'est urgent.*	say tewr-zhahn

Key Phrases: Health

doctor	*docteur*	dohk-tur
hospital	*hôpital*	oh-pee-tahl
pharmacy	*pharmacie*	far-mah-see
medicine	*médicament*	may-dee-kah-mahn
I am sick.	*Je suis malade.*	zhuh swee mah-lahd
I need a doctor (who speaks English).	*J'ai besoin d'un docteur (qui parle anglais).*	zhay buh-swan duhn dohk-tur (kee parl ahn-glay)
It hurts here.	*J'ai mal ici.*	zhay mahl ee-see

I need a doctor...	*J'ai besoin d'un docteur...*	zhay buh-swan duhn dohk-tur
We need a doctor...	*Nous avons besoin d'un docteur...*	nooz ah-vohn buh-swan duhn dohk-tur
...who speaks English.	*...qui parle anglais.*	kee parl ahn-glay
Please call a doctor.	*S'il vous plaît appelez un docteur.*	see voo play ah-puh-lay uhn dohk-tur
Could a doctor come here?	*Un docteur pourrait venir?*	uhn dohk-tur poo-ray vuh-neer
I am...	*Je suis...*	zhuh swee
He / She is...	*Il / Elle est...*	eel / ehl ay
...allergic to penicillin / sulfa.	*...allergique à la pénicilline / les sulfamides.*	ah-lehr-zheek ah lah pay-nee-see-leen / lay sool-fah-meed
I am diabetic.	*Je suis diabétique.*	zhuh swee dee-ah-bay-teek
I have cancer.	*J'ai le cancer.*	zhay luh kahn-say
I had a heart attack ___ years ago.	*J'ai eu une crise cardiaque il y a ___ ans.*	zhay uh ewn kreez kar-dee-ahk eel yah ___ ahn
It hurts here.	*J'ai mal ici.*	zhay mahl ee-see
I feel faint.	*Je me sens faible.*	zhuh muh sahn fay-bluh
It hurts to urinate.	*Uriner me fait mal.*	ew-ree-nay muh fay mahl
I have body odor.	*Je sens mauvais.*	zhuh sahn moh-vay
I'm going bald.	*Je deviens chauve.*	zhuh duh-vee-ahn shohv
Is it serious?	*C'est sérieux?*	say say-ree-uh
Is it contagious?	*C'est contagieux?*	say kohn-tah-zhee-uh
Aging sucks.	*Vieillir c'est la poisse.*	ve-yay-yeer say lah pwahs
Take one pill every ___ hours for ___ days before / with meals.	*Prendre un comprimé toutes les ___ heures pendant ___ jours avant / durant les repas.*	prahn-druh uhn kohn-pree-may toot lay ___ ur pahn-dahn ___ zhoor ah-vahn / doo-rahn lay ruh-pah
I need a receipt for my insurance.	*J'ai besoin d'un reçu pour mon assurance.*	zhay buh-swan duhn ruh-sew poor mohn ah-sew-rahns

Ailments

I have...	*J'ai...*	zhay
He / She has...	*Il / Elle a...*	eel / ehl ah
I need / We need medication for...	*J'ai / Nous avons besoin d'un médicament pour...*	zhay / nooz ah-vohn buh-swan duhn may-dee-kah-mahn poor
...arthritis.	*...l'arthrite.*	lar-treet
...asthma.	*...l'asthme.*	lahz-muh
...athlete's foot.	*...la mycose.*	lah mee-kohz
...bad breath.	*...mauvaise haleine.*	moh-vehz ah-leen
...blisters.	*...des ampoules.*	dayz ahm-pool
...bug bites.	*...des piqures d'insectes.*	day peek-ruh dan-sehkt
...a burn.	*...une brûlure.*	ewn brew-lewr
...chest pains.	*...maux de poitrine.*	mahl duh pwah-treen
...chills.	*...des frissons.*	day free-sohn
...a cold.	*...un rhume.*	uhn rewm
...congestion.	*...la congestion.*	lah kohn-zhehs-tee-ohn
...constipation.	*...la constipation.*	lah kohn-stee-pah-see-ohn
...a cough.	*...la toux.*	lah too
...cramps.	*...des crampes.*	day krahmp
...diabetes.	*...du diabète.*	doo dee-ah-beht
...diarrhea.	*...la diarrhée.*	lah dee-ah-ray
...dizziness.	*...le vertige.*	luh vehr-teezh
...earache.	*...mal aux oreilles.*	mahl ohz oh-ray
...epilepsy.	*...l'épilepsie.*	lay-pee-lehp-see
...a fever.	*...une fièvre.*	ewn fee-eh-vruh
...the flu.	*...la grippe.*	lah greep
...food poisoning.	*...empoisonement alimentaire.*	ahn-pwah-zuh-mahnt ah-lee-mahn-tair
...the giggles.	*...le fou rire.*	luh foo reer
...hay fever.	*...le rhume des foins.*	luh rewm day fwan
...a headache.	*...mal à la tête.*	mahl ah lah teht
...a heart condition.	*...problème cardiaque.*	proh-blehm kar-dee-ak
...hemorrhoids.	*...hémorroïdes.*	ay-mor-wahd
...high blood pressure.	*...de l'hypertension.*	duh lee-pehr-tahn-see-ohn
...indigestion.	*...une indigestion.*	ewn an-dee-zhuh-stee-ohn

...an infection.	*...une infection.*	ewn an-fehk-see-ohn
...inflammation.	*...une inflation.*	ewn an-flah-see-ohn
...a migraine.	*...une migraine.*	ewn mee-grayn
...nausea.	*...la nausée.*	lah noh-zay
...pneumonia.	*...la pneumonie.*	lah puh-noo-moh-nee
...a rash.	*...des boutons.*	day boo-tohn
...sinus problems.	*...problèmes de sinus.*	proh-blehm duh see-noo
...a sore throat.	*...mal à la gorge.*	mahl ah lah gorzh
...a stomachache.	*...mal à l'estomac.*	mahl ah luh-stoh-mah
...sunburn.	*...un coup de soleil.*	uhn koo duh soh-lay
...a swelling.	*...une enflure.*	ewn ahn-flewr
...a toothache.	*...mal aux dents.*	mahl oh dahn
...a urinary infection.	*...une infection urinarire.*	ewn an-fehk-see-ohn ew-ree-nah-reer
...a venereal disease.	*...une maladie vénérienne.*	ewn mah-lah-dee vay-nay-ree-ehn
...vicious sunburn.	*...un méchant coup de soleil.*	uhn may-shahn koo duh soh-lay
...vomiting.	*...le vomissement.*	luh voh-mee-suh-mahn
...worms.	*...des vers.*	day vehr

Women's Health

menstruation	*menstruation*	mahn-stroo-ah-see-ohn
menstrual cramps	*crampes de menstruation*	krahmp duh mahn-stroo-ah-see-ohn
period	*les règles*	lay reh-gluh
pregnancy (test)	*(test de) grossesse*	(tehst duh) groh-sehs
miscarriage	*fausse couche*	fohs koosh
abortion	*avortement*	ah-vor-tuh-mahn
birth control pill	*la pilule*	lah pee-lewl
diaphragm	*diaphragme*	dee-ah-frahm
I'd like to see a female...	*Je voudrais voir une femme-...*	zhuh voo-dray vwar ewn fahm-
...doctor.	*...docteur.*	dohk-tur
...gynecologist.	*...gynécologue.*	zhee-nay-koh-lohg
I've missed a period.	*J'ai du retard dans mes règles.*	zhay dew ruh-tar dahn may reh-gluh

English	French	Pronunciation
My last period started on ___.	*Mes dernières règles étaient le ___.*	may dehrn-yehr reh-gluh ay-tan luh
I am / She is... pregnant.	*Je suis / Elle est enceinte...*	zhuh swee / ehl ay ahn-sant
...___ months	*...de ___ mois.*	duh ___ mwah

Parts of the Body

English	French	Pronunciation
ankle	*cheville*	shuh-veel
arm	*bras*	brah
back	*dos*	doh
bladder	*vessie*	veh-see
breast	*seins*	san
buttocks	*fesses*	feh-say
chest	*poitrine*	pwah-treen
ear	*oreille*	oh-ray
elbow	*coude*	kood
eye / eyes	*oeil / yeux*	oy / yuh
face	*visage*	vee-sahzh
finger	*doigt*	dwat
foot	*pied*	pee-ay
hair	*cheveux*	shuh-vuh
hand	*main*	man
head	*tête*	teht
heart	*coeur*	koor
hip	*hanche*	ahnsh
intestines	*intestins*	an-tehs-tan
knee	*genou*	zhuh-noo
leg	*jambe*	zhahmb
lung	*poumon*	poo-mohn
mouth	*bouche*	boosh
neck	*cou*	koo
nose	*nez*	nay
penis	*pénis*	pay-nee
rectum	*rectum*	rehk-toom
shoulder	*épaule*	ay-pohl
stomach	*estomac*	ay-stoh-mah
teeth	*dents*	dahn

testicles	*testicules*	tehs-tee-kool
throat	*gorge*	gorzh
toe	*doigt de pied*	dwat duh pee-ay
urethra	*urèthre*	ew-reh-truh
uterus	*utérus*	ew-tay-rew
vagina	*vagin*	vah-zheen
waist	*taille*	tah-ee
wrist	*poignet*	pwahn-yay

For more anatomy lessons, see the illustrations on pages 510–511 in the appendix.

First-Aid Kit

antacid	*anti-acide*	ahn-tee-ah-seed
antibiotic	*antibiotique*	ahn-tee-bee-oh-teek
aspirin	*aspirine*	ah-spee-reen
non-aspirin substitute	*Tylenol*	tee-luh-nohl
bandage	*bandage*	bahn-dahzh
Band-Aids	*pansements*	pahn-suh-mahn
cold medicine	*remède contre le rhume*	ruh-mehd kohn-truh luh rewm
cough drops	*pastilles pour la toux*	pah-steel poor lah too
decongestant	*décongestant*	day-kohn-zhehs-tahn
disinfectant	*désinfectant*	day-zan-fehk-tahn
first-aid cream	*crème antiseptique*	krehm ahn-tee-sehp-teek
gauze / tape	*gaze / sparadra*	gahz / spah-rah-drah
laxative	*laxatif*	lahk-sah-teef
medicine for diarrhea	*médicament pour la diarrhée*	may-dee-kah-mahn poor lah dee-ah-ray
moleskin	*grain de beauté*	gran duh boh-tay
painkiller	*calmant*	kahl-mahn
Preparation H	*Préparation H* (no kidding)	pray-pah-rah-see-ohn ahsh
support bandage	*pansement élastique*	pahn-suh-mahn ay-lah-steek

thermometer	*thermomètre*	tehr-moh-meh-truh
Vaseline	*Vaseline*	vah-zuh-leen
vitamins	*vitamines*	vee-tah-meen

If you're feeling feverish, see the thermometer on page 514 in the appendix.

Toiletries

comb	*peigne*	pehn-yuh
conditioner for hair	*après-shampoing*	ah-preh-shahn-pwan
condoms	*préservatifs*	pray-zehr-vah-teef
dental floss	*fil dentaire*	feel dahn-tair
deodorant	*déodorant*	day-oh-doh-rahn
facial tissue	*kleenex*	klay-nehks
hairbrush	*brosse*	brohs
hand lotion	*crème pour les mains*	krehm poor lay man
lip salve	*beaume pour les lèvres*	bohm poor lay leh-vruh
mirror	*miroir*	meer-war
nail clipper	*clip-ongles*	kleep-ohn-gluh
razor	*rasoir*	rah-zwahr
sanitary napkins	*serviettes hygiéniques*	sehrv-yeht ee-zhay-neek
scissors	*ciseaux*	see-zoh
shampoo	*shampoing*	shahn-pwan
shaving cream	*mousse à raser*	moos ah rah-zehr
soap	*savon*	sah-vohn
sunscreen	*crème solaire*	krehm soh-layr
tampons	*tampons*	tahn-pohn
tissues	*mouchoirs en papier*	moosh-wahr ahn pahp-yay
toilet paper	*papier hygiénique*	pahp-yay ee-zhay-neek
toothbrush	*brosse à dents*	brohs ah dahn
toothpaste	*dentifrice*	dahn-tee-frees
tweezers	*pince à épiler*	pans ah ay-pee-lay

CHATTING

My name is ___.	*Je m'appelle ___.*	zhuh mah-pehl
What's your name?	*Quel est votre nom?*	kehl ay voh-truh nohn
Pleased to meet you.	*Enchanté.*	ahn-shahn-tay
This is ___.	*C'est ___.*	say
How are you?	*Comment allez-vous?*	koh-mahnt ah-lay-voo
Very well, thanks.	*Très bien, merci.*	treh bee-an mehr-see
Where are you from?	*D'où venez-vous?*	doo vuh-nay-voo
What city?	*Quelle ville?*	kehl veel
What country?	*Quel pays?*	kehl pay-ee
I am...	*Je suis...*	zhuh swee
...a male American.	*...américain.*	zah-may-ree-kan
...a female American.	*...américaine.*	zah-may-ree-kehn
...a male Canadian.	*...canadien.*	kah-nah-dee-an
...a female Canadian.	*...canadienne.*	kah-nah-dee-ehn
Where are you going?	*Où allez-vous?*	oo ah-lay-voo
I'm going to ___.	*Je vais à ___.*	zhuh vay ah
We're going to ___.	*Nous allons à ___.*	nooz ah-lohnz ah
Will you take my / our photo?	*Vous pouvez prendre ma / notre photo?*	voo-poo-vay prahn-druh mah / noh-truh foh-toh
Can I take a photo of you?	*Je peux prendre votre photo?*	zhuh puh prahn-druh noh-truh foh-toh
Smile!	*Souriez!*	soo-ree-ay

Key Phrases: Chatting

My name is ___.	*Je m'appelle ___.*	zhuh mah-pehl
What's your name?	*Quel est votre nom?*	kehl ay voh-truh nohn
Pleased to meet you.	*Enchanté.*	ahn-shahn-tay
Where are you from?	*D'où venez-vous?*	doo vuh-nay-voo
I'm from ___.	*Je viens de ___.*	zhuh vee-ahn duh
Where are you going?	*Où allez-vous?*	oo ah-lay-voo
I'm going to ___.	*Je vais à ___.*	zhuh vay ah
I like...	*J'aime...*	zhehm
Do you like...?	*Vous aimez...?*	vooz eh-may
Thank you very much.	*Merci beaucoup.*	mehr-see boh-koo
Have a good trip!	*Bon voyage!*	bohn voy-yahzh

Nothing More than Feelings...

I am / You are...	*Je suis / Vous êtes...*	zhuh swee / vooz eht
He / She is...	*Il / Elle est...*	eel / ehl ay
...happy. (m / f)	*...content / contente.*	kohn-tahn / kohn-tahnt
...sad.	*...triste.*	treest
...tired.	*...fatigué.*	fah-tee-gay
I am / You are...	*J'ai / Vous avez...*	zhay / vooz ah-vay
He / She is...	*Il / Elle a...*	eel / ehl ah
...hungry.	*...faim.*	fan
...thirsty.	*...soif.*	swahf
...lucky.	*...de la chance.*	duh lah shahns
...homesick.	*...le mal du pays.*	luh mahl dew pay-ee
...cold.	*...froid.*	frwah
...hot.	*...trop chaud.*	troh shoh

Who's Who

This is my friend.	*C'est mon ami.*	say mohn ah-mee
This is my... (m / f)	*C'est mon / ma...*	say mohn / mah
...boyfriend / girlfriend.	*...petit ami / petite amie.*	puh-teet ah-mee / puh-teet ah-mee

...husband / wife.	*...mari / femme.*	mah-ree / fahm
...son / daughter.	*...fils / fille.*	fees / fee
...brother / sister.	*...frère / soeur.*	frehr / sur
...father / mother.	*...père / mère.*	pehr / mehr
...uncle / aunt.	*...oncle / tante.*	ohn-kluh / tahnt
...nephew / niece.	*...neveu / nièce.*	nuh-vuh / nee-ehs
...male / female cousin.	*...cousin / cousine.*	koo-zan / koo-zeen
...grandfather / grandmother.	*...grand-père / grand-mère.*	grahn-pehr / grahn-mehr
...grandson / granddaughter.	*...petit-fils / petite-fille.*	puh-tee-fees / puh-teet-fee

Family

Are you married?	*Vous êtes marié?*	vooz eht mah-ree-ay
Do you have children?	*Vous avez des enfants?*	vooz ah-vay dayz ahn-fahn
How many boys / girls?	*Combien de garçons / filles?*	kohn-bee-an duh gar-sohn / feel
Do you have photos?	*Vous avez des photos?*	vooz ah-vay day foh-toh
How old is your child?	*Quel âge à votre enfant?*	kehl ahzh ah voh-truh ahn-fahn
Beautiful child!	*Quel bel enfant!*	kehl behl ahn-fahn
Beautiful children!	*Quels beaux enfants!*	kehl bohz ahn-fahn

Chatting with Children

What's your first name?	*Quel est ton prénom?*	kehl ay tohn pray-nohn
My name is ___.	*Je m'appelle ___.*	zhuh mah-pehl
How old are you?	*Quel âge as-tu?*	kehl ahzh ah-tew
Do you have brothers and sisters?	*Tu as des frères et soeurs?*	tew ahz day frehr ay sur
Do you like school?	*Tu aimes l'école?*	tew ehm lay-kohl
What are you studying?	*Tu étudies quoi?*	tew ay-tew-dee kwah

I'm studying ___.	*J'étudie ___.*	zhay-too-dee
What's your favorite subject?	*Quel est ton sujet préferé?*	kehl ay tohn soo-zhay pray-fuh-ray
Do you have pets?	*As-tu un animal chez toi?*	ah-tew uhn ah-nee-mahl shay twah
I have a...	*J'ai un...*	zhay uhn
We have a...	*Nous avons un...*	nooz ah-vohn uhn
...cat / dog / fish / bird.	*...chat / chien / poisson / oiseau.*	shah / shee-an / pwah-sohn / wah-zoh
What is this?	*Qu'est-ce que c'est?*	kes kuh say
Will you teach me...?	*Tu m'apprends...?*	tew mah-prahn
Will you teach us...?	*Tu nous apprend...?*	tew nooz ah-prahn
...some French words	*...quelques mots en français*	kehl-kuh moh ahn frahn-say
...a simple French song	*...une chanson française facile*	ewn shahn-sohn frahn-sehz fah-seel
Guess which country I live in.	*Devine mon pays.*	duh-veen mohn pay-ee
Guess which country we live in.	*Devine notre pays.*	duh-veen noh-truh pay-ee
How old am I?	*J'ai quel âge?*	zhay kehl ahzh
I'm ___ years old.	*J'ai ___ ans.*	zhay ___ ahn
Want to hear me burp?	*Veux-tu m'ententre roter?*	vuh-tew mahn-tahn-truh roh-tay
Teach me a fun game.	*Apprends-moi un jeu rigolo.*	ah-prahn-mwah uhn zhuh ree-goh-loh
Got any candy?	*Tu as des bonbons?*	tew ah day bohn-bohn
Want to arm wrestle?	*Tu veux faire un bras de fer?*	tew vuh fair uhn brah duh fehr
Gimme five.	*Tape là.*	tahp lah

If you want to do a "high five" with a kid, hold up your hand and say, "Tape là" (Hit me here). For a French sing-along, you'll find the words for "Happy Birthday" on page 25.

Travel Talk

I am / Are you...?	*Je suis / Vous êtes...?*	zhuh sweez / vooz eht
...on vacation	*...en vacances*	ahn vah-kahns
...on business	*...en voyage d'affaires*	ahn voy-yahzh dah-fair
How long have you been traveling?	*Il y a longtemps que vous voyagez?*	eel yah lohn-tahn kuh voo voy-yah-zhay
day / week	*jour / semaine*	zhoor / suh-mehn
month / year	*mois / année*	mwah / ah-nay
When are you going home?	*Quand allez-vous rentrer?*	kahn ah-lay-voo rahn-tray
This is my first time in ___.	*C'est ma première fois en ___.*	say mah pruhm-yehr fwah ahn
This is our first time in ___.	*C'est notre première fois en ___.*	say noh-truh pruhm-yehr fwah ahn
It's / It's not a tourist trap.	*C'est / Ce n'est pas un piège à touristes.*	say / suh nay pah uhn pee-ehzh ah too-reest
This is paradise.	*Ceci est le paradis.*	say-see ay luh pah-rah-deez
France is wonderful.	*La France est magnifique.*	lah frahns ay mahn-yee-feek
The French are friendly / boring / rude.	*Les Français sont gentils / ennuyeux / impolis.*	lay frahn-say sohn zhahn-tee / ahn-noo-yuh / an-poh-lee
So far...	*Jusqu'à maintenant...*	zhews-kah man-tuh-nahn
Today...	*Aujourd'hui...*	oh-zhoor-dwee
...I have / we have seen ___ and ___.	*...j'ai / nous avons vu ___ et ___.*	zhay / nooz ah-vohn vew ___ ay
Next...	*Après...*	ah-preh
Tomorrow...	*Demain...*	duh-man
...I will / we will see ___.	*...je vais / nous allons voir ___.*	zhuh vay / nooz ahl-lohn vwar
Yesterday...	*Hier...*	yehr
...I saw / we saw ___.	*...j'ai vu / nous avons vu ___.*	zhay vew / nooz ah-vohn vew

My / Our vacation is ___ days long, starting in ___ and ending in ___.	*J'ai / Nous avons ___ jours de vacances, qui commencent à ___ et qui finissent à ___*	zhay / nooz ah-vohn ___ zhoor duh vah-kahns kee kohn-mahn-sahn ah ___ ay kee fee-nee-sahn ah
To travel is to live.	*Voyager c'est vivre.*	voy-yah-zhay say vee-vruh
Travel is enlightening.	*Voyager ouvre l'esprit.*	voy-yah-zhay oo-vruh luh-spree
I wish all (American) politicians traveled.	*Je souhaite que tous les politiciens (américains). voyagent.*	zhuh soo-ayt kuh too lay poh-lee-tee-see-an (ah-may-ree-kan) voy-yah-zhahn
Have a good trip!	*Bon voyage!*	bohn voy-yahzh

Map Musings

Use the maps on pages 504–509 in the appendix to delve into family history and explore travel dreams.

I live here.	*J'habite ici.*	zhah-beet ee-see
We live here.	*Nous habitons ici.*	nooz ah-bee-tohn ee-see
I was born here.	*Je suis né là.*	zhuh swee nay lah
My ancestors came from ___.	*Mes ancêtres viennent de ___.*	mayz ahn-seh-truh vee-ehn duh
I've traveled to ___.	*J'ai visité à ___.*	zhay vee-zee-tay ah
We've traveled to ___.	*Nous avons visité à ___.*	nooz ah-vohn vee-zee-tay ah
Next I'll go to ___.	*Et puis je vais à ___.*	ay pwee zhuh vay ah
Next we'll go to ___.	*Et puis nous allons à ___.*	ay pwee nooz ahl-lohn ah
I'd like / We'd like to go to ___.	*Je voudrais / Nous voudrions aller à ___.*	zhuh voo-dray / noo voo-dree-ohn ah-lay ah
Where do you live?	*Où est-ce que vous vivez?*	oo ehs kuh voo vee-vay
Where were you born?	*Où êtes-vous né?*	oo eht-voo nay
Where did your ancestors come from?	*D'où viennent vos ancêtres?*	doo vee-ehn vohz ahn-seh-truh

Where have you traveled?	*Où avez-vous voyagé?*	oo ah-vay-voo voy-yah-zhay
Where are you going?	*Où allez-vous?*	oo ah-lay-voo
Where would you like to go?	*Où voudriez-vous voyager?*	oo voo-dree-yay-voo voy-yah-zhay

Weather

What's the weather tomorrow?	*Quel temps fera-t-il demain?*	kehl tahn fuh-rah-teel duh-man
sunny / cloudy	*ensoleillé / nuageux*	ahn-soh-lay-yay / nwah-zhuh
hot / cold	*chaud / froid*	shoh / frwah
muggy / windy	*humide / venteux*	oo-meed / vahn-tuh
rain / snow	*pluie / neige*	ploo-ee / nehzh
It's raining like cow's piss. (French saying)	*Il pleut comme vâche qui pisse.*	eel pluh kohm vahsh kee pees

Thanks a Million

Thank you very much.	*Merci beaucoup.*	mehr-see boh-koo
You are...	*Vous êtes...*	vooz eht
...helpful.	*...serviable.*	sehr-vee-ah-bluh
...wonderful.	*...magnifique.*	mahn-yee-feek
...generous. (m / f)	*...généreux / généreuse.*	zhay-nay-ruh / zhay-nay-ruhz
You spoil me / us.	*Vous me / nous gâtez.*	voo muh / noo gah-tay
You've been a great help!	*Vous m'avez beaucoup aider!*	voo mah-vay boh-koo ay-day
You are an angel from heaven.	*Vous êtes un ange venu du ciel.*	vooz eht uhn ahnzh vuh-new duh see-ehl
I will remember you...	*Je me souviendrai de vous...*	zhuh muh soov-yan-dreh duh voo
We will remember you...	*Nous nous souviendrons de vous...*	noo noo soov-yan-dreh duh voo

...always.	*...toujours.*	too-zhoor
...till Tuesday.	*...jusqu'à mardi.*	zhews-kah mar-dee

Responses for All Occasions

I like that.	*Ça me plaît.*	sah muh play
We like that.	*Ça nous plaît*	sah noo play
I like you.	*Je vous aime bien.*	zhuh vooz ehm bee-an
We like you.	*Nous vous aimons bien.*	noo vooz ehm-ohn bee-an
That's cool.	*C'est chouette.*	say shweht
Great!	*Formidable!*	for-mee-dah-bluh
What a nice place.	*Quell endroit sympa.*	kehl ahn-dwah sahn-pah
Perfect.	*Parfait.*	par-fay
Funny.	*Amusant.*	ah-mew-zahn
Interesting.	*Intéressant.*	an-tay-reh-sahn
Really?	*Vraiment?*	vray-mahn
Wow!	*Wow!*	"Wow"
Congratulations!	*Félicitations!*	fay-lee-see-tah-see-ohn
Well done!	*Bien joué!*	bee-an zhoo-ay
You're welcome.	*Je vous en prie.*	zhuh vooz ahn pree
It's nothing.	*De rien.*	duh ree-an
Bless you! (sneeze)	*À vos souhaits!*	ah voh sway
What a pity.	*Quel dommage.*	kehl doh-mahzh
That's life.	*C'est la vie.*	say lah vee
No problem.	*Pas de problème.*	pah duh proh-blehm
O.K.	*D'accord.*	dah-kor
This is the good life!	*Que la vie est belle!*	kuh lah vee ay behl
Have a good day!	*Bonne journée!*	buhn zhoor-nay
Good luck!	*Bonne chance!*	buhn shahns
Let's go!	*Allons-y!*	ah-lohn-zee

Conversing with Animals

rooster / cock-a-doodle-doo	*coq / cocorico*	kohk / koh-koh-ree-koh
bird / tweet tweet	*oiseau / cui cui*	wah-zoh / kwee kwee
cat / meow	*chat / miaou*	shah / mee-ah-oo

dog / woof woof — *chien / ouah ouah* — shee-an / wah wah
duck / quack quack — *canard / coin coin* — kah-nar / kwan kwan
cow / moo — *vache / meu* — vahsh / muh
pig / oink oink — *cochon / groin groin* — koh-shohn / grwan grwan

Profanity

People make animal noises, too. These words will help you understand what the more colorful locals are saying...

Damn! (Good God!) — *Bon Dieu!* — bohn dee-uh
bastard — *salaud* — sah-loh
bitch — *salope* — sah-lohp
breasts (colloq.) — *tétons* — tay-tohn
big breasts — *grands tétons* — grahn tay-tohn
penis (colloq.) — *bite* — beet
butthole — *sale con* — sahl kohn
drunk — *bourré* — boo-ray
idiot — *idiot* — ee-dee-oh
imbecile — *imbécile* — an-bay-seel
jerk — *connard* — kuh-nar
stupid — *stupide* — stew-peed
Did someone fart? — *Est-ce que quelqu'un à péter?* — ehs kuh kehl-kuhn ah pay-tay
I burped. — *J'ai roté.* — zhay roh-tay
This sucks. — *C'est dégueulasse.* — say day-gewl-ahs
Shit. — *Merde.* — mehrd
Bullshit. — *C'est de la merde.* — say duh lah mehrd
You are... — *Vous êtes...* — vooz eht
Don't be... — *Ne soyez pas...* — nuh soh-yay pah
...a son of a bitch. — *...un batard.* — uhn bah-tar
...an asshole. — *...un vieux con.* — uhn vee-uh kohn
...an idiot. — *...un idiot.* — uhn ee-dee-oh
...a creep. — *...un vicieux.* — uhn vee-see-uh
...a cretin. — *...un crétin.* — uhn kray-teen
...a pig. — *...un cochon.* — uhn koh-shohn

Sweet Curses

My goodness.	*Mon Dieu.*	mohn dee-uh
Goodness gracious.	*Mon bon Dieu.*	mohn bohn dee-uh
Oh, my gosh.	*Oh la la.*	oo lah lah
Shoot.	*Zut.*	zewt
Darn it!	*Mince!*	mans

CREATE YOUR OWN CONVERSATION

The French enjoy good conversations. Join in! You can mix and match these words into a conversation. Make it as deep or silly as you want.

Who

I / you	*je / vous*	zhuh / voo
he / she	*il / elle*	eel / ehl
we / they	*nous / ils*	noo / eel
my / your...	*mes / vos...*	may / voh
...parents / children	*...parents / enfants*	pah-rahn / zahn-fahn
men / women	*hommes / femmes*	ohm / fahm
rich / poor people	*riches / pauvres*	reesh / poh-vruh
young people	*jeunes*	zhuhn
middle-aged / old	*d'âge mur / vieux*	dahzh mewr / vee-uh
the French	*les Français*	lay frahn-say
the Austrians	*les Autrichiens*	layz oh-treesh-ee-an
the Belgians	*les Belges*	lay behlzh
the Czechs	*les Tchèques*	lay chehk
the Germans	*les Allemands*	layz ahl-mahn
the Italians	*les Italiens*	layz ee-tah-lee-an
the Spanish	*les Espagnols*	layz eh-spahn-yohl
the Swiss	*les Suisses*	lay swees
the Europeans	*les Européens*	layz ur-oh-pee-ehn
EU (European Union)	*UE (l'Union Européenne)*	ew uh (lewn-yun ur-oh-pee-ehn)
the Americans	*les Américains*	layz ah-may-ree-kan

liberals	*libéraux*	lee-bay-roh
conservatives	*conservateurs*	kohn-sehr-vah-tur
radicals	*radicaux*	rah-dee-koh
terrorists	*terroristes*	teh-roh-reest
politicians	*politiciens*	poh-lee-tee-see-an
big business	*grosses affaires*	grohs ah-fair
multinational corporations	*corporations multinationales*	kor-por-ah-see-ohn mewl-tee-nah-see-oh-nahl
military	*militaire*	mee-lee-tair
mafia	*mafia*	"mafia"
refugees	*réfugiés*	ray-few-zhee-ay
travelers	*voyageurs*	voy-yah-zhur
God	*Dieu*	dee-uh
Christian	*chrétien*	kray-tee-an
Catholic	*catholique*	kah-toh-leek
Protestant	*protestant*	proh-tehs-tahn
Jew	*juif*	zhweef
Muslim	*musulman*	mew-zewl-mahn
everyone	*tout le monde*	too luh mohnd

What

buy / sell	*acheter / vendre*	ah-shuh-tay / vahn-druh
have / lack	*avoir / manquer de*	ahv-wahr / mahn-kay duh
help / abuse	*aider / abuser*	ay-day / ah-boo-zay
learn / fear	*apprendre / craindre*	ah-prahn-druh / cran-druh
love / hate	*aimer / détester*	eh-may / day-tehs-tay
prosper / suffer	*prospérer / souffrir*	proh-spay-ray / soo-freer
take / give	*prendre / donner*	prahn-druh / duh-nay
want / need	*vouloir / avoir besoin de*	vool-wahr / ahv-wahr buh-swan duh
work / play	*travailler / jouer*	trah-vah-yay / zhoo-way

Why

(anti-) globalization	*(anti-) globalisation*	(ahn-tee-) gloh-bah-lee-zah-see-ohn
class warfare	*lutte sociale*	luht soh-see-ahl

corruption	*corruption*	koh-rewp-see-oh<u>n</u>
democracy	*démocratie*	day-moh-krah-tee
education	*éducation*	ay-dew-kah-see-oh<u>n</u>
family	*famille*	fah-mee-ee
food	*nourriture*	noo-ree-tewr
guns	*armes*	arm
happiness	*bonheur*	boh<u>n</u>-ur
health	*santé*	sah<u>n</u>-tay
hope	*espoir*	ehs-pwahr
imperialism	*impérialisme*	a<u>n</u>-pay-ree-ahl-eez-muh
lies	*mensonges*	mah<u>n</u>-soh<u>n</u>zh
love / sex	*amour / sexe*	ah-moor / "sex"
marijuana	*marijuana*	mah-ree-wah-nah
money / power	*argent / pouvoir*	ar-zhah<u>n</u> / poov-wahr
pollution	*pollution*	poh-lew-see-oh<u>n</u>
racism	*racisme*	rah-seez-muh
regime change	*changement de régime*	shah<u>n</u>-zhuh-mah<u>n</u> duh ray-zheem
relaxation	*relaxation*	ruh-lahk-sah-see-oh<u>n</u>
religion	*religion*	ruh-lee-zhee-oh<u>n</u>
respect	*respect*	ruh-speh
taxes	*taxes*	tahks
television	*télévision*	tay-lay-vee-zee-oh<u>n</u>
violence	*violence*	vee-oh-lah<u>n</u>s
war / peace	*guerre / paix*	gehr / peh
work	*travail*	trah-vah-ee
global perspective	*perspective globale*	pehr-spehk-teev gloh-bahl

You Be the Judge

(no) problem	*(pas de) problème*	(pah duh) proh-blehm
(not) good	*(pas) bon*	(pah) boh<u>n</u>
(not) dangerous	*(pas) dangereux*	(pah) dah<u>n</u>-zhay-ruh
(not) fair	*(pas) juste*	(pah) zhewst
(not) guilty	*(pas) coupable*	(pah) koo-pah-bluh
(not) powerful	*(pas) puissant*	(pah) pwee-sah<u>n</u>

(not) stupid	*(pas) stupide*	(pah) stew-peed
(not) happy	*(pas) content*	(pah) kohn-tahn
because / for	*parce que / pour*	pars kuh / poor
and / or / from	*et / ou / de*	ay / oo / duh
too much	*trop*	troh
(never) enough	*(jamais) assez*	(zhah-may) ah-say
same	*même*	mehm
better / worse	*mieux / pire*	mee-uh / peer
here / everywhere	*ici / partout*	ee-see / par-too

Beginnings and Endings

I like...	*J'aime...*	zhehm
We like...	*Nous aimons...*	nooz eh-mohn
I don't like...	*Je n'aime pas...*	zhuh nehm pah
We don't like...	*Nous n'aimons pas...*	noo neh-mohn pah
Do you like...?	*Vous aimez...?*	vooz eh-may
In the past...	*Dans le passé...*	dahn luh pah-say
When I was younger, I thought...	*Quand j'étais jeune, je pensais...*	kahn zhay-tay zhuhn zhuh pahn-say
Now, I think...	*Maintenant, je pense...*	man-tuh-nahn zhuh pahns
I am / Are you...?	*Je suis / Vous êtes...?*	zhuh swee / vooz eht
...optimistic / pessimistic	*...optimiste / pessimiste*	ohp-tee-meest / peh-see-meest
I believe...	*Je crois...*	zhuh krwah
I don't believe...	*Je ne crois pas...*	zhuh nuh krwah pah
Do you believe...?	*Croyez-vous...?*	krwah-yay-voo
...in God	*...en Dieu*	ahn dee-uh
...in life after death	*...en la vie après la mort*	ahn lah vee ah-preh lah mor
...in extraterrestrial life	*...dans la vie extraterrestre*	dahn lah vee ehk-strah-tuh-rehs-truh
...in Santa Claus	*...au Père Noël*	oh pehr noh-ehl
Yes. / No.	*Oui. / Non.*	wee / nohn
Maybe. / I don't know.	*Peut-être. / Je ne sais pas.*	puh-teh-truh / zhuh nuh say pah

What's most important in life?	*Quel est le plus important dans la vie?*	kehl ay luh plewz an-por-tahn dahn lah vee
The problem is...	*Le problème, c'est que...*	luh proh-blehm say kuh
The answer is...	*La solution, c'est...*	luh soh-lew-see-ohn say
We have solved the world's problems.	*Nous avons résolu les problèmes du monde.*	nooz ah-vohn ray-zoh-lew lay proh-blehm dew mohnd

AN AFFAIR TO REMEMBER

Words of Love

I / me / you / we	*je / moi / tu / nous*	zhuh / mwah / tew /noo
flirt	*flirter*	fleer-tay
kiss	*baiser*	bay-zay
hug	*se serrer dans les bras*	suh suh-ray dahn lay brah
love	*amour*	ah-moor
make love	*faire l'amour*	fair lah-moor
condom	*préservatif*	pray-zehr-vah-teef
contraceptive	*contraceptif*	kohn-trah-sehp-teef
safe sex	*safe sex*	"safe sex"
sexy	*sexy*	"sexy"
cozy	*douillet*	doo-yay
romantic	*romantique*	roh-mahn-teek
my angel	*mon ange*	mohn ahnzh
my doe	*ma biche*	mah beesh
my love	*mon amour*	mohn ah-moor
my little cabbage	*mon petit chou*	mohn puh-tee shoo
my flea (endearing)	*ma puce*	mah poos
my treasure	*mon trésor*	mohn tray-sor

Ah, Romance

What's the matter?	*Qu'est-ce qu'il y a?*	kehs keel yah
Nothing.	*Rien.*	ree-an
I am / Are you...?	*Je suis / Vous êtes...?*	zhuh swee / vooz eht
...gay	*...homosexual, gay*	oh-moh-sehk-soo-ehl, "gay"
...straight	*...hétéro*	ay-tay-roh
...bisexual	*...bisexuel*	bee-sehk-swehl
...undecided	*...indécis*	an-day-see
...prudish (m / f)	*...pudibond / pudibonde*	pew-dee-bohn / pew-dee-bohnd
...horny	*...excité*	ehk-see-tay
We are on our honeymoon.	*C'est notre lune de miel.*	say noh-truh lewn duh mee-ehl
I have a boyfriend.	*J'ai un petit ami.*	zhay uhn puh-teet ah-mee
I have a girlfriend.	*J'ai une petite amie.*	zhay ewn puh-teet ah-mee
I'm married.	*Je suis marié.*	zhuh swee mah-ree-ay
I'm married (but...).	*Je suis marié (mais...).*	zhuh swee mah-ree-ay (may)
I'm not married.	*Je ne suis pas marié.*	zhuh nuh swee pah mah-ree-ay
Do you have a boyfriend / a girlfriend?	*Vous avez un petit ami / une petite amie?*	vooz ah-vay uhn puh-teet ah-mee / ewn puh-teet ah-mee
I am adventurous. (m / f)	*Je suis aventureux / aventureuse.*	zhuh swee ah-vahn-too-ruh / ah-vahn-too-ruhz
I'm lonely (tonight).	*Je me sens seul (ce soir).*	zhuh muh sahn suhl (suh swar)
I am rich and single.	*Je suis riche et célibataire.*	zhuh swee reesh ay say-lee-bah-tair
Do you mind if I sit here?	*Ça vous embête si je m'assieds ici?*	sah vooz ahn-beht see zhuh mah-seed ee-see
Would you like a drink?	*Vous voulez un verre?*	voo voo-lay uhn vehr

Will you go out with me?	*Vous voulez sortir avec moi?*	voo voo-lay sor-teer ah-vehk mwah
Would you like to go out tonight for...?	*Vous voulez m'accompagner ce soir pour...?*	voo voo-lay mah-kohn-pahn-yay suh swar poor
...a walk	*...une promenade*	ewn proh-muh-nahd
...dinner	*...dîner*	dee-nay
...a drink	*...boire un pot*	bwar uhn poh
Where's the best place to dance nearby?	*Où est le meilleur endroit pour danser?*	oo ay luh meh-yur ahn-dwah poor dahn-say
Do you want to dance?	*Vous voulez danser?*	voo voo-lay dahn-say
Again?	*De nouveau?*	duh noo-voh
Let's celebrate!	*Faisons la fête!*	fay-zohn lah feht
Let's have fun like idiots!	*Amusons-nous comme des fous!*	ah-mew-zohn-noo kohm day foo
Let's have a wild and crazy night!	*On va s'éclater ce soir!*	ohn vah say-klah-tay suh swar
I have no diseases.	*Je n'ai pas de maladies.*	zhuh nay pah duh mah-lah-dee
I have many diseases.	*J'ai plusieurs maladies.*	zhay plewz-yur mah-lah-dee
I have only safe sex.	*Je pratique que le safe sex.*	zhuh prah-teek kuh luh "safe sex"
Can I take you home?	*Tu veux venir chez moi?*	tew vuh vuh-neer shay mwah
Why not?	*Pourquoi pas?*	poor-kwah pah
How can I change your mind?	*Qu'est-ce que je peux faire pour te faire changer d'avis?*	kehs kuh zhuh puh fair poor tuh fair shan-zhay dah-vee
Kiss me.	*Embrasse-moi.*	ahn-brah-say-mwah
May I kiss you?	*Je peux t'embrasser?*	zhuh puh tahn-brah-say
Can I see you again?	*On peut se revoir?*	ohn puh suh ruh-vwahr

CHATTING

Your place or mine?	*Chez toi ou chez moi?*	shay twah oo shay mwah
How does this feel?	*Comment tu te sens?*	koh-mahn tew tuh sahn
Is this an aphrodisiac?	*C'est un aphrodisiaque?*	sayt uhn ah-froh-dee-zee-yahk
This is my first time.	*C'est la première fois.*	seht lah pruhm-yehr fwah
This is not my first time.	*Ce n'est pas la première fois.*	seh nay pah lah pruhm-yehr fwah
You are my most beautiful souvenir.	*Tu es mon plus beau souvenir.*	tew ay mohn plew boh soo-vuh-neer
Do you do this often?	*Tu fais ça souvent?*	tew fay sah soo-vahn
How's my breath?	*Comment tu trouves mon haleine?*	koh-mahn tew troo-vay mohn ah-lehn
Let's just be friends.	*Soyons amis.*	swah-yohnz ah-mee
I'll pay for my share.	*Je paie mon partage.*	zhuh pay mohn par-tahzh
Would you like a massage...?	*Tu veux un massage...?*	tew vuh uhn mah-sahzh
...for your back	*...pour le dos*	poor luh doh
...for your feet	*...des pieds*	day pee-yay
Why not?	*Pourquoi pas?*	poor-kwah pah
Try it.	*Essaies.*	eh-say
That tickles.	*Ça chatouille.*	sah shah-too-ee
Oh my God.	*Mon Dieu.*	mohn dee-uh
I love you.	*Je t'aime.*	zhuh tehm
Darling, will you marry me?	*Chéri, tu veux m'épouser?*	shay-ree tew vuh may-poo-zay

ITALIAN

GETTING STARTED

User-friendly Italian

...is easy to get the hang of. Some Italian words are so familiar, you'd think they were English. If you can say ***pizza, lasagna,*** and ***spaghetti***, you can speak Italian.

Italian pronunciation differs from English in some key ways:

C usually sounds like C in cat.
  But C followed by E or I sounds like CH in chance.
CH sounds like C in cat.
E often sounds like AY in play.
G usually sounds like G in get.
  But G followed by E or I sounds like G in gentle.
GH sounds like G in spaghetti.
GLI sounds like LI in million. The G is silent.
GN sounds like GN in lasagna.
H is never pronounced.
I sounds like EE in seed.
R is rolled as in brrravo!
SC usually sounds like SK in skip.
  But SC followed by E or I sounds like SH in shape.
Z usually sounds like TS in hits, and sometimes like the sound of DZ in kids.

Have you ever noticed that most Italian words end in a vowel? It's ***o*** if the word is masculine and ***a*** if it's feminine. So a ***bambino*** gets blue and a ***bambina*** gets pink. A man is ***generoso*** (generous), a woman is ***generosa.*** A man will say, ***"Sono sposato"*** (I am married). A woman will say, ***"Sono sposata."*** In this book, we show gender-bender words like this: ***generoso[a].*** If you are speaking of a woman (which includes women speaking about themselves), use the ***a*** ending. It's always pronounced "ah." If a noun or adjective ends in ***e,*** such as ***cantante*** (singer) or ***gentile*** (kind), the same word applies to either sex.

Adjective endings agree with the noun. It's ***cara amica*** (a dear female friend) and ***caro amico*** (a dear male friend). Sometimes the adjective comes after the noun, as in ***vino rosso*** (red wine).

Plurals are formed by changing the final letter of the noun: ***a*** becomes ***e,*** and ***o*** becomes ***i.*** So it's one ***pizza*** and two ***pizze,*** and one cup of ***cappuccino*** and two cups of ***cappuccini.*** If you're describing any group of people that includes at least one male, the adjective should end with ***i.*** But if the group is female, the adjective ends with ***e.*** A handsome man is ***bello*** and an attractive group of men (or men and women) is ***belli.*** A beautiful woman is ***bella*** and a bevy of beauties is ***belle.*** In this book, you'll see plural adjective endings depicted like this: ***belli[e].***

Italians usually pronounce every letter in a word, so ***due*** (two) is **doo**-ay. Sometimes two vowels share one syllable. Piano sounds like pee**ah**-noh. The "pee**ah**" is one syllable. When one vowel in a pair should be emphasized, it will appear in bold letters: ***Italiano*** is ee-tah-lee**ah**-noh.

The key to Italian inflection is to remember this simple rule: most Italian words have their accent on the second-to-last syllable. To override this rule, Italians sometimes insert an accent: ***città*** (city) is pronounced chee-**tah**.

Italians are animated. You may think two Italians are arguing when in reality they're agreeing enthusiastically. Be confident and have fun communicating in Italian. The Italians really do want to understand you, and are forgiving of a yankee-fied version of their language.

Here's a quick guide to the phonetics used in this section:

ah like A in father.
ay like AY in play.
eh like E in let.
ee like EE in seed.
ehr sounds like "air."
g like G in go.
oh like O in note.
oo like OO in too.
or like OR in core.
ow like OW in now.
s like S in sun.
ts like TS in hits. It's a small explosive sound. Think of pizza (**pee**-tsah).

ITALIAN BASICS

In 800, Charlemagne traveled to Rome and became the Holy Roman Emperor using only these phrases.

Meeting and Greeting

Good day.	*Buon giorno.*	bwohn **jor**-noh
Good morning.	*Buon giorno.*	bwohn **jor**-noh
Good evening.	*Buona sera.*	**bwoh**-nah **say**-rah
Good night.	*Buona notte.*	**bwoh**-nah **noh**-tay
Hi / Bye. (informal)	*Ciao.*	chow
Welcome. (said to male / female / group)	*Benvenuto. / Benvenuta. / Benvenuti.*	behn-vay-**noo**-toh / behn-vay-**noo**-tah / behn-vay-**noo**-tee
Mr. / Mrs.	*Signore / Signora*	seen-**yoh**-ray / seen-**yoh**-rah
Miss	*Signorina*	seen-yoh-**ree**-nah
How are you?	*Come sta?*	**koh**-may stah
Very well.	*Molto bene.*	**mohl**-toh **behn**-ay
Thank you.	*Grazie.*	**graht**-seeay
And you?	*E lei?*	ay **leh**ee
My name is ___.	*Mi chiamo ___.*	mee kee**ah**-moh
What's your name?	*Come si chiama?*	**koh**-may see kee**ah**-mah
Pleased to meet you.	*Piacere.*	peeah-**chay**-ray
Where are you from?	*Di dove è?*	dee **doh**-vay eh
I am / We are / Are you...?	*Sono / Siamo / È...?*	**soh**-noh / see**ah**-moh / eh

...on vacation	*...in vacanza*	een vah-**kahnt**-sah
...on business	*...qui per lavoro*	kwee pehr lah-**voh**-roh
See you later.	*A più tardi.*	ah pew **tar**-dee
Goodbye.	*Arrivederci.*	ah-ree-vay-**dehr**-chee
Good luck!	*Buona fortuna!*	**bwoh**-nah for-**too**-nah
Have a good trip!	*Buon viaggio!*	bwohn veeah-joh

The greeting ***"Buon giorno"*** (Good day) turns to ***"Buona sera"*** (Good evening) in the late afternoon.

Essentials

Hello.	*Buon giorno.*	bwohn **jor**-noh
Do you speak English?	*Parla inglese?*	**par**-lah een-**glay**-zay
Yes. / No.	*Si. / No.*	see / noh
I don't speak Italian.	*Non parlo l'italiano.*	nohn **par**-loh lee-tah-lee**ah**-noh
I'm sorry.	*Mi dispiace.*	mee dee-spee**ah**-chay
Please.	*Per favore.*	pehr fah-**voh**-ray
Thank you.	*Grazie.*	**graht**-seeay
Thank you very much.	*Grazie mille.*	**graht**-seeay **mee**-lay
It's (not) a problem.	*(Non) c'è una problema.*	(nohn) cheh **oo**-nah proh-**blay**-mah
Good. / Great. / Excellent.	*Bene. / Benissimo. / Perfetto.*	**behn**-ay / behn-**ee**-see-moh / pehr-**feht**-toh
It's good.	*Va bene.*	vah **behn**-ay
You are very kind.	*Lei è molto gentile.*	**leh**ee eh **mohl**-toh jehn-**tee**-lay
Excuse me. (to get attention)	*Mi scusi.*	mee **skoo**-zee
Excuse me. (to pass)	*Permesso.*	pehr-**may**-soh
It doesn't matter.	*Non importa.*	nohn eem-**por**-tah
You're welcome.	*Prego.*	**pray**-goh

Sure.	*Certo.*	**chehr**-toh
O.K.	*Va bene.*	vah **behn**-ay
Let's go.	*Andiamo.*	ahn-deeah-moh
Goodbye!	*Arrivederci!*	ah-ree-vay-**dehr**-chee

Where?

Where is...?	*Dov'è...?*	doh-**veh**
...the tourist information office	*...l'ufficio informazioni*	loo-**fee**-choh een-for-maht-see**oh**-nee
...a cash machine	*...un bancomat*	oon **bahnk**-oh-maht
...the train station	*...la stazione*	lah staht-see**oh**-nay
...the bus station	*...la stazione degli autobus*	lah staht-see**oh**-nay **dayl**-yee **ow**-toh-boos
...the toilet	*...la toilette*	lah twah-**leht**-tay
men	*uomini, signori*	**woh**-mee-nee, seen-**yoh**-ree
women	*donne, signore*	**doh**-nay, seen-**yoh**-ray

You'll find some Italian words are similar to English if you're looking for a ***banca, farmacia, hotel, ristorante,*** or ***supermercato.***

How Much?

How much is it?	*Quanto costa?*	**kwahn**-toh **koh**-stah
Write it?	*Me lo scrive?*	may loh **skree**-vay
Is it free?	*È gratis?*	eh **grah**-tees
Is it included?	*È incluso?*	eh een-**kloo**-zoh
Do you have...?	*Ha...?*	ah
Where can I buy...?	*Dove posso comprare...?*	**doh**-vay **poh**-soh kohm-**prah**-ray
I would like...	*Vorrei....*	vor-**reh**ee
We would like...	*Vorremmo...*	vor-**ray**-moh
...this.	*...questo.*	**kweh**-stoh
...just a little.	*...un pochino.*	oon poh-**kee**-noh
...more.	*...di più.*	dee pew
...a ticket.	*...un biglietto.*	oon beel-**yay**-toh
...a room.	*...una camera.*	**oo**-nah **kah**-may-rah
...the bill.	*...il conto.*	eel **kohn**-toh

How Many?

one	*uno*	**oo**-noh
two	*due*	**doo**-ay
three	*tre*	tray
four	*quattro*	**kwah**-troh
five	*cinque*	**cheeng**-kway
six	*sei*	**seh**ee
seven	*sette*	**seht**-tay
eight	*otto*	**oh**-toh
nine	*nove*	**noh**-vay
ten	*dieci*	dee**ay**-chee

You'll find more to count on in the "Numbers" section on page 174.

When?

At what time?	*A che ora?*	ah kay **oh**-rah
open / closed	*aperto / chiuso*	ah-**pehr**-toh / keeoo-zoh
Just a moment.	*Un momento.*	oon moh-**mayn**-toh
Now.	*Adesso.*	ah-**dehs**-soh
Soon.	*Presto.*	**prehs**-toh
Later.	*Più tardi.*	pew **tar**-dee
Today.	*Oggi.*	**oh**-jee
Tomorrow.	*Domani.*	doh-**mah**-nee

Be creative! You can combine these phrases to say: "Two, please," or "No, thank you," or "Open tomorrow?" or "Please, where can I buy a ticket?" Please is a magic word in any language. If you want something and you don't know the word for it, just point and say "***Per favore***" (Please). If you know the word for what you want, such as the bill, simply say, "***Il conto, per favore***" (The bill, please).

Struggling

Do you speak English?	*Parla inglese?*	**par**-lah een-**glay**-zay
A teeny weeny bit?	*Nemmeno un pochino?*	nehm-**may**-noh oon poh-**kee**-noh

ITALIAN BASICS

Please speak English.	*Parli inglese, per favore.*	**par**-lee een-**glay**-zay pehr fah-**voh**-ray
You speak English well.	*Lei parla bene l'inglese.*	**leh**ee **par**-lah **behn**-ay leen-**glay**-zay
I don't speak Italian.	*Non parlo l'italiano.*	nohn **par**-loh lee-tah-lee**ah**-noh
We don't speak Italian.	*Non parliamo l'italiano.*	nohn par-lee**ah**-moh lee-tah-lee**ah**-noh
I speak a little Italian.	*Parlo un po' d'italiano.*	**par**-loh oon poh dee-tah-lee**ah**-noh
Sorry, I speak only English.	*Mi dispiace, parlo solo inglese.*	mee dee-spee**ah**-chay **par**-loh **soh**-loh een-**glay**-zay
Sorry, we speak only English.	*Mi dispiace, parliamo solo inglese.*	mee dee-spee**ah**-chay par-lee**ah**-moh **soh**-loh een-**glay**-zay
Does somebody nearby speak English?	*C'è qualcuno qui che parla inglese?*	cheh kwal-**koo**-noh kwee kay **par**-lah een-**glay**-zay
Who speaks English?	*Chi parla inglese?*	kee **par**-lah een-**glay**-zay
What does this mean?	*Cosa significa?*	**koh**-zah seen-**yee**-fee-kah
What is this in Italian / English?	*Come si dice questo in italiano / inglese?*	**koh**-may see **dee**-chay **kweh**-stoh een ee-tah-lee**ah**-noh / een-**glay**-zay
Repeat?	*Ripeta?*	ree-**pay**-tah
Speak slowly.	*Parli lentamente.*	**par**-lee layn-tah-**mayn**-tay
Slower.	*Più lentamente.*	pew layn-tah-**mayn**-tay
I understand.	*Capisco.*	kah-**pees**-koh
I don't understand.	*Non capisco.*	nohn kah-**pees**-koh
Do you understand?	*Capisce?*	kah-**pee**-shay
Write it?	*Me lo scrive?*	may loh **skree**-vay

Handy Questions

How much?	*Quanto?*	**kwahn**-toh
How many?	*Quanti?*	**kwahn**-tee
How long is the trip?	*Quanto tempo dura il viaggio?*	**kwahn**-toh **tehm**-poh **doo**-rah eel vee**ah**-joh
How many minutes?	*Quanti minuti?*	**kwahn**-tee mee-**noo**-tee
How many hours?	*Quante ore?*	**kwahn**-tay **oh**-ray
How far?	*Quanto dista?*	**kwahn**-toh **dee**-stah
How?	*Come?*	**koh**-may
Can you help me?	*Può aiutarmi?*	pwoh ah-yoo-**tar**-mee
Can you help us?	*Può aiutarci?*	pwoh ah-yoo-**tar**-chee
Can I / Can we...?	*Posso / Possiamo...?*	**poh**-soh / poh-see**ah**-moh
...have one	*...averne uno*	ah-**vehr**-nay **oo**-noh
...go in for free	*...andare senza pagare*	ahn-**dah**-ray **sehnt**-sah pah-**gah**-ray
...borrow that for a moment / an hour	*...prenderlo in prestito per un momento / un'ora*	prehn-**dehr**-loh een preh-**stee**-toh pehr oon moh-**mehn**-toh / oon-**oh**-rah
...use the toilet	*...usare la toilette*	oo-**zah**-ray lah twah-**leht**-tay
What? (didn't hear)	*Che cosa?*	kay **koh**-zah
What is this / that?	*Che cos'è questo / quello?*	kay koh-**zeh** **kweh**-stoh / **kway**-loh
What is better?	*Quale è meglio?*	**kwah**-lay eh **mehl**-yoh
What's going on?	*Cosa succede?*	**koh**-zah soo-**chay**-day
When?	*Quando?*	**kwahn**-doh
What time is it?	*Che ora è?*	kay **oh**-rah eh
At what time?	*A che ora?*	ah kay **oh**-rah
On time?	*Puntuale?*	poon-too**ah**-lay
Late?	*In ritardo?*	een ree-**tar**-doh
How long will it take?	*Quanto ci vuole?*	**kwahn**-toh chee voo**oh**-lay
When does this open / close?	*A che ora apre / chiude?*	ah kay **oh**-rah **ah**-pray / kee**oo**-day
Is this open daily?	*È aperto tutti i giorni?*	eh ah-**pehr**-toh **too**-tee ee **jor**-nee

What day is this closed?	*Che giorno chiudete?*	kay **jor**-noh keeoo-**day**-tay
Do you have...?	*Ha...?*	ah
Where is...?	*Dov'è...?*	doh-**veh**
Where are...?	*Dove sono...?*	**doh**-vay **soh**-noh
Where can I find / buy...?	*Dove posso trovare / comprare...?*	**doh**-vay **poh**-soh troh-**vah**-ray / kohm-**prah**-ray
Where can we find / buy...?	*Dove possiamo trovare / comprare...?*	**doh**-vay poh-see**ah**-moh troh-**vah**-ray / kohm-**prah**-ray
Is it necessary?	*È necessario?*	eh nay-chay-**sah**-reeoh
Is it possible...?	*È possibile...?*	eh poh-**see**-bee-lay
...to enter	*...entrare*	ehn-**trah**-ray
...to picnic here	*...mangiare al sacco qui*	mahn-**jah**-ray ahl **sah**-koh kwee
...to sit here	*...sedersi qui*	say-**dehr**-see kwee
...to look	*...guardare*	gwar-**dah**-ray
...to take a photo	*...fare una foto*	**fah**-ray **oo**-nah **foh**-toh
...to see this room	*...vedere questa camera*	vay-**day**-ray **kweh**-stah **kah**-may-rah
Who?	*Chi?*	kee
Why?	*Perchè?*	pehr-**keh**
Why not?	*Perchè no?*	pehr-**keh** noh
Yes or no?	*Si o no?*	see oh noh

To prompt a simple answer, ask, ***"Si o no?"*** (Yes or no?). To turn a word or sentence into a question, ask it in a questioning tone. ***"Va bene"*** (It's good) becomes ***"Va bene?"*** (Is it good?). An easy way to say, "Where is the toilet?" is to ask, ***"Toilette?"***

Yin and Yang

good / bad	*buono / cattivo*	**bwoh**-noh / kah-**tee**-voh
best / worst	*il migliore / il peggiore*	eel meel-**yoh**-ray / eel pay-**joh**-ray

a little / lots	*poco / tanto*	**poh**-koh / **tahn**-toh
more / less	*più / meno*	pew / **may**-noh
cheap / expensive	*economico / caro*	ay-koh-**noh**-mee-koh / **kah**-roh
big / small	*grande / piccolo*	**grahn**-day / **pee**-koh-loh
hot / cold	*caldo / freddo*	**kahl**-doh / **fray**-doh
warm / cool	*caldo / fresco*	**kahl**-doh / **fray**-skoh
open / closed	*aperto / chiuso*	ah-**pehr**-toh / kee**oo**-zoh
entrance / exit	*entrata / uscita*	ehn-**trah**-tah / oo-**shee**-tah
push / pull	*spingere / tirare*	**speen**-jay-ray / tee-**rah**-ray
arrive / depart	*arrivare / partire*	ah-ree-**vah**-ray / par-**tee**-ray
early / late	*presto / tardi*	**prehs**-toh / **tar**-dee
soon / later	*presto / più tardi*	**prehs**-toh / pew **tar**-dee
fast / slow	*veloce / lento*	vay-**loh**-chay / **lehn**-toh
here / there	*qui / lì*	kwee / lee
near / far	*vicino / lontano*	vee-**chee**-noh / lohn-**tah**-noh
indoors / outdoors	*dentro / fuori*	**dehn**-troh / foo-**oh**-ree
mine / yours	*mio / suo*	**mee**-oh / **soo**-oh
this / that	*questo / quello*	**kweh**-stoh / **kweh**-loh
everybody / nobody	*tutti / nessuno*	**too**-tee / nehs-**soo**-noh
easy / difficult	*facile / difficile*	**fah**-chee-lay / dee-**fee**-chee-lay
left / right	*sinistra / destra*	see-**nee**-strah / **dehs**-trah
up / down	*su / giú*	soo / joo
above / below	*sopra / sotto*	**soh**-prah / **soh**-toh
young / old	*giovane / anziano*	joh-**vah**-nay / ahnt-see**ah**-noh
new / old	*nuovo / vecchio*	**nwoh**-voh / **vehk**-eeoh
heavy / light	*pesante / leggero*	pay-**zahn**-tay / lay-**jay**-roh

dark / light	*scuro / chiaro*	**skoo**-roh / kee**ah**-roh
happy / sad	*felice / triste*	fee-**lee**-chay / **tree**-stay
beautiful / ugly	*bello[a] / brutto[a]*	**behl**-loh / **broo**-toh
nice / mean	*carino[a] / cattivo[a]*	kah-**ree**-noh / kah-**tee**-voh
smart / stupid	*intelligente / stupido[a]*	een-tehl-ee-**jayn**-tay / **stoo**-pee-doh
vacant / occupied	*libero / occupato*	**lee**-bay-roh / oh-koo-**pah**-toh
with / without	*con / senza*	kohn / **sehnt**-sah

Italian words marked with an [a] end with "a" if used to describe a female. A handsome man is ***bello,*** a beautiful woman is ***bella.***

Big Little Words

I	*io*	**ee**oh
you (formal)	*Lei*	**leh**ee
you (informal)	*tu*	too
we	*noi*	**noh**ee
he	*lui*	lwee
she	*lei*	**leh**ee
they	*loro*	**loh**-roh
and	*e*	ay
at	*a*	ah
because	*perchè*	pehr-**keh**
but	*ma*	mah
by (train, car, etc.)	*in*	een
for	*per*	pehr
from	*da*	dah
here	*qui*	kwee
if	*se*	say
in	*in*	een
it	*esso*	**ehs**-soh
not	*non*	nohn
now	*adesso*	ah-**dehs**-soh
only	*solo*	**soh**-loh

or	*o*	oh
that	*quello*	**kweh**-loh
this	*questo*	**kweh**-stoh
to	*a*	ah
very	*molto*	**mohl**-toh

Quintessential Expressions

Prego.	**pray**-goh	You're welcome. / Please. / All right. / Can I help you?
Pronto.	**prohn**-toh	Hello. (answering phone) / Ready. (other situations)
Ecco.	**ay**-koh	Here it is.
Dica.	**dee**-kah	Tell me.
Allora... (like our "uh" before a sentence)	ah-**loh**-rah	Well...
Senta.	**sayn**-tah	Listen.
Tutto va bene.	**too**-toh vah **behn**-ay	Everything's fine.
Basta.	**bah**-stah	That's enough.
È tutto.	eh **too**-toh	That's all.
la dolce vita	lah **dohl**-chay **vee**-tah	the sweet life
il dolce far niente	eel **dohl**-chay far neee**ehn**-tay	the sweetness of doing nothing
...issimo[a] ("bravo" means good, "bravissimo" means very good)	...**ee**-see-moh	very

COUNTING

NUMBERS

0	*zero*	**zay**-roh
1	*uno*	**oo**-noh
2	*due*	**doo**-ay
3	*tre*	tray
4	*quattro*	**kwah**-troh
5	*cinque*	**cheeng**-kway
6	*sei*	**seh**ee
7	*sette*	**seht**-tay
8	*otto*	**oh**-toh
9	*nove*	**noh**-vay
10	*dieci*	dee**ay**-chee
11	*undici*	**oon**-dee-chee
12	*dodici*	**doh**-dee-chee
13	*tredici*	**tray**-dee-chee
14	*quattordici*	kwah-**tor**-dee-chee
15	*quindici*	**kween**-dee-chee
16	*sedici*	**say**-dee-chee
17	*diciassette*	dee-chah-**seht**-tay
18	*diciotto*	dee-**choh**-toh
19	*diciannove*	dee-chahn-**noh**-vay
20	*venti*	**vayn**-tee
21	*ventuno*	vayn-**too**-noh
22	*ventidue*	vayn-tee-**doo**-ay
23	*ventitrè*	vayn-tee-**tray**

30	*trenta*	**trayn**-tah
31	*trentuno*	trayn-**too**-noh
40	*quaranta*	kwah-**rahn**-tah
41	*quarantuno*	kwah-rahn-**too**-noh
50	*cinquanta*	cheeng-**kwahn**-tah
60	*sessanta*	say-**sahn**-tah
70	*settanta*	say-**tahn**-tah
80	*ottanta*	oh-**tahn**-tah
90	*novanta*	noh-**vahn**-tah
100	*cento*	**chehn**-toh
101	*centouno*	chehn-toh-**oo**-noh
102	*centodue*	chehn-toh-**doo**-ay
200	*duecento*	doo-ay-**chehn**-toh
1000	*mille*	**mee**-lay
2000	*duemila*	doo-ay-**mee**-lah
2001	*duemilauno*	doo-ay-mee-lah-**oo**-noh
2002	*duemiladue*	doo-ay-mee-lah-**doo**-ay
2003	*duemilatre*	doo-ay-mee-lah-**tray**
2004	*duemila-quattro*	doo-ay-mee-lah-**kwah**-troh
2005	*duemila-cinque*	doo-ay-mee-lah-**cheeng**-kway
2006	*duemilasei*	doo-ay-mee-lah-**seh**ee
2007	*duemilasette*	doo-ay-mee-lah-**seht**-tay
2008	*duemilaotto*	doo-ay-mee-lah-**oh**-toh
2009	*duemilanove*	doo-ay-mee-lah-**noh**-vay
2010	*duemila-dieci*	doo-ay-mee-lah-dee**ay**-chee
million	*milione*	mee-lee**oh**-nay
billion	*miliardo*	meel-**yar**-doh
number one	*numero uno*	**noo**-may-roh **oo**-noh
first	*primo*	**pree**-moh
second	*secondo*	say-**kohn**-doh
third	*terzo*	**tehrt**-soh
once / twice	*una volta / due volte*	**oo**-nah **vohl**-tah / **doo**-ay **vohl**-tay
a quarter	*un quarto*	oon **kwar**-toh

a third	*un terzo*	oon **tehrt**-soh
half	*mezzo*	**mehd**-zoh
this much	*tanto così*	**tahn**-toh koh-**zee**
a dozen	*una dozzina*	**oo**-nah dohd-**zee**-nah
some	*un po'*	oon poh
enough	*abbastanza*	ah-bah-**stahnt**-sah
a handful	*una manciata*	**oo**-nah mah<u>n</u>-**chah**-tah
50%	*cinquanta per cento*	cheeng-**kwahn**-tah pehr **chehn**-toh
100%	*cento per cento*	**chehn**-toh pehr **chehn**-toh

MONEY

Where is a cash machine?	*Dov'è un bancomat?*	doh-**veh** oon **bahnk**-oh-maht
My ATM card has been...	*La mia tessera bancomat è stata...*	lah **mee**-ah teh-**say**-rah **bahnk**-oh-maht eh **stah**-tah
...demagnetized.	*...demagnetizzata.*	day-man-yeht-eed-**zah**-tah
...stolen.	*...rubata.*	roo-**bah**-tah
...eaten by the machine.	*...trattenuta dal bancomat.*	trah-tay-**noo**-tah dahl **bahnk**-oh-maht

Key Phrases: Money

euro (€)	*euro*	ay-**oo**-roh
money	*soldi, denaro*	**sohl**-dee, day-**nah**-roh
cash	*contante*	koh<u>n</u>-**tahn**-tay
credit card	*carta di credito*	**kar**-tah dee **kray**-dee-toh
bank	*banca*	**bahn**-kah
cash machine	*bancomat*	**bahnk**-oh-maht
Where is a cash machine?	*Dov'è un bancomat?*	doh-**veh** oon **bahnk**-oh-maht
Do you accept credit cards?	*Accettate carte di credito?*	ah-chay-**tah**-tay **kar**-tay dee **kray**-dee-toh

Do you accept credit cards?	*Accettate carte di credito?*	ah-chay-**tah**-tay **kar**-tay dee **kray**-dee-toh
Can you change dollars?	*Può cambiare dollari?*	pwoh kahm-bee**ah**-ray **dol**-lah-ree
What is your exchange rate for dollars...?	*Qual'è il cambio del dollaro...?*	kwah-**leh** eel **kahm**-beeoh dayl **dol**-lah-roh
...in traveler's checks	*...per traveler's checks*	pehr "traveler's checks"
What is the commission?	*Quant'è la commissione?*	kwahn̲-**teh** lah koh-mee-see**oh**-nay
Any extra fee?	*C'è un sovrapprezzo?*	cheh oon soh-vrah-**prehd**-zoh
Can you break this? (big bill into smaller bills)	*Mi può cambiare questo?*	mee pwoh kahm-bee**ah**-ray **kweh**-stoh
I would like...	*Vorrei....*	vor-**reh**ee
...small bills.	*...banconote di piccolo taglio.*	bahn̲-koh-**noh**-tay dee **pee**-koh-loh **tahl**-yoh
...large bills.	*...banconote di grosso taglio.*	bahn̲-koh-**noh**-tay dee **groh**-soh **tahl**-yoh
...coins.	*...monete.*	moh-**nay**-tay
€50	*cinquanta euro*	cheeng-**kwahn**-tah ay-**oo**-roh
Is this a mistake?	*Questo è un errore?*	**kweh**-stoh eh oon eh-**roh**-ray
This is incorrect.	*Questo non è corretto.*	**kweh**-stoh nohn̲ eh kor-**reht**-toh
Did you print these today?	*Le ha stampate oggi?*	lay ah stahm-**pah**-tay **oh**-jee
I'm broke.	*Sono al verde.*	**soh**-noh ahl **vehr**-day
I'm poor.	*Sono povero[a].*	**soh**-noh **poh**-vay-roh
I'm rich.	*Sono ricco[a].*	**soh**-noh **ree**-koh
I'm Bill Gates.	*Sono Bill Gates.*	**soh**-noh "Bill Gates"
Where is the nearest casino?	*Dov'è il casinò più vicino?*	doh-**veh** eel kah-zee-**noh** pew vee-**chee**-noh

Italy uses the euro currency. Euros (€) are divided into 100 cents. Use your common cents—cents are like pennies, and the euro has coins like nickels, dimes, and half-dollars.

Money Words

euro (€)	*euro*	ay-**oo**-roh
cents	*centesimi*	chehn-**tay**-zee-mee
money	*soldi, denaro*	**sohl**-dee, day-**nah**-roh
cash	*contante*	kohn-**tahn**-tay
cash machine	*bancomat*	**bahnk**-oh-maht
bank	*banca*	**bahn**-kah
credit card	*carta di credito*	**kar**-tah dee **kray**-dee-toh
change money	*cambiare dei soldi*	kahm-bee**ah**-ray **deh**ee **sohl**-dee
exchange	*cambio*	**kahm**-beeoh
buy / sell	*comprare / vendere*	kohm-**prah**-ray / vehn-**day**-ray
commission	*commissione*	koh-mee-see**oh**-nay
traveler's check	*traveler's check*	"traveler's check"
cash advance	*prelievo*	pray-lee**ay**-voh
cashier	*cassiere*	kah-see**ay**-ray
bills	*banconote*	bahn-koh-**noh**-tay
coins	*monete*	moh-**nay**-tay
receipt	*ricevuta*	ree-chay-**voo**-tah

All cash machines are multilingual. On the small chance you'd need to conduct your transaction in Italian, you'd use these buttons: ***esatto*** (correct), ***conferma*** (confirm), and ***annullare*** (cancel). Your PIN code is a ***codice segreto.***

TIME

What time is it?	*Che ore sono?*	kay **oh**-ray **soh**-noh
It's...	*Sono...*	**soh**-noh
...8:00 in the morning.	*...le otto di mattina.*	lay **oh**-toh dee mah-**tee**-nah

Key Phrases: Time

minute	*minuto*	mee-**noo**-toh
hour	*ora*	**oh**-rah
day	*giorno*	**jor**-noh
week	*settimana*	say-tee-**mah**-nah
What time is it?	*Che ore sono?*	kay **oh**-ray **soh**-noh
It's...	*Sono...*	**soh**-noh
...8:00.	*...le otto.*	lay **oh**-toh
...16:00.	*...le sedici.*	lay **say**-dee-chee
When does this open / close?	*A che ora apre / chiude?*	ah kay **oh**-rah **ah**-pray / kee**oo**-day

...16:00.	*...le sedici.*	lay **say**-dee-chee
...4:00 in the afternoon.	*...le quattro del pomeriggio.*	lay **kwah**-troh dayl poh-may-**ree**-joh
...10:30 in the evening.	*...le dieci e mezza di sera.*	lay dee**ay**-chee ay **mehd**-zah dee **say**-rah
...a quarter past nine.	*...le nove e un quarto.*	lay **noh**-vay ay oon **kwar**-toh
...a quarter to eleven.	*...le undici meno un quarto.*	lay **oon**-dee-chee **may**-noh oon **kwar**-toh
It's...	*È...*	eh
...noon.	*...mezzogiorno.*	mehd-zoh-**jor**-noh
...midnight.	*...mezzanotte.*	mehd-zah-**noh**-tay
...early / late.	*...presto / tardi.*	**prehs**-toh / **tar**-dee
...on time.	*...puntuale.*	poon-too**ah**-lay
...sunrise.	*...alba.*	**ahl**-bah
...sunset.	*...tramonto.*	trah-**mohn**-toh
It's my bedtime.	*Per me è ora di andare a dormire.*	pehr may eh **oh**-rah dee ahn-**dah**-ray ah dor-**mee**-ray

Timely Expressions

I'll return / We'll return...	*Torno / Torniamo...*	**tor**-noh / tor-nee**ah**-moh

COUNTING

...at 11:20.	*...alle undici e venti.*	**ah**-lay **oon**-dee-chee ay **vayn**-tee
I'll arrive / We'll arrive...	*Arrivo / Arriviamo...*	ah-**ree**-voh / ah-ree-vee**ah**-moh
...by 18:00.	*...per le diciotto.*	pehr lay dee-**choh**-toh
When is checkout time?	*A che ora bisogna liberare la camera?*	ah kay **oh**-rah bee-**sohn**-yah lee-bay-**rah**-ray lah **kah**-may-rah
At what time...?	*A che ora...?*	ah kay **oh**-rah
...does this open / close	*...apre / chiude*	**ah**-pray / kee**oo**-day
...does the train / bus leave for ___	*...parte il treno / l'autobus per ___*	**par**-tay eel **tray**-noh / **low**-toh-boos pehr
...the next train / the bus leave for ___	*...parte il prossimo treno / autobus per ___*	**par**-tay eel **proh**-see-moh **tray**-noh / **ow**-toh-boos pehr
...the train / the bus arrive in ___	*...arriva a ___ il treno / l'autobus?*	ah-**ree**-vah ah ___ eel **tray**-noh / **low**-toh-boos
I / We want to take the 16:30 train.	*Vorrei / Vorremmo prendere il treno delle sedici e trenta.*	vor-**reh**ee / vor-**ray**-moh **prehn**-day-ray eel **tray**-noh **dehl**-lay **say**-dee-chee ay **trayn**-tah
Is the train / the bus...?	*È... il treno / l'autobus?*	eh... eel **tray**-noh / **low**-toh-boos
...early / late	*...in anticipo / in ritardo*	een ahn-tee-**chee**-poh / een ree-**tar**-doh
...on time	*...in orario*	een oh-**rah**-reeoh

In Italy, the 24-hour clock (or military time) is used by hotels, for opening/closing hours of stores, and for train, bus, and ferry schedules. Friends use the same "clock" we do. You'd meet a friend at 3:00 in the afternoon (***tre del pomeriggio***) to catch a train that leaves at 15:15. In Italy, the ***pomeriggio*** (afternoon) turns to ***sera*** (evening) generally about 5:00 P.M. (5:30 P.M. is ***cinque e mezza di sera***).

About Time

minute	*minuto*	mee-**noo**-toh
hour	*ora*	**oh**-rah
in the morning	*di mattina*	dee mah-**tee**-nah
in the afternoon	*di pomeriggio*	dee poh-may-**ree**-joh
in the evening	*di sera*	dee **say**-rah
at night	*di notte*	dee **noh**-tay
at 6:00 sharp	*alle sei in punto*	**ah**-lay **seh**ee een **poon**-toh
from 8:00 to 10:00	*dalle otto alle dieci*	**dah**-lay **oh**-toh **ah**-lay dee**ay**-chee
in half an hour	*tra mezz'ora*	trah mehd-**zoh**-rah
in one hour	*tra un'ora*	trah oon-**oh**-rah
in three hours	*tra tre ore*	trah tray **oh**-ray
anytime	*a qualsiasi ora*	ah kwahl-see**ah**-zee **oh**-rah
immediately	*immediata-mente*	ee-may-deeah-tah-**mayn**-tay
every hour	*ogni ora*	**ohn**-yee **oh**-rah
every day	*ogni giorno*	**ohn**-yee **jor**-noh
daily	*giornaliero*	jor-nahl-**yehr**-oh
last	*passato*	pah-**sah**-toh
this	*questo*	**kweh**-stoh
next	*prossimo*	**proh**-see-moh
May 15	*il quindici maggio*	eel **kween**-dee-chee **mah**-joh
in the future	*in futuro*	een foo-**too**-roh
in the past	*nel passato*	nehl pah-**sah**-toh

The Day

day	*giorno*	**jor**-noh
today	*oggi*	**oh**-jee
yesterday	*ieri*	**yay**-ree
tomorrow	*domani*	doh-**mah**-nee
tomorrow morning	*domani mattina*	doh-**mah**-nee mah-**tee**-nah
day after tomorrow	*dopodomani*	doh-poh-doh-**mah**-nee

The Week

week	*settimana*	say-tee-**mah**-nah
last week	*la settimana scorsa*	lah say-tee-**mah**-nah **skor**-sah
this week	*questa settimana*	**kweh**-stah say-tee-**mah**-nah
next week	*la settimana prossima*	lah say-tee-**mah**-nah **proh**-see-mah
Monday	*lunedì*	loo-nay-**dee**
Tuesday	*martedì*	mar-tay-**dee**
Wednesday	*mercoledì*	mehr-koh-lay-**dee**
Thursday	*giovedì*	joh-vay-**dee**
Friday	*venerdì*	vay-nehr-**dee**
Saturday	*sabato*	**sah**-bah-toh
Sunday	*domenica*	doh-**may**-nee-kah

The Month

month	*mese*	**may**-zay
January	*gennaio*	jay-**nah**-yoh
February	*febbraio*	fay-**brah**-yoh
March	*marzo*	**mart**-soh
April	*aprile*	ah-**pree**-lay
May	*maggio*	**mah**-joh
June	*giugno*	**joon**-yoh
July	*luglio*	**lool**-yoh
August	*agosto*	ah-**goh**-stoh
September	*settembre*	say-**tehm**-bray
October	*ottobre*	oh-**toh**-bray
November	*novembre*	noh-**vehm**-bray
December	*dicembre*	dee-**chehm**-bray

The Year

year	*anno*	**ahn**-noh
spring	*primavera*	pree-mah-**vay**-rah
summer	*estate*	ay-**stah**-tay
fall	*autunno*	ow-**too**-noh
winter	*inverno*	een-**vehr**-noh

Holidays and Happy Days

holiday	*festa*	**fehs**-tah
national holiday	*festa nazionale*	**fehs**-tah naht-seeoh-**nah**-lay
religious holiday	*festa religiosa*	**fehs**-tah ray-lee-**joh**-zah
Is today / tomorrow a holiday?	*Oggi / Domani è festa?*	**oh**-jee / doh-**mah**-nee eh **fehs**-tah
Is a holiday coming up soon? When?	*Siamo vicini a una festa? Quand'è?*	see**ah**-moh vee-**chee**-nee ah **oo**-nah **fehs**-tah kwahn-**deh**
What is the holiday?	*Che festa è?*	kay **fehs**-tah eh
Merry Christmas!	*Buon Natale!*	bwohn nah-**tah**-lay
Happy New Year!	*Felice anno nuovo!*	fay-**lee**-chay **ahn**-noh **nwoh**-voh
Easter	*Pasqua*	**pahs**-kwah
Happy (wedding) anniversary!	*Buon anniversario (di matrimonio).*	bwohn ah-nee-vehr-**sah**-reeoh (dee mah-tree-**moh**-neeoh)
Happy birthday!	*Buon compleanno!*	bwohn kohm-play-**ahn**-noh

Italians celebrate birthdays with the same "Happy Birthday" tune that we do. The Italian words mean "Best wishes to you": ***"Tanti auguri a te, tanti auguri a te, tanti auguri, caro[a] ___, tanti auguri a te!"***

Holidays during tourist season are April 25 (Liberation Day), May 1 (Labor Day), June 24 (***San Giovanni,*** northern Italy), August 15 (***Ferragosto,*** or Assumption of Mary), and November 1 (All Saints Day). In Italy, every saint gets a holiday—celebrated in local communities throughout the year.

TRAVELING

TRAINS

The Train Station

Where is the...?	*Dov'è la...?*	doh-**veh** lah
...train station	*...stazione*	staht-see**oh**-nay
Italian State Railways	*Ferrovie dello Stato (FS)*	fay-**roh**-veeay **dehl**-loh **stah**-toh
train information	*informazioni sui treni*	een-for-maht-see**oh**-nee **soo**ee **tray**-nee
train	*treno*	**tray**-noh
fast train	*inter-city (IC, EC)*	"inter-city"
fastest train	*Eurostar (ES)*	**yoo**-roh-star
fast / faster	*veloce / più veloce*	vay-**loh**-chay / pew vay-**loh**-chay
arrival	*arrivo*	ah-**ree**-voh
departure	*partenza*	par-**tehnt**-sah
delay	*ritardo*	ree-**tar**-doh
toilet	*toilette*	twah-**leht**-tay
waiting room	*sala di attesa, sala d'aspetto*	**sah**-lah dee ah-**tay**-zah, **sah**-lah dah-**spay**-toh
lockers	*armadietti*	ar-mah-dee**ay**-tee
baggage check room	*deposito bagagli, consegna*	day-**poh**-zee-toh bah-**gahl**-yee, kohn-**sayn**-yah

Key Phrases: Trains

train station	*stazione*	staht-see**oh**-nay
train	*treno*	**tray**-noh
ticket	*biglietto*	beel-**yay**-toh
transfer (verb)	*cambiare*	kahm-bee**ah**-ray
supplement	*supplemento*	soo-play-**mehn**-toh
arrival	*arrivo*	ah-**ree**-voh
departure	*partenza*	par-**tehnt**-sah
platform, track	*binario*	bee-**nah**-reeoh
train car	*vagone*	vah-**goh**-nay
A ticket to ___.	*Un biglietto per ___.*	oon beel-**yay**-toh pehr
Two tickets to ___.	*Due biglietti per ___.*	doo-ay beel-**yay**-tee pehr
When is the next train?	*Quando è il prossimo treno?*	**kwahn**-doh eh eel **proh**-see-moh **tray**-noh
Where does the train leave from?	*Da dove parte il treno?*	dah **doh**-vay **par**-tay eel **tray**-noh
Which train to ___?	*Quale treno per ___?*	**kwah**-lay **tray**-noh pehr

lost and found office	*ufficio oggetti smarriti*	oo-**fee**-choh oh-**jeht**-tee smah-**ree**-tee
tourist information	*informazioni per turisti*	een-for-maht-see**oh**-nee pehr too-**ree**-stee
to the platforms	*ai binari*	**ah**ee bee-**nah**-ree
platform, track	*binario*	bee-**nah**-reeoh
to the trains	*ai treni*	**ah**ee **tray**-nee
train car	*vagone*	vah-**goh**-nay
dining car	*carrozza ristorante*	kar-**rohd**-zah ree-stoh-**rahn**-tay
sleeper car	*carrozza letto*	kar-**rohd**-zah **leht**-toh
conductor	*capotreno*	kah-poh-**tray**-noh

Some Italian train stations have wonderful (and fun) schedule computers. Once you've mastered these (start by punching the

"English" button), you'll save lots of time figuring out the right train connections.

You'll encounter several types of trains in Italy. Along with the various local and milk-run (***locale***) trains, you'll see:

- the slow ***diretto*** trains
- the medium-speed ***espresso*** and ***InterRegionale*** trains
- the fast ***rapido*** trains such as the ***IC*** and ***IC Plus*** (***InterCity***, domestic routes), plus the ***EC*** (***EuroCity***, international routes)
- the super-fast ***Cisalpino*** trains (from Florence, Milan, or Venice to Switzerland and Stuttgart)
- the super-duper-fast ***Eurostar Italia***, Italy's bullet train

If you have a railpass, you will need to pay a reservation fee for the ***Eurostar Italia***, ***Cisalpino***, and ***IC Plus***, as well as for many ***IC*** and ***EC*** trains, when indicated in schedules.

Getting a Ticket

Where can I buy a ticket?	*Dove posso comprare un biglietto?*	**doh**-vay **poh**-soh kohm-**prah**-ray oon beel-**yay**-toh
A ticket to ___.	*Un biglietto per ___.*	oon beel-**yay**-toh pehr
Where can we buy tickets?	*Dove possiamo comprare i biglietti?*	**doh**-vay poh-see**ah**-moh kohm-**prah**-ray ee beel-**yay**-tee
Two tickets to ___.	*Due biglietti per ___.*	**doo**-ay beel-**yay**-tee pehr
Is this the line for...?	*È questa la fila per...?*	eh **kweh**-stah lah **fee**-lah pehr
...tickets	*...biglietti*	beel-**yay**-tee
...reservations	*...prenotazioni*	pray-noh-taht-see**oh**-nee
How much is the fare to ___?	*Quant'è la tariffa per ___?*	kwahn-**teh** lah tah-**ree**-fah pehr
Is this ticket valid for ___?	*Questo biglietto è valido per ___?*	**kwehs**-toh beel-**yay**-toh eh **vah**-lee-doh pehr

How long is this ticket valid?	*Per quanto tempo è valido questo biglietto?*	pehr **kwahn**-toh **tehm**-poh eh **vah**-lee-doh **kwehs**-toh beel-**yay**-toh
When is the next train?	*Quando è il prossimo treno?*	**kwahn**-doh eh eel **proh**-see-moh **tray**-noh
Do you have a schedule for all trains departing for ___ today / tomorrow?	*Ha un orario di tutti i treni in partenza per ___ oggi / domani?*	ah oon oh-**rah**-reeoh dee **too**-tee ee **tray**-nee een par-**tehnt**-sah pehr ___ **oh**-jee / doh-**mah**-nee
I'd like to leave...	*Vorrei partire...*	vor-**reh**ee par-**tee**-ray
We'd like to leave...	*Vorremmo partire...*	vor-**ray**-moh par-**tee**-ray
I'd like to arrive...	*Vorrei arrivare...*	vor-**reh**ee ah-ree-**vah**-ray
We'd like to arrive...	*Vorremmo arrivare...*	vor-**ray**-moh ah-ree-**vah**-ray
...by ___.	*...per le ___.*	pehr lay
...in the morning.	*...di mattina.*	dee mah-**tee**-nah
...in the afternoon.	*...di pomeriggio.*	dee poh-may-**ree**-joh
...in the evening.	*...di sera.*	dee **say**-rah
Is there a...?	*C'è un...?*	cheh oon
...earlier train	*...treno prima*	**tray**-noh **pree**-mah
...later train	*...treno più tardi*	**tray**-noh pew **tar**-dee
...overnight train	*...treno notturno*	**tray**-noh noh-**toor**-noh
...cheaper train	*...treno più economico*	**tray**-noh pew ay-koh-**noh**-mee-koh
...a cheaper option	*...una possibilità più economica*	**oo**-nah poh-see-bee-lee-**tah** pew ay-koh-**noh**-mee-kah
...local train	*...treno locale*	**tray**-noh loh-**kah**-lay
...express train	*...treno espresso*	**tray**-noh ehs-**pray**-soh
What track does it leave from?	*Da che binario parte?*	dah kay bee-**nah**-reeoh **par**-tay
What track?	*Quale binario?*	**kwah**-lay bee-**nah**-reeoh
On time?	*È puntuale?*	eh poon-too**ah**-lay
Late?	*In ritardo?*	een ree-**tar**-doh

Reservations, Supplements, and Discounts

Is a reservation required?	*Ci vuole la prenotazione?*	chee **vwoh**-lay lah pray-noh-taht-see**oh**-nay
I'd like to reserve...	*Vorrei prenotare...*	vor-**reh**ee pray-noh-**tah**-ray
...a seat.	*...un posto.*	oon **poh**-stoh
...a couchette.	*...una cuccetta.*	**oo**-nah koo-**chay**-tah
...a sleeper.	*...un posto in vagone letto.*	oon **poh**-stoh een vah-**goh**-nay **leht**-toh
...the entire train.	*...tutto il treno.*	**too**-toh eel **tray**-noh
We'd like to reserve...	*Vorremmo prenotare...*	vor-**ray**-moh pray-noh-**tah**-ray
...two seats.	*...due posti.*	**doo**-ay **poh**-stee
...two couchettes.	*...due cuccette.*	**doo**-ay koo-**chay**-tay
...a sleeper compartment with two beds.	*...un vagone letto da due letti.*	oon vah-**goh**-nay **leht**-toh dah doo-ay **leht**-tee
Is there a supplement?	*C'è un supplemento?*	cheh oon soo-play-**mehn**-toh
Does my railpass cover the supplement?	*Il mio railpass include il supplemento?*	eel **mee**-oh **rayl**-pahs een-**kloo**-day eel soo-play-**mehn**-toh
Is there a discount for...?	*Fate sconti per...?*	**fah**-tay **skohn**-tee pehr
...youth	*...giovani*	joh-**vah**-nee
...seniors	*...anziani*	ahnt-see**ah**-nee
...families	*...famiglie*	fah-**meel**-yay

Ticket Talk

ticket window	*Biglietteria*	beel-yeht-ay-**ree**-ah
reservations window	*Prenotazioni*	pray-noh-taht-see**oh**-nay
national	*nazionali*	naht-seeoh-**nah**-lee
international	*internazionali*	een-tehr-naht-seeoh-**nah**-lee

ticket	*biglietto*	beel-**yay**-toh
one way	*andata*	ahn̲-**dah**-tah
roundtrip	*andata e ritorno*	ahn̲-**dah**-tah ay ree-**tor**-noh
first class	*prima classe*	**pree**-mah **klah**-say
second class	*seconda classe*	say-**kohn**-dah **klah**-say
validate	*timbrare, obliterare*	teem-**brah**-ray, oh-blee-tay-**rah**-ray
schedule	*orario*	oh-**rah**-reeoh
departure	*partenza*	par-**tehnt**-sah
direct	*diretto*	dee-**reht**-toh
transfer (verb)	*cambiare*	kahm-bee**ah**-ray
connection	*coincidenza*	koh-een-chee-**dehnt**-sah
with supplement	*con supplemento*	kohn̲ soo-play-**mehn**-toh
reservation	*prenotazione*	pray-noh-taht-see**oh**-nay
seat...	*posto...*	**poh**-stoh
...by the window	*...vicino al finestrino*	vee-**chee**-noh ahl fee-nay-**stree**-noh
...on the aisle	*...vicino al corridoio*	vee-**chee**-noh ahl koh-ree-**doh**-yoh
berth...	*cuccetta...*	koo-**chay**-tah
...upper	*...di sopra*	dee **soh**-prah
...middle	*...in mezzo*	een **mehd**-zoh
...lower	*...di sotto*	dee **soh**-toh
refund	*rimborso*	reem-**bor**-soh
reduced fare	*tariffa ridotta*	tah-**ree**-fah ree-**doh**-tah

Changing Trains

Is it direct?	*È diretto?*	eh dee-**reht**-toh
Must I transfer?	*Devo cambiare?*	**day**-voh kahm-bee**ah**-ray
Must we transfer?	*Dobbiamo cambiare?*	doh-bee**ah**-moh kahm-bee**ah**-ray
When? Where?	*Quando? Dove?*	**kwahn**-doh **doh**-vay
Do I change / Do we change here for ___?	*Cambio / Cambiamo qui per ___?*	**kahm**-beeoh / kahm-bee**ah**-moh kwee pehr

Where do I change / do we change for ___?	*Dove cambio / cambiamo per ___?*	**doh**-vay **kahm**-beeoh / kahm-bee**ah**-moh pehr
At what time?	*A che ora?*	ah kay **oh**-rah
From what track does my / our connecting train leave?	*Da che binario parte la mia / la nostra coincidenza?*	dah kay bee-**nah**-reeoh **par**-tay lah **mee**-ah / lah **noh**-strah koh-een-chee-**dehnt**-sah
How many minutes in ___ to change trains?	*Quanti minuti a ___ per prendere coincidenza?*	**kwahn**-tee mee-**noo**-tee ah ___ pehr **prehn**-day-ray lah koh-een-chee-**dehnt**-sah

On the Platform

Where is...?	*Dov'è...?*	doh-**veh**
Is this...?	*Questo è...?*	**kwehs**-toh eh
...the train to ___	*...il treno per ___*	eel **tray**-noh pehr
Which train to ___?	*Quale treno per ___?*	**kwah**-lay **tray**-noh pehr
Which train car for ___?	*Quale vagone per ___?*	**kwah**-lay vah-**goh**-nay pehr
Where is first class?	*Dov'è la prima classe?*	doh-**veh** lah **pree**-mah **klah**-say
...front / middle / back	*...in testa / in centro / in coda*	een **tehs**-tah / een **chehn**-troh / een **koh**-dah
Where can I validate my ticket?	*Dove posso timbrare il biglietto?*	**doh**-vay **poh**-soh teem-**brah**-ray eel beel-**yay**-toh

You must validate (***timbrare***) your train ticket prior to boarding the train. Look for the yellow machines on the platform and insert your ticket—watch others and imitate.

On the Train

Is this (seat) free?	*È libero?*	eh **lee**-bay-roh
May I / May we...?	*Posso / Possiamo...?*	**poh**-soh / poh-see**ah**-moh

...sit here (me / we)	*...sedermi / sederci qui*	say-**dehr**-mee / say-**dehr**-chee kwee
...open the window	*...aprire il finestrino*	ah-**pree**-ray eel fee-nay-**stree**-noh
...eat your food	*...mangiare il suo cibo*	mahn-**jah**-ray eel **soo**-oh **chee**-boh
Save my place?	*Mi tiene il posto?*	mee tee**ay**-nay eel **poh**-stoh
Save our places?	*Ci tiene il posto?*	chee tee**ay**-nay eel **poh**-stoh
That's my seat.	*È il mio posto.*	eh eel **mee**-oh **poh**-stoh
These are our seats.	*Sono i nostri posti.*	**soh**-noh ee **noh**-stree **poh**-stee
Where are you going?	*Dove va?*	**doh**-vay vah
I'm going to ___.	*Vado a ___.*	**vah**-doh ah
We're going to ___.	*Andiamo a ___.*	ahn-dee**ah**-moh ah
Tell me when to get off?	*Mi dice quando devo scendere?*	mee **dee**-chay **kwahn**-doh **day**-voh **shehn**-day-ray
Tell us when to get off?	*Ci dice quando dobbiamo scendere?*	chee **dee**-chay **kwahn**-doh doh-bee**ah**-moh **shehn**-day-ray
Where is a (good-looking) conductor?	*Dov'è un (bel) capotreno?*	doh-**veh** oon (behl) kah-poh-**tray**-noh
Does this train stop in ___?	*Questo treno si ferma a ___?*	**kwehs**-toh **tray**-noh see **fehr**-mah ah
When will it arrive in ___?	*Quando arriva a ___?*	**kwahn**-doh ah-**ree**-vah ah
When will it arrive?	*Quando arriva?*	**kwahn**-doh ah-**ree**-vah

Reading Train and Bus Schedules

a	to
arrivi	arrivals
arrivo	arrival (also abbreviated "a")

Major Transportation Lines In Italy

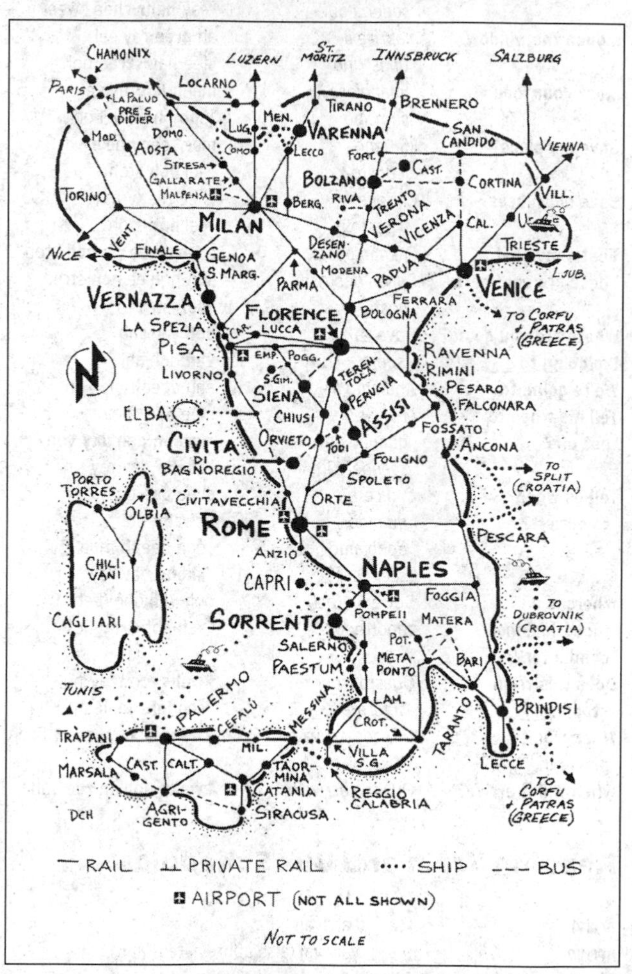

binario	track
da	from
destinazione	destination
domenica	Sunday
eccetto	except
feriali	weekdays including Saturday
ferma a tutte le stazioni	stops at all the stations
festivi	Sundays and holidays
fino	until
giorni	days
giornaliero	daily
in ritardo	late
non ferma a ___	doesn't stop in ___
ogni	every
partenza	departure (also abbreviated "p")
partenze	departures
per	for
sabato	Saturday
si effettua anche ___	it also runs ___
solo	only
tutti i giorni	daily
vacanza	holiday
1-5	Monday-Friday
6, 7	Saturday, Sunday

European schedules use the 24-hour clock. It's like American time until noon. After that, subtract twelve and add P.M. So 13:00 is 1 P.M., 20:00 is 8 P.M., and 24:00 is midnight. If your train is scheduled to depart at 00:01, it'll leave one minute after midnight.

Going Places

Italy	*Italia*	ee-**tahl**-yah
Austria	*Austria*	**ow**-streeah
Belgium	*Belgio*	**behl**-joh
Czech Republic	*Repubblica Ceca*	reh-**poo**-blee-kah **cheh**-kah

England	*Inghilterra*	een-geel-**tehr**-rah
France	*Francia*	**frahn**-chah
Paris	*Parigi*	pah-**ree**-jee
Germany	*Germania*	jehr-**mahn**-yah
Munich	*Monaco di Baviera*	**moh**-nah-koh dee bah-vee**ay**-rah
Greece	*Grecia*	**gray**-chah
Ireland	*Irlanda*	eer-**lahn**-dah
Netherlands	*Paesi Bassi*	pah-**ay**-zee **bah**-see
Portugal	*Portogallo*	por-toh-**gah**-loh
Scandinavia	*Paesi Scandinavi*	pah-**ay**-zee skahn-dee-**nah**-vee
Spain	*Spagna*	**spahn**-yah
Switzerland	*Svizzera*	**sveet**-say-rah
Turkey	*Turchia*	**toor**-keeah
Europe	*Europa*	ay-oo-**roh**-pah
EU (European Union)	*UE (Unione Europeo)*	oo ay (oon-ee-**ohn**-ay ay-oo-roh-**pay**-oh)
Russia	*Russia*	**roo**-see**ah**
Africa	*Africa*	**ahf**-ree-kah
United States	*Stati Uniti*	**stah**-tee oo-**nee**-tee
Canada	*Canada*	kah-nah-**dah**
world	*mondo*	**mohn**-doh

Local Places

Bologna	*Bologna*	boh-**lohn**-yah
Cinque Terre	*Cinque Terre*	**cheeng**-kway **tehr**-ray
Civita	*Civita*	chee-**vee**-tah
Florence	*Firenze*	fee-**rehn**-tsay
Italian Riviera	*Riviera Ligure*	reev-**yehr**-rah lee-**goo**-ray
Lake Como	*Lago di Como*	**lah**-goh dee **koh**-moh
Milan	*Milano*	mee-**lah**-noh
Naples	*Napoli*	**nah**-poh-lee
Orvieto	*Orvieto*	or-vee**ay**-toh

Pisa	*Pisa*	**pee**-zah
Rome	*Roma*	**roh**-mah
San Gimignano	*San Gimignano*	sahn jee-meen-**yah**-noh
Sicily	*Sicilia*	see-**chee**-leeah
Siena	*Siena*	see-**ehn**-ah
Sorrento	*Sorrento*	sor-**rehn**-toh
Varenna	*Varenna*	vah-**rehn**-nah
Vatican City	*Città del Vaticano*	cheet-**tah** dayl vah-tee-**kah**-noh
Venice	*Venezia*	vay-**nayt**-seeah
Vernazza	*Vernazza*	vehr-**naht**-tsah

BUSES AND SUBWAYS

At the Bus or Subway Station

ticket	*biglietto*	beel-**yay**-toh
city bus	*autobus*	**ow**-toh-boos
long-distance bus	*pullman, corriera*	**pool**-mahn, koh-ree-**ehr**-ah
bus stop	*fermata*	fehr-**mah**-tah
bus station	*stazione degli autobus*	staht-see**oh**-nay **dayl**-yee **ow**-toh-boos
subway	*metropolitana*	may-troh-poh-lee-**tah**-nah
subway station	*stazione della metropolitana*	staht-see**oh**-nay **day**-lah may-troh-poh-lee-**tah**-nah
subway map	*cartina*	kar-**tee**-nah
subway entrance	*entrata*	ayn-**trah**-tah
subway stop	*fermata*	fehr-**mah**-tah
subway exit	*uscita*	oo-**shee**-tah
direct	*diretto*	dee-**reht**-toh
connection	*coincidenza*	koh-een-chee-**dehnt**-sah
pickpocket	*borsaiolo*	bor-sah-**yoh**-loh

Most big cities offer deals on transportation, such as one-day tickets (***biglietto giornaliero***) and cheaper fares for youths and seniors. On a map, ***voi siete qui*** means "you are here." Venice has boats instead of buses. Zip around on ***traghetti*** (gondola ferries) and ***vaporetti*** (motorized ferries).

Taking Buses and Subways

How do you get to___?	*Come si va a ___?*	**koh**-may see vah ah
How much is a ticket?	*Quanto costa un biglietto?*	**kwahn**-toh **koh**-stah oon beel-**yay**-toh
Where can I buy a ticket?	*Dove posso comprare un biglietto?*	**doh**-vay **poh**-soh kohm-**prah**-ray oon beel-**yay**-toh
Where can we buy tickets?	*Dove possiamo comprare i biglietti?*	**doh**-vay poh-see**ah**-moh kohm-**prah**-ray ee beel-**yay**-tee
One ticket, please.	*Un biglietto, per favore*	oon beel-**yay**-toh pehr fah-voh-ray
Two tickets.	*Due biglietti.*	**doo**-ay beel-**yay**-tee
Is this ticket valid (for ___)?	*Questo biglietto è valido (per ___)?*	**kwehs**-toh beel-**yay**-toh eh **vah**-lee-doh (pehr ___)
Is there a one-day pass?	*C'è un biglietto giornaliero?*	cheh oon beel-**yay**-toh jor-nahl-**yay**-roh
Which bus to ___?	*Quale autobus per ___?*	**kwah**-lay **ow**-toh-boos pehr

Key Phrases: Buses and Subways

bus	*autobus*	**ow**-toh-boos
subway	*metropolitana*	may-troh-poh-lee-**tah**-nah
ticket	*biglietto*	beel-**yay**-toh
How do you get to ___?	*Come si va a ___?*	**koh**-may see vah ah
Which stop for ___?	*Qual'è la fermata per___?*	kwah-**leh** lah fehr-**mah**-tah pehr
Tell me when to get off?	*Mi dice quando devo scendere?*	mee **dee**-chay **kwahn**-doh **day**-voh **shehn**-day-ray

Does it stop at ___?	*Si ferma a ___?*	see **fehr**-mah ah
Which metro stop for ___?	*Qual'è la fermata per___?*	kwah-**leh** lah fehr-**mah**-tah pehr
Which direction for ___?	*Da che parte è ___?*	dah kay **par**-tay eh
Must I transfer?	*Devo cambiare?*	**day**-voh kahm-bee**ah**-ray
Must we transfer?	*Dobbiamo cambiare?*	doh-bee**ah**-moh kahm-bee**ah**-ray
When does... leave?	*Quando parte...?*	**kwahn**-doh **par**-tay
...the first	*...il primo*	eel **pree**-moh
...the next	*...il prossimo*	eel **proh**-see-moh
...the last	*...l'ultimo*	**lool**-tee-moh
...bus / subway	*...autobus / metropolitana*	**ow**-toh-boos / may-troh-poh-lee-**tah**-nah
What's the frequency per hour / day?	*Quante volte passa all'ora / al giorno?*	**kwahn**-tay **vohl**-tay **pah**-sah ah-**loh**-rah / ahl **jor**-noh
Where does it leave from?	*Da dove parte?*	dah **doh**-vay **par**-tay
What time does it leave?	*A che ora parte?*	ah kay **oh**-rah **par**-tay
I'm going to ___.	*Vado a ___.*	**vah**-doh ah
We're going to ___.	*Andiamo a ___.*	ahn-dee**ah**-moh ah
Tell me when to get off?	*Mi dice quando devo scendere?*	mee **dee**-chay **kwahn**-doh **day**-voh **shehn**-day-ray
Tell us when to get off?	*Ci dice quando dobbiamo scendere?*	chee **dee**-chay **kwahn**-doh doh-bee**ah**-moh **shehn**-day-ray

TAXIS

Getting a Taxi

Taxi!	*Taxi!*	**tahk**-see
Can you call a taxi?	*Può chiamare un taxi?*	pwoh kee-ah-**mah**-ray oon **tahk**-see
Where is a taxi stand?	*Dov'è una fermata dei taxi?*	doh-veh **oo**-nah fehr-**mah**-tah **deh**ee **tahk**-see
Where can I get a taxi?	*Dov'è posso prendere un taxi?*	doh-veh **poh**-soh **prehn**-day-ray oon **tahk**-see
Where can we get a taxi?	*Dov'è possiamo prendere un taxi?*	doh-veh poh-see**ah**-moh **prehn**-day-ray oon **tahk**-see
Are you free?	*È libero?*	eh **lee**-bay-roh
Occupied.	*Occupato.*	oh-koo-**pah**-toh
To ___, please.	*A ___, per favore.*	ah ___ pehr fah-**voh**-ray
To this address.	*A questo indirizzo.*	ah **kwehs**-toh een-dee-**reed**-zoh
Take me to ___.	*Mi porti a ___.*	mee **por**-tee ah
Take us to ___.	*Ci porti a ___.*	chee **por**-tee ah
Approximately how much will it cost to go...?	*Quanto costa più o meno fino...?*	**kwahn**-toh **koh**-stah pew oh **may**-noh **fee**-noh
...to ___	*...a ___*	ah

Key Phrases: Taxis

Taxi!	*Taxi!*	**tahk**-see
Are you free?	*È libero?*	eh **lee**-bay-roh
To ___, please.	*A ___, per favore.*	ah ___ pehr fah-**voh**-ray
meter	*tassametro*	tah-sah-**may**-troh
Stop here.	*Si fermi qui.*	see **fehr**-mee kwee
Keep the change.	*Tenga il resto.*	**tayn**-gah eel **rehs**-toh

...to the airport	*...all'aeroporto*	ah-lah-ay-roh-**por**-toh
...to the train station	*...alla stazione ferroviaria*	**ah**-lah staht-see**oh**-nay fay-roh-vee-**ah**-reeah
...to this address	*...a questo indirizzo*	ah **kweh**-stoh een-dee-**reed**-zoh
Any extra supplement?	*C'è qualche supplemento?*	cheh **kwahl**-kay soo-play-**mehn**-toh
Too much.	*Troppo.*	**troh**-poh
Can you take ___ people?	*Può portare ___ persone?*	pwoh por-**tah**-reh ___ pehr-**soh**-nay
Any extra fee?	*C'è un sovrapprezzo?*	cheh oon soh-vrah-**prehd**-zoh
Do you have an hourly rate?	*Ha una tariffa oraria?*	ah **oo**-nah tah-**ree**-fah oh-**rah**-reeah
How much for a one-hour city tour?	*Quant'è per un giro della città di un'ora?*	kwahn-**teh** pehr oon **jee**-roh **day**-lah chee-**tah** dee oon-**oh**-rah

Cab fares are reasonable, and most drivers are honest. Expect a charge for luggage. Three or more tourists are usually better off hailing a cab than messing with city buses in Italy. If you're having a tough time hailing a taxi, ask for the nearest taxi stand (***fermata dei taxi***). The simplest way to tell a cabbie where you want to go is by stating your destination followed by "please" (***"Uffizi, per favore"***). Tipping isn't expected, but it's polite to round up.

In the Taxi

The meter, please.	*Il tassametro, per favore.*	eel tah-sah-**may**-troh pehr fah-**voh**-ray
Where is the meter?	*Dov'è il tassametro?*	doh-**veh** eel tah-sah-**may**-troh
I'm / We're in a hurry.	*Sono / Siamo di fretta.*	**soh**-noh / see**ah**-moh dee **fray**-tah
Slow down.	*Rallenti.*	rah-**lehn**-tee
If you don't slow down, I'll throw up.	*Se non rallenta, vomito.*	say nohn rah-**lehn**-tah **voh**-mee-toh

Left / Right / Straight.	*A sinistra / A destra / Diritto.*	ah see-**nee**-strah / ah **dehs**-trah / dee-**ree**-toh
I'd like to stop here briefly.	*Vorrei fermarmi un momento.*	vor-**reh**ee fehr-**mar**-mee oon moh-**mehn**-toh
We'd like to stop here briefly.	*Vorremmo fermarci un momento.*	vor-**ray**-moh fehr-**mar**-chee oon moh-**mehn**-toh
Please stop here for __ minutes.	*Si fermi qui per __ minuti, per favore.*	see **fehr**-mee kwee pehr __ mee-**noo**-tee pehr fah-**voh**-ray
Can you wait?	*Può aspettare?*	pwoh ah-spay-**tah**-ray
Crazy traffic, isn't it?	*Un traffico incredibile, vero?*	oon **trah**-fee-koh een-kray-**dee**-bee-lay **vay**-roh
You drive like...	*Guida come...*	**gwee**-dah **koh**-may
...a madman!	*...un pazzo!*	oon **pahd**-zoh
...Michael Schumacher.	*...Michele Schumacher.*	mee-**kay**-lay "Schumacher"
You drive very well.	*Guida molto bene.*	**gwee**-dah **mohl**-toh **behn**-ay
Where did you learn to drive?	*Ma dove ha imparato a guidare?*	mah **doh**-vay ah eem-pah-**rah**-toh ah gwee-**dah**-ray
Stop here.	*Si fermi qui.*	see **fehr**-mee kwee
Here is fine.	*Va bene qui.*	vah **behn**-ay kwee
At this corner.	*A questo angolo.*	ah **kwehs**-toh **ahn**-goh-loh
The next corner.	*Al prossimo angolo.*	ahl **proh**-see-moh **ahn**-goh-loh
My change, please.	*Il resto, per favore.*	eel **rehs**-toh pehr fah-**voh**-ray
Keep the change.	*Tenga il resto.*	**tayn**-gah eel **rehs**-toh
This ride is / was more fun than Disneyland.	*Questo viaggio è / è stato più divertente di Disneyland.*	**kwehs**-toh vee**ah**-joh eh / eh **stah**-toh pew dee-vehr-**tehn**-tay dee "Disneyland"

DRIVING

Rental Wheels

car rental agency	*agenzia di autonoleggio*	ah-**jehnt**-seeah dee ow-toh-noh-**leh**-joh
I'd like to rent...	*Vorrei noleggiare...*	vor-**reh**ee noh-leh-**jah**-ray
We'd like to rent...	*Vorremmo noleggiare...*	vor-**ray**-moh noh-leh-**jah**-ray
...a car.	*...una macchina.*	**oo**-nah **mah**-kee-nah
...a station wagon.	*...una station wagon.*	**oo**-nah **staht**-see-ohn **wah**-gohn
...a van.	*...un monovolume.*	oon moh-noh-voh-**loo**-may
...a motorcycle.	*...una motocicletta.*	**oo**-nah moh-toh-chee-**klay**-tah
...a motor scooter.	*...un motorino.*	oon moh-toh-**ree**-noh
How much...?	*Quanto...?*	**kwahn**-toh
...per hour	*...all'ora*	ah-**loh**-rah
...per half day	*...per mezza giornata*	pehr **mehd**-zah jor-**nah**-tah
...per day	*...al giorno*	ahl **jor**-noh
...per week	*...alla settimana*	**ah**-lah say-tee-**mah**-nah
Unlimited mileage?	*Chilometraggio illimitato?*	kee-loh-may-**trah**-joh eel-lee-mee-**tah**-toh
When must I bring it back?	*Quando devo riportarla?*	**kwahn**-doh **day**-voh ree-por-**tar**-lah
Is there...?	*C'è...?*	cheh
...a helmet	*...un casco*	oon **kah**-skoh
...a discount	*...uno sconto*	**oo**-noh **skohn**-toh
...a deposit	*...una caparra*	**oo**-nah kah-**pah**-rah
...insurance	*...l'assicurazione*	lah-see-koo-raht-see**oh**-nay

Key Phrases: Driving

car	*macchina*	**mah**-kee-nah
gas station	*benzinaio*	baynd-zee-**nah**-yoh
parking lot	*parcheggio*	par-**kay**-joh
accident	*incidente*	een-chee-**dehn**-tay
left / right	*sinistra / destra*	see-**nee**-strah / **dehs**-trah
straight ahead	*sempre diritto*	**sehm**-pray dee-**ree**-toh
downtown	*centro*	**chehn**-troh
How do you get to ___?	*Come si va a ___?*	**koh**-may see vah ah
Where can I park?	*Dove posso parcheggiare?*	**doh**-vay **poh**-soh par-kay-**jah**-ray

Parking

parking lot	*parcheggio*	par-**kay**-joh
parking garage	*garage*	gah-**rahj**
Is parking nearby?	*È vicino il parcheggio?*	eh vee-**chee**-noh eel par-**kay**-joh
Can I park here?	*Posso parcheggiare qui?*	**poh**-soh par-kay-**jah**-ray kwee
Is this a safe place to park?	*È sicuro parcheggiare qui?*	eh see-**koo**-roh par-kay-**jah**-ray kwee
How long can I park here?	*Per quanto tempo posso parcheggiare qui?*	pehr **kwahn**-toh **tehm**-poh **poh**-soh par-kay-**jah**-ray kwee
Must I pay to park here?	*È a pagamento questo parcheggio?*	eh ah pah-gah-**mayn**-toh **kweh**-stoh par-**kay**-joh
How much per hour / day?	*Quanto costa all'ora / al giorno?*	**kwahn**-toh **koh**-stah ahl-**loh**-rah / ahl **jor**-noh

Parking in Italian cities is expensive and hazardous. Plan to pay to use a parking garage in big cities. Leave nothing in your car at night. Always ask at your hotel about safe parking. Take restrictions seriously to avoid getting fines and having your car towed (an interesting but costly experience).

FINDING YOUR WAY

I'm going to ___.	*Vado a ___.*	**vah**-doh ah
We're going to ___.	*Andiamo a ___.*	ahn-dee**ah**-moh ah
How do you get to ___?	*Come si va a ___?*	**koh**-may see vah ah
Do you have a...?	*Ha una...?*	ah **oo**-nah
...city map	*...cartina della città*	kar-**tee**-nah **day**-lah chee-**tah**
...road map	*...cartina stradale*	kar-**tee**-nah strah-**dah**-lay
How many minutes...?	*Quanti minuti...?*	**kwahn**-tee mee-**noo**-tee
How many hours...?	*Quante ore...?*	**kwahn**-tay **oh**-ray
...on foot	*...a piedi*	ah pee**ay**-dee
...by bicycle	*...in bicicletta*	een bee-chee-**klay**-tah
...by car	*...in macchina*	een **mah**-kee-nah
How many kilometers to...?	*Quanti chilometri per...?*	**kwahn**-tee kee-**loh**-may-tree pehr
What is the... route to Rome?	*Qual'è la strada... per andare a Roma?*	kwah-**leh** lah **strah**-dah... pehr ahn-**dah**-ray ah **roh**-mah
...most scenic	*...più panoramica*	pew pah-noh-**rah**-mee-kah
...fastest	*...più veloce*	pew vay-**loh**-chay
...most interesting	*...più interessante*	pew een-tay-ray-**sahn**-tay
Point it out?	*Me lo mostra?*	may loh **mohs**-trah
I'm lost.	*Mi sono perso[a].*	mee **soh**-noh **pehr**-soh
Where am I?	*Dove sono?*	**doh**-vay **soh**-noh
Where is...?	*Dov'è...?*	doh-**veh**
The nearest...?	*Il più vicino...?*	eel pew vee-**chee**-noh
Where is this address?	*Dov'è questo indirizzo?*	doh-**veh** **kweh**-stoh een-dee-**reed**-zoh

Route-Finding Words

map	*cartina*	kar-**tee**-nah
road map	*cartina stradale*	kar-**tee**-nah strah-**dah**-lay
downtown	*centro*	**chehn**-troh
straight ahead	*sempre diritto*	**sehm**-pray dee-**ree**-toh
left	*sinistra*	see-**nee**-strah
right	*destra*	**dehs**-trah
first	*prima*	**pree**-mah
next	*prossima*	**proh**-see-mah
intersection	*incrocio*	een-**kroh**-choh
corner	*angolo*	**ahn**-goh-loh
block	*isolato*	ee-zoh-**lah**-toh
roundabout	*rotonda*	roh-**tohn**-dah
stoplight	*semaforo*	say-mah-**foh**-roh
(main) square	*piazza (principale)*	pee**aht**-sah (preen-chee-**pah**-lay)
street	*strada, via*	**strah**-dah, **vee**-ah
bridge	*ponte*	**pohn**-tay
tunnel	*tunnel*	**toon**-nehl
highway	*autostrada*	ow-toh-**strah**-dah
freeway	*superstrada*	soo-pehr-**strah**-dah
north	*nord*	nord
south	*sud*	sood
east	*est*	ayst
west	*ovest*	**oh**-vehst

In Italy, the shortest distance between any two points is the ***autostrada***. Tolls are not cheap (about a dollar for every 10 minutes), and there aren't as many signs as we are used to, so stay alert or you may miss your exit. Italy's ***autostrada*** rest stops are among the best in Europe.

The Police

As in any country, the flashing lights of a patrol car are a sure sign that someone's in trouble. If it's you, try this handy phrase: ***"Mi dispiace, sono un turista"*** (Sorry, I'm a tourist). Or, for the adventurous: ***"Se non le piace come guido, si tolga dal marciapiede"*** (If you don't like how I drive, stay off the sidewalk).

I'm late for my tour.	*Sono in ritardo per il tour.*	**soh**-noh een ree-**tar**-doh pehr eel toor
Can I buy your hat?	*Mi vende il suo cappello?*	mee **vehn**-day eel **soo**-oh kah-**pehl**-loh
What seems to be the problem?	*Quale sarebbe il problema?*	**kwah**-lay sah-**reh**-bay eel proh-**blay**-mah

Reading Road Signs

alt / stop	stop
carabinieri	police
centro, centrocittà	to the center of town
circonvallazione	ring road
dare la precedenza	yield
deviazione	detour
entrata	entrance
lavori in corso	road work ahead
prossima uscita	next exit
rallentare	slow down
senso unico	one-way street
tutti le (altre) destinazioni	to all (other) destinations
uscita	exit
zona pedonale	pedestrian zone

You'll find more common road signs on page 512 in the appendix.

Other Signs You May See

acqua non potabile	undrinkable water
affittasi, in affitto	for rent or for hire
aperto	open
aperto da ___ a ___	open from ___ to ___
attenzione	caution
bagno, gabinetto, toilette, toletta, WC	toilet

cagnaccio	mean dog
camere libere	vacancy
chiuso	closed
chiuso per ferie	closed for vacation
chiuso per restauro	closed for restoration
completo	no vacancy
donne	women
entrata libera	free admission
entrata vietata	no entry
fuori servizio / guasto	out of service
non toccare	do not touch
occupato	occupied
parcheggio vietato	no parking
pericolo	danger
proibito	prohibited
saldo	sale
sciopero	on strike
signore	women
signori	men
spingere / tirare	push / pull
torno subito	I'll return soon (sign on store)
uomini	men
uscita d'emergenza	emergency exit
vendesi, in vendita	for sale
vietato	forbidden
vietato fumare	no smoking
vietato l'accesso	keep out

SLEEPING

Places to Stay

hotel	*hotel, albergo*	**oh**-tehl, ahl-**behr**-goh
small hotel (often family-run)	*pensione, locanda*	payn-see**oh**-nay, loh-**kahn**-dah
rooms for rent	*affita camere*	ah-**fee**-tah **kah**-may-ray
youth hostel	*ostello della gioventù*	oh-**stehl**-loh **dehl**-lah joh-vehn-**too**
vacancy	*camere libere*	**kah**-may-ray **lee**-bay-ray
no vacancy	*completo*	kohm-**play**-toh

Reserving a Room

I like to reserve rooms a few days in advance as I travel. But if my itinerary is set, I reserve before I leave home. To reserve from home by email or fax, use the handy form in the appendix (online at www.ricksteves.com/reservation).

Hello.	*Buon giorno.*	bwohn **jor**-noh
Do you speak English?	*Parla inglese?*	**par**-lah een-**glay**-zay
Do you have a room for...?	*Avete una camera per...?*	ah-**vay**-tay **oo**-nah **kah**-may-rah pehr
...one person	*...una persona*	**oo**-nah pehr-**soh**-nah
...two people	*...due persone*	**doo**-ay pehr-**soh**-nay
...tonight	*...stanotte*	stah-**noh**-tay

Key Phrases: Sleeping

I want to make / confirm a reservation.	*Vorrei fare / confermare una prenotazione.*	vor-**reh**ee **fah**-ray / kohn-fehr-**mah**-ray **oo**-nah pray-noh-taht-see**oh**-nay
I'd like a room (for two people), please.	*Vorrei una camera (per due persone), per favore.*	vor-**reh**ee **oo**-nah **kah**-may-rah (pehr **doo**-ay pehr-**soh**-nay) pehr fah-**voh**-ray
...with / without / and	*...con / senza / e*	kohn / **sehnt**-sah / ay
...toilet	*...toilette*	twah-**leht**-tay
...shower	*...doccia*	**doh**-chah
Can I see the room?	*Posso vedere la camera?*	**poh**-soh vay-**day**-ray lah **kah**-may-rah
How much is it?	*Quanto costa?*	**kwahn**-toh **koh**-stah
Credit card O.K.?	*Carta di credito è O.K.?*	**kar**-tah dee **kray**-dee-toh eh "O.K."

...two nights	*...due notti*	**doo**-ay **noh**-tee
...Friday	*...venerdì*	vay-nehr-**dee**
...June 21	*...il ventuno giugno*	eel vayn-**too**-noh **joon**-yoh
Yes or no?	*Si o no?*	see oh noh
I'd like...	*Vorrei...*	vor-**reh**ee
We'd like...	*Vorremmo...*	vor-**ray**-moh
...a private bathroom.	*...un bagno completo.*	oon **bahn**-yoh kohm-**play**-toh
...your cheapest room.	*...la camera più economica.*	lah **kah**-may-rah pew ay-koh-**noh**-mee-kah
...___ bed (beds) for ___ people in ___ room (in ___ rooms).	*...___ letto (letti) per ___ persone nella ___ camera (nelle ___ camere).*	___ **leht**-toh (**leht**-tee) pehr ___ pehr-**soh**-nay **nay**-lah ___ **kah**-may-rah (**nay**-lay ___ **kah**-may-ray)
How much is it?	*Quanto costa?*	**kwahn**-toh **koh**-stah
Anything cheaper?	*Niente di più economico?*	nee-**ehn**-tay dee pew ay-koh-**noh**-mee-koh
I'll take it.	*La prendo.*	lah **prehn**-doh

My name is ___.	*Mi chiamo ___.*	mee kee**ah**-moh
I'll stay / We'll stay...	*Starò / Staremo...*	stah-**roh** / stah-**ray**-moh
...for ___ night (nights).	*...per ___ notte (notti).*	pehr ___ **noh**-tay (**noh**-tee)
I'll come / We'll come...	*Arriverò / Arriveremo...*	ah-ree-vay-**roh** / ah-ree-vay-**ray**-moh
...in the morning.	*...la mattina.*	lah mah-**tee**-nah
...in the afternoon.	*...il pomeriggio.*	eel poh-may-**ree**-joh
...in the evening.	*...la sera.*	lah **say**-rah
...in one hour.	*...tra un'ora.*	trah oon-**oh**-rah
...before 16:00.	*...prima delle sedici.*	**pree**-mah **dehl**-lay **say**-dee-chee
...Friday before 6 P.M.	*...venerdí entro le sei di sera.*	vay-nehr-**dee** **ehn**-troh lay **seh**ee dee **say**-rah
Thank you.	*Grazie.*	**graht**-seeay

Using a Credit Card

If you need to secure your reservation with a credit card, here's the lingo.

Is a deposit required?	*Bisogna lasciare una caparra?*	bee-**sohn**-yah lah-**shah**-ray **oo**-nah kah-**pah**-rah
Credit card O.K.?	*Carta di credito è O.K.?*	**kar**-tah dee **kray**-dee-toh eh "O.K."
credit card	*carta di credito*	**kar**-tah dee **kray**-dee-toh
debit card	*bancomat*	**bahnk**-oh-maht
The name on the card is ___.	*Il nome sulla carta è ___.*	il **noh**-may **soo**-lah **kar**-tah eh
The credit card number is...	*Il numero della carta di credito è...*	eel **noo**-may-roh **dehl**-lah **kar**-tah dee **kray**-dee-toh eh
0	*zero*	**zay**-roh
1	*uno*	**oo**-noh
2	*due*	**doo**-ay
3	*tre*	tray
4	*quattro*	**kwah**-troh
5	*cinque*	**cheeng**-kway
6	*sei*	**seh**ee

7	*sette*	**seht**-tay
8	*otto*	**oh**-toh
9	*nove*	**noh**-vay
The expiration date is...	*La data di scadenza è...*	lah **dah**-tah dee shah-**dehnt**-sah eh
January	*gennaio*	jay-**nah**-yoh
February	*febbraio*	fay-**brah**-yoh
March	*marzo*	**mart**-soh
April	*aprile*	ah-**pree**-lay
May	*maggio*	**mah**-joh
June	*giugno*	**joon**-yoh
July	*luglio*	**lool**-yoh
August	*agosto*	ah-**goh**-stoh
September	*settembre*	say-**tehm**-bray
October	*ottobre*	oh-**toh**-bray
November	*novembre*	noh-**vehm**-bray
December	*dicembre*	dee-**chehm**-bray
2009	*duemilanove*	doo-ay-mee-lah-**noh**-vay
2010	*duemila-dieci*	doo-ay-mee-lah-deeay-chee
2011	*duemila-undici*	doo-ay-mee-lah-**oon**-dee-chee
2012	*duemila-dodici*	doo-ay-mee-lah-**doh**-dee-chee
2013	*duemila-tredici*	doo-ay-mee-lah-**tray**-dee-chee
2014	*duemila-quattordici*	doo-ay-mee-lah-kwah-**tor**-dee-chee
2015	*duemila-quindici*	doo-ay-mee-lah-**kween**-dee-chee
2016	*duemila-sedici*	doo-ay-mee-lah-**say**-dee-chee
Can I reserve with a credit card and pay in cash?	*Posso prenotare con la carta di credito e pagare in contanti?*	**poh**-soh pray-noh-**tah**-ray kohn lah **kar**-tah dee **kray**-dee-toh ay pah-**gah**-ray een kohn-**tahn**-tee
I have another card.	*Ho un'altra carta.*	oh oo-**nahl**-trah **kar**-tah

If your ***carta di credito*** (credit card) is not approved, you can say ***"Ho un'altra carta"*** (I have another card)—if you do.

The Alphabet

If phoning, you can use the code alphabet below to spell out your name if necessary. Unless you're giving the hotelier your name as it appears on your credit card, consider using a shorter version of your name to make things easier.

a	ah	*Ancona*	ahn-**koh**-nah
b	bee	*Bologna*	boh-**lohn**-yah
c	chee	*Como*	**koh**-moh
d	dee	*Domodossola*	doh-moh-**doh**-soh-lah
e	ay	*Empoli*	**ehm**-poh-lee
f	**ehf**-ay	*Firenze*	fee-**rehn**-tsay
g	jee	*Genova*	**jay**-noh-vah
h	ah-kah	*Hotel, "acca"*	**oh**-tehl, **ah**-kah
i	ee	*Imola*	ee-moh-lah
j	ee **loon**-gah	*i lunga*	ee **loon**-gah
k	**kahp**-ah	*"kappa"*	**kah**-pah
l	**ehl**-ay	*Livorno*	lee-**vor**-noh
m	**ehm**-ay	*Milano*	mee-**lah**-noh
n	**ehn**-ay	*Napoli*	**nah**-poh-lee
o	oh	*Otranto*	oh-**trahn**-toh
p	pee	*Palermo*	pah-**lehr**-moh
q	koo	*quaranta (40)*	kwah-**rahn**-tah
r	**ehr**-ay	*Rovigo*	roh-**vee**-goh
s	**ehs**-ay	*Savona*	sah-**voh**-nah
t	tee	*Treviso*	tray-**vee**-zoh
u	oo	*Urbino*	oor-**bee**-noh
v	vee	*Venezia*	vay-**nayt**-seeah
w	**dohp**-yah voo	*"doppia vu"*	**dohp**-yah voo
x	eeks	*"ics"*	eeks
y	**eep**-see-lohn	*"ispilon"*	**eep**-see-lohn
z	**zeht**-ah	*Zara*	**tsah**-rah

Just the Fax, Ma'am

If you're booking a room by fax...

I want to send a fax.	*Vorrei mandare un fax.*	vor-**reh**ee mahn-**dah**-ray oon fahks
What is your fax number?	*Qual è il suo numero di fax?*	kwahl eh eel **soo**-oh **noo**-may-roh dee fahks
Your fax number is not working.	*Il suo numero di fax non funziona.*	eel **soo**-oh **noo**-may-roh dee fahks nohn foont-see**oh**-nah
Please turn on your fax machine.	*Per favore accendere il fax.*	pehr fah-**voh**-ray ah-**chehn**-day-ray eel fahks

Getting Specific

I'd like a room...	*Vorrei una camera...*	vor-**reh**ee **oo**-nah **kah**-may-rah
We'd like a room...	*Vorremmo una camera...*	vor-**ray**-moh **oo**-nah **kah**-may-rah
...with / without / and	*...con / senza / e*	kohn / **sehnt**-sah / ay
...toilet	*...toilette*	twah-**leht**-tay
...shower	*...doccia*	**doh**-chah
...shower down the hall	*...doccia in fondo al corridoio*	**doh**-chah een **fohn**-doh ahl kor-ree-**doh**-yoh
...bathtub	*...vasca da bagno*	**vah**-skah dah **bahn**-yoh
...double bed	*...letto matrimoniale*	**leht**-toh mah-tree-moh-nee**ah**-lay
...twin beds	*...letti singoli*	**leht**-tee **seeng**-goh-lee
...balcony	*...balcone*	bahl-**koh**-nay
...view	*...vista*	**vee**-stah
...only a sink	*...solo un lavandino*	**soh**-loh oon lah-vahn-**dee**-noh
...on the ground floor	*...al piano terra*	ahl pee**ah**-noh **tay**-rah
...television	*...televisione*	tay-lay-vee-zee**oh**-nay
...telephone	*...telefono*	tay-**lay**-foh-noh
...air conditioning	*...aria condizionata*	**ah**-reeah kohn-deet-see-oh-**nah**-tah

...kitchenette	*...cucina*	koo-**chee**-nah
Do you have...?	*Avete...?*	ah-**vay**-tay
...an elevator	*...l'ascensore*	lah-shehn-**soh**-ray
...a swimming pool	*...la piscina*	lah pee-**shee**-nah
I arrive Monday, depart Wednesday.	*Arrivo lunedì, parto mercoledì.*	ah-**ree**-voh loo-nay-**dee** **par**-toh mehr-koh-lay-**dee**
We arrive Monday, depart Wednesday.	*Arriviamo lunedì, partiamo mercoledì.*	ah-ree-vee**ah**-moh loo-nay-**dee** par-tee**ah**-moh mehr-koh-lay-**dee**
I am desperate.	*Sono disperato[a].*	**soh**-noh dee-spay-**rah**-toh
We are desperate.	*Siamo disperati.*	see**ah**-moh dee-spay-**rah**-tee
I will / We will sleep anywhere.	*Posso / Possiamo dormire ovunque.*	**poh**-soh / poh-see**ah**-moh dor-**mee**-ray oh-**voon**-kway
I have a sleeping bag.	*Ho un sacco a pelo.*	oh oon **sah**-koh ah **pay**-loh
We have sleeping bags.	*Abbiamo i sacchi a pelo.*	ah-bee**ah**-moh ee **sah**-kee ah **pay**-loh
Will you call another hotel for me?	*Chiamerebbe un altro albergo per me?*	keeah-may-**reh**-bay oon **ahl**-troh ahl-**behr**-goh pehr may

Families

Do you have...?	*Avete...?*	ah-**vay**-tay
...a room for families	*...una camera grande per una famiglia*	**oo**-nah **kah**-may-rah **grahn**-day pehr **oo**-nah fah-**meel**-yah
...a family rate	*...una tariffa per famiglie*	**oo**-nah tah-**ree**-fah pehr fah-**meel**-yay
...a discount for children	*...uno sconto per i bambini*	**oo**-noh **skohn**-toh pehr ee bahm-**bee**-nee
I / We have...	*Ho / Abbiamo...*	oh / ah-bee**ah**-moh
...one child, age ___ months / years.	*...un bambino di ___ mesi / anni.*	oon bahm-**bee**-noh dee ___ **may**-zee / **ahn**-nee

...two children, ages ___ and ___ years.	*...due bambini, di ___ e ___ anni.*	**doo**-ay bahm-**bee**-nee dee ___ ay ___ **ahn**-nee
I'd like...	*Vorrei...*	vor-**reh**ee
We'd like...	*Vorremmo...*	vor-**ray**-moh
...a crib.	*...una culla.*	**oo**-nah **koo**-lah
...a small extra bed.	*...un letto singolo in più.*	oon **leht**-toh **seeng**-goh-loh een pew
...bunk beds.	*...letti a castello.*	**lay**-tee ah kah-**stehl**-loh
babysitting service	*servizio di baby sitter*	sehr-**veet**-seeoh dee **bay**-bee **see**-tehr
Is a... nearby?	*C'è.... qui vicino?*	cheh... kwee vee-**chee**-noh
...park	*...un parco*	oon **par**-koh
...playground	*...un parco giochi*	oon **par**-koh **joh**-kee
...swimming pool	*...una piscina*	**oo**-nah pee-**shee**-nah

For fun, Italians call kids ***marmocchi*** (munchkins).

Confirming, Changing, and Canceling Reservations

Use this template for your telephone call.

I have / We have a reservation.	*Ho / Abbiamo una prenotazione.*	oh / ah-bee**ah**-moh **oo**-nah pray-noh-taht-see**oh**-nay
My name is ___.	*Mi chiamo ___.*	mee kee**ah**-moh
I'd like to... my reservation.	*Vorrei fare... una prenotazione.*	vor-**reh**ee **fah**-ray... **oo**-nah pray-noh-taht-see**oh**-nay
...confirm	*...confermare*	kohn-fehr-**mah**-ray
...reconfirm	*...riconfermare*	ree-kohn-fehr-**mah**-ray
...cancel	*...annullare*	ah-noo-**lah**-ray
...change	*...cambiare*	kahm-bee**ah**-ray
The reservation is / was for...	*La prenotazione è / era per...*	lah pray-noh-taht-see**oh**-nay eh / **ehr**-ah pehr
...one person	*...una persona*	**oo**-nah pehr-**soh**-nah
...two people	*...due persone*	**doo**-ay pehr-**soh**-nay
...today / tomorrow	*...oggi / domani*	**oh**-jee / doh-**mah**-nee

...the day after tomorrow	*...dopodomani*	doh-poh-doh-**mah**-nee
...August 13	*...il tredici agosto*	eel **tray**-dee-chee ah-**goh**-stoh
...one night / two nights	*...una notte / due notti*	**oo**-nah **noh**-tay / **doo**-ay **noh**-tee
Can you find my / our reservation?	*Può trovare la mia / nostra prenotazione?*	pwoh troh-**vah**-ray lah **mee**-ah / **noh**-strah pray-noh-taht-see**oh**-nay
What is your cancellation policy?	*Qual è il vostro regolamento riguardo alla cancellazione delle prenotazioni?*	kwahl eh eel **voh**-stroh ray-goh-lah-**mehn**-toh ree-**gwar**-doh **ahl**-lah kahn-chehl-aht-see**oh**-nay **dehl**-lay pray-noh-taht-see**oh**-nee
Will I be billed for the first night if I can't make it?	*Mi addebitate la prima notte se non ce la faccio?*	mee ah-day-bee-**tah**-tay lah **pree**-mah **noh**-tay say nohn chay lah **fah**-choh
I'd like to arrive instead on...	*Invece vorrei arrivare...*	een-**vay**-chay voh-**reh**ee ah-ree-**vah**-ray
We'd like to arrive instead on...	*Invece vorremmo arrivare...*	een-**vay**-chay vor-**ray**-moh ah-ree-**vah**-ray
Is everything O.K.?	*Va bene?*	vah **behn**-ay
Thank you. I'll see you then.	*Grazie. Ci vediamo al mio arrivo.*	**graht**-seeay chee vay-dee**ah**-moh ahl **mee**-oh ah-**ree**-voh
We'll see you then.	*Ci vediamo al nostro arrivo.*	chee vay-dee**ah**-moh ahl **noh**-stroh ah-**ree**-voh
I'm sorry I need to cancel.	*Mi dispiace ma devo annullare.*	mee dee-spee**ah**-chay mah **day**-voh ah-noo-**lah**-ray

Nailing Down the Price

How much is...?	*Quanto costa...?*	**kwahn**-toh **koh**-stah
...a room for ___ people	*...una camera per ___ persone*	**oo**-nah **kah**-may-rah pehr ___ pehr-**soh**-nay

...your cheapest room	*...la camera più economica*	lah **kah**-may-rah pew ay-koh-**noh**-mee-kah
Is breakfast included?	*La colazione è inclusa?*	lah koh-laht-see**oh**-nay eh een-**kloo**-zah
Is breakfast required?	*È obbligatoria la colazione?*	eh oh-blee-gah-**toh**-reeah lah koh-laht-see**oh**-nay
How much without breakfast?	*Quant'è senza la colazione?*	kwahn-**teh sehnt**-sah lah koh-laht-see**oh**-nay
Is half-pension required?	*È obbligatoria la mezza pensione?*	eh oh-blee-gah-**toh**-reeah lah **mehd**-zah pehn-see**oh**-nay
Complete price?	*Prezzo completo?*	**prehd**-zoh kohm-**play**-toh
Is it cheaper for three-night stays?	*È più economico se mi fermo tre notti?*	eh pew ay-koh-**noh**-mee-koh say mee **fehr**-moh tray **noh**-tee
I will stay three nights.	*Mi fermo tre notti.*	mee **fehr**-moh tray **noh**-tee
We will stay three nights.	*Ci fermiamo tre notti.*	chee fehr-mee**ah**-moh tray **noh**-tee
Is it cheaper if I pay in cash?	*È più economico se pago in contanti?*	eh pew ay-koh-**noh**-mee-koh say **pah**-goh een kohn-**tahn**-tee
What is the cost per week?	*Quanto costa a settimana?*	**kwahn**-toh **koh**-stah ah say-tee-**mah**-nah

Italian hotels almost always have larger rooms to fit three to six people. Your price per person plummets as you pack more into a room. Breakfasts are usually basic (coffee, rolls and marmalade) and expensive (about €6). They're often optional.

In resort towns, some hotels offer ***mezza pensione*** (half-pension), consisting of two meals per day served at the hotel: breakfast and your choice of lunch or dinner. The price for half-pension is often listed per person rather than per room. Hotels that offer half-pension often require it in summer. The meals are usually good, but if you want the freedom to forage for food, look for hotels that don't push half-pension.

Choosing a Room

Can I see the room?	*Posso vedere la camera?*	**poh**-soh vay-**day**-ray lah **kah**-may-rah
Can we see the room?	*Possiamo vedere la camera?*	poh-see**ah**-moh vay-**day**-ray lah **kah**-may-rah
Show me another room?	*Mi mostra un'altra camera?*	mee **moh**-strah oo-**nahl**-trah **kah**-may-rah
Show us another room?	*Ci mostra un'altra camera?*	chee **moh**-strah oo-**nahl**-trah **kah**-may-rah
Do you have something...?	*Avete qualcosa...?*	ah-**vay**-tay kwahl-**koh**-zah
...larger / smaller	*...più grande / più piccola*	pew **grahn**-day / pew **pee**-koh-lah
...better / cheaper	*...più bella / più economica*	pew **behl**-lah / pew ay-koh-**noh**-mee-kah
...brighter	*...più luminosa*	pew loo-mee-**noh**-zah
...in the back	*...al di dietro*	ahl dee dee**ay**-troh
...quieter	*...più tranquilla*	pew trahn-**kwee**-lah
Sorry, it's not right for me.	*Mi dispiace, non mi va.*	mee dee-spee**ah**-chay nohn mee vah
Sorry, it's not right for us.	*Mi dispiace, non va per noi.*	mee dee-spee**ah**-chay nohn vah pehr **noh**ee
I'll take it.	*La prendo.*	lah **prehn**-doh
We'll take it.	*La prendiamo.*	lah prehn-dee**ah**-moh
My key, please.	*La mia chiave, per favore.*	lah **mee**-ah kee**ah**-vay pehr fah-**voh**-ray
Sleep well.	*Sogni d'oro.*	**sohn**-yee **doh**-roh
Good night.	*Buona notte.*	**bwoh**-nah **noh**-tay

Breakfast

Is breakfast included?	*La colazione è inclusa?*	lah koh-laht-see**oh**-nay eh een-**kloo**-zah
How much is breakfast?	*Quanto costa la colazione?*	**kwahn**-toh **koh**-stah lah koh-laht-see**oh**-nay
When does breakfast start?	*Quando comincia la colazione?*	**kwahn**-doh koh-**meen**-chah lah koh-laht-see**oh**-nay

When does breakfast end?	*Quando finisce la colazione?*	**kwahn**-doh fee-**nee**-shay lah koh-laht-see**oh**-nay
Where is breakfast served?	*Dove è servita la colazione?*	**doh**-vay eh sehr-**vee**-tah lah koh-laht-see**oh**-nay

Hotel Help

I'd like...	*Vorrei...*	vor-**reh**ee
We'd like...	*Vorremmo...*	vor-**ray**-moh
...a / another...	*...un / un altro...*	oon / oon **ahl**-troh
...towel.	*...asciugamano.*	ah-shoo-gah-**mah**-noh
...a clean bath towel / clean bath towels.	*...un asciugamano pulito / degli asciugamani puliti.*	oon ah-shoo-gah-**mah**-noh poo-**lee**-toh / **day**-lee ah-shoo-gah-**mah**-nee poo-**lee**-tee
...pillow.	*...cuscino.*	koo-**shee**-noh
...clean sheets.	*...lenzuola pulite.*	lehnt-soo**oh**-lah poo-**lee**-tay
...blanket.	*...coperta.*	koh-**pehr**-tah
...glass.	*...bicchiere.*	bee-kee**ay**-ray
...sink stopper.	*...tappo.*	**tah**-poh
...soap.	*...sapone.*	sah-**poh**-nay
...toilet paper.	*...carta igienica.*	**kar**-tah ee-**jay**-nee-kah
...electrical adapter.	*...adattatore elettrico.*	ah-dah-tah-**toh**-ray ay-**leht**-ree-koh
...brighter light bulb.	*...lampadina più potente.*	lahm-pah-**dee**-nah pew poh-**tehn**-tay
...lamp.	*...lampada.*	lahm-**pah**-dah
...chair.	*...sedia.*	say-**dee**-ah
...table.	*...tavolo.*	**tah**-voh-loh
...Internet access.	*...l'accesso a Internet.*	lah-**chay**-soh ah **een**-tehr-neht
...different room.	*...altra camera.*	**ahl**-trah **kah**-may-rah
...silence.	*...silenzio.*	see-**lehnt**-seeoh
...to speak to the manager.	*...parlare con il direttore.*	par-**lah**-ray kohn eel dee-reht-**toh**-ray

How can I make the room cooler / warmer?	*Come faccio a rinfrescare / riscaldare la camera?*	**koh**-may **fah**-choh ah reen-frehs-**kah**-ray / rees-kahl-**dah**-ray lah **kah**-may-rah
Where can I...?	*Dove posso...?*	**doh**-vay **poh**-soh
...wash my laundry	*...fare del bucato*	**fah**-ray dayl boo-**kah**-toh
...hang my laundry	*...stendere il bucato*	**stehn**-day-ray eel boo-**kah**-toh
Is a full-service laundry nearby?	*C'è una lavanderia qui vicino?*	cheh **oo**-nah lah-vahn-deh-**ree**ah kwee vee-**chee**-noh
Is a self-service laundry nearby?	*C'è una lavanderia automatica qui vicino?*	cheh **oo**-nah lah-vahn-deh-**ree**ah ow-toh-**mah**-tee-kah kwee vee-**chee**-noh
I'd like to stay another night.	*Vorrei fermarmi un'altra notte.*	vor-**reh**ee fehr-**mar**-mee oo-**nahl**-trah **noh**-tay
We'd like to stay another night.	*Vorremmo fermarci un'altra notte.*	vor-**ray**-moh fehr-**mar**-chee oo-**nahl**-trah **noh**-tay
Where can I park?	*Dove posso parcheggiare?*	**doh**-vay **poh**-soh par-kay-**jah**-ray
When do you lock up?	*A che ora chiude?*	ah kay **oh**-rah kee**oo**-day
Please wake me at 7:00.	*Mi svegli alle sette, per favore.*	mee **zvayl**-yee **ah**-lay **seht**-tay pehr fah-**voh**-ray

Hotel Hassles

Come with me.	*Venga con me.*	**vayn**-gah kohn may
I have / We have a problem in the room.	*Ho / Abbiamo un problema con la camera.*	oh / ah-bee**ah**-moh oon proh-**blay**-mah kohn lah **kah**-may-rah
bad odor	*cattivo odore*	kah-**tee**-voh oh-**doh**-ray
bugs	*insetti*	een-**seht**-tee
mice	*topi*	**toh**-pee

cockroaches	*scarafaggi*	skah-rah-**fah**-jee
prostitutes	*prostitute*	proh-stee-**too**-tay
I'm covered with bug bites.	*Sono pieno[a] di punture di insetti.*	**soh**-noh pee**ay**-noh dee poon-**too**-ray dee een-**seht**-tee
The bed is too soft / hard.	*Il letto è troppo morbido / duro.*	eel **leht**-toh eh **troh**-poh **mor**-bee-doh / **doo**-roh
I can't sleep.	*Non riesco a dormire.*	nohn ree**ay**-skoh ah dor-**mee**-ray
The room is too...	*La camera è troppo...*	lah **kah**-may-rah eh **troh**-poh
...hot / cold.	*...calda / fredda.*	**kahl**-dah / **fray**-dah
...noisy / dirty.	*...rumorosa / sporca.*	roo-moh-**roh**-zah / **spor**-kah
I can't open...	*Non riesco ad aprire...*	nohn ree**ay**-skoh ahd ah-**pree**-ray
I can't shut...	*Non riesco a chiudere...*	nohn ree**ay**-skoh ah keeoo-**day**-ray
...the door / the window.	*...la porta / la finestra.*	lah **por**-tah / lah fee-**nay**-strah
Air conditioner...	*Condizionatore...*	kohn-deet-see-oh-nah-**toh**-ray
Lamp...	*Lampada...*	lahm-**pah**-dah
Lightbulb...	*Lampadina...*	lahm-pah-**dee**-nah
Electrical outlet...	*Presa...*	**pray**-zah
Key...	*Chiave...*	kee**ah**-vay
Lock...	*Serratura...*	say-rah-**too**-rah
Window...	*Finestra...*	fee-**nay**-strah
Faucet...	*Rubinetto...*	roo-bee-**nay**-toh
Sink...	*Lavabo...*	**lah**-vah-boh
Toilet...	*Toilette...*	twah-**leht**-tay
Shower...	*Doccia...*	**doh**-chah
...doesn't work.	*...non funziona.*	nohn foont-see**oh**-nah
There is no hot water.	*Non c'è acqua calda.*	nohn cheh **ah**-kwah **kahl**-dah
When is the water hot?	*A che ora è calda l'acqua?*	ah kay **oh**-rah eh **kahl**-dah **lah**-kwah

Checking Out

When is check-out time?	*A che ora devo lasciare la camera?*	ah kay **oh**-rah **day**-voh lah-**shah**-ray lah **kah**-may-rah
I'll leave...	*Parto...*	**par**-toh
We'll leave...	*Partiamo...*	par-tee**ah**-moh
...today / tomorrow.	*...oggi / domani.*	**oh**-jee / doh-**mah**-nee
...very early.	*...molto presto.*	**mohl**-toh **prehs**-toh
Can I pay now?	*Posso pagare subito?*	**poh**-soh pah-**gah**-ray **soo**-bee-toh
Can we pay now?	*Possiamo pagare subito?*	poh-see**ah**-moh pah-**gah**-ray **soo**-bee-toh
The bill, please.	*Il conto, per favore.*	eel **kohn**-toh pehr fah-**voh**-ray
Credit card O.K.?	*Carta di credito è O.K.?*	**kar**-tah dee **kray**-dee-toh eh "O.K."
Everything was great.	*Tutto magnifico.*	**too**-toh mahn-**yee**-fee-koh
I slept like a rock.	*Ho dormito come un sasso.*	oh dor-**mee**-toh **koh**-may oon **sah**-soh
Will you call my next hotel...?	*Può chiamare il mio prossimo hotel...?*	pwoh kee-**mah**-ray eel **mee**-oh **proh**-see-moh **oh**-tehl
...for tonight	*...per stasera*	pehr stah-**say**-rah
...to make a reservation	*...per fare una prenotazione*	pehr **fah**-ray **oo**-nah pray-noh-taht-see**oh**-nay
...to confirm a reservation	*...per confermare una prenotazione*	pehr kohn-fehr-**mah**-ray **oo**-nah pray-noh-taht-see**oh**-nay
I will pay for the call.	*Pago la chiamata.*	**pah**-goh lah keeah-**mah**-tah
Can I...?	*Posso...?*	**poh**-soh
Can we...?	*Possiamo...?*	poh-see**ah**-moh
...leave baggage here until ___	*...lasciare il bagaglio qui fino a ___*	lah-**shah**-ray eel bah-**gahl**-yoh kwee **fee**-noh ah

I never tip beyond the included service charges in hotels or for hotel services.

Camping

camping	*campeggio*	kahm-**pay**-joh
campsite	*piazzuola*	pee-ahd-**zwoh**-lah
tent	*tenda*	**tayn**-dah
The nearest campground?	*Il campeggio più vicino?*	eel kahm-**pay**-joh pew vee-**chee**-noh
Can I...?	*Posso...?*	**poh**-soh
Can we...?	*Possiamo...?*	poh-see**ah**-moh
...camp here for one night	*...campeggiare qui per una notte*	kahm-pay-**jah**-ray kwee pehr **oo**-nah **noh**-tay
Do showers cost extra?	*Costano extra le docce?*	koh-**stah**-noh **ehk**-strah lay **doh**-chay
shower token	*gettone per la doccia*	jeht-**toh**-nay pehr lah **doh**-chah

In some Italian campgrounds and youth hostels, you must buy a ***gettone*** (token) to activate a coin-operated hot shower. It has a timer inside, like a parking meter. To avoid a sudden cold rinse, buy at least two ***gettoni*** before getting undressed.

EATING

RESTAURANTS

Types of Restaurants

Italian food is one of life's great pleasures. The Italians have an expression: ***"A tavola non si invecchia"*** (At the table, one does not age). Below is a guideline for restaurant types. Note that the first few names are sometimes interchangeable, and a ***trattoria*** can occasionally be more expensive than a ***ristorante.*** Always check the menu posted outside a restaurant to be sure.

Ristorante—A fine-dining establishment
Trattoria—Typically a family-owned place that serves home-cooked meals at moderate prices
Osteria—More informal, with large shared tables, good food, and wine
Pizzeria—A casual pizza joint that also offers pasta and more
Pizza Rustica—A cheap pizza shop that sells pizza by the weight or slice (often take-out only)
Rosticceria—A take-out or sit-down shop specializing in roasted meats
Tavola calda—Inexpensive hot/cold buffet-style restaurant
Bar—The neighborhood hangout that serves coffee, soft drinks, beer, liquor, snacks, and ready-made sandwiches
Enoteca—Wine shop or wine bar that also serves snacks
Freeflow—A self-serve cafeteria

Autogrill—Cafeteria and snack bar, found at freeway rest stops and often in city centers (Ciao is a popular chain)

Locanda—A countryside restaurant serving simple local specialties

Finding a Restaurant

Where's a good... restaurant nearby?	*Dov'è un buon ristorante... qui vicino?*	doh-**veh** oon bwohn ree-stoh-**rahn**-tay... kwee vee-**chee**-noh
...cheap	*...economico*	ay-koh-**noh**-mee-koh
...local-style	*...con cucina casereccia*	kohn koo-**chee**-nah kah-zay-**ray**-chah
...untouristy	*...non per turisti*	nohn pehr too-**ree**-stee
...vegetarian	*...vegetariano*	vay-jay-tah-ree**ah**-noh
...fast food (Italian-style)	*...tavola calda*	**tah**-voh-lah **kahl**-dah
...self-service buffet	*...self-service*	sehlf-**sehr**-vees
...Chinese	*...cinese*	chee-**nay**-zay
with terrace	*con terrazza*	kohn tay-**rahd**-zah
with a salad bar	*con un banco delle insalate*	kohn oon **bahn**-koh **dehl**-lay een-sah-**lah**-tay
with candles	*con candele*	kohn kahn-**day**-lay
romantic	*romantico*	roh-**mahn**-tee-koh
moderate price	*a buon mercato*	ah bwohn mer-**kah**-toh
to splurge	*fare sfoggio*	**fah**-ray **sfoh**-joh
Is it better than McDonald's?	*È migliore di McDonald's?*	eh meel-**yoh**-ray dee "McDonald's"

Getting a Table

What time does this open / close?	*A che ora apre / chiude?*	ah kay **oh**-rah **ah**-pray / kee**oo**-day
Are you open...?	*È aperto...?*	eh ah-**pehr**-toh
...today / tomorrow	*...oggi / domani*	**oh**-jee / doh-**mah**-nee
...for lunch / dinner	*...per pranzo / cena*	pehr **prahnt**-soh / **chay**-nah

Key Phrases: Restaurants

Where's a good restaurant nearby?	*Dov'è un buon ristorante qui vicino?*	doh-**veh** oon bwohn ree-stoh-**rahn**-tay kwee vee-**chee**-noh
I'd like...	*Vorrei...*	vor-**reh**ee
We'd like...	*Vorremmo...*	vor-**ray**-moh
...a table for one / two.	*...una tavola per uno / due.*	**oo**-nah **tah**-voh-lah pehr **oo**-noh / **doo**-ay
...inside / outside	*...dentro / fuori*	**dehn**-troh / **fwoh**-ree
...with a view.	*...con la vista.*	kohn lah **vee**-stah
Is this seat free?	*È libero questo posto?*	eh **lee**-bay-roh **kwehs**-toh **poh**-stoh
The menu (in English), please.	*Il menù (in inglese), per favore.*	eel may-**noo** (een een-**glay**-zay) pehr fah-**voh**-ray
Bill, please.	*Conto, per favore.*	**kohn**-toh pehr fah-**voh**-ray
Credit card O.K.?	*Carta di credito è O.K.?*	**kar**-tah dee **kray**-dee-toh eh "O.K."

Should I / we make reservations?	*Mi / Ci consiglia prenotare una tavola?*	mee / chee kohn-**seel**-yah pray-noh-**tah**-ray **oo**-nah **tah**-voh-lah
I'd like...	*Vorrei...*	vor-**reh**ee
We'd like...	*Vorremmo...*	vor-**ray**-moh
...a table for one / two.	*...una tavola per uno / due.*	**oo**-nah **tah**-voh-lah pehr **oo**-noh / **doo**-ay
...to reserve a table for two people...	*...prenotare un tavola per due persone...*	pray-noh-**tah**-ray oon **tah**-voh-lah pehr **doo**-ay pehr-**soh**-nay
...for today / tomorrow	*...per oggi / domani*	pehr **oh**-jee / doh-**mah**-nee
...at 8:00 P.M.	*...alle venti*	**ah**-lay **vayn**-tee
My name is ___.	*Mi chiamo ___.*	mee kee**ah**-moh

EATING

I have a reservation for ___ people.	*Ho una prenotazione per ___ persone.*	oh **oo**-nah pray-noh-taht-see**oh**-nay pehr ___ pehr-**soh**-nay
I'd like to sit...	*Vorrei sedermi...*	vor-**reh**ee say-**dehr**-mee
We'd like to sit...	*Vorremmo sederci...*	vor-**ray**-moh say-**dehr**-chee
...inside / outside.	*...dentro / fuori.*	**dehn**-troh / **fwoh**-ree
...by the window.	*...vicino alla finestra.*	vee-**chee**-noh **ah**-lah fee-**nay**-strah
...with a view.	*...con la vista.*	koh<u>n</u> lah **vee**-stah
...where it's quiet.	*...a una tavola tranquilla.*	ah **oo**-nah **tah**-voh-lah trah<u>n</u>-**kee**-lah
Is this table free?	*È libero questa tavola?*	eh **lee**-behr-oh **kwehs**-tah **tah**-voh-lah
Can I sit here?	*Posso sedermi qui?*	**poh**-soh say-**dehr**-mee kwee
Can we sit here?	*Possiamo sederci qui?*	poh-see**ah**-moh say-**dehr**-chee kwee

Better restaurants routinely take telephone reservations. Guidebooks include phone numbers, and the process is simple. If you want to eat at a normal European dinnertime (later than 7:30 P.M.), it's smart to call and reserve a table. Many of my favorite restaurants are filled with Americans at 7:30 P.M. and can feel like tourist traps. But if you drop in at (or reserve ahead for) 8:30 or 9:00 P.M., when the Italians are eating, they feel completely local.

The Menu

menu	*menù*	may-**noo**
tourist menu	*menù turistico*	may-**noo** too-**ree**-stee-koh
specialty of the house	*specialità della casa*	spay-chah-lee-**tah** **dehl**-lah **kah**-zah
breakfast	*colazione*	koh-laht-see**oh**-nay
lunch	*pranzo*	**prahnt**-soh
dinner	*cena*	**chay**-nah
appetizers	*antipasti*	ah<u>n</u>-tee-**pah**-stee

sandwiches	*panini*	pah-**nee**-nee
bread	*pane*	**pah**-nay
salad	*insalata*	een-sah-**lah**-tah
soup	*minestra, zuppa*	mee-**nehs**-trah, **tsoo**-pah
first course *(pasta, soup)*	*primo piatto*	**pree**-moh pee**ah**-toh
main course *(meat, fish)*	*secondo piatto*	say-**kohn**-doh pee**ah**-toh
side dishes	*contorni*	kohn-**tor**-nee
meat	*carni*	**kar**-nee
poultry	*pollame*	poh-**lah**-may
fish	*pesce*	**peh**-shay
seafood	*frutti di mare*	**froo**-tee dee **mah**-ray
vegetables	*legumi*	lay-**goo**-mee
cheeses	*formaggi*	for-**mah**-jee
desserts	*dolci*	**dohl**-chee
munchies (tapas)	*spuntini*	spoon-**tee**-nee
beverages	*bevande, bibite*	bay-**vahn**-day, **bee**-bee-tay
beer	*birra*	**beer**-rah
wines	*vini*	**vee**-nee
cover charge	*coperto*	koh-**pehr**-toh
service included	*servizio incluso*	sehr-**veet**-seeoh een-**kloo**-zoh
service not included	*servizio non incluso*	sehr-**veet**-seeoh nohn een-**kloo**-zoh
hot / cold	*caldo / freddo*	**kahl**-doh / **fray**-doh
with / and / or / without	*con / e / o / senza*	kohn / ay / oh / **sehnt**-sah

Without the money-saving words in this chapter, Italy is a very expensive place to eat. You'll do best in places with no or minimal service and cover charges, and by sticking to the ***primo piatto*** (first course) dishes. A hearty minestrone and/or pasta fills the average American, and some pricier restaurants don't allow you to eat without ordering the more expensive ***secondo*** course (often consisting of just the entrée listed, with no vegetables). Try a ***menù del giorno*** (menu of the day), with a choice of appetizer, entrée, and dessert (plus sometimes wine or mineral water) at a fixed price.

Ordering

waiter	*cameriere*	kah-may-ree**ay**-ray
waitress	*cameriera*	kah-may-ree**ay**-rah
I'm ready / We're ready to order.	*Sono pronto / Siamo pronti per ordinare.*	**soh**-noh **prohn**-toh / see**ah**-moh **prohn**-tee pehr or-dee-**nah**-ray
I'd like / We'd like...	*Vorrei / Vorremmo...*	vor-**reh**ee / vor-**ray**-moh
...just a drink.	*...soltanto qualcosa da bere.*	sohl-**tahn**-toh kwahl-**koh**-zah dah **bay**-ray
...a snack.	*...uno spuntino.*	**oon**-oh spoon-**tee**-noh
...just a salad.	*...solo un'insalata.*	**soh**-loh oon-een-sah-**lah**-tah
...a half portion.	*...una mezza porzione.*	**oo**-nah **mehd**-zah port-see**oh**-nay
...only a pasta dish.	*...solo un primo piatto.*	**soh**-loh oon **pree**-moh pee**ah**-toh
...a tourist *menù*. (fixed-price menu)	*...un menù turistico.*	oon may-**noo** too-**ree**-stee-koh
...to see the menu.	*...vedere il menù.*	vay-**day**-ray eel may-**noo**
...to order.	*...ordinare.*	or-dee-**nah**-ray
...to pay.	*...pagare.*	pah-**gah**-ray
...to throw up.	*...vomitare.*	voh-mee-**tah**-ray
Do you have...?	*Avete...?*	ah-**vay**-tay
...a menu in English	*...un menù in inglese*	oon may-**noo** een een-**glay**-zay
...a lunch special	*...un piatto speciale per il pranzo*	oon pee**ah**-toh spay-chee**ah**-lay pehr eel **prahnt**-soh
What do you recommend?	*Che cosa raccomanda?*	kay **koh**-zah rah-koh-**mahn**-dah

What's your favorite dish?	*Qual'è il suo piatto preferito?*	kwah-**leh** eel **soo**-oh peeah-toh preh-feh-**ree**-toh
Is it...?	*È...?*	eh
...good	*...buono*	**bwoh**-noh
...expensive	*...caro*	**kah**-roh
...light	*...leggero*	lay-**jay**-roh
...filling	*...sostanzioso*	soh-stahnt-see**oh**-zoh
What is that?	*Che cosa è quello?*	kay **koh**-zah eh **kway**-loh
What is...?	*Che cosa c'è...?*	kay **koh**-zah cheh
...local	*...di locale*	dee loh-**kah**-lay
...fresh	*...di fresco*	dee **fray**-skoh
...cheap and filling	*...di economico e sostanzioso*	dee ay-koh-**noh**-mee-koh ay soh-stahnt-see**oh**-zoh
...fast	*...di veloce*	dee vay-**loh**-chay
Can we split this and have an extra plate?	*Possiamo dividerlo e avere un altro piatto?*	poh-see**ah**-moh dee-vee-**dehr**-loh ay ah-**vay**-ray oon **ahl**-troh pee**ah**-toh
I've changed my mind.	*Ho cambiato idea.*	oh kahm-bee**ah**-toh ee-**day**-ah
Can I substitute (something) for the ___?	*Posso sostituire (qualcosa d'altro) per il ___?*	**poh**-soh soh-stee-**twee**-ray (kwahl-**koh**-zah **dahl**-troh) pehr eel
Can I / Can we get it "to go"?	*Posso / Possiamo averlo da portar via?*	**poh**-soh / poh-see**ah**-moh ah-**vehr**-loh dah **por**-tar **vee**-ah
"To go"?	*Da portar via?* ("for the road")	dah **por**-tar **vee**-ah

To summon a waiter, ask *"Per favore?"* (Please?). The waiter brings a menu (*menù*) and asks what you'd like to drink (*Da bere?*). When ready to take your order, the waiter will ask, *"Prego?"* He'll often expect you to order multiple courses (he'll ask *"E dopo?"*—"And then?"), but it's O.K. to just get one course—just say *"È tutto."* (That's all). When you're finished, place your utensils on your plate with the handles pointing to your right as the Italians do. This tells the waiter you're done. He'll confirm by asking if you're finished (*Finito?*). He'll usually ask if you'd like dessert (*Qualcosa di dolce?*) and coffee (*Un caffè?*), and if you want anything else (*Altro?*). You ask for the bill: *"Il conto, per favore."*

Tableware and Condiments

plate	*piatto*	pee**ah**-toh
extra plate	*un altro piatto*	oon **ahl**-troh pee**ah**-toh
napkin	*tovagliolo*	toh-vahl-**yoh**-loh
silverware	*posate*	poh-**zah**-tay
knife	*coltello*	kohl-**tehl**-loh
fork	*forchetta*	for-**kay**-tah
spoon	*cucchiaio*	koo-kee**ah**-yoh
cup	*tazza*	**tahd**-zah
glass	*bicchiere*	bee-kee**ay**-ray
carafe	*caraffa*	kah-**rah**-fah
water	*acqua*	**ah**-kwah
bread	*pane*	**pah**-nay
breadsticks	*grissini*	gree-**see**-nee
butter	*burro*	**boo**-roh
margarine	*margarina*	mar-gah-**ree**-nah
salt / pepper	*sale / pepe*	**sah**-lay / **pay**-pay
sugar	*zucchero*	**tsoo**-kay-roh
artificial sweetener	*dolcificante*	dohl-chee-fee-**kahn**-tay
honey	*miele*	mee**ay**-lay
mustard	*senape*	**say**-nah-pay
ketchup	*ketchup*	"ketchup"
mayonnaise	*maionese*	mah-yoh-**nay**-zay
toothpick	*stuzzicadente*	stood-see-kah-**dehn**-tay

The Food Arrives

Is this included with the meal?	*È incluso nel pasto questo?*	eh een-**kloo**-zoh nayl **pah**-stoh **kweh**-stoh
I did not order this.	*Io questo non l'ho ordinato.*	**ee**oh **kweh**-stoh nohn loh or-dee-**nah**-toh

We did not order this.	*Noi questo non l'abbiamo ordinato.*	**noh**ee **kweh**-stoh nohn lah-bee**ah**-moh or-dee-**nah**-toh
Heat it up?	*Lo può scaldare?*	loh pwoh skahl-**dah**-ray
A little.	*Un po'.*	oon poh
More. / Another.	*Un altro po'. / Un altro.*	oon **ahl**-troh poh / oon **ahl**-troh
The same.	*Lo stesso.*	loh **stehs**-soh
Enough.	*Basta.*	**bah**-stah
Finished.	*Finito.*	fee-**nee**-toh
I'm full.	*Sono sazio.*	soh-noh **saht**-seeoh

After bringing your meal, your server might wish you a cheery "***Buon appetito!***" (pronounced bwohn ah-pay-**tee**-toh).

Compliments to the Chef

Yummy!	*Buono!*	**bwoh**-noh
Delicious!	*Delizioso!*	day-leet-see**oh**-zoh
Divinely good!	*Una vera bontà!*	**oo**-nah **vay**-rah bohn-**tah**
My compliments to the chef!	*Complimenti al cuoco!*	kohm-plee-**mayn**-tee ahl koo**oh**-koh
I love Italian food / this food.	*Adoro la cucina italiana / questo piatto.*	ah-**doh**-roh lah koo-**chee**-nah ee-tah-lee**ah**-nah / **kwehs**-toh pee**ah**-toh
Better than mom's cooking.	*Meglio della cucina di mia mamma.*	**mehl**-yoh **dehl**-lah koo-**chee**-nah dee **mee**-ah **mah**-mah

Paying for Your Meal

The bill, please.	*Il conto, per favore.*	eel **kohn**-toh pehr fah-**voh**-ray
Together.	*Conto unico.*	**kohn**-toh **oo**-nee-koh
Separate.	*Conto separato.*	**kohn**-toh say-pah-**rah**-toh
Credit card O.K.?	*Carta di credito è O.K.?*	**kar**-tah dee **kray**-dee-toh eh "O.K."

Is there a cover charge?	*Si paga per il coperto?*	see **pah**-gah pehr eel koh-**pehr**-toh
Is service included?	*È incluso il servizio?*	eh een-**kloo**-zoh eel sehr-**veet**-seeoh
This is not correct.	*Questo non è giusto.*	**kweh**-stoh nohn eh **joo**-stoh
Explain it?	*Lo può spiegare?*	loh pwoh speeay-**gah**-ray
Can you explain / itemize the bill?	*Può spiegare / dettagliare il conto?*	pwoh speeay-**gah**-ray / day-tahl-**yah**-ray eel **kohn**-toh
Is tipping expected?	*Bisogna lasciare una mancia?*	bee-**sohn**-yah lah-**shah**-ray **oo**-nah **mahn**-chah
What percent?	*Che percentuale?*	kay pehr-chehn-too**ah**-lay
tip	*mancia*	**mahn**-chah
Keep the change.	*Tenga il resto.*	**tayn**-gah eel **rehs**-toh
This is for you.	*Questo è per lei.*	**kweh**-stoh eh pehr **leh**ee
Could I have a receipt, please?	*Posso avere una ricevuta, per favore?*	**poh**-soh ah-**vay**-ray **oo**-nah ree-chay-**voo**-tah pehr fah-**voh**-ray

Most menus list the ***coperto*** (cover) and ***servizio*** (service) charge. There's no need to tip beyond that, but if the service was good, toss in a euro per person. If there's no service charge, consider tipping 5 to 10 percent. If you're uncertain, ask another customer if tipping is expected (***Bisogna lasciare una mancia?***). In Italian bars and freeway rest stops, pay first at the ***cassa*** (cash register), then take your receipt to the counter to get your food. There's no need to tip.

SPECIAL CONCERNS

In a Hurry

I'm / We're in a hurry.	*Sono / Siamo di fretta.*	**soh**-noh / see**ah**-moh dee **fray**-tah
I need to be served quickly. Is that a problem?	*Ho bisogno di essere servito[a] rapidamente. È un problema?*	oh bee-**zohn**-yoh dee eh-**say**-ray sehr-**vee**-toh rah-pee-dah-**mehn**-tay eh oon proh-**blay**-mah

EATING

We need to be served quickly. Is that a problem?	*Avremmo bisogno di essere serviti rapidamente. È un problema?*	ah-**vray**-moh bee-**zohn**-yoh dee eh-**say**-ray sehr-**vee**-tee rah-pee-dah-**mehn**-tay eh oon proh-**blay**-mah
When will the food be ready?	*Tra quanto è pronto il cibo?*	trah **kwahn**-toh eh **prohn**-toh eel **chee**-boh

Dietary Restrictions

I'm allergic to...	*Sono allergico[a] al...*	**soh**-noh ahl-**lehr**-jee-koh ahl
I cannot / He cannot / She cannot eat...	*Non posso / Lui non può / lei non può mangiare...*	nohn **poh**-soh / lwee nohn pwoh / **leh**ee nohn pwoh mahn-**jah**-ray
...dairy products.	*...latticini.*	lah-tee-**chee**-nee
...wheat.	*...frumento.*	froo-**mehn**-toh
...meat / pork.	*...carne / maiale.*	**kar**-nay / mah-**yah**-lay
...salt / sugar.	*...sale / zucchero.*	**sah**-lay / **tsoo**-kay-roh
...shellfish.	*...molluschi e crostacei.*	moh-**loos**-kee ay kroh-**stah**-chayee
...spicy foods.	*...cibo piccante.*	**chee**-boh pee-**kahn**-tay
...nuts.	*...noci e altra frutta secca.*	**noh**-chee ay **ahl**-trah **froo**-tah **say**-kah
I am diabetic.	*Ho il diabete.*	oh eel deeah-**bay**-tay
No caffeine.	*Senza caffeina.*	**sehnt**-sah kah-fay**ee**-nah
No alcohol.	*Niente alcool.*	nee**ehn**-tay **ahl**-kohl
I'm a...	*Sono un...*	**soh**-noh oon
...vegetarian.	*...vegetariano[a].*	vay-jay-tah-ree**ah**-noh
...strict vegetarian.	*...strettamente vegetariano[a].*	stray-tah-**mayn**-tay vay-jay-tah-ree**ah**-noh
...carnivore.	*...carnivoro[a].*	kar-**nee**-voh-roh
...big eater.	*...mangione.*	mahn-jee**oh**-nay
Is any meat or animal fat used in this?	*Contiene carne o grassi animali?*	kohn-tee**ay**-nay **kar**-nay oh **grah**-see ah-nee-**mah**-lee

Children

Do you have...?	*Avete...?*	ah-**vay**-tay
...a children's portions	*...un platto per i bambini*	oon peeah-toh pehr ee bahm-**bee**-nee
...a half portion	*...una mezza porzione*	**oo**-nah **mehd**-zah port-see**oh**-nay
...a high chair / booster seat	*...un seggiolone / seggiolino*	oon seh-joh-**loh**-nay / seh-joh-**lee**-noh
plain noodles	*della pasta in bianco*	**dehl**-lah **pah**-stah een bee**ahn**-koh
plain rice	*del riso in bianco*	dehl **ree**-zoh een bee**ahn**-koh
with butter	*con il burro*	koh<u>n</u> eel **boo**-roh
no sauce	*senza sugo*	**sehnt**-sah **soo**-goh
with sauce / dressing	*con il sugo / il condimento*	koh<u>n</u> eel **soo**-goh / eel koh<u>n</u>-dee-**mehn**-toh
on the side	*a parte*	ah **par**-tay
Nothing spicy.	*Niente di piccante.*	nee**ehn**-tay dee pee-**kahn**-tay
Not too hot.	*Non troppo caldo.*	noh<u>n</u> **troh**-poh **kahl**-doh
Please keep the food separate on the plate.	*Per favore tenete separato il cibo nel piatto.*	pehr fah-**voh**-ray tay-**nay**-tay say-pah-**rah**-toh eel **chee**-boh nehl pee**ah**-toh
He / She will share our meal.	*Lui / Lei mangia parte del nostro pasto.*	lwee / **leh**ee **mahn**-jah **par**-tay dehl **noh**-stroh **pah**-stoh
They will share our meal.	*Loro mangiano parte del nostro pasto.*	**loh**-roh mah<u>n</u>-**jah**-noh **par**-tay dehl **noh**-stroh **pah**-stoh
Please bring the food quickly.	*Per favore ci porti da mangiare velocemente.*	pehr fah-**voh**-ray chee **por**-tee dah mah<u>n</u>-**jah**-ray vay-loh-chay-**mehn**-tay
Can I / Can we have an extra...?	*Potrei / Potremmo avere un altro...*	poh-**tray**ee / poh-**tray**-moh ah-**vay**-ray oon **ahl**-troh
...plate	*...piatto*	pee**ah**-toh

...cup	*...tazza*	**tahd**-zah
...spoon / fork	*...cucchiaio / forchetta*	koo-kee**ah**-yoh / for-**kay**-tah
Can I / Can we have two extra...?	*Potrei / Potremmo avere altri due...?*	poh-**tray**ee / poh-**tray**-moh ah-**vay**-ray **ahl**-tree **doo**-ay
...plates	*...piatti*	pee**ah**-tee
...cups	*...tazze*	**tahd**-zay
...spoons / forks	*...cucchiai / forchette*	koo-kee**ah**-ee / for-**kay**-tay
Small milk (in a plastic cup).	*Un po di latte (in una tazza di plastica).*	oon poh dee **lah**-tay (een **oo**-nah **tahd**-zah dee **plah**-stee-kah
straw / straws	*cannuccia / cannucce*	kah-**noo**-chah / kah-**noo**-chay
More napkins, please.	*Degli altri tovaglioli, per favore.*	**day**-lee **ahl**-tree toh-vahl-**yoh**-lee pehr fah-**voh**-ray
Sorry for the mess.	*Scusi per il pasticcio.*	**skoo**-zee pehr eel pah-**stee**-choh

Don't expect to find peanut butter sandwiches in Italy. Italian kids would rather have a sandwich with Nutella (***un panino con la Nutella***), the popular chocolate-hazelnut spread.

WHAT'S COOKING?

Breakfast

breakfast	*colazione*	koh-laht-see**oh**-nay
bread	*pane*	**pah**-nay
roll	*brioche*	bree-**ohsh**
croissant	*cornetto*	kor-**nay**-toh
toast	*toast*	"toast"
butter	*burro*	**boo**-roh
jam	*marmellata*	mar-mehl-**lah**-tah
jelly	*gelatina*	jay-lah-**tee**-nah
milk	*latte*	**lah**-tay
coffee / tea (see Drinking)	*caffè / tè*	kah-**feh** / teh

Is breakfast included?	*La colazione è inclusa?*	lah koh-laht-see**oh**-nay eh een-**kloo**-zah

Italian breakfasts, like Italian bath towels, are small: coffee and a roll with butter and marmalade. The strong coffee is often mixed about half-and-half with milk. At your hotel, refills are usually free. The delicious red orange juice is made from Sicilian blood oranges (***arancia tarocco***). Local open-air markets thrive in the morning, and a picnic breakfast followed by a ***cappuccino*** in a bar is a good option.

Snacks and Quick Meals

For fresh, fast, and frugal pizza, ***pizza rustica*** shops offer the cheapest hot meal in any Italian town, selling pizza by the slice (***pezzo***) or weight (***etto*** = 100 grams, around a quarter pound). ***Due etti*** (200 grams) makes a good light lunch. You can always get it to go (***"Da portar via"***—for the road), or, if there are seats, you can

Key Phrases: What's Cooking?

food	*cibo*	**chee**-boh
breakfast	*colazione*	koh-laht-see**oh**-nay
lunch	*pranzo*	**prahnt**-soh
dinner	*cena*	**chay**-nah
bread	*pane*	**pah**-nay
cheese	*formaggio*	for-**mah**-joh
soup	*minestra, zuppa*	mee-**nehs**-trah, **tsoo**-pah
salad	*insalata*	een-sah-**lah**-tah
meat	*carni*	**kar**-nee
chicken	*pollo*	**poh**-loh
fish	*pesce*	**peh**-shay
fruit	*frutta*	**froo**-tah
vegetables	*legumi*	lay-**goo**-mee
dessert	*dolci*	**dohl**-chee
Delicious!	*Delizioso!*	day-leet-see**oh**-zoh

eat it on the spot. For handier pizza, nearly any bar has lousy, microwavable pizza snacks. To get cold pizza warmed up, say, ***"Calda, per favore"*** (Hot, please). To get an extra plate, ask for ***"Un altro piatto."*** Here are some pizza words:

acciughe	ah-**choo**-gay	anchovies
alla diavola	**ah**-lah dee**ah**-voh-lah	spicy
bianca, ciaccina	bee**ahn**-kah, chah-**chee**-nah	"white" pizza (no tomato sauce)
calzone	kahlt-**soh**-nay	folded pizza with various fillings
capricciosa	kah-pree-**choh**-zah	means "chef's choice"—usually ham, mushrooms, olives, and artichokes
carciofi	kar-**choh**-fee	artichokes
funghi	**foong**-gee	mushrooms
Margherita	mar-gehr-**ee**-tah	cheese and tomato sauce
melanzane	may-lahnt-**sah**-nay	eggplant
Napoletana	nah-poh-lay-**tah**-nah	cheese, anchovies, and tomato sauce
peperoni	pay-pehr-**oh**-nee	green or red peppers (not sausage!)
porcini	pohr-**chee**-nee	porcini mushrooms
prosciutto	proh-**shoo**-toh	ham
quattro stagioni	**kwah**-troh stah-jee**oh**-nee	four toppings on separate quarters of a pizza
ripieno	ree-pee**ay**-noh	stuffed
salame piccante	sah-**lah**-may pee-**kahn**-tay	pepperoni
salsiccia	sahl-**see**-chah	sausage
Siciliana	see-chee-lee**ah**-nah	capers and olives
vegetariana, ortolana	vay-jay-tah-ree**ah**-nah or-toh-**lah**-nah	veggie

For other quick, tasty meals, drop by a ***rosticceria*** deli, where you'll find a cafeteria-style display of reasonably priced food. Get it "to go" or grab a seat and eat.

EATING

Sandwiches

I'd like a sandwich.	*Vorrei un panino.*	vor-**reh**ee oon pah-**nee**-noh
We'd like two sandwiches.	*Vorremmo due panini.*	vor-**ray**-moh doo-ay pah-**nee**-nee
small sandwiches	*tramezzini*	trah-mehd-**zee**-nee
toasted ham and cheese	*toast*	"toast"
toasted	*tostato*	toh-**stah**-toh
cheese	*formaggio*	for-**mah**-joh
chicken	*pollo*	**poh**-loh
egg salad	*insalata con uova*	een-sah-**lah**-tah kohn **woh**-vah
fish	*pesce*	**peh**-shay
ham	*prosciutto*	proh-**shoo**-toh
pork	*porchetta*	por-**kay**-tah
salami	*salame*	sah-**lah**-may
tuna	*tonno*	**toh**-noh
turkey	*tacchino*	tah-**kee**-noh
lettuce	*lattuga*	lah-**too**-gah
mayonnaise	*maionese*	mah-yoh-**nay**-zay
tomatoes	*pomodori*	poh-moh-**doh**-ree
mustard	*senape*	**say**-nah-pay
ketchup	*ketchup*	"ketchup"
onions	*cipolle*	chee-**poh**-lay
Does this come cold or warm?	*Si mangia freddo o caldo?*	see **mahn**-jah **fray**-doh oh **kahl**-doh

Many bars sell small, ready-made sandwiches called ***tramezzini.*** These crustless white bread sandwiches, displayed behind glass, come with a variety of fillings (such as shrimp) mixed with a mayonnaise dressing. Two or three make a fast, easy meal. ***Panini,*** made from heartier bread with meat, cheese, and veggie combinations, can be delicious toasted. Say, ***"Calda, per favore"*** (Heated, please). Prices are usually posted. Pay the cashier for the sandwich and your beverage, then give your receipt to the person behind the bar to get your food.

In central Italy, ***porchetta*** stands serve tasty rolls stuffed with slices of roasted suckling pig.

If You Knead Bread

bread	*pane*	**pah**-nay
whole-grain bread	*pane integrale*	**pah**-nay een-tay-**grah**-lay
olive bread	*pane di olive*	**pah**-nay dee oh-**lee**-vay
rye bread	*pane di segale*	**pah**-nay dee say-**gah**-lay
brown bread	*pane scuro*	**pah**-nay skoo-roh
Tuscan bread (unsalted)	*pane Toscano*	**pah**-nay toh-**skah**-noh
breadsticks	*grissini*	gree-**see**-nee

Every region of Italy has its own bread, highly prized by the locals. We say "good as gold," but the Italians say, "good as bread."

Say Cheese

cheese	*formaggio*	for-**mah**-joh
fresh, mild, and soft	*fresco*	**fray**-skoh
aged, sharp, and hard	*stagionato*	stah-joh-**nah**-toh
cheese plate	*piatto di formaggi misti*	pee**ah**-toh dee for-**mah**-jee **mee**-stee
Can I try a taste?	*Posso avere un'assagio?*	**poh**-soh ah-**vay**-ray oo-nah-**sah**-joh

Soups and Salads

soup	*minestra, zuppa*	mee-**nehs**-trah, **tsoo**-pah
soup of the day	*zuppa del giorno*	**tsoo**-pah dayl **jor**-noh
broth...	*brodo...*	**broh**-doh
...chicken	*...di pollo*	dee **poh**-loh
...beef	*...di carne*	dee **kar**-nay
...vegetable	*...di verdura*	dee vehr-**doo**-rah
...with noodles	*...con pastina*	koh<u>n</u> pah-**stee**-nah
...with rice	*...con riso*	koh<u>n</u> **ree**-zoh
vegetable soup	*minestrone*	mee-nay-**stroh**-nay

salad...	*insalata...*	een-sah-**lah**-tah
...green	*...verde*	**vehr**-day
...mixed	*...mista*	**mee**-stah
...with ham and cheese	*...con prosciutto e formaggio*	kohn proh-**shoo**-toh ay for-**mah**-joh
...with egg	*...con uova*	kohn **woh**-vah
lettuce	*lattuga*	lah-**too**-gah
tomatoes	*pomodori*	poh-moh-**doh**-ree
onion	*cipolla*	chee-**poh**-lah
cucumbers	*cetrioli*	chay-tree**oh**-lee
oil / vinegar	*olio / aceto*	**oh**-leeoh / ah-**chay**-toh
What is in this salad?	*Che cosa c'è in questa insalata?*	kay **koh**-zah cheh een **kweh**-stah een-sah-**lah**-tah
dressing on the side	*condimento a parte*	kohn-dee-**mehn**-toh ah **par**-tay

Created in Tuscany, ***ribollita*** is a stew of white beans, veggies, and olive oil, layered with day-old bread.

In Italy, salad dressing is usually just the oil and vinegar at the table (if it's missing, ask for the ***oliera***). Salad bars at fast food restaurants and ***autostrada*** rest stops can be a good budget bet.

Seafood

seafood	*frutti di mare*	**froo**-tee dee **mah**-ray
assorted seafood	*misto di frutti di mare*	**mee**-stoh dee **froo**-tee dee **mah**-ray
fish	*pesce*	**peh**-shay
anchovies	*acciughe*	ah-**choo**-gay
barnacles	*balani*	bah-**lah**-nee
bream (fish)	*orata*	oh-**rah**-tah
clams	*vongole*	**vohn**-goh-lay
cod	*merluzzo*	mehr-**lood**-zoh
crab	*granchio*	**grahn**-keeoh
crayfish	*gambero, aragosta*	gahm-**bay**-roh, ah-rah-**goh**-stah
cuttlefish	*seppie*	**sehp**-eeay

herring	*aringa*	ah-**reeng**-gah
lobster	*aragosta*	ah-rah-**goh**-stah
mussels	*cozze*	kohd-zay
octopus	*polipo, polpo*	**poh**-lee-poh, **pohl**-poh
oysters	*ostriche*	**ohs**-tree-kay
prawns	*scampi, gamberi*	**skahm**-pee, gahm-**bay**-ree
salmon	*salmone*	sahl-**moh**-nay
sardines	*sardine*	sar-**dee**-nay
scad (like mackerel)	*sgombro*	**sgohm**-broh
scallops	*capesante*	kah-pay-**zahn**-tay
sea bass	*branzino*	brahnt-**see**-noh
shrimp	*gamberetti*	gahm-bay-**ray**-tee
sole	*sogliola*	sohl-**yoh**-lah
squid	*calamari*	kah-lah-**mah**-ree
swordfish	*pesce spada*	**peh**-shay **spah**-dah
tiger shrimp	*gamberoni*	gahm-bay-**roh**-nee
trout	*trota*	**troh**-tah
tuna	*tonno*	**toh**-noh
How much for a portion?	*Quanto per una porzione?*	**kwahn**-toh pehr **oo**-nah port-see**oh**-nay
What's fresh today?	*Cosa c'è di fresco oggi?*	**koh**-zah cheh dee **fray**-skoh **oh**-jee
Do you eat this part?	*Si mangia anche questa parte?*	see **mahn**-jah **ahn**-kay **kweh**-stah **par**-tay
Just the head, please.	*Solo la testa, per favore.*	**soh**-loh lah **tehs**-tah pehr fah-**voh**-ray

Italians like to stuff seafood with delicious herbs, breadcrumbs, and cheese, be it mussels, sardines, or anchovies. Most fish are served grilled and whole. Seafood is sometimes sold by the weight; if you see ***100 g*** or ***l'etto*** by the price on the menu, that's the price you'll pay per 100 grams, about a quarter pound. To find out how much a typical portion costs, ask, ***"Quanto per una porzione?"***

Poultry

poultry	*pollame*	poh-**lah**-may
chicken	*pollo*	**poh**-loh
duck	*anatra*	**ah**-nah-trah
turkey	*tacchino*	tah-**kee**-noh
How long has this been dead?	*Da quanto tempo è morto questo?*	dah **kwahn**-toh **tehm**-poh eh **mor**-toh **kweh**-stoh

Meat

meat	*carne*	**kar**-nay
beef	*manzo*	**mahnt**-soh
beef steak	*bistecca di manzo*	bee-**stay**-kah dee **mahnt**-soh
sirloin steak	*entrecote*	ayn-tray-**koh**-tay
ribsteak	*costata*	koh-**stah**-tah
roast beef	*roast beef*	"roast beef"
brains	*cervella*	chehr-**vehl**-lah
bunny	*coniglio*	koh-**neel**-yoh
cutlet (veal)	*cotoletta*	koh-toh-**lay**-tah
goat, baby	*capretto*	kah-**pray**-toh
ham	*prosciutto*	proh-**shoo**-toh
cooked ham	*prosciutto cotto*	proh-**shoo**-toh **koh**-toh
dried, air-cured ham	*prosciutto crudo*	proh-**shoo**-toh **kroo**-doh
lamb	*agnello*	ahn-**yehl**-loh
liver	*fegato*	**fay**-gah-toh
meat stew	*stufato di carne*	stoo-**fah**-toh dee **kar**-nay
pork	*maiale*	mah-**yah**-lay
salt-cured bacon	*pancetta*	pahn-**chay**-tah
sausage	*salsiccia*	sahl-**see**-chah
snails	*lumache*	loo-**mah**-chay
suckling pig	*porchetta*	por-**kay**-tah
sweetbreads (calf pancreas)	*animelle di vitello*	ah-nee-**mehl**-lay dee vee-**tehl**-loh

Avoiding Mis-Steaks

alive	*vivo*	**vee**-voh
raw	*crudo*	**kroo**-doh
very rare	*molto al sangue*	**mohl**-toh ahl **sahn**-gway
rare	*al sangue*	ahl **sahn**-gway
medium	*cotto*	**koh**-toh
well-done	*ben cotto*	bayn **koh**-toh
very well-done	*completamente cotto*	kohm-play-tah-**mehn**-tay **koh**-toh
almost burnt	*quasi bruciato*	**kwah**-zee broo-**chah**-toh

tongue	*lingua*	**leeng**-gwah
tripe	*trippa*	**tree**-pah
veal	*vitello*	vee-**tehl**-loh
thin-sliced veal	*scaloppine*	skah-loh-**pee**-nay
wild boar	*cinghiale*	cheeng-**gah**-lay

On a menu, the price of steak is often listed per ***etto*** (100 grams, about a quarter of a pound). When ordering ***bistecca*** (steak) in a restaurant, it is most common to order four or five ***ettos*** and share it.

How Food is Prepared

assorted	*assortiti*	ah-sor-**tee**-tee
baked	*al forno*	ahl **for**-noh
boiled	*bollito, lesso*	boh-**lee**-toh, **lay**-soh
braised	*brasato*	brah-**zah**-toh
broiled	*alla graticola*	**ah**-lah grah-tee-**koh**-lah
cold	*freddo*	**fray**-doh
cooked	*cotto*	**koh**-toh
deep-fried	*fritto*	**free**-toh
fillet	*filetto*	fee-**lay**-toh
fresh	*fresco*	**fray**-skoh
fried	*fritto*	**free**-toh

fried with breadcrumbs	*alla Milanese*	**ah**-lah mee-lah-**nay**-zay
grilled	*alla griglia*	**ah**-lah **greel**-yah
homemade	*casalingo*	kah-zah-**leen**-goh
hot	*caldo*	**kahl**-doh
in cream sauce	*con panna*	kohn **pah**-nah
medium	*medio*	**may**-deeoh
microwave	*forno a microonde*	**for**-noh ah mee-kroh-**ohn**-day
mild	*non piccante*	nohn pee-**kahn**-tay
mixed	*misto*	**mee**-stoh
poached	*affogato*	ah-foh-**gah**-toh
rare	*al sangue*	ahl **sahn**-gway
raw	*crudo*	**kroo**-doh
roasted	*arrosto*	ah-**roh**-stoh
sautéed	*saltato in padella*	sahl-**tah**-toh een pah-**dehl**-lah
smoked	*affumicato*	ah-foo-mee-**kah**-toh
sour	*agro*	**ah**-groh
spicy hot	*piccante*	pee-**kahn**-tay
steamed	*al vapore*	ahl vah-**poh**-ray
steamed in parchment	*al cartoccio*	ahl kar-**toh**-choh
stuffed	*ripieno*	ree-pee**ay**-noh
sweet	*dolce*	**dohl**-chay
well-done	*ben cotto*	bayn **koh**-toh
with cheese and breadcrumbs	*alla Parmigiana*	**ah**-lah par-mee-**jah**-nah
with rice	*con il riso*	kohn eel **ree**-zoh

Veggies

vegetables	*legumi, verdure*	lay-**goo**-mee, vehr-**doo**-ray
mixed vegetables	*misto di verdure*	**mee**-stoh dee vehr-**doo**-ray
artichoke	*carciofo*	kar-**choh**-foh
giant artichoke	*mame*	**mah**-may

asparagus	*asparagi*	ah-spah-**rah**-jee
beans	*fagioli*	fah-**joh**-lee
beets	*barbabietole*	bar-bah-beeay-**toh**-lay
broccoli	*broccoli*	**broh**-koh-lee
cabbage	*verza*	**vehrt**-sah
carrots	*carote*	kah-**roh**-tay
cauliflower	*cavolfiore*	kah-vohl-fee**oh**-ray
corn	*granturco*	grahn-**toor**-koh
cucumber	*cetrioli*	chay-tree**oh**-lee
eggplant	*melanzana*	may-lahnt-**sah**-nah
fennel	*finocchio*	fee-**noh**-keeoh
French fries	*patate fritte*	pah-**tah**-tay **free**-tay
garlic	*aglio*	**ahl**-yoh
green beans	*fagiolini*	fah-joh-**lee**-nee
lentils	*lenticchie*	lehn-**tee**-keeay
mushrooms	*funghi*	**foong**-gee
olives	*olive*	oh-**lee**-vay
onions	*cipolle*	chee-**poh**-lay
peas	*piselli*	pee-**zehl**-lee
peppers...	*peperoni*	pay-pay-**roh**-nee
...green / red	*...verdi / rossi*	**vehr**-dee / **roh**-see
pickles	*cetriolini*	chay-treeoh-**lee**-nee
potatoes	*patate*	pah-**tah**-tay
rice	*riso*	**ree**-zoh
spinach	*spinaci*	spee-**nah**-chee
tomatoes	*pomodori*	poh-moh-**doh**-ree
truffles	*tartufi*	tar-**too**-fee
zucchini	*zucchine*	tsoo-**kee**-nay

Vegetables are often ordered as a ***contorno*** (side dish) with a ***secondo*** course. Common side dishes include ***patate fritte*** or ***patate arrosto*** (potatoes fried or roasted), ***spinaci*** (spinach), ***fagioli*** (green beans), ***asparagi*** (asparagus) and ***insalate verde*** or ***insalate mista*** (green salad or mixed with carrots and tomato). Sometimes more elaborate choices are available, such as ***fiore di zucca*** (fried zucchini blossoms stuffed with mozzarella). Although the Italians are experts at cooking pasta, they tend to overcook vegetables.

Fruits

apple	*mela*	**may**-lah
apricot	*albicocca*	ahl-bee-**koh**-kah
banana	*banana*	bah-**nah**-nah
berries	*frutti di bosco*	**froo**-tee dee **bohs**-koh
cantaloupe	*melone*	may-**loh**-nay
cherry	*ciliegia*	chee-lee**ay**-jah
dates	*datteri*	**dah**-tay-ree
fig	*fico*	**fee**-koh
fruit	*frutta*	**froo**-tah
grapefruit	*pompelmo*	pohm-**pehl**-moh
grapes	*uva*	**oo**-vah
honeydew melon	*melone verde*	may-**loh**-nay **vehr**-day
lemon	*limone*	lee-**moh**-nay
orange	*arancia*	ah-**rahn**-chah
peach	*pesca*	**pehs**-kah
pear	*pera*	**pay**-rah
pineapple	*ananas*	**ah**-nah-nahs
plum	*susina*	soo-**zee**-nah
prune	*prugna*	**proon**-yah
raspberry	*lampone*	lahm-**poh**-nay
strawberry	*fragola*	**frah**-goh-lah
tangerine	*mandarino*	mahn-dah-**ree**-noh
watermelon	*cocomero*	koh-koh-**may**-roh

On a menu, you might see ***frutta fresca di stagione*** (fresh fruit of the season). Mixed berries are called ***frutti di bosco*** (forest fruits). If you ask for ***sottobosco*** (under the forest), you'll get a bowl of mixed berries with lemon and sugar.

Nuts

almond	*mandorle*	mahn-**dor**-lay
chestnut	*castagne*	kah-**stahn**-yay
coconut	*noce di cocco*	**noh**-chay dee **koh**-koh
hazelnut	*nocciola*	noh-**choh**-lah
peanuts	*arachidi*	ah-**rah**-kee-dee
pine nuts	*pinoli*	pee-**noh**-lee

EATING

pistachio	*pistacchio*	pee-**stah**-keeoh
walnut	*noce*	**noh**-chay

Just Desserts

dessert	*dolci*	**dohl**-chee
cake	*torta*	**tor**-tah
fruit cup	*macedonia senza zucchero*	mah-chay-**doh**-neeah **sehnt**-sah **tsoo**-kay-roh
fruit salad	*macedonia*	mah-chay-**doh**-neeah
fruit with ice cream	*coppa di frutta*	**koh**-pah dee **froo**-tah
tart	*tartina*	tar-**tee**-nah
pie	*crostata*	kroh-**stah**-tah
whipped cream	*panna*	**pah**-nah
chocolate mousse	*mousse*	moos
pudding	*budino*	boo-**dee**-noh
pastry	*pasticceria*	pah-stee-**chay**-ree-ah
strudel	*strudel*	"strudel"
cookies	*biscotti*	bee-**skoh**-tee
candies	*caramelle*	kah-rah-**mehl**-lay
low calorie	*poche calorie*	**poh**-kay kah-loh-**ree**-ay
homemade	*casalingo*	kah-zah-**leen**-goh
We'll split one.	*Ne dividiamo uno.*	nay dee-vee-dee**ah**-moh **oo**-noh
Two forks / spoons, please.	*Due forchette / cucchiai, per favore.*	**doo**-ay for-**kay**-tay / koo-kee**ah**-yee pehr fah-**voh**-ray
I shouldn't, but...	*Non dovrei, ma...*	nohn doh-**vreh**ee mah
Exquisite!	*Squisito!*	skwee-**zee**-toh
It's heavenly!	*Da sogno!*	dah **sohn**-yoh
I'm a glutton for chocolate.	*Sono golosa per cioccolato.*	**soh**-noh goh-**loh**-zah pehr choh-koh-**lah**-toh
Better than sex.	*Meglio del sesso.*	**mehl**-yoh dehl **say**-soh
Just looking at it fattens you.	*Fa ingrassare solo a guardarlo.*	fah een-grah-**sah**-ray **soh**-loh ah gwar-**dar**-loh
Sinfully good.	*Un peccato di gola.* ("a sin of the throat")	oon pay-**kah**-toh dee **goh**-lah

So good I even licked my moustache.	*Così buono che mi sono leccato anche i baffi.*	koh-**zee bwoh**-noh kay mee **soh**-noh lay-**kah**-toh **ahn**-kay ee **bah**-fee

There are also hundreds of different cookies made in Italy, especially in the Veneto region. Every holiday is an excuse to celebrate with a new tasty treat. ***Bussoli*** are for Easter. ***Frittole*** (small doughnuts) are eaten during ***Carnevale.*** Even Romeo and Juliet have their own special sweets named for them: ***baci di Giulietta*** (vanilla meringues, literally "Juliet's kisses") and ***sospiri di Romeo*** (hazelnut and chocolate cookies, literally "Romeo's sighs").

Bacio (chocolate hazelnut) also means "kiss." ***Baci*** (kisses) are Italy's version of Chinese fortune cookies. The poetic fortunes, wrapped around chocolate balls, are written by people whose love of romance exceeds their grasp of English.

Ice Cream

ice cream	*gelato*	jay-**lah**-toh
sherbet	*sorbetto*	sor-**bay**-toh
cone / cup	*cono / coppa*	**koh**-noh / **koh**-pah
one scoop	*una pallina*	**oo**-nah pah-**lee**-nah
two scoops	*due palline*	**doo**-ay pah-**lee**-nay
with whipped cream	*con panna*	kohn **pah**-nah
A little taste?	*Un assaggio?*	oon ah-**sah**-joh
How many flavors can I get per scoop?	*Quanti gusti posso avere per pallina?*	**kwahn**-tee **goo**-stee **poh**-soh ah-**vay**-ray pehr pah-**lee**-nah
apricot	*albicocca*	ahl-bee-**koh**-kah
berries	*frutti di bosco*	**froo**-tee dee **bohs**-koh
blueberry	*mirtillo*	meer-**tee**-loh
cantaloupe	*melone*	may-**loh**-nay
coconut	*cocco*	**koh**-koh
chocolate	*cioccolato*	choh-koh-**lah**-toh
super chocolate	*tartufo*	tar-**too**-foh
vanilla and chocolate chips	*stracciatella*	strah-chah-**tehl**-lah

chocolate hazelnut	*bacio*	**bah**-choh
chocolate and mint	*After Eight*	"After Eight"
coffee	*caffè*	kah-**feh**
hazelnut	*nocciola*	noh-**choh**-lah
lemon	*limone*	lee-**moh**-nay
milk	*fior di latte*	**fee**or dee **lah**-tay
mint	*menta*	**mayn**-tah
orange	*arancia*	ah-**rahn**-chah
peach	*pesca*	**pehs**-kah
pear	*pera*	**pay**-rah
pineapple	*ananas*	**ah**-nah-nahs
raspberry	*lampone*	lahm-**poh**-nay
rice	*riso*	**ree**-zoh
strawberry	*fragola*	**frah**-goh-lah
vanilla	*crema*	**kray**-mah
yogurt	*yogurt*	**yoh**-goort

DRINKING

Water, Milk, and Juice

mineral water...	*acqua minerale...*	**ah**-kwah mee-nay-**rah**-lay
...with / without gas	*...gassata / non gassata*	gah-**sah**-tah / nohn gah-**sah**-tah
tap water	*acqua del rubinetto*	**ah**-kwah dayl roo-bee-**nay**-toh
whole milk	*latte intero*	**lah**-tay een-**tay**-roh
skim milk	*latte magro*	**lah**-tay **mah**-groh
fresh milk	*latte fresco*	**lah**-tay **fray**-skoh
milk shake	*frappè*	frah-**peh**
hot chocolate...	*cioccolata calda...*	choh-koh-**lah**-tah **kahl**-dah
...with whipped cream	*...con panna*	kohn **pah**-nah
orange soda	*aranciata*	ah-rahn-**chah**-tah
lemon soda	*limonata*	lee-moh-**nah**-tah
juice...	*succo di...*	**soo**-koh dee
...fruit	*...frutta*	**froo**-tah

...apple	*...mela*	**may**-lah
...apricot	*...albicocca*	ahl-bee-**koh**-kah
...grapefruit	*...pompelmo*	pohm-**pehl**-moh
...orange	*...arancia*	ah-**rahn**-chah
...peach	*...pesca*	**pehs**-kah
...pear	*...pera*	**pay**-rah
freshly-squeezed orange juice	*spremuta d'arancia*	spray-**moo**-tah dah-**rahn**-chah
100% juice	*succo al cento per cento*	**soo**-koh ahl **chehn**-toh pehr **chehn**-toh
with / without...	*con / senza...*	kohn / **sehnt**-sah
...sugar	*...zucchero*	**tsoo**-kay-roh
...ice	*...ghiaccio*	gee**ah**-choh
glass / cup	*bicchiere / tazza*	bee-kee**ay**-ray / **tahd**-zah
bottle...	*bottiglia...*	boh-**teel**-yah
...small / large	*...piccola / grande*	**pee**-koh-lah / **grahn**-day
Is this water safe to drink?	*È potabile quest'acqua?*	eh poh-**tah**-bee-lay kweh-**stah**-kwah

I drink the tap water in Italy (Venice's is piped in from a mountain spring, and Florence's is very chlorinated), but it's good style and never expensive to order a ***litro*** (liter) or ***mezzo litro*** (half liter) of bottled water with your meal.

Coffee and Tea

coffee...	*caffè...*	kah-**feh**
...with milk	*...latte*	**lah**-tay
...with whipped cream	*...con panna*	kohn **pah**-nah
...with water	*...lungo*	**loon**-goh
...iced	*...freddo*	**fray**-doh
...instant	*...solubile*	soo-**loo**-bee-lay
...American-style	*...Americano*	ah-may-ree-**kah**-noh
coffee with foamy milk	*cappuccino*	kah-poo-**chee**-noh
decaffeinated	*decaffeinato, Haag*	day-kah-fay-**nah**-toh, hahg

black	*nero*	**nay**-roh
milk...	*latte...*	**lah**-tay
...with a little coffee	*...macchiato*	mah-kee**ah**-toh
sugar	*zucchero*	**tsoo**-kay-roh
hot water	*acqua calda*	**ah**-kwah **kahl**-dah
tea / lemon	*tè / limone*	teh / lee-**moh**-nay
herbal tea	*tisana*	tee-**zah**-nah
tea bag	*bustina di tè*	boo-**stee**-nah dee teh
fruit tea	*tè alla frutta*	teh **ah**-lah **froo**-tah
mint tea	*tè alla menta*	teh **ah**-lah **mehn**-tah
iced tea	*tè freddo*	teh **fray**-doh
small / large	*piccola / grande*	**pee**-koh-lah / **grahn**-day
Another cup.	*Un'altra tazza.*	oo-**nahl**-trah **tahd**-zah
Same price if I sit or stand?	*Costa uguale al tavolo o al banco?*	**koh**-stah oo-**gwah**-lay ahl **tah**-voh-loh oh ahl **bahn**-koh

Caffè is espresso served in a teeny tiny cup. Foamy ***cappuccino*** was named after the monks with their brown robes and frothy cowls. A ***caffè corretto*** (literally "coffee corrected") is coffee and firewater. In a bar, you'll pay at the ***cassa***, then take your receipt to the person who makes the coffee. Refills are never free, except at hotel breakfasts.

When you're ordering coffee in bars in bigger cities, you'll notice that the price board (***lista dei prezzi***) clearly lists two price levels: the cheaper level for the stand-up bar and the more expensive for the ***tavola*** (table) or ***terrazza*** (out on the terrace or sidewalk).

Wine

I would like...	*Vorrei....*	vor-**reh**ee
We would like...	*Vorremo...*	vor-**ray**-moh
...a glass...	*...un bicchiere...*	oon bee-kee**ay**-ray
...a quarter liter...	*...un quarto litro...*	oon **kwar**-toh **lee**-troh
...a half liter...	*...un mezzo litro...*	oon **mehd**-zoh **lee**-troh
...a carafe...	*...una caraffa...*	**oo**-nah kah-**rah**-fah
...a half bottle...	*...una mezza bottiglia...*	**oo**-nah **mehd**-zah boh-**teel**-yah

Key Phrases: Drinking

drink	*bibite*	bee-**bee**-tay
(mineral) water	*acqua (minerale)*	**ah**-kwah (mee-nay-**rah**-lay)
tap water	*acqua del rubinetto*	**ah**-kwah dayl roo-bee-**nay**-toh
milk	*latte*	**lah**-tay
juice	*succo*	**soo**-koh
coffee	*caffè*	kah-**feh**
tea	*tè*	teh
wine	*vino*	**vee**-noh
beer	*birra*	**bee**-rah
Cheers!	*Cin cin!*	cheen cheen

...a bottle...	*...una bottiglia...*	**oo**-nah boh-**teel**-yah
...a 5-liter jug...	*...una damigiana da cinque litri...*	**oo**-nah dah-mee-**jah**-nah dah **cheeng**-kway **lee**-tree
...a barrel...	*...un barile...*	oon bah-**ree**-lay
...a vat...	*...un tino...*	oon **tee**-noh
...of red wine.	*...di rosso.*	dee **roh**-soh
...of white wine.	*...di bianco.*	dee bee**ahn**-koh
...of rosé wine.	*...di rosato.*	dee roh-**zah**-toh
...the wine list.	*...la lista dei vini.*	lah **lee**-stah **deh**ee **vee**-nee

Galileo once wrote, "Wine is light held together by water." It is certainly a part of the Italian culinary trinity—the vine, olive, and wheat. Visit an ***enoteca*** (wine shop or bar) to sample a variety of regional wines.

Wine Words

Italian wines are named by grape, place, descriptive term, or a combination of these. The following list will help you identify what you're looking for in a wine and where to find it.

wine / wines	*vino / vini*	**vee**-noh / **vee**-nee
select wine (good year)	*vino selezionato*	**vee**-noh say-layt-seeoh-**nah**-toh
table wine	*vino da tavola*	**vee**-noh dah **tah**-voh-lah
house wine	*vino della casa*	**vee**-noh **dehl**-lah **kah**-zah
local	*locale*	loh-**kah**-lay
of the region	*della regione*	**dehl**-lah ray-**joh**-nay
red	*rosso*	**roh**-soh
white	*bianco*	bee**ahn**-koh
rosé	*rosato*	roh-**zah**-toh
sparkling	*frizzante*	freed-**zahn**-tay
fruity	*amabile*	ah-**mah**-bee-lay
light / heavy	*leggero / pesante*	lay-**jay**-roh / pay-**zahn**-tay
sweet	*dolce, abbocato*	**dohl**-chay, ah-boh-**kah**-toh
medium	*medio*	**may**-deeoh
semi-dry	*semi-secco*	say-mee-**say**-koh
dry	*secco*	**say**-koh
very dry	*molto secco*	**mohl**-toh **say**-koh
full-bodied	*pieno, corposo*	pee**ay**-noh, kor-**poh**-zoh
mature	*maturo*	mah-**too**-roh
cork	*tappo*	**tah**-poh
corkscrew	*cavitappi*	kah-vee-**tah**-pee
grapes	*uva*	**oo**-vah
vintage	*annata*	ah-**nah**-tah
vineyard	*vigneto*	veen-**yay**-toh
wine-tasting	*degustazione*	day-goo-staht-see**oh**-nay
What is a good year?	*Qual'è una buon'annata?*	kwah-**leh oo**-nah bwoh-nah-**nah**-tah
What do you recommend?	*Cosa raccomanda?*	**koh**-zah rah-koh-**mahn**-dah

Wine Labels

DOCG	meets national standards for highest-quality wine (permitted grapes, minimum alcohol content)
DOC	meets national standards for high-quality wine

EATING

IGT	meets regional standards
riserva	DOCG or DOC wine matured for a longer, specified time
classico	from a defined, select area
annata	year of harvest
vendemmia	harvest
imbottigliato dal produttore all'origin	bottled by producers

To save money, order ***"Una caraffa di vino della casa"*** (a carafe of house wine). Many smaller hotels have a cellar or cantina that they are proud to show off. For a memorable and affordable adventure in Venice, have a "pub crawl" dinner. While ***cicchetti*** (bar munchies) aren't as common as they used to be, many bars (called ***cicchetteria***) are still popular for their wide selection of tasty hors d'oeuvres. Ask for ***un'ombra*** (a small glass of wine) to wash them down.

Beer

beer	*birra*	**bee**-rah
bar	*bar*	bar
from the tap	*alla spina*	**ah**-lah **spee**-nah
glass of draft beer	*una birra alla spina*	**oo**-nah **bee**-rah **ah**-lah **spee**-nah
20 cl draft beer	*una birra piccola*	**oo**-nah **bee**-rah **pee**-koh-lah
33 cl draft beer	*una birra media*	**oo**-nah **bee**-rah **may**-deeah
50 cl draft beer	*una birra grande*	**oo**-nah **bee**-rah **grahn**-day
1 liter draft beer	*un litro di birra alla spina*	oon **lee**-troh dee **bee**-rah **ah**-lah **spee**-nah
bottle	*bottiglia*	boh-**teel**-yah
light / dark	*chiara / scura*	kee**ah**-rah / **skoo**-rah
local / imported	*locale / importata*	loh-**kah**-lay / eem-por-**tah**-tah
Italian beer	*birra nazionale*	**bee**-rah naht-seeoh-**nah**-lay

German beer	*birra tedesca*	**bee**-rah tay-**dehs**-kah
Irish beer	*birra irlandese*	**bee**-rah eer-lahn-**day**-zay
small / large	*piccola / grande*	**pee**-koh-lah / **grahn**-day
low calorie	*leggera*	lay-**jay**-rah
cold	*fredda*	**fray**-dah
colder	*più fredda*	pew **fray**-dah

Bar Talk

Shall we go for a drink?	*Andiamo a prendere qualcosa da bere?*	ahn-dee**ah**-moh ah **prehn**-day-ray kwahl-**koh**-zah dah **bay**-ray
I'll buy you a drink.	*Ti offro una bevanda.*	tee **oh**-froh **oo**-nah bay-**vahn**-dah
It's on me.	*Pago io.*	**pah**-goh **ee**oh
The next one's on me.	*Offro io la prossima.*	**oh**-froh **ee**oh lah **proh**-see-mah
What would you like?	*Che cosa prende?*	kay **koh**-zah **prehn**-day
I'll have...	*Prendo...*	**prehn**-doh
I don't drink.	*Non bevo.*	nohn **bay**-voh
alcohol-free	*analcolica*	ahn-ahl-**koh**-lee-kah
What is the local specialty?	*Qual'è la specialità locale?*	kwah-**leh** lah spay-chah-lee-**tah** loh-**kah**-lay
What is a good drink for a man / for a woman?	*Qual'è una buona bevanda per un uomo / per una donna?*	kwah-**leh** **oo**-nah **bwoh**-nah bay-**vahn**-dah pehr oon **woh**-moh / pehr **oo**-nah **doh**-nah
Straight.	*Liscio.*	**lee**-shoh
With / Without...	*Con / Senza...*	kohn / **sehnt**-sah
...alcohol.	*...alcool.*	**ahl**-kohl
...ice.	*...ghiaccio.*	gee**ah**-choh
One more.	*Un altro.*	oon **ahl**-troh
Cheers!	*Cin cin!*	cheen cheen
To your health!	*Salute!*	sah-**loo**-tay
Long life!	*Lunga vita!*	**loong**-gah **vee**-tah

Long live Italy!	*Viva l'Italia!*	**vee**-vah lee-**tahl**-yah
I'm feeling...	*Mi sento...*	mee **sehn**-toh
...tipsy.	*...brillo[a].*	**bree**-loh
...a little drunk.	*...un po' ubriaco[a].*	oon poh oo-bree**ah**-koh
...wasted.	*...ubriaco[a] fradicio[a].*	oo-bree**ah**-koh **frah**-dee-choh
I'm hung over.	*Ho la sbornia.*	oh lah **sbor**-neeah

PICNICKING

At the Grocery

Is it self-service?	*È self-service?*	eh sehlf-**sehr**-vees
Ripe for today?	*Da mangiare oggi?*	dah mahn-**jah**-ray **oh**-jee
Does it need to be cooked?	*Bisogna cucinarlo prima di mangiarlo?*	bee-**zohn**-yah koo-chee-**nar**-loh **pree**-mah dee mahn-**jar**-loh
A little taste?	*Un assaggio?*	oon ah-**sah**-joh
Fifty grams.	*Cinquanta grammi.*	cheeng-**kwahn**-tah **grah**-mee
One hundred grams.	*Un etto.*	oon **eht**-toh
More. / Less.	*Più. / Meno.*	pew / **may**-noh
A piece.	*Un pezzo.*	oon **pehd**-zoh
A slice.	*Una fetta.*	**oo**-nah **fay**-tah
Four slices.	*Quattro fette.*	**kwah**-troh **fay**-tay
Sliced (fine).	*Tagliato (a fette sottili).*	tahl-**yah**-toh (ah **fay**-tay soh-**tee**-lee)
Half.	*Metà.*	may-**tah**
A small bag.	*Un sacchettino.*	oon sah-keht-**tee**-noh
A bag, please.	*Un sacchetto, per favore.*	oon sah-**keht**-toh pehr fah-**voh**-ray
Will you make... for me / us?	*Mi / Ci può fare...?*	mee / chee pwoh **fah**-ray
...a sandwich	*...un panino*	oon pah-**nee**-noh
...two sandwiches	*...due panini*	**doo**-ay pah-**nee**-nee
To take out.	*Da portar via.*	dah **por**-tar **vee**-ah

Can I / Can we use...?	*Posso / Possiamo usare...?*	**poh**-soh / poh-see**ah**-moh oo-**zah**-ray
...the microwave	*...il forno a microonde*	eel **for**-noh ah mee-kroh-**ohn**-day
May I borrow a...?	*Posso prendere in prestito...?*	**poh**-soh **prehn**-day-ray een preh-**stee**-toh
Do you have a...?	*Ha per caso...?*	ah pehr **kah**-zoh
Where can I buy / find a...?	*Dove posso comprare / trovare un...?*	**doh**-vay **poh**-soh kohm-**prah**-ray / troh-**vah**-ray oon
...corkscrew	*...cavatappi*	kah-vah-**tah**-pee
...can opener	*...apriscatole*	ah-pree-skah-**toh**-lay
Is there a park nearby?	*C'è un parco qui vicino?*	cheh oon **par**-koh kwee vee-**chee**-noh
Where is a good place to picnic?	*Dov'è un bel posto per fare un picnic?*	doh-**veh** oon behl **poh**-stoh pehr **fah**-ray oon **peek**-neek
Is picnicking allowed here?	*Va bene fare un picnic qui?*	vah **behn**-nay **fah**-ray oon **peek**-neek kwee
Enjoy your meal!	*Buon appetito!*	bwohn ah-pay-**tee**-toh

Tasty Picnic Words

picnic	*picnic*	**peek**-neek
open air market	*mercato*	mehr-**kah**-toh
grocery store	*alimentari*	ah-lee-mayn-**tah**-ree
supermarket	*supermercato*	soo-pehr-mehr-**kah**-toh
delicatessen	*salumeria*	sah-loo-may-**ree**-ah
bakery	*panetteria, forno*	pah-nay-tay-**ree**-ah, **for**-noh
sandwich shop	*paninoteca*	pah-nee-noh-**tay**-kah
pastry shop	*pasticceria*	pah-stee-chay-**ree**-ah
sandwich or roll	*panino*	pah-**nee**-noh
bread	*pane*	**pah**-nay
cured ham (pricey)	*prosciutto crudo*	proh-**shoo**-toh **kroo**-doh
cooked ham	*prosciutto cotto*	proh-**shoo**-toh **koh**-toh
sausage	*salsiccia*	sahl-**see**-chah
cheese	*formaggio*	for-**mah**-joh

mustard...	*senape...*	**say**-nah-pay
mayonnaise...	*maionese...*	mah-yoh-**nay**-zay
...in a tube	*...in tubetto*	een too-**bay**-toh
yogurt	*yogurt*	**yoh**-goort
fruit	*frutta*	**froo**-tah
box of juice	*cartone di succo di frutta*	kar-**toh**-nay dee **soo**-koh dee **froo**-tah
straw / straws	*cannuccia / cannucce*	kah-**noo**-chah / kah-**noo**-chay
spoon / fork...	*cucchiaio / forchetta...*	koo-kee**ah**-yoh / for-**kay**-tah
...made of plastic	*...di plastica*	dee **plah**-stee-kah
cup / plate...	*bicchiere / piatto...*	bee-kee**ay**-ray / pee**ah**-toh
...made of paper	*...di carta*	dee **kar**-tah

Make your own sandwiches by getting the ingredients at a market. Order meat and cheese by the gram. One hundred grams (what the Italians call an ***etto***) is about a quarter pound, enough for two sandwiches.

MENU DECODER

ITALIAN/ENGLISH

This handy decoder won't list every word on the menu, but it will help you get ***trota*** (trout) instead of ***tripa*** (tripe).

abbacchio	lamb (Rome)
abbacchio alla Romana	roasted spring lamb
abbocato	sweet (wine)
acciughe	anchovies
aceto	vinegar
acqua	water
acqua del rubinetto	tap water
acqua minerale	mineral water
affogato	poached
affumicato	smoked
After Eight	chocolate and mint (gelato)
aglio	garlic
agnello	lamb
agro	sour
ai funghi	with mushrooms
al cartoccio	steamed in parchment
al dente	not overcooked (pasta)
al forno	baked
al sangue	rare (meat)

al vapore	steamed
albicocca	apricot
alcool	alcohol
alfredo	butter, cream, cheese sauce
all'arrabbiata	with bacon, tomato–spicy hot
alla cacciatora	"hunter's style," with olive oil, rosemary, garlic, tomato
alla diavola	spicy
alla graticola	broiled
alla Parmigiana	with cheese and breadcrumbs
alla spina	from the tap (beer)
amabile	fruity (wine)
amatriciana	with bacon, tomato, and spices
analcolica	alcohol-free
ananas	pineapple
anatra	duck
animelle di vitello	sweetbreads
annata	vintage (wine)
antipasti	appetizers
antipasto misto	salami and marinated vegetables
arachidi	peanuts
aragosta	lobster
arancia	orange
aranciata	orange soda
aringa	herring
arrabiata	spicy tomato-chili sauce
arrosto	roasted
asiago	hard and spicy cheese
asparagi	asparagus
assortiti	assorted
assortito di carne arrosto	roasted assortment of meats
astice	male lobster
bacio	chocolate hazelnut candy
balani	barnacles
barbabietole	beets
basilico	basil
ben cotto	well-done (meat)

bevande	beverages
bianca, pizza	"white" pizza (no tomato sauce)
bianco	white
bibite	beverages
bicchiere	glass
bignole	cream puffs (Florence)
biologico	organic
birra	beer
biscotti	cookies
bistecca	steak
bistecca alle Fiorentina	T-bone steak
bocconcini	small balls of mozzarella
bollente	boiling hot
bollito	boiled
bollito misto	various boiled meats with sauces
Bolognese	meat and tomato sauce
bottiglia	bottle
branzino	bass
brasato	braised
brioche	roll
brodo	broth
bruschetta	toast with tomatoes and basil
bucatini	hollow, thick spaghetti
budino	pudding
burro	butter
burro d'arachidi	peanut butter
bustina di tè	tea bag
caciucco	Tuscan fish soup
caffè	coffee
caffè Americano	American-style coffee
caffè con panna	coffee with whipped cream
caffè corretto	coffee and firewater
caffè freddo	iced coffee
caffè latte	coffee with milk
caffè lungo	coffee with water
caffè macchiato	coffee with a little milk
caffè solubile	instant coffee

caffeina	caffeine
calamari	squid
caldo	hot
calzone	folded pizza
cannelloni	large tube-shaped noodles
cannoli	fried pastry tubes filled with ricotta, fruit, and chocolate
cantucci	Tuscan almond cookies
capesante	scallops
cappuccino	coffee with foam
capra	goat
caprese	mozzarella and tomato salad
capretto	baby goat
capricciosa	chef's choice
caprino	goat cheese
capriolo	venison
caraffa	carafe
caramelle	candy
carbonara	with meat sauce
carciofo	artichoke
carne	meat
carote	carrots
carpaccio	thinly sliced air-cured meat
casa	house
casalingo	homemade
cassa	cash register
cassata siciliana	Sicilian sponge cake
castagne	chestnut
cavatappi	corkscrew
cavolfiore	cauliflower
cavolini de Bruxelles	Brussels sprouts
cavolo	cabbage
ceci	chickpeas
cena	dinner
cereali	cereal
cervella	brains
cervo	venison

cetrioli	cucumber
cetriolini	pickles
ciabatta	crusty, flat, rustic bread
ciaccina, pizza	"white" pizza (no tomato sauce)
cibo	food
ciccheti	small appetizers
ciliegia	cherry
cinese	Chinese
cinghiale	wild boar
cioccolata	chocolate
cipolle	onions
cocomero	watermelon
colazione	breakfast
con	with
con panna	with whipped cream
coniglio	rabbit
cono	cone
contorni	side dishes
coperto	cover charge
coppa	small bowl
corretto	coffee and firewater
cornetto	croissant
corposo	full-bodied (wine)
costata	rib steak
cotoletta	cutlet
cotto	cooked; medium (meat)
cozze	mussels
crema	vanilla
crème caramel	caramelized topped custard
crescenza	mild cheese
crostata	pie with jam
crostini	toast with paté
crudo	raw
cucina	cuisine
cuoco	chef
da portar via	"to go"
datteri	dates

decaffeinato	decaffeinated
del giorno	of the day
della casa	of the house
di	of
digestivo	after-dinner drink
dolce	sweet
dolci	desserts
dragoncello	tarragon
e	and
emmenthal	Swiss cheese
entrecote	sirloin steak
erbe	herb
etto	one hundred grams
fagiano	pheasant
fagioli	beans
fagiolini	green beans
farcito	stuffed
farfalle	butterfly-shaped pasta
farinata	porridge
fatto in casa	homemade
fegato	liver
fegato alla Veneziana	liver and onions
fettina	slice
fettucine	long, flat noodles
fico	fig
filetto	fillet
filone	large unsalted bread
finocchio	fennel
fior di latte	milk (gelato flavor)
focaccia	flat bread
fontina	creamy, nutty, gruyere-style cheese
formaggio	cheese
fragola	strawberry
frangelico	hazelnut liqueur
frappè	milkshake
freddo	cold
fresco	fresh

frittata	omelet
fritto	fried
fritto misto	fried seafood
frizzante	sparkling
frumento	wheat
frutta	fruit
frutti di bosco	berries
frutti di mare	seafood
funghi	mushrooms
gamberetti	small shrimp
gamberi	shrimp
gamberoni	big shrimp
gassata	carbonated
gelatina	jelly
gelato	Italian ice cream
Genovese	with pesto sauce
ghiaccio	ice
giorno	day
gnocchi	potato noodles
gorgonzola	bleu cheese
granchione	crab
grande	large
granita	snow cone
granturco	corn
grappa	firewater
griglia	grilled
grissini	breadsticks
groviera	Swiss cheese
gusti	flavors
Haag	decaffeinated coffee
importata	imported
incluso	included
insalata	salad
insalata con uova	egg salad
insalata di mare	seafood salad
involtini	meat or fish filets with fillings
kasher	kosher

lampone	raspberry
latte	milk
latte fresco	fresh milk
latte intero	whole milk
latte macchiato	milk with a little coffee
latte magro	skim milk
latticini	small mozzarella balls
lattuga	lettuce
leggero	light
legumi	vegetables
lenticchie	lentils
lepre	hare
limonata	lemon soda
limone	lemon
lingua	tongue
linguine	thin, flat noodles
locale	local
lumache	snails
maccheroni	tube-shaped pasta
macedonia	fresh fruit salad
maiale	pork
maionese	mayonnaise
mame	giant artichokes
mandarino	tangerine
mandorle	almond
manzo	beef
margarina	margarine
Margherita	with cheese and tomato sauce (pizza)
marinara	tomato and garlic sauce
marmellata	jam
mascarpone	sweet, buttery dessert cheese
maturo	mature (wine)
mela	apple
melanzana	eggplant
melone	cantaloupe
melone verde	honeydew melon

menta	mint
menù del giorno	menu of the day
menù turistico	fixed-price meal
mercato	open-air market
merluzzo	cod
mezzo	half
miele	honey
Milanese	fried in breadcrumbs
millefoglie	layers of sweet, buttery pastry
minerale-acqua	mineral water
minestra	soup
minestrone	vegetable soup
mirtillo	blueberry
misto	mixed
molto	very
molto al sangue	very rare (meat)
mozzarella	handmade water-buffalo cheese
Napoletana	with cheese, anchovies, and tomato sauce (pizza)
nero	black
nero di seppie e polenta	cuttlefish cooked in its own ink
nocciola	hazelnut
noccioline americana	peanut
noce	walnut
noce di cocco	coconut
nocino	walnut liqueur
non	not
non fumare	non-smoking
non fumatori	non-smoking
o	or
olio	oil
olive	olives
omelette	omelet
orata	bream (fish)
orecchiette	small, ear-shaped pasta
organico	organic
ortolana	vegetarian (pizza)

ossobuca alla Genovese	veal shank braised in broth
ossobuco	bone marrow
ostriche	oysters
pallina	scoop
pancetta	salt-cured bacon
pane	bread
pane aromatico	herb or vegetable bread
pane casereccia	home-style bread
pane di olive	olive bread
pane di segale	rye bread
pane integrale	whole grain bread
pane scuro	brown bread
pane Toscano	rustic bread made without salt
paneficio	bakery
panettone	Milanese yeast fruitcake
panforte	fruitcake
panino	roll, sandwich
panna	cream, whipped cream
panna cotta	cooked cream with berries
pansotti	pasta stuffed with veggies
panzanella	bread and vegetable salad
parmigiano	Parmesan cheese
pasticceria	pastry shop; pastry
pasticcini	pastries
pastina	noodles
patate	potatoes
patate fritte	French fries
pecorino	sheep's cheese
penne	tube-shaped noodles
pepato	with pepper
pepe	pepper
peperonata	peppers with tomato sauce
peperoncino	paprika
peperoni	bell peppers
pera	pear
percorino	sheep cheese
pesante	heavy (wine)

pesca	peach
pescatora	seafood sauce
pesce	fish
pesce spada	swordfish
pesto	basil, pine nut, olive oil paste
petto (di___)	breast (of___)
pezzo	piece
piadina	stuffed, soft, flat bread
piatto	plate
piatto di formaggi misti	cheese plate
piccante	spicy hot
piccolo	small
pici	rough-cut thick twisted pasta
pieno	full-bodied (wine)
pinioli	pine nuts
piselli	peas
pistacchio	pistachio
poche calorie	low calorie
polenta	moist cornmeal
polipo	octopus
pollame	poultry
pollo	chicken
pollo alla cacciatora	chicken with olive oil, rosemary, garlic, and tomato
polpo	octopus
pomodoro	tomato
pompelmo	grapefruit
porchetta	roast suckling pig
porcini	porcini mushrooms
pranzo	lunch
prezzemolo	parsley
prima colazione	breakfast
primo piatto	first course
profiterole	cream-filled pastry with chocolate sauce
prosciutto	cured ham
prosciutto cotto	cooked ham

prosciutto crudo	dried, air-cured ham
prosciutto e melone / fichi	air-cured ham wrapped around melon / fresh figs
provolone	rich, firm aged cow's cheese
prugna	prune
puttanesca	zesty sauce
quattro	four
quattro formaggi	four cheeses
quattro stagioni	with four separate toppings (pizza)
radiattore	radiator-shaped pasta
ragù	meat and tomato sauce
ribollita	hearty bread and vegetable soup
ricivuta	receipt
ricotta	soft, airy cheese
rigatoni	tube-shaped noodles
ripieno	stuffed
riso	rice
risotto	saffron-flavored rice
rosato	rosé (wine)
rosmarino	rosemary
rosso	red
rotelli	wheel-shaped pasta
salame	pork sausage
salamino piccante	pepperoni
salato	salty
sale	salt
salmone	salmon
salsiccia	sausage
saltimbocca alla Romana	veal cutlet sautéed with sage, *prosciutto*, and white wine
salumi misti	assortment of sliced, cured meats
salvia	sage
sambuca	anise (licorice) liqueur
saporito	mild
sarde	sardines
scaloppine	thin-sliced veal
scampi	prawns

schiacciata	pizza-like flatbread
sciacchetra	sweet desert wine
secco	dry (wine)
secondo piatto	second course
selvaggina	game
senape	mustard
senza	without
seppie	cuttlefish, sometimes squid
servizio	service charge
servizio incluso	service included
servizio non incluso	service not included
sfogliatella	pastry filled with sweetened ricotta
sgombro	scad (like mackerel)
Siciliana	with capers and olives (pizza)
sogliola	sole
sono pieno	I'm stuffed
sorbetto	sherbet
specialità	specialty
spezzatino	meat, potato, tomato stew
spiedini alla griglia	grilled seafood on a skewer
spinaci	spinach
spizziccare	snack
spremuta	freshly squeezed juice
spuntino	snack
stagionato	aged, sharp, and hard (cheese)
stagioni	seasons (and pizza toppings)
stracchino	spreadable cheese
stracciatella	chocolate chips w/vanilla (gelato)
strangolapreti	twisted pasta
strapazzate	scrambled
stufato	stew
stuzzicadente	toothpick
succo	juice
sugo	sauce, usually tomato
susina	plum
tacchino	turkey
tagliatelle	flat noodles

taleggio	rich, creamy cheese
tartina	tart
tartufi	truffles
tartufo	super-chocolate ice cream
tavola calda	buffet-style
tavola	table
tazza	cup
tè	tea
tè alla frutta	fruit tea
tè alla menta	mint tea
tè freddo	iced tea
tiramisú	espresso-soaked cake with chocolate, cream, and marsala
tisana	herbal tea
tonno	tuna
torta	cake
torte	pie
tortellini	stuffed noodles
tovagliolo	napkin
tramezzini	small, crustless sandwiches
trippa	tripe
trota	trout
uova	eggs
uova fritte	fried eggs
uova strapazzate	scrambled eggs
uovo alla coque (molle / sodo)	boiled egg (soft / hard)
uva	grapes
vegetariano	vegetarian
veloce	fast
vendemmia	harvest (wine)
verde	green
verdure	vegetables
verza	cabbage
vigneto	vineyard
vino	wine
vino da tavola	table wine

vino della casa	house wine
vino selezionato	select wine (good year)
vino sfuso	house wine in a jug
vitello	veal
vitello tonato	thinly sliced veal with tuna-caper mayonnaise
vongole	clams
wurstel	hot dogs
zabaglione	egg and liquor cream
zucchero	sugar
zuppa	soup
zuppa di pesce	fish soup or stew
zuppa inglese	trifle

ACTIVITIES

SIGHTSEEING

Where?

Where is...?	*Dov'è...?*	doh-**veh**
...the best view	*...la vista più bella*	lah **vee**-stah pew **behl**-lah
...the main square	*...la piazza principale*	lah pee**aht**-sah preen-chee-**pah**-lay
...the old town center	*...il centro storico*	eel **chehn**-troh **stoh**-ree-koh
...the museum	*...il museo*	eel moo-**zay**-oh
...the castle	*...il castello*	eel kah-**stehl**-loh
...the palace	*...il palazzo*	eel pah-**lahd**-zoh
...the ruins	*...le rovine*	lay roh-**vee**-nay
...an amusement park	*...un parco dei divertimenti*	oon **par**-koh **deh**ee dee-vehr-tee-**mehn**-tee
...tourist information	*...l'ufficio informazioni*	loo-**fee**-choh een-for-maht-see**oh**-nee
...the toilet	*...la toilette*	lah twah-**leht**-tay
...the entrance / exit	*...l'entrata / l'uscita*	lehn-**trah**-tah / loo-**shee**-tah
Is there a festival nearby?	*C'è un festival qui vicino?*	cheh oon fehs-tee-**vahl** kwee vee-**chee**-noh

Key Phrases: Sightseeing

Where is ___?	*Dov'è ___?*	doh-**veh**
How much is it?	*Quanto costa?*	**kwahn**-toh **koh**-stah
What time does this open / close?	*A che ora apre / chiude?*	ah kay **oh**-rah **ah**-pray / kee**oo**-day
Do you have a guided tour?	*Avete un tour guidato?*	ah-**vay**-tay oon toor gwee-**dah**-toh
When is the next tour in English?	*Quando è il prossimo tour in inglese?*	**kwahn**-doh eh eel **proh**-see-moh toor een een-**glay**-zay

At the Sight

Do you have...?	*Avete...?*	ah-**vay**-tay
...information...	*...informazioni...*	een-for-maht-see**oh**-nee
...a guidebook...	*...una guida...*	**oo**-nah **gwee**-dah
...in English	*...in inglese*	een een-**glay**-zay
Is it free?	*È gratis?*	eh **grah**-tees
How much is it?	*Quanto costa?*	**kwahn**-toh **koh**-stah
Is (the ticket) valid all day?	*È valido per tutto il giorno?*	eh **vah**-lee-doh pehr **too**-toh eel **jor**-noh
Can I get back in?	*Posso rientrare?*	**poh**-soh ree-ehn-**trah**-ray
What time does this open / close?	*A che ora apre / chiude?*	ah kay **oh**-rah **ah**-pray / kee**oo**-day
What time is the last entry?	*Quand'è l'ultima entrata?*	kwahn-**deh lool**-tee-mah ayn-**trah**-tah

Please

PLEASE let me / us in.	*PER FAVORE, mi / ci faccia entrare.*	pehr fah-**voh**-ray mee / chee **fah**-chah ayn-**trah**-ray
I've traveled all the way from ___.	*Sono venuto[a] qui da ___.*	**soh**-noh vay-**noo**-toh kwee dah
We've traveled all the way from ___.	*Siamo venuti[e] qui da ___.*	see**ah**-moh vay-**noo**-tee kwee dah

ACTIVITIES

I must leave tomorrow.	*Devo partire domani.*	**day**-voh par-**tee**-ray doh-**mah**-nee
We must leave tomorrow.	*Dobbiamo partire domani.*	doh-bee**ah**-moh par-**tee**-ray doh-**mah**-nee
I promise I'll be fast.	*Prometto che sarò veloce.*	proh-**meht**-toh kay sah-**roh** vay-**loh**-chay
We promise we'll be fast.	*Promettiamo che saremo veloci.*	proh-meht-tee**ah**-moh kay sah-**ray**-moh vay-**loh**-chee
It was my mother's dying wish that I see this.	*Ho promesso a mia madre sul letto di morte che avrei visto questo.*	oh proh-**mehs**-soh ah **mee**-ah **mah**-dray sool **leht**-toh dee **mor**-tay kay ah-**vray**ee **vee**-stoh **kweh**-stoh
I've / We've always wanted to see this.	*Ho / Abbiamo sempre desiderato vedere questo.*	oh / ah-bee**ah**-moh **sehm**-pray day-zee-day-**rah**-toh vay-**dehr**-ay **kweh**-stoh

Tours

Do you have...?	*Avete...?*	ah-**vay**-tay
...an audioguide	*...un'audioguida*	oo-now-deeoh-**gwee**-dah
...a guided tour	*...un tour guidato*	oon toor gwee-**dah**-toh
...a city walking tour	*...una visita guidata della città*	**oo**-nah vee-**zee**-tah gwee-**dah**-tah **dehl**-lah chee-**tah**
...in English	*...in inglese*	een een-**glay**-zay
When is the next tour in English?	*Quando è il prossimo tour in inglese?*	**kwahn**-doh eh eel **proh**-see-moh toor een een-**glay**-zay
Is it free?	*È gratis?*	eh **grah**-tees
How much is it?	*Quanto costa?*	**kwahn**-toh **koh**-stah
How long does it last?	*Quanto dura?*	**kwahn**-toh **doo**-rah
Can I / Can we join a tour in progress?	*Posso / Possiamo unirci ad un tour già iniziato?*	**poh**-soh / poh-see**ah**-moh oon-**eer**-chee ahd oon toor jah ee-neet-see**ah**-toh

Entrance Signs

adulti	adults
giro guidato, tour	guided tour
mostra	special exhibit
siete qui	you are here (on map)

Discounts

You may be eligible for discounts at tourist sights, hotels, or on buses and trains—ask.

Is there a discount for...?	*Fate sconti per...?*	**fah**-tay **skohn**-tee pehr
...youth	*...giovani*	joh-**vah**-nee
...students	*...studenti*	stoo-**dehn**-tee
...families	*...famiglie*	fah-**meel**-yay
...seniors	*...anziani*	ahnt-seeah-nee
...groups	*...comitive*	koh-mee-**tee**-vay
I am...	*Sono...*	**soh**-noh
He / She is...	*Lui / Lei ha...*	lwee / **leh**ee ah
... ___ years old.	*... ___ anni.*	___ **ahn**-nee
...extremely old.	*...vecchissimo[a].*	vehk-**ee**-see-moh

In the Museum

Where is...?	*Dov'è...?*	doh-**veh**
I'd / We'd like to see...	*Mi / Ci piacerebbe vedere...*	mee / chee peeah-chay-**ray**-bay vay-**dehr**-ay
Photo / video O.K.?	*Foto / video è O.K.?*	**foh**-toh / **vee**-day-oh eh "O.K."
No flash / tripod.	*Vietato usare flash / trepiede.*	veeay-**tah**-toh oo-**zah**-ray flahsh / tray-pee**ay**-day
I like it.	*Mi piace.*	mee pee**ah**-chay
It's so...	*È così...*	eh koh-**zee**
...beautiful.	*...bello.*	**behl**-loh
...ugly.	*...brutto.*	**broo**-toh
...strange.	*...strano.*	**strah**-noh

...boring.	*...noioso.*	noh-**yoh**-zoh
...interesting.	*...interessante.*	een-tay-ray-**sahn**-tay
...pretentious.	*...presuntuoso.*	pray-zoon-**twoh**-zoh
It's thought-provoking.	*Fa pensare.*	fah pehn-**sah**-ray
It's B.S.	*È una stronzata.*	eh **oo**-nah strohnt-**sah**-tah
I don't get it.	*Non capisco.*	nohn kah-**pees**-koh
Is it upside down?	*È rovesciato?*	eh roh-vay-**shah**-toh
Who did this?	*Chi l'ha fatto?*	kee lah **fah**-toh
How old is this?	*Quanti anni ha?*	**kwahn**-tee **ah**-nee ah
Wow!	*Wow!*	"Wow"
My feet hurt!	*Mi fanno male i piedi!*	mee **fah**-noh **mah**-lay ee peeay-dee
I'm exhausted!	*Sono stanco[a] morto[a]!*	**soh**-noh **stahn**-koh **mor**-toh
We're exhausted!	*Siamo stanchi[e] morti[e].*	seeah-moh **stahn**-kee **mor**-tee

Be careful when planning your sightseeing. Many museums close in the afternoon from 1:00 P.M. until 3:00 or 4:00 P.M., and are closed all day on a weekday, usually Monday. Museums often stop selling tickets 45 minutes before closing. Historic churches usually open much earlier than museums.

SHOPPING

Shops

Where is a...?	*Dov'è un...?*	doh-**veh** oon
antique shop	*negozio di antiquariato*	nay-**goht**-seeoh dee ahn-tee-kwah-ree**ah**-toh
art gallery	*galleria d'arte*	gah-lay-**ree**-ah **dar**-tay
bakery	*panificio*	pah-nee-**fee**-choh
barber shop	*barbiere*	bar-bee**ay**-ray
beauty salon	*parrucchiere*	pah-roo-kee**ay**-ray
book shop	*libreria*	lee-bray-**ree**-ah

Key Phrases: Shopping

Where can I buy...?	*Dove posso comprare...?*	**doh**-vay **poh**-soh kohm-**prah**-ray
Where is a...?	*Dov'è un...?*	doh-**veh** oon
grocery store	*alimentari*	ah-lee-mayn-**tah**-ree
department store	*grande magazzino*	**grahn**-day mah-gahd-**zee**-noh
pharmacy	*farmacia*	far-mah-**chee**-ah
How much is it?	*Quanto costa?*	**kwahn**-toh **koh**-stah
I'm just browsing.	*Sto solo guardando.*	stoh **soh**-loh gwar-**dahn**-doh

camera shop	*foto-ottica*	foh-toh-**oh**-tee-kah
cell phone shop	*negozio di cellulari*	nay-**goht**-seeoh dee chehl-loo-**lah**-ree
clothing boutique	*boutique di abbigliamento*	boo-**teek** dee ah-beel-yah-**mehn**-toh
coffee shop	*bar*	bar
department store	*grande magazzino*	**grahn**-day mah-gahd-**zee**-noh
delicatessen	*salumeria*	sah-loo-may-**ree**-ah
flea market	*mercato delle pulci*	mehr-**kah**-toh **dehl**-lay **pool**-chee
flower market	*mercato dei fiori*	mehr-**kah**-toh **deh**ee fee-**oh**-ree
grocery store	*alimentari*	ah-lee-mayn-**tah**-ree
hardware store	*ferramenta*	fehr-rah-**mehn**-tah
Internet café	*Internet café*	**een**-tehr-neht kah-**fay**
jewelry shop	*gioielliera*	joh-yay-lee**ay**-rah
launderette	*lavanderia*	lah-vahn-day-**ree**-ah
leather shop	*pelletteria*	pehl-leht-teh-**ree**-ah
newsstand	*giornalaio*	jor-nah-**lah**-yoh
office supplies	*cartoleria*	kar-toh-lay-**ree**-ah
open air market	*mercato*	mehr-**kah**-toh
optician	*ottico*	**oh**-tee-koh

pastry shop	*pasticceria*	pah-stee-chay-**ree**-ah
pharmacy	*farmacia*	far-mah-**chee**-ah
photocopy shop	*copisteria*	koh-pee-stay-**ree**-ah
pottery shop	*negozio di ceramica*	nay-**goht**-seeoh dee chay-**rah**-mee-kah
shopping mall	*centro commerciale*	**chehn**-troh koh-mehr-**chah**-lay
souvenir shop	*negozio di souvenir*	nay-**goht**-seeoh dee **soo**-vay-neer
supermarket	*supermercato*	soo-pehr-mehr-**kah**-toh
sweets shop	*negozio di dolciumi, pasticceria*	nay-**goht**-seeoh dee dohl-chee**oo**-mee, pah-stee-chay-**ree**-ah
toy store	*negozio di giocattoli*	nay-**goht**-seeoh dee joh-**kah**-toh-lee
travel agency	*agenzia di viaggi*	ah-jehnt-**see**-ah dee vee**ah**-jee
used bookstore	*negozio di libri usati*	nay-**goht**-seeoh dee **lee**-bree oo-**zah**-tee
...with books in English	*...che vende libri in inglese*	kay **vehn**-dray **lee**-bree een een-**glay**-zay
wine shop	*negozio di vini*	nay-**goht**-seeoh dee **vee**-nee

Most businesses are closed daily from 1:00 P.M. until 3:00 or 4:00 P.M. Many stores in the larger cities close for all or part of August—not a good time to plan a shopping spree.

Shop Till You Drop

opening hours	*orario d'apertura*	oh-**rah**-reeoh dah-pehr-**too**-rah
sale	*saldo*	**sahl**-doh
I'd like / We'd like...	*Vorrei / Vorremmo...*	vor-**reh**ee / vor-**ray**-moh
Where can I buy...?	*Dove posso comprare...?*	**doh**-vay **poh**-soh kohm-**prah**-ray
Where can we buy...?	*Dove possiamo comprare...?*	**doh**-vay poh-see**ah**-moh kohm-**prah**-ray

How much is it?	*Quanto costa?*	**kwahn**-toh **koh**-stah
I'm / We're...	*Sto / Stiamo...*	stoh / stee**ah**-moh
...just browsing.	*...solo guardando.*	**soh**-loh gwar-**dahn**-doh
Do you have something...?	*Avete qualcosa di...?*	ah-**vay**-tay kwahl-**koh**-zah dee
...cheaper	*...meno caro*	**may**-noh **kah**-roh
...better	*...miglior qualità*	**meel**-yor kwah-lee-**tah**
Better quality, please.	*Qualcosa di migliore qualità, per favore.*	kwahl-**koh**-zah dee **meel**-yoh-ray kwah-lee-**tah** pehr fah-**voh**-ray
genuine / imitation	*autentico / imitazione*	ow-**tehn**-tee-koh / ee-mee-taht-see**oh**-nay
Can I / Can we see more?	*Posso / Possiamo vederne ancora?*	**poh**-soh / poh-see**ah**-moh vay-**dehr**-nay ahn-**koh**-rah
This one.	*Questo qui.*	**kweh**-stoh kwee
Can I try it on?	*Lo posso provare?*	loh **poh**-soh proh-**vah**-ray
Do you have a mirror?	*Ha uno specchio?*	ah **oo**-noh **spay**-keeoh
Too...	*Troppo...*	**troh**-poh
...big.	*...grande.*	**grahn**-day
...small.	*...piccolo.*	**pee**-koh-loh
...expensive.	*...caro.*	**kah**-roh
It's too...	*È troppo...*	eh **troh**-poh
...short / long.	*...corto / lungo.*	**kor**-toh / **loon**-goh
...tight / loose.	*...stretto / largo.*	**streht**-toh / **lar**-goh
...dark / light.	*...scuro / chiaro.*	**skoo**-roh / kee**ah**-roh
What is it made of?	*Di che cosa è fatto?*	dee kay **koh**-zah eh **fah**-toh
Is it machine washable?	*Si può lavare in lavatrice?*	see pwoh lah-**vah**-ray een lah-vah-**tree**-chay
Will it shrink?	*Si ritira?*	see ree-**tee**-rah
Will it fade in the wash?	*Scolora quando si lava?*	skoh-**loh**-rah **kwahn**-doh see **lah**-vah
Credit card O.K.?	*Carta di credito è O.K.?*	**kar**-tah dee **kray**-dee-toh eh "O.K."
Can you ship this?	*Può spedirmelo?*	pwoh spay-**deer**-may-loh
Tax-free?	*Esente da tasse?*	ay-**zehn**-tay dah **tah**-say

I'll think about it.	*Ci penserò.*	chee pehn-say-**roh**
What time do you close?	*A che ora chiudete?*	ah kay **oh**-rah keeoo-**day**-tay
What time do you open tomorrow?	*A che ora aprite domani?*	ah kay **oh**-rah ah-**pree**-tay doh-**mah**-nee

Street Markets

Did you make this?	*L'avete fatto voi questo?*	lah-**vay**-tay **fah**-toh **voh**ee **kweh**-stoh
Is that your final price?	*È questo il prezzo finale?*	eh **kweh**-stoh eel **prehd**-zoh fee-**nah**-lay
Cheaper?	*Me lo dà a meno?*	may loh dah ah **may**-noh
My last offer.	*La mia ultima offerta.*	lah **mee**-ah **ool**-tee-mah oh-**fehr**-tah
Good price.	*Buon prezzo.*	bwohn **prehd**-zoh
I'll take it.	*Lo prendo.*	loh **prehn**-doh
I'm nearly broke.	*Sono quasi al verde.*	**soh**-noh **kwah**-zee ahl **vehr**-day
My male friend...	*Il mio amico...*	eel **mee**-oh ah-**mee**-koh
My female friend...	*La mia amica...*	lah **mee**-ah ah-**mee**-kah
My husband...	*Mio marito...*	**mee**-oh mah-**ree**-toh
My wife...	*Mia moglie...*	**mee**-ah **mohl**-yay
...has the money.	*...ha i soldi.*	ah ee **sohl**-dee

At street markets, it's common to bargain.

Clothes

For...	*Per...*	pehr
...a male / a female baby.	*...un neonato / una neonata.*	oon nay-oh-**nah**-toh / **oo**-nah nay-oh-**nah**-tah
...a male / a female child.	*...un bambino / una bambina.*	oon bahm-**bee**-noh / **oo**-nah bahm-**bee**-nah
...a male / a female teenager.	*...un ragazzo / una ragazza.*	oon rah-**gahd**-zoh / **oo**-nah rah-**gahd**-zah
...a man.	*...un uomo.*	oon **woh**-moh

...a woman.	*...una donna.*	**oo**-nah **doh**-nah
bathrobe	*accappatoio*	ah-kah-pah-**toh**-yoh
bib	*bavaglino*	bah-vahl-**yee**-noh
belt	*cintura*	cheen-**too**-rah
bra	*reggiseno*	ray-jee-**zay**-noh
clothing	*vestiti*	vehs-**tee**-tee
dress	*vestito da donna*	vehs-**tee**-toh dah **doh**-nah
flip-flops	*ciabatte da piscina*	chah-**bah**-tay dah pee-**shee**-nah
gloves	*guanti*	**gwahn**-tee
hat	*cappello*	kah-**pehl**-loh
jacket	*giacca*	**jah**-kah
jeans	*jeans*	"jeans"
nightgown	*vestaglia*	vehs-**tahl**-yah
nylons	*collant*	koh-**lahnt**
pajamas	*pigiama*	pee-**jah**-mah
pants	*pantaloni*	pahn-tah-**loh**-nee
raincoat	*impermeabile*	eem-pehr-may-**ah**-bee-lay
sandals	*sandali*	sahn-**dah**-lee
scarf	*sciarpa, foulard*	**shar**-pah, foo-**lard**
shirt...	*camicia...*	kah-**mee**-chah
...long-sleeved	*...a maniche lunghe*	ah mah-**nee**-kay **loong**-gay
...short-sleeved	*...a maniche corte*	ah mah-**nee**-kay **kor**-tay
...sleeveless	*...senza maniche*	**sehnt**-sah mah-**nee**-kay
shoelaces	*lacci da scarpe*	**lah**-chee dah **skar**-pay
shoes	*scarpe*	**skar**-pay
shorts	*pantaloni corti*	pahn-tah-**loh**-nee **kor**-tee
skirt	*gonna*	**goh**-nah
sleeper (for baby)	*tutina (da neonato)*	too-**tee**-nah (dah nay-oh-**nah**-toh)
slip	*sottoveste*	soh-toh-**vehs**-tay
slippers	*ciabatte, pantofole*	chah-**bah**-tay, pahn-**toh**-foh-lay
socks	*calzini*	kahlt-**see**-nee

sweater	*maglione*	mahl-yee**oh**-nay
swimsuit	*costume da bagno*	kohs-**too**-may dah **bahn**-yoh
tennis shoes	*scarpe da ginnastica*	**skar**-pay dah jee-**nah**-stee-kah
T-shirt	*maglietta*	mahl-**yay**-tah
underwear	*mutande*	moo-**tahn**-day
vest	*gilè*	jee-**lay**

Colors

black	*nero*	**nay**-roh
blue	*azzurro*	ahd-**zoo**-roh
brown	*marrone*	mah-**roh**-nay
gray	*grigio*	**gree**-joh
green	*verde*	**vehr**-day
orange	*arancio*	ah-**rahn**-choh
pink	*rosa*	**roh**-zah
purple	*viola*	vee**oh**-lah
red	*rosso*	**roh**-soh
white	*bianco*	bee**ahn**-koh
yellow	*giallo*	**jah**-loh
dark / light	*scuro / chiaro*	**skoo**-roh / kee**ah**-roh
lighter	*più chiaro*	pew kee**ah**-roh
brighter	*più brillante*	pew bree-**lahn**-tay
darker	*più scuro*	pew **skoo**-roh

Materials

brass	*ottone*	oh-**toh**-nay
bronze	*bronzo*	**brohnt**-soh
ceramic	*ceramica*	chay-**rah**-mee-kah
copper	*rame*	**rah**-may
cotton	*cotone*	koh-**toh**-nay
glass	*vetro*	**vay**-troh
gold	*oro*	**oh**-roh
lace	*pizzo*	**peed**-zoh
leather	*cuoio / pelle*	**kwoh**-yoh / **pehl**-lay
linen	*lino*	**lee**-noh

marble	*marmo*	**mar**-moh
metal	*metallo*	may-**tah**-loh
nylon	*nylon*	**nee**-loh<u>n</u>
paper	*carta*	**kar**-tah
pewter	*peltro*	**pehl**-troh
plastic	*plastica*	**plah**-stee-kah
polyester	*polyestere*	poh-lee-ehs-**tay**-ray
porcelain	*porcellana*	por-chay-**lah**-nah
silk	*seta*	**say**-tah
silver	*argento*	ar-**jehn**-toh
velvet	*velluto*	vay-**loo**-toh
wood	*legno*	**layn**-yoh
wool	*lana*	**lah**-nah

Jewelry

bracelet	*bracciale*	brah-chee**ah**-lay
brooch	*spilla*	**spee**-lah
earrings	*orecchini*	oh-ray-**kee**-nee
jewelry	*gioielli*	joh-**yeh**-lee
necklace	*collana*	koh-**lah**-nah
ring	*anello*	ah-**nehl**-loh
Is this...?	*Questo è...?*	**kwehs**-toh eh
...sterling silver	*...argento sterling*	ar-**jehn**-toh **stehr**-leeng
...real gold	*...oro zecchino*	**oh**-roh tseh-**kee**-noh
...stolen	*...rubato*	roo-**bah**-toh

SPORTS

Bicycling

bicycle	*bicicletta*	bee-chee-**klay**-tah
mountain bike	*mountain bike*	"mountain bike"
I'd like to rent a bicycle.	*Vorrei noleggiare una bicicletta.*	vor-**reh**ee noh-leh-**jah**-ray **oo**-nah bee-chee-**klay**-tah
We'd like to rent two bicycles.	*Vorremmo noleggiare due biciclette.*	vor-**ray**-moh noh-leh-**jah**-ray **doo**-ay bee-chee-**klay**-tay

How much...?	*Quanto...?*	**kwahn**-toh
...per hour	*...all'ora*	ah-**loh**-rah
...per half day	*...per mezza giornata*	pehr **mehd**-zah jor-**nah**-tah
...per day	*...al giorno*	ahl **jor**-noh
Is a deposit required?	*Ci vuole un deposito?*	chee **vwoh**-lay oon day-**poh**-zee-toh
deposit	*deposito*	day-**poh**-zee-toh
helmet	*casco*	**kahs**-koh
lock	*lucchetto*	loo-**keht**-toh
air / no air	*aria / senza aria*	**ah**-reeah / **sehnt**-sah **ah**-reeah
tire	*gomma*	**goh**-mah
pump	*pompa*	**pohm**-pah
map	*cartina*	kar-**tee**-nah
How many gears?	*Quante marce?*	**kwahn**-tay **mar**-kay
What is a... route of about ___ kilometers?	*Mi può indicare un percorso... di circa ___ chilometri?*	mee pwoh een-dee-**kah**-ray oon pehr-**kor**-soh... dee **cheer**-kah ___ kee-**loh**-may-tree
...good	*...bello*	**behl**-loh
...scenic	*...panoramico*	pah-noh-**rah**-mee-koh
...interesting	*...interessante*	een-tay-ray-**sahn**-tay
...easy	*...facile*	**fah**-chee-lay
How many minutes / How many hours by bicycle?	*Quanti minuti / Quante ore in bicicletta?*	**kwahn**-tee mee-**noo**-tee / **kwahn**-tay **oh**-ray een bee-chee-**klay**-tah
I (don't) like hills.	*(Non) mi piacciono le salite.*	(nohn) mee peeah-**choh**-noh lay sah-**lee**-tay

For more on route-finding, see "Finding Your Way," beginning on page 203 in the Italian Traveling chapter.

Swimming and Boating

Where can I / can we rent...?	*Dove posso / possiamo noleggiare...?*	**doh**-vay **poh**-soh / poh-see**ah**-moh noh-leh-**jah**-ray
...a paddleboat	*...un pedalò*	oon pay-dah-**loh**
...a rowboat	*...una barca a remi*	**oo**-nah **bar**-kah ah **ray**-mee
...a boat	*...una barca*	**oo**-nah **bar**-kah
...a sailboat	*...una barca a vela*	**oo**-nah **bar**-kah ah **vay**-lah
How much...?	*Quanto...?*	**kwahn**-toh
...per hour	*...all'ora*	ah-**loh**-rah
...per half day	*...per mezza giornata*	pehr **mehd**-zah jor-**nah**-tah
...per day	*...al giorno*	ahl **jor**-noh
beach	*spiaggia*	spee**ah**-jah
nude beach	*spiaggia nudista*	spee**ah**-jah noo-**dee**-stah
Where's a good beach?	*Mi può indicare una bella spiaggia?*	mee pwoh een-dee-**kah**-ray **oo**-nah **behl**-lah spee**ah**-jah
Is it safe for swimming?	*È sicura per nuotare?*	eh see-**koo**-rah pehr nwoh-**tah**-ray
flip-flops	*ciabatte da piscina*	chah-**bah**-tay dah pee-**shee**-nah
pool	*piscina*	pee-**shee**-nah
snorkel and mask	*boccaglio e maschera*	boh-**kahl**-yoh ay mahs-**kay**-rah
sunglasses	*occhiali da sole*	oh-kee**ah**-lee dah **soh**-lay
sunscreen	*protezione solare*	proh-teht-see**oh**-nay soh-**lah**-ray
surfboard	*tavola da surf*	**tah**-voh-lah dah soorf
surfer	*surfer*	**soorf**-er
swimsuit	*costume da bagno*	kohs-**too**-may dah **bahn**-yoh
towel	*asciugamano*	ah-shoo-gah-**mah**-noh

waterskiing	*sci acquatico*	shee ah-**kwah**-tee-koh
windsurfing	*windsurf*	**weend**-soorf

In Italy, nearly any beach is topless, but if you want a nude beach, keep your eyes peeled for a ***spiaggia nudista.***

Sports Talk

sports	*gli sport*	**lee**yee sport
game	*partita*	par-**tee**-tah
team	*squadra*	**skwah**-drah
championship	*campionato*	kahm-peeoh-**nah**-toh
soccer	*football, calcio*	**foot**-bahl, **kahl**-choh
basketball	*basket*	**bah**-skeht
hockey	*hockey*	**oh**-kee
American football	*football Americano*	**foot**-bahl ah-may-ree-**kah**-noh
baseball	*baseball*	**bahs**-bahl
tennis	*tennis*	**tehn**-nees
golf	*golf*	gohlf
skiing	*sci*	shee
gymnastics	*ginnastica*	jee-**nah**-stee-kah
Olympics	*le Olimpiadi*	lay oh-leem-pee**ah**-dee
medal...	*medaglia...*	may-**dahl**-yah
...gold / silver / bronze	*...oro / argento / bronzo*	**oh**-roh / ar-**jehn**-toh / **brohnt**-soh
Which is your favorite sport / athlete?	*Qual'è il suo sport / giocatore?*	kwah-**leh** eel **soo**-oh sport / joh-kah-**toh**-ray
Which is your favorite team?	*Qual'è la sua squadra?*	kwah-**leh** lah **soo**-ah **skwah**-drah
Where can I see a game?	*Dove posso vedere una partita?*	**doh**-vay **poh**-soh vay-**day**-ray **oo**-nah par-**tee**-tah
jogging	*jogging*	**joh**-geeng
Where's a good place to jog?	*Dov'è un buon luogo per fare jogging?*	doh-**veh** oon bwohn loo**oh**-goh pehr **fah**-ray **joh**-geeng

ENTERTAINMENT

What's happening tonight?	*Che cosa succede stasera?*	kay **koh**-zah soo-**chay**-day stah-**zay**-rah
What do you recommend?	*Che cosa raccomanda?*	kay **koh**-zah rah-koh-**mahn**-dah
Where is it?	*Dov'è?*	doh-**veh**
How do you get there?	*Come ci si arriva?*	**koh**-may chee see ah-**ree**-vah
Is it free?	*È gratis?*	eh **grah**-tees
Are there seats available?	*Ci sono ancora dei posti?*	chee **soh**-noh ahn-**koh**-rah **deh**ee **poh**-stee
Where can I buy a ticket?	*Dove si comprano i biglietti?*	**doh**-vay see kohm-**prah**-noh ee beel-**yay**-tee
Do you have tickets for today / tonight?	*Ha dei biglietti per oggi / stasera?*	ah **deh**ee beel-**yay**-tee pehr **oh**-jee / stah-**zay**-rah
When does it start?	*A che ora comincia?*	ah kay **oh**-rah koh-**meen**-chah
When does it end?	*A che ora finisce?*	ah kay **oh**-rah fee-**nee**-shay
Where's the best place to dance nearby?	*Qual'è il posto migliore per ballare qui vicino?*	kwah-**leh** eel **poh**-stoh meel-**yoh**-ray pehr bah-**lah**-ray kwee vee-**chee**-noh
Where do people stroll?	*Dov'è la passeggiata?*	doh-**veh** lah pah-say-**jah**-tah

Entertaining Words

movie...	*cinema...*	**chee**-nay-mah
...original version	*...versione originale*	vehr-see**oh**-nay oh-ree-jee-**nah**-lay
...in English	*...in inglese*	een een-**glay**-zay
...with subtitles	*...con sottotitoli*	kohn soh-toh-**tee**-toh-lee
...dubbed	*...doppiato*	doh-pee**ah**-toh
music...	*musica...*	**moo**-zee-kah
...live	*...dal vivo*	dahl **vee**-voh
...classical	*...classica*	**klah**-see-kah

...folk	*...folk*	fohlk
...opera	*...lirica*	**lee**-ree-kah
...symphony	*...sinfonica*	seen-**foh**-nee-kah
...choir	*...corale*	koh-**rah**-lay
...traditional	*...tradizionale*	trah-deet-seeoh-**nah**-lay
old rock	*rock vecchio stile*	rohk **vehk**-eeoh **stee**-lay
jazz / blues	*jazz / blues*	jahz / "blues"
singer	*cantante*	kahn-**tahn**-tay
concert	*concerto*	kohn-**chehr**-toh
show	*spettacolo*	speht-**tah**-koh-loh
dancing	*ballare*	bah-**lah**-ray
folk dancing	*danze popolari*	**dahnt**-say poh-poh-**lah**-ree
disco	*discoteca*	dee-skoh-**tay**-kah
bar with live music	*locale con musica dal vivo*	loh-**kah**-lay kohn **moo**-zee-kah dahl **vee**-voh
nightclub	*locale notturno*	loh-**kah**-lay noh-**toor**-noh
no cover charge	*ingresso libero*	een-**gray**-soh **lee**-bay-roh
sold out	*tutto esaurito*	**too**-toh ay-zow-**ree**-toh

For cheap entertainment, take a ***passeggiata*** (stroll) through town with the locals. As you bump shoulders in the crowd, you'll know why it's also called ***struscio*** (rubbing). This is Italy on parade. If ever you could enjoy being forward, this is the time. Whispering a breathy ***bella*** (cute girl) or ***bello*** (cute guy) feels natural.

CONNECT

PHONING

I'd like to buy a...	*Vorrei comprare una...*	voh-**reh**ee kohm-**prah**-ray **oo**-nah
...telephone card.	*...carta telefonica.*	**kar**-tah tay-lay-**foh**-nee-kah
...cheap international telephone card.	*...carta telefonica prepagate internazionali.*	**kar**-tah tay-lay-**foh**-nee-kah pray-pah-**gah**-tay een-tehr-naht-seeoh-**nah**-lee
Where is the nearest phone?	*Dov'è il telefono più vicino?*	doh-**veh** eel tay-**lay**-foh-noh pew vee-**chee**-noh
It doesn't work.	*Non funziona.*	nohn foont-see**oh**-nah
May I use your phone?	*Posso usare il telefono?*	**poh**-soh oo-**zah**-ray eel tay-**lay**-foh-noh
Can you talk for me?	*Può parlare per me?*	pwoh par-**lah**-ray pehr may
It's busy.	*È occupato.*	eh oh-koo-**pah**-toh
Will you try again?	*Può riprovare?*	pwoh ree-proh-**vah**-ray
Wait a moment.	*Un momento.*	oon moh-**mayn**-toh
Hello. (on phone)	*Pronto.*	**prohn**-toh
My name is ___.	*Mi chiamo ___.*	mee kee**ah**-moh

Sorry, I speak only a little Italian.	*Mi dispiace, parlo solo un po' d'italiano.*	mee dee-spee**ah**-chay **par**-loh **soh**-loh oon poh dee-tah-lee**ah**-noh
Speak slowly and clearly.	*Parli lentamente e chiaramente.*	**par**-lee layn-tah-**mayn**-tay ay keeah-rah-**mayn**-tay

In this section, you'll find phrases to reserve a hotel room (page 207) or a table at a restaurant (page 224). To spell your name over the phone, refer to the code alphabet on page 211.

Make your calls using handy phone cards sold at post offices, train stations, ***tabacchi*** (tobacco shops), and from machines near phone booths. There are two kinds:

1) an insertable card (***carta telefonica***) that you slide into a phone in a phone booth (tear the corner off your phone card before using), and...

2) a cheaper-per-minute international phone card (with a scratch-off PIN code) that you can use from any phone, usually even from your hotel room. If a phone balks, change its setting from pulse to tone.

At phone booths, you'll encounter these words on the display: ***sganciare*** (which means either hang onto the phone...or hang up), ***inserire una carta*** (insert a card), ***carta telefonica*** (the phone acknowledges that you've inserted a phone card), then ***selezionare*** or ***digitare numero*** (dial your number). ***Occupato*** means busy. You'll see the ***credito*** (card value) tick down after you connect. When you hang up, you'll see ***attendere prego*** (please wait), ***ritirare la carta*** (retrieve your card), and again ***sganciare*** (you're done or you can start again). There are some regional differences in the various messages, but the sequence is the same.

Italian phones are temperamental. While you're dialing, you may hear a brusque recording: "***Telecom Italia informazione gratuita: Il numero selezionato è inesistente***" (Telecom Italia free information: The number you're dialing is nonexistent). If you get this message, try dialing again, slowly, as though the phone doesn't understand numbers very well. For more tips, see "Let's Talk Telephones" on page 501 in the appendix.

Telephone Words

telephone	*telefono*	tay-**lay**-foh-noh
telephone card	*carta telefonica*	**kar**-tah tay-lay-**foh**-nee-kah
cheap international telephone card	*carta telefonica prepagate internazionali*	**kar**-tah tay-lay-**foh**-nee-kah pray-pah-**gah**-tay een-tehr-naht-seeoh-**nah**-lee
PIN code	*PIN*	peen
phone booth	*cabina telefonica*	kah-**bee**-nah tay-lay-**foh**-nee-kah
out of service	*guasto*	goo**ah**-stoh
metered phone	*telefono a scatti*	tay-**lay**-foh-noh ah **skah**-tee
phone office	*posto telefonico pubblico*	**poh**-stoh tay-lay-**foh**-nee-koh **poob**-lee-koh
operator	*centralinista*	chayn-trah-lee-**nee**-stah
international assistance	*assistenza per chiamate internazionali*	ah-see-**stehnt**-sah pehr keeah-**mah**-tay een-tehr-naht-seeoh-**nah**-lee
international call	*telefonata internazionale*	tay-lay-foh-**nah**-tah een-tehr-naht-seeoh-**nah**-lay
collect call	*telefonata a carico del desinatario*	tay-lay-foh-**nah**-tah ah **kah**-ree-koh dayl dehs-tee-nah-**tah**-reeoh
credit card call	*telefonata con la carta di credito*	tay-lay-foh-**nah**-tah kohn lah **kar**-tah dee **kray**-dee-toh
toll-free	*numero verde*	**noo**-may-roh **vehr**-day
fax	*fax*	fahks
country code	*prefisso per il paese*	pray-**fee**-soh pehr eel pah-**ay**-zay
area code	*prefisso*	pray-**fee**-soh
extension	*numero interno*	**noo**-may-roh een-**tehr**-noh
telephone book	*elenco telefonico*	ay-**lehn**-koh tay-lay-**foh**-nee-koh
yellow pages	*pagine gialle*	**pah**-jee-nay **jah**-lay

Cell Phones

Where is a cell phone shop?	*Dov'è un negozio di cellulari?*	doh-**veh** oon nay-**goht**-seeoh dee chehl-loo-**lah**-ree
I'd like / We'd like...	*Vorrei / Vorremmo*	vor-**reh**ee / vor-**ray**-moh
...a cell phone.	*...un telefono cellulare.*	oon tay-**lay**-foh-noh chehl-loo-**lah**-ray
...a chip.	*...una scheda.*	**oo**-nah **skay**-dah
...to buy more time.	*...una ricarica.*	**oo**-nah ree-**kah**-ree-kah
How do you...?	*Come si fa a...?*	**koh**-may see fah ah
...make calls	*...fare una chiamata*	**fah**-ray **oo**-nah keeah-**mah**-tah
...receive calls	*...ricevere una chiamata*	ree-**chay**-vay-ray **oo**-nah keeah-**mah**-tah
Will this work outside this country?	*Funziona anche all'estero?*	foont-see**oh**-nah **ahn**-kay ah-lehs-**tay**-roh
Where can I buy a chip for this service / phone?	*Dove posso comprare una scheda per questo gestore / telefono?*	**doh**-vay **poh**-soh kohm-**prah**-ray **oo**-nah **skay**-dah pehr **kweh**-stoh jehs-**toh**-ray / tay-**lay**-foh-noh

CONNECT

EMAIL AND THE WEB

Email

My email address is ___.	*Il mio indirizzo di posta elettronica è ___.*	eel **mee**-oh een-dee-**reed**-zoh dee **poh**-stah ay-leht-**troh**-nee-kah eh
What's your email address?	*Qual è il suo indirizzo di posta elettronica?*	kwahl eh eel **soo**-oh een-dee-**reed**-zoh dee **poh**-stah ay-leht-**troh**-nee-kah

Key Phrases: Email and the Web

email	*posta elettronica*	**poh**-stah ay-leht-**troh**-nee-kah
Internet	*Internet*	**een**-tehr-neht
Where is the nearest Internet access point?	*Dov'è l'Internet più vicino?*	doh-**veh** **leen**-tehr-neht pew vee-**chee**-noh
I'd like to check my email.	*Vorrei controllare la mia posta elettronica.*	vor-**reh**ee kohn-troh-**lah**-ray lah **mee**-ah **poh**-stah ay-leht-**troh**-nee-kah

Can I use this computer to check my email?	*Posso usare il computer per controllare mia posta elettronica?*	**poh**-soh oo-**zah**-ray eel kohm-**poo**-ter pehr kohn-troh-**lah**-ray **mee**-ah **poh**-stah ay-leht-**troh**-nee-kah
Where can I / can we access the Internet?	*C'è un posto dove posso / possiamo accedere a Internet?*	cheh oon **poh**-stoh **doh**-vay **poh**-soh / poh-see**ah**-moh ah-**chay**-day-ray ah **een**-tehr-neht
Where is an Internet café?	*Dov'è un Internet café?*	doh-**veh** oon **een**-tehr-neht kah-**fay**
How much for...minutes?	*Quanto costa per... minuti?*	**kwahn**-toh **koh**-stah pehr... mee-**noo**-tee
...10	*...dieci*	dee**ay**-chee
...15	*...quindici*	**kween**-dee-chee
...30	*...trenta*	**trayn**-tah
...60	*...sessanta*	say-**sahn**-tah
Help me, please.	*Mi aiuti, per favore.*	mee ah-**yoo**-tee pehr fah-**voh**-ray
How do I...	*Come si fa a...*	**koh**-may see fah ah
...start this?	*...accendere questo?*	ah-**chehn**-day-ray **kweh**-stoh

CONNECT

...send a file?	*...mandare un file?*	mahn̲-**dah**-ray oon **fee**-lay
...print out a file?	*...stampare un file?*	stahm-**pah**-ray oon **fee**-lay
...make this symbol?	*...fare questo simbolo?*	**fah**-ray **kweh**-stoh **seem**-boh-loh
...type @?	*...fare la chiocciola?*	fah-ray lah kee**oh**-choh-lah
This isn't working.	*Non funziona.*	nohn̲ foont-see**oh**-nah

Web Words

email	*posta elettronica*	**poh**-stah ay-leht-**troh**-nee-kah
email address	*indirizzo di posta elettronica*	een-dee-**reed**-zoh dee **poh**-stah ay-leht-**troh**-nee-kah
website	*sito Internet*	**see**-toh **een**-tehr-neht
Internet	*Internet*	**een**-tehr-neht
surf the Web	*navigare su Internet*	nah-vee-**gah**-ray soo **een**-tehr-neht
download	*scaricare*	shah-ree-**kah**-ray
@ sign	*chiocciola*	kee**oh**-choh-lah
dot	*punto*	**poon**-toh
hyphen (-)	*trattino*	trah-**tee**-noh
underscore (_)	*linea bassa*	**lee**-nay-ah **bah**-sah
Wi-Fi	*Wi-Fi*	**wee**-fee

On Screen

aprire	open	salvare	save
cancellare	delete	stampare	print
documento	file	scrivere	write
inviare	send	rispondere	reply
messaggio	message		

CONNECT

MAILING

Where is the post office?	*Dov'è la Posta?*	doh-**veh** lah **poh**-stah
Which window for...?	*Qual'è lo sportello per...?*	kwah-**leh** loh spor-**tehl**-loh pehr
Is this the line for...?	*È questa la fila per...?*	eh **kweh**-stah lah **fee**-lah pehr
...stamps	*...francobolli*	frahn-koh-**boh**-lee
...packages	*...pacchi*	**pah**-kee
To the United States...	*Per Stati Uniti...*	pehr **stah**-tee oo-**nee**-tee
...by air mail.	*...per via aerea.*	pehr **vee**-ah ah-**ay**-ray-ah
...by surface mail.	*...via terra.*	**vee**-ah **tehr**-rah
How much is it?	*Quanto costa?*	**kwahn**-toh **koh**-stah
How much to send a letter / postcard to...?	*Quanto costa mandare una lettera / una cartolina a...?*	**kwahn**-toh **koh**-stah mahn-**dah**-ray **oo**-nah leht-**tay**-rah / **oo**-nah kar-toh-**lee**-nah ah

CONNECT

Key Phrases: Mailing

post office	*ufficio postale*	oo-**fee**-choh poh-**stah**-lay
stamp	*francobollo*	frahn-koh-**boh**-loh
postcard	*cartolina*	kar-toh-**lee**-nah
letter	*lettera*	**leht**-tay-rah
air mail	*per via aerea*	pehr **vee**-ah ah-**ay**-ray-ah
Where is the post office?	*Dov'è la Posta?*	doh-**veh** lah **poh**-stah
I need stamps for ___ postcards / letters to America.	*Ho bisogno di francobolli per ___ cartoline / lettere per gli Stati Uniti.*	oh bee-**zohn**-yoh dee frahn-koh-**boh**-lee pehr ___ kar-toh-**lee**-nay / **leht**-tay-ray pehr **lee**yee **stah**-tee oo-**nee**-tee

I need stamps for ___ postcards to...	*Ho bisogno di francobolli per ___ cartoline per...*	oh bee-**zohn**-yoh dee frahn-koh-**boh**-lee pehr ___ kar-toh-**lee**-nay pehr
...America / Canada.	*...gli Stati Uniti / il Canada.*	**lee**yee **stah**-tee oo-**nee**-tee / eel kah-nah-**dah**
Pretty stamps, please.	*Dei bei francobolli, per favore.*	**deh**ee **beh**ee frahn-koh-**boh**-lee pehr fah-**voh**-ray
I always choose the slowest line.	*Scelgo sempre la fila più lenta.*	**shehl**-goh **sehm**-pray lah **fee**-lah pew **lehn**-tah
How many days will it take?	*Quanti giorni ci vogliono?*	**kwahn**-tee **jor**-nee chee **vohl**-yoh-noh

In Italy, you can often get stamps at the corner ***tabacchi*** (tobacco shop). As long as you know which stamps you need, this is a great convenience. Unless you like to gamble, avoid mailing packages from Italy. The most reliable post offices are in the Vatican City.

Licking the Postal Code

Post & Telegraph Office	*Poste e Telegrafi*	**poh**-stay ay tay-**lay**-grah-fee
post office	*ufficio postale*	oo-**fee**-choh poh-**stah**-lay
stamp	*francobollo*	frahn-koh-**boh**-loh
postcard	*cartolina*	kar-toh-**lee**-nah
letter	*lettera*	**leht**-tay-rah
envelope	*busta*	**boo**-stah
package	*pacco*	**pah**-koh
box...	*scatola...*	**skah**-toh-lah
...cardboard	*...de cartone*	day kar-**toh**-nay
string	*filo*	**fee**-loh
tape	*scotch*	"scotch"
mailbox	*cassetta postale*	kah-**say**-tah poh-**stah**-lay
air mail	*per via aerea*	pehr **vee**-ah ah-**ay**-ray-ah
express	*espresso*	eh-**sprehs**-soh
surface mail	*via terra*	**vee**-ah **tehr**-rah

slow and cheap	*lento e economico*	**lehn**-toh ay ay-koh-**noh**-mee-koh
book rate	*prezzo di listino*	**prehd**-zoh dee lee-**stee**-noh
weight limit	*limite di peso*	lee-**mee**-tay dee **pay**-zoh
registered	*raccomandata*	rah-koh-mahn-**dah**-tah
insured	*assicurato*	ah-see-koo-**rah**-toh
fragile	*fragile*	frah-**jee**-lay
contents	*contenuto*	kohn-tay-**noo**-toh
customs	*dogana*	doh-**gah**-nah
sender	*mittente*	mee-**tehn**-tay
destination	*destinatario*	dehs-tee-nah-**tah**-reeoh
to / from	*da / a*	dah / ah
address	*indirizzo*	een-dee-**reed**-zoh
zip code	*codice postale*	koh-**dee**-chay poh-**stah**-lay
general delivery	*fermo posta*	**fehr**-moh **poh**-stah

HELP!

Help!	*Aiuto!*	ah-**yoo**-toh
Call a doctor!	*Chiamate un dottore!*	keeah-**mah**-tay oon doh-**toh**-ray
Call...	*Chiamate...*	keeah-**mah**-tay
...the police.	*...la polizia.*	lah poh-leet-**see**-ah
...an ambulance.	*...un'ambulanza.*	oo-nahm-boo-**lahnt**-sah
...the fire department.	*...i vigili del fuoco.*	ee **vee**-jee-lee dehl **fwoh**-koh
I'm lost.	*Mi sono perso[a].*	mee **soh**-noh **pehr**-soh
We're lost.	*Ci siamo persi[e].*	chee see**ah**-moh **pehr**-see
Thank you for your help.	*Grazie dell'aiuto.*	**graht**-seeay dehl-ah-**yoo**-toh
You are very kind.	*Lei è molto gentile.*	**leh**ee eh **mohl**-toh jehn-**tee**-lay

In Italy, call 118 if you have a medical emergency.

Theft and Loss

Stop, thief!	*Fermatelo! Al ladro!*	fehr-**mah**-tay-loh ahl **lah**-droh
I have been robbed.	*Sono stato[a] derubato[a].*	**soh**-noh **stah**-toh day-roo-**bah**-toh
We have been robbed.	*Siamo stati[e] derubati[e].*	see**ah**-moh **stah**-tee day-roo-**bah**-tee

A thief took...	*Un ladro ha preso...*	oon **lah**-droh ah **pray**-zoh
Thieves took...	*I ladri hanno preso...*	ee **lah**-dree **ah**-noh **pray**-zoh
I have lost my money.	*Ho perso i soldi.*	oh **pehr**-soh ee **sohl**-dee
We have lost our money.	*Abbiamo perso i soldi.*	ah-bee**ah**-moh **pehr**-soh ee **sohl**-dee
I've lost my...	*Ho perso il mio...*	oh **pehr**-soh eel **mee**-oh
...passport.	*...passaporto.*	pah-sah-**por**-toh
...ticket.	*...biglietto.*	beel-**yay**-toh
...baggage.	*...bagaglio.*	bah-**gahl**-yoh
...wallet.	*...portafoglio.*	por-tah-**fohl**-yoh
I've lost...	*Ho perso...*	oh **pehr**-soh
...my purse.	*...la mia borsa.*	la **mee**-ah **bor**-sah
...my faith in humankind.	*...la fiducia nel prossimo.*	lah fee-**doo**-chah nayl **proh**-see-moh
We've lost our...	*Abbiamo perso i nostri...*	ah-bee**ah**-moh **pehr**-soh ee **noh**-stree
...passports.	*...passaporti.*	pah-sah-**por**-tee
...tickets.	*...biglietti.*	beel-**yay**-tee
...baggage.	*...bagagli.*	bah-**gahl**-yee
I want to contact my embassy.	*Vorrei contattare la mia ambasciata.*	vor-**reh**ee kohn-tah-**tah**-ray lah **mee**-ah ahm-bah-shee**ah**-tah
I need to file a police report for my insurance.	*Devo fare una denuncia per la mia assicurazione.*	**day**-voh **fah**-ray **oo**-nah day-**noon**-chah pehr lah **mee**-ah ah-see-koo-raht-see**oh**-nay

Dialing 113 will connect you to English-speaking police help. See page 503 in the appendix for US embassies in Italy.

Helpful Words

ambulance	*ambulanza*	ahm-boo-**lahnt**-sah
accident	*incidente*	een-chee-**dehn**-tay

Key Phrases: Help!

accident	*incidente*	een-chee-**dehn**-tay
emergency	*emergenza*	ay-mehr-**jehnt**-sah
police	*polizia*	poh-leet-**see**-ah
Help!	*Aiuto!*	ah-**yoo**-toh
Call a doctor / the police!	*Chiamate un dottore / la polizia!*	keeah-**mah**-tay oon doh-**toh**-ray / lah poh-leet-**see**-ah
Stop, thief!	*Fermatelo! Al ladro!*	fehr-**mah**-tay-loh ahl **lah**-droh

injured	*ferito*	fay-**ree**-toh
emergency	*emergenza*	ay-mehr-**jehnt**-sah
emergency room	*pronto soccorso*	**prohn**-toh soh-**kor**-soh
fire	*fuoco*	**fwoh**-koh
police	*polizia*	poh-leet-**see**-ah
smoke	*fumo*	**foo**-moh
thief	*ladro*	**lah**-droh
pickpocket	*borsaiolo*	bor-sah-**yoh**-loh

Help for Women

Leave me alone.	*Mi lasci in pace.*	mee **lah**-shee een **pah**-chay
I want to be alone.	*Voglio stare sola.*	**vohl**-yoh **stah**-ray **soh**-lah
I'm not interested.	*Non sono interessata.*	nohn **soh**-noh een-tay-ray-**sah**-tah
I'm married.	*Sono sposata.*	**soh**-noh spoh-**zah**-tah
I'm a lesbian.	*Sono lesbica.*	**soh**-noh **lehz**-bee-kah
I have a contagious disease.	*Ho una malattia contagiosa.*	oh **oo**-nah mah-lah-**tee**-ah kohn-tah-**joh**-zah
You are bothering me.	*Mi sta importunando.*	mee stah eem-por-too-**nahn**-doh

This man is bothering me.	*Questo uomo mi importuna.*	**kweh**-stoh **woh**-moh mee eem-por-**too**-nah
You are intrusive.	*Mi sta dando fastidio.*	mee stah **dahn**-doh fah-**stee**-deeoh
Don't touch me.	*Non mi tocchi.*	nohn mee **toh**-kee
You're disgusting.	*Tu sei disgustoso.*	too **seh**ee dees-goo-**stoh**-zoh
Stop following me.	*La smetta di seguirmi.*	lah **smay**-tah dee say-gweer-mee
Stop it!	*La smetta!*	lah **smay**-tah
Enough!	*Basta!*	**bah**-stah
Go away.	*Se ne vada.*	say nay **vah**-dah
Get lost!	*Sparisca!*	spah-**ree**-skah
Drop dead!	*Crepi!*	**kray**-pee
I'll call the police.	*Chiamo la polizia.*	kee**ah**-moh lah poh-leet-**see**-ah

Whenever macho males threaten to make leering a contact sport, local women stroll arm-in-arm or holding hands. Wearing conservative clothes and avoiding smiley eye contact also convey a "don't hustle me" message.

SERVICES

Laundry

Is a... nearby?	*C'è una... qui vicino?*	cheh **oo**-nah... kwee vee-**chee**-noh
...self-service laundry	*...lavanderia self-service*	lah-vahn-day-**ree**-ah sehlf-**sehr**-vees
...full-service laundry	*...lavanderia*	lah-vahn-day-**ree**-ah
Help me, please.	*Mi aiuti, per favore.*	mee ah-**yoo**-tee pehr fah-**voh**-ray
How does this work?	*Come funziona?*	**koh**-may foont-see**oh**-nah
Where is the soap?	*Dov'è il detersivo?*	doh-**veh** eel day-tehr-**see**-voh
Are these yours?	*Sono suoi questi?*	**soh**-noh **swoh**-ee **kweh**-stee
This stinks.	*Questo puzza.*	**kweh**-stoh **pood**-zah
Smells...	*Sente...*	**sehn**-tay
...like spring time.	*...del profumo di primavera.*	dehl proh-**foo**-moh dee pree-mah-**vay**-rah
...like a locker room.	*...d'uno spogliatoio.*	**doo**-noh spohl-yah-**toh**-yoh
...like cheese.	*...del formaggio.*	dehl for-**mah**-joh
I need change.	*Ho bisogno di moneta.*	oh bee-**zohn**-yoh dee moh-**nay**-tah
Same-day service?	*Servizio in giornata?*	sehr-**veet**-seeoh een jor-**nah**-tah

By when do I need to drop off my clothes?	*Quando devo portare qui i miei panni?*	**kwahn**-doh **day**-voh por-**tah**-ray kwee ee mee-**ay**ee **pah**-nee
When will they be ready?	*Quando saranno pronti?*	**kwahn**-doh sah-**rah**-noh **prohn**-tee
Dried?	*Asciutti?*	ah-**shoo**-tee
Folded?	*Piegati?*	peeay-**gah**-tee
Hey there, what's spinning?	*Salve, come gira?*	**sahl**-vay **koh**-may **jee**-rah

Clean Words

wash / dry	*lavare / asciugare*	lah-**vah**-ray / ah-shoo-**gah**-ray
washer / dryer	*lavatrice / asciugatrice*	lah-vah-**tree**-chay / ah-shoo-gah-**tree**-chay
detergent	*detersivo da bucato*	day-tehr-**see**-voh dah boo-**kah**-toh
token	*gettone*	jeht-**toh**-nay
whites	*il bianco*	eel bee**ahn**-koh
colors	*il colore*	eel koh-**loh**-ray
delicates	*delicato*	day-lee-**kah**-toh
handwash	*lavare a mano*	lah-**vah**-ray ah **mah**-noh

Haircuts

Where is a barber / hair salon?	*Dov'è un barbiere / parrucchiere?*	doh-**veh** oon bar-bee**ay**-ray / pah-roo-kee**ay**-ray
I'd like...	*Vorrei...*	vor-**reh**ee
...a haircut.	*...un taglio.*	oon **tahl**-yoh
...a permanent.	*...una permanente.*	**oo**-nah pehr-mah-**nehn**-tay
...just a trim.	*...solo una spuntatina.*	**soh**-loh **oo**-nah spoon-tah-**tee**-nah
Cut about this much off.	*Tagli tanto così.*	**tahl**-yee **tahn**-toh **koh**-zee
Cut my bangs here.	*Mi tagli la frangia qui.*	mee **tahl**-yee lah **frahn**-jah kwee
Longer here.	*Più lunghi qui.*	pew **loong**-gee kwee

SERVICES

Shorter here.	*Più corti qui.*	pew **kor**-tee kwee
I'd like my hair...	*Vorrei...*	vor-**reh**ee
...short.	*...tagliarmi i capelli.*	tahl-**yar**-mee ee kah-**pay**-lee
...colored.	*...tingermi i capelli.*	teen-**jehr**-mee ee kah-**pay**-lee
...shampooed.	*...fare uno shampoo.*	**fah**-ray **oo**-noh **shahm**-poo
...blow dried.	*...una piega a phon.*	**oo**-nah pee**ay**-gah ah fohn
It looks good.	*Sta bene.*	stah **behn**-ay

Repair

These handy lines can apply to any repair, whether it's a ripped rucksack, bad haircut, or crabby camera.

This is broken.	*Questo è rotto.*	**kweh**-stoh eh **roh**-toh
Can you fix it?	*Lo può aggiustare?*	loh pwoh ah-joo-**stah**-ray
Just do the essentials.	*Faccia solamente le cose essenziali.*	**fah**-chah soh-lah-**mayn**-tay lay **koh**-zay ay-saynt-see**ah**-lee
How much will it cost?	*Quanto costa?*	**kwahn**-toh **koh**-stah
When will it be ready?	*Quando sarà pronta?*	**kwahn**-doh sah-**rah** **prohn**-tah
I need it by ___.	*Ne ho bisogno entro ___.*	nay oh bee-**zohn**-yoh **ayn**-troh
We need it by ___.	*Ci serve per___.*	chee **sehr**-vay pehr
Without it, I'm...	*Senza sono...*	**sehn**-sah **soh**-noh
...lost.	*...perso.*	**pehr**-soh
...ruined.	*...rovinato.*	roh-vee-**nah**-toh
...finished.	*...finito.*	fee-**nee**-toh

SERVICES

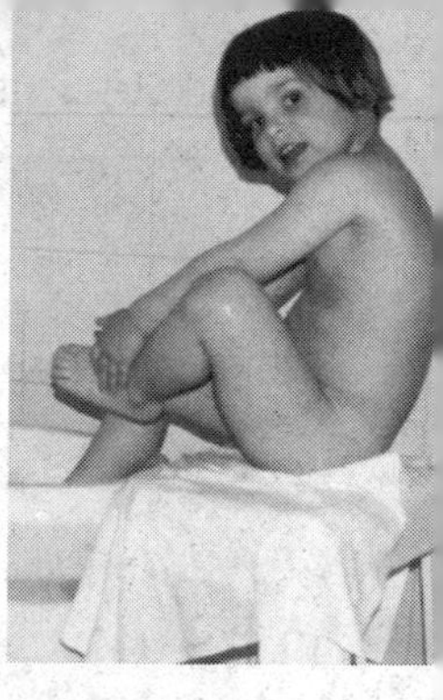

HEALTH

I am sick.	*Sto male.*	stoh **mah**-lay
I feel (very) sick.	*Mi sento (molto) male.*	mee **sehn**-toh (**mohl**-toh) **mah**-lay
My husband / My wife...	*Mio marito / Mia moglie...*	**mee**-oh mah-**ree**-toh / **mee**-ah **mohl**-yay
My son / My daughter...	*Mio figlio / Mia figlia...*	**mee**-oh **feel**-yoh / **mee**-ah **feel**-yah
My male friend / My female friend...	*Il mio amico / La mia amica...*	eel **mee**-oh ah-**mee**-koh / lah **mee**-ah ah-**mee**-kah
...feels (very) sick.	*...si sente (molto) male.*	see **sehn**-tay (**mohl**-toh) **mah**-lay
It's urgent.	*È urgente.*	eh oor-**jehn**-tay
I / We need a doctor...	*Ho / Abbiamo bisogno di un dottore...*	oh / ah-bee**ah**-moh bee-**zohn**-yoh dee oon doh-**toh**-ray
...who speaks English.	*...che parli inglese.*	kay **par**-lee een-**glay**-zay
Please call a doctor.	*Per favore, chiami un dottore.*	pehr fah-**voh**-ray kee**ah**-mee oon doh-**toh**-ray
Could a doctor come here?	*Puo venire qua un dottore?*	pwoh vay-**nee**-ray kwah oon doh-**toh**-ray
I am...	*Sono...*	**soh**-noh
He / She is...	*Lui / Lei è...*	lwee / **leh**ee eh

Key Phrases: Health

doctor	*dottore*	doh-**toh**-ray
hospital	*ospedale*	oh-spay-**dah**-lay
pharmacy	*farmacia*	far-mah-**chee**-ah
medicine	*medicina*	may-dee-**chee**-nah
I am sick.	*Mi sento male.*	mee **sehn**-toh **mah**-lay
I need a doctor (who speaks English).	*Ho bisogno di un dottore (che parli inglese).*	oh bee-**zohn**-yoh dee oon doh-**toh**-ray (kay **par**-lee een-**glay**-zay)
It hurts here.	*Fa male qui.*	fah **mah**-lay kwee

...allergic to penicillin / sulfa.	*...allergico[a] alla pennicillina / ai sulfamidici.*	ah-**lehr**-jee-koh **ah**-lah pehn-nee-chee-**lee**-nah / **ah**ee sool-fah-mee-**dee**-chee
I am diabetic.	*Ho il diabete.*	oh eel deeah-**bay**-tay
I have cancer.	*Ho il cancro.*	oh eel **kahn**-kroh
I had a heart attack ___ years ago.	*Ho avuto un infarto ___ anni fa.*	oh ah-**voo**-toh oon een-**far**-toh ___ **ah**-nee fah
It hurts here.	*Fa male qui.*	fah **mah**-lay kwee
I feel faint.	*Mi sento svenire.*	mee **sehn**-toh svay-**nee**-ray
It hurts to urinate.	*Fa male urinare.*	fah **mah**-lay oo-ree-**nah**-ray
I have body odor.	*Puzzo.*	**pood**-zoh
I'm going bald.	*Perdo i capelli.*	**pehr**-doh ee kah-**pay**-lee
Is it serious?	*È grave?*	eh **grah**-vay
Is it contagious?	*È contagioso?*	eh kohn-tah-**joh**-zoh
Aging sucks.	*Che schifo, invecchiare!*	kay **skee**-foh een-vehk-kee**ah**-ray
Take one pill every ___ hours for ___ days before meals / with meals.	*Prenda una pillola ogni ___ ore per ___ giorni prima dei pasti / con i pasti.*	**prehn**-dah **oo**-nah peel-**oh**-lah **ohn**-yee ___ **oh**-ray pehr ___ **jor**-nee **pree**-mah **de**hee **pah**-stee / kohn ee **pah**-stee

I need a receipt for my insurance.	*Ho bisogno di una ricevuta per la mia assicurazione.*	oh bee-**zohn**-yoh dee **oo**-nah ree-chay-**voo**-tah pehr lah **mee**-ah ah-see-koo-raht-see**oh**-nay

Ailments

I have...	*Ho...*	oh
He / She has...	*Lui / Lei ha...*	lwee / **leh**ee ah
I / We need medication for...	*Ho / Abbiamo bisogno di un farmaco per...*	oh / ah-bee**ah**-moh bee-**zohn**-yoh dee oon far-**mah**-koh pehr
...arthritis.	*...l'artrite.*	lar-**tree**-tay
...asthma.	*...l'asma.*	**lahz**-mah
...athelete's foot (fungus).	*...piede d'atleta (fungo).*	pee**ay**-day daht-**lay**-tah (**foong**-goh)
...bad breath.	*...l'alito cattivo.*	lah-**lee**-toh kah-**tee**-voh
...blisters.	*...vesciche.*	vay-**shee**-kay
...bug bites.	*...le punture d'insetto.*	lay poon-**too**-ray deen-**seht**-toh
...a burn.	*...una bruciatura.*	**oo**-nah broo-chah-**too**-rah
...chest pains.	*...dolore al petto.*	doh-**loh**-ray ahl **peht**-toh
...chills.	*...i brividi.*	ee bree-**vee**-dee
...a cold.	*...un raffreddore.*	oon rah-fray-**doh**-ray
...congestion.	*...una congestione.*	**oo**-nah koh<u>n</u>-jehs-tee**oh**-nay
...constipation.	*...la stitichezza.*	lah stee-tee-**kayd**-zah
...a cough.	*...la tosse.*	lah **toh**-say
...cramps.	*...i crampi*	ee krahm-pee
...diabetes.	*...il diabete.*	eel dee-ah-**bay**-tay
...diarrhea.	*...la diarrea.*	lah dee-ah-**ray**-ah
...dizziness.	*...capogiri.*	kah-poh-**jee**-ree
...earache.	*...il mal d'orecchi.*	eel mahl doh-**ray**-kee
...epilepsy.	*...l'epilessia.*	lay-pee-**lay**-seeah
...a fever.	*...la febbre.*	lah **feh**-bray
...the flu.	*...l'influenza.*	leen-floo-**ehnt**-sah
...food poisoning.	*...l'avvelenamento da cibo.*	lah-vehl-ehn-ah-**mehn**-toh dah **chee**-boh

...the giggles.	*...la ridarella.*	lah ree-dah-**ray**-lah
...hay fever.	*...il raffreddore da fieno.*	eel rah-fray-**doh**-ray dah fee**ay**-noh
...a headache.	*...un mal di testa.*	oon mahl dee **tehs**-tah
...a heart condition.	*...i disturbi cardiaci.*	ee dee-**stoor**-bee kar-dee**ah**-chee
...hemorrhoids.	*...le emorroidi.*	lay ay-moh-roh**ee**-dee
...high blood pressure.	*...la pressione alta.*	lah pray-see**oh**-nay **ahl**-tah
...indigestion.	*...una indigestione.*	**oo**-nah een-dee-jay-stee**oh**-nay
...an infection.	*...una infezione.*	**oo**-nah een-feht-see**oh**-nay
...inflammation.	*...una infiammazione.*	**oo**-nah een-feeah-maht-see**oh**-nay
...a migraine.	*...l'emicrania.*	lay-mee-**krah**-nee-ah
...nausea.	*...la nausea.*	lah **now**-zee-ah
...pneumonia.	*...la bronco-polmonite.*	lah brohn-koh-pohl-moh-**nee**-tay
...a rash.	*...un'irritazione della pelle.*	oo-nee-ree-taht-see**oh**-nay **dehl**-lah **pehl**-lay
...sinus problems.	*...disturbi sinusali.*	dee-**stoor**-bee see-noo-**zah**-lee
...a sore throat.	*...il mal di gola.*	eel mahl dee **goh**-lah
...a stomachache.	*...il mal di stomaco.*	eel mahl dee **stoh**-mah-koh
...sunburn.	*...una scottatura solare.*	**oo**-nah skoh-tah-**too**-rah soh-**lah**-ray
...swelling.	*...un gonfiore.*	oon gohn-fee**oh**-ray
...a toothache.	*...mal di denti.*	mahl dee **dehn**-tee
...a urinary infection.	*...infezione urinaria.*	een-feht-see**oh**-nay oo-ree-**nah**-reeah
...a venereal disease.	*...una malattia venerea.*	**oo**-nah mah-lah-**tee**-ah vay-nay-ray-ah
...vicious sunburn.	*...una grave scottatura solare.*	oo-nah **grah**-vay skoh-tah-**too**-rah soh-**lah**-ray
...vomiting.	*...il vomito*	eel **voh**-mee-toh
...worms.	*...vermi.*	**vehr**-mee

HEALTH

Women's Health

menstruation, period	*le mestruazioni*	lay may-stroo-aht-see**oh**-nee
menstrual cramps	*i dolori mestruali*	ee doh-**loh**-ree may-stroo-**ah**-lee
pregnancy (test)	*(test di) gravidanza*	(tehst dee) grah-vee-**dahnt**-sah
miscarriage	*aborto spontaneo*	ah-**bor**-toh spohn-**tah**-nay-oh
abortion	*aborto*	ah-**bor**-toh
birth control pills	*pillole anti-concezionali*	peel-**oh**-lay ahn-tee-kohn-chayt-seeoh-**nah**-lee
diaphragm	*diaframma*	deeah-**frah**-mah
condoms	*preservativi*	pray-zehr-vah-**tee**-vee
I'd like to see...	*Vorrei vedere...*	vor-**reh**ee vay-**dehr**-ay
...a female doctor.	*...una dottoressa.*	**oo**-nah doh-toh-**ray**-sah
...a female gynecologist.	*...una ginecologa.*	oo-nah jee-nay-koh-**loh**-gah
I've missed a period.	*Ho saltato il ciclo mestruale.*	oh sahl-**tah**-toh eel **chee**-kloh may-stroo-**ah**-lay
My last period started on ___.	*L'ultima mestruazione è cominciata il ___.*	**lool**-tee-mah may-stroo-aht-see**oh**-nay eh koh-meen-**chah**-tah eel
I am / She is... pregnant.	*Sono / È incinta...*	**soh**-noh / eh een-**cheen**-tah
...___ months	*...di ___ mesi.*	dee ___ **may**-zee

Parts of the Body

ankle	*caviglia*	kah-**veel**-yah
arm	*braccio*	**brah**-choh
back	*schiena*	skee**ay**-nah
bladder	*vescica*	vay-**shee**-kah
breast	*seno*	**say**-noh
buttocks	*glutei*	**gloo**-tehee
chest	*petto*	**pay**-toh

ear	*orecchio*	oh-**ray**-keeoh
elbow	*gomito*	goh-**mee**-toh
eye	*occhio*	**oh**-keeoh
face	*faccia*	**fah**-chah
finger	*dito*	**dee**-toh
foot	*piede*	pee**ay**-day
hair (head / body)	*capelli / peli*	kah-**pay**-lee / **pay**-lee
hand	*mano*	**mah**-noh
head	*testa*	**tehs**-tah
heart	*cuore*	**kwoh**-ray
intestines	*intestino*	een-tehs-**tee**-noh
knee	*ginocchio*	jee-**noh**-keeoh
leg	*gamba*	**gahm**-bah
lung	*polmone*	pohl-**moh**-nay
mouth	*bocca*	**boh**-kah
neck	*collo*	**koh**-loh
nose	*naso*	**nah**-zoh
penis	*pene*	**pay**-nay
rectum	*retto*	**ray**-toh
shoulder	*spalla*	**spah**-lah
stomach	*stomaco*	**stoh**-mah-koh
teeth	*denti*	**dehn**-tee
testicles	*testicoli*	tehs-**tee**-koh-lee
throat	*gola*	**goh**-lah
toe	*alluce*	ah-**loo**-chay
urethra	*uretra*	oo-**reht**-rah
uterus	*utero*	**oo**-tay-roh
vagina	*vagina*	vah-**jee**-nah
waist	*vita*	**vee**-tah
wrist	*polso*	**pohl**-soh

For more anatomy lessons, see the illustrations on pages 510-511 in the appendix.

First-Aid Kit

antacid	*antiacido*	ahn-teeah-**chee**-doh
antibiotic	*antibiotici*	ahn-tee-bee**oh**-tee-chee
aspirin	*aspirina*	ah-spee-**ree**-nah
non-aspirin substitute	*Saridon*	**sah**-ree-dohn
bandage	*benda*	**behn**-dah
Band-Aids	*cerotti*	chay-**roh**-tee
cold medicine	*medicina per il raffreddore*	may-dee-**chee**-nah pehr eel rah-fray-**doh**-ray
cough drops	*sciroppo per la tosse*	skee-**roh**-poh pehr lah **toh**-say
decongestant	*decongestionante*	day-kohn-jehs-teeoh-**nahn**-tay
disinfectant	*disinfettante*	dee-seen-feht-**tahn**-tay
first-aid cream	*pomata antistaminica*	proh-**mah**-tah ahn-tee-stah-**mee**-nee-kah
gauze / tape	*garza / nastro*	**gart**-sah / **nah**-stroh
laxative	*lassativo*	lah-sah-**tee**-voh
medicine for diarrhea	*farmaco per la diarrea*	far-**mah**-koh pehr lah dee-ah-**ray**-ah
moleskin	*feltro, moleskin*	**fehl**-troh, "moleskin"
painkiller	*analgesico*	ah-nahl-**jehz**-ee-koh
Preparation H	*Preparazione H*	pray-pah-raht-see**oh**-nay **ah**-kah
support bandage	*fascia di sostegno*	**fah**-shah dee soh-**stehn**-yoh
thermometer	*termometro*	tehr-moh-**may**-troh
Vaseline	*vaselina*	vah-zay-**lee**-nah
vitamins	*vitamine*	vee-tah-**mee**-nay

If you're feeling feverish, see the thermometer on page 514 in the appendix.

Toiletries

comb	*pettine*	pay-**tee**-nay
conditioner for hair	*balsamo*	**bahl**-sah-moh
condoms	*preservativi*	pray-zehr-vah-**tee**-vee
dental floss	*filo interdentale*	**fee**-loh een-tehr-dayn-**tah**-lay
deodorant	*deodorante*	day-oh-doh-**rahn**-tay
facial tissue	*fazzoletto di carta*	fahd-zoh-**lay**-toh dee **kar**-tah
hairbrush	*spazzola per capelli*	spahd-**zoh**-lah pehr kah-**pay**-lee
hand lotion	*crema per le mani*	**kray**-mah pehr lay **mah**-nee
lip salve	*burro di cacao*	**boo**-roh dee kah-**kah**-oh
mirror	*specchio*	**spay**-keeoh
nail clippers	*tagliaunghie*	tahl-yah-**oong**-geeay
razor	*rasoio*	rah-**zoh**-yoh
sanitary napkins	*assorbenti igienici*	ah-sor-**bayn**-tee ee-jay-**nee**-chee
scissors	*forbici*	for-**bee**-chee
shampoo	*shampoo*	**shahm**-poo
shaving cream	*crema da barba*	**kray**-mah dah **bar**-bah
soap	*sapone*	sah-**poh**-nay
sunscreen	*protezione solare*	proh-tayt-see**oh**-nay soh-**lah**-ray
suntan lotion	*crema abbronzante*	**kray**-mah ah-brohnt-**sahn**-tay
tampons	*assorbenti interni*	ah-sor-**bayn**-tee een-**tehr**-nee
tissues	*fazzoletti di carta*	fahd-zoh-**leht**-tee dee **kar**-tah
toilet paper	*carta igienica*	**kar**-tah ee-**jay**-nee-kah
toothbrush	*spazzolino da denti*	spahd-zoh-**lee**-noh dah **dayn**-tee
toothpaste	*dentifricio*	dayn-tee-**free**-choh
tweezers	*pinzette*	peent-**say**-tay

CHATTING

My name is ___.	*Mi chiamo ___.*	mee kee**ah**-moh
What's your name?	*Come si chiama?*	**koh**-may see kee**ah**-mah
This is...	*Le presento...*	lay pray-**zehn**-toh
Pleased to meet you.	*Piacere.*	peeah-**chay**-ray
How are you?	*Come sta?*	**koh**-may stah
Very well, thanks.	*Molto bene, grazie.*	**mohl**-toh **behn**-ay **graht**-seeay
Where are you from?	*Di dove è?*	dee **doh**-vay eh
What city?	*Da che città?*	dah kay chee-**tah**
What country?	*Da che paese?*	dah kay pah-**ay**-zay
I'm...	*Sono...*	**soh**-noh
...American.	*...Americano[a].*	ah-may-ree-**kah**-noh
...Canadian.	*...Canadese.*	kah-nah-**day**-zay
Where are you going? (singular / plural)	*Dove va? / Dove andate?*	**doh**-vay vah / **doh**-vay ahn-**dah**-tay
I'm going / We're going to ___.	*Vado / Andiamo a ___.*	**vah**-doh / ahn-dee**ah**-moh ah
Will you take my / our photo?	*Mi / ci fa una foto?*	mee / chee fah **oo**-nah **foh**-toh
Can I take a photo of you?	*Posso fare le una foto?*	**poh**-soh **fah**-ray lay **oo**-nah **foh**-toh

Key Phrases: Chatting

My name is ___.	*Mi chiamo ___.*	mee kee**ah**-moh
What's your name?	*Come si chiama?*	**koh**-may see kee**ah**-mah
Pleased to meet you.	*Piacere.*	peeah-**chay**-ray
Where are you from?	*Di dove è?*	dee **doh**-vay eh
I'm from ___.	*Sono da ___.*	**soh**-noh dah
Where are you going? (singular / plural)	*Dove va? / Dove andate?*	**doh**-vay vah / **doh**-vay ahn-**dah**-tay
I'm going to ___.	*Vado a ___.*	**vah**-doh ah
I like...	*Mi piace...*	mee pee**ah**-chay
Do you like...?	*Le piace...?*	lay pee**ah**-chay
Thank you very much.	*Molte grazie.*	**mohl**-tay **graht**-seeay
Have a good trip!	*Buon viaggio!*	bwohn vee**ah**-joh

Nothing More Than Feelings...

I am / You are...	*Sono / È...*	**soh**-noh / eh
He / She is...	*Lui / Lei è...*	lwee / **leh**ee eh
...happy.	*...felice.*	fay-**lee**-chay
...sad.	*...triste.*	**tree**-stay
...tired.	*...stanco[a].*	**stahn**-koh
...lucky.	*...fortunato[a].*	for-too-**nah**-toh
I am / You are...	*Ho / Ha...*	oh / ah
He / She is...	*Lui / Lei ha...*	lwee / **leh**ee ah
...hungry.	*...fame.*	**fah**-may
...thirsty.	*...sete.*	**say**-tay
...homesick.	*...nostalgia.*	noh-**stahl**-jah
...cold.	*...freddo.*	**fray**-doh
...too warm.	*...troppo caldo.*	**troh**-poh **kahl**-doh

Who's Who

My... (m / f)	*Mio / Mia...*	**mee**-oh / **mee**-ah
...friend (m / f).	*...amico / amica.*	ah-**mee**-koh / ah-**mee**-kah
...boyfriend / girlfriend.	*...ragazzo / ragazza.*	rah-**gahd**-zoh / rah-**gahd**-zah
...husband / wife.	*...marito / moglie.*	mah-**ree**-toh / **mohl**-yay
...son / daughter.	*...figlio / figlia.*	**feel**-yoh / **feel**-yah
...brother / sister.	*...fratello / sorella.*	frah-**tehl**-loh / soh-**rehl**-lah
...father / mother.	*...padre / madre.*	**pah**-dray / **mah**-dray
...uncle / aunt.	*...zio / zia.*	**tsee**oh / **tsee**ah
...nephew or niece.	*...nipote.*	nee-**poh**-tay
...male / female cousin.	*...cugino / cugina.*	koo-**jee**-noh / koo-**jee**-nah
...grandfather / grandmother.	*...nonno / nonna.*	**noh**-noh / **noh**-nah
...grandchild.	*...nipote.*	nee-**poh**-tay

Family

Are you married? (to a woman / a man)	*È sposata? / È sposato?*	eh spoh-**zah**-tah / eh spoh-**zah**-toh
Do you have children?	*Ha bambini?*	ah bahm-**bee**-nee
How many boys and girls?	*Quanti maschi e femmine?*	**kwahn**-tee **mahs**-kee ay fehm-**mee**-nay
Do you have photos?	*Ha delle foto?*	ah **dehl**-lay **foh**-toh
How old is your child?	*Quanti anni ha il suo bambino?*	**kwahn**-tee **ahn**-nee ah eel **soo**-oh bahm-**bee**-noh
Beautiful baby boy!	*Bel bambino!*	behl bahm-**bee**-noh
Beautiful baby girl!	*Bella bambina!*	**behl**-lah bahm-**bee**-nah
Beautiful children!	*Bei bambini!*	**beh**ee bahm-**bee**-nee

Chatting with Children

My name is ___.	*Mi chiamo ___.*	mee kee**ah**-moh
How old are you?	*Quanti anni hai?*	**kwahn**-tee **ahn**-nee **ah**ee

Do you have brothers and sisters?	*Hai fratelli e sorelle?*	**ah**ee frah-**tehl**-lee ay soh-**rehl**-lay
Do you like school?	*Ti piace la scuola?*	tee pee**ah**-chay lah **skwoh**-lah
What are you studying?	*Che cosa stai studiando?*	kay **koh**-zah **stah**ee stoo-dee**ahn**-doh
I'm studying ___.	*Sto studiando ___.*	stoh stoo-dee**ahn**-doh
What's your favorite subject?	*Qual'è la tua materia preferita?*	kwah-**leh** lah **too**-ah mah-tay-**ree**-ah pray-fay-**ree**-tah
Do you have pets?	*Hai animali domestici?*	**ah**ee ah-nee-**mah**-lee doh-mehs-**tee**-chee
I have / We have a...	*Ho / Abbiamo un...*	oh / ah-bee**ah**-moh oon
...cat / dog / fish / bird.	*...gatto / cane / pesce / uccello.*	**gah**-toh / **kah**-nay / **peh**-shay / oo-**cheh**-loh
What is this / that?	*Che cos'è questo / quello?*	kay koh-**zeh kweh**-stoh / **kweh**-loh
Will you teach me / us...?	*Mi / Ci insegni...?*	mee / chee een-**sayn**-yee
...some Italian words	*...delle parole in italiano*	**dehl**-lay pah-**roh**-lay een ee-tah-lee**ah**-noh
...a simple Italian song	*...una canzone italiana facile*	**oo**-nah kahnt-**soh**-nay ee-tah-lee**ah**-nah **fah**-chee-lay
Guess which country I live in / we live in.	*Indovina in quale paese vivo / viviamo.*	een-doh-**vee**-nah een **kwah**-lay pah-**ay**-zay **vee**-voh / vee-vee**ah**-moh
How old am I?	*Quanti anni ho?*	**kwahn**-tee **ahn**-nee oh
I'm ___ years old.	*Ho ___ anni.*	oh ___ **ahn**-nee
Teach me a fun game.	*Mi insegni un gioco divertente.*	mee een-**sayn**-yee oon **joh**-koh dee-vehr-**tehn**-tay
Got any candy?	*Hai una caramella?*	**ah**ee **oo**-nah kah-rah-**mehl**-lah
Want to thumb-wrestle?	*Vuoi fare la lotta con i pollici?*	**vwoh**ee **fah**-ray lah **loh**-tah kohn ee poh-**lee**-chee

Gimme five. (hold up your hand)	*Dammi un cinque.*	**dah**-mee oon **cheeng**-kway

Travel Talk

I am / Are you...?	*Sono / È...?*	**soh**-noh / eh
...on vacation	*...in vacanza*	een vah-**kahnt**-sah
...on business	*...qui per lavoro*	kwee pehr lah-**voh**-roh
How long have you been traveling?	*Da quanto tempo è in viaggio?*	dah **kwahn**-toh **tehm**-poh eh een vee**ah**-joh
day / week	*giorno / settimana*	**jor**-noh / say-tee-**mah**-nah
month / year	*mese / anno*	**may**-zay / **ahn**-noh
When are you going home?	*Quando ritorna a casa?*	**kwahn**-doh ree-**tor**-nah ah **kah**-zah
This is my first time in ___.	*Questa è la mia prima volta in ___.*	**kweh**-stah eh lah **mee**-ah **pree**-mah **vohl**-tah een
This is our first time in ___.	*Questa è la nostra prima volta in ___.*	**kweh**-stah eh lah **noh**-strah **pree**-mah **vohl**-tah een
It is (not) a tourist trap.	*(Non) è una trappola per turisti.*	(nohn) eh **oo**-nah trah-**poh**-lah pehr too-**ree**-stee
The Italians are friendly / boring / rude.	*Gli italiani sono amichevoli / noiosi / maleducati.*	**lee**yee ee-tah-lee**ah**-nee **soh**-noh ah-mee-kay-**voh**-lee / noh-**yoh**-zee / mah-lay-doo-**kah**-tee
Italy is fantastic.	*L'Italia è fantastica.*	lee-**tahl**-yah eh fahn-**tah**-stee-kah
So far...	*Finora...*	fee-**noh**-rah
Today...	*Oggi...*	**oh**-jee
...I have / we have seen ___ and ___.	*...ho / abbiamo visto ___ e ___.*	oh / ah-bee**ah**-moh **vee**-stoh ___ ay
Next...	*Dopo...*	**doh**-poh
Tomorrow...	*Domani...*	doh-**mah**-nee
...I will see / we will see ___.	*...vedrò / vedremo ___.*	vay-**droh** / vay-**dray**-moh
Yesterday...	*Ieri....*	**yay**-ree

...I saw / we saw ___.	*...ho visto / abbiamo visto ___.*	oh **vee**-stoh / ah-bee**ah**-moh **vee**-stoh
My / Our vacation is ___ days long. It began in ___ and finishes in ___.	*La mia / La nostra vacanza dura ___ giorni. Comincia a ___ e finisce a ___.*	lah **mee**-ah / lah **noh**-strah vah-**kahnt**-sah **doo**-rah ___ **jor**-nee koh-**meen**-chah ah ___ ay fee-**nee**-shay ah
I'm happy here.	*Sono felice qui.*	**soh**-noh fay-**lee**-chay kwee
This is paradise.	*Questo è il paradiso.*	**kweh**-stoh eh eel pah-rah-**dee**-zoh
To travel is to live.	*Viaggiare è vivere.*	veeah-**jah**-ray eh vee-**vay**-ray
Travel is enlightening.	*Viaggiare illumina.*	veeah-**jah**-ray ee-**loo**-mee-nah
I wish all (American) politicians traveled.	*Vorrei che tutti i politici (americani) viaggiassero.*	vor-**reh**ee kay **too**-tee ee poh-**lee**-tee-chee (ah-may-ree-**kah**-nee) veeah-jah-**say**-roh
Have a good trip!	*Buon viaggio!*	bwohn vee**ah**-joh

Map Musings

These phrases and the maps on pages 504–509 in the appendix will help you delve into family history and explore your travel dreams.

I live here.	*Abito qui.*	ah-**bee**-toh kwee
We live here.	*Abitiamo qui.*	ah-bee-tee**ah**-moh kwee
I was born here.	*Sono nato[a] qui.*	**soh**-noh **nah**-toh kwee
My ancestors came from ___.	*I miei antenati vennero da ___.*	ee mee**ay**-ee ahn-tay-**nah**-tee vay-**nay**-roh dah
I've traveled to ___.	*Sono stato[a] a ___.*	**soh**-noh **stah**-toh ah
We've traveled to ___.	*Siamo stati[e] a ___.*	see**ah**-moh **stah**-tee ah
Next I'll go to ___.	*Poi andrò a ___.*	**poh**ee ahn-**droh** ah
Next we'll go to ___.	*Poi andremo a ___.*	**poh**ee ahn-**dray**-moh ah
I'd like / We'd like to go to ___.	*Vorrei / Vorremmo andare a ___.*	vor-**reh**ee / vor-**ray**-moh ahn-**dah**-ray ah

Where do you live?	*Dove abita?*	**doh**-vay ah-**bee**-tah
Where were you born?	*Dove è nato[a]?*	**doh**-vay eh **nah**-toh
Where did your ancestors come from?	*Da dove vennero i suoi antenati?*	dah **doh**-vay vay-**nay**-roh ee **swoh**-ee ahn-tay-**nah**-tee
Where have you traveled?	*Dove è stato[a]?*	**doh**-vay eh **stah**-toh
Where are you going?	*Dove va?*	**doh**-vay vah
Where would you like to go?	*Dove vorrebbe andare?*	**doh**-vay voh-**ray**-bay ahn-**dah**-ray

Weather

What will the weather be like tomorrow?	*Come sarà il tempo domani?*	**koh**-may sah-**rah** eel **tehm**-poh doh-**mah**-nee
sunny / cloudy	*bello / nuvoloso*	**behl**-loh / noo-voh-**loh**-zoh
hot / cold	*caldo / freddo*	**kahl**-doh / **fray**-doh
muggy / windy	*umido / ventoso*	**oo**-mee-doh / vehn-**toh**-zoh
rain / snow	*pioggia / neve*	pee**oh**-jah / **nay**-vay
Should I bring a jacket?	*Devo portare una giacca?*	**day**-voh por-**tah**-ray **oo**-nah **jah**-kah

Thanks a Million

Thank you very much.	*Molte grazie.*	**mohl**-tay **graht**-seeay
A thousand thanks.	*Grazie mille.*	**graht**-seeay **mee**-lay
This is great fun.	*È un vero divertimento.*	eh oon **vay**-roh dee-vehr-tee-**mayn**-toh
You are...	*Lei è...*	**leh**ee eh
...helpful.	*...di aiuto.*	dee ah-**yoo**-toh
...wonderful.	*...meraviglioso[a].*	may-rah-veel-**yoh**-zoh
...generous.	*...generoso[a].*	jay-nay-**roh**-zoh
...kind.	*...gentile.*	jayn-**tee**-lay

You spoil me / us.	*Mi / Ci viziate.*	mee / chee veet-see**ah**-tay
You've been a great help.	*Lei è un grande aiuto.*	**leh**ee eh oon **grahn**-day ah-**yoo**-toh
You are a saint.	*Lei è un[a] santo[a].*	**leh**ee eh oon **sahn**-toh
I will remember you...	*Mi ricorderò di Lei...*	mee ree-kor-day-**roh** dee **leh**ee
We will remember you...	*Ci ricorderemo di Lei...*	chee ree-kor-day-**ray**-moh dee **leh**ee
...always.	*...sempre.*	**sehm**-pray
...till Tuesday.	*...fino a martedì.*	**fee**-noh ah mar-tay-**dee**

Responses for All Occasions

I like that.	*Mi piace.*	mee pee**ah**-chay
We like that.	*Ci piace.*	chee pee**ah**-chay
I like you.	*Lei mi piace.*	**leh**ee mee pee**ah**-chay
We like you.	*Lei ci piace.*	**leh**ee chee pee**ah**-chay
Great!	*Ottimo!*	**oh**-tee-moh
Fantastic!	*Fantastico!*	fahn-**tah**-stee-koh
What a nice place.	*Che bel posto.*	kay behl **poh**-stoh
Perfect.	*Perfetto.*	pehr-**feht**-toh
Funny.	*Divertente.*	dee-vehr-**tehn**-tay
Interesting.	*Interessante.*	een-tay-ray-**sahn**-tay
Really?	*Davvero?*	dah-**vay**-roh
Wow!	*Wow!*	"Wow"
Congratulations!	*Congratulazioni!*	kohn-grah-too-laht-see**oh**-nee
Well done!	*Bravo[a]!*	**brah**-voh
You're welcome.	*Prego.*	**pray**-goh
Bless you! (after sneeze)	*Salute!*	sah-**loo**-tay
What a pity.	*Che peccato.*	kay pehk-**kah**-toh
That's life.	*È la vita!*	eh lah **vee**-tah
No problem.	*Non c'è problema.*	nohn cheh proh-**blay**-mah
O.K.	*Va bene.*	vah **behn**-ay
This is the good life!	*Questa sì che è vita!*	**kweh**-stah see kay eh **vee**-tah
I feel like a pope! (happy)	*Sto come un papa!*	stoh **koh**-may oon **pah**-pah

Have a good day!	*Buona giornata!*	**bwoh**-nah jor-**nah**-tah
Good luck!	*Buona fortuna!*	**bwoh**-nah for-**too**-nah
Let's go!	*Andiamo!*	ahn-deeah-moh
stoned	*fumato, fatto*	foo-**mah**-toh, **fah**-toh
Wow!	*Wow!*	"Wow"

Conversing with Animals

rooster / cock-a-doodle-doo	*gallo / chicchirichì*	**gah**-loh / kee-kee-ree-**kee**
bird / tweet tweet	*uccello / cip cip*	oo-**chehl**-loh / cheep cheep
cat / meow	*gatto / miao*	**gah**-toh / **mee**-ow
dog / bark bark	*cane / bau bau*	**kah**-nay / bow bow
duck / quack quack	*oca / quac quac*	**oh**-kah / kwahk kwahk
cow / moo	*mucca / muu*	**moo**-kah / moo
pig / oink oink	*maiale / oinc oinc*	mah-**yah**-lay / oynk oynk

Profanity

People make animal noises, too. These words will help you understand what the more colorful locals are saying.

Go to hell!	*Vai al diavolo!*	**vah**ee ahl dee**ah**-voh-loh
Damn it.	*Dannazione.*	dah-naht-see**oh**-nay
bastard	*bastardo*	bah-**star**-doh
bitch	*cagna, troia*	**kahn**-yah, **troh**-yah
breasts (colloq.)	*tete*	**tay**-tay
penis (colloq.)	*cazzo*	**kahd**-zoh
butthole	*stronzo*	**strohnt**-soh
drunk	*ubriaco*	oo-bree**ah**-koh
idiot	*idiota*	ee-dee**oh**-tah
imbecile	*imbecille*	eem-bay-**chee**-lay
jerk	*scemo*	**shay**-moh
stupid	*stupido*	**stoo**-pee-doh
Did someone fart?	*Ma qualcuno ha fatto una scoreggia?*	mah kwahl-**koo**-noh ah **fah**-toh **oo**-nah skoh-**ray**-jah

I burped.	*Ho ruttato.*	oh roo-**tah**-toh
This sucks.	*Questo fa schifo.*	**kweh**-stoh fah **skee**-foh
Screw it.	*Vaffanculo.*	vah-fahn-**koo**-loh
Go take a shit.	*Va'a cagare.*	**vah**-ah kah-**gah**-ray
Shit.	*Merda.*	**mehr**-dah
Bullshit.	*Balle.*	**bah**-lay
Shove it up your ass.	*Mettitelo nel culo.*	meht-tee-**tay**-loh nayl **koo**-loh
Stick it between your teeth.	*Ficcatelo tra i denti.*	fee-kah-**tay**-loh trah ee **dayn**-tee
You are...	*Sei...*	seh**ee**
Don't be...	*Non essere...*	nohn ehs-**say**-ray
...a son of a whore.	*...un figlio di puttana.*	oon **feel**-yoh dee poo-**tah**-nah
...an asshole.	*...uno stronzo.*	**oo**-noh **strohnt**-soh
...an idiot.	*...un idiota.*	oon ee-dee**oh**-tah
...a creep.	*...un deficiente.*	oon day-fee-chee-**ehn**-tay
...a cretin.	*...un cretino.*	oon kray-**tee**-noh
...a pig.	*...un porco.*	oon **por**-koh

Sweet Curses

My goodness.	*Mamma mia.*	**mah**-mah **mee**-ah
Good heavens.	*Santo cielo.*	**sahn**-toh cheeay-loh
Shoot.	*Cavolo.*	**kah**-voh-loh
Darn it!	*Accidenti.*	ah-chee-**dehn**-tee

CREATE YOUR OWN CONVERSATION

You can mix and match these words into a conversation. Make it as deep or silly as you want.

Who

I / you	*io / Lei*	**ee**oh / **leh**ee
he / she	*lui / lei*	lwee / **leh**ee
we / they	*noi / loro*	**noh**ee / **loh**-roh

my / your...	*mio / suo...*	**mee**-oh / **soo**-oh
...parents / children	*...genitori / figli*	jay-nee-**toh**-ree / **feel**-yee
men / women	*uomini / donne*	woh-**mee**-nee / **doh**-nay
rich / poor people	*ricchi / poveri*	**ree**-kee / **poh**-vay-ree
young / old people	*giovani / anziani*	joh-**vah**-nee / ahn̲t-see**ah**-nee
middle-aged people	*persone di mezza èta*	pehr-**soh**-nay dee **mehd**-za ay-**tah**
Italians	*italiani*	ee-tah-lee**ah**-nee
Austrians	*austriaci*	ow-stree**ah**-chee
Belgians	*belgi*	**bayl**-jee
Czech	*cechi*	**chay**-kee
French	*francesi*	frahn̲-**chay**-zee
Germans	*tedeschi*	tay-**dehs**-kee
Spanish	*spagnoli*	span-**yoh**-lee
Swiss	*svizzeri*	sveed-**zeh**-ree
Europeans	*europei*	ay-oo-roh-**pay**-ee
EU (European Union)	*UE (Unione Europeo)*	oo ay (oon-ee-**ohn**-ay ay-oo-roh-**pay**-oh)
Americans	*americani*	ah-may-ree-**kah**-nee
liberals	*liberali*	lee-bay-**rah**-lee
conservatives	*conservatori*	kohn̲-sehr-vah-**toh**-ree
radicals	*radicali*	rah-dee-**kah**-lee
terrorists	*terroristi*	tehr-roh-**ree**-stee
politicians	*politici*	poh-**lee**-tee-chee
big business	*grande affare*	**grahn**-day ah-**fah**-ray
multinational corporations	*multi-nazionale*	mool-tee-naht-seeoh-**nah**-lay
military	*militare*	mee-lee-**tah**-ray
mafia	*mafia*	"mafia"
refugees	*profughi*	proh-**foo**-gee
travelers	*viaggiatori*	veeah-jah-**toh**-ree
God	*Dio*	**dee**oh
Christian	*cristiano*	kree-stee**ah**-noh
Catholic	*cattolico*	kah-**toh**-lee-koh

Protestant	*protestante*	proh-tay-**stahn**-tay
Jew	*ebreo*	ay-**bray**-oh
Muslim	*musulmano*	moo-sool-**mah**-noh
everyone	*tutti*	**too**-tee

What

buy / sell	*comprare / vendere*	kohm-**prah**-ray / vehn-**day**-ray
have / lack	*avere / non avere*	ah-**vay**-ray / nohn ah-**vay**-ray
help / abuse	*aiutare / abusare*	ah-yoo-**tah**-ray / ah-boo-**zah**-ray
learn / fear	*imparare / temere*	eem-pah-**rah**-ray / tay-**may**-ray
love / hate	*amare / odiare*	ah-**mah**-ray / oh-dee**ah**-ray
prosper / suffer	*prosperare / soffrire*	proh-spay-**rah**-ray / soh-**free**-ray
take / give	*prendere / dare*	**prehn**-day-ray / **dah**-ray
want / need	*volere / aver bisogno*	voh-**lay**-ray / **ah**-vehr bee-**zohn**-yoh
work / play	*lavorare / giocare*	lah-voh-**rah**-ray / joh-**kah**-ray

Why

(anti-) globalization	*(anti-) globalizzazione*	(**ahn**-tee-)gloh-bah-leed-zaht-see**oh**-nay
class warfare	*conflitto di classe*	kohn-**flee**-toh dee **klah**-say
corruption	*corruzione*	koh-root-see**oh**-nay
democracy	*democrazia*	day-moh-kraht-**see**-ah
education	*istruzione*	een-stroot-see**oh**-nay
family	*famiglia*	fah-**meel**-yah
food	*cibo*	**chee**-boh
guns	*armi*	**ar**-mee
happiness	*felicità*	fay-lee-chee-**tah**
health	*salute*	sah-**loo**-tay

hope	*speranza*	spay-**rahnt**-sah
imperialism	*imperialismo*	eem-pehr-eeahl-**ees**-moh
lies	*bugie*	boo-**jee**-ay
love / sex	*amore / sesso*	ah-**moh**-ray / **sehs**-soh
marijuana	*marijuana*	mah-ree-**wahn**-nah
money / power	*denaro / potere*	day-**nah**-roh / poh-**tay**-ray
pollution	*inquinamento*	een-kwee-nah-**mayn**-toh
racism	*razzismo*	rahd-**zeez**-moh
regime change	*cambio di regime*	**kahm**-beeoh dee ray-**jee**-may
relaxation	*rilassamento*	ree-lah-sah-**mayn**-toh
religion	*religione*	ray-lee-**joh**-nay
respect	*rispetto*	ree-**spay**-toh
taxes	*tasse*	**tah**-say
television	*televisione*	tay-lay-vee-zee**oh**-nay
violence	*violenza*	vee-oh-**lehnt**-sah
work	*lavoro*	lah-**voh**-roh
war / peace	*guerra / pace*	**gwehr**-rah / **pah**-chay
global perspective	*prospettiva globale*	proh-spay-**tee**-vah gloh-**bah**-lay

You Be the Judge

(no) problem	*(non c'è) problema*	(nohn cheh) proh-**blay**-mah
(not) good	*(non) bene*	(nohn) **behn**-ay
(not) dangerous	*(non) pericoloso*	(nohn) pay-ree-koh-**loh**-zoh
(not) fair	*(non) giusto*	(nohn) **joo**-stoh
(not) guilty	*(non) colpevole*	(nohn) kohl-pay-**voh**-lay
(not) powerful	*(non) potente*	(nohn) poh-**tehn**-tay
(not) stupid	*(non) stupido*	(nohn) **stoo**-pee-doh
(not) happy	*(non) felice*	(nohn) fay-**lee**-chay
because / for	*perchè / per*	pehr-**keh** / pehr
and / or / from	*e / o / da*	ay / oh / dah
too much	*troppo*	**troh**-poh

(never) enough	*(mai) abbastanza*	(**mah**ee) ah-bah-**stahnt**-sah
same	*stesso*	**stay**-soh
better / worse	*meglio / peggio*	**mehl**-yoh / **peh**-joh
here / everywhere	*qui / ovunque*	kwee / oh-**voon**-kway

Beginnings and Endings

I like...	*Mi piace...*	mee pee**ah**-chay
We like...	*Ci piace...*	chee pee**ah**-chay
I don't like...	*Non mi piace...*	nohn mee pee**ah**-chay
We don't like...	*Non ci piace...*	nohn chee pee**ah**-chay
Do you like...?	*Le piace...?*	lay pee**ah**-chay
In the past...	*In passato...*	een pah-**sah**-toh
When I was younger, I thought...	*Quando ero più giovane, credevo...*	**kwahn**-doh **ay**-roh pew joh-**vah**-nay cray-**day**-voh
Now, I think...	*Ora penso...*	**oh**-rah **pehn**-soh
I am / Are you...?	*Sono / È...?*	**soh**-noh / eh
...an optimist / pessimist	*...ottimista / pessimista*	oh-tee-**mee**-stah / pay-see-**mee**-stah
I believe...	*Credo...*	**kray**-doh
I don't believe...	*Non credo...*	nohn **kray**-doh
Do you believe...?	*Lei crede...?*	**leh**ee **kray**-day
...in God	*...in Dio*	een **dee**oh
...in life after death	*...nella vita ultraterrena*	**nay**-lah **vee**-tah ool-trah-tay-**ray**-nah
...in extraterrestrial life	*...negli extraterrestri*	**nayl**-yee ehk-strah-tehr-**rehs**-tree
...in Santa Claus	*...in Babbo Natale*	een **bah**-boh nah-**tah**-lay
Yes. / No.	*Si. / No.*	see / noh
Maybe. / I don't know.	*Forse. / Non lo so.*	**for**-say / nohn loh soh
What's most important in life?	*Qual'è la cosa più importante nella vita?*	kwah-**leh** lah **koh**-zah pew eem-por-**tahn**-tay **nay**-lah **vee**-tah
The problem is...	*Il problema è...*	eel proh-**blay**-mah eh

The answer is...	*La risposta è...*	lah ree-**spoh**-stah eh
We have solved the world's problems.	*Abbiamo risolto i problemi del mondo.*	ah-bee**ah**-moh ree-**zohl**-toh ee proh-**blay**-mee dayl **mohn**-doh

AN AFFAIR TO REMEMBER

Words of Love

I / me / you / we	*io / mi / ti / noi*	**ee**oh / mee / tee / **noh**ee
flirt	*flirtare*	fleer-**tah**-ray
kiss	*bacio*	**bah**-choh
hug	*abbraccio*	ah-**brah**-choh
love	*amore*	ah-**moh**-ray
make love	*fare l'amore*	**fah**-ray lah-**moh**-ray
condom	*preservativo*	pray-zehr-vah-**tee**-voh
contraceptive	*contraccetivo*	kohn-trah-chay-**tee**-voh
safe sex	*sesso sicuro*	**sehs**-soh see-**koo**-roh
sexy	*sensuale*	sayn-soo**ah**-lay
cozy	*accogliente*	ah-kohl-**yehn**-tay
romantic	*romantico*	roh-**mahn**-tee-koh
honey bunch	*dolce come il miele*	**dohl**-chay **koh**-may eel mee**ay**-lay
cupcake	*pasticcino*	pah-stee-**chee**-noh
sugar pie	*zuccherino*	tsoo-kay-**ree**-noh
pussy cat	*gattino[a]*	gah-**tee**-noh

Ah, Romance

What's the matter?	*Qual'è il problema?*	kwah-**leh** eel proh-**blay**-mah
Nothing.	*Niente.*	nee**ehn**-tay
I am / Are you...?	*Sono / È...?*	**soh**-noh / eh
...straight	*...normale*	nor-**mah**-lay
...gay	*...gay*	gay
...bisexual	*...bisessuale*	bee-sehs-soo**ah**-lay

...undecided	*...indeciso[a]*	een-day-**chee**-zoh
...prudish	*...pudico[a]*	**poo**-dee-koh
...horny	*...allupato[a]*	ah-loo-**pah**-toh
We are on our honeymoon.	*Siamo in luna di miele.*	see**ah**-moh een **loo**-nah dee mee**ay**-lay
I have...	*Ho...*	oh
...a boyfriend.	*...il ragazzo.*	eel rah-**gahd**-zoh
...a girlfriend.	*...la ragazza.*	lah rah-**gahd**-zah
I'm married.	*Sono sposato[a].*	**soh**-noh spoh-**zah**-toh
I'm married (but...).	*Sono sposato[a] (ma...).*	**soh**-noh spoh-**zah**-toh (mah)
I'm not married.	*Non sono sposato[a].*	nohn **soh**-noh spoh-**zah**-toh
Do you have a boyfriend / a girlfriend?	*Ha il ragazzo / la ragazza?*	ah eel rah-**gahd**-zoh / lah rah-**gahd**-zah
I'm adventurous.	*Sono avventuroso.*	**soh**-noh ah-vehn-too-**roh**-zoh
I'm lonely.	*Sono solo[a].*	**soh**-noh **soh**-loh
I'm lonely tonight.	*Sono solo[a] stasera.*	**soh**-noh **soh**-loh stah-**zay**-rah
I'm rich and single.	*Sono ricco[a] e single.*	**soh**-noh **ree**-koh ay **seeng**-glay
Do you mind if I sit here?	*Le dispiace se mi siedo qui?*	lay dee-spee**ah**-chay say mee see**ay**-doh kwee
Would you like a drink?	*Vuole qualcosa da bere?*	**vwoh**-lay kwahl-**koh**-zah dah **bay**-ray
Will you go out with me?	*Vuole uscire con me?*	**vwoh**-lay oo-**shee**-ray kohn may
Would you like to go out tonight for...?	*Vuole uscire stasera per...?*	**vwoh**-lay oo-**shee**-ray stah-**zay**-rah pehr
...a walk	*...una passeggiata*	**oo**-nah pah-say-**jah**-tah
...dinner	*...cena*	**chay**-nah
...a drink	*...qualcosa da bere*	kwahl-**koh**-zah dah **bay**-ray
Where's the best place to dance nearby?	*C'è un bel locale da ballo qui vicino?*	cheh oon behl loh-**kah**-lay dah **bah**-loh kwee vee-**chee**-noh

Do you want to dance?	*Vuole ballare?*	**vwoh**-lay bah-**lah**-ray
I have no diseases.	*Non ho malattie.*	nohn oh mah-lah-**tee**-ay
I have many diseases.	*Ho molte malattie.*	oh **mohl**-tay mah-lah-**tee**-ay
I have only safe sex.	*Faccio solo sesso sicuro.*	**fah**-choh **soh**-loh **sehs**-soh see-**koo**-roh
Let's have a wild and crazy night!	*Passiamo una notte di fuoco!*	pah-see**ah**-moh **oo**-nah **noh**-tay dee **fwoh**-koh
Can I take you home?	*Posso accompagnarti a casa?*	**poh**-soh ah-kohm-pahn-**yar**-tee ah **kah**-zah
Why not?	*Perché no?*	pehr-**kay** noh
How can I change your mind?	*Posso farti cambiare idea?*	**poh**-soh **far**-tee kahm-bee**ah**-ray ee-**day**-ah
Kiss me.	*Baciami.*	bah-chee**ah**-mee
May I kiss you?	*Posso baciarti?*	**poh**-soh bah-chee-**ar**-tee
Can I see you again?	*Ti posso rivedere?*	tee **poh**-soh ree-vay-**day**-ray
Your place or mine?	*A casa tua o a casa mia?*	ah **kah**-zah **too**-ah oh ah **kah**-zah **mee**-ah
How does this feel?	*Ti piace questo?*	tee pee**ah**-chay **kweh**-stoh
Is this an aphrodisiac?	*È un afrodisiaco questo?*	eh oon ah-froh-dee-**zee**-ah-koh **kweh**-stoh
This is (not) my first time.	*Questa (non) è* la mia *prima volta.*	**kweh**-stah (nohn) eh lah **mee**-ah **pree**-mah **vohl**-tah
You are my most beautiful souvenir.	*Sei il mio più bel ricordo.*	**seh**ee eel **mee**-oh pew behl ree-**kor**-doh
Do you do this often?	*Lo fai spesso?*	loh **fah**ee **speh**-soh
How's my breath?	*Com'è il mio alito?*	koh-**meh** eel **mee**-oh ah-**lee**-toh
Let's just be friends.	*Solo amici.*	**soh**-loh ah-**mee**-chee

I'll pay for my share.	*Pago per la mia parte.*	**pah**-goh pehr lah **mee**-ah **par**-tay
Would you like a massage...?	*Vorresti un massaggio...?*	vor-**ray**-stee oon mah-**sah**-joh
...for your back	*...alla schiena*	**ah**-lah sheeay-nah
...for your feet	*...ai piedi*	**ah**ee peeay-dee
Why not?	*Perchè no?*	pehr-**keh** noh
Try it.	*Provalo.*	**proh**-vah-loh
It tickles.	*Fa solletico.*	fah soh-**lay**-tee-koh
Oh my God!	*Oh mio Dio!*	oh **mee**-oh **dee**-oh
I love you.	*Ti amo.*	tee **ah**-moh
Darling, will you marry me?	*Cara, mi vuoi sposare?*	**kah**-rah mee **vwoh**ee spoh-**zah**-ray

GERMAN

GETTING STARTED

Versatile, Entertaining German

...is spoken throughout Germany, Austria, and most of Switzerland. In addition, German rivals English as the handiest second language in Scandinavia, the Netherlands, Eastern Europe, and Turkey.

German is kind of a "lego language." Be on the look-out for fun combination words. A ***Fingerhut*** (finger hat) is a thimble, a ***Halbinsel*** (half island) is a peninsula, a ***Stinktier*** (stinky animal) is a skunk, and a ***Dummkopf*** (dumb head) is... um... uh...

German pronunciation differs from English in some key ways:

CH sounds like the guttural CH in Scottish loch.
J sounds like Y in yes.
K is never silent.
S can sound like S in sun or Z in zoo.
SCH sounds like SH in shine.
TH sounds like T in top.
V sounds like F in fun.
W sounds like V in volt.
Z sounds like TS in hits.
ÄU and **EU** sound like OY in joy.
E sounds like A in cake.
O always sounds like O in note (never like O in not).
U always sounds like U in flute (never like U in hut or U in cute).

EI sounds like I in light.
I and **IE** sound like EE in seed.

German has a few unusual signs and sounds. The letter *ß* is not a letter B at all–it's interchangeable with "ss." Some of the German vowels are double-dotted with an umlaut. The *ä* has a sound like E in "men." The *ö* has a sound uncommon in English. To make the *ö* sound, round your lips to say "o," but say "ee." To say *ü*, pucker your lips to make an "oo" sound, but say "e." The German *ch* has a clearing-your-throat sound. Say *Achtung!*

Here's a guide to the phonetics in this section:

ah like A in father.
a like AR in far.
ay like AY in play.
ee like EE in seed.
eh like E in get.
ehr sounds like "air."
er like ER in mother.
ew pucker your lips and say "ee."
g like G in go.
kh like the guttural CH in Achtung.
i like I in hit.
ī like I in light.
o like O in cost.
oh like O in note.
or like OR in core.
oo like OO in moon.
ow like OW in now.
oy like OY in toy.
s like S in sun.
u like U in put.
uh like U in but.
ur like UR in purr.
ts like TS in hits. It's a small explosive sound.

In German, the verb is often at the end of the sentence–it's where the action is. Germans capitalize all nouns. Each noun has a gender, which determines which "the" you'll use (***der*** man, ***die*** woman, and ***das*** neuter). No traveler is expected to remember which is which. It's O.K. to just grab whichever "the" (***der, die, das***) comes to mind. In the interest of simplicity, we've occasionally left out the articles. Also for simplicity, we often drop the all-important "please." Please use "please" (***bitte***, pronounced **bit**-teh) liberally.

Each German-speaking country has a distinct dialect. The Swiss speak a lilting Swiss-German around the home, but in schools and at work they speak and write in the same standard German used in Germany and Austria (called "High" German, or ***Hochdeutsch***). The multilingual Swiss greet you with a cheery "***Grüetzi***," (pron. **grewt**-see), thank you by saying "***Merci,***" (pron. **mehr**-see), and bid goodbye with "***Ciao***" (pron. chow). Both Austrians and Bavarians speak in a sing-song dialect, and greet one another with "***Grüss Gott***" (pron. grews goht) which means "May God greet you".

GERMAN BASICS

While he used a tank instead of a Eurailpass, General Patton made it all the way to Berlin using only these phrases.

Meeting and Greeting

Good day.	*Guten Tag.*	**goo**-tehn tahg
Good morning.	*Guten Morgen.*	**goo**-tehn **mor**-gehn
Good evening.	*Guten Abend.*	**goo**-tehn **ah**-behnt
Good night.	*Gute Nacht.*	**goo**-teh nahkht
Hi. (informal)	*Hallo.*	**hah**-loh
Welcome!	*Willkommen!*	vil-**koh**-mehn
Mr.	*Herr*	hehr
Ms.	*Frau*	frow
Miss (under 18)	*Fräulein*	**froy**-līn
How are you?	*Wie geht's?*	vee gayts
Very well, thanks.	*Sehr gut, danke.*	zehr goot **dahng**-keh
And you?	*Und Ihnen?*	oont **ee**-nehn
My name is ___.	*Ich heiße ___.*	ikh **hī**-seh
What's your name?	*Wie heißen Sie?*	vee **hī**-sehn zee
Pleased to meet you.	*Sehr erfreut.*	zehr ehr-**froyt**
Where are you from?	*Woher kommen Sie?*	voh-hehr **koh**-mehn zee
I am / We are...	*Ich bin / Wir sind...*	ikh bin / veer zint
Are you...?	*Sind Sie...?*	zint zee
...on vacation	*...auf Urlaub*	...owf **oor**-lowp

...on business	*...auf Geschäftsreise*	...owf geh-**shehfts**-rī-zeh
See you later!	*Bis später!*	bis **shpay**-ter
So long! (informal)	*Tschüss!*	chewss
Goodbye.	*Auf Wiedersehen.*	owf **vee**-der-zayn
Good luck!	*Viel Glück!*	feel glewk
Have a good trip!	*Gute Reise!*	**goo**-teh **rī**-zeh

People use the greeting "***Guten Morgen***" (Good morning) until noon, and "***Guten Tag***" (Good day) switches to "***Guten Abend***" (Good evening) around 6 P.M.

Essentials

Good day.	*Guten Tag.*	**goo**-tehn tahg
Do you speak English?	*Sprechen Sie Englisch?*	**shprehkh**-ehn zee **ehng**-lish
Yes. / No.	*Ja. / Nein.*	yah / nīn
I don't speak German.	*Ich spreche nicht Deutsch.*	ikh **shprehkh**-eh nikht doych
I'm sorry.	*Es tut mir leid.*	ehs toot meer līt
Please.	*Bitte.*	**bit**-teh
Thank you.	*Danke.*	**dahng**-keh
Thank you very much.	*Vielen Dank.*	**fee**-lehn dah_n_gk
No problem.	*Kein Problem.*	kīn proh-**blaym**
Good.	*Gut.*	goot
Very good.	*Sehr gut.*	zehr goot
Excellent.	*Ausgezeichnet.*	ows-geht-**sīkh**-neht
You are very kind.	*Sie sind sehr freundlich.*	zee zint zehr **froynd**-likh
Excuse me. (to pass or get attention)	*Entschuldigung.*	ehnt-**shool**-dig-oong
It doesn't matter.	*Macht's nichts.*	mahkhts nikhts
You're welcome.	*Bitte.*	**bit**-teh
Sure.	*Sicher.*	**zikh**-er
O.K.	*In Ordnung.*	in **ord**-noong
Let's go.	*Auf geht's.*	owf gayts
Goodbye.	*Auf Wiedersehen.*	owf **vee**-der-zayn

Where?

Where is...?	*Wo ist...?*	voh ist
...the tourist information office	*...das Touristen-informations-büro*	dahs too-**ris**-tehn-in-for-maht-see-**ohns** **bew**-roh
...a cash machine	*...ein Bankomat*	**īn bahnk**-oh-maht
...the train station	*...der Bahnhof*	dehr **bahn**-hohf
...the bus station	*...der Busbahnhof*	dehr **boos**-bahn̲-hohf
...the toilet	*...die Toilette*	dee toh-**leh**-teh
men / women	*Herren / Damen*	**hehr**-ehn / **dah**-mehn

You'll find some German words are similar to English if you're looking for a ***Bank, Hotel, Restaurant,*** or ***Supermarkt.***

How Much?

How much is it?	*Wie viel kostet das?*	vee feel **kohs**-teht dahs
Write it down?	*Aufschreiben?*	**owf**-shrī-behn
Is it free?	*Ist es umsonst?*	ist ehs oom-**zohnst**
Included?	*Inklusive?*	in-kloo-**zee**-veh
Do you have...?	*Haben Sie...?*	**hah**-behn zee
Where can I buy...?	*Wo kann ich... kaufen?*	voh kahn̲ ikh... **kow**-fehn
I'd like...	*Ich hätte gern...*	ikh **heh**-teh gehrn
We'd like...	*Wir hätten gern...*	veer **heh**-tehn gehrn
...this.	*...dies.*	deez
...just a little.	*...nur ein bißchen.*	noor īn **bis**-yehn
...more.	*...mehr.*	mehr
...a ticket.	*...eine Karte.*	**ī**-neh **kar**-teh
...a room.	*...ein Zimmer.*	īn **tsim**-mer
...the bill.	*...die Rechnung.*	dee **rehkh**-noong

How Many?

one	*eins*	īns
two	*zwei*	tsvī
three	*drei*	drī
four	*vier*	feer

five	*fünf*	fewnf
six	*sechs*	zehkhs
seven	*sieben*	**zee**-behn
eight	*acht*	ahkht
nine	*neun*	noyn
ten	*zehn*	tsayn

You'll find more to count on in the "Numbers" section (page 347).

When?

At what time?	*Um wie viel Uhr?*	oom vee feel oor
open	*geöffnet*	geh-**urf**-neht
closed	*geschlossen*	geh-**shloh**-sehn
Just a moment.	*Moment.*	moh-**mehnt**
Now.	*Jetzt.*	yehtst
Soon.	*Bald.*	bahlt
Later.	*Später.*	**shpay**-ter
Today.	*Heute.*	**hoy**-teh
Tomorrow.	*Morgen.*	**mor**-gehn

Be creative! You can combine these phrases to say: "Two, please," or "No, thank you," or "Open tomorrow?" or "Please, where can I buy a ticket?" Please is a magic word in any language. If you want something and you don't know the word for it, just point and say, "***Bitte***" (Please). If you know the word for what you want, such as the bill, simply say, "***Rechnung, bitte***" (Bill, please).

Struggling

Do you speak English?	*Sprechen Sie Englisch?*	**shprehkh**-ehn zee **ehng**-lish
A teeny weeny bit?	*Ein ganz klein bißchen?*	īn gahnts klīn **bis**-yehn
Please speak English.	*Bitte sprechen Sie Englisch.*	**bit**-teh **shprehkh**-ehn zee **ehng**-lish
You speak English well.	*Ihr Englisch ist sehr gut.*	eer **ehng**-lish ist zehr goot

I don't speak German.	*Ich spreche nicht Deutsch.*	ikh **shprehkh**-eh nikht doych
We don't speak German.	*Wir sprechen nicht Deutsch.*	veer **shprehkh**-ehn nikht doych
I speak a little German.	*Ich spreche ein bißchen Deutsch.*	ikh **shprehkh**-eh īn **bis**-yehn doych
Sorry, I speak only English.	*Es tut mir leid, ich spreche nur Englisch.*	ehs toot meer līt ikh **shprehkh**-eh noor **ehng**-lish
Sorry, we speak only English.	*Es tut mir leid, wir sprechen nur Englisch.*	ehs toot meer līt veer **shprehkh**-ehn noor **ehng**-lish
Does somebody nearby speak English?	*Spricht jemand in der Nähe Englisch?*	shprikht **yay**-mahnt in dehr **nay**-heh **ehng**-lish
Who speaks English?	*Wer kann Englisch?*	vehr kahn **ehng**-lish
What does this mean?	*Was bedeutet das?*	vas beh-**doy**-teht dahs
What is this in German / English?	*Wie heißt das auf Deutsch / Englisch?*	vee hīst dahs owf doych / **eng**-lish
Repeat?	*Noch einmal?*	nohkh **īn**-mahl
Please speak slowly.	*Bitte sprechen Sie langsam.*	**bit**-teh **shprehkh**-ehn zee **lahng**-zahm
Slower.	*Langsamer.*	**lahng**-zah-mer
I understand.	*Ich verstehe.*	ikh fehr-**shtay**-heh
I don't understand.	*Ich verstehe nicht.*	ikh fehr-**shtay**-heh nikht
Do you understand?	*Verstehen Sie?*	fehr-**shtay**-hehn zee
Write it down?	*Aufschreiben?*	**owf**-shrī-behn

Handy Questions

How much?	*Wie viel?*	vee feel
How many?	*Wie viele?*	vee **fee**-leh
How long...?	*Wie lange...?*	vee lahng-eh
...is the trip	*...dauert die Reise*	**dow**-ert dee **rī**-zeh
How many minutes / hours?	*Wie viele Minuten / Stunden?*	vee **fee**-leh mee-**noo**-tehn / **shtoon**-dehn

How far?	*Wie weit?*	vee vīt
How?	*Wie?*	vee
Can you help me?	*Können Sie mir helfen?*	**kurn**-nehn zee meer **hehlf**-ehn
Can you help us?	*Können Sie uns helfen?*	**kurn**-nehn zee oons **hehlf**-ehn
Can I...?	*Kann ich...?*	kahn ikh
Can we...?	*Können wir...?*	**kurn**-nehn veer
...have one	*...eins haben*	īns **hah**-behn
...go in for free	*...umsonst rein*	oom-**zohnst** rīn
...borrow that for a moment	*...das für eine Moment leihen*	dahs fewr **ī**-neh moh-**mehnt lī**-hehn
...borrow that for an hour	*...das für eine Stunde leihen*	dahs fewr **ī**-neh **shtoon**-deh **lī**-hehn
...use the toilet	*...die Toilette benützen*	dee toh-**leh**-teh beh-**newts**-ehn
What? (didn't hear)	*Wie bitte?*	vee **bit**-teh
What is this / that?	*Was ist dies / das?*	vahs ist deez / dahs
What is better?	*Was ist besser?*	vahs ist **behs**-ser
What's going on?	*Was ist los?*	vahs ist lohs
When?	*Wann?*	vahn
What time is it?	*Wie spät ist es?*	vee shpayt ist ehs
At what time?	*Um wie viel Uhr?*	oom vee feel oor
On time? / Late?	*Pünktlich? / Spät?*	**pewnkt**-likh / shpayt
How long will it take?	*Wie lange dauert es?*	vee **lahng**-eh **dow**-ert ehs
When does this open / close?	*Wann ist hier geöffnet / geschlossen*	vahn ist heer geh-**urf**-neht / geh-**shloh**-sehn
Is this open daily?	*Ist es täglich offen?*	ist ehs **tayg**-likh **oh**-fehn
What day is this closed?	*An welchem Tag ist es geschlossen?*	ahn **vehlkh**-ehm tahg ist ehs geh-**shloh**-sehn
Do you have...?	*Haben Sie...?*	**hah**-behn zee
Where is...?	*Wo ist...?*	voh ist
Where are...?	*Wo sind...?*	voh zint
Where can I find / buy...?	*Wo kann ich... finden / kaufen?*	voh kahn ikh... **fin**-dehn / **kow**-fehn

Where can we find / buy...?	*Wo können wir... finden / kaufen?*	vo **kurn**-ehn veer... **fin**-dehn / **kow**-fehn
Is it necessary?	*Ist das nötig?*	ist dahs **nur**-tig
Is it possible...?	*Ist es möglich...?*	ist ehs **mur**-glikh
...to enter	*...hinein zu gehen*	hin-**īn** tsoo **gay**-hehn
...to picnic here	*...hier zu picknicken*	heer tsoo **pik**-nik-ehn
...to sit here	*...hier zu sitzen*	heer tsoo **zit**-sehn
...to look	*...anzusehen*	**ahn**-tsoo-zay-hehn
...to take a photo	*...ein Foto zu machen*	īn **foh**-toh tsoo **mahkh**-ehn
...to see a room	*...ein Zimmer zu sehen*	īn **tsim**-mer tsoo **zay**-hehn
Who?	*Wer?*	vehr
Why?	*Warum?*	vah-**room**
Why not?	*Warum nicht?*	vah-**room** nikht
Yes or no?	*Ja oder nein?*	yah **oh**-der nīn

To prompt a simple answer, ask, "***Ja oder nein?***" (Yes or no?). To turn a word or sentence into a question, ask it in a questioning tone. An easy way to ask, "Where is the toilet?" is to say, "***Toilette?***"

Yin and Yang

good / bad	*gut / schlecht*	goot / shlehkht
best / worst	*beste / schlechteste*	**bes**-teh / **shlehkh**-tehs-teh
a little / lots	*wenig / viel*	**vay**-nig / feel
more / less	*mehr / weniger*	mehr / **vay**-nig-er
cheap / expensive	*billig / teuer*	**bil**-lig / **toy**-er
big / small	*groß / klein*	grohs / klīn
hot / cold	*heiß / kalt*	hīs / kahlt
warm / cool	*warm / kühl*	varm / kewl
open / closed	*geöffnet / geschlossen*	geh-**urf**-neht / geh-**shloh**-sehn
entrance / exit	*Eingang / Ausgang*	**īn**-gahng / **ows**-gahng
push / pull	*drücken / ziehen*	**drewk**-ehn / **tsee**-hehn

arrive / depart	*ankommen / abfahren*	**ahn**-koh-mehn / **ahp**-fah-rehn
early / late	*früh / spät*	frew / shpayt
soon / later	*bald / später*	bahlt / **shpay**-ter
fast / slow	*schnell / langsam*	shnehl / **lahng**-zahm
here / there	*hier / dort*	heer / dort
near / far	*nah / fern*	nah / fayrn
indoors / outdoors	*drinnen / draussen*	**drin**-nehn / **drow**-sehn
mine / yours	*mein / Ihr*	mīn / eer
this / that	*dies / das*	deez / dahs
everybody / nobody	*jeder / keiner*	**yay**-der / **kī**-ner
easy / difficult	*leicht / schwierig*	līkht / **shvee**-rig
left / right	*links / rechts*	links / rehkhts
up / down	*hoch / unter*	hohkh / **oon**-ter
beautiful / ugly	*schön / häßlich*	shurn / **hehs**-likh
nice / mean	*nett / gemein*	neht / geh-**mīn**
smart / stupid	*klug / dumm*	kloog / doom
vacant / occupied	*frei / besetzt*	frī / beh-**zehtst**
with / without	*mit / ohne*	mit / **oh**-neh

Big Little Words

I	*ich*	ikh
you (formal)	*Sie*	zee
you (informal)	*du*	doo
we	*wir*	veer
he	*er*	ehr
she	*sie*	zee
they	*sie*	zee
and	*und*	oont
at	*bei*	bī
because	*weil*	vīl
but	*aber*	**ah**-ber
by (train, car, etc.)	*mit*	mit
for	*für*	fewr
from	*von*	fohn
here	*hier*	heer

if	*ob*	ohp
in	*in*	in
it	*es*	ehs
not	*nicht*	nikht
now	*jetzt*	yehtst
only	*nur*	noor
or	*oder*	**oh**-der
this / that	*dies / das*	deez / dahs
to	*nach*	nahkh
very	*sehr*	zehr

Quintessential Expressions

Ach so.	ahkh zoh	I see.
Achtung.	**ahkh**-toong	Attention. / Watch out.
Alles klar.	**ah**-lehs klar	Everything is clear. / I get it.
Ausgezeichnet.	ows-geht-**sīkh**-neht	Excellent.
Bitte.	**bit**-teh	Please. / You're welcome.
Kann ich Ihnen helfen?	Kahn ikh **een**-ehn **helf**-ehn	Can I help you?
Es geht.	ehs gayt	So-so.
Gemütlich.	geh-**mewt**-likh	Cozy.
Gemütlichkeit.	geh-**mewt**-likh-kīt	Coziness.
Genau.	geh-**now**	Exactly.
Halt.	hahlt	Stop.
Hoppla!	**hohp**-lah	Oops!
Kein Wunder.	kīn **voon**-der	No wonder.
Mach schnell!	mahkh shnehl	Hurry up!
Macht's nichts.	mahkhts nikhts	It doesn't matter.
Natürlich.	nah-**tewr**-likh	Naturally.
Sonst noch etwas?	zohnst nohkh **eht**-vahs	Anything else?
Stimmt.	shtimt	Correct.
Super.	**zoo**-pehr	Great.
Warum nicht?	vah-**room** nikht	Why not?

Was ist los?	vahs ist lohs	What's going on?
Wie geht's?	vee gayts	How's it going?

Gemütlich (the adjective) and ***Gemütlichkeit*** (the noun) refer to a special local coziness. A candlelit dinner, a friendly pub, a strolling violinist under a grape arbor on a balmy evening...this is ***gemütlich***.

COUNTING

NUMBERS

The number ***zwei*** (two) is sometimes pronounced "tsvoh" to help distinguish it from the similar sound of ***eins*** (one).

Remember the nursery rhyme about the four-and-twenty blackbirds? That's how Germans say the numbers from 21 to 99 (e.g., 59 = ***neunundfünfzig*** = nine-and-fifty).

0	*null*	nool
1	*eins*	īns
2	*zwei*	tsvī
3	*drei*	drī
4	*vier*	feer
5	*fünf*	fewnf
6	*sechs*	zehkhs
7	*sieben*	**zee**-behn
8	*acht*	ahkht
9	*neun*	noyn
10	*zehn*	tsayn
11	*elf*	ehlf
12	*zwölf*	tsvurlf
13	*dreizehn*	**drī**-tsayn
14	*vierzehn*	**feer**-tsayn
15	*fünfzehn*	**fewnf**-tsayn
16	*sechzehn*	**zehkh**-tsayn

17	*siebzehn*	**zeeb**-tsayn
18	*achtzehn*	**ahkht**-tsayn
19	*neunzehn*	**noyn**-tsayn
20	*zwanzig*	**tsvahn**-tsig
21	*einundzwanzig*	**ī n**-oont-tsvahn-tsig
22	*zweiundzwanzig*	**tsvī**-oont-tsvahn-tsig
23	*dreiundzwanzig*	**drī**-oont-tsvahn-tsig
30	*dreißig*	**drī**-sig
31	*einunddreißig*	**īn**-oont-drī-sig
40	*vierzig*	**feer**-tsig
41	*einundvierzig*	**īn**-oont-feer-tsig
50	*fünfzig*	**fewnf**-tsig
60	*sechzig*	**zehkh**-tsig
70	*siebzig*	**zeeb**-tsig
80	*achtzig*	**ahkht**-tsig
90	*neunzig*	**noyn**-tsig
100	*hundert*	**hoon**-dert
101	*hunderteins*	hoon-dert-**īns**
102	*hundertzwei*	hoon-dert-**tsvī**
200	*zweihundert*	**tsvī**-hoon-dert
1000	*tausend*	**tow**-zehnd
2000	*zweitausend*	**tsvī**-tow-zehnd
2001	*zweitausendeins*	**tsvī**-tow-zehnd-**īns**
2002	*zweitausendzwei*	**tsvī**-tow-zehnd-**tsvī**
2003	*zweitausenddrei*	**tsvī**-tow-zehnd-**drī**
2004	*zweitausendvier*	**tsvī**-tow-zehnd-**feer**
2005	*zweitausendfünf*	**tsvī**-tow-zehnd-**fewnf**
2006	*zweitausendsechs*	**tsvī**-tow-zehnd-**zehkhs**
2007	*zweitausendsieben*	**tsvī**-tow-zehnd-**zee**-behn
2008	*zweitausendacht*	**tsvī**-tow-zehnd-**ahkht**
2009	*zweitausendneun*	**tsvī**-tow-zehnd-**noyn**
2010	*zweitausendzehn*	**tsvī**-tow-zehnd-**tsayn**
million	*eine Million*	ī-neh mil-**yohn**
billion	*eine Milliarde*	ī-neh mil-**yar**-deh
number one	*Nummer eins*	**noo**-mer **īns**
first	*erste*	**ehr**-steh
second	*zweite*	**tsvī**-teh

third	*dritte*	**drit**-teh
once / twice	*ein Mal / zwei Mal*	īn mahl / tsvī mahl
a quarter	*ein Viertel*	īn **feer**-tehl
a third	*ein Drittel*	īn **drit**-tehl
half	*Halb*	hahlp
this much	*so viel*	zoh feel
a dozen	*ein Dutzend*	īn **doot**-tsehnd
some	*einige*	**ī**-ni-geh
enough	*genug*	geh-**noog**
a handful	*eine Hand voll*	**ī**-neh hahn̲t fohl
50%	*fünfzig Prozent*	**fewnf**-tsig proh-**tsehnt**
100%	*hundert Prozent*	**hoon**-dert proh-**tsehnt**

MONEY

Where is a cash machine?	*Wo ist ein Geldautomat?*	voh ist īn **gelt**-ow-toh-maht
My ATM card has been...	*Meine Kontokarte wurde...*	**mī**-neh **kohn**-toh-kar-teh **voor**-deh
...demagnetized.	*...entmagnetisiert.*	ehnt-mahg-neh-teh-**zeert**
...stolen.	*...gestohlen.*	geh-**shtoh**-lehn
...eaten by the machine.	*...von der Maschine geschluckt.*	fohn̲ dehr mahs-**shee**-neh geh-**shlookt**
Do you accept credit cards?	*Akzeptieren Sie Kreditkarten?*	ahk-tsehp-**teer**-ehn zee kreh-**deet**-kar-tehn
Can you change dollars?	*Können Sie Dollar wechseln?*	**kurn**-nehn zee **dohl**-lar **vehkh**-sehln
What is your exchange rate for dollars...?	*Was ist ihr Wechselkurs für Dollars...?*	vahs ist eer **vehkh**-sehl-koors fewr **dohl**-lars
...in traveler's checks	*...in Reiseschecks*	in **rī**-zeh-shehks
What is the commission?	*Wie viel ist die Kommission?*	vee feel ist dee koh-mis-see-**ohn**
Any extra fee?	*Extra Gebühren?*	**ehx**-trah geh-**bew**-rehn
Can you break this? (big bills into smaller bills)	*Können Sie dies wechseln?*	**kurn**-nehn zee deez **vehkh**-sehln

Key Phrases: Money

euro (€)	*Euro*	**oy**-roh
money	*Geld*	gehlt
cash	*Bargeld*	**bar**-gehlt
credit card	*Kreditkarte*	kreh-**deet**-kar-teh
bank	*Bank*	bahnk
cash machine	*Geldautomat, Bankomat*	**gelt**-ow-toh-maht, **bahnk**-oh-maht
Where is a cash machine?	*Wo ist ein Bankomat?*	voh ist īn **bahnk**-oh-maht
Do you accept credit cards?	*Akzeptieren Sie Kreditkarten?*	ahk-tsehp-**teer**-ehn zee kreh-**deet**-kar-tehn

I would like...	*Ich hätte gern...*	ikh **heht**-teh gehrn
...small bills.	*...kleine Banknoten.*	**klī**-neh **bahnk**-noh-tehn
...large bills.	*...große Banknoten.*	**groh**-seh **bahnk**-noh-tehn
...coins.	*...Münzen.*	**mewn**-tsehn
€50	*fünfzig Euro*	**fewnf**-tsig **oy**-roh
Is this a mistake?	*Ist das ein Fehler?*	ist dahs īn **fay**-ler
This is incorrect.	*Das stimmt nicht.*	dahs shtimt nikht
Did you print these today?	*Haben Sie die heute gedruckt?*	**hah**-ben zee dee **hoy**-teh geh-**drookt**
I'm broke / poor / rich.	*Ich bin pleite / arm / reich.*	ikh bin **plī**-teh / arm / rīkh
I'm Bill Gates.	*Ich bin Bill Gates.*	ikh bin "Bill Gates"
Where is the nearest casino?	*Wo ist das nächste Kasino?*	voh ist dahs **nehkh**-steh kah-**see**-noh

Germany and Austria use the euro currency. Euros (€) are divided into 100 cents. Switzerland has held fast to its francs (Fr), which are divided into 100 centimes (c) or rappen (Rp). Use your common cents—cents and centimes are like pennies, and the euro and franc currency each have coins like nickels, dimes, and half-dollars.

Money Words

euro (€)	*Euro*	**oy**-roh
cents	*Cent*	sehnt
money	*Geld*	gehlt
cash	*Bargeld*	**bar**-gehlt
cash machine	*Geldautomat, Bankomat*	**gelt**-ow-toh-maht, **bahnk**-oh-maht
bank	*Bank*	bahnk
credit card	*Kreditkarte*	kreh-**deet**-kar-teh
change money	*Geld wechseln*	gehlt **vehkh**-sehln
exchange	*Wechsel*	**vehkh**-sehl
buy / sell	*kaufen / verkaufen*	**kow**-fehn / fehr-**kow**-fehn
commission	*Kommission*	koh-mis-see-**ohn**
cash advance	*Vorschuß in Bargeld*	**for**-shoos in **bar**-gehlt
cashier	*Kassierer*	kahs-**seer**-er
bills	*Banknoten*	**bahnk**-noh-tehn
coins	*Münzen*	**mewn**-tsehn
receipt	*Beleg*	beh-**lehg**

Every cash mashine (***Geldautomat*** in Germany, ***Bankomat*** in Austria and Switzerland) is multilingual, but if you want to be adventuresome, ***Bestätigung*** means confirm, ***Korrektur*** means change or correct, and ***Abbruch*** is cancel. Your PIN code is a ***Geheimnummer***.

TIME

What time is it?	*Wie spät ist es?*	vee shpayt ist ehs
It's...	*Es ist...*	ehs ist
...8:00 in the morning.	*...acht Uhr morgens.*	ahkht oor **mor**-gehns
...16:00.	*...sechzehn Uhr.*	**zehkh**-tsayn oor
...4:00 in the afternoon.	*...vier Uhr nachmittags.*	feer oor **nahkh**-mit-tahgs
...10:30 in the evening.	*...halb elf Uhr abends.* ("half-eleven")	hahlp ehlf oor **ah**-behnts

COUNTING

Key Phrases: Time

minute	*Minute*	mee-**noo**-teh
hour	*Stunde*	**shtoon**-deh
day	*Tag*	tahg
week	*Woche*	**vohkh**-eh
What time is it?	*Wie spät ist es?*	vee shpayt ist ehs
It's...	*Es ist...*	ehs ist
...8:00.	*...acht Uhr.*	ahkht oor
...16:00.	*...sechzehn Uhr.*	**zehkh**-tsayn oor
When does this open / close?	*Wann ist hier geöffnet / geschossen?*	vahn ist heer geh-**urf**-neht / geh-**shloh**-sehn

...a quarter past nine.	*...Viertel nach neun.*	**feer**-tehl nahkh noyn
...a quarter to eleven.	*...Viertel vor elf.*	**feer**-tehl for ehlf
...noon.	*...Mittag.*	**mit**-tahg
...midnight.	*...Mitternacht*	**mit**-ter-nahkht
...early / late.	*...früh / spät.*	frew / shpayt
...on time.	*...pünktlich.*	**pewnkt**-likh
...sunrise.	*...Sonnenaufgang.*	zoh-nehn-**owf**-gahng
...sunset.	*...Sonnenuntergang.*	zoh-nehn-**oon**-ter-gahng
It's my bedtime.	*Es ist meine Zeit fürs Bett.*	ehs ist **mī**-neh tsīt fewrs beht

Timely Expressions

I will / We will....	*Ich bin / Wir sind...*	ikh bin / veer zint
...be back at 11:20.	*...um elf Uhr zwanzig zurück.*	oom ehlf oor **tsvahn**-tsig tsoo-**rewk**
I will / We will...	*Ich bin / Wir sind...*	ikh bin / veer zint
...be there by 18:00.	*...um achtzehn Uhr dort.*	oom **ahkht**-tsayn oor dort
When is check-out time?	*Wann muß ich das Zimmer verlassen?*	vahn mus ikh dahs **tsim**-mer fehr-**lah**-sehn

When does this open / close?	*Wann ist hier geöffnet / geschossen*	vahn ist heer geh-**urf**-neht / geh-**shloh**-sehn
When...?	*Wann...?*	vahn
...does this train / bus leave for ___	*...geht der Zug / Bus nach ___*	gayt dehr tsoog / boos nahkh
...does the next train / bus leave for ___	*...geht der nächste Zug / Bus nach ___*	gayt dehr **nehkh**-steh tsoog / boos nahkh
...does the train / bus arrive in ___	*...kommt der Zug / Bus in ___ an*	kohmt dehr tsoog / boos in ___ ahn
I want / We want...	*Ich möchte / Wir möchten...*	ikh **merkh**-teh / veer **merkh**-tehn
...to take the 16:30 train.	*...den Zug um sechzehn Uhr dreißig nehmen.*	dehn tsoog oom **zehkh**-tsayn oor **drī**-sig **nay**-mehn
Is the train / bus...?	*Ist der Zug / Bus...?*	ist dehr tsoog / boos
...early / late	*...früh / spät*	frew / shpayt
...on time	*...pünktlich*	**pewnkt**-likh

In Germany, Austria, and Switzerland, the 24-hour clock (or military time) is used by hotels, for the opening and closing hours of museums, and for train, bus, and boat schedules. Informally, Europeans usually use the same 12-hour clock we use.

About Time

minute	*Minute*	mee-**noo**-teh
hour	*Stunde*	**shtoon**-deh
in the morning	*am Morgen*	ahm **mor**-gehn
in the afternoon	*am Nachmittag*	ahm **nahkh**-mit-tahg
in the evening	*am Abend*	ahm **ah**-behnt
at night	in der *Nacht*	in dehr nahkht
at 6:00 sharp	*Punkt sechs Uhr*	poonkt zehkhs oor
from 8:00 to 10:00	*von acht bis zehn*	fohn ahkht bis tsayn
in half an hour	*in einer halben Stunde*	in **ī**-ner **hahl**-behn **shtoon**-deh

in one hour	*in einer Stunde*	in ī-ner **shtoon**-deh
in three hours	*in drei Stunden*	in drī **shtoon**-dehn
anytime	*jederzeit*	yay-der-**tsīt**
immediately	*jetzt*	yehtst
every hour	*jede Stunde*	**yay**-deh **shtoon**-deh
every day	*jeden Tag*	**yay**-dehn tahg
daily	*täglich*	**tay**-glikh
last	*letzte*	**lehts**-teh
this	*diese*	**dee**-zeh
next	*nächste*	**nehkh**-steh
May 15	*fünfzehnten Mai*	**fewnf**-tsayn-tehn mī
high season	*Hochsaison*	**hohkh**-zay-zohn
low season	*Nebensaison*	**neh**-behn-zay-zohn
in the future	*in Zukunft*	in **tsoo**-koonft
in the past	*in der Vergangenheit*	in dehr fehr-**gahng**-ehn-hīt

The Day

day	*Tag*	tahg
today	*heute*	**hoy**-teh
yesterday	*gestern*	**geh**-stern
tomorrow	*morgen*	**mor**-gehn
tomorrow morning	*morgen früh*	**mor**-gehn frew
day after tomorrow	*übermorgen*	**ew**-ber-mor-gehn

The Week

week	*Woche*	**vohkh**-eh
last / this / next week	*letzte / diese / nächste Woche*	**lehts**-teh / **dee**-zeh / **nehkh**-steh **vohkh**-eh
Monday	*Montag*	**mohn**-tahg
Tuesday	*Dienstag*	**deen**-stahg
Wednesday	*Mittwoch*	**mit**-vohkh
Thursday	*Donnerstag*	**dohn**-ner-stahg
Friday	*Freitag*	**frī**-tahg
Saturday	*Samstag, Sonnabend*	**zahm**-stahg, **zohn**-ah-behnt
Sunday	*Sonntag*	**zohn**-tahg

The Month

month	*Monat*	**moh**-naht
January	*Januar*	**yah**-noo-ar
February	*Februar*	**fay**-broo-ar
March	*März*	mehrts
April	*April*	ah-**pril**
May	*Mai*	mī
June	*Juni*	**yoo**-nee
July	*Juli*	**yoo**-lee
August	*August*	ow-**goost**
September	*September*	zehp-**tehm**-ber
October	*Oktober*	ohk-**toh**-ber
November	*November*	noh-**vehm**-ber
December	*Dezember*	day-**tsehm**-ber

For dates, take any number, add the sound "-ten" to the end, then say the month. June 19 is ***neunzehnten Juni.***

The Year

year	*Jahr*	yar
spring	*Frühling*	**frew**-ling
summer	*Sommer*	**zohm**-mer
fall	*Herbst*	hehrpst
winter	*Winter*	**vin**-ter

Holidays and Happy Days

holiday	*Feiertag*	**fī**-er-tahg
national holiday	*staatlicher Feiertag*	**shtaht**-likh-er **fī**-er-tahg
school holiday	*Schulferien*	**shool**-fehr-ee-ehn
religious holiday	*religiöser Feiertag*	reh-lig-ee-**ur**-zer **fī**-er-tahg
Is today / tomorrow a holiday?	*Ist heute / morgen ein Feiertag?*	ist **hoy**-teh / **mor**-gehn īn **fī**-er-tahg
Is a holiday coming up soon?	*Ist bald ein Feiertag?*	ist bahlt īn **fī**-er-tahg

When?	*Wann?*	vahn
What is the holiday?	*Welcher Feiertag ist das?*	**vehlkh**-er **fī**-er-tahg ist dahs
Merry Christmas!	*Fröhliche Weihnachten!*	**frur**-likh-eh **vī**-nahkh-tehn
Happy New Year!	*Glückliches Neues Jahr!*	**glewk**-likh-ehs **noy**-ehs yar
Easter	*Ostern*	**ohs**-tern
Happy anniversary!	*Herzlichen Glückwunsch!*	**hehrts**-likh-ehn **glewk**-voonsh
Happy birthday!	*Herzlichen Glückwunsch zum Geburtstag!*	**hehrts**-likh-ehn **glewk**-voonsh tsoom geh-**boorts**-tahg

German-speakers sing "Happy Birthday" to the tune we use, sometimes even in English. The German version means "On your birthday, best wishes": ***Zum Geburtstag, viel Glück, Zum Geburtstag, viel Glück, Zum Geburtstag, liebe ___, Zum Geburtstag, viel Glück.***

Traditional Germanic celebrations include ***Karneval*** (a.k.a ***Fascnacht, Fasnet,*** or ***Fasching***), a week-long festival of parades and partying that happens before Lent in February, and the centers of revelry are Köln (Germany), Mainz (Germany), and Basel (Switzerland), though celebrations happen in cities and towns throughout southern Germany, western Austria, and northern Switzerland. ***Christi Himmelfahrt,*** or the Ascension of Christ, comes in May, and doubles for Father's Day. You'll see men in groups on pilgrimages through the countryside, usually carrying beer or heading toward it.

Germany's national holiday is October 3, Austria's is October 26, and Switzerland's is August 1.

TRAVELING

The German word for journey or trip is ***Fahrt.*** Many tourists enjoy nice, relaxing ***Fahrts.*** In German-speaking areas, you'll see signs for ***Einfahrt*** (entrance), ***Rundfahrt*** (round trip), ***Rückfahrt*** (return trip), ***Panoramafahrt*** (scenic journey), ***Zugfahrt*** (train trip), ***Ausfahrt*** (trip out), and throughout your trip, people will smile and wish you a ***"Gute Fahrt."***

TRAINS

The Train Station

Where is the...?	*Wo ist der...?*	voh ist dehr
...(central) train station	*...(Haupt-)Bahnhof*	(**howpt**-)**bahn**-hohf
German Railways	*Deutsche Bahn (DB)*	**doy**-cheh bahn (day bay)
Swiss Railways	*Schweizer Bundesbahn (SBB)*	**shvīt**-ser **boon**-dehs-bahn (ehs bay bay)
Austrian Railways	*Österreichische Bundesbahn (ÖBB)*	**urs**-ter-**rīkh**-is-sheh **boon**-dehs-bahn (ur bay bay)
train information	*Zugauskunft*	tsoog-**ows**-koonft
train	*Zug*	tsoog
high-speed train	*Intercity, Schnellzug*	"inter-city," **shnehl**-tsoog

highest-speed train	*ICE*	ee tsay ay
fast / faster	*schnell / schneller*	shnehl / **shnehl**-ler
arrival	*Ankunft*	**ahn**-koonft
departure	*Abfahrt*	**ahp**-fart
delay	*Verspätung*	fehr-**shpay**-toong
toilet	*Toilette*	toh-**leh**-teh
waiting room	*Wartesaal*	**var**-teh-zahl
lockers	*Schließfächer*	**shlees**-fehkh-er
baggage check room	*Gepäckaufgabe*	geh-**pehk**-owf-gah-beh
lost and found office	*Fundbüro*	**foond**-bew-roh
tourist information	*Touristen-information*	too-**ris**-tehn-in-for-maht-see-**ohn**
platform	*Bahnsteig*	**bahn**-shtīg
to the trains	*zu den Zugen*	tsoo dayn **tsoo**-gehn
track	*Gleis*	glīs
train car	*Wagen*	**vah**-gehn
dining car	*Speisewagen*	**shpī**-zeh-vah-gehn
sleeper car	*Liegewagen*	**lee**-geh-vah-gehn
conductor	*Schaffner*	**shahf**-ner

You'll encounter several types of trains in Germany. Along with the various local and milk-run trains, there are the:

- slow ***RB*** (***RegionalBahn***) and ***RE*** (***RegionalExpress***) trains,
- the medium-speed ***IR*** (***InterRegio***) and ***IRE*** (***InterRegioExpress***)trains,
- the fast ***IC*** (***InterCity***, domestic routes) and ***EC*** (***EuroCity***, international routes) trains, and
- the super-fast ***ICE*** trains (***InterCityExpress***).

Railpasses cover travel on all of these trains, and reservations are rarely required on daytime trains. Railpasses are not valid on the rare ***Metropolitan*** train between Köln and Hamburg.

Getting a Ticket

Where can I buy a ticket?	*Wo kann ich eine Fahrkarte kaufen?*	voh kahn ikh ī-neh **far**-kar-teh **kow**-fehn
A ticket to ___.	*Eine Fahrkarte nach ___.*	ī-neh **far**-kar-teh nahkh
Where can we buy tickets?	*Wo können wir Fahrkarten kaufen?*	voh **kurn**-nehn veer **far**-kar-tehn **kow**-fehn
Two tickets to ___.	*Zwei Fahrkarten nach ___.*	tsvī **far**-kar-tehn nahkh
Is this the line for...?	*Ist das die Schlange für...?*	ist dahs dee **shlahng**-eh fewr
...tickets	*...Fahrkarten*	**far**-kar-tehn
...reservations	*...Reservierungen*	reh-zer-**feer**-oong-ehn
How much is a ticket to ___?	*Wie viel kostet eine Fahrkarte nach ___?*	vee feel **kohs**-teht ī-neh **far**-kar-teh nahkh
Is this ticket valid for ___?	*Ist diese Fahrkarte gültig für ___?*	ist **dee**-zeh **far**-kar-teh **gewl**-tig fewr
How long is this ticket valid?	*Wie lange ist diese Fahrkarte gültig?*	vee **lahng**-eh ist **dee**-zeh **far**-kar-teh **gewl**-tig
When is the next train?	*Wann ist der nächste Zug?*	vahn ist dehr **nehkh**-steh tsoog
Do you have a schedule for all trains departing today / tomorrow for ___?	*Haben Sie einen Fahrplan für alle Züge heute / morgen nach ___?*	**hah**-behn zee ī-nehn **far**-plahn fewr **ahl**-leh **tsew**-geh **hoy**-teh / **mor**-gehn nahkh
I'd like to leave...	*Ich möchte... abfahren.*	ikh **murkh**-teh... **ahp**-fah-rehn
We'd like to leave...	*Wir möchten... abfahren.*	veer **murkh**-tehn... **ahp**-fah-rehn
I'd like to arrive...	*Ich möchte... ankommen.*	ikh **murkh**-teh... **ahn**-koh-mehn
We'd like to arrive...	*Wir möchten... ankommen.*	veer **murkh**-tehn... **ahn**-koh-mehn
...by ___	*...vor ___*	for
...in the morning.	*...am Morgen*	ahm **mor**-gehn

...in the afternoon.	*...am Nachmittag*	ahm **nahkh**-mit-tahg
...in the evening.	*...am Abend*	ahm **ah**-behnt
Is there a...?	*Gibt es einen...?*	gipt ehs **ī**-nehn
...later train	*...späterer Zug*	**shpay**-ter-er tsoog
...earlier train	*...früherer Zug*	**frew**-her-er tsoog
...overnight train	*...Nachtzug*	**nahkht**-tsoog
...cheaper train	*...billigere Zug*	**bil**-lig-er-eh tsoog
...cheaper option	*...billigere Möglichkeit*	**bil**-lig-er-eh **murg**-likh-kīt
...local train	*...Regionalzug*	reh-gee-oh-**nahl**-tsoog
...express train	*...Schnellzug*	**shnehl**-tsoog
What track does the train leave from?	*Von welches Gleis fährt er ab?*	fohn **vehlkh**-ehs glīs fayrt ehr ahp
On time?	*Pünktlich?*	**pewnkt**-likh
Late?	*Spät?*	shpayt

Reservations, Supplements, and Discounts

Is a reservation required?	*Brauche ich eine Platzkarte?*	**browkh**-eh ikh **ī**-neh **plahts**-kar-teh
I'd like to reserve...	*Ich möchte... reservieren.*	ikh **murkh**-teh... reh-zer-**vee**-rehn
...a seat.	*...einen Sitzplatz*	**ī**-nehn **zits**-plahts
...a berth.	*...einen Liegewagenplatz*	**ī**-nehn **lee**-geh-vah-gehn-plahts
...a sleeper.	*...einen Schlafwagenplatz*	**ī**-nehn **shlahf**-vah-gehn-plahts
...the entire train.	*...den ganzen Zug*	dayn **gahn**-tsehn tsoog
We'd like to reserve...	*Wir möchten... reservieren.*	veer **murkh**-tehn... reh-zer-**vee**-rehn
...two seats.	*...zwei Sitzplätze*	tsvī **zits**-pleht-seh
...two couchettes.	*...zwei Liegewagen-plätze*	tsvī **lee**-geh-vah-gehn-pleht-seh
...two sleepers.	*...zwei Schlafwagen-plätze*	tsvī **shlahf**-vah-gehn-pleht-seh
Is there a supplement?	*Kostet das einen Zuschlag?*	**kohs**-teht dahs **ī**-nehn **tsoo**-shlahg

Does my railpass cover the supplement?	*Ist der Zuschlag in meinem Railpass enthalten?*	ist dehr **tsoo**-shlahg in **mī**-nehm **rayl**-pahs ehnt-**hahl**-tehn
Is there a discount for...?	*Gibt es eine Ermäßigung für...?*	gipt ehs **ī**-neh ehr-**may**-see-goong fewr
...youths	*...Jugendliche*	**yoo**-gehnd-likh-eh
...seniors	*...Senioren*	zehn-**yor**-ehn
...families	*...Familien*	fah-**mee**-lee-ehn

Ticket Talk

ticket window	*Fahrscheine*	far-**shī**-neh
reservations window	*Reservierungen*	reh-zer-**feer**-oong-ehn
national / international	*Inland / Ausland*	**in**-lahnt / **ows**-lahnt
ticket	*Fahrkarte*	**far**-kar-teh
one-way ticket	*Hinfahrkarte*	**hin**-far-kar-teh
roundtrip ticket	*Rückfahrkarte*	**rewk**-far-kar-teh
first class	*erste Klasse*	**ehr**-steh **klah**-seh
second class	*zweite Klasse*	**tsvī**-teh **klah**-seh
non-smoking	*Nichtraucher*	**nikht**-rowkh-er
validate	*abstempeln*	**ahp**-shtehm-pehln
schedule	*Fahrplan*	**far**-plahn
departure	*Abfahrtszeit*	**ahp**-farts-tsīt
direct	*Direkt*	dee-**rehkt**
transfer (verb)	*umsteigen*	**oom**-shtī-gehn
connection	*Anschluß*	**ahn**-shloos
with supplement	*mit Zuschlag*	mit **tsoo**-shlahg
reservation	*Platzkarte*	**plahts**-kar-teh
seat	*Platz*	plahts
window seat	*Fensterplatz*	**fehn**-ster-plahts
aisle seat	*Platz am Gang*	plahts ahm gahng
berth...	*Liege...*	**lee**-geh
...upper	*...obere*	**oh**-ber-eh
...middle	*...mittlere*	**mit**-leh-reh
...lower	*...untere*	**oon**-ter-eh
refund	*Rückvergütung*	**rewk**-fehr-gew-toong
reduced fare	*verbilligte Karte*	fehr-**bil**-lig-teh **kar**-teh

Key Phrases: Trains

(central) train station	*(Haupt-) Bahnhof*	(**howpt**-) **bahn**-hohf
train	*Zug*	tsoog
ticket	*Fahrkarte*	**far**-kar-teh
transfer (verb)	*umsteigen*	**oom**-shtī-gehn
supplement	*Zuschlag*	**tsoo**-shlahg
arrival	*Ankunft*	**ahn**-koonft
departure	*Abfahrt*	**ahp**-fart
platform	*Bahnsteig*	**bahn**-shtīg
track	*Gleis*	glīs
train car	*Wagen*	**vah**-gehn
A ticket to ___.	*Eine Fahrkarte nach ___.*	ī-neh **far**-kar-teh nahkh
Two tickets to ___.	*Zwei Fahrkarten nach ___.*	tsvī **far**-kar-tehn nahkh
When is the next train?	*Wann ist der nächste Zug?*	vahn ist dehr **nehkh**-steh tsoog
Where does the train leave from?	*Von wo fährt der Zug ab?*	fohn voh fayrt dehr tsoog ahp
Which train to ___?	*Welcher Zug nach ___?*	**vehlkh**-er tsoog nahkh

TRAVELING

Changing Trains

Is it direct?	*Direktverbindung?*	dee-**rehkt**-fehr-bin-doong
Must I transfer?	*Muß ich umsteigen?*	mus ikh **oom**-shtī-gehn
Must we transfer?	*Müssen wir umsteigen?*	**mew**-sehn veer **oom**-shtī-gehn
When? / Where?	*Wann? / Wo?*	vahn / voh
Do I / Do we change here for ___?	*Muß ich / Müssen wir hier umsteigen nach ___?*	mus ikh / **mew**-sehn veer heer **oom**-shtī-gehn nahkh

Where do I / do we change for ___?	*Wo muß ich / müssen wir umsteigen für ___?*	voh mus ikh / **mew**-sehn veer **oom**-shtī-gehn fewr
At what time?	*Um wie viel Uhr?*	oom vee feel oor
From what track does my / our connecting train leave ?	*Auf welchem Gleis fährt mein / unser Verbindungszug?*	owf **wehlkh**-ehm glīs fayrt mīn / **oon**-ser fehr-**bin**-doongs-tsoog
How many minutes in ___ to change trains?	*Wie viele Minuten zum Umsteigen in ___?*	vee **fee**-leh mee-**noo**-tehn tsoom **oom**-shtī-gehn in

On the Platform

Where is...?	*Wo ist...?*	voh ist
Is this...?	*Ist das...?*	ist dahs
...the train to ___	*...der Zug nach ___*	dehr tsoog nahkh
Which train to ___?	*Welcher Zug nach ___?*	**vehlkh**-er tsoog nahkh
Which train car to ___?	*Welcher Wagen nach ___?*	**vehlkh**-er **vah**-gehn nahkh
Where is first class?	*Wo ist die erste Klasse?*	voh ist dee **ehr**-steh **klah**-seh
...front / middle / back	*...vorne / mitte / hinten*	**for**-neh / **mit**-teh / **hin**-tehn
Where can I validate my ticket?	*Wo kann ich meine Fahrkarte abstempeln?*	voh kahn̲ ikh **mī**-neh **far**-kar-teh **ahp**-shtehm-pehln

At the platform, you'll often see a sign that says ***Etwa 10 Min. später.*** This means that the train is running about (***etwa***) 10 minutes later (***später***) than expected.

On the Train

Is this seat free?	*Ist dieser Platz frei?*	ist **dee**-zer plahts frī
May I / May we...?	*Darf ich / Dürfen wir...?*	darf ikh / **dewr**-fehn veer
...sit here	*...hier sitzen*	heer **zit**-sehn

TRAVELING

Major Transportation Lines in Germany, Austria, and Switzerland

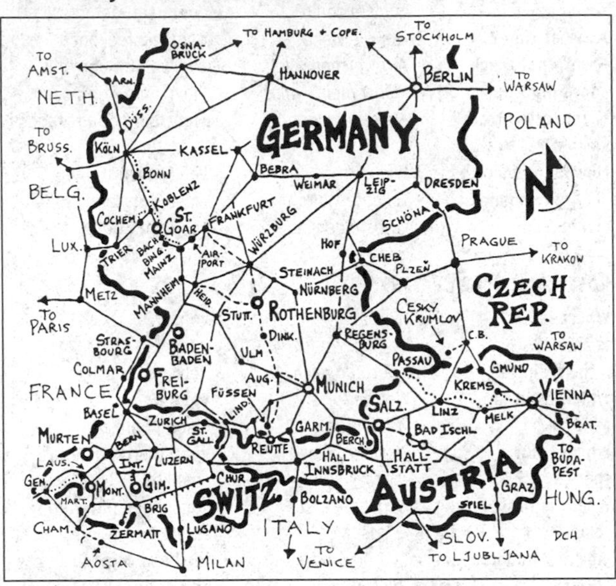

...open the window	*...das Fenster öffnen*	dahs **fehn**-ster **urf**-nehn
...eat your meal	*...Ihre Mahlzeit essen*	**eer**-eh **mahl**-tsīt **ehs**-sehn
Save my place?	*Halten Sie meinen Platz frei?*	**hahl**-tehn zee **mī**-nehn plahts frī
Save our places?	*Halten Sie unsere Plätze frei?*	**hahl**-tehn zee **oon**-zer-eh **pleht**-seh frī
That's my seat.	*Das ist mein Platz.*	dahs ist mīn plahts
These are our seats.	*Das sind unsere Plätze.*	dahs zint **oon**-zer-eh **pleht**-seh
Where are you going?	*Wohin fahren Sie?*	voh-hin **far**-ehn zee
I'm going to ___.	*Ich fahre nach ___.*	ikh **far**-eh nahkh

We're going to ___.	*Wir fahren nach ___.*	veer **far**-ehn nahkh
Can you tell me / us when to get off?	*Können Sie mir / uns Bescheid sagen?*	**kurn**-nehn zee meer / oons beh-**shīt** zah-gehn
Where is a (good-looking) conductor?	*Wo ist ein (hübscher) Schaffner?*	voh ist īn (**hewb**-sher) **shahf**-ner
Does this train stop in ___?	*Hält dieser Zug in ___?*	hehlt **dee**-zer tsoog in
When will it arrive in ___?	*Wann kommt er in ___ an?*	vahn kohmt ehr in ___ ahn
When will it arrive?	*Wann kommt er an?*	vahn kohmt ehr ahn

As you approach a station on the train, you will hear an announcement such as: ***In wenigen Minuten erreichen wir in München*** (In a few minutes, we will arrive in Munich).

Reading Train and Bus Schedules

European schedules use the 24-hour clock. It's like American time until noon. After that, subtract twelve and add P.M. So 13:00 is 1 P.M., 20:00 is 8 P.M., and 24:00 is midnight. One minute after midnight is 00:01.

Abfahrt	departure
Ankunft	arrival
auch	also
außer	except
bis	until
Feiertag	holiday
Gleis	track
jeden	every
nach	to
nicht	not
nur	only
Richtung	direction
Samstag	Saturday
Sonntag	Sunday

täglich (tgl.)	daily
tagsüber	days
über	via
verspätet	late
von	from
Werktags	Monday-Saturday (workdays)
Wochentags	weekdays
Zeit	time
Ziel	destination
1-5, 6, 7	Monday-Friday, Saturday, Sunday

Going Places

Germany	*Deutschland*	**doych**-lahn̲d
Munich	*München*	**mewnkh**-ehn
Bavaria	*Bayern*	**bī**-ehrn
Black Forest	*Schwarzwald*	**shvahrts**-vahlt
Danube	*Donau*	**doh**-now
Austria	*Österreich*	**urs**-ter-rīkh
Vienna	*Wien*	veen
Switzerland	*Schweiz*	shvītz
Belgium	*Belgien*	**behl**-gee-ehn
Czech Republic	*Tschechien*	**shehkh**-ee-ehn
Prague	*Prag*	prahk
Denmark	*Dänemark*	**deh**-neh-mark
France	*Frankreich*	**frahnk**-rīkh
Great Britain	*Großbritannien*	grohs-brit-**ahn**-ee-ehn
Greece	*Griechenland*	**greekh**-ehn-lahn̲d
Ireland	*Irland*	**ihr**-lahn̲d
Italy	*Italien*	i-**tah**-lee-ehn
Venice	*Venedig*	veh-**neh**-dig
Netherlands	*Niederlande*	**nee**-der-lahn̲-deh
Norway	*Norwegan*	**nor**-vay-gehn
Portugal	*Portugal*	**pohr**-too-gahl
Scandinavia	*Skandinavien*	shkahn̲-dee-**nah**-vee-ehn
Spain	*Spanien*	**shpahn**-ee-ehn
Sweden	*Schweden*	**shvay**-dehn
Turkey	*Türkei*	tewr-**kī**

Europe	*Europa*	oy-**roh**-pah
EU (European Union)	*EU*	ay oo
Russia	*Rußland*	**roos**-lahnd
Africa	*Afrika*	**ah**-free-kah
United States	*USA* (Vereinigten Staaten)	oo ehs ah (fehr-**ī**-nig-tehn **shtah**-tehn)
Canada	*Kanada*	**kah**-nah-dah
world	*Welt*	vehlt

Local Places

Here are a few more place names:

Bacharach (Ger.)	**bahkh**-ah-rahkh
Jungfrau (Switz.)	**yoong**-frow
Kleine Scheidegg (Switz.)	**klī**-neh **shī**-dehg
Köln (Ger.)	kurln
Mosel (Ger.)	**moh**-zehl
Neuschwanstein (Ger.)	noysh-**vahn**-shtīn
Reutte (Aus.)	**roy**-teh
Rothenburg (Ger.)	**roh**-tehn-boorg

BUSES AND SUBWAYS

At the Bus or Subway Station

ticket	*Fahrkarte*	**far**-kar-teh
day ticket	*Tageskarte*	**tahg**-ehs-kar-teh
short-ride ticket	*Kurzstrecke*	**koorts**-streh-keh
city bus	*Linienbus*	**lee**-nee-ehn-boos
regional / long-distance bus	*Regionalbus / Fernbus*	reh-gee-ohn-**ahl**-boos / **fayrn**-boos
bus stop	*Bushaltestelle*	**boos**-hahl-teh-**shtehl**-leh
bus station	*Busbahnhof*	**boos**-bahn-hohf
subway	*U-Bahn*	**oo**-bahn
subway station	*U-Bahn-Station*	**oo**-bahn-stah-tsee-ohn

subway map	*U-Bahn-Streckenplan*	**oo**-bahn-**shtrehk**-ehn-plahn
subway entrance	*U-Bahn-Eingang*	**oo**-bahn-**īn**-gahng
subway stop	*U-Bahn-Haltestelle*	**oo**-bahn-**hahl**-teh-shtehl-leh
subway exit	*U-Bahn-Ausgang*	**oo**-bahn-**ows**-gahng
direct	*Direkt*	dee-**rehkt**
direction	*Richtung*	**rikh**-toong
connection	*Anschluß*	**ahn**-shlus
pickpocket	*Taschendieb*	**tahsh**-ehn-deep

Most big cities offer deals on transportation, such as one-day tickets, cheaper fares for youths and seniors, or a discount for buying a batch of tickets (which you can share with friends). If you're taking a short trip (usually four stops or fewer), buy a discounted ***Kurzstrecke*** ("short stretch" ticket). Major cities in Germany, such as Munich and Berlin, have an ***U-Bahn*** (subway) and an ***S-Bahn*** (urban rail system). If your Eurailpass is valid on the day you're traveling, you can use the ***S-Bahn*** for free. On a map, ***Standort*** means "You are here."

Taking Buses and Subways

How do I get to ___?	*Wie komme ich zu ___?*	vee **koh**-meh ikh tsoo
How do we get to ___?	*Wie kommen wir zu ___?*	vee **koh**-mehn veer tsoo
How much is a ticket?	*Wie viel kostet eine Fahrkarte?*	vee feel **kohs**-teht ī-neh **far**-kar-teh
Where can I buy a ticket?	*Wo kaufe ich eine Fahrkarte?*	voh **kow**-feh ikh ī-neh **far**-kar-teh
Where can we buy tickets?	*Wo kaufen wir Fahrkarten?*	voh **kow**-fehn veer **far**-kar-tehn
One ticket, please.	*Eine Fahrkarte, bitte.*	ī-neh **far**-kar-teh **bit**-teh
Two tickets.	*Zwei Fahrkarten.*	tsv**ī** **far**-kar-tehn
Is this ticket valid (for ___)?	*Ist diese Fahrkarte gültig (für ___)?*	ist **dee**-zeh **far**-kar-teh **gewl**-tig (fewr ___)

Key Phrases: Buses and Subways

bus	*Bus*	boos
subway	*U-Bahn*	**oo**-bahn
ticket	*Fahrkarte*	**far**-kar-teh
How do I get to ___?	*Wie komme ich zu ___?*	vee **koh**-meh ikh tsoo
How do we get to ___?	*Wie kommen wir zu ___?*	vee **koh**-mehn veer tsoo
Which stop for ___?	*Welche Haltestelle für ___?*	**vehlkh**-eh **hahl**-teh-shtehl-leh fewr
Can you tell me / us when to get off?	*Können Sie mir / uns Bescheid sagen?*	**kurn**-nehn zee meer / oons beh-**shīt** zah-gehn

Is there a...?	*Gibt es eine...?*	gipt ehs **ī**-neh
...one-day pass	*...Tageskarte*	**tahg**-ehs-kar-teh
...discount if I buy more tickets	*...Preisnachlaß, wenn ich mehrere Fahrkarten kaufe*	prīs-**nahkh**-lahs vehn ikh **meh**-reh-reh **far**-kar-tehn **kow**-feh
Which bus to ___?	*Welcher Bus nach ___?*	**vehlkh**-er boos nahkh
Does it stop at ___?	*Hält er in ___?*	hehlt ehr in
Which bus stop for ___?	*Welche Haltestelle für ___?*	**vehlkh**-eh **hahl**-teh-shtehl-leh fewr
Which metro stop for ___?	*Welcher Halt für ___?*	**vehlkh**-er hahlt fewr
Which direction for ___?	*Welche Richtung nach ___?*	**vehlkh**-eh **rikh**-toong nahkh
Must I transfer?	*Muß ich umsteigen?*	mus ikh **oom**-shtī-gehn
Must we transfer?	*Müssen wir umsteigen?*	**mew**-sehn veer **oom**-shtī-gehn
When is the...?	*Wann fährt der... ab?*	vahn fayrt dehr... ahp

...first / next / last	*...erste / nächste / letzte*	**ehr**-steh / **nehkh**-steh / **lehts**-teh
...bus / subway	*...Bus / U-Bahn*	boos / **oo**-bahn
What's the frequency per hour / day?	*Wie oft pro Stunde / Tag?*	vee ohft pro **shtoon**-deh / tahg
Where does it leave from?	*Von wo fährt er ab?*	fohn voh fayrt ehr ahp
What time does it leave?	*Um wie viel Uhr fährt er ab?*	oom vee feel oor fayrt ehr ahp
I'm going to ___.	*Ich fahre nach ___.*	ikh **far**-eh nahkh
We're going to ___.	*Wir fahren nach ___.*	veer **far**-ehn nahkh
Can you tell me / us when to get off?	*Können Sie mir / uns Bescheid sagen?*	**kurn**-nehn zee meer / oons beh-**shīt** zah-gehn

TAXIS

Getting a Taxi

Taxi!	*Taxi!*	**tahk**-see
Can you call a taxi?	*Können Sie mir ein Taxi rufen?*	**kurn**-nehn zee meer īn **tahk**-see **roo**-fehn
Where can I get a taxi?	*Wo finde ich ein Taxi?*	voh fin-deh ikh īn **tahk**-see
Where can we get a taxi?	*Wo finden wir ein Taxi?*	voh fin-dehn veer īn **tahk**-see
Where is a taxi stand?	*Wo ist ein Taxistand?*	voh ist īn **tahk**-see-sht**ahn**t
Are you free?	*Sind Sie frei?*	zint zee frī
Occupied.	*Besetzt.*	beh-**zehtst**
To ___, please.	*Zu ___, bitte.*	tsoo ___ **bit**-teh
To this address.	*Zu dieser Adresse.*	tsoo **dee**-zer ah-**dreh**-seh
Take me / us to ___.	*Bringen Sie mich / uns zu ___.*	**bring**-ehn zee mikh / oons tsoo
Approximately how much will it cost for a trip...?	*Wie viel ungefähr kostet die Fahrt...?*	vee feel **oon**-geh-fehr **kohs**-teht dee fart

Key Phrases: Taxis

Taxi!	*Taxi!*	**tahk**-see
Are you free?	*Sind Sie frei?*	zint zee frī
To __, please.	*Zu __, bitte.*	tsoo __ **bit**-teh
meter	*Zähler*	**tsay**-ler
Stop here.	*Halten Sie hier.*	**hahl**-tehn zee heer
Keep the change.	*Stimmt so.*	shtimt zoh

...to __	*...zu __*	tsoo
...to the airport	*...zum Flughafen*	tsoom **floog**-hah-fehn
...to the train station	*...zum Bahnhof*	tsoom **bahn**-hohf
...to this address	*...zu dieser Adresse*	tsoo **dee**-zer ah-**dreh**-seh
No extra supplements?	*Keine Zuschläge?*	**kī**-neh **tsoo**-shleh-geh
Too much.	*Zu viel.*	tsoo feel
Can you take __ people?	*Können Sie __ Personen mitnehmen?*	**kurn**-nehn zee __ pehr-**zoh**-nehn **mit**-nay-mehn
Any extra fee?	*Extra Gebühren?*	**ex**-trah geh-**bew**-rehn
Do you have an hourly rate?	*Haben Sie einen Stundenansatz?*	**hah**-behn zee **ī**-nehn **shtoon**-dehn-**ahn**-zahts
How much for a one-hour city tour?	*Wie viel für eine Stunde Stadtbesichtigung?*	vee feel fewr **ī**-neh **shtoon**-deh **shtaht**-beh-**sikh**-ti-goong

Ride in style in a German taxi—usually a BMW or Mercedes. If you're having a tough time hailing a taxi, ask for the nearest taxi stand (***Taxistand***). The simplest way to tell a cabbie where you want to go is by stating your destination followed by "please" ("***Hofbräuhaus, bitte***"). Tipping isn't expected, but it's polite to round up. So if the fare is €19, round to €20.

In the Taxi

The meter, please.	*Den Zähler, bitte.*	dayn **tsay**-ler **bit**-teh
Where is the meter?	*Wo ist der Zähler?*	voh ist dehr **tsay**-ler
I'm in a hurry.	*Ich bin in Eile.*	ikh bin in **ī**-leh
We're in a hurry.	*Wir sind in Eile.*	veer zint in **ī**-leh
Slow down.	*Fahren Sie langsamer.*	**fahr**-ehn zee **lahng**-zah-mer
If you don't slow down, I'll throw up.	*Wenn Sie nicht langsamer fahren, muß ich kotzen.*	vehn zee nikht **lahng**-zah-mer **far**-ehn mus ikh **koht**-sehn
Left / Right / Straight.	*Links / Rechts / Geradeaus.*	links / rehkhts / geh-rah-deh-**ows**
I'd like / We'd like to stop here briefly.	*Ich möchte / Wir möchten hier kurz anhalten.*	ikh **murkh**-teh / veer **murkh**-tehn heer koorts **ahn**-hahl-tehn
Please stop here for ___ minutes.	*Bitte halten Sie hier für ___ Minuten.*	**bit**-teh **hahl**-tehn zee heer fewr ___ mee-**noo**-tehn
Can you wait?	*Können Sie warten?*	**kurn**-nehn zee **var**-tehn
Crazy traffic, isn't it?	*Verrückter Verkehr, nicht wahr?*	fehr-**rewk**-ter fehr-**kehr** nikht var
You drive like...	*Sie fahren wie...*	zee **far**-ehn vee
...a madman!	*...ein Verrückter!*	īn fehr-**rewk**-ter
...Michael Schumacher.	*...Michael Schumacher.*	mee-kay-ehl "Schumacher"
You drive very well.	*Sie fahren sehr gut.*	zee **far**-ehn zehr goot
Where did you learn to drive?	*Wo haben Sie Auto fahren gelernt?*	voh **hah**-behn zee **ow**-toh **far**-ehn geh-**lehrnt**
Stop here.	*Halten Sie hier.*	**hahl**-tehn zee heer
Here is fine.	*Hier ist gut.*	heer ist goot
At this corner.	*An dieser Ecke.*	ahn̲ **dee**-zer **ehk**-eh
The next corner.	*An der nächsten Ecke.*	ahn̲ dehr **nehkh**-stehn **ehk**-eh
My change, please.	*Mein Wechselgeld, bitte.*	mīn **vehkh**-sehl-gehlt **bit**-teh
Keep the change.	*Stimmt so.*	shtimt zoh

This ride is / was more fun than Disneyland.	*Diese Fahrt ist / war lustiger als Disneyland.*	**dee**-zer fart ist / var **loos**-ti-ger ahls "Disneyland"

DRIVING

Rental Wheels

car rental agency	*Autovermietung*	**ow**-toh-fehr-**mee**-toong
I'd like to rent a...	*Ich möchte ein... mieten.*	ikh **murkh**-teh īn... **mee**-tehn
We'd like to rent a...	*Wir möchten ein... mieten.*	veer **murkh**-tehn īn... **mee**-tehn
...car.	*...Auto*	**ow**-toh
...station wagon.	*...Kombi*	**kohm**-bee
...van.	*...Kleinbus*	**klīn**-boos
...motorcycle.	*...Motorrad*	**moh**-tor-raht
...motor scooter.	*...Motorroller*	**moh**-tor-roh-ler
...tank.	*...Panzer*	**pahn**-tser
How much per...?	*Wie viel pro...?*	vee feel proh
...hour	*...Stunde*	**shtoon**-deh
...half day	*...halben Tag*	**hahl**-behn tahg

Key Phrases: Driving

car	*Auto*	**ow**-toh
gas station	*Tankstelle*	**tahnk**-shtehl-leh
parking lot	*Parkplatz*	**park**-plahts
accident	*Unfall*	**oon**-fahl
left / right	*links / rechts*	links / rehkhts
straight ahead	*geradeaus*	geh-rah-deh-**ows**
downtown	*Zentrum*	**tsehn**-troom
How do I get to ___?	*Wie komme ich nach ___?*	vee **koh**-meh ikh nahkh
Where can I park?	*Wo kann ich parken?*	voh kahn ikh **par**-ken

...day	*...Tag*	tahg
...week	*...Woche*	**vohkh**-eh
Unlimited mileage?	*Unbegrenzte Kilometer?*	oon-beh-**grents**-teh kee-loh-**may**-ter
When must I bring it back?	*Wann muß ich es zurückbringen?*	vahn mus ikh ehs tsoo-**rewk**-bring-ehn
Is there a...?	*Gibt es eine...?*	gipt ehs **ī**-neh
...helmet	*...Helm*	hehlm
...discount	*...Ermäßigung*	ehr-**may**-see-goong
...deposit	*...Kaution*	kowt-see-**ohn**
...insurance	*...Versicherung*	fehr-**zikh**-er-oong

Parking

parking lot	*Parkplatz*	**park**-plahts
parking garage	*Garage*	gah-**rah**-zheh
parking meter	*Parkuhr*	**park**-oor
parking clock (to put on dashboard)	*Parkscheibe*	**park**-shī-beh
Where can I park?	*Wo kann ich parken?*	voh kahn ikh **par**-kehn
Is parking nearby?	*Gibt es Parkplätze in der Nähe?*	gipt ehs **park**-pleht-seh in dehr **nay**-heh
Can I park here?	*Darf ich hier parken?*	darf ikh heer **par**-kehn
Is this a safe place to park?	*Ist dies ein sicherer Parkplatz?*	ist deez īn **zikh**-her-er **park**-plahts
How long can I park here?	*Wie lange darf ich hier parken?*	vee **lahng**-eh darf ikh heer **par**-kehn
Must I pay to park here?	*Kostet Parken hier etwas?*	**kohs**-teht **par**-kehn heer **eht**-vahs
How much per hour / day?	*Wie viel pro Stunde / Tag?*	vee feel proh **shtoon**-deh / tahg

Free but time-limited parking spaces use the "cardboard clock" (***Parkscheibe***), usually found in your rental car. Put the clock on your dashboard with your arrival time so parking attendants can see you've been there less than the posted maximum stay. At metered spaces, you'll pre-pay for the length of your stay. Find the meter (usually about one or two per block), pay for the time you need, then put the ticket (***Parkschein***) on your dashboard. If you're not sure what to do, check the dashboards of the cars around you.

FINDING YOUR WAY

I'm going on foot to ___.	*Ich gehe nach ___.*	ikh **gay**-heh nahkh
We're going on foot to ___.	*Wir gehen nach ___.*	veer **gay**-hehn nahkh
I'm going to ___. (by car)	*Ich fahre nach ___.*	ikh **fah**-reh nahkh
We're going to ___. (by car)	*Wir fahren nach ___.*	veer **fah**-rehn nahkh
How do I get to ___?	*Wie komme ich nach ___?*	vee **koh**-meh ikh nahkh ___
How do we get to ___?	*Wie kommen wir nach ___?*	vee **koh**-mehn veer nahkh ___
Do you have a...?	*Haben Sie eine...?*	**hah**-behn zee **ī**-neh
...city map	*...Stadtplan*	**shtaht**-plahn
...road map	*...Straßenkarte*	**shtrah**-sehn-kar-teh
How many minutes / hours...?	*Wie viele Minuten / Stunden...?*	vee **fee**-leh mee-**noo**-tehn / **shtoon**-dehn
...on foot	*...zu Fuß*	tsoo foos
...by bicycle	*...mit dem Rad*	mit daym raht
...by car	*...mit dem Auto*	mit daym **ow**-toh
How many kilometers to ___?	*Wie viele Kilometer sind es nach ___?*	vee **fee**-leh kee-loh-**may**-ter zint ehs nahkh
What's the... route to Berlin?	*Was ist der... Weg nach Berlin?*	vahs ist dehr... vehg nahkh behr-**leen**
...most scenic	*...schönste*	**shurn**-steh
...fastest	*...schnellste*	**shnehl**-steh
...most interesting	*...interessanteste*	in-ter-ehs-**sahn**-tehs-teh
Point it out?	*Zeigen Sie es mir?*	**tsī**-gehn zee ehs meer

I'm lost.	*Ich habe mich verlaufen.*	ikh **hah**-beh mikh fehr-**lowf**-ehn
We're lost.	*Wir haben uns verlaufen.*	veer **hah**-behn oons fehr-**lowf**-ehn
Where am I?	*Wo bin ich?*	voh bin ikh
Where is...?	*Wo ist...?*	voh ist
The nearest...?	*Der nächste...?*	dehr **nehkh**-steh
Where is this address?	*Wo ist diese Adresse?*	voh ist **dee**-zeh ah-**drehs**-seh

Route-Finding Words

city map	*Stadtplan*	**shtaht**-plahn
road map	*Straßenkarte*	**shtrah**-sehn-kar-teh
downtown	*Zentrum, Stadtzentrum*	**tsehn**-troom, **shtaht**-tsehn-troom
straight ahead	*geradeaus*	geh-rah-deh-**ows**
left	*links*	links
right	*rechts*	rehkhts
first	*erste*	**ehr**-steh
next	*nächste*	**nehkh**-steh
intersection	*Kreuzung*	**kroy**-tsoong
corner	*Ecke*	**ehk**-eh
block	*Häuserblock*	**hoy**-zer-blohk
roundabout	*Kreisel*	**krī**-zehl
ring road	*Ringstraße*	**ring**-shtrah-seh
stoplight	*Ampel*	**ahm**-pehl
(main) square	*(Markt-)platz*	(**markt**-)plahts
street	*Straße*	**shtrah**-seh
bridge	*Brücke*	**brew**-keh
tunnel	*Tunnel*	**too**-nehl
highway	*Landstraße*	**lahnd**-shtrah-seh
national highway	*Fernstraße*	**fayrn**-shtrah-seh
freeway	*Autobahn*	**ow**-toh-bahn
north	*Nord*	nord
south	*Süd*	zewd
east	*Ost*	ohst
west	*West*	vehst

The shortest distance between two points is the ***Autobahn.*** The right to no speed limit is as close to the average German driver's heart as the right to bear arms is to many American hearts. To survive, never cruise in the passing lane. While all roads seem to lead to the little town of ***Ausfahrt,*** that is the German word for exit. The ***Autobahn*** information magazine, available at any ***Autobahn Tankstelle*** (gas station), lists all road signs, interchanges, and the hours and facilities of various rest stops. Missing a turnoff can cost you lots of time and miles—be alert for ***Autobahn Kreuz*** (interchange) signs.

The Police

As in any country, the flashing lights of a patrol car are a sure sign that someone's in trouble. If it's you, try this handy phrase: "***Entschuldigung, ich bin Tourist***" (Sorry, I'm a tourist). Or, for the adventurous: "***Wenn es Ihnen nicht gefällt, wie ich Auto fahre, gehen Sie doch vom Gehweg runter.***" (If you don't like how I drive, stay off the sidewalk.)

I'm late for my tour.	*Ich bin zu spät für meine Gruppenreise.*	ikh bin tsoo shpayt fewr **mī**-neh **groop**-ehn-**rī**-zeh
Can I buy your hat?	*Kann ich Ihren Hut kaufen?*	kahn ikh **eer**-ehn hoot **kowf**-ehn
What seems to be the problem?	*Was ist los?*	vas ist lohs
Sorry, I'm a tourist.	*Entschuldigung, ich bin Tourist.*	ehnt-**shool**-dig-oong ikh bin **too**-rist

Reading Road Signs

Alle Richtungen	Out of town (all destinations)
Ausfahrt	Exit
Autobahn Kreuz	Freeway interchange
Baustelle	Construction
Dreieck ("three-corner")	fork
Einbahnstraße	One-way street
Einfahrt	Entrance

TRAVELING

Fußgänger	Pedestrians
Gebühr	Toll
Langsam	Slow down
Nächste Ausfart	Next exit
Parken verboten	No parking
Stadtmitte	To the center of town
Stopp	Stop
Straßenarbeiten	Road workers ahead
Umleitung	Detour
Vorfahrt beachten	Yield
Zentrum	To the center of town

You'll find more common road signs in the graphic on page 512 in the appendix.

Other Signs You May See

Belegt	No vacancy
Besetzt	Occupied
Bissiger Hund	Mean dog
Damen	Ladies
Drücken / Ziehen	Push / Pull
Einfahrt freihalten	Keep entrance clear
Eintritt frei	Free admission
Fahrrad	Bicycle
Gefahr	Danger
Geöffnet von ___ bis ___	Open from ___ to ___
Geöffnet	Open
Geschlossen	Closed
Herren	Men
Kein Eingang, Keine Einfahrt	No entry
Kein Trinkwasser	Undrinkable water
Keine Werbung	No soliciting
Lebensgefährlich	Extremely dangerous
Nicht rauchen	No smoking
Notausgang	Emergency exit
Ruhetag ("quiet day")	Closed

Stammtisch	Reserved table for regulars
Toiletten	Toilets
Verboten	Forbidden
Vorsicht	Caution
WC	Toilet
Wegen Umbau geschlossen	Closed for restoration
Wegen Ferien geschlossen	Closed for vacation
Ziehen / Drücken	Pull / Push
Zimmer frei	Rooms available
Zu verkaufen	For sale
Zu vermieten	For rent or for hire
Zugang verboten	Keep out

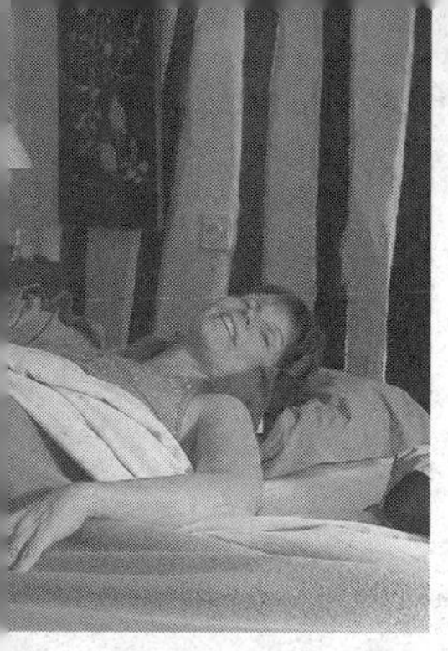

SLEEPING

Places to Stay

hotel	*Hotel*	hoh-**tehl**
small hotel	*Pension*	pehn-see-**ohn**
country inn	*Gasthaus, Gasthof*	**gahst**-hows, **gahst**-hohf
family-run place	*Familienbetrieb*	fah-**mee**-lee-ehn-beh-treeb
room in a home, bed & breakfast	*Gästezimmer, Fremdenzimmer*	**gehs**-teh-tsim-mer, **frehm**-dehn-tsim-mer
youth hostel	*Jugendherberge*	**yoo**-gehnd-hehr-behr-geh
vacancy	*Zimmer frei*	**tsim**-mer frī
no vacancy	*belegt*	beh-**lehgt**

The word ***garni*** in a hotel name means "without restaurant."

Reserving a Room

I like to reserve rooms a few days in advance as I travel. But if my itinerary is set, I reserve before I leave home. To reserve from home by fax or email, use the handy form in the appendix (online at www.ricksteves.com/reservation).

Hello.	*Guten Tag.*	**goo**-tehn tahg
Do you speak English?	*Sprechen Sie Englisch?*	**shprehkh**-ehn zee **ehng**-lish
Do you have a room for...?	*Haben Sie ein Zimmer für...?*	**hah**-behn zee īn **tsim**-mer fewr
...one person	*...eine Person*	ī-neh pehr-**zohn**

Key Phrases: Sleeping

I want to make / confirm a reservation.	*Ich möchte eine Reservierung machen / bestätigen.*	ikh **murkh**-teh **ī**-neh reh-zer-**feer**-oong **mahkh**-ehn / beh-**shtay**-teh-gehn
I'd like a room (for two people), please.	*Ich möchte ein Zimmer (für zwei Personen), bitte.*	ikh **murkh**-teh īn **tsim**-mer (fewr tsvī pehr-**zoh**-nehn) **bit**-teh
...with/without/and	*...mit / ohne / und*	mit / **oh**-neh / oont
...toilet	*...Toilette*	toh-**leh**-teh
...shower	*...Dusche*	**doo**-sheh
Can I see the room?	*Kann ich das Zimmer sehen?*	kahn̲ ikh dahs **tsim**-mer **zay**-hehn
How much is it?	*Wie viel kostet das?*	vee feel **kohs**-teht dahs
Credit card O.K.?	*Kreditkarte O.K.?*	kreh-**deet**-kar-teh "O.K."

...two people	*...zwei Personen*	tsvī pehr-**zoh**-nehn
...tonight	*...heute Abend*	**hoy**-teh **ah**-behnt
...two nights	*...zwei Nächte*	tsvī **naykh**-teh
...Friday	*...Freitag*	**frī**-tahg
...June 21	*...einundzwanzigsten Juni*	**īn**-oont-tsvahn̲-tsig-stehn **yoo**-nee
Yes or no?	*Ja oder nein?*	yah **oh**-der nīn
I'd like...	*Ich möchte...*	ikh **murkh**-teh
We'd like...	*Wir möchten...*	veer **murkh**-tehn
...a private bathroom.	*...eigenes Bad.*	**ī**-geh-nehs baht
...your cheapest room.	*...ihr billigstes Zimmer.*	eer **bil**-lig-stehs **tsim**-mer
...___ bed(s) for ___ people in ___ room(s).	*...___ Bett(en) für ___ Personen in ___ Zimmer(n).*	beht-(tehn) fewr pehr-**zoh**-nehn in **tsim**-mer(n)
How much is it?	*Wie viel kostet das?*	vee feel **kohs**-teht dahs
Anything cheaper?	*Etwas Billigeres?*	**eht**-vahs **bil**-lig-er-ehs

I'll take it.	*Ich nehme es.*	ikh **nay**-meh ehs
My name is ___.	*Ich heiße ___.*	ikh **hī**-seh
I'll stay...	*Ich bleibe...*	ikh **blī**-beh
We'll stay...	*Wir bleiben...*	veer **blī**-behn
...for one night.	*...für eine Nacht.*	fewr **ī**-neh nahkht
...for ___ nights.	*...für ___ Nächte.*	fewr ___ **nehkh**-teh
I'll come...	*Ich komme...*	ikh **koh**-meh
We'll come...	*Wir kommen...*	veer **koh**-mehn
...in the morning.	*...am Morgen.*	ahm **mor**-gehn
...in the afternoon.	*...am Nachmittag.*	ahm **nahkh**-mit-tahg
...in the evening.	*...am Abend.*	ahm **ah**-behnt
...in one hour.	*...in einer Stunde.*	in **ī**-ner **shtoon**-deh
...before 4:00 in the afternoon.	*...vor vier Uhr abends.*	for feer oor **ah**-behnts
...Friday before 6 p.m.	*...Freitag vor sechs Uhr abends.*	**frī**-tahg for zehx oor **ah**-behnts
Thank you.	*Danke.*	**dahng**-keh

Using a Credit Card

If you need to secure your reservation with a credit card, here's the lingo.

Do you need a deposit?	*Brauchen Sie eine Anzahlung?*	**browkh**-ehn zee **ī**-neh **ahn**-tsahl-oong
Credit card O.K.?	*Kreditkarte O.K.?*	kreh-**deet**-kar-teh "O.K."
credit card	*Kreditkarte*	kreh-**deet**-kar-teh
debit card	*Kontokarte*	**kohn**-toh-kar-teh
The name on the card is	*Der Name auf der Karte ist ___.*	der **nah**-meh owf dehr **kar**-teh ist
The credit card number is...	*Die Kreditkarten-nummer ist...*	dee kreh-**deet**-kar-tehn-**noo**-mer ist
0	*null*	nool
1	*eins*	īns
2	*zwei*	tsvī
3	*drei*	drī
4	*vier*	feer

5	*fünf*	fewnf
6	*sechs*	zehx
7	*sieben*	**zee**-behn
8	*acht*	ahkht
9	*neun*	noyn
Valid until ___.	*Gültig bis ___.*	**gool**-tig bis
January	*Januar*	**yah**-noo-ar
February	*Februar*	**fay**-broo-ar
March	*März*	mehrts
April	*April*	ah-**pril**
May	*Mai*	mī
June	*Juni*	**yoo**-nee
July	*Juli*	**yoo**-lee
August	*August*	ow-**goost**
September	*September*	zehp-**tehm**-ber
October	*Oktober*	ohk-**toh**-ber
November	*November*	noh-**vehm**-ber
December	*Dezember*	day-**tsehm**-ber
2009	*zweitausendneun*	**tsvī**-tow-zehnd-**noyn**
2010	*zweitausendzehn*	**tsvī**-tow-zehnd-**tsayn**
2011	*zweitausendelf*	**tsvī**-tow-zehnd-**elf**
2012	*zweitausendzwölf*	**tsvī**-tow-zehnd-**tsvurlf**
2013	*zweitausenddreizehn*	**tsvī**-tow-zehnd-**drī**-tsayn
2014	*zweitausendvierzehn*	**tsvī**-tow-zehnd-**feer**-tsayn
2015	*zweitausend-fünfzehn*	**tsvī**-tow-zehnd-**fewnf**-tsayn
2016	*zweitausend-sechzehn*	**tsvī**-tow-zehnd-**zehkh**-tsayn
Can I reserve with a credit card and pay in cash?	*Kann ich mit der Karte reservieren und bar zahlen?*	kahn ikh mit dehr **kar**-teh reh-ser-**veer**-ehn und bar **tsah**-lehn
I have another card.	*Ich habe eine andere Karte.*	ikh **hah**-beh **ī**-neh **ahn**-deh-reh **kar**-teh

If your ***Kreditkarte*** (credit card) is not approved, you can say "***Ich habe eine andere Karte***" (I have another card)—if you do.

The Alphabet

If phoning, you can use the code alphabet below to spell out your name if necessary. Unless you're giving the hotelier your name as it appears on your credit card, consider using a shorter version of your name to make things easier.

a	ah	*Anna*	**ah**-nah
ä	ay	*Ärger (anger)*	**ehr**-ger
b	bay	*Bertha*	**behr**-tah
c	tsay	*Cäsar*	**tseh**-zar
d	day	*Daniel*	**dah**-nee-ehl
e	ay	*Emil*	**eh**-meel
f	"f"	*Friedrich*	**freed**-rikh
g	gay	*Gustav*	**goo**-stahf
h	hah	*Heinrich*	**hīn**-rikh
i	ee	*Ida*	**ee**-dah
j	yot	*Jakob*	**yah**-kohp
k	kah	*Kaiser (emperor)*	**kī**-zer
l	"l"	*Leopold*	**lay**-oh-pohld
m	"m"	*Martha*	**mar**-tah
n	"n"	*Niklaus*	**nik**-lows
o	"o"	*Otto*	**oh**-toh
ö	ur	*Ökonom*	urk-oh-**nohm**
p	pay	*Peter*	**pay**-ter
q	koo	*Quelle*	**kveh**-leh
r	ehr	*Rosa*	**roh**-zah
s	"s"	*Sophie*	zoh-**fee**
t	tay	*Theodor*	**tay**-oh-dor
u	oo	*Ulrich*	**ool**-rikh
ü	ew	*Übel (evil)*	**ew**-behl
v	fow	*Viktor*	**veek**-tor
w	vay	*Wilhelm*	**vil**-hehlm
x	eeks	*Xaver*	**ksah**-ver
y	**ewp**-sil-lohn	*Ypsilon*	**ewp**-sil-lohn
z	tseht	*Zeppelin*	**tseh**-peh-lin
ß	**es**-tseht	*Ziss*	tsis

Just the Fax, Ma'am

If you're booking a room by fax...

I want to send a fax.	*Ich möchte einen Fax senden.*	ikh **murkh**-teh ī-nehn fahx **zehn**-dehn
What is your fax number?	*Was ist Ihre Faxnummer?*	vahs ist **eer**-eh **fahx**-noo-mer
Your fax number is not working.	*Ihre Faxnummer funktioniert nicht.*	**eer**-eh **fahx**-noo-mer foonk-tsee-ohn̲-**eert** nikht
Please turn on your fax machine.	*Bitte stellen Sie Ihren Fax an.*	**bit**-teh **shtehl**-lehn zee **eer**-ehn fahx ahn̲

Getting Specific

I'd like a room...	*Ich möchte ein Zimmer...*	ikh **murkh**-teh īn **tsim**-mer
We'd like a room...	*Wir möchten ein Zimmer...*	veer **murkh**-tehn īn **tsim**-mer
...with / without / and	*...mit / ohne / und*	mit / **oh**-neh / oont
...toilet	*...Toilette*	toh-**leh**-teh
...shower	*...Dusche*	**doo**-sheh
...shower down the hall	*...Dusche im Gang*	**doo**-sheh im gahn̲g
...bathtub	*...Badewanne*	**bah**-deh-vah-neh
...double bed	*...Doppelbett*	**doh**-pehl-beht
...twin beds	*...Einzelbetten*	**īn**-tsehl-beht-tehn
...balcony	*...Balkon*	bahl-**kohn**
...view	*...Ausblick*	**ows**-blick
...with only a sink	*...nur mit Waschbecken*	noor mit **vahsh**-behk-ehn
...on the ground floor	*...im Erdgeschoß*	im **ehrd**-geh-shohs
...television	*...Fernsehen*	**fehrn**-zay-hehn
...telephone	*...Telefon*	tehl-eh-**fohn**
...air conditioning	*...Klimaanlage*	**klee**-mah-ahn̲-lah-geh
...kitchenette	*...Kleinküche*	**klīn**-kewkh-eh

Is there an elevator?	*Gibt es einen Fahrstuhl?*	gipt ehs ī-nehn **far**-shtool
Do you have a swimming pool?	*Haben Sie einen Pool?*	**hah**-behn zee ī-nehn pool
I arrive Monday, depart Wednesday.	*Ich komme am Montag, und reise am Mittwoch ab.*	ikh **koh**-meh ahm **mohn**-tahg oont **rī**-zeh ahm **mit**-vohkh ahp
We arrive Monday, depart Wednesday.	*Wir kommen am Montag, und reisen am Mittwoch ab.*	veer **koh**-mehn ahm **mohn**-tahg oont **rī**-zehn ahm **mit**-vohkh ahp
I'm desperate.	*Ich bin am Verzweifeln.*	ikh bin ahm fehr-**tsvī**-fehln
We're desperate.	*Wir sind am Verzweifeln.*	veer zint ahm fehr-**tsvī**-fehln
I'll sleep anywhere.	*Ich kann irgendwo schlafen.*	ikh kahn **ir**-gehnd-voh **shlah**-fehn
We'll sleep anywhere.	*Wir können irgendwo schlafen.*	veer **kurn**-nehn **ir**-gehnd-voh **shlah**-fehn
I have a sleeping bag.	*Ich habe einen Schlafsack.*	ikh **hah**-beh ī-nehn **shlahf**-zahk
We have sleeping bags.	*Wir haben Schlafsäcke.*	veer **hah**-behn **shlahf**-zehk-eh
Will you please call another hotel for me?	*Rufen Sie bitte in einem anderen Hotel für mich an?*	**roo**-fehn zee **bit**-teh in ī-nehm **ahn**-der-ehn hoh-**tehl** fewr meekh ahn

SLEEPING

Families

Do you have a...?	*Haben Sie ein...?*	**hah**-behn zee īn
...family room	*...Familienzimmer*	fah-**mee**-lee-ehn-**tsim**-mer
...family discount	*...Familienrabatt*	fah-**mee**-lee-ehn-rah-**baht**
...discount for children	*...Rabatt für Kinder*	rah-**baht** fewr **kin**-der
I have / We have...	*Ich habe / Wir haben...*	ikh **hah**-beh / veer **hah**-behn

...one child, ___ months / years old.	*...ein Kind, ___ Monate / Jahre alt.*	īn kint ___ moh-**nah**-teh / **yar**-eh ahlt
...two children, ___ and ___ years old.	*...zwei Kinder, ___ und ___ Jahre alt.*	tsvī **kin**-der ___ oont ___ **yar**-eh ahlt
I'd like...	*Ich hätte gern...*	ikh **heht**-teh gehrn
We'd like...	*Wir hätten gern...*	veer **heht**-tehn gehrn
...a crib.	*...ein Kinderbett.*	īn **kin**-der-beht
...a small extra bed.	*...ein kleines Extrabett.*	īn **klī**-nehs **ehk**-strah-beht
...bunk beds.	*...Kojen.*	**koh**-yehn
babysitting service	*Kinderaufsicht*	**kin**-der-**owf**-zikht
Is a... nearby?	*Ist ein... in der Nähe?*	ist īn... in dehr **nay**-heh
...park	*...Park*	park
...playground	*...Spielplatz*	**shpeel**-plahts
...swimming pool	*...Schwimmbad*	**shvim**-baht

For fun, Germans call little boys ***Lausbub*** (kid with lice) and little girls ***Göre*** (brat).

Confirming, Changing, and Canceling Reservations

You can use this template for your telephone call.

I have a reservation.	*Ich habe eine Reservierung.*	ikh **hah**-beh **ī**-neh reh-zer-**feer**-oong
We have a reservation.	*Wir haben eine Reservierung.*	veer **hah**-behn **ī**-neh reh-zer-**feer**-oong
My name is ___.	*Ich heiße ___.*	ikh **hī**-seh ___
I'd like to... my reservation.	*Ich möchte meine Reservierung...*	ikh **murkh**-teh **mī**-neh reh-zer-**feer**-oong
...confirm	*...bestätigen*	beh-**shtay**-teh-gehn
...reconfirm	*...nochmals bestätigen.*	**nohkh**-mahls beh-**shtay**-tig-ehn
...cancel	*...annullieren*	ah-nool-**eer**-ehn
...change	*...ändern*	**ehn**-dern

The reservation is / was for...	*Die Reservierung ist / war für...*	dee reh-zer-**feer**-oong ist / var fewr
...one person	*...eine Person*	ī-neh pehr-**zohn**
...two people	*...zwei Personen*	tsvī pehr-**zoh**-nehn
...today / tomorrow	*...heute / morgen*	**hoy**-teh / **mor**-gehn
...the day after tomorrow	*...übermorgen*	**ew**-ber-**mor**-gehn
...August 13	*dreizehnten August*	**drī**-tsayn-tehn ow-**goost**
...one night / two nights	*...eine Nacht / zwei Nächte*	ī-neh nahkht / tsvī **naykh**-teh
Did you find my / our reservation?	*Haben Sie meine / unsere Reservierung gefunden?*	**hah**-behn zee **mī**-neh / **oon**-zer-eh reh-zer-**feer**-oong geh-**foon**-dehn
What is your cancellation policy?	*Wie ist es mit einer Annulierung?*	vee ist ehs mit **ī**-ner ah-nool-**eer**-oong
Will I be billed for the first night if I can't make it?	*Werde ich für die erste Nacht belastet, wenn ich nicht kommen kann?*	**vehr**-deh ikh fewr dee **ehr**-steh nahkht beh-**lah**-steht vehn ikh nikht **koh**-mehn kahn
I'd like to arrive instead on ___.	*Ich möchte lieber am ___ kommen.*	ikh **murkh**-teh **lee**-ber ahm ___ **koh**-mehn
We'd like to arrive instead on ___.	*Wir möchten lieber am ___ kommen.*	veer **murkh**-tehn **lee**-ber ahm ___ **koh**-mehn
Is everything O.K.?	*Ist alles in Ordnung?*	ist **ahl**-lehs in **ord**-noong
Thank you. See you then.	*Vielen Dank. Bis dann.*	**fee**-lehn dahngk bis dahn
I'm sorry, I need to cancel.	*Ich bedauere, aber ich muß annullieren.*	ikh beh-**dow**-eh-reh **ah**-ber ikh moos ah-nool-**eer**-ehn

Nailing Down the Price

How much is...?	*Wie viel kostet...?*	vee feel **kohs**-teht
...a room for ___ people	*...ein Zimmer für ___ Personen*	īn **tsim**-mer fewr ___ pehr-**zoh**-nehn
...your cheapest room	*...Ihr billigstes Zimmer*	eer **bil**-lig-stehs **tsim**-mer

Breakfast included?	*Frühstück inklusive?*	**frew**-shtewk in-kloo-**zee**-veh
Is half-pension required?	*Ist Halbpension Bedingung?*	ist **halb**-pehn-see-oh<u>n</u> beh-**ding**-oong
Complete price?	*Vollpreis?*	**fohl**-prīs
Is it cheaper if I stay three nights?	*Ist es billiger, wenn ich drei Nächte bleibe?*	ist ehs **bil**-lig-er vehn ikh drī**naykh**-teh **blī**-beh
I'll stay three nights.	*Ich werde drei Nächte bleiben.*	ikh **vehr**-deh drī **naykh**-teh **blī**-behn
We will stay three nights.	*Wir werden drei Nächte bleiben.*	veer **vehr**-dehn drī **naykh**-teh **blī**-behn
Is it cheaper if I pay cash?	*Ist es billiger, wenn ich bar zahle?*	ist ehs **bil**-lig-er vehn ikh bar **tsah**-leh
What is the cost per week?	*Was ist der Wochenpreis?*	vahs ist dehr **vohkh**-ehn-prīs

Choosing a Room

Can I see the room?	*Kann ich das Zimmer sehen?*	kah<u>n</u> ikh dahs **tsim**-mer **zay**-hehn
Can we see the room?	*Können wir das Zimmer sehen?*	**kurn**-nehn veer dahs **tsim**-mer **zay**-hehn
Show me / us another room?	*Zeigen Sie mir / uns ein anderes Zimmer?*	**tsī**-gehn zee meer / oons īn **ahn**-der-ehs **tsim**-mer
Do you have something...?	*Haben Sie etwas...?*	**hah**-behn zee **eht**-vahs
...larger / smaller	*...größeres / kleineres*	**grur**-ser-ehs / **klī**-ner-ehs
...better / cheaper	*...besseres / billigeres*	**behs**-ser-ehs / **bil**-lig-er-ehs
...brighter	*...helleres*	**hehl**-ler-ehs
...in the back	*...nach hinten hinaus*	nahkh **hin**-tehn hin-**ows**
...quieter	*...ruhigeres*	**roo**-i-ger-ehs
Sorry, it's not right for me / us.	*Tut mir leid, es ist nicht das Richtige für mich / uns.*	toot meer līt ehs ist nikht dahs **rikh**-tig-eh fewr mikh / oons

SLEEPING

I'll take it.	*Ich nehme es.*	ikh **nay**-meh ehs
We'll take it.	*Wir nehmen es.*	veer **nay**-mehn ehs
My key, please.	*Mein Schlüssel, bitte.*	mīn **shlew**-sehl **bit**-teh
Sleep well.	*Schlafen Sie gut.*	**shlah**-fehn zee goot
Good night.	*Gute Nacht.*	**goo**-teh nahkht

Breakfast

When does breakfast start?	*Wann beginnt das Frühstück?*	vahn beh-**gint** dahs **frew**-shtewk
When does breakfast end?	*Wann endet das Frühstück?*	vahn **ehn**-deht dahs **frew**-shtewk
Where is breakfast served?	*Wo wird Frühstück serviert?*	voh virt **frew**-shtewk zer-**veert**

Breakfast is normally included in the price of your room. For a list of breakfast words, see page 406.

Hotel Help

I'd like...	*Ich hätte gern...*	ikh **heht**-teh gehrn
We'd like...	*Wir hätten gern...*	veer **heht**-tehn gehrn
...a / another	*...ein / noch ein*	īn / nohkh īn
...towel.	*...Handtuch.*	**hahnd**-tookh
...clean bath towel / clean bath towels	*...sauberes Badetuch / saubere Badetücher.*	**zow**-ber-ehs **bah**-deh-tookh / **zow**-ber-eh **bah**-deh-tewkh-er
...pillow.	*...Kissen.*	**kis**-sehn
...clean sheets.	*...saubere Bettwäsche.*	**zow**-ber-eh **beht**-veh-sheh
...blanket.	*...Decke.*	**dehk**-eh
...glass.	*...Glas.*	glahs
...sink stopper.	*...Abflußstöpsel.*	**ahp**-floos-shturp-zehl
...soap.	*...Seife.*	**zī**-feh
...toilet paper.	*...Klopapier.*	**kloh**-pah-peer
...electrical adapter.	*...Stromwandler.*	**strohm**-vahnd-ler
...brighter light bulb.	*...hellere Glühbirne.*	**hehl**-eh-reh **gloo**-bir-neh

...lamp.	*...Lampe.*	**lahm**-peh
...chair.	*...Stuhl.*	shtool
...table.	*...Tisch.*	tish
...Internet access.	*...Internetanschluß.*	**in**-tehr-neht-**ahn**-shloos
...different room.	*...anderes Zimmer.*	**ahn**-der-ehs **tsim**-mer
...silence.	*...Ruhe.*	**roo**-heh
...to speak to the manager.	*...mit dem Chef sprechen.*	mit daym shehf **shprekh**-ehn
I've fallen and I can't get up.	*Ich bin gefallen und kann nicht aufstehen.*	ikh bin geh-**fahl**-lehn oont kahn nikht **owf**-shtay-hehn
How can I make the room...?	*Wie kann ich das Zimmer... machen?*	vee kahn ikh dahs **tsim**-mer...**mahkh**-ehn
...cooler / warmer?	*...kühler / wärmer*	**kewl**-er / **vehrm**-er
Where can I wash / hang my laundry?	*Wo kann ich meine Wäsche waschen / aufhängen?*	voh kahn ikh **mī**-neh **vehsh**-eh **vahsh**-ehn / **owf**-hehng-ehn
Is a... laundry nearby?	*Ist ein Waschsalon... in der Nähe?*	ist īn **vahsh**-sah-lohn in dehr **nay**-heh
...self-service	*...mit Selbstbedienung*	...mit zehlpst-beh-**dee**-noong
...full service	*...mit Dienstleistung*	mit **deenst**-līs-toong
I'd like / We'd like...	*Ich möchte / Wir möchten...*	ikh **murkh**-teh / veer **murkh**-tehn
...to stay another night.	*...noch eine Nacht bleiben.*	nokh **ī**-neh nahkht **blī**-behn
Where can I park?	*Wo soll ich parken?*	voh zohl ikh **par**-kehn
What time do you lock up?	*Um wie viel Uhr schließen Sie ab?*	oom vee feel oor **shlee**-sehn zee ahp
Please wake me at 7:00.	*Wecken Sie mich um sieben Uhr, bitte.*	**vehk**-ehn zee mikh oom **zee**-behn oor **bit**-teh
Where do you go to eat lunch / eat dinner / drink coffee?	*Wo gehen Sie zum Mittag essen / Abend essen / Kaffee trinken?*	voh **gay**-hehn zee tsoom **mit**-tahg **eh**-sehn / **ah**-behnt **eh**-sehn / kah-**fay** **trink**-ehn

Hotel Hassles

Come with me.	*Kommen Sie mit mir.*	**koh**-mehn zee mit meer
There is a problem in my room.	*Es gibt ein Problem mit meinem Zimmer.*	ehs gipt īn proh-**blaym** mit **mī**-nehm **tsim**-mer
It smells bad.	*Es stinkt.*	ehs shtinkt
bedbugs	*Wanzen*	**vahn**-tsehn
mice	*Mäuse*	**moy**-zeh
cockroaches	*Kakerlaken*	**kah**-ker-**lahk**-ehn
prostitutes	*Freudenmädchen*	**froy**-dehn-**mayd**-tyehn
I'm covered with bug bites.	*Ich bin mit Wanzenbissen übersäht.*	ikh bin mit **vahn**-tsehn-**bis**-sehn ew-ber-**zayt**
The bed is too soft / hard.	*Das Bett ist zu weich / hart.*	dahs beht ist tsoo vīkh / hart
I can't sleep.	*Ich kann nicht schlafen.*	ikh kahn nikht **shlah**-fehn
The room is too...	*Das Zimmer ist zu...*	dahs **tsim**-mer ist tsoo
...hot / cold.	*...heiß / kalt.*	hīs / kahlt
...noisy / dirty.	*...laut / schmutzig.*	lowt / **shmoot**-sig
I can't open / shut...	*Ich kann... nicht öffnen / schliessen.*	ikh kahn... nikht **urf**-nehn / **shlees**-ehn
...the door / the window.	*...die Tür / das Fenster*	dee tewr / dahs **fehn**-ster
Air conditioner...	*Klimaanlage...*	**klee**-mah-ahn-lah-geh
Lamp...	*Lampe...*	**lahm**-peh
Lightbulb...	*Birne...*	**bir**-neh
Electrical outlet...	*Steckdose...*	**shtehk**-doh-zeh
Key...	*Schlüssel...*	**shlew**-sehl
Lock...	*Schloß...*	shlohs
Window...	*Fenster...*	**fehn**-ster
Faucet...	*Wasserhahn...*	**vah**-ser-hahn
Sink...	*Waschbecken...*	**vahsh**-behk-ehn
Toilet...	*Toilette...*	toh-**leh**-teh
Shower...	*Dusche...*	**doo**-sheh
...doesn't work.	*...ist kaputt.*	ist kah-**poot**

There is no hot water.	*Es gibt kein warmes Wasser.*	ehs gipt kīn **var**-mehs **vahs**-ser
When is the water hot?	*Wann wird das Wasser warm?*	vahn̲ virt dahs **vahs**-ser varm

Checking Out

When is check-out time?	*Wann muß ich das Zimmer verlassen?*	vahn̲ mus ikh dahs **tsim**-mer fehr-**lah**-sehn
I'll leave...	*Ich fahre... ab.*	ikh **fah**-reh... ahp
We'll leave...	*Wir fahren... ab.*	veer **fah**-rehn... ahp
...today / tomorrow	*...heute / morgen*	**hoy**-teh / **mor**-gehn
...very early	*...sehr früh*	zehr frew
Can I pay now?	*Kann ich jetzt zahlen?*	kahn̲ ikh yetzt **tsah**-lehn
Can we pay now?	*Können wir jetzt zahlen?*	**kurn**-nehn veer yetzt **tsah**-lehn
Bill, please.	*Rechnung, bitte.*	**rehkh**-noong **bit**-teh
Credit card O.K.?	*Kreditkarte O.K.?*	kreh-**deet**-kar-teh "O.K."
Everything was great.	*Alles war gut.*	**ahl**-lehs var goot
I slept like a bear.	*Ich habe wie ein Bär geschlafen.*	ikh **hah**-beh vee īn bayr geh-**shlahf**-ehn
Will you call my next hotel...?	*Können Sie mein nächstes Hotel anrufen...?*	**kurn**-nehn zee mīn **nehkh**-stehs hoh-**tehl** **ahn**-roo-fehn
...for tonight	*...für heute Abend*	fewr **hoy**-teh **ah**-behnt
...to make a reservation	*...zum reservieren*	tsoom reh-ser-**veer**-ehn
...to confirm a reservation	*...zum bestätigen*	tsoom beh-**shtay**-teh-gehn
I will pay for the call.	*Ich bezahle für den Anruf.*	ikh beh-**tsah**-leh fewr dayn **ahn**-roof
Can I...?	*Kann ich...?*	kahn̲ ikh
Can we...?	*Können wir...?*	**kurn**-nehn veer
...leave baggage here until ___	*...das Gepäck hier lassen bis ___*	dahs geh-**pehk** heer **lah**-sehn bis

I never tip beyond the included service charges in hotels or for hotel services.

Camping

camping	*Camping*	**kahm**-ping
campsite	*Zeltstelle*	**tsehlt**-shtehl-leh
tent	*Zelt*	tsehlt
The nearest campground?	*Der nächste Campingplatz?*	dehr **nehkh**-steh **kahm**-ping-plahts
Can I...?	*Kann ich...?*	kahn ikh
Can we...?	*Können wir...?*	**kurn**-nehn veer
...camp here for one night	*...hier eine Nacht zelten*	heer **ī**-neh nahkht **tsehl**-tehn
Are showers included?	*Duschen eingeschlossen?*	**doo**-shehn **īn**-geh-shlohs-sehn

EATING

RESTAURANTS

Types of Restaurants

Here are several types of eateries and some variations you'll find per country:

Restaurant—Primarily fine dining with formal service
Ratskeller—Atmospheric restaurant cellar with food of varying quality
Gasthaus, Gasthof, or ***Wirtschaft***—Country inn serving fine meals
Gaststätte or ***Gaststube***—Informal restaurant
Heurigen—Austrian wine bar that serves food (see "Wine," 420)
Kneipe—German bar
Weinstübli or ***Bierstübli***—Wine bar or tavern in Switzerland
Café or ***Konditorei***—Pastry and coffee shop that sometimes serves light lunches (**Mittagessen**)
Schnell Imbiß—Small fast-food stand

Finding a Restaurant

Where's a good... restaurant nearby?	*Wo ist hier ein gutes... Restaurant?*	voh ist heer īn **goo**-tehs... rehs-tow-**rahnt**
...cheap	*...billiges*	**bil**-lig-ehs
...local-style	*...einheimisches*	īn-**hī**-mish-ehs

...untouristy	*...nicht für Touristen gedachtes*	nikht fewr too-**ris**-tehn geh-**dahkh**-tehs
...vegetarian	*...vegetarisches*	vehg-eht-**ar**-ish-ehs
...fast food	*...Schnellimbiß*	shnehl-**im**-bis
...self-service buffet	*...Selbstbedienungs-Buffet*	zehlpst-beh-**dee**-noongs-boo-fay
...Italian	*...italienisches*	i-tahl-**yehn**-ish-ehs
...Turkish	*...türkisches*	**tewrk**-ish-ehs
...Chinese	*...chinesisches*	khee-**nayz**-ish-ehs
beer garden	*Biergarten*	**beer**-gar-tehn
with terrace	*mit Terrasse*	mit tehr-**rahs**-seh
with a salad bar	*mit Salatbar*	mit **zah**-laht-bar
with candles	*bei Kerzenlicht*	bī **kehr**-tzehn-likht
romantic	*romantisch*	roh-**mahn**-tish
moderate price	*günstig*	**gewn**-stig
splurge	*zum Verwöhnen*	tsoom fehr-**vur**-nehn
Is it better than McDonald's?	*Ist es besser als McDonald's?*	ist ehs behs-ser ahls "McDonald's"

German restaurants close one day a week. It's called ***Ruhetag*** (quiet day). Before tracking down a recommended restaurant, call to make sure it's open.

EATING

Getting a Table

When does this open / close?	*Wann ist hier geöffnet / geschlossen?*	vahn ist heer geh-**urf**-neht / geh-**shlohs**-sehn
Are you open...?	*Sind Sie... geöffnet?*	zint see... geh-**urf**-neht
...today / tomorrow	*...heute / morgen*	**hoy**-teh / **mor**-gehn
...for lunch / dinner	*...zum Mittagessen / Abendessen*	tsoom **mit**-tahg-eh-sehn / **ah**-behnt-eh-sehn
Are reservations recommended?	*Soll mann reservieren?*	zohl mahn reh-zer-**feer**-ehn
I'd like...	*Ich hätte gern...*	ikh **heh**-teh gehrn
We'd like...	*Wir hätten gern...*	veer **heh**-tehn gehrn
...a table for one / two.	*...einen Tisch für ein / zwei.*	**ī**-nehn tish fewr īn / tsvī

...to reserve a table for two people...	*...einen Tisch für zwei reserviert...*	ī-nehn tish fewr tsvī reh-ser-**veert**
...for today / tomorrow	*...für heute / morgen*	fewr **hoy**-teh / **mor**-gehn
...at 8 p.m.	*...um zwanzig Uhr*	oom **tsvahn**-tsig oor
My name is ___.	*Ich heiße ___.*	ikh **hī**-seh
I have a reservation for ___ people.	*Ich habe eine Reservierung für ___ Personen.*	ikh **hah**-beh **ī**-neh reh-zer-**feer**-oong fewr___pehr-**zohn**-ehn
I'd like to sit...	*Ich möchte... sitzen.*	ikh **murkh**-teh... **zit**-sehn
We'd like to sit...	*Wir möchten... sitzen.*	veer **murkh**-tehn... **zit**-sehn
...inside / outside.	*...drinn / draussen*	drin / **drow**-sehn
...by the window.	*...beim Fenster*	bīm **fehn**-ster
...with a view.	*...mit Aussicht*	mit **ows**-zikht
...where it's quiet.	*...im Ruhigen*	im **roo**-hig-ehn
Non-smoking (if possible).	*Nichtraucher (wenn möglich).*	**nikht**-rowkh-er (vehn **mur**-glikh)
Is this table free?	*Ist dieser Tisch frei?*	ist **dee**-zer tish frī
Can I sit here?	*Kann ich hier sitzen?*	kahn ikh heer **zit**-sehn
Can we sit here?	*Können wir hier sitzen?*	**kurn**-ehn veer heer **zit**-sehn

Germans eat meals about when we do. In many bars and restaurants, you'll see tables with little signs that say ***Stammtisch*** ("This table reserved for our regulars"). Don't sit there unless you're invited by a local.

EATING

The Menu

menu	*Karte, Speisekarte*	**kar**-teh, **shpī**-zeh-**kar**-teh
fixed-price meal	*Touristenmenü*	too-**ris**-tehn-meh-**new**
fast service special	*Schnellbedienung*	shnehl-beh-**dee**-noong
self-service	*Selbstbedienung*	sehlbst-beh-**dee**-noong
specialty of the house	*Spezialität des Hauses*	**shpayt**-see-ahl-ee-**tayt** dehs **how**-zehs
breakfast	*Frühstück*	**frew**-shtewk

Key Phrases: Restaurants

Where's a good restaurant nearby?	*Wo ist hier ein gutes Restaurant?*	voh ist heer īn **goo**-tehs rehs-tow-**rahnt**
I'd like...	*Ich hätte gern...*	ikh **heh**-teh gehrn
We'd like...	*Wir hätten gern...*	veer **heh**-tehn gehrn
...a table for one / two.	*...einen Tisch für ein / zwei.*	**ī**-nehn tish fewr īn / tsvī
...non-smoking (if possible).	*...nichtraucher (wenn möglich).*	**nikht**-rowkh-er (vehn **mur**-glikh)
Is this seat free?	*Ist hier frei?*	ist heer frī
Menu (in English), please.	*Speisekarte (auf Englisch), bitte.*	**shpī**-zeh-kar-teh (owf **ehng**-lish) **bit**-teh
Bill, please.	*Rechnung, bitte.*	**rehkh**-noong **bit**-teh
Credit card O.K.?	*Kreditkarte O.K.?*	kreh-**deet**-kar-teh "O.K."

lunch	*Mittagessen*	**mit**-tahg-eh-sehn
dinner	*Abendessen*	**ah**-behnt-eh-sehn
appetizers	*Vorspeise*	**for**-shpī-zeh
cold plates	*kalte Gerichte*	**kahl**-teh geh-**rikh**-teh
sandwiches	*Brotzeiten*	**broht**-tsī-tehn
bread	*Brot*	broht
salad	*Salat*	zah-**laht**
soup	*Suppe*	**zup**-peh
first course	*erster Gang*	**ehr**-ster gahng
main course	*Hauptgerichte*	**howpt**-geh-rikh-teh
meat	*Fleisch*	flīsh
poultry	*Geflügel*	geh-**flew**-gehl
fish	*Fisch*	fish
seafood	*Meeresfrüchte*	**meh**-rehs-frewkh-teh
children's plate	*Kinderteller*	**kin**-der-tehl-ler
side dishes	*Beilagen*	**bī**-lah-gehn
vegetables	*Gemüse*	geh-**mew**-zeh
cheese	*Käse*	**kay**-zeh
dessert	*Nachspeise*	**nahkh**-shpī-zeh

munchies	*zum Knabbern*	tsoom **knahb**-bern
beverages	*Getränke*	geh-**trehnk**-eh
drink menu	*Getränkekarte*	geh-**trehnk**-eh-**kar**-teh
beer	*Bier*	beer
wine	*Wein*	vīn
cover charge	*Eintritt*	**īn**-trit
service included	*Trinkgeld inklusive*	**trink**-gehlt in-kloo-**zee**-veh
service not included	*Trinkgeld nicht inklusive*	**trink**-gehlt nikht in-kloo-**zee**-veh
hot / cold	*warm / kalt*	varm / kahlt
with / and / or / without	*mit / und / oder / ohne*	mit / oont / **oh**-der / **oh**-neh

Save money by ordering a ***halbe Portion*** (half portion) or a ***Tageskarte*** (menu of the day).

Ordering

waiter	*Kellner*	**kehl**-ner
waitress	*Kellnerin*	**kehl**-ner-in
I'm ready to order.	*Ich möchte bestellen.*	ikh **murkh**-teh beh-**shtehl**-lehn
We're ready to order.	*Wir möchten bestellen.*	veer **murkh**-tehn beh-**shtehl**-lehn
I'd like...	*Ich möchte...*	ikh **murkh**-teh
We'd like...	*Wir möchten...*	veer **murkh**-tehn
...just a drink.	*...nur etwas zu trinken.*	noor **eht**-vahs tsoo **trink**-ehn
...a snack.	*...eine Kleinigkeit.*	**ī**-neh **klī**-nig-kīt
...just a salad.	*...nur einen Salat.*	noor **ī**-nehn zah-**laht**
...a half portion.	*...eine halbe Portion.*	**ī**-neh **hahl**-beh por-tsee-**ohn**
...to see the menu.	*...die Karte sehen.*	dee **kar**-teh **zay**-hehn
...to order.	*...bestellen.*	beh-**shtehl**-lehn
...to pay.	*...zahlen.*	**tsahl**-ehn
...to throw up.	*...mich übergeben.*	mikh **ew**-ber-gay-behn
What is fast?	*Was geht schnell?*	vahs gayt shnehl

Do you have...?	*Haben Sie...?*	**hah**-behn zee
...an English menu	*...eine Speisekarte auf Englisch*	ī-neh **shpī**-zeh-kar-teh owf **ehng**-lish
...a lunch special	*...ein Mittagsmenü*	īn **mit**-tahgs-meh-**new**
What do you recommend?	*Was schlagen Sie vor?*	vahs **shlah**-gehn zee for
What's your favorite dish?	*Was ist Ihr Lieblingsessen?*	vahs ist eer **leeb**-lings-eh-sehn
Is it...?	*Ist es...?*	ist ehs
...good	*...gut*	goot
...expensive	*...teuer*	**toy**-er
...light	*...leicht*	līkht
...filling	*...sättigend*	**seht**-tee-gehnd
What is...?	*Was ist...?*	vahs ist
...that	*...das*	dahs
...local	*...typisch*	**tew**-pish
...fresh	*...frisch*	frish
...cheap	*...billig*	**bil**-lig
Can we split this and have an extra plate?	*Können wir das teilen und noch einen Teller haben?*	**kurn**-nehn veer dahs **tī**-lehn oont nohkh ī-nehn **tehl**-ler **hah**-behn
I've changed my mind.	*Ich habe es mir anders überlegt.*	ikh **hah**-beh ehs meer **ahn**-ders ew-ber-**laygt**
Can I substitute (anything) for the ___?	*Kann ich (etwas anderes) statt ___ haben?*	kahn ikh (**eht**-vahs **ahn**-der-ehs) shtaht ___ **hah**-behn
Can I / Can we get it to go?	*Kann ich / Können wir das mitnehmen?*	kahn ikh / **kurn**-nehn veer dahs **mit**-nay-mehn
To go?	*Zum Mitnehmen?*	tsoom **mit**-nay-mehn

To get the waiter's attention, ask "***Bitte?***" (Please?). The waiter will give you a menu (***Speisekarte***) and then ask if you'd like something to drink (***Etwas zu trinken?***). When ready to take your order, the waiter simply says, "***Bitte?***" After the meal, he'll ask if the meal tasted good (***Hat's gut geschmeckt?***), if you'd like dessert (***Möchten Sie eine Nachspeise?***), and if you'd like anything else (***Sonstnoch etwas?***). You ask for the bill (***Die Rechnung, bitte***).

Tableware and Condiments

plate	*Teller*	**tehl**-ler
extra plate	*Extrateller*	**ehk**-strah-tehl-ler
napkin	*Serviette*	zer-vee-**eht**-teh
silverware	*Besteck*	beh-**shtehk**
knife	*Messer*	**mehs**-ser
fork	*Gabel*	**gah**-behl
spoon	*Löffel*	**lurf**-fehl
cup	*Tasse*	**tah**-seh
glass	*Glas*	glahs
carafe	*Karaffe*	kah-**rah**-feh
water	*Wasser*	**vah**-ser
bread	*Brot*	broht
large pretzel	*Brezel*	**breht**-sehl
butter	*Butter*	**boo**-ter
margarine	*Margarine*	mar-gah-**ree**-neh
salt / pepper	*Salz / Pfeffer*	zahlts / **pfehf**-fer
sugar	*Zucker*	**tsoo**-ker
artificial sweetener	*Süßstoff*	**sews**-shtohf
honey	*Honig*	**hoh**-nig
mustard...	*Senf...*	zehnf
...mild / sharp / sweet	*...mild / scharf / süß*	meelt / sharf / zews
ketchup	*Ketchup*	"ketchup"
mayonnaise	*Mayonnaise*	mah-yoh-**nay**-zeh
toothpick	*Zahnstocher*	**tsahn**-shtohkh-er

The Food Arrives

Is it included?	*Ist es inbegriffen?*	ist ehs **in**-beh-grif-ehn
I did not order this.	*Dies habe ich nicht bestellt.*	deez **hah**-beh ikh nikht beh-**shtehlt**
We did not order this.	*Dies haben wir nicht bestellt.*	deez **hah**-behn veer nikht beh-**shtehlt**
Please heat this up?	*Bitte aufwärmen?*	**bit**-teh **owf**-vehr-mehn
A little.	*Ein bißchen.*	īn **bis**-yehn
More. / Another.	*Mehr. / Noch ein.*	mehr / nohkh īn

The same.	*Das gleiche.*	dahs **glīkh**-eh
Enough.	*Genug.*	geh-**noog**
Finished.	*Fertig.*	**fehr**-tig
I'm full.	*Ich bin satt.*	ikh bin zaht

After bringing the meal, your server might wish you a cheery "***Guten Appetit!***" (pronounced **goo**-tehn ah-peh-**teet**).

Compliments to the Chef

Yummy!	*Mmmh!*	mmm
Delicious!	*Lecker!*	**lehk**-er
Excellent!	*Ausgezeichnet!*	ows-geh-**tsīkh**-neht
It tastes very good!	*Schmeckt sehr gut!*	shmehkt zehr goot
I love German / this food.	*Ich liebe deutsches / dieses Essen.*	ikh **lee**-beh **doy**-chehs / **dee**-zehs **eh**-sehn
Better than mom's cooking.	*Besser als bei Muttern.*	**behs**-ser ahls bī **moo**-tern
My compliments to the chef!	*Kompliment an den Koch!*	kohmp-li-**mehnt** ahn dayn kohkh

Paying for Your Meal

The bill, please.	*Die Rechnung, bitte.*	dee **rehkh**-noong **bit**-teh
Together.	*Zusammen.*	tsoo-**zah**-mehn
Separate checks.	*Getrennte Rechnung.*	geh-**trehn**-teh **rehkh**-noong
Credit card O.K.?	*Kreditkarte O.K.?*	kreh-**deet**-kar-teh "O.K."
This is not correct.	*Dies stimmt nicht.*	deez shtimt nikht
Please explain.	*Erklären Sie, bitte.*	ehr-**klehr**-ehn zee **bit**-teh
Can you explain / itemize the bill?	*Können Sie die Rechnung einzeln / erklären?*	**kurn**-nehn zee dee **rehkh**-noong **īn**-tsehln / ehr-**klehr**-ehn
What if I wash the dishes?	*Und wenn ich die Teller wasche?*	oont vehn ikh dee **tehl**-ler **vah**-sheh
Is tipping expected?	*Wird ein Trinkgeld erwartet?*	virt īn **trink**-gehlt ehr-**var**-teht
What percent?	*Wie viel Prozent?*	vee feel proh-**tsehnt**

tip	*Trinkgeld*	**trink**-gehlt
Keep the change.	*Stimmt so.*	shtimt zoh
This is for you.	*Dies ist für Sie.*	deez ist fewr zee
Could I have a receipt, please?	*Kann ich bitte einen Beleg haben?*	kahn̲ ikh **bit**-teh ī-nehn beh-**lehg hah**-behn

When you're ready for the bill, ask for the ***Rechnung*** (reckoning). A service charge is nearly always included. Tipping is not expected beyond that, though it's polite to round up to the next big coin. If you're uncertain whether to tip, ask another customer if it's expected (***Wird ein Trinkgeld erwartet?***). Rather than leave the tip on the table, it's better style to say the total amount you want to pay (including the tip) when you give the waiter your money.

In Austria, a cover charge (***Gedeck***) is added at finer dining establishments. If the restaurant doesn't include a cover charge, the bread placed on your table usually costs extra. Ask to make sure you're not charged for food you don't want: "***Ist es inbegriffen?***" (Is it included?).

SPECIAL CONCERNS

In a Hurry

I'm in a hurry.	*Ich bin in Eile.*	ikh bin in **ī**-leh
We're in a hurry.	*Wir sind in Eile.*	veer zint in **ī**-leh
Will the food be ready soon?	*Ist das Essen bald bereit?*	ist dahs **eh**-sehn bahlt beh-**rīt**
I need / We need to be served quickly. Is that O.K.?	*Ich muß / Wir müssen schnell bedient werden. Geht das?*	ikh mus / veer **mews**-sehn shnehl beh-**deent** **vehr**-dehn gayt dahs

Dietary Restrictions

I'm allergic to...	*Ich bin allergisch auf...*	ikh bin ah-**lehr**-gish **owf**
I / he / she cannot eat...	*Ich / er / sie darf kein...essen.*	ikh / ehr / zee darf kīn... **eh**-sehn
...dairy products.	*...Milchprodukte*	**milkh**-proh-dook-teh

EATING

...wheat.	*...Weizen*	vī-tsehn
...meat / pork.	*...Fleisch / Schweinefleisch*	flīsh / **shvī**-neh-flīsh
...salt / sugar.	*...Salz / Zucker*	zahlts / **tsoo**-ker
...shellfish.	*...Meeresfrüchte*	**meh**-rehs-**frewkh**-teh
...spicy foods.	*...scharfe Gewürze*	**shar**-feh geh-**vewr**-tseh
...nuts.	*...Nüsse*	**new**-seh
I'm a diabetic.	*Ich bin Diabetiker.**	ikh bin dee-ah-**beht**-ik-er
No caffeine.	*Koffeinfrei.*	koh-fay-**een**-frī
No alcohol.	*Kein Alkohol.*	kīn **ahl**-koh-hohl
I'm a...	*Ich bin...*	ikh bin
...vegetarian.	*...Vegetarier.**	veh-geh-**tar**-ee-er
...strict vegetarian.	*...strenger Vegetarier.**	**shtrehng**-er veh-geh-**tar**-ee-er
...carnivore.	*...Fleischesser.*	**flīsh**-ehs-ser
...big eater.	*...grosser Esser.*	**groh**-ser **ehs**-ser
Is any meat or animal fat used in this?	*Hat es Fleisch oder tierische Fette drin?*	haht ehs flīsh **oh**-der **teer**-ish-eh **feht**-teh drin

* If you're female, add "in" to the end of these words if you're describing yourself, like this: ***Diabetikerin*** and ***Vegetarierin***.

Children

Do you have...?	*Haben Sie...?*	**hah**-behn zee
...a children's portion	*...eine Kinderportion*	**ī**-neh **kin**-der-por-tsee-**ohn**
...a half portion	*...eine halbe Portion*	**ī**-neh **hahl**-beh por-tsee-**ohn**
...a high chair / booster seat	*...einen Kinderhocker/ Kindersitz*	**ī**-nehn **kin**-der-**hoh**-ker **kin**-der-zits
plain noodles / rice	*Nudeln / Reis ohne alles*	**noo**-dehln / rīs **oh**-neh **ahl**-lehs
with butter	*mit Butter*	mit **boo**-ter
no sauce	*ohne Sauce*	**oh**-neh **zoh**-seh

English	German	Pronunciation
sauce / dressing on the side	*Sauce / Salatsoße separat*	**zoh**-seh / zah-**laht**-zoh-seh zeh-par-**aht**
Nothing spicy.	*Nicht scharf gewürzt.*	nikht sharf geh-**vewrtst**
Not too hot.	*Nicht zu heiß.*	nikht tsoo hīs
He will / She will / They will share our meal.	*Er wird / Sie wird / Sie werden unser Essen teilen.*	ehr virt / zee virt / zee **vehr**-dehn **oon**-ser **eh**-sehn **tī**-lehn
Please bring the food quickly.	*Bitte schnell servieren.*	**bit**-teh shnehl zer-**veer**-ehn
Can I / Can we have an extra...?	*Kann ich / Können wir ein zusätzliche... haben?*	kahn ikh / **kurn**-nehn veer īn tsoo-**zehts**-likh-eh... **hah**-behn
...plate	*...Teller*	**tehl**-ler
...cup	*...Schale, Becher*	**shah**-leh, **behkh**-er
...spoon / fork	*...Löffel / Gabel*	**lurf**-fehl / **gah**-behl
Can I / Can we have two extra...?	*Kann ich / Können wir zwei zusätzliche... haben?*	kahn ikh / **kurn**-nehn veer tsvī tsoo-**zehts**-likh-eh... **hah**-behn
...plates	*...Teller*	**tehl**-ler
...cups	*...Schalen, Becher*	**shah**-lehn, **behkh**-er
...spoons / forks	*...Löffel / Gabeln*	**lurf**-fehl / **gah**-behln
A small milk (in a plastic cup).	*Eine kleine Portion Milch (in einem plastikbecher).*	ī-neh klī-neh por-tsee-ohn milkh (in ī-nehm plah-steek-behkh-er)
More napkins, please.	*Mehr Servietten, bitte.*	mehr zer-vee-**eht**-tehn **bit**-teh
Sorry for the mess.	*Entschuldigen Sie die Unordnung.*	ehnt-**shool**-dig-oong zee dee oon-**ord**-noong

WHAT'S COOKING?

Breakfast

breakfast	*Frühstück*	**frew**-shtewk
bread	*Brot*	broht
roll	*Brötchen, Semmel*	**brurt**-syehn, **zehm**-mehl
toast	*Toast*	tohst
butter	*Butter*	**boo**-ter
jelly	*Marmelade*	mar-meh-**lah**-deh
pastry	*Kuchen, Gebäck*	**kookh**-ehn, geh-**behk**
croissant	*Gipfel*	**gip**-fehl
omelet	*Omelett*	**ohm**-leht
egg / eggs	*Ei / Eier*	ī / **ī**-er
fried eggs	*Spiegeleier*	**shpee**-gehl-ī-er
scrambled eggs	*Rühreier*	**rew**-rī-er
soft boiled / hard boiled	*weichgekocht / hartgekocht*	**vīkh**-geh-kohkht / **hart**-geh-kohkht

Key Phrases: What's Cooking?

food	*Essen*	**eh**-sehn
breakfast	*Frühstück*	**frew**-shtewk
lunch	*Mittagessen*	**mit**-tahg-eh-sehn
dinner	*Abendessen*	**ah**-behnt-eh-sehn
bread	*Brot*	broht
cheese	*Käse*	**kay**-zeh
soup	*Suppe*	**zup**-peh
salad	*Salat*	zah-**laht**
meat	*Fleisch*	flīsh
chicken	*Hähnchen*	**hayn**-syen
fish	*Fisch*	fish
fruit	*Obst*	ohpst
vegetables	*Gemüse*	geh-**mew**-zeh
dessert	*Nachspeise*	**nahkh**-shpī-zeh
Delicious!	*Lecker!*	**lehk**-er

ham	*Schinken*	**shink**-ehn
bacon	*Speck*	shpehk
cheese	*Käse*	**kay**-zeh
yogurt	*Joghurt*	**yoh**-gurt
cereal	*Cornflakes*	"cornflakes"
granola cereal	*Müsli*	**mews**-lee
milk	*Milch*	milkh
fruit juice	*Fruchtsaft*	**frookht**-zahft
orange juice (fresh)	*Orangensaft (frischgepreßt)*	oh-**rahn**-zhehn-zahft (frish-geh-**prehst**)
hot chocolate	*heiße Schokolade*	**hī**-seh shoh-koh-**lah**-deh
coffee / tea	*Kaffee / Tee*	kah-**fay** / tay
Breakfast included?	*Frühstück inklusive?*	**frew**-shtewk in-kloo-**zee**-veh

Frühstück is almost always included with your room and is your chance to fuel up for the day with pots of coffee, bread, rolls, cheese, ham, eggs, and sometimes local specialties. For a hearty cereal, try ***Bircher Müsli***, a healthy mix of oats, nuts, yogurt, and fruit. If breakfast is optional, take a walk to the ***Bäckerei-Konditorei*** (bakery). Germany and Austria are famous for this special cultural attraction—more varieties of bread, pastries, and cakes than you ever imagined, baked fresh every morning and throughout the day. Sometimes a café is part of a ***Konditorei***.

Snacks and Quick Meals

Bündnerfleisch	**bewnt**-ner-flīsh	dried beef, thinly sliced
Wurstplatte, Schlachtplatte ("slaughterplate")	**voorst**-plah-teh, **shlahkht**-plah-teh	assorted cold cuts (sausages, ham, liver paté, cow's tongue...)
Sauerkrautplatte	**zow**-er-krowt-**plah**-teh	assorted cold cuts with sauerkraut
Käsebrot	**kay**-zeh-broht	bread with cheese
Frikadelle	frik-ah-**dehl**-leh	large meatball / hamburger
Bauernomelette	**bow**-ern-ohm-leht	omelet with bacon and onion

Rollmops	**rohl**-mohps	pickled herring
Brezel	**breht**-sehl	pretzel
Toast mit Schinken und Käse	tohst mit **shink**-ehn oont **kay**-zeh	toast with ham and cheese

Sandwiches

I'd like a sandwich.	*Ich hätte gern ein Sandwich.*	ikh **heh**-teh gehrn īn **zahnd**-vich
We'd like two sandwiches.	*Wir hätten gern zwei Sandwiche.*	veer **heh**-tehn gehrn tvsī **zahnd**-vich-eh
toasted	*getoastet*	geh-**tohst**-eht
cheese	*Käse*	**kay**-zeh
chicken	*Hähnchen*	**hayn**-syen
egg salad	*Eiersalat*	**ī**-er-zah-laht
fish	*Fisch*	fish
ham	*Schinken*	**shink**-ehn
jelly	*Marmelade*	mar-meh-**lah**-deh
peanut butter	*Erdnußbutter*	**ehrd**-noos-boo-ter
pork sandwich	*Schweinefleisch Sandwich*	**shvīn**-flīsh **zahnd**-vich
salami	*Salami*	zah-**lah**-mee
tuna	*Thunfisch*	**toon**-fish
turkey	*Truthahn, Pute*	**troot**-hahn, **poo**-teh
lettuce	*Kopfsalat*	**kohpf**-zah-laht
mayonnaise	*Mayonnaise*	mah-yoh-**nay**-zeh
tomatoes	*Tomaten*	toh-**mah**-tehn
mustard	*Senf*	zehnf
onions	*Zwiebeln*	**tsvee**-behln
Does this come cold or warm?	*Wird das kalt oder warm serviert?*	virt dahs kahlt **oh**-der varm zer-**veert**
Heated, please.	*Erwärmt, bitte.*	ehr-**vehrmt bit**-teh

If You Knead Bread

bread	*Brot*	broht
dark bread	*dunkles Brot*	**doon**-klehs broht
three-grain bread	*Dreikornbrot*	**drī**-korn-broht

rye bread	*Roggenmischbrot*	**roh**-gehn-mish-broht
dark rye bread	*Schwarzbrot*	**shvarts**-broht
whole grain bread	*Vollkornbrot*	**fohl**-korn-broht
light bread	*Weißbrot*	**vīs**-broht
wimpy white bread	*Toast*	tohst
French bread	*Baguette*	bah-**geht**
roll (Germany, Austria)	*Brötchen, Semmel*	**brurt**-khehn, **zehm**-mehl
roll (Switz)	*Brötli*	**brurt**-lee

There are hundreds of different kinds of local breads in Germany, Austria, and Switzerland. Add a visit to the neighborhood ***Bäckerei*** to your touring schedule and look for their specialties (***Spezialitäten***). ***Stollen*** (pron. **shtohl**-lehn) is a sweet Christmas bread with raisins and nuts, topped with powdered sugar.

Say Cheese

cheese	*Käse*	**kay**-zeh
mild / sharp	*mild / scharf*	meelt / sharf
cheese plate	*Käseplatte, Käseteller*	**kay**-zeh-**plah**-teh, **kay**-zeh-**tehl**-ler
Can I try a taste?	*Kann ich es probieren?*	kahn̲ ikh ehs **proh**-beer-ehn

The holes in Swiss cheese are made during fermentation—the more symmetrical the holes, the more expert the fermentation.

Two of Switzerland's best-known specialties are cheese-based: ***Käse Fondue*** is Emmentaler and Gruyère melted with white wine and garlic. Eat this tasty treat by dipping bread into it. Lose your bread in the pot and you have to kiss all the men (or women) at the table. ***Raclette*** is melted cheese from Valais. A special appliance slowly melts the bottom of the brick of cheese. Just scrape off a mound and eat it with potatoes, pickled onions, and gherkins.

Soups and Salads

soup (of the day)	*Suppe (des Tages)*	**zup**-peh (dehs **tahg**-ehs)
chicken broth...	*Hühnerbrühe...*	**hew**-ner-brew-heh
beef broth...	*Rinderbrühe...*	**rin**-der-brew-heh
...with noodles	*...mit Nudeln*	mit **noo**-dehln
...with rice	*...mit Reis*	mit rīs
stew	*Eintopf*	**īn**-tohpf
vegetable soup	*Gemüsesuppe*	geh-**mew**-zeh-zup-peh
spicy goulash soup	*Gulaschsuppe*	**goo**-lahsh-zup-peh
liver dumpling soup	*Leberknödelsuppe*	**lay**-ber-kuh-nur-dehl-zup-peh
split pea soup	*Erbsensuppe*	**ehrb**-sehn-zup-peh
oxtail soup	*Ochsenschwanzsuppe*	**okh**-sehn-shvants-zup-peh
cabbage and sausage soup	*Bauernsuppe*	**bow**-ern-zup-peh
Serbian-style bean soup	*Serbische Bohnensuppe*	**zehr**-bi-sheh **boh**-nehn-zup-peh
salad	*Salat*	zah-**laht**
green salad	*grüner Salat*	**grew**-ner zah-**laht**
mixed salad	*gemischter Salat*	geh-**mish**-ter zah-**laht**
potato salad	*Kartoffelsalat*	kar-**tohf**-fehl-zah-laht
Greek salad	*griechischer Salat*	**greekh**-ish-er zah-**laht**
chef's salad...	*gemischter Salat des Hauses...*	geh-**mish**-ter zah-**laht** dehs **how**-zehs
...with ham and cheese	*...mit Schinken und Käse*	mit **shink**-ehn oont **kay**-zeh
...with egg	*...mit Ei*	mit ī
plate of various salads	*Salatteller*	zah-**laht**-tehl-ler
cold cuts mixed with pickles and mayonnaise	*Fleischsalat*	**flīsh**-zah-laht
vegetable platter	*Gemüseplatte, Gemüseteller*	geh-**mew**-zeh-plah-teh, geh-**mew**-zeh-tehl-ler
lettuce	*Salat*	zah-**laht**
tomato	*Tomate*	toh-**mah**-teh

onion	*Zwiebel*	**tsvee**-behl
cucumber	*Gurken*	**gur**-kehn
oil / vinegar	*Öl / Essig*	url / **ehs**-sig
salad dressing	*Salatsoße*	zah-**laht**-zoh-seh
dressing on the side	*Salatsoße separat*	zah-**laht**-zoh-seh zeh-par-**aht**
What is in this salad?	*Was ist in diesem Salat?*	vahs ist in **dee**-zehm zah-**laht**

In Germany, soup is often served as a first course to the large midday meal (***Mittagessen***). Typical German salads usually consist of a single ingredient with dressing, such as ***Gurkensalat*** (sliced cucumber marinated in a sweet vin-aigrette) and ***Tomatensalat*** (tomatoes in vinaigrette with dill). For a meaty salad, try a Fleischsalat (**flīsh**-zah-laht)—chopped cold cuts mixed with pickles and mayonnaise.

The ***Salatbar*** (salad bar) is becoming a global phenomenon. You're normally charged by the size of the plate for one trip. Choose a ***Teller*** (plate) that is ***kleiner*** (small), ***mittlerer*** (medium), or ***großer*** (large). Budget travelers eat a cheap and healthy lunch by stacking a small plate high.

Seafood

seafood	*Meeresfrüchte*	**meh**-rehs-**frewkh**-teh
assorted seafood	*gemischte Meeresfrüchte*	geh-**mish**-teh **meh**-rehs-**frewkh**-teh
fish	*Fisch*	fish
clams	*Muscheln*	**moo**-shehln
cod	*Dorsch*	dorsh
herring	*Hering*	**hehr**-ing
pike	*Hecht*	hehkht
salmon	*Lachs*	lahkhs
trout	*Forelle*	foh-**rehl**-leh
tuna	*Thunfisch*	**toon**-fish
What's fresh today?	*Was ist heute frisch?*	vahs ist **hoy**-teh frish
Do you eat this part?	*Ißt man diesen Teil?*	ist mahn **dee**-zehn tīl

Poultry

poultry	*Geflügel*	geh-**flew**-gehl
chicken	*Hähnchen*	**hayn**-syehn
roast chicken	*Brathähnchen*	**braht**-hayn-syehn
duck	*Ente*	**ehn**-teh
turkey	*Truthahn, Pute*	**troot**-hahn, **poo**-teh
How long has this been dead?	*Wie lange ist dieses Tier schon tot?*	vee **lahng**-eh ist **dee**-zehs teer shohn toht

Meat

meat	*Fleisch*	flīsh
bacon	*Speck*	shpehk
beef	*Rindfleisch*	**rint**-flīsh
beef steak	*Beefsteak*	**beef**-shtayk
brains	*Hirn*	hehrn
bunny	*Kaninchen*	kah-**neen**-syehn
cutlet	*Kotelett*	**koht**-leht
ham	*Schinken*	**shink**-ehn
lamb	*Lamm*	lahm
liver	*Leber*	**lay**-ber
mixed grill	*Grillteller*	**gril**-tehl-ler
organs	*Innereien*	in-neh-**rī**-ehn
pork	*Schweinefleisch*	**shvī**-neh-flīsh
roast beef	*Rinderbraten*	**rin**-der-brah-tehn
sausage	*Wurst*	voorst
tripe	*Kutteln*	**kut**-tehln
veal	*Kalbfleisch*	**kahlp**-flīsh

EATING

How Food is Prepared

assorted	*gemischte*	geh-**mish**-teh
baked	*gebacken*	geh-**bah**-kehn
boiled	*gekocht*	geh-**kohkht**
braised	*geschmort*	geh-**shmort**
broiled	*ofengegrillt*	**ohf**-ehn-geh-grilt
cold	*kalt*	kahlt

Avoiding Mis-Steaks

tenderloin	*Filet mignon*	"filet mignon"
T-bone	*T-bone*	**tay**-bohn
tenderloin of T-bone	*Lendenstück*	**lehn**-dehn-shtewk
raw	*roh*	roh
very rare	*blutig*	**bloo**-tig
rare	*rot*	roht
medium	*halbgar*	**hahlp**-gar
well-done	*gar, durchgebraten*	gar, **durkh**-geh-brah-tehn
very well-done	*ganz gar*	gahnts gar
almost burnt	*fast verkohlt*	fahst fehr-**kohlt**

cooked	*gekocht*	geh-**kohkht**
deep-fried	*frittiert*	frit-**eert**
fillet	*Filet*	fi-**lay**
fresh	*frisch*	frish
fried	*gebraten*	geh-**brah**-tehn
grilled	*gegrillt*	geh-**grilt**
homemade	*hausgemacht*	**hows**-geh-mahkht
hot	*heiß*	hīs
in cream sauce	*in Rahmsauce*	in **rahm**-zoh-seh
medium	*halbgar*	**hahlp**-gar
microwave	*Mikrowelle*	**mee**-kroh-vehl-leh
mild	*mild*	meelt
mixed	*gemischte*	geh-**mish**-teh
poached	*pochierte*	pohkh-ee-**ehr**-teh
rare	*rot*	roht
raw	*roh*	roh
roast	*Braten*	**brah**-tehn
roasted	*geröstet*	geh-**rurs**-teht
sautéed	*pfannengebraten*	**pfahn**-nehn-geh **braht**-ehn
smoked	*geräuchert*	geh-**roykh**-ert

sour	*sauer*	**zow**-er
spicy hot	*scharf*	sharf
steamed	*gedünstet*	geh-**dewn**-steht
stuffed	*gefüllt*	geh-**fewlt**
sweet	*süß*	zews
topped with cheese	*mit Käseschicht*	mit **kay**-zeh-shnit
well-done	*gar*	gar
with rice	*mit Reis*	mit rīs

Veggies

vegetables	*Gemüse*	geh-**mew**-zeh
mixed vegetables	*gemischtes Gemüse*	geh-**mish**-tehs geh-**mew**-zeh
with vegetables	*mit Gemüse*	mit geh-**mew**-zeh
artichoke	*Artischocke*	art-i-**shoh**-keh
asparagus	*Spargel*	**shpar**-gehl
beans	*Bohnen*	**boh**-nehn
beets	*Rüben*	**rew**-behn
broccoli	*Brokkoli*	**brohk**-koh-lee
cabbage	*Kohl*	kohl
carrots	*Karotten*	kah-**roht**-tehn
cauliflower	*Blumenkohl*	**bloo**-mehn-kohl
corn	*Mais*	mīs
cucumber	*Gurken*	**goor**-kehn
eggplant	*Auberginen*	oh-ber-**zhee**-nehn
garlic	*Knoblauch*	kuh-**noh**-blowkh
green beans	*grüne Bohnen*	**grew**-neh **boh**-nehn
leeks	*Lauch*	lowkh
lentils	*Linsen*	**lin**-zehn
mushrooms	*Pilze*	**pilt**-seh
olives	*Oliven*	oh-**leev**-ehn
onions	*Zwiebeln*	**tsvee**-behln
peas	*Erbsen*	**ehrb**-zehn
pepper...	*Paprika...*	**pah**-pree-kah
...green / red / yellow	*...grün / rot / gelb*	grewn / roht / gehlp
pickles	*Essiggurken*	**ehs**-sig-goor-kehn

potatoes	*Kartoffeln*	kar-**tof**-fehln
radishes	*Radieschen*	rah-**dee**-shyehn
spinach	*Spinat*	shpee-**naht**
tomatoes	*Tomaten*	toh-**mah**-tehn
zucchini	*Zucchini*	tsoo-**kee**-nee

Fruits

apple	*Apfel*	**ahp**-fehl
apricot	*Aprikose*	ahp-ri-**koh**-zeh
banana	*Banane*	bah-**nah**-neh
berries	*Beeren*	**behr**-ehn
blackberries	*Brombeeren*	**brohm**-behr-ehn
canteloupe	*Melone*	meh-**loh**-neh
cherry	*Kirsche*	**keer**-sheh
cranberries	*Preiselbeeren*	**prī**-sehl-behr-ehn
date	*Dattel*	**daht**-tehl
fig	*Feige*	**fī**-geh
fruit	*Obst*	ohpst
grapefruit	*Pampelmuse, Grapefruit*	pahm-pehl-**moo**-zeh, **grahp**-froot
grapes	*Trauben*	**trow**-behn
lemon	*Zitrone*	tsee-**troh**-neh
orange	*Apfelsine, Orange*	ahp-fehl-**zee**-neh, oh-**rahn**-zheh
peach	*Pfirsich*	**pfeer**-zikh
pear	*Birne*	**beer**-neh
pineapple	*Ananas*	**ahn**-ahn-ahs
plum	*Pflaume, Zwetsche*	**pflow**-meh, **tsveht**-sheh
prune	*Backpflaume*	**bahk**-pflow-meh
raspberries	*Himbeeren*	**him**-behr-ehn
red currants	*Johannisbeeren*	yoh-**hahn**-nis-behr-ehn
strawberries	*Erdbeeren*	**ehrt**-behr-ehn
tangerine	*Mandarine*	mahn-dah-**ree**-neh
watermelon	*Wassermelone*	**vah**-ser-meh-loh-neh

Nuts

nut	*Nuß*	noos
almond	*Mandel*	**mahn**-dehl
chestnut	*Kastanie*	**kahs**-tahn-yeh
coconut	*Kokosnuß*	**koh**-kohs-noos
hazelnut	*Haselnuß*	**hah**-zehl-noos
peanut	*Erdnuß*	**ehrd**-noos
pistachio	*Pistazien*	pis-**tahts**-ee-ehn
walnut	*Walnuß*	**vahl**-noos

Just Desserts

dessert	*Nachspeise, Nachtisch*	**nahkh**-shpī-zeh, **nahkh**-tish
strudel	*Strudel*	**shtroo**-dehl
cake	*Kuchen*	**kookh**-ehn
a piece of cake	*ein Stück Kuchen*	īn stewk **kookh**-ehn
sherbet	*Sorbet*	zor-**beht**
fruit cup	*Früchtebecher*	**frewkh**-teh-behkh-er
fruit salad	*Obstsalat*	**ohpst**-zah-laht
tart	*Törtchen*	**turt**-shyehn
pie	*Torte*	**tor**-teh
cream	*Sahne, Rahm*	**zah**-neh, rahm
whipped cream	*Schlagsahne*	**shlahg**-zah-neh
chocolate	*Schokolade*	shoh-koh-**lah**-deh
chocolate mousse	*Mousse*	moos
pudding	*Pudding*	"pudding"
pastry	*Gebäck*	geh-**behk**
cookies	*Kekse*	**kayk**-zeh
candy	*Bonbons*	**bon**-bonz
low calorie	*kalorienarm*	kah-loh-**ree**-ehn-arm
homemade	*hausgemacht*	**hows**-geh-mahkht
We'll split one.	*Wir teilen eine.*	veer **tī**-lehn **ī**-neh
Two forks / spoons, please.	*Zwei Gabeln / Löffel, bitte.*	tsvī **gah**-behln / **lurf**-fehl **bit**-teh
I shouldn't, but...	*Ich sollte nicht, aber...*	ikh **zohl**-teh nikht **ah**-ber
Delicious!	*Köstlich! Lecker!*	**kurst**-likh / **lehk**-er

Heavenly.	*Himmlisch.*	**him**-lish
Death by chocolate.	*Tod durch Schokolade.*	tohd durkh shoh-koh-**lah**-deh
Better than sex.	*Besser als Sex.*	**behs**-ser ahls zehx
A moment on the lips, forever on the hips.	*Ein Weilchen auf der Zunge, ewig auf der Hüfte.*	īn **vīl**-shyehn owf dehr **tsoong**-eh **eh**-vig owf dehr **hewf**-teh
I'm in seventh heaven.	*Ich bin im siebten Himmel.*	ikh bin im **zeeb**-tehn **him**-mehl

Ice Cream

ice cream	*Eis*	īs
scoop	*Kugel*	**koog**-ehl
cone	*Waffel*	**vah**-fehl
small bowl	*Schale*	**shah**-leh
chocolate	*Schokolade*	shoh-koh-**lah**-deh
vanilla	*Vanille*	vah-**nil**-leh
strawberry	*Erdbeer*	**ehrt**-behr
lemon	*Zitrone*	tsee-**troh**-neh
rum-raisin	*Malaga*	**mah**-lah-gah
hazelnut	*Haselnuß*	**hah**-zehl-noos
Can I taste it?	*Kann ich probieren?*	kahn ikh **proh**-beer-ehn

Two great dessert specialties are Vienna's famous super-chocolate cake, ***Sachertorte,*** and Germany's Black Forest cherry cake, called ***Schwarzwälder Kirschtorte.*** This diet-killing chocolate cake with cherries and rum can be found all over Germany. For a little bit of Italy, try ***Gelato*** (Italian ice cream) at a ***gelateria.***

In Germany at Christmas time, look for the spiced gingerbread, ***Lebkuchen,*** packaged inside tins shaped like cottages, bells, animals, and fanciful Christmas designs.

The Swiss changed the world in 1875 with their invention of milk chocolate. Nestlé, Suchard, and Lindt are the major producers and sometimes offer factory tours—and samples, of course. ***Nußnougat Crème*** (milk chocolate hazelnut) is a popular spread all over Europe, especially the Italian brand, Nutella. Anything dipped in Nutella becomes a tasty cultural experience.

DRINKING

Water, Milk, and Juice

mineral water...	*Mineralwasser...*	min-eh-**rahl**-vah-ser
...with / without gas	*...mit / ohne Gas*	mit / **oh**-neh gahs
mixed with mineral water	*gespritzt*	geh-**shpritst**
tap water	*Leitungswasser*	**lī**-toongs-vah-ser
fruit juice	*Fruchtsaft*	**frookht**-zahft
100% juice	*reiner Fruchtsaft*	**rī**-ner **frookht**-zahft
orange juice	*Orangensaft*	oh-**rahn**-zhehn-zahft
freshly squeezed	*frischgepreßt*	frish-geh-**prehst**
apple juice	*Apfelsaft*	**ahp**-fehl-zahft
grapefruit juice	*Grapefruitsaft*	**grahp**-froot-zahft
clear soda	*Limonade*	lee-moh-**nah**-deh
with / without...	*mit / ohne...*	mit / **oh**-neh
...sugar	*...Zucker*	**tsoo**-ker
...ice	*...Eis*	īs
glass / cup	*Glas / Tasse*	glahs / **tah**-seh
small / large	*kleine / große*	**klī**-neh / **groh**-seh
bottle	*Flasche*	**flah**-sheh
Is the water safe to drink?	*Ist das Trinkwasser?*	ist dahs **trink**-vahs-ser
milk	*Milch*	milkh
whole milk	*Vollmilch*	**fohl**-milkh
skim milk	*Magermilch*	**mah**-ger-milkh
fresh milk	*frische Milch*	**frish**-eh milkh
acidophilus	*Acidophilus, Kefir*	ah-**see**-doh-fi-lus, **keh**-feer
buttermilk	*Buttermilch*	**boo**-ter-milkh
chocolate milk	*Schokomilch*	**shoh**-koh-milkh
hot chocolate	*heiße Schokolade, Kakao*	**hī**-seh shoh-koh-**lah**-deh, kah-**kow**
Ovaltine	*Ovomaltine*	oh-voh-mahl-**tee**-neh
milkshake	*Milchshake*	**milkh**-shayk

EATING

On a menu, you'll find drinks listed under ***Getränkekarte*** (drink menu). If you ask for ***Wasser*** in a restaurant, you'll be served mineral water. Germans rarely drink tap water at the table; develop a taste for the inexpensive and classier ***Mineralwasser***. Bubbly mineral water might be listed on menus or in stores as "***mit Kohlensäure***" (with carbon dioxide) or "***mit Sprudel***" (with bubbles). But when you're requesting it, the easy-to-remember "***mit Gas***" will do the trick. To get water without bubbles, look for "***ohne Kohlensäure / Sprudel / Gas.***" If you have your heart set on free tap water, ask for ***Leitungswasser*** and be persistent.

Soda-lovers seek out the Fanta/Coke blend called ***Mezzo Mix*** or ***Spezi. Rivella*** is a dairy-based Swiss soft drink. To get a diet drink, use the word "light" instead of "diet" (for instance, Diet Coke is called "Coke Light").

Coffee and Tea

coffee	*Kaffee*	kah-**fay**
espresso	*Espresso*	ehs-**prehs**-soh
cappuccino	*Cappuccino*	kah-poo-**chee**-noh
decaffeinated	*koffeinfrei, Haag*	koh-fay-**in**-frī, hahg
instant coffee	*Pulverkaffee, Nescafe*	pool-ver-kah-**fay**, "Nescafe"
black	*schwarz*	shvarts
with cream / milk	*mit Sahne / Milch*	mit **zah**-neh / milkh
with sugar	*mit Zucker*	mit **tsoo**-ker
iced coffee or coffee w/ ice cream	*Eiskaffee*	**īs**-kah-fay
hot water	*heißes Wasser*	**hī**-sehs **vah**-ser
tea / lemon	*Tee / Zitrone*	tay / tsee-**troh**-neh
tea bag	*Teebeutel*	**tay**-boy-tehl
iced tea	*Eistee*	**īs**-tay
herbal tea	*Kräutertee*	**kroy**-ter-tay
peppermint tea	*Pfefferminztee*	**pfeh**-fer-mints-tay
fruit tea	*Früchte Tee*	**frewkh**-teh tay
little pot	*Kännchen*	**kehn**-shyehn
Another cup.	*Noch eine Tasse.*	nohkh **ī**-neh **tah**-seh

Key Phrases: Drinking

drink	*Getränk*	geh-**traynk**
(mineral) water	*(Mineral-) Wasser*	(min-eh-**rahl**-) **vah**-ser
tap water	*Leitungswasser*	**lī**-toongs-vah-ser
milk	*Milch*	milkh
juice	*Saft*	zahft
coffee	*Kaffee*	kah-**fay**
tea	*Tee*	tay
wine	*Wein*	vīn
beer	*Bier*	beer
Cheers!	*Prost!*	prohst

Wine

I would like...	*Ich hätte gern...*	ikh **heh**-teh gehrn
We would like...	*Wir hätten gern...*	veer **heh**-tehn gehrn
...a glass...	*...ein Glas...*	īn glahs
...an eighth liter...	*...ein Achtel...*	īn **ahkh**-tehl
...a quarter liter...	*...ein Viertel...*	īn **feer**-tehl
...a carafe...	*...eine Karaffe...*	ī-neh kah-**rah**-feh
...a half bottle...	*...eine halbe Flasche...*	ī-neh **hahl**-beh **flah**-sheh
...a bottle...	*...eine Flasche...*	ī-neh **flah**-sheh
...a five-liter jug...	*...einen fünf-Liter Krug...*	ī-nehn **fewnf**-lee-ter kroog
...a barrel...	*...ein Faß...*	īn fahs
...a vat...	*...ein Riesenfaß...*	īn **rī**-zehn-fahs
...of red wine.	*...Rotwein.*	**roht**-vīn
...of white wine.	*...Weißwein.*	**vīs**-vīn
...the wine list.	*...die Weinkarte.*	dee **vīn**-kar-teh

Three-quarters of German, Austrian, and Swiss wines are white. As you travel through wine-growing regions, you'll see ***Probieren*** signs inviting you in for a free (or nearly free) wine tasting.

White wines to look for in Germany are ***Riesling*** (fruity and fragrant), ***Müller Thurgau*** (best when young, smooth, and sweet), ***Gewürztraminer*** (intense and spicy), and ***Grauburgunder*** (soft, full-bodied white—known as ***Pinot Gris*** or ***Grigio*** in other countries). In Austria, consider ***Grüner Veltliner*** (dry, light), ***Riesling***, ***Pinot Blanc*** (semi-dry, fruity nose), and ***Heuriger*** wine (new wine). In Switzerland, try the tart, white ***Fendant*** and the lovely, fruity ***St. Saphorin*** from the slopes above Lake Geneva.

Typically, you order a glass of wine by saying ***Ein Viertel*** (a quarter liter) or ***Ein Achtel*** (an eighth liter). In Switzerland, a ***Pfiff*** is two deciliters of red wine, and a ***Bocalino*** is a small, decorated ceramic jug with two deciliters of a light Swiss red wine called ***Dole***.

Wine Words

wine	*Wein*	vīn
red wine	*Rotwein*	**roht**-vīn
white wine	*Weißwein*	**vīs**-vīn
rosé	*Rosé*	roh-**zay**
table wine	*Tafelwein*	**tah**-fehl-vīn
house wine	*Hausmarke*	**hows**-mar-keh
local	*einheimisch*	**īn**-hī-mish
of the region	*regional*	reh-gee-oh<u>n</u>-**ahl**
sparkling	*sprudelnd*	**shproo**-dehlnt
fruity	*fruchtig*	**frookh**-tig
light / heavy	*leicht / schwer*	līkht / shvehr
sweet	*süß, lieblich*	zews, **leeb**-likh
medium	*halbsüß*	**hahlp**-zews
semi-dry	*halbtrocken*	**hahlp**-trohk-ehn
dry	*trocken*	**trohk**-ehn
very dry	*sehr trocken*	zehr **trohk**-ehn
full-bodied	*vollmundig*	fohl-**moon**-dig
mature	*trinkreif*	**trink**-rīf
wine spritzer	*Wein gespritzt*	vīn geh-**shpritst**
cork	*Korken*	**kor**-kehn
corkscrew	*Korkenzieher*	**kor**-kehn-tsee-her

grapes	*Weintrauben*	**vīn**-trow-behn
vintage	*Weinlese*	**vīn**-lay-zeh
vineyard	*Weinberg*	**vīn**-behrg
wine-tasting	*Weinprobe*	**vīn**-proh-beh
What is a good year (vintage)?	*Welcher Jahrgang (Weinlese) ist gut?*	**vehlkh**-er **yar**-gahng (**vīn**-lay-zeh) ist goot
What do you recommend?	*Was empfehlen Sie?*	vahs ehmp-**fay**-lehn zee

Unfermented wine is called ***Most.*** Partially fermented wine is called ***Federweißer*** (pron. **feh**-der-vī-ser) in Germany, ***Suuser*** (pron. **zoo**-ser) in Switzerland, and ***Sturm*** (pron. shtoorm) in Austria. ***Staubiger*** (pron. **shtow**-big-er) is a cloudy, fully fermented Austrian wine.

Wine Labels

As with most European countries, Germany has a strict set of rules dictating how quality wine is produced: the higher the percentage of natural grape sugar, the higher the alcohol content, the higher the rating. You can identify the origin of German wine by the color or shape of the bottle: brown (Rhine), green (Mosel), or jug-shaped (Franconian). The ***Weinsiegel*** (wine seal) on the neck of the bottle is also color-coded—yellow for dry, green for semi-dry, and red for sweet. Switzerland and Austria produce less wine than Germany but follow similar standards. Listed below are terms to help you decipher all of the information on a German, Austrian, or Swiss wine label.

Spätlese, Auslese, Beerenauslese, Trockenbeeren Auslese, Eiswein	late harvest wines (listed in order of grape sugar content from high to highest)
Kabinett	select wine
Qualitätswein	better quality wine
QmP (Qualitätswein mit Prädikat)	quality wine of distinction
QbA (Qualitätswein bestimmter Anbaugebiete)	quality wine of a specific region

Heuriger	new wine (Austria)
Landwein	country wine, dry to semi-dry
Gutsabfüllung	estate bottled
Tafelwein	table wine–lowest category

Beer

beer	*Bier*	beer
bar	*Kneipe (Germany), Beisl (Austria), Baiz (Switzerland)*	ku-**nī**-peh, **bī**-zehl, bīts
from the tap	*vom Faß*	fom fahs
bottle	*Flasche*	**flah**-sheh
light–but not "lite"	*Helles*	**hehl**-lehs
dark	*Dunkles*	**doonk**-lehs
local / imported	*einheimisch / importiert*	**īn**-hī-mish / im-por-tee-**ehrt**
small / large	*kleines / großes*	**klī**-nehs / **groh**-sehs
half-liter	*Halbes*	**hahl**-behs
liter (Bavarian)	*Maß*	mahs
low calorie	*Light*	"light"
cold	*kalt*	kahlt
colder	*kälter*	**kehl**-ter

Germany is Europe's beer capital. Its beer is regulated by the German Purity law (***Reinheitsgebot***), the oldest food and beverage law in the world. Only four ingredients may be used in German beer: malt, yeast, hops, and water. Pils is a bottom-fermented, full beer and ***Weizen*** is wheat-based. ***Malzbier*** is the non-alcoholic malt beer that children drink. The barely alcoholic ***Nährbier***, considered healthy and caloric, is for fattening up skinny kids. ***Radler*** (which means biker) is a refreshing mix of beer and lemon soda, invented in Munich for cyclists on hot days. A ***Berliner Weisse mit Schuß*** is a wheat beer with a shot of fruit syrup. ***Bockbier***, from Bavaria, is a strong amber called "liquid bread" and is consumed mostly at Easter and Christmas. ***Märzen*** is a light beer brewed in March (***März***), then stored for ***Oktoberfest***.

Drink menus list exactly how many deciliters you'll get in your glass. A "5 dl" beer is half a liter, or about a pint. When you order beer, ask for "*Ein Halbes*" for a half liter or "*Ein Maß*" for a whole liter (about a quart). Some beer halls serve beer only by the liter! Children are welcome in beer halls.

In Austria, order "*ein Bier*" and you get a light, basic beer in a standard beer mug. Order a *Pils* and you get a more flavorful, stronger beer in a tulip glass. A *Dunkel* is the darkest, served in a straight, tall glass. In the German-speaking regions of Switzerland, a *Stange* is a *Pils* in a tall, fluted glass. The popular *Weizenbier*, which is poured slowly to build its frothy head thick and high, is served in a large rounded-top glass with a wedge of lemon.

Bar Talk

Let's go out for a drink.	*Komm, wir gehen aus für ein Drink.*	kohm veer **gay**-hehn ows fewr īn drink
May I buy you a drink?	*Kann ich dir ein Drink spendieren?*	kahn ikh deer īn drink shpehn-**deer**-ehn
My treat.	*Ich lade ein.*	ikh **lah**-deh īn
The next one's on me.	*Die nächste Runde geht auf mich.*	dee **nehkh**-steh **roon**-deh gayt owf mikh
What would you like?	*Was hättest du gern?*	vahs **heh**-tehst doo gehrn
I'll have a ___.	*Ich nehme ein ___.*	ikh **nay**-meh īn
I don't drink.	*Ich trinke keinen Alcohol.*	ikh **trink**-eh **kīn**-ehn **ahl**-koh-hohl
alcohol-free	*alkoholfrei*	**ahl**-koh-hohl-**frī**
What is the local specialty?	*Was ist die Spezialität hier?*	vahs ist dee **shpayt**-see-ahl-ee-**tayt** heer
What is a good man's / woman's drink?	*Was ist ein gutes Männer-/Damen-Getränk?*	vahs ist īn **goo**-tehs **meh**-ner / dah-mehn geh-**trehnk**
Straight.	*Pur.*	poor
With / Without...	*Mit / Ohne...*	mit / **oh**-neh
...alcohol.	*...Alkohol.*	**ahl**-koh-hohl
...ice.	*...Eis.*	īs

One more.	*Noch eins.*	nokh īns
Cheers!	*Prost!*	prohst
To your health!	*Auf Ihre Gesundheit!*	owf **eer**-eh geh-**zoond**-hīt
To you!	*Zum Wohl!*	tsoom vohl
Long life!	*Langes Leben!*	**lahng**-ehs **lay**-behn
I'm...	*Ich bin...*	ikh bin
...tipsy.	*...beschwippst.*	beh-**shvipst**
...a little drunk.	*...ein bißchen betrunken.*	īn **bis**-yehn beh-**troonk**-ehn
...wasted.	*...völlig blau.* ("completely blue")	**furl**-lig blow
...a boozehound.	*...Schnapshund.*	**shnahps**-hoont
I'm hung over.	*Ich hab' ein Kater.* ("I have a tomcat.")	ikh hahp īn **kah**-ter

The bartender will often throw a coaster (***Bierdeckel***) down at your place and keep track of your bill by keeping a stroke tally on the coaster. To get your bill, hand the bartender your coaster.

PICNICKING

At the Grocery

Self-service?	*Selbstbedienung?*	**zehlpst**-beh-dee-noong
Ripe for today?	*Jetzt reif?*	yehtst rīf
Does this need to be cooked?	*Muß man das kochen?*	mus mah<u>n</u> dahs **kohkh**-ehn
Can I taste it?	*Kann ich probieren?*	kah<u>n</u> ikh proh-**beer**-ehn
Fifty grams.	*Fünfzig Gramm.*	**fewnf**-tsig grahm
One hundred grams.	*Hundert Gramm.*	**hoon**-dert grahm
More. / Less.	*Mehr. / Weniger.*	mehr / **vay**-nig-er
A piece.	*Ein Stück.*	īn shtewk
A slice.	*Eine Scheibe.*	ī-neh **shī**-beh
Four slices.	*Vier Scheiben.*	feer **shī**-behn
Sliced.	*In Scheiben.*	in **shī**-behn
Half.	*Halb.*	hahlp
A small bag.	*Eine kleine Tüte.*	ī-neh **klīn**-eh **tew**-teh
A bag, please.	*Eine Tüte, bitte.*	īn **tew**-teh **bit**-teh

Can you make me / us...?	*Können Sie mir / uns... machen?*	**kurn**-nehn zee meer / oons... **mahkh**-ehn
...a sandwich	*...ein Sandwich*	īn **zahnd**-vich
...two sandwiches	*...zwei Sandwiche*	tsvī **zahnd**-vich-eh
To take out.	*Zum Mitnehmen.*	tsoom **mit**-nay-mehn
Can I use the microwave?	*Kann ich die Mikrowelle benutzen?*	kahn ikh dee mee-kroh-**vehl**-leh beh-**noot**-sehn
May I borrow a...?	*Kann ich ein... leihen?*	kahn ikh īn... **lī**-hehn
Do you have a...?	*Haben Sie ein...?*	**hah**-behn zee īn
Where can I buy / find a...?	*Wo kann ich ein... kaufen / finden?*	voh kahn ikh īn... **kow**-fehn / **fin**-dehn
...corkscrew	*...Korkenzieher*	**kor**-kehn-tsee-her
...can opener	*...Dosenöffner*	**doh**-zehn-urf-ner
Is there a park nearby?	*Gibt es einen Park in der Nähe?*	gipt ehs **ī**-nehn park in dehr **nay**-heh
Where is a good place to picnic?	*Wo ist gut zu picknicken?*	voh ist goot tsoo **pik**-nik-ehn
Is picnicking allowed here?	*Darf man hier picknicken?*	darf mahn heer **pik**-nik-ehn

Tasty Picnic Words

EATING

picnic	*Picknick*	**pik**-nik
open air market	*Markt*	markt
grocery store	*Lebensmittel-geschäft*	**lay**-behns-mit-tehl-geh-**shehft**
supermarket	*Supermarkt*	**zoo**-per-markt
delicatessen	*Feinkostgeschäft*	**fīn**-kohst-geh-**shehft**
bakery	*Bäckerei*	behk-eh-**rī**
pastry shop	*Konditorei, Patisserie*	kohn-dee-toh-**rī**, pah-tis-er-**ee**
cheese shop	*Käserei*	kay-zeh-**rī**
sandwich	*Sandwich*	**zahnd**-vich
bread	*Brot*	broht
roll	*Brötchen, Semmel*	**brurt**-shyehn, **zehm**-mehl
ham	*Schinken*	**shink**-ehn

sausage	*Wurst*	voorst
cheese	*Käse*	**kay**-zeh
mustard...	*Senf...*	zehnf
mayonnaise...	*Mayonnaise...*	mah-yoh-**nay**-zeh
...in a tube	*...in der Tube*	in dehr **too**-beh
mild / sharp / sweet	*mild / scharf / süß*	meelt / sharf / zews
yogurt	*Joghurt*	"yogurt"
fruit	*Obst*	ohpst
juice	*Saft*	zaft
cold drinks	*kalte Getränke*	**kahl**-teh geh-**trehnk**-eh
straw(s)	*Halm(e)*	hahlm(eh)
plastic...	*Plastik...*	**plah**-steek
...spoon / fork	*...Löffel / Gabel*	**lurf**-fehl / **gah**-behl
paper...	*Papier...*	pah-**peer**
...plate / cup	*...teller / becher*	**tehl**-ler / **behkh**-er

Assemble your picnic at a ***Markt*** (open-air market) or ***Supermarkt*** (supermarket)—or get a fast snack at an ***Obst*** (fruit stand) or ***Imbiß*** (fast-food stand).

At the grocery, you buy meat and cheese by the gram. One hundred grams is about a quarter pound, enough for two sandwiches. To weigh and price your produce, put it on the scale, push the photo or number (keyed to the bin it came from), and then stick your sticker on the food. To get real juice, look for 100% or ***kein Zucker*** on the label. ***Drink*** or ***Trink*** is soda. ***Bio*** means organically grown, and a ***Bioladen*** (***Bioläderli*** in Switzerland) is a store that sells organic products.

MENU DECODER

GERMAN/ENGLISH

This handy decoder won't list every word on the menu, but it'll get you ***Bratwurst*** (pork sausage) instead of ***Blutwurst*** (blood sausage).

Abendessen	dinner
Achtel	eighth liter
Allgäuer Bergkäse	hard, mild cheese with holes
Altenburger	soft, mild goat cheese
Ananas	pineapple
Apfel	apple
Apfelsaft	apple juice
Apfelsine	orange
Apfelstrudel	apples and raisins in puff pastry
Appenzeller	sharp, hard Swiss cheese
Appenzeller Alpenbitter	digestif (alcohol) made from flower and roots
Aprikose	apricot
Artischocke	artichoke
Aubergine	eggplant
Bäckerei	bakery
Backpflaume	prune
Banane	banana

Bauern	farmer-style (from the garden)
Bauernsuppe	cabbage and sausage soup
Becher	small glass
Bedienung	service
Beere	berry
Beilagen	side dishes
Beinwurst	smoked pork, herb sausage
Berliner	raspberry-filled doughnut
Bier	beer
biologisch / bio	organic
Birne	pear
Blumenkohl	cauliflower
Blutwurst	blood sausage
Bockbier	Bavarian amber beer
Bockwurst	white pork sausage
Bohnen	beans
Braten	roast
Brathähnchen	roast chicken
Bratwurst	pork sausage
Brezel	pretzel
Brokkoli	broccoli
Brombeere	blackberry
Brot	bread
Brötchen	roll
Brotzeit	snack
Bündnerfleisch	air-cured beef
Burewurst	boiled *Bratwurst*
Butterhörnchen	croissant
Champignon	mushroom
chinesisch	Chinese
Churer Fleischtorte	meat pie (Switz.)
Cremeschnitte	Napoleon
Currywurst	curry-flavored *Burewurst*
Dattel	date
Debreziner	spicy Hungarian sausage
Dorsch	cod
Dreikornbrot	three-grain bread

dunkel	dark
durchgebraten	well-done
Edelpilzkäse	mild blue cheese
Ei	egg
Eier	eggs
Eierlikör	eggnog-like liqueur
einheimisch	local
Eintopf	stew
Eintritt	cover charge
Eis	ice cream; ice
Eiskaffee	iced coffee, coffee with ice cream
Eistee	iced tea
Emmentaler	hard, mild Swiss cheese
Ente	duck
Erbsen	peas
Erbsensuppe	split pea soup
Erdbeere	strawberry
Erdnuß	peanut
erster Gang	first course
Essen	food
Essig	vinegar
Essiggurken	pickles
Feige	fig
Feinkostgeschäft	delicatessen
Fett	fat
Fisch	fish
Flasche	bottle
Fleisch	meat
Fleischsalat	cubed deli-meat salad
Forelle	trout
französisch	French
Frikadelle	large meatball, hamburger
frisch	fresh
frischgepreßt	freshly squeezed
Frischkäse	soft curd cheese with herbs
Frittaten	sliced pancakes
frittiert	deep-fried

Früchtebecher	fruit cup
fruchtig	fruity (wine)
Fruchtsaft	fruit juice
Frühstück	breakfast
Gang	course
ganz gar	very well-done
gar	well-done
Gas	carbonation
Gasthaus, Gasthof	country inn and restaurant
Gaststätte, Gaststube	informal restaurant
Gebäck	pastry
gebraten	baked
gedünstet	steamed
Geflügel	poultry
gefüllt	stuffed
gegrillt	grilled
gekocht	cooked
gemischt	mixed
gemischter Salat	mixed salad
Gemüse	vegetables
Gemüseplatte/-teller	vegetable platter
Gemüsesuppe	vegetable soup
geräuchert	smoked
Germknödel	sourdough dumplings
geröstet	roasted
geschmort	braised
Geschnetzeltes	meat slivers in a rich sauce with noodles or Rösti
gespritzt	with mineral water
Getränke	beverages
Getränkekarte	drink menu
Glas	glass
Glühwein	hot spiced wine
Graubrot	whole wheat bread
Grillteller	mixed grill
groß	big
grün	green

grüner Salat	green salad
Gruyère	strong-flavored Swiss cheese
Gulasch	spicy stew (goulash)
Gurken	cucumber
Gutsabfüllung	estate bottled (wine)
Hähnchen	chicken
halb	half
halbgar	medium
halbsüß	semi-sweet, medium (wine)
halbtrocken	semi-dry (wine)
hartgekocht	hard-boiled
Haselnuß	hazelnut
Hauptspeise	main course
Haus	house
Hausfrauen Art	housewife-style (apples, onions, and sour cream)
hausgemacht	homemade
heiß	hot
heiße Schockolade	hot chocolate
helles	light (beer)
Hering	herring
Heurigen	young wine; wine bar with food
Himbeere	raspberry
Honig	honey
Hühnerbrühe	chicken broth
importiert	imported
inklusive	included
Innereien	organs
italienisch	Italian
Jagdwurst	smoked pork, garlic, and mustard sausage
Jäger	hunter-style (with mushrooms and gravy)
Jägermeister	anise and herb digestif
Jägertee	tea with brandy and rum
Joghurt	yogurt
Johannisbeere	red currant

Kaffee	coffee
Kaiserschmarren	shredded pancakes with raisins, sugar, and cinnamon
Kakao	cocoa
Kalbfleisch	veal
kalt	cold
Kaninchen	bunny
Kännchen	small pot of tea
Karaffe	carafe
Karotte	carrot
Karte	menu
Kartoffel	potato
Kartoffelsalat	potato salad
Käse	cheese
Käse Fondue	melted Swiss cheeses eaten with cubes of bread
Käsebrot	cheese with bread
Käsekrainer	sausage mixed with cheese
Käseplatte/-teller	cheese platter
Käserei	cheese shop
Kastanie	chestnut
Kekse	cookies
Kinderteller	children's portion
Kirsche	cherry
klein	small
Kleinigkeit	snack
Kneipe	bar, tavern
Knoblauch	garlic
Knödel	dumpling
Kohl	cabbage
Kohlensäure	carbonation
Kohlroulade	stuffed cabbage leaves
Kokosnuß	coconut
Konditerei	pastry shop
Korkenzieher	corkscrew
koscher	kosher
köstlich	delicious

Kotelett	cutlet
Kraut	sauerkraut
Kräutertee	herbal tea
Kugel	scoop
Kutteln	tripe
Lamm	lamb
Leber	liver
Leberkäse	pork liver meatloaf
Leberknödelsuppe	liver dumpling soup
Leberwurst	liverwurst
Lebkuchen	gingerbread
leicht	light
lieblich	sweet (wine)
Limburger	strong-smelling, soft cheese with herbs
limonade	clear soda or lemonade
Linsen	lentils
Linzertorte	almond cake with raspberry
Mais	corn
Malaga	rum-raisin flavor
Malzbier	non-alcoholic kids' beer
Mandarine	tangerine
Mandel	almond
Mandelgipfli	almond croissant (Switz.)
Marmelade	jelly
Maß	liter of beer
Matjesfilet	herring filets
Maultaschen	ravioli
Meeresfrüchte	seafood
Melone	cantaloupe
Mettwurst	spicy, soft sausage spread
Miesmuscheln	mussels
Mikrowelle	microwave
Milch	milk
mild	mild
Mineralwasser	mineral water
mit	with

Mittagessen	lunch
Mohnkuchen	poppy-seed cake
Mohr im Hemd	chocolate pudding with chocolate sauce
Möhre	carrot
Muscheln	clams
Müsli	granola cereal
Nachspeise	dessert
Nachtisch	dessert
Nudel	noodle
Obst	fruit
Obstler	fruit brandy
Obstsalat	fruit salad
Ochsenschwanzsuppe	oxtail soup
oder	or
ohne	without
Öl	oil
Oliven	olives
Omelett	omelet
Orangensaft	orange juice
Pampelmuse	grapefruit
Paprika	bell pepper
Pfannekuchen	pancakes
Pfeffer	pepper
Pfefferminz	peppermint
Pfirsich	peach
Pflaume	plum
Pflümli	plum *Schnaps*
Pistazien	pistachio
pochieren	poached
Pommes (frites)	French fries
Preiselbeere	cranberry
Pute	turkey
Quark	smooth curd cheese
Quittung	receipt
Raclette	melted cheese with vegetable side dishes (Switz.)

Radiesch	radish
Radler	beer and lemon soda
Rahmsauce	cream sauce
Ratsheerentopf	roasted meats and potato stew
Ratskeller	cellar restaurant
Rinderbraten	roast beef
Rinderbrühe	beef broth
Rindfleisch	beef
Rissoles	pear tarts
Roggenmischbrot	rye bread
roh	raw
Rollmops	pickled herring
Rösti	hash browns (Switz.)
Rote Grütze	raspberry and currant pudding
Rotwein	red wine
Rotweiß	with ketchup and mayonnaise (Wurst)
Rüben	beets
Rühreier	scrambled eggs
Sachertorte	chocolate cake layered with chocolate cream
Sahne	cream
Salat	salad
Salatsoße	salad dressing
Salatteller	plate of various salads
Salz	salt
Salzburger Nockerl	fluffy, baked pudding/flan
sättigend	filling
Sauce	sauce
Sauerbraten	braised beef
Schalentiere	shellfish
scharf	spicy
Scheibe	slice
Schinken	ham
Schlachtplatte	assorted cold meats
Schlagsahne	whipped cream
schnell	fast
Schnellimbiß	fast-food stand

Schnitzel	thinly sliced pork or veal
Schokolade	chocolate
Schwarzbrot	dark rye bread
Schwarzwälder Kirschtorte	Black Forest cake–chocolate, cherries, and cream
Schweinebraten	roasted pork with gravy
Schweinefleisch	pork
sehr	very
Semmel	roll
Senf	mustard
Serbische Bohnensuppe	bean soup (Aus.)
Sorbet	sherbet
Soße	sauce
Spargel	asparagus (usually white)
Spätzle	German-style noodles
Speck	bacon
Spezialität	specialty
Spiegeleier	fried eggs
Spinat	spinach
Sprudel	carbonation (bubbles)
sprudelnd	sparkling
Stollen	Christmas bread with fruit and nuts
Stolzer Heinrich	pork sausage fried in beer
Streußelkuchen	coffeecake squares
Stück	piece
Suppe	soup
süß	sweet
Tafelspitz	boiled beef with apples and horseradish
Tafelwein	table wine
Tage	day
Tageskarte, Tagesgericht	menu of the day
Tasse	cup
Tee	tea
Teller	plate
Thunfisch	tuna

Tilsiter	mild, tangy, firm cheese
Tiroler Bauernschmaus	various meats with sauerkraut, potatoes, and dumplings
Tirolerwurst	Austrian smoked sausage
Tomaten	tomatoes
Törtchen	tart
Torte	cake
Traube	grape
trocken	dry
Truthahn	turkey
typisch	local
und	and
Vanille	vanilla
Vegetarier	vegetarian
Vermicell	noodle-shaped chestnut mousse
Viertel	quarter liter
Vollkornbrot	dark bread, whole wheat
vollmundig	full-bodied (wine)
vom Faß	on tap (beer)
Vorspeise	appetizers
Waffel	cone
Walnuß	walnut
Wasser	water
Wassermelone	watermelon
weichgekocht	soft-boiled
Wein	wine
Weinberg	vineyard
Weinkarte	wine list
Weinlese	vintage (wine)
Weinprobe	wine tasting
Weintrauben	grapes (wine)
weiß	white
Weißbrot	light bread
Weißwein	white wine
Weißwurst	boiled veal sausage
Weizen	wheat
Weizenbier	wheat beer

Wiener	Viennese style—breaded and fried
Wiener Schnitzel	breaded, pan-fried veal
Wienerli	thin frankfurter (hot dog)
Wurst	sausage
Zahnstocher	toothpick
Zitrone	lemon
Zucchini	zucchini
Zucker	sugar
zum Mitnehmen	"to go"
Zwetschge	plum
Zwetschgenknödel	fried plum dumplings
Zwiebel	onion
Zwiebelbraten	pot roast with onions
Zwiebelwurst	liver and onion sausage

ACTIVITIES

SIGHTSEEING

Where?

Where is...?	*Wo ist...?*	voh ist
...the tourist information office	*...das Touristeninformationsbüro*	dahs too-**ris**-tehn-in-for-maht-see-**ohns**-bew-roh
...the best view	*...der beste Ausblick*	dehr **behs**-teh **ows**-blick
...the main square	*...der Hauptplatz*	dehr **howpt**-plahts
...the old town center	*...die Altstadt*	dee **ahlt**-shtaht
...the town hall	*...das Rathaus*	dahs **raht**-hows
...the museum	*...das Museum*	dahs moo-**zay**-um
...the castle	*...die Burg*	dee boorg
...the palace	*...das Schloß*	dahs shlohs
...the ruins	*...die Ruine*	dee roo-**ee**-neh
...an amusement park	*...einen Vergnügungspark*	ī-nehn fehrg-**new**-goongs-park
...the entrance / exit	*...der Eingang / Ausgang*	dehr **īn**-gahng / **ows**-gahng
...the toilet	*...die Toilette*	dee toh-**leh**-teh
Nearby is there a...?	*Gibt es in der Nähe ein...?*	gipt ehs in dehr **nay**-heh īn
...fair (rides, games)	*...Kirmes*	**keer**-mehs
...festival (music)	*...Festival*	fehs-tee-**vahl**

Key Phrases: Sightseeing

Where is...?	*Wo ist...?*	voh ist
How much is it?	*Wie viel kostet das?*	vee feel **kohs**-teht dahs
What time does this...?	*Um wie viel Uhr ist hier...?*	oom vee feel oor ist heer
...open / close	*...geöffnet / geschlossen*	geh-**urf**-neht / geh-**shloh**-sehn
Do you have a guided tour?	*Haben Sie eine geführte Tour?*	**hah**-behn zee **ī**-neh geh-**fewr**-teh toor
When is the next tour in English?	*Wann ist die nächste Tour auf Englisch?*	vahn̲ ist dee **nehkh**-steh toor owf **ehng**-lish

At the Sight

Do you have...?	*Haben Sie...?*	**hah**-behn zee
...information...	*...Auskunft...*	**ows**-koonft
...a guidebook...	*...einen Stadtführer / ein Reisebuch...*	**ī**-nehn **shtaht**-fewr-er / īn **rī**-zeh-bookh
...in English	*...auf Englisch*	owf **ehng**-lish
Is it free?	*Ist es umsonst?*	ist ehs oom-**zohnst**
How much is it?	*Wie viel kostet das?*	vee feel **kohs**-teht dahs
Is the ticket good all day?	*Gilt der Schein den ganzen Tag lang?*	gilt dehr shīn dayn **gahn**-tsehn tahg lahn̲g
Can I get back in?	*Kann ich wieder hinein?*	kahn̲ ikh **vee**-der hin-**īn**
What time does this open / close?	*Um wie viel Uhr ist hier geöffnet / geschlossen?*	oom vee feel oor ist heer geh-**urf**-neht / geh-**shloh**-sehn
When is the last entry?	*Wann ist letzter Einlaß?*	vahn̲ ist **lehts**-ter **īn**-lahs

Please

PLEASE let me / us in!	*BITTE, lassen Sie mich / uns hinein!*	**bit**-teh **lah**-sehn zee mikh / oons hin-**īn**

I've / We've traveled all the way from ___.	*Ich bin / Wir sind extra aus ___ gekommen.*	ikh bin / veer zint **ehk**-strah ows ___ geh-**koh**-mehn
I must / We must leave tomorrow.	*Ich muß / Wir müssen morgen abreisen.*	ikh mus / veer **mew**-sehn **mor**-gehn **ahp**-rī-zehn
I promise I'll / we'll be fast.	*Ich verspreche, mich / uns zu beeilen.*	ikh fehr-**shprehkh**-eh mikh / oons tsoo beh-**ī**-lehn
I promised my mother on her deathbed that I'd see this.	*Ich habe meiner Mutter am Sterbebett versprochen, das zu sehen.*	ikh **hah**-beh **mī**-ner **moo**-ter ahm **shtehr**-beh-beht fehr-**shprohkh**-ehn dahs tsoo **zay**-hehn
I've always wanted to see this.	*Ich wollte das schon immer sehen.*	ikh **vohl**-teh dahs shoh<u>n</u> **im**-mehr **zay**-hen

Tours

Do you have...?	*Haben Sie...?*	**hah**-behn zee
...an audioguide	*...einen Tonbandführer*	**ī**-nehn **tohn**-bah<u>n</u>t-fewr-er
...a guided tour	*...eine geführte Tour*	**ī**-neh geh-**fewr**-teh toor
...a city walking tour	*...eine geführte Stadtbesichtigung*	**ī**-neh geh-**fewr**-teh shtaht-beh-**zikh**-tig-oong
...in English	*...auf Englisch*	owf **ehng**-lish
When is the next tour in English?	*Wann ist die nächste Führung auf Englisch?*	vah<u>n</u> ist dee **nehkh**-steh **few**-roong owf **ehng**-lish
Is it free?	*Ist es umsonst?*	ist ehs oom-**zohnst**
How much is it?	*Wie viel kostet das?*	vee feel **kohs**-teht dahs
How long does it last?	*Wie lange dauert es?*	vee **lahng**-eh **dow**-ert ehs
Can I / Can we join a tour in progress?	*Kann ich / Können wir mit der angefangenen Führung gehen?*	kah<u>n</u> ikh / **kurn**-nehn veer mit dehr ah<u>n</u>-geh-**fahng**-ehn-ehn **few**-roong **gay**-hehn

Entrance Signs

Erwachsene	adults
kombinierter Eintritt	combo-ticket
Führung	guided tour
Ausstellung	exhibit
Standort	you are here (on map)

Discounts

You may be eligible for a discount at tourist sights, in hotels, or on buses and trains—ask.

Is there a discount for...?	*Gibt es eine Ermäßigung für...?*	gipt ehs **ī**-neh ehr-**may**-see-goong fewr
...youth	*...Kinder*	**kin**-der
...students	*...Studenten*	shtoo-**dehn**-tehn
...families	*...Familien*	fah-**meel**-yehn
...seniors	*...Senioren*	zehn-**yor**-ehn
...groups	*...Gruppen*	**groop**-ehn
I am...	*Ich bin...*	ikh bin
He / She is...	*Er / Sie ist...*	ehr / zee ist
...___ years old.	*...___ Jahre alt.*	___ **yah**-reh ahlt
...extremely old.	*...extrem alt.*	ehx-**trehm ahlt**

In the Museum

Where is...?	*Wo ist...?*	voh ist
I'd like to see...	*Ich möchte gerne... sehen.*	ikh **murkh**-teh **gehr**-neh... **zay**-hehn
We'd like to see...	*Wir möchten gerne... sehen.*	veer **murkh**-tehn **gehr**-neh... **zay**-hehn
Photo / Video O.K.?	*Fotografieren / Videofilmen O.K.?*	foh-toh-grah-**feer**-ehn / **vee**-deh-oh-fil-mehn "O.K."
No flash.	*Kein Blitz.*	kīn blits
No tripod.	*Stativ verboten.*	shtah-**teef** fehr-**boh**-tehn
I like it.	*Es gefällt mir.*	ehs geh-**fehlt** meer
It's so...	*Es ist so...*	ehs ist zoh
...beautiful.	*...schön.*	shurn

...ugly.	*...häßlich.*	**hehs**-likh
...strange.	*...seltsam.*	**zehlt**-zahm
...boring.	*...langweilig.*	**lahng**-vī-lig
...interesting.	*...interessant.*	in-tehr-ehs-**sahnt**
...pretentious.	*...angeberisch.*	**ahn**-gay-ber-ish
...thought-provoking.	*...Gedanken anregend.*	geh-**dahnk**-ehn **ahn**-ray-gehnt
...B.S.	*...Blödsinn.*	**blurd**-zin
I don't get it.	*Kapier' ich nicht.*	kah-**peer** ikh nikht
Is it upside down?	*Ist es verkehrt?*	ist ehs fehr-**kehrt**
Who did this?	*Wer hat das gemacht?*	vehr haht dahs geh-**mahkht**
How old is this?	*Wie alt ist das?*	vee ahlt ist dahs
Wow!	*Fantastisch! Toll!*	fahn-**tahs**-tish / tohl
My feet have had it!	*Meine Füße sind ganz plattgelaufen!*	**mī**-neh **few**-seh zint gahnts **plaht**-geh-lowf-ehn
I'm exhausted!	*Ich bin fix und fertig!*	ikh bin fix oont **fehr**-tig
We're exhausted!	*Wir sind fix und fertig!*	veer zint fix oont **fehr**-tig

Be careful when planning your sightseeing. Many museums close one day a week, and many stop selling tickets 45 minutes or so before they close. Some sights are tourable only by groups with a guide. Individuals usually end up with the next German escort. To get an English tour, call in advance to see if one's scheduled. Individuals can often tag along with a large tour group.

SHOPPING

Shops

Where is a...?	*Wo ist ein...?*	voh ist īn
antique shop	*Antiquitäten-laden*	ahn-tee-kvee-**tay**-tehn-**lah**-dehn
art gallery	*Kunstgalerie*	koonst-gah-leh-**ree**
bakery	*Bäckerei*	behk-eh-**rī**

Key Phrases: Shopping

Where can I buy...?	*Wo kann ich... kaufen?*	voh kahn̲ ikh... **kow**-fehn
Where is a...?	*Wo ist ein...?*	voh ist īn
grocery store	*Lebensmittel-geschäft*	**lay**-behns-mit-tehl-geh-**shehft**
department store	*Kaufhaus*	**kowf**-hows
Internet café	*Internetcafé*	**in**-tehr-neht-kah-**fay**
launderette	*Waschsalon*	**vahsh**-zah-lohn̲
pharmacy	*Apotheke*	ah-poh-**tay**-keh
How much is it?	*Wie viel kostet das?*	vee feel **kohs**-teht dahs
I'm just browsing.	*Ich sehe mich nur um.*	ikh **zay**-heh mikh noor oom

barber shop	*Herrenfrisör*	hehr-rehn-friz-**ur**
beauty salon	*Frisiersalon, Haarsalon*	friz-**eer**-zah-lohn̲, **har**-zah-lohn̲
book shop	*Buchladen*	**bookh**-lah-dehn
camera shop	*Photoladen*	**foh**-toh-lah-dehn
cell phone shop	*Handyladen*	**han**-dee-lah-dehn
cheese shop	*Käserei*	kay-zeh-**rī**
clothing boutique	*Kleiderladen*	**klī**-der-lah-dehn
coffee shop	*Kaffeeladen*	**kah**-fay-lah-dehn
delicatessen	*Feinkostgeschäft*	**fīn**-kohst-geh-**shehft**
department store	*Kaufhaus*	**kowf**-hows
flea market	*Flohmarkt*	**floh**-markt
flower market	*Blumenmarkt*	**bloo**-mehn-markt
grocery store	*Lebensmittel-geschäft*	**lay**-behns-mit-tehl-geh-**shehft**
hardware store	*Eisenwaren-geschäft*	ī-zehn-**vah**-rehn-geh-**shehft**
Internet café	*Internetcafé*	**in**-tehr-neht-kah-**fay**
jewelry shop	*Schmuckladen*	**shmook**-lah-dehn
launderette	*Waschsalon*	**vahsh**-zah-lohn̲

newsstand	*Kiosk, Zeitungsstand*	**kee**-ohsk, **tsī**-toongs-shtahn̲t
office supplies	*Bürobedarf*	**bew**-roh-beh-darf
open-air market	*Markt*	markt
optician	*Optiker*	**ohp**-ti-ker
pastry shop	*Konditorei, Zuckerbäcker*	kohn̲-dee-toh-**rī**, **tsoo**-ker-bayk-er
pharmacy	*Apotheke*	ah-poh-**tay**-keh
photocopy shop	*Copyshop*	"copy shop"
shopping mall	*Einkaufszentrum*	**īn**-kowfs-tsehn-troom
souvenir shop	*Souvenirladen*	zoo-veh-**neer**-lah-den
supermarket	*Supermarkt*	**zoo**-per-markt
sweets shop	*Süßwarengeschäft*	**zoos**-vah-rehn-geh-**shehft**
toy store	*Spielzeugladen*	**shpeel**-tsoyg-lah-dehn
travel agency	*Reiseagentur*	**rī**-zeh-ah-gehn-tur
used bookstore	*Bücher aus zweiter Hand, Antiquariat*	**bookh**-er ows **tsvī**-ter hahn̲t, ahn̲-teek-vah-**ree**-aht
...with books in English	*...mit englischen Büchern*	mit **ehng**-lish-ehn **bewkh**-ern
wine shop	*Weinhandlung*	**vīn**-hahn̲t-loong

Many businesses close from 12:00 to 15:00 on weekday afternoons and all day on Sundays. Typical hours are Monday through Friday 9:00 to 18:00 or 20:00, Saturday 9:00 to 13:00.

Shop Till You Drop

opening hours	*Öffnungszeiten*	urf-noongs-**tsī**-tehn
sale	*Schlussverkauf*	**shloos**-fehr-kowf
special	*Angebot*	**ahn**-geh-boht
good value	*preiswert*	**prīs**-vehrt
I'd like...	*Ich hätte gern...*	ikh **heh**-teh gehrn
We'd like...	*Wir hätten gern...*	veer **heh**-tehn gehrn
Where can I buy...?	*Wo kann ich... kaufen?*	voh kahn̲ ikh... **kow**-fehn

Where can we buy...?	*Wo können wir... kaufen?*	voh **kurn**-ehn veer... **kow**-fehn
How much is it?	*Wie viel kostet das?*	vee feel **kohs**-teht dahs
I'm just browsing.	*Ich sehe mich nur um.*	ikh **zay**-heh mikh noor oom
We're just browsing.	*Wir sehen uns nur um.*	veer **zay**-hehn oons noor oom
Do you have something cheaper?	*Haben Sie etwas Billigeres?*	**hah**-behn zee **eht**-vahs **bil**-lig-er-ehs
Better quality, please.	*Bessere Qualität, bitte.*	**behs**-ser-er kvah-lee-**tayt bit**-teh
genuine / imitation	*echt / imitation*	ehkht / im-i-taht-see-**ohn**
Can I see more?	*Kann ich mehr sehen?*	kahn̲ ikh mehr **zay**-hehn
Can we see more?	*Können wir mehr sehen?*	**kurn**-ehn veer mehr **zay**-hehn
This one.	*Dieses.*	**dee**-zehs
Can I try it on?	*Kann ich es anprobieren?*	kahn̲ ikh ehs **ahn**-proh-beer-ehn
Do you have a mirror?	*Haben Sie einen Spiegel?*	**hah**-behn zee **ī**-nehn **shpee**-gehl
Too...	*Zu...*	tsoo
...big.	*...groß.*	grohs
...small.	*...klein.*	klīn
...expensive.	*...teuer.*	**toy**-er
It's too...	*Es ist zu...*	ehs ist tsoo
...short / long.	*...kurz / lang.*	koorts / lahn̲g
...tight / loose.	*...eng / weit.*	ehng / vīt
...dark / light.	*...dunkel / hell.*	**doon**-kehl / hehl
What is it made of?	*Was ist das für Material?*	vahs ist dahs fewr mah-tehr-ee-**ahl**
Is it machine washable?	*Ist es waschmaschinenfest?*	ist ehs **vahsh**-mah-sheen-ehn-fehst
Will it shrink?	*Läuft es ein?*	loyft ehs īn
Is it color-fast?	*Ist es farbenfest?*	ist ehs **far**-behn-fehst
Credit card O.K.?	*Kreditkarte O.K.?*	kreh-**deet**-kar-teh "O.K."
Can you ship this?	*Können Sie das versenden?*	**kurn**-nehn zee dahs fehr-**zehn**-dehn

Tax-free?	*Steuerfrei?*	**shtoy**-er-frī
I'll think about it.	*Ich denke drüber nach.*	ikh **dehnk**-eh **drew**-ber nahkh
What time do you close?	*Um wie viel Uhr schließen Sie?*	oom vee feel oor **shlee**-sehn zee
What time do you open tomorrow?	*Wann öffnen Sie morgen?*	vahn **urf**-nehn zee **mor**-gehn

Street Markets

Did you make this?	*Haben Sie das gemacht?*	**hah**-behn zee dahs geh-**mahkht**
Is that your lowest price?	*Ist das der günstigste Preis?*	ist dahs dehr **gewn**-stig-steh prīs
Cheaper?	*Billiger?*	**bil**-ig-er
Good price.	*Guter Preis.*	**goo**-ter prīs
My last offer.	*Mein letztes Angebot.*	mīn **lehts**-tehs **ahn**-geh-boht
I'll take it.	*Ich nehme es.*	ikh **nay**-meh ehs
We'll take it.	*Wir nehmen es.*	veer **nay**-mehn ehs
I'm nearly broke.	*Ich bin fast pleite.*	ikh bin fahst **plī**-teh
We're nearly broke.	*Wir sind fast pleite.*	veer zint fahst **plī**-teh
My male friend...	*Mein Freund...*	mīn froynd
My female friend...	*Meine Freundin...*	**mī**-neh **froyn**-din
My husband...	*Mein Mann...*	mīn mahn
My wife...	*Meine Frau...*	**mī**-neh frow
...has the money.	*...hat das Geld.*	haht dahs gehlt

Clothes

For...	*Für...*	fewr
...a baby.	*...ein Baby.*	īn **bay**-bee
...a male / a female child.	*...einen Buben / ein Mädchen.*	ī-nehn **boo**-behn / īn **mayd**-khehn
...a male / a female teenager.	*...einen Jungen / ein Fräulein.*	ī-nehn **yoong**-ehn / īn **froy**-līn
...a man.	*...einen Herren.*	ī-nehn **hehr**-ehn
...a woman.	*...eine Dame.*	ī-neh **dah**-meh
bathrobe	*Bademantel*	**bah**-deh-mahn-tehl

bib	*Latz*	lahts
belt	*Gurt*	goort
bra	*BH (Büstenhalter)*	bay hah (**bewst**-ehn-hahl-ter)
clothing	*Kleider*	**klī**-der
dress	*Kleid*	klīt
flip-flops	*Strandsandalen*	**shtrahnt**-zahn-dah-lehn
gloves	*Handschuhe*	**hahnt**-shoo-heh
hat	*Hut*	hoot
jacket	*Jacke*	**yah**-keh
jeans	*Jeans*	"jeans"
nightgown	*Nachthemd*	**nahkht**-hehmt
nylons	*Strümpfe*	**shtrewmp**-feh
pajamas	*Pyjama*	pew-**jah**-mah
pants	*Hosen*	**hoh**-zehn
raincoat	*Regenmantel*	**ray**-gehn-mahn-tehl
sandals	*Sandalen*	zahn-**dah**-lehn
scarf	*Schal*	shahl
shirt...	*Hemd...*	hehmt
...long-sleeved	*...mit langen Ärmeln*	mit **lahng**-ehn **ehr**-mehln
...short-sleeved	*...mit kurzen Ärmeln*	mit **koorts**-ehn **ehr**-mehln
...sleeveless	*...ohne Ärmel*	**oh**-neh **ehr**-mehl
shoelaces	*Schnürsenkel*	**shnewr**-zehn-kehl
shoes	*Schuhe*	**shoo**-heh
shorts	*kurze Hosen*	**koorts**-eh **hoh**-zehn
skirt	*Rock*	rohk
sleeper (for baby)	*Kindereinteiler*	**kin**-der-**īn**-tī-ler
slip	*Unterrock*	**oon**-ter-rohk
slippers	*Pantoffeln*	pahn-**tohf**-ehln
socks	*Socken*	**zohk**-ehn
sweater	*Pullover, Pulli*	"pullover," **poo**-lee
swimsuit	*Badeanzug*	**bah**-deh-ahn-tsoog
tennis shoes	*Tennisschuhe*	**teh**-nis-shoo-heh
tights	*Strümpfe*	**shtrewmp**-feh
T-shirt	*T-shirt, Hemdchen*	**tay**-shirt, **hehmt**-shyehn
underwear	*Unterhosen*	**oon**-ter-hoh-zehn
vest	*Weste*	**veh**-steh

Colors

black	*schwarz*	shvarts
blue	*blau*	blow (rhymes with cow)
brown	*braun*	brown
gray	*grau*	grow (rhymes with cow)
green	*grün*	grewn
orange	*orange*	oh-**rahn**-zheh
pink	*rosa*	**roh**-sah
purple	*lila*	**lee**-lah
red	*rot*	roht
white	*weiß*	vīs
yellow	*gelb*	gehlp
dark / light	*dunkel / hell*	**doon**-kehl / hehl
A lighter...	*Eine hellere...*	**ī**-neh **hehl**-er-eh
A brighter...	*Eine farbigere...*	**ī**-neh **far**-big-er-eh
A darker...	*Eine dunklere...*	**ī**-neh **doon**-kler-eh
...shade.	*...Schattierung.*	shaht-**eer**-oong

Materials

brass	*Messing*	**mehs**-sing
bronze	*Bronze*	**brohn**-seh
ceramic	*Keramik*	keh-**rah**-mik
copper	*Kupfer*	**koop**-fer
cotton	*Baumwolle*	**bowm**-voh-leh
glass	*Glas*	glahs
gold	*Gold*	gohlt
lace	*Spitze*	**shpit**-seh
leather	*Leder*	**lay**-der
linen	*Leinen*	**lī**-nehn
marble	*Marmor*	**mar**-mor
metal	*Metall*	meh-**tahl**
nylon	*Nylon*	**nee**-loh<u>n</u>
paper	*Papier*	pah-**peer**
pewter	*Zinn*	tsin
plastic	*Plastik*	**plah**-stik
polyester	*Polyester*	poh-lee-**ehs**-ter

porcelain	*Porzellan*	por-tsehl-**lahn**
silk	*Seide*	**zī**-deh
silver	*Silber*	**zil**-ber
velvet	*Samt*	zahmt
wood	*Holz*	hohlts
wool	*Wolle*	**voh**-leh

Jewelry

jewelry	*Schmuck*	shmook
bracelet	*Armband*	**arm**-bahn̲t
brooch	*Brosche*	**broh**-sheh
earrings	*Ohrringe*	**or**-ring-eh
necklace	*Halsband*	**hahls**-bahn̲t
ring	*Ring*	ring
Is this...?	*Ist das...?*	ist dahs
...sterling silver	*...echt Silber*	ehkht **zil**-ber
...real gold	*...echt Gold*	ehkht gohlt
...stolen	*...gestohlen*	geh-**shtoh**-lehn

SPORTS

Bicycling

bicycle	*Fahrrad, Velo (Switz.)*	**far**-raht, **feh**-loh
mountain bike	*Mountainbike*	"mountain bike"
I'd like to rent a bicycle.	*Ich möchte ein Fahrrad mieten.*	ikh **murkh**-teh īn **far**-raht **mee**-tehn
We'd like to rent two bicycles.	*Wir möchten zwei Fahrrähder mieten.*	veer **murkh**-tehn tsvī **far**-ray-der **mee**-tehn
How much per...?	*Wie viel pro...?*	vee feel proh
...hour	*...Stunde*	**shtoon**-deh
...half day	*...halben Tag*	**hahl**-behn tahg
...day	*...Tag*	tahg
Is a deposit required?	*Brauchen Sie eine Anzahlung?*	**browkh**-ehn zee **ī**-neh **ahn**-tsahl-oong
deposit	*Anzahlung*	**ahn**-tsahl-oong
helmet	*Helm*	hehlm

lock	*Schloß*	shlohs
air / no air	*Luft / keine Luft*	looft / **kī**-neh looft
tire	*Reifen*	**rī**-fehn
pump	*Pumpe*	**poom**-peh
map	*Karte*	**kar**-teh
How many gears?	*Wie viele Gänge?*	vee **fee**-leh **gayng**-eh
What is a... route of about ___ kilometers?	*Was ist eine... Strecke von etwas___ Kilometer?*	vahs ist **ī**-neh... **shtreh**-keh fohn **eht**-vahs ___ kee-loh-**may**-ter
...good	*...gute*	**goo**-teh
...scenic	*...schöne*	**shurn**-eh
...interesting	*...interessante*	in-tehr-ehs-**sahn**-teh
...easy	*...leichte*	**līkh**-teh
How many minutes / hours by bicycle?	*Wie viele Minuten / Stunden mit dem Rad?*	vee **fee**-leh mee-**noo**-tehn / **shtoon**-dehn mit daym raht
I (don't) like hills.	*Ich mag (keine) Hügel.*	ikh mahg (**kī**-neh) **hew**-gehl
I brake for bakeries.	*Ich bremse für Bäckereien.*	ikh **brehm**-zeh fewr behk-eh-**rī**-ehn

For more route-finding words, see "Finding Your Way," beginning on page 375 in the German Traveling chapter.

Swimming and Boating

Where can I rent a...?	*Wo kann ich ein... mieten?*	voh kahn ikh īn... **mee**-tehn
Where can we rent a...?	*Wo können wir ein... mieten?*	voh **kurn**-ehn veer īn... **mee**-tehn
...paddleboat	*...Wasserfahrrad*	**vah**-ser-fah-raht
...rowboat	*...Ruderboot*	**roo**-der-boot
...boat	*...Boot*	boot
...sailboat	*...Segelboot*	**zay**-gehl-boot
How much per...?	*Wie viel pro...?*	vee feel proh
...hour	*...Stunde*	**shtoon**-deh

...half day	*...halben Tag*	**hahl**-behn tahg
...day	*...Tag*	tahg
beach	*Strand*	shtrahn̲t
nude beach	*FKK-Strand*	ehf-kah-kah-shtrahn̲t
Where's a good beach?	*Wo ist ein guter Strand?*	voh ist īn **goo**-ter shtrahn̲t
Is it safe for swimming?	*Ist Schwimmen ohne Gefahr?*	ist **shvim**-mehn **oh**-neh geh-**far**
flip-flops	*Sandalen*	zahn̲-**dah**-lehn
pool	*Schwimmbad*	**shvim**-baht
snorkel and mask	*Schnorchel und Maske*	**shnorkh**-ehl oont **mah**-skeh
sunglasses	*Sonnenbrille*	**zohn**-nehn-bril-leh
sunscreen	*Sonnenschutz*	**zohn**-nehn-shoots
surfboard	*Surfboard*	"surfboard"
surfer	*Wellenreiter*	**veh**-lehn-rī-ter
swimsuit	*Badeanzug*	**bah**-deh-ahn̲-tsoog
towel	*Badetuch*	**bah**-deh-tookh
waterskiing	*Wasserskifahren*	**vah**-ser-shi-**far**-ehn
windsurfing	*Windsurfen*	**vint**-zoorf-ehn

Germans are pioneers in the field of nudity—they're internationally known for letting it all hang out. Pretty much any beach in Germany can be topless, but if you want a true nude beach, look for ***FKK***, which stands for ***Freikörper Kultur*** (Free Body Culture). You'll also stumble into plenty of nude sunbathers (more men than women) on sunny days at any big-city park or riverbank.

Sports Talk

sports	*Sport*	shport
game	*Spiel*	shpeel
team	*Mannschaft*	**mahn**-shahft
championship	*Meisterschaft*	**mī**-ster-shahft
soccer	*Fußball*	**foos**-bahl
basketball	*Basketball, Korbballspiel*	**bahs**-keht-bahl, **kor**-bahl-shpeel
hockey	*Hockey*	**hoh**-kee

American football	*Football*	**foot**-bahl
tennis	*Tennis*	**teh**-nees
golf	*Golf*	gohlf
skiing	*Skifahren*	**shee**-far-ehn
gymnastics	*Gymnastik*	gewm-**nah**-steek
Olympics	*Olympiade*	oh-lewm-pee-**ah**-deh
gold / silver / bronze...	*Gold-/Silber-/Ehren...*	gohlt / **zil**-ber / **eh**-rehn
...medal	*...Medaille*	**meh**-dahl-yeh
What sport athlete / team do you like?	*Sportler / Team haben Sie am liebsten?*	**shport**-ler / "team" **hah**-behn zee ahm **leeb**-stehn
Where can I see a game?	*Wo kann ich ein Spiel sehen?*	voh kahn̲ ikh īn shpeel **zay**-hehn
jogging	*Jogging*	"jogging"
Where's a good place to jog?	*Wo geht man gut Jogging?*	voh gayt mahn̲ goot "jogging"

ENTERTAINMENT

What's happening tonight?	*Was ist heute abend los?*	vahs ist **hoy**-teh **ah**-behnt lohs
What do you recommend?	*Was empfehlen Sie?*	vahs ehmp-**fay**-lehn zee
Where is it?	*Wo ist es?*	voh ist ehs
How do I get there?	*Wie komme ich hin?*	vee **koh**-meh ikh hin
How do we get there?	*Wie kommen wir hin?*	vee **koh**-mehn veer hin
Is it free?	*Ist es umsonst?*	ist ehs oom-**zohnst**
Are there seats available?	*Gibt es noch Platz?*	gipt ehs nohkh plahts
Where can I buy a ticket?	*Wo kann ich eine Karte kaufen?*	voh kahn̲ ikh ī-neh **kar**-teh **kowf**-ehn
Do you have tickets for today / tonight?	*Haben Sie Karten für heute / heute Abend?*	**hah**-behn zee **kar**-tehn **hah**-behn zee **kar**-tehn fewr **hoy**-teh / **hoy**-teh **ah**-behnt

When does it start?	*Wann fängt es an?*	vahn fehngt ehs ahn
When does it end?	*Wann endet es?*	vahn **ehn**-deht ehs
Where's the best place to dance nearby?	*Wo geht man hier am besten Tanzen?*	voh gayt mahn heer ahm **behs**-tehn **tahn**-tsehn
Where do people stroll?	*Wo geht man hier Promenieren?*	voh gayt mahn heer proh-meh-**neer**-ehn

Entertaining Words

movie...	*Film...*	film
...original version	*...im Original*	im oh-rig-ee-**nahl**
...in English	*...auf Englisch*	owf **ehng**-lish
...with subtitles	*...mit Untertiteln*	mit **oon**-ter-tee-tehln
...dubbed	*...synchronisiert*	zewn-kroh-nee-**zeert**
music...	*Musik...*	moo-**zeek**
...live	*...live*	"live"
...classical	*...klassisch*	**klahs**-sish
...opera	*...Oper*	**oh**-per
...symphony	*...Symphonie*	zewm-foh-**nee**
...choir	*...Chor*	kor
folk music	*Volksmusik*	**fohlks**-moo-zeek
rock / jazz / blues	*Rock-N-Roll / Jazz / Blues*	"rock-n-roll" / "jazz" / "blues"
male singer	*Sänger*	**zehng**-er
female singer	*Sängerin*	**zehng**-er-in
concert	*Konzert*	kohn-**tsehrt**
show	*Vorführung*	**for**-few-roong
dancing	*Tanzen*	**tahn**-tsehn
folk dancing	*Volkstanz*	**fohlks**-tahnts
disco	*Disko*	**dis**-koh
bar with live music	*Bar mit Live-Musik*	bar mit "live" moo-**zeek**
nightclub	*Nachtklub*	**nahkht**-kloob
(no) cover charge	*(kein) Eintritt*	(kīn) **īn**-trit
sold out	*ausverkauft*	**ows**-fehr-kowft

Oktoberfest, the famous Munich beer festival, fills Bavaria's capital with the sounds of ***"Prost!"***, carnival rides, sizzling ***Bratwurst,*** and oompah bands. The party starts the third Saturday in September and lasts for 16 days. The ***Salzburger Festspiele*** (Salzburg's music festival) treats visitors to the sound of music from late July to the end of August.

CONNECT

PHONING

I'd like to buy a...	*Ich möchte eine... kaufen.*	ikh **murkh**-teh ī-neh... **kow**-fehn
...telephone card.	*...Telefonkarte*	tehl-eh-**fohn**-kar-teh
...cheap international telephone card.	*...billige internationale Telefonkarte*	**bil**-lig-geh in-tehr-naht-see-oh-**nah**-leh tehl-eh-**fohn**-kar-teh
Where is the nearest phone?	*Wo ist das nächste Telefon?*	voh ist dahs **nehkh**-steh tehl-eh-**fohn**
It doesn't work.	*Es ist außer Betrieb.*	ehs ist **ow**-ser beh-**treep**
May I use your phone?	*Darf ich Ihr Telefon benutzen?*	darf ikh eer tehl-eh-**fohn** beh-**noot**-sehn
Can you talk for me?	*Können Sie für mich sprechen?*	**kurn**-nehn zee fewr mikh **shprehkh**-ehn
It's busy.	*Besetzt.*	beh-**zehtst**
Will you try again?	*Noch einmal versuchen?*	nohkh **īn**-mahl fehr-**zookh**-ehn
My name is ___.	*Ich heiße ___.*	ikh **hī**-seh
Sorry, I speak only a little German.	*Tut mir leid, ich spreche nur ein bißchen deutsch.*	toot meer līt ikh **shprehkh**-eh noor īn **bis**-yehn doych
Speak slowly and clearly.	*Sprechen Sie langsam und. deutlich*	**shprehkh**-ehn zee **lahng**-zahm oont **doyt**-likh
Wait a moment.	*Moment mal.*	moh-**mehnt** mahl

Telephone Words

telephone	*Telefon*	tehl-eh-**fohn**
telephone card	*Telefonkarte*	tehl-eh-**fohn**-kar-teh
cheap international telephone card	*billige internationale Telefonkarte*	**bil**-lig-geh in-tehr-naht-see-oh-**nah**-leh tehl-eh-**fohn**-kar-teh
PIN code	*Geheimnummer*	geh-**hīm**-noo-mer
phone booth	*Telefonkabine*	tehl-eh-**fohn**-kah-bee-neh
out of service	*außer Betrieb*	**ow**-ser beh-**treep**
post office	*Post*	pohst
operator	*Vermittlung*	fehr-**mit**-loong
international assistance	*internationale Auskunft*	in-tehr-naht-see-oh-**nah**-leh **ows**-koonft
international call	*Auslandsgespräch*	**ows**-lahnts-geh-shpraykh
collect call	*R-gespräch*	**ehr**-geh-shpraykh
credit card call	*Kreditkartenge-spräch*	kreh-**deet**-kar-tehn-geh-shpraykh
toll-free	*gebührenfrei*	geh-**bew**-rehn-frī
fax	*Fax*	fahx
country code	*Landesvorwahl*	**lahn**-dehs-for-vahl
area code	*Vorwahl*	**for**-vahl
extension	*Intern*	in-**tehrn**
telephone book	*Telefonbuch*	tehl-eh-**fohn**-bookh
yellow pages	*gelbe Seiten*	**gehl**-beh **zī**-tehn

In German-speaking countries, it's polite to identify yourself by name at the beginning of every phone conversation. For domestic calls, make your calls from phone booths with an insertable card (sold at newsstands, handier than coins—except in Austria, where coin phones are more common). For international calls, ask at the newsstand for the cheapest deal for calling home (***Was ist die billigste Möglichkeit für den Anruf Amerika/Kanada?***)—you'll get a PIN code and access number, either printed on your receipt, or on a scratch-off card.

At phone booths, you'll encounter these words: ***Kartentelefon*** (accepts cards, sometimes coins), ***Ganzein-schieben*** (insert completely), ***Bitte wählen*** (please dial), and ***Guthaben*** (the value left on your card). If the number you're calling is out of service, you'll hear a recording: "***Kein Anschluß unter dieser Nummer.***" For more tips, see "Let's Talk Telephones" on page 501 in the appendix.

Cell Phones

Where is a cell phone shop?	*Wo is ein Handyladen?*	voh ist īn **han**-dee-lah-dehn
I'd like...	*Ich möchte...*	ikh **murkh**-teh
We'd like...	*Wir möchten...*	veer **murkh**-tehn
...a cell phone.	*...ein Handy.*	īn "handy"
...a chip.	*...eine Chipkarte.*	**ī**-neh **chip**-kar-teh
...to buy more time.	*...mehr Sprechzeit kaufen.*	mehr **shprehkh**-tsīt **kow**-fehn
How do you...?	*Wie kann man...?*	vee kahn mahn
...make calls	*...telefonieren*	teh-leh-fohn-**eer**-ehn
...receive calls	*...abnehmen*	**ahp**-nay-mehn
Will this work outside this country?	*Geht das im Ausland?*	gayt dahs im **ows**-lahnt
Where can I buy a chip for this this phone / this service?	*Wo kann ich einen Microchip kaufen für dieses Telefon / diesen Dienst?*	voh kahn ikh **ī**-nehn **meek**-roh-chip **kow**-fehn fewr **dee**-zehs teh-leh-**fohn** / **dee**-zehn deenst

EMAIL AND THE WEB

Email

My email address is ___.	*Meine E-mail-Adresse ist ___.*	**mī**-neh "email" ah-**dreh**-seh ist
What's your email address?	*Was ist Ihre E-mail-Adresse?*	vahs ist **ee**-reh "email" ah-**dreh**-seh
Can we check our email?	*Können wir unser E-mail nachlesen?*	**kurn**-nehn veer **oon**-ser "email" **nahkh**-lay-zehn

Key Phrases: Email and the Web

email	*E-Mail*	"email"
Internet	*Internet*	"internet"
Where is the nearest Internet café?	*Wo ist das nächste Internetcafé?*	voh ist dahs **naykh**-steh "internet café"
I'd like to check my email.	*Ich möchte mein E-mail nachlesen.*	ikh **murkh**-teh mīn "email" **nahkh**-lay-zehn

May I use this computer to check my email?	*Darf ich diesen Computer benutzen um mein E-Mail nachzulesen?*	darf ikh **dee**-zehn kohm-**pew**-ter beh-**noot**-sehn oom mīn "email" **nahkh**-tsoo-lay-zehn
Where is there access to the Internet?	*Wo gibt es einen Internet zugang?*	voh gipt ehs **ī**-nehn "internet" **tsoo**-gahng
Where is an Internet café?	*Wo ist ein Internetcafé?*	voh ist īn "internet café"
How much for... minutes?	*Wie viel für... Minuten?*	vee feel fewr... mee-**noo**-tehn
...10	*...zehn*	tsayn
...15	*...fünfzehn*	**fewnf**-tsayn
...30	*...dreißig*	**drī**-sig
Help me, please.	*Hilfen Sie mir, bitte.*	**hil**-fehn zee meer **bit**-teh
How do I...	*Wie...*	vee
...start this?	*...fange ich an?*	**fahng**-eh ikh ahn
...send a file?	*...sende ich einen Anhang?*	**zehn**-deh ikh **ī**-nehn **ahn**-hahng
...print out a file?	*...drucke ich einen Text?*	**droo**-keh ikh **ī**-nehn tehkst
...type @?	*...geht A-Affenschwanz?*	gayt ah-**ah**-fehn-shvants
This isn't working.	*Das funktioniert nicht.*	dahs foonk-tsee-ohn-**eert** nikht

Web Words

email	*E-Mail*	"email"
email address	*E-Mail-Adresse*	"email" ah-**dreh**-seh
website	*Internetseite*	**in**-tehr-neht-**zī**-teh
Internet	*Internet*	"internet"
surf the Web	*im Internet schwimmen*	im "internet" **shvim**-mehn
download	*herunterladen*	hehr-**oon**-ter-lah-dehn
@ sign	*A-Affenschwanz* ("A-monkey tail")	ah-**ah**-fehn-shvants
dot	*Punkt*	poonkt
hyphen (-)	*Bindestrich*	**bin**-deh-shtrikh
underscore (_)	*Großstrich*	**grohs**-shtrikh
Wi-Fi	*WLAN*	**vay**-lahn

On Screen

Ansicht	view	öffnen	open
bearbeiten	edit	Ordner	folder
drucken	print	Post	mail
löschen	delete	senden	send
Mitteilung	message	speichern	save

MAILING

Where is the post office?	*Wo ist die Post?*	voh ist dee pohst
Which window for...?	*An welchem Schalter ist...?*	ahn **vehlkh**-ehm **shahl**-ter ist
Is this the line for...?	*Ist das die Schlange für...?*	ist dahs dee **shlahng**-eh fewr
...stamps	*...Briefmarken*	**breef**-mar-kehn
...packages	*...Pakete*	pah-**kay**-teh
To the USA....	*In die USA...*	in dee oo ehs ah
...by air mail.	*...mit Luftpost.*	mit **looft**-pohst
...by surface mail.	*...per Schiff.*	pehr shif
...slow and cheap.	*...langsam und billig.*	**lahng**-zahm oont **bil**-lig

CONNECT

Key Phrases: Mailing

post office	*Post(-amt)*	**pohst** (-ahmt)
stamp	*Briefmarke*	**breef**-mar-keh
postcard	*Postkarte*	**pohst**-kar-teh
letter	*Brief*	breef
airmail	*Luftpost*	**looft**-pohst
Where is the post office?	*Wo ist die Post?*	voh ist dee pohst
I need stamps for ___ postcards / letters to America.	*Ich brauche Briefmarken für ___ Postkarten / Briefe nach Amerika.*	ikh **browkh**-eh **breef**-mar-kehn fewr ___ **pohst**-kar-tehn / **breef**-eh nahkh ah-**mehr**-ee-kah

How much is it?	*Wie viel kostet das?*	vee feel **kohs**-teht dahs
How much to send a letter / postcard to ___?	*Wie viel ist ein Brief / Postkarte nach ___?*	vee feel ist īn breef / **pohst**-kar-teh nahkh
I need stamps for ___ postcards to...	*Ich brauche Briefmarken für ___ Postkarten nach...*	ikh **browkh**-eh **breef**-mar-kehn fewr ___ **pohst**-kar-tehn nahkh
...America / Canada.	*...Amerika / Kanada.*	ah-**mehr**-ee-kah / **kah**-nah-dah
Pretty stamps, please.	*Hübsche Briefmarken, bitte.*	**hewb**-sheh **breef**-mar-kehn **bit**-teh
I always choose the slowest line.	*Ich wähle immer die langsamste Schlange.*	ikh **vay**-leh **im**-mer dee **lahng**-zahm-steh **shlahng**-eh
How many days will it take?	*Wie viele Tage braucht das?*	vee **fee**-leh **tahg**-eh browkht dahs

In Germany, Austria, and Switzerland, you can often get stamps at a ***Kiosk*** (newsstand), stamp machine (yellow, marked ***Briefmarken***), or ***Tabak*** (tobacco shop). As long as you know which stamps you need, this is a great convenience. At the post office, the window labeled ***Alle Leistungen*** handles everything.

German mailboxes often come in pairs: the box for local mail is labeled with its range of zip codes, and the other box (labeled ***Andere PLZ***) is for everything else.

Licking the Postal Code

German Postal Service	*Deutsche Bundespost*	**doy**-cheh **boon**-dehs-pohst
post office	*Post(-amt)*	**pohst** (-ahmt)
stamp	*Briefmarke*	**breef**-mar-keh
postcard	*Postkarte*	**pohst**-kar-teh
letter	*Brief*	breef
envelope	*Umschlag*	**oom**-shlahg
package	*Paket*	pah-**kayt**
box	*Karton / Schachtel*	kar-**tohn** / **shahkh**-tehl
string	*Schnur*	shnoor
tape	*Klebeband*	**klay**-beh-bahnd
mailbox	*Briefkasten*	**breef**-kahs-tehn
airmail	*Luftpost*	**looft**-pohst
express mail	*Eilpost*	**īl**-pohst
slow and cheap	*langsam und billig*	**lahng**-zahm oont **bil**-lig
book rate	*Büchersendung*	**bewkh**-er-zehn-doong
weight limit	*Gewichtsbe-grenzung*	geh-**vikhts**-beh-grehn-tsoong
registered	*Einschreiben*	**īn**-shrī-behn
insured	*versichert*	fehr-**zikh**-ert
fragile	*zerbrechlich*	tsehr-**brehkh**-likh
contents	*Inhalt*	**in**-hahlt
customs	*Zoll*	tsohl
to / from	*nach / von*	nahkh / fohn
address	*Adresse*	ah-**dreh**-seh
zip code	*Postleitzahl*	**pohst**-līt-sahl
general delivery	*postlagernd*	**pohst**-lahg-ernt

HELP!

Help!	*Hilfe!*	**hil**-feh
Help me!	*Helfen Sie mir!*	**hehl**-fehn zee meer
Call a doctor!	*Rufen Sie einen Arzt!*	**roo**-fehn zee ī-nehn artst
Call...	*Rufen Sie...*	**roo**-fehn zee
...the police.	*...die Polizei.*	dee poh-leet-**sī**
...an ambulance.	*...den Krankenwagen.*	dayn **krahnk**-ehn-vah-gehn
...the fire dept.	*...die Feuerwehr.*	dee **foy**-er-vehr
I'm lost. (on foot)	*Ich habe mich verlaufen.*	ikh **hah**-beh mikh fehr-**lowf**-ehn
We're lost. (on foot)	*Wir haben uns verlaufen.*	veer **hah**-behn oons fehr-**lowf**-ehn
I'm lost. (by car)	*Ich habe mich verfahren.*	ikh **hah**-beh mikh fehr-**far**-ehn
Thank you for your help.	*Danke für Ihre Hilfe.*	**dahng**-keh fewr **ee**-reh **hil**-feh
You are very kind.	*Sie sind sehr freundlich*	zee zint zehr **froynd**-likh

Theft and Loss

I've been robbed.	*Ich bin beraubt worden.*	ikh bin beh-**rowbt vor**-dehn
We've been robbed.	*Wir sind beraubt worden.*	veer zint beh-**rowbt vor**-dehn
Stop, thief!	*Halt, Dieb!*	hahlt deep
A thief took...	*Ein Dieb hat... genommen.*	īn deep haht... geh-**noh**-mehn

Key Phrases: Help!

accident	*Unfall*	**oon**-fahl
emergency	*Notfall*	**noht**-fahl
police	*Polizei*	poh-leet-**sī**
Help!	*Hilfe!*	**hil**-feh
Call a doctor / the police!	*Rufen Sie einen Arzt / die Polizei!*	**roo**-fehn zee **ī**-nehn artst / dee poh-leet-**sī**
Stop, thief!	*Halt, Dieb!*	hahlt deep

I've lost...	*Ich habe... verloren.*	**hah**-beh... fehr-**lor**-ehn
...my money.	*...mein Geld*	mīn gehlt
...my passport.	*...meinen Paß*	**mī**-nehn pahs
...my train ticket / plane ticket.	*...meine Fahrkarte / Flugkarte*	**mī**-neh **far**-kar-teh / **floog**-kar-teh
...my baggage.	*...mein Gepäck*	mīn geh-**pehk**
...my purse.	*...meine Handtasche*	**mī**-neh **hahnt**-tahsh-eh
...my wallet.	*...meine Brieftasche*	**mī**-neh **breef**-tahsh-eh
We've lost our...	*Wir haben unsere... verloren.*	veer **hah**-behn **oon**-zer-eh... fehr-**lor**-ehn
...passports.	*...Pässe*	**peh**-seh
...train tickets / plane tickets.	*...Fahrkarten / Flugkarten*	**far**-kar-tehn / **floog**-kar-tehn
...baggage.	*...Gepäck*	geh-**pehk**
I want to contact my embassy.	*Ich möchte meine Botschaft kontaktieren.*	ikh **murkh**-teh **mī**-neh **boht**-shahft koh<u>n</u>-tahk-**tee**-rehn
I need to file a police report for my insurance.	*Ich muß einen Polizeireport für meine Versicherung erstellen.*	ikh mus **ī**-nehn poh-leet-**sī**-reh-port fewr **mī**-neh fehr-**zikh**-er-oong ehr-**shteh**-lehn

See page 503 in the appendix for information on US embassies in Germany, Austria, and Switzerland.

Helpful Words

ambulance	*Krankenwagen*	**krahnk**-ehn-vah-gehn
accident	*Unfall*	**oon**-fahl
injured	*verletzt*	fehr-**lehtst**
emergency	*Notfall*	**noht**-fahl
emergency room	*Notfallaufnahme*	noht-fahl-**owf**-nah-meh
fire	*Feuer*	**foy**-er
police	*Polizei*	poh-leet-**sī**
smoke	*Rauch*	rowkh
thief	*Dieb*	deep
pickpocket	*Taschendieb*	**tahsh**-ehn-deep

Help for Women

Leave me alone.	*Lassen Sie mich in Ruhe.*	**lah**-sehn zee mikh in **roo**-heh
I want to be alone.	*Ich möchte alleine sein.*	ikh **murkh**-teh ah-**lī**-neh zīn
I'm not interested.	*Ich habe kein Interesse.*	ikh **hah**-beh kīn in-tehr-**ehs**-seh
I'm married.	*Ich bin verheiratet.*	ikh bin fehr-**hī**-rah-teht
I'm a lesbian.	*Ich bin lesbisch.*	ikh bin **lehz**-bish
You are bothering me.	*Sie sind mir lästig.*	zee zint meer **lehs**-tig
He is bothering me.	*Er belästigt mich.*	ehr beh-**lehs**-tigt mikh
Don't touch me.	*Fassen Sie mich nicht an.*	**fah**-sehn zee mikh nikht ahn
You're disgusting.	*Sie sind eklig.*	zee zint **ehk**-lig
Stop following me.	*Hör auf, mir nachzulaufen.*	hur owf meer **nahkh**-tsoo-**lowf**-ehn
Stop it!	*Hören Sie auf!*	**hur**-ehn zee owf
Enough!	*Das reicht!*	dahs rīkht
Go away.	*Gehen Sie weg.*	**gay**-ehn zee vayg
Get lost!	*Hau ab!*	how ahp
Drop dead!	*Verschwinde!*	fehr-**shvin**-deh
I'll call the police.	*Ich rufe die Polizei.*	ikh **roo**-feh dee poh-leet-**sī**

SERVICES

Laundry

Is a... laundry nearby?	*Ist ein Waschsalon... in der Nähe?*	ist īn **vahsh**-zah-lohn... in dehr **nay**-heh
...self-service	*...mit Selbstbedienung*	mit zehlpst-beh-**dee**-noong
...full service	*...mit Dienstleistung*	mit **deenst**-līs-toong
Help me, please.	*Hilfen Sie mir, bitte.*	**hil**-fehn zee meer **bit**-teh
How does this work?	*Wie funktioniert das?*	vee foonk-tsee-ohn-**eert** dahs
Where is the soap?	*Wo ist das Waschmittel?*	voh ist dahs **vahsh**-mit-tehl
Are these yours?	*Sind das Ihre?*	zint dahs **ee**-reh
This stinks.	*Das stinkt.*	dahs shtinkt
Smells like...	*Riecht wie...*	rīkht vee
...spring time.	*...Frühling.*	**frew**-ling
...a locker room.	*...eine Turnhalle.*	**ī**-neh **toorn**-hah-leh
...cheese.	*...Käse.*	**kay**-zeh
I need change.	*Ich brauche Kleingeld.*	ikh **browkh**-eh **klīn**-gehlt
Same-day service?	*Noch am selben Tag?*	nohkh ahm **zehl**-behn tahg
By when do I need to drop off my clothes?	*Bis wann kann ich meine Wäsche vorbeibringen?*	bis vahn kahn ikh **mī**-neh **veh**-sheh for-**bī**-bring-ehn
When will my clothes be ready?	*Wann wird meine Wäsche fertig sein?*	vahn virt **mī**-neh **veh**-sheh **fehr**-tig zīn
Dried?	*Getrocknet?*	geh-**trohk**-neht

Folded?	*Gefaltet?*	geh-**fahl**-teht
Hey there, what's spinning?	*Hey, worum dreht's sich?*	hay **voh**-room drayts zikh

Clean Words

full-service laundry	*Waschsalon mit Dienstleisung*	**vahsh**-zah-lohn mit **deenst**-līs-toong
self-service laundry	*Waschsalon mit Selbstbedienung*	**vahsh**-zah-lohn mit zehlpst-beh-**dee**-noong
wash / dry	*waschen / trocknen*	**vahsh**-ehn / **trohk**-nehn
washer / dryer	*Waschmaschine / Trockner*	**vahsh**-mahs-shee-neh / **trohk**-ner
detergent	*Waschmittel*	**vahsh**-mit-tehl
token	*Zahlmarke, Jeton*	**tsahl**-mar-keh, **yeh**-tohn
whites	*Helles*	**hehl**-lehs
colors	*Buntwäsche*	**boont**-veh-sheh
delicates	*Feinwäsche*	**fīn**-veh-sheh
handwash	*von Hand waschen*	fohn hahnt **vah**-shehn

Haircuts

Where is a barber / hair salon?	*Wo ist ein Herrenfrisör / Friseursalon?*	voh ist īn heh-rehn-friz-**ur** / friz-**oor**-zah-lohn
I'd like...	*Ich möchte...*	ikh **murkh**-teh
...a haircut.	*...meine Haare schneiden.*	**mī**-neh **hah**-reh **shnī**-dehn
...a permanent.	*...eine Dauerwelle.*	**ī**-neh **dow**-er-veh-leh
...just a trim.	*...nur stutzen.*	noor **shtoot**-sehn
Cut about this much off.	*Etwa so viel kürzen.*	**eht**-vah zo feel **kewrt**-sehn
Cut my bangs here.	*Meine Stirnhaare hier kürzen.*	**mī**-neh **shteern**-hah-reh heer **kewrt**-sehn
Longer / shorter here.	*Hier länger / kürzer.*	heer **layng**-er / **kewrt**-ser
I'd like my hair...	*Ich möchte meine Haare..*	ikh **murkh**-teh **mī**-neh **hah**-reh

...short.	*...kurz.*	koorts
...colored.	*...gefärbt.*	geh-**fayrbt**
...shampooed.	*...gewaschen.*	geh-**vahsh**-ehn
...blow dried.	*...getrocknet.*	geh-**trohk**-neht
It looks good.	*Es sieht gut aus.*	ehs zeet goot ows

Repair

These handy lines can apply to any repair, whether it's a ripped rucksack, broken camera, or bad haircut.

This is broken.	*Das hier ist kaputt.*	dahs heer ist kah-**poot**
Can you fix it?	*Können Sie das reparieren?*	**kurn**-nehn zee dahs reh-pah-**reer**-ehn
Just do the essentials.	*Machen Sie nur das Nötigste.*	**mahkh**-ehn zee noor dahs **nur**-tig-steh
How much will it cost?	*Wie viel kostet das?*	vee feel **kohs**-teht-dahs
When will it be ready?	*Wann ist es fertig?*	vahn ist ehs **fehr**-tig
I need it by ___.	*Ich brauche es bis ___.*	ikh **browkh**-eh ehs bis
We need it by ___.	*Wir brauchen es bis ___.*	veer **browkh**-ehn ehs bis
Without it, I'm...	*Ohne bin ich...*	**oh**-neh bin ikh
...helpless.	*...hilflos.*	**hilf**-lohs
...a mess.	*...aufgeschmissen.* ("all thrown up in the air")	**owf**-geh-shmis-sehn
...done for.	*...erledigt.*	ehr-**lay**-digt

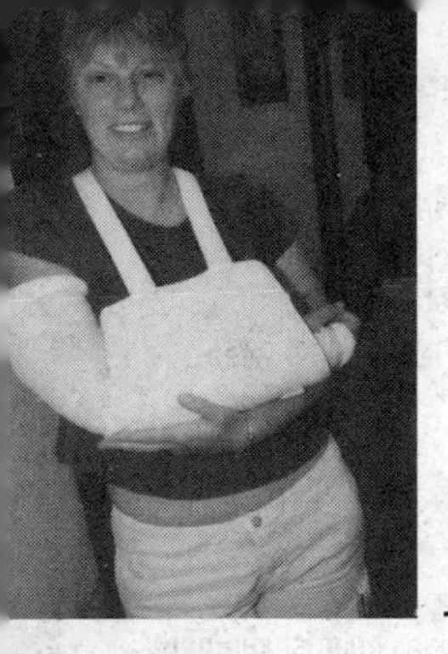

HEALTH

I am sick.	*Ich bin krank.*	ikh bin krahn̲k
I feel (very) sick.	*Ich fühle mich (sehr) schlecht.*	ikh **few**-leh mikh (zehr) shlehkht
It hurts here.	*Hier tut es weh.*	heer toot ehs vay
My husband / My wife...	*Mein Mann / Meine Frau...*	mīn mahn̲ / **mī**-neh frow
My son / My daughter...	*Mein Sohn / Meine Tochter...*	mīn zohn̲ / **mī**-neh **tohkh**-ter
My male friend / My female friend...	*Mein Freund / Meine Freundin...*	mīn froynt / **mī**-neh **froyn**-din
...feels (very) sick.	*...fühlt sich (sehr) schlecht.*	fewlt zikh (zehr) shlehkht
It's urgent.	*Es ist dringend.*	ehs ist **dring**-ehnt
I need a doctor...	*Ich brauche einen Arzt...*	ikh **browkh**-eh **ī**-nehn artst
We need a doctor...	*Wir brauchen einen Arzt...*	veer **browkh**-ehn **ī**-nehn artst
...who speaks English.	*...der Englisch spricht.*	dehr **ehng**-lish shprikht
Please call a doctor.	*Bitte rufen Sie einen Arzt.*	**bit**-teh **roo**-fehn zee **ī**-nehn artst
Could a doctor come here?	*Kann der Arzt hier kommen?*	kahn̲ dehr artst heer **koh**-mehn
I am...	*Ich bin...*	ikh bin
He / She is...	*Er / Sie ist...*	ehr / zee ist

Key Phrases: Health

doctor	*Arzt*	artst
hospital	*Krankenhaus*	**krahn**-kehn-hows
pharmacy	*Apotheke*	ah-poh-**tay**-keh
medicine	*Medikament*	meh-dee-kah-**mehnt**
I am sick.	*Ich bin krank.*	ikh bin krahnk
I need a doctor (who speaks English).	*Ich brauche einen Arzt (der Englisch spricht).*	ikh **browkh**-eh ī-nehn artst (dehr **ehng**-lish shprikht)
It hurts here.	*Hier tut es weh.*	heer toot ehs vay

...allergic to penicillin / sulfa.	*...allergisch auf Penizillin / Sulfa.*	ah-**lehr**-gish owf pehn-ee-tsee-**leen** / **zool**-fah
I am diabetic.	*Ich bin Diabetiker.*	ikh bin dee-ah-**beht**-ee-ker
I have cancer.	*Ich habe Krebs.*	ikh **hah**-beh krehbs
I had a heart attack ___ years ago.	*Ich hatte einen Herzschlag vor ___ Jahren.*	ikh **hah**-teh ī-nehn **hayrts**-shlahg for ___ **yah**-rehn
I feel faint.	*Ich fühle mich schwach.*	ikh **few**-leh mikh shvahkh
It hurts to urinate.	*Urinieren schmerzt.*	oo-rin-**eer**-ehn shmehrtst
I have body odor.	*Ich habe Körpergeruch.*	ikh **hah**-beh **kur**-per-geh-rookh
I'm going bald.	*Mir fallen die Haare aus.*	meer **fah**-lehn dee **hah**-reh ows
Is it serious?	*Ist es ernst?*	ist ehs ehrnst
Is it contagious?	*Ist es ansteckend?*	ist ehs **ahn**-shtehk-ehnt
Aging sucks.	*Altern stinkt.*	**ahl**-tern shtinkt
Take one pill every ___ hours for ___ days.	*Alle ___ Stunden eine Pille einnehmen während ___ Tagen.*	**ah**-leh ___ **shtoon**-dehn ī-neh **pil**-leh **īn**-nay-mehn **vehr**-ehnt ___ **tah**-gehn

I need a receipt for my insurance.	*Ich brauche eine Quittung für meine Versicherung.*	ikh **browkh**-eh **ī**-neh **kvit**-toong fewr **mī**-neh fehr-**zikh**-eh-roong

Ailments

I have...	*Ich habe...*	ikh **hah**-beh
He / She has...	*Er / Sie hat...*	ehr / zee haht
I need / We need medication for...	*Ich brauche / Wir brauchen Medikament für...*	ikh **browkh**-eh / veer **browkh**-ehn meh-dee-kah-**mehnt** fewr
...arthritis.	*...Gelenk-entzündung.*	geh-**lehnk**-ehnt-tsewn-doong
...asthma.	*...Asthma.*	**ahst**-mah
...athlete's foot.	*...Fußpilz.*	**foos**-pilts
...bad breath.	*...schlechten Atem.*	**shlehkh**-tehn **ah**-tehm
...blisters.	*...Blasen.*	**blah**-zehn
...bug bites.	*...Instektenstiche.*	in-**zehk**-tehn-shtikh-eh
...a burn.	*...eine Verbrennung.*	**ī**-neh fehr-**breh**-noong
...chest pains.	*...Schmerzen in der Brust.*	**shmehrts**-ehn in dehr broost
...chills.	*...Kälteschauer.*	**kehl**-teh-show-ehr
...a cold.	*...eine Erkältung.*	**ī**-neh ehr-**kehl**-toong
...congestion.	*...Nasenver-stopfung.*	**nah**-zehn-fehr-**shtohp**-foong
...constipation.	*...Verstopfung.*	fehr-**shtohp**-foong
...a cough.	*...einen Husten.*	**ī**-nehn **hoo**-stehn
...cramps.	*...Krämpfe.*	**krehmp**-feh
...diabetes.	*...Zuckerkrankheit.*	**tsoo**-ker-krahnk-hīt
...diarrhea.	*...Durchfall.*	**doorkh**-fahl
...dizziness.	*...Schwindel.*	**shvin**-dehl
...earache.	*...Ohrenschmerzen.*	**or**-ehn-shmehrts-ehn
...epilepsy.	*...Epilepsie.*	eh-pil-ehp-**see**
...a fever.	*...Fieber.*	**fee**-ber
...the flu.	*...die Grippe.*	dee **grip**-peh
...food poisoning.	*...Lebensmittel-vergiftung.*	**lay**-behns-mit-tehl-fehr-**gift**-oong

HEALTH

...giggles.	*...einen Lachanfall.*	ī-nehn **lahkh**-ahn-fahl
...hay fever.	*...Heuschnupfen.*	**hoy**-shnoop-fehn
...a headache.	*...Kopfschmerzen.*	**kohpf**-shmehrts-ehn
...a heart condition.	*...Herzbeschwerden.*	**hayrts**-beh-shvehr-dehn
...hemorrhoids.	*...Hämorrhoiden.*	heh-mor-oh-**ee**-dehn
...high blood pressure.	*...Bluthochdruck.*	**bloot**-hohkh-drook
...indigestion.	*...Verdauungs-störung.*	fehr-**dow**-oongs-shtur-oong
...an infection.	*...eine Infektion.*	ī-neh in-fehk-tsee-**ohn**
...a migraine.	*...Migräne.*	mee-**gray**-neh
...nausea.	*...Übelkeit.*	**ew**-behl-kīt
...inflammation.	*...eine Entzündung.*	ī-neh ehnt-**tsewn**-doong
...pneumonia.	*...Lungen-entzündung.*	**loong**-ehn-ehnt-**tsewn**-doong
...a rash.	*...einen Ausschlag.*	ī-nehn **ows**-shlahg
...sinus problems.	*...Schleimhaut-entzündung.*	**shlīm**-howt-ehnt-**tsewn**-doong
...a sore throat.	*...Halsschmerzen.*	**hahls**-shmehrts-ehn
...a stomachache.	*...Magenschmerzen.*	**mah**-gehn-shmehrts-ehn
...sunburn.	*...Sonnenbrand.*	**zoh**-nehn-brahnt
...a swelling.	*...eine Schwellung.*	ī-neh **shvehl**-loong
...a toothache.	*...Zahnschmerzen.*	**tsahn**-shmehrts-ehn
...urinary infection.	*...Harnröhren-entzündung.*	**harn**-rur-rehn-ehnt-**tsewn**-doong
...a venereal disease.	*...eine Geschlechts-krankheit.*	ī-neh geh-**shlehkhts**-krahnk-hīt
...vicious sunburn.	*...üblen Sonnenbrand.*	**ew**-blehn **zoh**-nehn-brahnt
...vomiting.	*...Übergeben.*	ew-ber-**gay**-behn
...worms.	*...Würmer.*	**vewr**-mer

Women's Health

menstruation	*Menstruation*	mehn-stroo-ah-see-**ohn**
menstrual cramps	*Monatskrämpfe*	**moh**-nahts-krehmp-feh
period	*Periode*	pehr-ee-**oh**-deh
pregnancy (test)	*Schwanger-schaft(-stest)*	**shvahng**-er-shahft(-stehst)

miscarriage	*Fehlgeburt*	**fayl**-geh-boort
abortion	*Abtreibung*	**ahp**-trī-boong
birth control pills	*Verhütungspille*	fehr-**hewt**-oongs-pil-leh
diaphragm	*Spirale*	shpee-**rah**-leh
I'd like to see a female...	*Ich möchte gern zu einer...*	ikh **murkh**-teh gehrn tsoo **ī**-ner
...doctor.	*...Ärztin.*	**ayrts**-tin
...gynecologist.	*...Gynäkologin.*	gewn-eh-koh-**loh**-gin
I've missed a period.	*Ich habe meine Tage nicht bekommen.*	ikh **hah**-beh **mī**-neh **tahg**-eh nikht beh-**kohm**-mehn
My last period started on ___.	*Meine letzte Periode fing am ___ an.*	**mī**-neh **lehts**-teh pehr-ee-**oh**-deh fing ahm ___ ahn
I am / She is... pregnant.	*Ich bin / Sie ist... schwanger.*	ikh bin / zee ist... **shvahng**-er
...___ months	*...im ___ Monat*	im ___ **moh**-naht

HEALTH

Parts of the Body

ankle	*Fußgelenk*	**foos**-geh-lehnk
arm	*Arm*	arm
back	*Rücken*	**rew**-kehn
bladder	*Blase*	**blah**-zeh
breast	*Busen*	**boo**-sehn
buttocks	*Hinterbacken*	**hin**-ter-bahk-ehn
chest	*Brust*	broost
ear	*Ohr*	or
elbow	*Ellbogen*	**ehl**-boh-gehn
eye	*Auge*	**ow**-geh
face	*Gesicht*	geh-**zikht**
finger	*Finger*	**fing**-er
foot	*Fuß*	foos
hair	*Haare*	har-reh
hand	*Hand*	hahnt
head	*Kopf*	kohpf
heart	*Herz*	hayrts

hip	*Hüfte*	**hewf**-teh
intestines	*Därme*	**dayr**-meh
knee	*Knie*	kuh-**nee**
leg	*Bein*	bīn
lung	*Lunge*	**loong**-eh
mouth	*Mund*	moont
neck	*Nacken*	**nahk**-ehn
nose	*Nase*	**nah**-zeh
penis	*Penis*	**peh**-nees
rectum	*Anus*	**ah**-noos
shoulder	*Schulter*	**shool**-ter
stomach	*Magen*	**mah**-gehn
teeth	*Zähne*	**tsay**-neh
testicles	*Hoden*	**hoh**-dehn
throat	*Hals*	hahls
toe	*Zehe*	**tsay**-heh
urethra	*Harnröhre*	**harn**-rur-eh
uterus	*Gebärmutter*	geh-**bayr**-moo-ter
vagina	*Vagina*	vah-**gee**-nah
waist	*Bund*	boont
wrist	*Handgelenk*	**hahnt**-geh-lehnk

For more anatomy lessons, see the illustrations on pages 510–511 in the appendix.

First-Aid Kit

antacid	*Mittel gegen Magenbrennen*	**mit**-tehl **gay**-gehn **mah**-gehn-breh-nehn
antibiotic	*Antibiotika*	ahn̲-tee-bee-**oh**-tee-kah
aspirin	*Aspirin*	ah-spir-**een**
non-aspirin substitute	*Ben-u-ron*	**behn**-oo-rohn̲
bandage	*Verband*	fehr-**bahnt**
Band-Aids	*Pflaster*	**pflahs**-ter
cold medicine	*Grippemittel*	**grip**-eh-mit-tehl
cough drops	*Hustenbonbons*	**hoo**-stehn-bohn̲-bohn̲s

disinfectant	*Desinfektionsmittel*	dehs-in-fehk-tsee-**ohns**-mit-tehl
first-aid cream	*Erste-Hilfe-Salbe*	**ehrst**-eh-**hil**-feh-**zahl**-beh
gauze / tape	*Verband*	fehr-**bahnt**
laxative	*Laxativ*	lahks-ah-**teef**
medicine for diarrhea	*Durchfallmedikament*	**doorkh**-fahl-meh-dee-kah-**mehnt**
moleskin	*Pflaster gegen Blasen*	**pflahs**-ter **gay**-gehn **blah**-zehn
painkiller	*Schmerzmittel*	**shmehrts**-mit-tehl
Preparation H	*Hämorrhoiden Salbe*	heh-mor-oh-**ee**-dehn **zahl**-beh
support bandage	*Stützverband*	**shtewts**-fehr-bahnt
thermometer	*Thermometer*	tehr-moh-**may**-ter
Vaseline	*Vaseline, Mineralsalbe*	vah-zeh-**lee**-neh, min-eh-**rahl**-zahl-beh
vitamins	*Vitamine*	vee-tah-**mee**-neh

If you're feeling feverish, see the thermometer on page 514 in the appendix.

Toiletries

comb	*Kamm*	kahm
conditioner for hair	*Haarfestiger*	**har**-fehs-tig-er
condoms	*Kondome*	kohn-**doh**-meh
dental floss	*Zahnseide*	**tsahn**-zī-deh
deodorant	*Deodorant*	deh-oh-doh-**rahnt**
facial tissue	*Papiertuch*	pah-**peer**-tookh
hairbrush	*Haarbürste*	**har**-bewr-steh
hand lotion	*Handlotion*	**hahnt**-loh-tsee-ohn
lip salve	*Lippenbalsam*	**lip**-pehn-bahl-zahm
mirror	*Spiegel*	**shpee**-gehl
nail clipper	*Nagelschere*	**nah**-gehl-sheh-reh
razor	*Rasierapparat*	rah-**zeer**-ahp-ar-aht
sanitary napkins	*Damenbinden*	**dah**-mehn-bin-dehn

scissors	*Schere*	**sheh**-reh
shampoo	*Shampoo*	**shahm**-poo
shaving cream	*Rasierschaum*	rah-**zeer**-showm
soap	*Seife*	**zī**-feh
sunscreen	*Sonnenschutz*	**zoh**-nehn-shoots
suntan lotion	*Sonnenöl*	**zoh**-nehn-url
tampons	*Tampons*	**tahm**-pohns
tissues	*Taschentücher*	**tah**-shehn-tewkh-er
toilet paper	*Klopapier*	kloh-pah-**peer**
toothbrush	*Zahnbürste*	**tsahn**-bewr-steh
toothpaste	*Zahnpasta*	**tsahn**-pah-stah
tweezers	*Pinzette*	pin-**tseh**-teh
baby food	*Babynahrung*	**bay**-bee-nah-roong
bib	*Latz*	lahts
bottle	*Flasche*	**flah**-sheh
diapers	*Windeln*	**vin**-dehln
diaper wipes	*Feuchtigkeitstücher*	**foykh**-tig-kīts-tewkh-er
diaper ointment	*Babysalbe*	**bay**-bee-zahl-beh
formula...	*Babynahrung...*	**bay**-bee-nah-roong
...powdered	*...in Pulver*	in **pool**-ver
...liquid	*...flüssig*	**flew**-sig
...soy	*...mit Soya*	mit **zoh**-yah
medication for...	*Medikament für...*	meh-dee-kah-**mehnt** fewr
...diaper rash	*...Windeldermatitis*	vin-del-dehr-ma-**tee**-tis
...teething	*...Zahnen*	**tsahn**-ehn
nipple	*Nippel*	**nip**-pehl
pacifier	*Nuggel*	**noog**-gehl
Will you refrigerate this?	*Können Sie das kühl stellen?*	**kurn**-nehn zee dahs kewl **shteh**-lehn
Will you warm... for a baby?	*Können Sie... fürs Baby wärmen?*	**kurn**-nehn zee... fewrs **bay**-bee **vayrm**-ehn
...this	*...das*	dahs
...some water	*...etwas Wasser*	**eht**-vahs **vah**-ser
...some milk	*...etwas Milch*	**eht**-vahs milkh
Not too hot, please.	*Nicht zu heiß, bitte.*	nikht tsoo hīs **bit**-teh

HEALTH

CHATTING

My name is ___.	*Ich heiße ___.*	ikh **hī**-seh
What's your name?	*Wie heißen Sie?*	vee **hī**-sehn zee
Pleased to meet you.	*Freut mich.*	froyt mikh
This is ___.	*Das ist ___.*	dahs ist
How are you?	*Wie geht's?*	vee gayts
Very well, thanks.	*Sehr gut, danke.*	zehr goot **dahng**-keh
Where are you from?	*Woher kommen Sie?*	**voh**-hehr **koh**-mehn zee
What...?	*Von welcher...?*	foh<u>n</u> **vehlkh**-er
...city	*...Stadt*	shtaht
...country	*...Land*	lah<u>n</u>t
...planet	*...Planet*	plah<u>n</u>-**ayt**
I'm from...	*Ich bin aus...*	ikh bin ows
...America.	*...Amerika.*	ah-**mehr**-ee-kah
...Canada.	*...Kanada.*	**kah**-nah-dah
Where are you going?	*Wo hin gehen Sie?*	voh hin **gay**-hehn zee
I'm going to ___.	*Ich gehe nach ___.*	ikh **gay**-heh nahkh
We're going to ___.	*Wir gehen nach ___.*	veer **gay**-hehn nahkh
Will you take my / our photo?	*Machen Sie ein Foto von mir / uns?*	**mahkh**-ehn zee īn **foh**-toh **fohn meer** / **oons**
Can I take a photo of you?	*Kann ich ein Foto von Ihnen machen?*	kah<u>n</u> ikh īn **foh**-toh foh<u>n</u> **ee**-nehn **mahkh**-ehn
Smile!	*Lächeln!*	**laykh**-ehln

Key Phrases: Chatting

My name is ___.	*Ich heiße ___.*	ikh **hī**-seh
What's your name?	*Wie heißen Sie?*	vee **hī**-sehn zee
Pleased to meet you.	*Freut mich.*	froyt mikh
Where are you from?	*Woher kommen Sie?*	**voh**-hehr **koh**-mehn zee
I'm from ___.	*Ich bin aus ___.*	ikh bin ows
Where are you going?	*Wohin gehen Sie?*	voh-hin **gay**-hehn zee
I'm going to ___.	*Ich gehe nach ___.*	ikh **gay**-heh nahkh
I like...	*Ich mag...*	ikh mahg
Do you like...?	*Mögen Sie...?*	**mur**-gehn zee
Thank you very much.	*Vielen Dank.*	**fee**-lehn dahngk
Have a good trip!	*Gute Reise!*	**goo**-teh **rī**-zeh

Nothing More Than Feelings...

I am / You are...	*Ich bin / Sie sind...*	ikh bin / zee zint
He / She is...	*Er / Sie ist...*	ehr / zee ist
...happy.	*...glücklich.*	**glewk**-likh
...sad.	*...traurig.*	**trow**-rig
...tired.	*...müde.*	**mew**-deh
...hungry.	*...hungrig.*	**hoon**-grig
...thirsty.	*...durstig.*	**door**-stig
I'm hot.	*Mir ist zu warm.*	meer ist tsoo varm
I'm cold.	*Mir ist kalt.*	meer ist kahlt
I'm homesick.	*Ich habe Heimweh.*	ikh **hah**-beh **hīm**-vay
I'm lucky.	*Ich habe Glück.*	ikh **hah**-beh glewk

Who's Who

This is... of mine.	*Das ist... von mir.*	dahs ist... fohn meer
...a male friend	*...ein Freund*	īn froynt
...a female friend	*...eine Freundin*	**ī**-neh **froyn**-din
This is my... (male / female)	*Das ist mein / meine...*	dahs ist mīn / **mī**-neh

...boyfriend / girlfriend.	*...Freund / Freundin.*	froynt / **froyn**-din
...husband / wife.	*...Mann / Frau.*	mahn / frow
...son / daughter.	*...Sohn / Tochter.*	zohn / **tohkh**-ter
...brother / sister.	*...Bruder / Schwester.*	**broo**-der / **shvehs**-ter
...father / mother.	*...Vater / Mutter.*	**fah**-ter / **moo**-ter
...uncle / aunt.	*...Onkel / Tante.*	**ohn**-kehl / **tahn**-teh
...nephew / niece.	*...Neffe / Nichte.*	**nehf**-feh / **neekh**-teh
...male / female cousin.	*...Vetter / Base.*	**feh**-ter / **bah**-zeh
...grandfather / grandmother.	*...Großvater / Großmutter.*	**grohs**-fah-ter / **grohs**-moo-ter
...grandson / granddaughter.	*...Enkel / Enkelin.*	**ehn**-kehl / **ehn**-kehl-in

Family

Are you married?	*Sind Sie verheiratet?*	zint zee fehr-**hī**-rah-teht
Do you have children?	*Haben Sie Kinder?*	**hah**-behn zee **kin**-der
How many boys / girls?	*Wie viele Jungen / Mädchen?*	vee **fee**-leh **yoong**-ehn / **mayd**-khehn
Do you have photos?	*Haben Sie Fotos?*	**hah**-behn zee **foh**-tohs
How old is your child?	*Wie alt ist Ihr Kind?*	vee ahlt ist eer kint
Beautiful child!	*Schönes Kind!*	**shur**-nehs kint
Beautiful children!	*Schöne Kinder!*	**shur**-neh **kin**-der

Chatting with Children

What's your name?	*Wie heißt du?*	vee hīst doo
My name is ___.	*Ich heiße ___.*	ikh **hī**-seh
How old are you?	*Wie alt bist du?*	vee ahlt bist doo
How old am I?	*Wie alt bin ich?*	vee ahlt bin ikh
I'm ___ years old.	*Ich bin ___ Jahre alt.*	ikh bin ___ **yah**-reh ahlt
Do you have siblings?	*Hast du Geschwister?*	hahst doo geh-**shvis**-ter
Do you like school?	*Magst du die Schule?*	mahgst doo dee **shoo**-leh

What are you studying?	*Was studierst du?*	vahs shtoo-**deerst** doo
What's your favorite subject?	*Was ist dein Lieblingsfach?*	vahs ist dīn **lee**-blings-fahkh
What is this?	*Was ist das?*	vahs ist dahs
Will you teach me / us some German words?	*Bringst du mir / uns einige deutsche Wörter bei?*	bringst doo meer / oons **ī**-nig-eh **doy**-cheh **vur**-ter bī
Will you teach me / us a simple German song?	*Kannst du mir / uns ein einfaches deutsches Lied beibringen?*	kahn͟st doo meer / oons īn **īn**-fahkh-ehs **doy**-chehs leet **bī**-bring-ehn
Guess which country I live / we live in.	*Rate mal, in welchem Land ich wohne / wir wohnen.*	**rah**-teh mahl in **vehlkh**-ehm lahn͟t ikh **voh**-neh / veer **voh**-nehn
Do you have pets?	*Hast du Haustiere?*	hahst doo **hows**-teer-eh
I have...	*Ich habe...*	ikh **hah**-beh
We have...	*Wir haben...*	veer **hah**-behn
...a cat / a dog / a fish / a bird	*...eine Katze / einen Hund / einen Fisch / einen Vogel*	**ī**-neh **kaht**-seh / **ī**-nehn hoont / **ī**-nehn fish / **ī**-nehn **voh**-gehl
Want to hear me burp?	*Willst du meinen Rülpser hören?*	vilst doo **mī**-nehn **rewlp**-zer **hur**-ehn
Teach me a fun game.	*Bringe mir ein lustiges Spiel bei.*	**bring**-eh meer īn **loo**-shtig-ehs shpeel bī
Got any candy?	*Hast du Süßigkeiten?*	hahst doo **zew**-sig-kī-tehn
Want to thumb-wrestle?	*Willst du Daumenziehen?*	vilst doo **dow**-mehn-tsee-hehn
Give me a handshake.	*Handschlag.*	**hahnt**-shlahg

If you do break into song, you'll find the words for "Happy Birthday" on page 356.

German kids usually shake hands instead of doing a "high five," but teaching them can be a fun icebreaker. Just say

"*So machen wir das in Amerika*" ("This is how we do it in America") and give 'em five!

Travel Talk

I am / Are you...?	*Ich bin / Sind Sie...?*	ikh bin / zint zee
...on vacation	*...auf Urlaub*	owf **oor**-lowp
...on business	*...auf Geschäftsreise*	owf geh-**shehfts**-rī-zeh
How long have you been traveling?	*Wie lange sind Sie schon unterwegs?*	vee **lahng**-eh zint zee shohn oont-er-**vehgs**
day / week	*Tag / Woche*	tahg / **vohkh**-eh
month / year	*Monat / Jahr*	**moh**-naht / yar
When are you going home?	*Wann fahren Sie zurück?*	vahn **far**-ehn zee tsoo-**rewk**
This is my first time in ___.	*Ich bin zum ersten Mal in ___.*	ikh bin tsoom **ehr**-stehn mahl in
This is our first time in ___.	*Wir sind zum ersten Mal in ___.*	veer zint tsoom **ehr**-stehn mahl in
It's (not) a tourist trap.	*Es ist (nicht) nur für Touristen.*	ehs ist (nikht) noor fewr too-**ris**-tehn
This is paradise.	*Das ist das Paradies.*	dahs ist dahs **pah**-rah-dees
This is a wonderful country.	*Dies ist ein wunderbares Land.*	deez ist īn **voon**-dehr-bah-rehs lahnt
The Germans / Austrians / Swiss...	*Die Deutschen / Österreicher / Schweizer...*	dee **doy**-chehn / **urs**-teh-rīkh-er / **shvīt**-ser
...are friendly / boring / rude.	*...sind freundlich / langweilig / unhöflich.*	zint **froynd**-likh / **lahng**-vī-lig / oon-**hurf**-likh
So far...	*Bis jetzt...*	bis yehtst
Today...	*Heute...*	**hoy**-teh
...I have seen ___ and ___.	*...habe ich ___ und ___ gesehen.*	**hah**-beh ikh ___ oont ___ geh-**zay**-hehn
...we have seen ___.	*...haben wir ___ gesehen.*	**hah**-behn veer ___ geh-**zay**-hehn

Next...	*Nächste...*	**nehkh**-steh
Tomorrow...	*Morgen...*	**mor**-gehn
...I will see ___.	*...werde ich ___ sehen.*	**vehr**-deh ikh ___ **zay**-hehn
...we will see ___.	*...werden wir ___ sehen.*	**vehr**-dehn veer ___ **zay**-hehn
Yesterday...	*Gestern...*	**geh**-stern
...I saw ___.	*...habe ich ___ gesehen.*	**hah**-beh ikh ___ geh-**zay**-hehn
...we saw ___.	*...haben wir ___ gesehen.*	**hah**-behn veer ___ geh-**zay**-hehn
My / Our vacation is ___ days long, starting in ___ and ending in ___.	*Meine / Unsere Ferien dauern ___ Tage, fangen in ___ an und enden in ___.*	**mī**-neh / **oon**-zer-eh **fay**-ree-ehn **dow**-ern ___ **tah**-geh **fahng**-ehn in ___ ahn oont **ehn**-dehn in
Travel is enlightening.	*Reisen ist aufschlußreich.*	**rī**-zehn ist **owf**-schloos-rīkh
I wish all (American) politicians traveled.	*Ich wünschte alle (amerikanischen) Politiker würden reisen.*	ikh **vewnsh**-teh **ah**-leh (ah-mehr-i-**kahn**-ish-ehn) poh-**lee**-tik-er vewr-dehn **rī**-zehn
Have a good trip!	*Gute Reise!*	**goo**-teh **rī**-zeh
To travel is to live.	*Reisen heißt leben.*	**rī**-zehn hīst **lay**-behn

Map Musings

The maps on pages 504–509 in the appendix will help you delve into family history and explore travel dreams.

I live here.	*Ich wohne hier.*	ikh **voh**-neh heer
We live here.	*Wir wohnen hier.*	veer **voh**-nehn heer
I was born here.	*Ich bin hier geboren.*	ikh bin heer geh-**boh**-rehn
My ancestors came from ___.	*Meine Vorfahren kamen aus ___.*	**mī**-neh **for**-far-ehn **kah**-mehn ows
I'd like/We'd like to go to ___.	*Ich möchte / Wir möchten nach ___ gehen.*	ich **murkh**-teh / veer **murkh**-tehn nahkh ___ **gay**-hehn

I've / We've traveled to ___.	*Ich bin / Wir sind in ___ gewesen.*	ikh bin / veer zint in ___ geh-**vay**-zehn
Next I'll go to ___.	*Als Nächstes gehe ich nach ___.*	als **nehkh**-stehs **gay**-heh ikh nahkh
Next we'll go to ___.	*Als Nächstes gehen wir nach ___.*	als **nehkh**-stehs **gay**-hehn veer nahkh
Where do you live?	*Wo wohnen Sie?*	voh **voh**-nehn zee
Where were you born?	*Wo sind Sie geboren?*	voh zint zee geh-**boh**-rehn
Where did your ancestors come from?	*Woher kommen Ihre Vorfahren?*	voh-hehr **koh**-mehn **ee**-reh **for**-far-ehn
Where have you traveled?	*Wo sind Sie schon gewesen?*	voh zint zee shohn geh-**vay**-zehn
Where are you going?	*Wohin gehen Sie?*	voh-hin **gay**-hehn zee
Where would you like to go?	*Wohin möchten Sie?*	voh-hin **murkh**-tehn zee

Weather

What's the weather tomorrow?	*Wie wird das Wetter morgen?*	vee virt dahs **veh**-ter **mor**-gehn
sunny / cloudy	*sonnig / bewölkt*	**zoh**-nig / beh-**vurlkt**
hot / cold	*heiß / kalt*	hīs / kahlt
muggy / windy	*schwül / windig*	shvewl / **vin**-dig
rain / snow	*Regen / Schnee*	**ray**-gehn / shnay
Should I bring a jacket?	*Soll ich eine Jacke mitbringen?*	zohl ikh **ī**-neh **yah**-keh **mit**-bring-ehn
It's raining buckets.	*Es regnet wie aus Kübeln.*	ehs **rayg**-neht vee ows **kew**-behln
The fog is like milk soup.	*Das ist eine Milchsuppe.*	dahs ist **ī**-neh **milkh**-zoo-peh
It's so hot you can boil an egg on the sidewalk.	*Es ist so heiß, daß man Eier auf dem Gehsteig braten kann.*	es ist zo hīs dahs mahn **ī**-er owf daym **geh**-shtīg **brah**-tehn kahn

The wind could blow your ears off.	*Der Wind könnte mir die Ohren wegblasen.*	dehr vint **kurn**-teh meer dee **or**-ehn **vehg**-blah-zehn

Thanks a Million

Thank you very much.	*Vielen Dank.*	**fee**-lehn dahngk
This is great fun.	*Das ist ein Riesenspaß.*	dahs ist īn **ree**-zehn-shpahs
You are...	*Sie sind...*	zee zint
...helpful.	*...hilfreich.*	**hilf**-rīkh
...wonderful.	*...wunderbar.*	**voon**-der-bar
...generous.	*...großzügig.*	**grohs**-tsew-gig
You spoil me / us.	*Sie verwöhnen mich / uns.*	zee fehr-**vur**-nehn mikh / oons
You've been a great help.	*Sie waren sehr hilfreich.*	zee **vah**-rehn zehr **hilf**-rīkh
You are an angel from God.	*Sie sind ein Engel, von Gott gesandt.*	zee zint īn **ehng**-ehl fohn goht geh-**zahndt**
I will remember you...	*Ich werde Sie... in Erinnerung behalten.*	ikh **vehr**-deh zee... in eh-**rin**-er-oong beh-**hahl**-tehn
We will remember you...	*Wir werden Sie... in Erinnerung behalten.*	veer **vehr**-dehn zee... in eh-**rin**-er-oong beh-**hahl**-tehn
...always.	*...immer*	**im**-mer
...till Tuesday.	*...bis Dienstag*	bis **deen**-stahg

Responses for All Occasions

I like that.	*Das gefällt mir.*	dahs geh-**fehlt** meer
We like that.	*Das gefällt uns.*	dahs geh-**fehlt** oons
I like you.	*Sie gefallen mir.*	zee geh-**fah**-lehn meer
We like you.	*Sie gefallen uns.*	zee geh-**fah**-lehn oons
That's cool!	*Hey, cool! Toll!*	"hey, cool," tohl
Excellent!	*Ausgezeichnet!*	ows-geh-**tsīkh**-neht
What a nice place.	*Was für ein herrlicher Ort.*	vahs fewr īn **hehr**-likh-er ort

CHATTING

Perfect.	*Perfekt.*	pehr-**fehkt**
Funny.	*Komisch.*	**koh**-mish
Interesting.	*Interessant.*	in-tehr-eh-**sahnt**
Really?	*Wirklich?*	**virk**-likh
Wow!	*Woah!*	woh-**ah**
Congratulations!	*Herzlichen Glückwunsch!*	**hehrts**-likh-ehn **glewk**-voonsh
Well done!	*Gut gemacht!*	goot geh-**mahkht**
You're welcome.	*Bitte schön.*	**bit**-teh shurn
Bless you! (after sneeze)	*Gesundheit!*	geh-**zoond**-hīt
What a pity.	*Wie schade.*	vee **shah**-deh
That's life.	*So geht's eben.*	zoh gayts **ay**-behn
No problem.	*Kein Problem.*	kīn proh-**blaym**
O.K.	*O.K.*	"O.K."
This is the good life!	*So läßt es sich leben!*	zoh lehst ehs zikh **lay**-ben
Have a good day!	*Schönen Tag!*	**shurn**-ehn tahg
Good luck!	*Viel Glück!*	feel glewk
Let's go!	*Auf geht's!*	owf gayts

Conversing with Animals

rooster / cock-a-doodle-doo	*Hahn / kikeriki*	hahn / kee-keh-ree-**kee**
bird / tweet tweet	*Vogel / piep piep*	**foh**-gehl / peep peep
cat / meow	*Katze / miau*	**kaht**-seh / mee-**ow**
dog / woof woof	*Hund / wuff wuff*	hoont / vuff vuff
duck / quack quack	*Ente / quak quak*	**ehn**-teh / kvahk kvahk
cow / moo	*Kuh / muh*	koo / moo
pig / oink oink	*Schwein / nöff nöff*	shvīn / nurf nurf

Profanity

People make animal noises too. These words will help you understand what the more colorful locals are saying...

Go to hell!	*Geh zur Hölle!*	gay tsur **hurl**-leh

Damn it.	*Verdammt.*	fehr-**dahmt**
bastard (pig-dog)	*Schweinehund*	**shvī**-neh-hoont
bitch (goat)	*Ziege*	**tsee**-geh
breasts (colloq.)	*Titten*	**tit**-ehn
penis (colloq.)	*Schwanz*	shvahnts
butthole	*Arschloch*	**arsh**-lohkh
drunk	*besoffen*	beh-**zohf**-fehn
idiot	*Idiot*	id-ee-**oht**
imbecile	*Trottel*	**troh**-tehl
jerk	*Blödmann*	**blurd**-mahn
stupid (dumb head)	*Dummkopf*	**doom**-kohpf
This sucks.	*Das ödet an.*	dahs **ur**-deht ahn
Shit.	*Scheiße.*	**shī**-seh
Bullshit.	*Blödsinn.*	**blurd**-zin
Sit on it.	*Am Arsch.*	ahm arsh
Shit on it.	*Scheiß drauf.*	shīs drowf
You are...	*Du bist...*	doo bist
Don't be...	*Sei kein...*	zī kīn
...a "shit guy."	*...Scheißkerl.*	**shīs**-kehrl
...an asshole.	*...Arschloch.*	**arsh**-lohkh
...an idiot.	*...Idiot.*	id-ee-**oht**
...a creep.	*...Psychopath.*	**psew**-koh-paht
...a cretin.	*...Blödmann.*	**blurd**-mahn
...a pig.	*...Schwein.*	shvīn

Sweet Curses

My goodness.	*Meine Güte.*	**mī**-neh **gew**-teh
Goodness gracious.	*Ach du liebe Zeit.*	ahkh doo **lee**-beh tsīt
Oh, my gosh.	*Oh, Jemine.*	oh **yeh**-mee-neh
Shoot.	*Scheibenkleister.*	**shī**-behn-klī-ster
Darn it!	*Verflixt!*	fehr-**flikst**

CREATE YOUR OWN CONVERSATION

You can mix and match these words into a conversation. Make it as deep or silly as you want.

Who

I / you	*ich / Sie*	ikh / zee
he / she	*er / sie*	ehr / zee
we / they	*wir / sie*	veer / zee
my / your...	*mein / Ihr...*	mīn / eer
...parents / children	*...Eltern / Kinder*	**ehl**-tern / **kin**-der
men / women	*Männer / Frauen*	**mehn**-ner / **frow**-ehn
rich / poor people	*Reichen / Armen*	**rīkh**-ehn / **ar**-mehn
young / old people	*Junge / Alte*	**yoong**-eh /**ahl**-teh
middle-aged people	*Mittelalterliche*	**mit**-ehl-ahl-ter-likh-eh
Germans	*Deutschen*	**doy**-chehn
Austrians	*Österreicher*	**urs**-teh-rīkh-er
Swiss	*Schweizer*	**shvīt**-ser
Czechs	*Tschechen*	**chehkh**-ehn
French	*Franzosen*	frahn-**tsoh**-zehn
Italians	*Italiener*	i-tah-lee-**ehn**-er
Europeans	*Europäer*	oy-roh-**pay**-er
EU (European Union)	*EU*	ay oo
Americans	*Amerikaner*	ah-mehr-ee-**kahn**-er
liberals	*Liberale*	lib-eh-**rah**-leh
conservatives	*Konservative*	kohn-zehr-vah-**teev**-eh
radicals	*Radikale*	rah-di-**kah**-leh
terrorists	*Terroristen*	tehr-or-**ist**-ehn
politicians	*Politiker*	poh-**lee**-tik-er
big business	*Großkapital*	**grohs**-kahp-i-**tahl**
multinational corporations	*Multis*	**mool**-tees
military	*Militär*	mil-ee-**tehr**
mafia	*Mafia*	"mafia"
Neo-Nazis	*Neonazis*	"Neo-Nazis"
eastern Germany	*Ostdeutschland*	**ohst**-doych-lahnt
western Germany	*Westen von Deutschland*	**vehs**-tehn fohn **doych**-lahnt

CHATTING

eastern / western Germans	*Ostdeutscher/ Westdeutscher*	**ohst**-doy-cher/ **vehst**-doy-cher
refugees	*Flüchtlinge*	**flewkht**-ling-eh
travelers	*Reisende*	**rī**-zehn-deh
God	*Gott*	goht
Christians	*Christen*	**kris**-tehn
Catholics	*Katholiken*	kah-**toh**-li-kehn
Protestants	*Protestanten*	proh-tehs-**tahn**-tehn
Jews	*Juden*	**yoo**-dehn
Muslims	*Moslems*	**mohz**-lehms
everyone	*alle Leute*	**ah**-leh **loy**-teh

What

buy / sell	*kaufen / verkaufen*	**kow**-fehn / fehr-**kow**-fehn
have / lack	*haben / haben nicht*	**hah**-behn / **hah**-behn nikht
help / abuse	*helfen / mißbrauchen*	**hehl**-fehn / mis-**browkh**-ehn
learn / fear	*lernen / fürchten*	**lehrn**-ehn / **fewrkh**-tehn
love / hate	*lieben / hassen*	**lee**-behn / **hah**-sehn
prosper / suffer	*florieren / leiden*	floh-**ree**-rehn / **lī**-dehn
take / give	*nehmen / geben*	**nay**-mehn / **gay**-behn
want / need	*wollen / brauchen*	**vol**-lehn / **browkh**-ehn
work / play	*arbeiten / spielen*	**ar**-bīt-ehn / **shpeel**-ehn

Why

(anti-) globalization	*(Anti-) Globalisierung*	(**ahn**-tee-) gloh-bahl-is-**eer**-oong
class warfare	*Klassenkampf*	**klahs**-ehn-kahmpf
corruption	*Korruption*	kor-rupt-see-**ohn**
democracy	*Demokratie*	day-moh-krah-**tee**
education	*Ausbildung*	**ows**-bil-doong
family	*Familie*	fah-**mee**-lee-eh
food	*Essen*	**eh**-sehn
guns	*Waffen*	**vah**-fehn
happiness	*Glück*	glewk

health	*Gesundheit*	geh-**zoond**-hīt
hope	*Hoffnung*	**hohf**-noong
imperialism	*Kolonisation*	koh-loh-nee-saht-see-**ohn**
lies	*Lügen*	**lew**-gehn
love / sex	*Liebe / Sex*	**lee**-beh / zehx
marijuana	*Marihuana*	mah-ri-**wah**-nah
money / power	*Geld / Macht*	gehlt / mahkht
pollution	*Umweltverschmutzung*	**oom**-vehlt-fehr-**shmut**-tsoong
racism	*Rassismus*	rah-**sis**-moos
regime change	*Regimewechsel*	reh-**zheem**-vehkh-sehl
relaxation	*Entspannung*	ehnt-**shpah**-noong
religion	*Religion*	reh-leeg-ee-**ohn**
respect	*Respekt*	rehs-**pehkt**
reunification	*Wiedervereinigung*	**vee**-dehr-fehr-**īn**-i-goong
taxes	*Steuern*	**shtoy**-ern
television	*Fernsehen*	**fehrn**-zay-hehn
violence	*Gewalt*	geh-**vahlt**
war / peace	*Krieg / Frieden*	kreeg / **free**-dehn
work	*Arbeit*	**ar**-bīt
global perspective	*Gesamtperspektive*	geh-**zahmt**-per-spehk-**tee**-veh

CHATTING

You Be the Judge

(no) problem	*(kein) Problem*	(kīn) proh-**blaym**
(not) good	*(nicht) gut*	(nikht) goot
(not) dangerous	*(nicht) gefährlich*	(nikht) geh-**fehr**-likh
(not) fair	*(nicht) fair*	(nikht) "fair"
(not) guilty	*(nicht) schuldig*	(nikht) **shool**-dig
(not) powerful	*(nicht) mächtig*	(nikht) **mehkh**-tig
(not) stupid	*(nicht) dumm*	(nikht) doom
(not) happy	*(nicht) glücklich*	(nikht) **glewk**-likh
because / for	*weil / wegen*	vīl / **vay**-gehn
and / or / from	*und / oder / von*	oont / **oh**-dehr / fohn
too much	*zu viel*	tsoo feel
(never) enough	*(nie) genug*	(nee) geh-**noog**

same	*gleich*	glīkh
better / worse	*besser / schlechter schlechter*	**behs**-ser / **shlehkh**-ter **shlehkh**-ter

Beginnings and Endings

I like...	*Ich mag...*	ikh mahg
We like...	*Wir mögen...*	veer **mur**-gehn
I don't like...	*Ich mag... nicht.*	ikh mahg... nikht
We don't like...	*Wir mögen... nicht.*	veer **mur**-gehn... nikht
Do you like...?	*Mögen Sie...?*	**mur**-gehn zee
In the past...	*Früher...*	**frew**-her
When I was younger, I thought...	*Als ich jünger war, dachte ich...*	ahls ikh **yewng**-er var **dahkh**-teh ikh
Now, I think...	*Jetzt denke ich...*	yetst **dehnk**-eh ikh
I am / Are you...?	*Ich bin / Sind Sie...?*	ikh bin / zint zee
...an optimist / pessimist	*...ein Optimist / Pessimist*	īn **ohp**-ti-meest / **pehs**-i-meest
I believe in...	*Ich glaube an...*	ikh **glow**-beh ahn
I don't believe in...	*Ich glaube nicht an...*	ikh **glow**-beh nikht ahn
Do you believe in...?	*Glauben Sie an...?*	**glow**-behn zee ahn
...God	*...Gott*	goht
...life after death	*...Leben nach dem Tod*	**lay**-behn nahkh daym tohd
...extraterrestrial life	*...Leben im Weltall*	**lay**-behn im **vehlt**-ahl
...Santa Claus	*...Weihnachtsmann*	**vī**-nahkhts-mahn
Yes. / No.	*Ja. / Nein.*	yah / nīn
Maybe. / I don't know.	*Vielleicht. / Ich weiß nicht.*	fee-**līkht** / ikh vīs nikht
What is most important in life?	*Was ist das Wichtigste im Leben?*	vahs ist dahs **vikh**-tig-steh im **lay**-behn
The problem is...	*Das Problem ist...*	dahs proh-**blaym** ist
The answer is...	*Die Antwort ist...*	dee **ahnt**-vort ist
We have solved the world's problems.	*Wir haben die Probleme der Welt gelöst.*	veer **hah**-behn dee proh-**blay**-meh dehr vehlt geh-**lurst**

AN AFFAIR TO REMEMBER

Words of Love

I / me / you / we	*ich / mich / dich / wir*	ikh / mikh / dikh / veer
flirt	*flirten*	**flir**-tehn
kiss	*Kuß*	kus
hug	*Umarmung*	oom-**arm**-oong
love	*Liebe*	**lee**-beh
make love (sleep together)	*miteinander schlafen*	mit-īn-**ahn**-dehr **shlah**-fehn
condom	*Kondom, Präservativ*	**kon**-dohm, pray-zehr-fah-**tif**
contraceptive	*Verhütungs-mittel*	fehr-**hew**-toongs-**mit**-tehl
safe sex	*safe sex*	"safe sex"
sexy	*sexy*	"sexy"
cozy	*gemütlich*	geh-**mewt**-likh
romantic	*romantisch*	roh-**mahn**-tish
cupcake	*Schnuckel*	**shnook**-ehl
little rabbit	*Häschen*	**hay**-shyehn
little sugar mouse	*Zuckermäuschen*	**tsoo**-ker-**moy**-shyehn
pussy cat	*Miezekatze*	**meets**-eh-**kaht**-seh
baby	*Baby*	"baby"

Ah, Romance

What's the matter?	*Was ist los?*	vahs ist lohs
Nothing.	*Nichts.*	nikhts
I am / Are you...?	*Ich bin / Sind Sie...?*	ikh bin / zint zee
...straight	*...hetero*	**hay**-ter-oh
...gay	*...schwul*	shvul
...bisexual	*...bisexual*	bee-zeks-oo-**ahl**
...undecided	*...mir nicht sicher*	meer nikht **zikh**-er
...prudish	*...verklemmt*	fehr-**klehmt**
...horny	*...geil*	gīl
We are on our honeymoon.	*Wir sind auf unserer Hochzeitsreise.*	veer zint owf **oon**-zer-er **hohkh**-tsīts-rī-zeh

CHATTING

I have...	*Ich habe...*	ikh **hah**-beh
...a boyfriend.	*...einen Freund.*	**ī**-nehn froynt
...a girlfriend.	*...eine Freundin.*	**ī**-neh **froyn**-din
I'm married, but...	*Ich bin verheiratet, aber...*	ikh bin fehr-**hī**-rah-teht **ah**-ber
I'm not married.	*Ich bin nicht verheiratet.*	ikh bin nikht fehr-**hī**-rah-teht
Do you have a boyfriend / a girlfriend?	*Haben Sie einen Freund / eine Freundin?*	**hah**-behn zee **ī**-nehn froynt / **ī**-neh **froyn**-din
I'm adventurous.	*Ich bin auf Abenteuer aus.*	ikh bin owf **ah**-behn-toy-er ows
I'm lonely (tonight).	*Ich bin einsam (heut' Nacht).*	ikh bin **īn**-zahm (hoyt nahkht)
I'm rich and single.	*Ich bin reich und zu haben.*	ikh bin rīkh oont tsoo **hah**-behn
Do you mind if I sit here?	*Stört es Sie, wenn ich hier sitze?*	shturt ehs zee vehn ikh heer **zit**-seh
Would you like a drink?	*Möchten Sie einen Drink?*	**murkh**-tehn zee **ī**-nehn drink
Will you go out with me?	*Gehen Sie mit mir aus?*	**gay**-hehn zee mit meer ows
Would you like to go out tonight for...?	*Möchten Sie heute ausgehen für...?*	**murkh**-tehn zee **hoy**-teh **ows**-gay-hehn fewr
...a walk	*...einen Spaziergang*	**ī**-nehn shpaht-**seer**-gahng
...dinner	*...ein Abendessen*	īn **ah**-behnt-eh-sehn
...a drink	*...einen Drink*	īn drink
Where's the best place to dance nearby?	*Wo geht man hier am besten Tanzen?*	voh gayt mahn heer ahm **beh**-stehn **tahn**-tsehn
Do you want to dance?	*Möchten Sie tanzen?*	**murkh**-tehn zee **tahn**-tsehn
Again?	*Noch einmal?*	nokh **īn**-mahl
Let's party!	*Feiern wir!*	**fī**-ern veer
Let's have fun like idiots!	*Feiern wir wie blöd!*	**fī**-ern veer vee blurd

Let's have a wild and crazy night!	*Machen wir einen 'drauf!*	**mahkh**-ehn veer ī-nehn drowf
I have no diseases.	*Ich habe keine Krankheiten.*	ikh **hah**-behh **kī**-neh **krahnk**-hī-tehn
I have many diseases.	*Ich habe viele Krankheiten.*	ikh **hah**-beh **fee**-leh **krahnk**-hī-tehn
I have only safe sex.	*Mit mir nur safe sex.*	mit meer noor "safe sex"
Can I take you home?	*Kann ich Sie nach Hause bringen?*	kahn ikh zee nahkh **how**-zeh **bring**-ehn
Why not?	*Warum nicht?*	vah-**room** nikht
How can I change your mind?	*Wie kann ich Sie umstimmen?*	vee kahn ikh zee **oom**-shtim-mehn
Kiss me.	*Küß mich.*	kews mikh
May I kiss you?	*Darf ich dich küssen?*	darf ikh dikh **kews**-ehn
Can I see you again?	*Können wir uns wiedersehen?*	**kurn**-nehn veer oons **vee**-der-zayn
Your place or mine?	*Bei dir oder bei mir?*	bī deer **oh**-der bī meer
How does this feel?	*Wie fühlt sich das an?*	vee fewlt zikh dahs ahn
Is this an aphrodisiac?	*Ist dies ein Aphrodisiakum?*	ist deez īn ah-froh-dee-zee-**ahk**-oom
This is (not) my first time.	*Dies ist für mich (nicht) das erste Mal.*	deez ist fewr mikh (nikht) dahs **ehr**-steh mahl
You are my most beautiful souvenir.	*Du bist mein schönstes Andenken.*	doo bist mīn **shurn**-stehs **ahn**-dehnk-ehn
Do you do this often?	*Machst du das oft?*	mahkhst doo dahs oft
Do I have bad breath?	*Habe ich Mundgeruch?*	**hah**-beh ikh **moont**-geh-rookh
Let's just be friends.	*Wir können doch einfach Freunde sein.*	veer **kurn**-nehn dohkh **īn**-fahkh **froyn**-deh zīn
I'll pay for my share.	*Ich bezahle meinen Anteil.*	ikh beht-**sah**-leh **mī**-nehn **ahn**-tīl

Would you like a... massage?	*Darf ich dir den... massieren?*	darf ikh deer dayn... mah-**see**-rehn
...back	*...Rücken*	**rew**-kehn
...foot	*...Fuß*	foos
Why not?	*Warum nicht?*	vah-**room** nikht
Try it.	*Versuch's doch mal.*	fehr-**zookhs** dokh mahl
That tickles.	*Das kitzelt.*	dahs **kit**-sehlt
Oh my God!	*Oh mein Gott!*	oh mīn goht
I love you.	*Ich liebe dich.*	ikh **lee**-beh dikh
Darling, marry me!	*Liebling, heirate mich!*	**lee**-bleeng **hī**-rah-teh mikh

TIPS FOR HURDLING THE LANGUAGE BARRIER

Don't Be Afraid to Communicate

Even the best phrase book won't satisfy your needs in every situation. To really hurdle the language barrier, you need to leap beyond the printed page, and dive into contact with the locals. Never allow your lack of foreign language skills to isolate you from the people and cultures you traveled halfway around the world to experience. Remember that in every country you visit, you're surrounded by expert, native-speaking tutors. Spend bus and train rides letting them teach you.

Start conversations by asking politely in the local language, "Do you speak English?" When you speak English with someone from another country, talk slowly, clearly, and with carefully chosen words. Use what the Voice of America calls "simple English." You're talking to people who are wishing it was written down, hoping to see each letter as it tumbles out of your mouth. Pronounce each letter, avoiding all contractions and slang. For bad examples, listen to other tourists.

Keep things caveman-simple. Make single nouns work as entire sentences ("Photo?"). Use internationally-understood words ("Self-service" works in Paris, Rome, or Berlin). Butcher the language if you must. The important thing is to make the effort. To get air mail stamps, you can flap your wings and say "tweet, tweet." If you want milk, moo and pull two imaginary udders. Risk looking like a fool.

If you're short on words, make your picnic a potluck. Pull out a map and point out your journey. Draw what you mean. Bring photos from home and introduce your family. Play cards or toss a Frisbee. Fold an origami bird for kids or dazzle 'em with sleight-of-hand magic.

Go ahead and make educated guesses. Many situations are easy-to-fake multiple choice questions. Practice. Read timetables, concert posters and newspaper headlines. Listen to each language on a multilingual tour. Be melodramatic. Exaggerate the local accent. Self-consciousness is the deadliest communication-killer.

Choose multilingual people to communicate with, such as students, business people, urbanites, young well-dressed people, or anyone in the tourist trade. Use a small note pad to jot down handy phrases and to help you communicate more clearly with the locals by scribbling down numbers, maps, and so on. Some travelers carry important messages written on a small card: allergic to nuts, strict vegetarian, your finest ice cream.

International Words

As our world shrinks, more and more words hop across their linguistic boundaries and become international. Savvy travelers develop a knack for choosing words most likely to be universally understood ("auto" instead of "car," "kaput" instead of "broken," "photo," not "picture"). Internationalize your pronunciation. "University," if you play around with its sound (oo-nee-vehr-see-tay), will be understood anywhere. The average American is a real flunky in this area. Be creative.

You'll find some internationally understood words listed on the next page. Remember, cut out the Yankee accent and give each word a pan-European sound.

Amigo
Attila (mean, crude)
Auto
Autobus ("booos")
Bank
Beer
Bill Gates
Bon voyage
Bye-bye
Camping
Casanova (romantic)
Central
Chocolate
Ciao
Coffee
Coke, Coca-Cola
Communist
Computer
Disco
Disneyland (wonderland)
Elephant (big clod)
English ("Engleesh")
Europa
Fascist
Hello
Hercules (strong)
Hotel
Information
Internet
Kaput
Mama mia
Mañana
McDonald's
Michelangelo (artistic)
Moment
No
No problem
Nuclear
OK
Oo la la
Pardon
Passport
Photo
Photocopy
Picnic
Police
Post
Rambo
Restaurant
Rock 'n' roll
Self-service
Sex / Sexy
Sport
Stop
Super
Taxi
Tea
Telephone
Toilet
Tourist
US profanity
University
Vino
Yankee, Americano

Numbers and Stumblers

- Europeans write a few of their numbers differently than we do. 1=1, 4=4, 7=7.
- Europeans write the date in this order: day/month/year.
- Commas are decimal points and decimals are commas. A dollar and a half is 1,50 and there are 5.280 feet in a mile.
- The European "first floor" isn't the ground floor, but the first floor up.
- When counting with your fingers, start with your thumb. If you hold up only your first finger, you'll probably get two of something.

TONGUE TWISTERS

Tongue twisters are a great way to practice a language and break the ice with locals. Here are a few that are sure to challenge you, and amuse your hosts.

French *(Tire-langues)*

Bonjour madame la saucissonière!
Hello, madame sausage-seller!

Combien sont ces six saucissons-ci?
How much are these six sausages?

Ces six saucissons-ci sont six sous.
These six sausages are six cents.

Si ces saucissons-ci sont six sous, ces six saucissons-ci sont trop chers.
If these are six cents, these six sausages are too expensive.

Je veux et j'exige qu'un chasseur sachant chasser sans ses èchasses sache chasser sans son chien de chasse.
I want and demand that a hunter who knows how to hunt without his stilts knows how to hunt without his hunting dog.

Ce sont seize cent jacynthes sèches dans seize cent sachets secs.
These are 600 dry hyacinths in 600 dry sachets.

Ce sont trois très gros rats dans trois très gros trous roulant trois gros rats gris morts.
These are three very fat rats in three very fat rat-holes rolling three fat gray dead rats.

Italian *(Scioglilingue)*

Trentatrè trentini arrivarono a Trento tutti e trentatrè trottorellando.
Thirty-three people from Trent arrived in Trent, all thirty-three trotting.

Chi fù quel barbaro barbiere che barberò così barbaramente a Piazza Barberini quel povero barbaro di Barbarossa?
Who was that barbarian barber in Barberini Square who shaved that poor barbarian Barbarossa?

Sopra la panca la capra canta, sotto la panca la capra crepa.
On the bench the goat sings, under the bench the goat dies.

German *(Zungenbrecher)*

Zehn zahme Ziegen zogen Zucker zum Zoo.	Ten domesticated goats pulled sugar to the zoo.
Blaukraut bleibt Blaukraut und Brautkleid bleibt Brautkleid.	Bluegrass remains bluegrass and a wedding dress remains a wedding dress.
Fischers Fritze fischt frische Fische, frische Fische fischt Fischers Fritze.	Fritz Fischer catches fresh fish, fresh fish Fritz Fisher catches.
Die Katze trapst die Treppe rauf.	The cat is walking up the stairs.
Ich komme über Oberammergau, oder komme ich über Unterammergau?	I am coming via Oberammergau, or am I coming via Unterammergau?

English

After your European friends have laughed at you, let them try these tongue twisters in English:

Soldiers' shoulders.

If neither he sells seashells, nor she sells seashells, who shall sell seashells? Shall seashells be sold?

I'm a pleasant mother pheasant plucker. I pluck mother pheasants. I'm the most pleasant mother pheasant plucker that ever plucked a mother pheasant.

Thieves seize skis.

Peter Piper picked a peck of pickled peppers.

Rugged rubber baby buggy bumpers.

Red bug's blood and black bug's blood.

The sixth sick sheik's sixth sheep's sick.

APPENDIX

LET'S TALK TELEPHONES

Making Calls within a European Country: About half of all European countries use area codes (like we do); the other half uses a direct-dial system without area codes.

To make calls within a country that uses a direct-dial system (Belgium, Czech Republic, Denmark, France, Greece, Italy, Norway, Poland, Portugal, Spain, and Switzerland), you dial the same number whether you're calling across the country or across the street.

In countries that use area codes (such as Austria, Britain, Croatia, Finland, Germany, Ireland, the Netherlands, Slovakia, Slovenia, and Sweden), you dial the local number when calling within a city and you add the area code if calling long-distance within the country.

Making International Calls: You always start with the international access code (011 if you're calling from America or Canada, or 00 from Europe), then dial the country code of the country you're calling (see codes on following page).

What you dial next depends on the system of the country you're calling. If the country uses area codes, drop the initial zero of the area code, then dial the rest of the number.

Countries that use direct-dial (no area codes) vary in how they're accessed internationally by phone. Always start by dialing the international access code, then the country code. If you're calling the

Czech Republic, Denmark, Italy, Norway, Portugal, or Spain, simply dial the phone number in its entirety. But if you're calling Belgium, France, Poland, or Switzerland, drop the initial zero of the number.

Country Codes

After you've dialed the international access code, dial the code of the country you're calling.

Austria—43
Belgium—32
Bosnia-Herzegovina—387
Britain—44
Canada—1
Croatia—385
Czech Rep.—420
Denmark—45
Estonia—372
Finland—358
France—33
Germany—49
Gibraltar—350
Greece—30
Hungary—36
Ireland—353
Italy—39
Montenegro—382
Morocco—212
Netherlands—31
Norway—47
Poland—48
Portugal—351
Slovakia—421
Slovenia—386
Spain—34
Sweden—46
Switzerland—41
Turkey—90
United States—1

Cell Phones

Many travelers now buy cell phones in Europe to make both local and international calls. You'll pay under $100 for a "locked" phone that works only in the country you buy it in (includes about $20 worth of calls). You can buy additional time at a newsstand or cell phone shop. An "unlocked" phone is more expensive, but it works all over Europe: when you cross a border, buy a SIM card (about $25) at a cell phone shop and insert the pop-out chip, which comes with a new phone number. Pricier tri-band phones (***tribande*** in France, ***telefono tri–banda*** in Italy, and ***Triband Handys*** in Germany) also work in North America.

Directory Assistance

Austria: national—16, international—08, train info—051717
France: 12 (some English spoken)
Germany: national—11833, international—11834, train info—11861, German tourist offices—dial area code, then 19433
Italy: 12 (for €0.50, a computer gives the number twice, in Italian)
Switzerland: national—111, international—191, train info—0900-300-3004

US Embassies and Consulates

AUSTRIA

- Tel. 01/313-390
- Bolzmannga, **Vienna**
- www.usembassy.at

FRANCE

- tel. 01 43 12 22 22
- 4 avenue Gabriel, **Paris**
- Métro stop: Concorde
- http://france.usembassy.gov

GERMANY

- Tel. 089/28880
- Königinstrasse 5, **Munich**

- Tel. 030/832-9233
- Clayallee 170, **Berlin**
- www.usembassy.de

ITALY

- Tel. 06-46741
- Via Vittorio Veneto 121, **Rome**
- http://rome.usembassy.gov

- Tel. 055-266-951
- Lungarno Vespucci 38, **Florence**

SWITZERLAND

- Tel. 031-357-7234
- Jubilaeumsstraße 93, **Bern**
- http://bern.usembassy.gov

MAPS

If you want to show anyone where you're from, where you're going, or where you're hoping to visit, these maps can come in handy.

Europe

APPENDIX

France

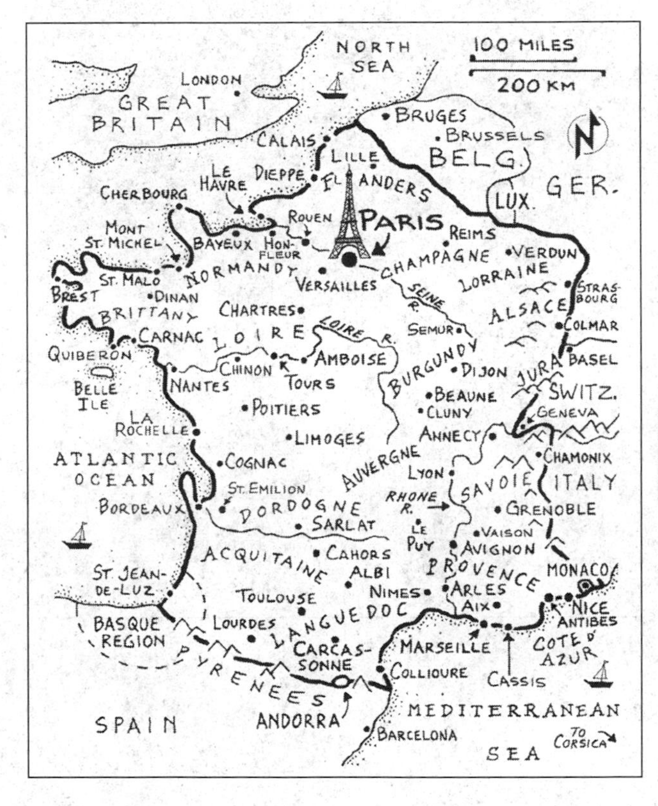

APPENDIX

Italy

AUSTRIA
100 MILES
100 KM
BERN
INNS-BRUCK
SWITZ.
MT. BLANC
BOLZANO
DOLOMITES
LJUBLJANA
LAKE DISTRICT
UDINE
SLOV.
AOSTA
COMO
TRENTO
TRIESTE
MILAN
LOMBARDY
VENETO
VERONA
VENICE
CROATIA
FRANCE
TURIN
PIEDMONT
PO R.
EMILIA-ROMAGNA
BOLOGNA
BOSNIA & HERZE-GOVINA
GENOA
RAVENNA
ZADAR
LIGURIA
CINQUE TERRE
LA SPEZIA
LUCCA
SAN MARINO
FLORENCE
NICE
LIGURIAN SEA
PISA
ARNO R.
SPLIT
ANCONA
TUSCANY
PERUGIA
SIENA
ASSISI
UMBRIA
ADRIATIC SEA
MONT.
ELBA
ORVIETO
ABRUZZI
PESCARA
DUBROVNIK
CORSICA (FR.)
LAZIO
TIBER
GARGANO PEN.
ROME
BARI
CAMPANIA
MT. VESUVIUS
NAPLES
POMPEII
PUGLIA
BRINDISI
OLBIA
TYRRHENIAN SEA
CAPRI
MATERA
PAESTUM
LECCE
AMALFI COAST
SARDINIA
CALABRIA
CAGLIARI
LIPARI ISLANDS
IONIAN SEA
MEDITERRANEAN SEA
PALERMO
TRAPANI
REGGIO
CEFALU
TAORMINA
MT. ETNA
AGRIGENTO
SYRACUSE
ALG.
TUNIS
TUNISIA
SICILY
DCH

Germany

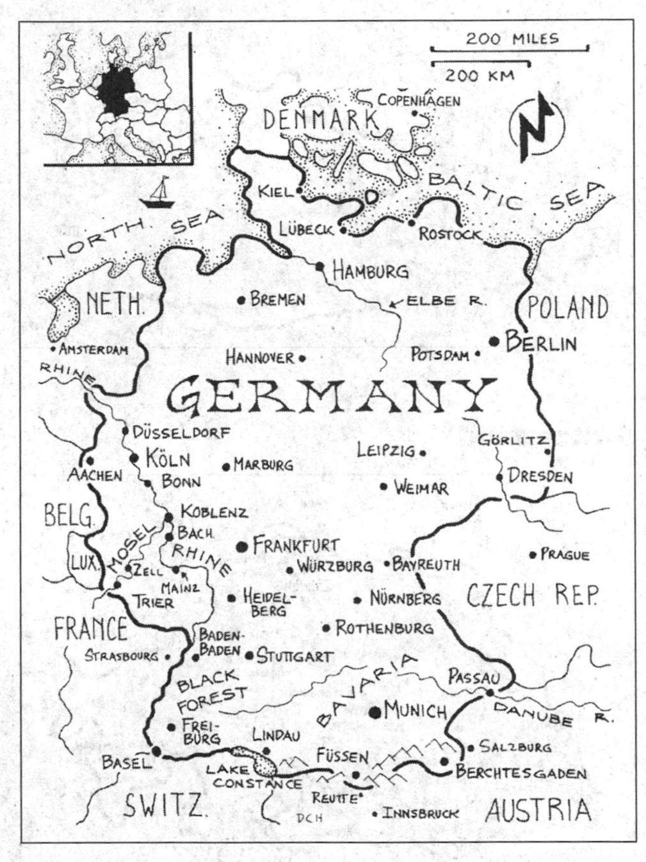

200 MILES
200 KM
COPENHAGEN
DENMARK
BALTIC SEA
KIEL
LÜBECK
ROSTOCK
NORTH SEA
HAMBURG
BREMEN
ELBE R.
NETH.
POLAND
BERLIN
AMSTERDAM
HANNOVER
POTSDAM
RHINE
GERMANY
DÜSSELDORF
GÖRLITZ
LEIPZIG
KÖLN
MARBURG
AACHEN
BONN
DRESDEN
WEIMAR
BELG.
KOBLENZ
BACH
MOSEL
FRANKFURT
PRAGUE
RHINE
LUX.
ZELL
WÜRZBURG
BAYREUTH
MAINZ
TRIER
HEIDEL-
BERG
NÜRNBERG
CZECH REP.
FRANCE
ROTHENBURG
BADEN-
BADEN
STRASBOURG
STUTTGART
BAVARIA
PASSAU
BLACK
FOREST
MUNICH
DANUBE R.
FREI-
BURG
LINDAU
SALZBURG
BASEL
FÜSSEN
BERCHTESGADEN
LAKE
CONSTANCE
REUTTE
SWITZ.
DCH
INNSBRUCK
AUSTRIA

Austria

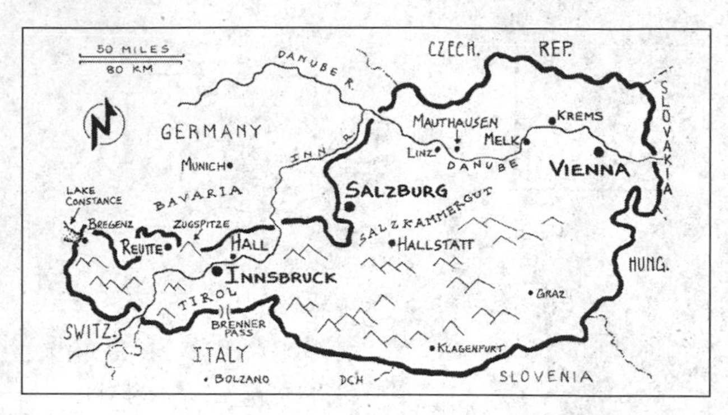

Switzerland

The United States

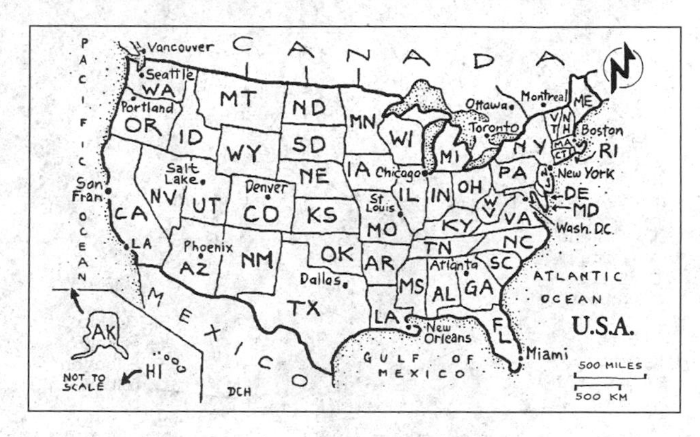

The World

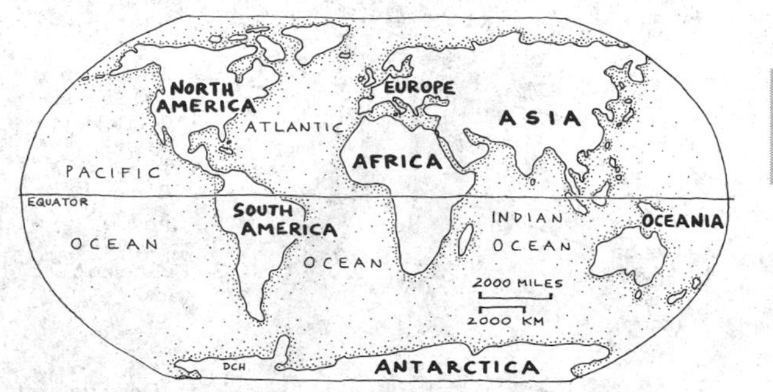

Parts of the Body

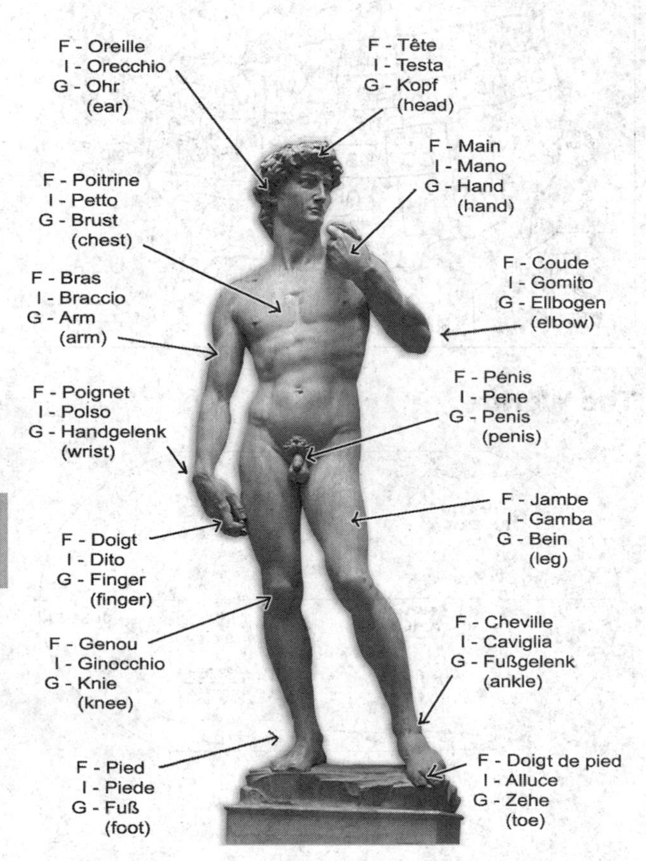
F - Oreille
I - Orecchio
G - Ohr
(ear)
F - Tête
I - Testa
G - Kopf
(head)
F - Main
I - Mano
G - Hand
(hand)
F - Poitrine
I - Petto
G - Brust
(chest)
F - Coude
I - Gomito
G - Ellbogen
(elbow)
F - Bras
I - Braccio
G - Arm
(arm)
F - Pénis
I - Pene
G - Penis
(penis)
F - Poignet
I - Polso
G - Handgelenk
(wrist)
F - Jambe
I - Gamba
G - Bein
(leg)
F - Doigt
I - Dito
G - Finger
(finger)
F - Cheville
I - Caviglia
G - Fußgelenk
(ankle)
F - Genou
I - Ginocchio
G - Knie
(knee)
F - Pied
I - Piede
G - Fuß
(foot)
F - Doigt de pied
I - Alluce
G - Zehe
(toe)

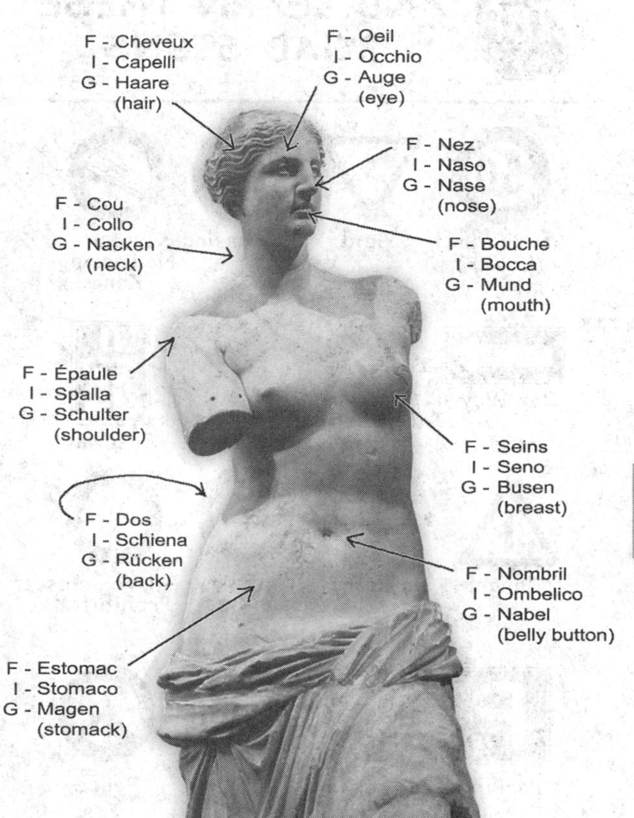
F - Cheveux
I - Capelli
G - Haare
(hair)
F - Oeil
I - Occhio
G - Auge
(eye)
F - Nez
I - Naso
G - Nase
(nose)
F - Cou
I - Collo
G - Nacken
(neck)
F - Bouche
I - Bocca
G - Mund
(mouth)
F - Épaule
I - Spalla
G - Schulter
(shoulder)
F - Seins
I - Seno
G - Busen
(breast)
F - Dos
I - Schiena
G - Rücken
(back)
F - Nombril
I - Ombelico
G - Nabel
(belly button)
F - Estomac
I - Stomaco
G - Magen
(stomack)

Standard Road Signs

AND LEARN THESE ROAD SIGNS

Speed Limit (km/hr)

Yield

No Passing

End of No Passing Zone

One Way

Intersection

Main Road

Freeway

Danger

No Entry

No Entry for Cars

All Vehicles Prohibited

Parking

No Parking

Customs

Peace

APPENDIX

Chill Out

Many hotel rooms in the Mediterranean part of Europe have air-conditioning—often controlled via a remote (like a TV). Various remotes have basically the same features:

- fan icon (to toggle through fans speed from light to gale)
- louver icon (for choosing steady air flow or waves)
- snow and sun icons (heat or cold, generally just one or the other is possible: cool air in summer, heat in winter)
- two clock settings (to determine how long the A/C will stay on before turning off, or stay off before turning on)
- temperature control (20° or 21° is comfortable in Celsius)

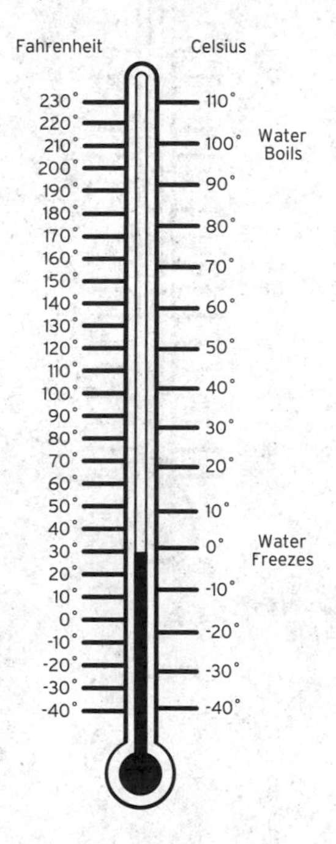

Medical Thermometer

French	*thermomètre*	tehr-moh-meh-truh
Italian	*termometro*	tehr-moh-**may**-troh
German	*thermometer*	tehr-moh-**may**-ter

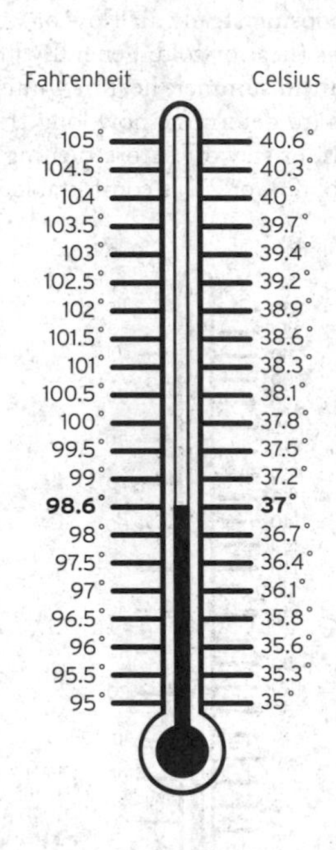

French Tear-Out Cheat Sheet

Keep these survival phrases in your pocket, handy to memorize or use if you're caught without your phrase book.

Good day.	*Bonjour.*	bohn-zhoor
Do you speak English?	*Parlez-vous anglais?*	par-lay-voo ahn-glay
Yes. / No.	*Oui. / Non.*	wee / nohn
I don't understand.	*Je ne comprends pas.*	zhuh nuh kohn-prahn pah
Please.	*S'il vous plaît.*	see voo play
Thank you.	*Merci.*	mehr-see
You're welcome.	*De rien.*	duh ree-an
I'm sorry.	*Désolé.*	day-zoh-lay
Excuse me (to get attention).	*Excusez-moi.*	ehk-skew-zay-mwah
Excuse me (to pass).	*Pardon.*	pahr-dohn
No problem.	*Pas de problème.*	pah duh proh-blehm
Very good.	*Très bon.*	tray bohn
Goodbye.	*Au revoir.*	oh reh-vwahr
How much is it?	*C'est combien?*	kohn-bee-an
Write it?	*Ecrivez?*	ay-kree-vay
euro (€)	*euro*	oo-roo
one / two	*un / deux*	uhn / duh
three / four	*trois / quatre*	twah / kah-truh
five / six	*cinq / six*	sank / sees
seven / eight	*sept / huit*	seht / weet
nine / ten	*neuf / dix*	nuhf / dees
20	*vingt*	van
30	*trente*	trahnt
40	*quarante*	kah-rahnt
50	*cinquante*	san-kahnt
60	*soixante*	swah-sahnt
70	*soixante-dix*	swah-sahnt-dees
80	*quatre-vingts*	kah-truh-van
90	*quatre-vingt-dix*	kah-truh-van-dees

100	*cent*	sahn
I'd like...	*Je voudrais...*	zhuh voo-dray
We'd like...	*Nous voudrions...*	noo voo-dree-ohn
...this.	*...ceci.*	suh-see
...more.	*...plus.*	ploo
...a ticket.	*...un billet.*	uhn bee-yay
...a room.	*...une chambre.*	ewn shahn-bruh
...the bill.	*...l'addition.*	lah-dee-see-ohn
Is it possible?	*C'est possible?*	say poh-see-bluh
Where are the toilets?	*Où sont les toilettes?*	oo sohn lay twah-leht
men / women	*hommes / dames*	ohm / dahm
entrance / exit	*entrée / sortie*	ahn-tray / sor-tee
no entry	*défense d'entrer*	day-fahns dahn-tray
open / closed	*ouvert / fermé*	oo-vehr / fehr-may
At what time does this open / close?	*À quelle heure c'est ouvert / fermé?*	ah kehl ur say oo-vehr / fehr-may
Just a moment.	*Un moment.*	uhn moh-mahn
Now.	*Maintenant.*	man-tuh-nahn
Soon.	*Bientôt.*	bee-an-toh
Later.	*Plus tard.*	plew tar
Today.	*Aujourd'hui.*	oh-zhoor-dwee
Tomorrow.	*Demain.*	duh-man
Monday	*lundi*	luhn-dee
Tuesday	*mardi*	mar-dee
Wednesday	*mercredi*	mehr-kruh-dee
Thursday	*jeudi*	zhuh-dee
Friday	*vendredi*	vahn-druh-dee
Saturday	*samedi*	sahm-dee
Sunday	*dimanche*	dee-mahnsh

Italian Tear-Out Cheat Sheet

Keep these survival phrases in your pocket, handy to memorize or use if you're caught without your phrase book.

Good day.	*Buon giorno.*	bwoh<u>n</u> **jor**-noh
Do you speak English?	*Parla inglese?*	**par**-lah een-**glay**-zay
Yes. / No.	*Si. / No.*	see / noh
I don't understand.	*Non capisco.*	noh<u>n</u> kah-**pees**-koh
Please.	*Per favore.*	pehr fah-**voh**-ray
Thank you.	*Grazie.*	**graht**-seeay
You're welcome.	*Prego.*	**pray**-goh
I'm sorry.	*Mi dispiace.*	mee dee-spee**ah**-chay
Excuse me. (to get attention)	*Mi scusi.*	mee **skoo**-zee
Excuse me. (to pass)	*Permesso.*	pehr-**may**-soh
(No) problem.	*(Non) c'è un problema.*	(noh<u>n</u>) cheh oon proh-**blay**-mah
It's good.	*Va bene.*	vah **behn**-ay
Goodbye.	*Arrivederci.*	ah-ree-vay-**dehr**-chee
How much is it?	*Quanto costa?*	**kwahn**-toh **koh**-stah
Write it?	*Me lo scrive?*	may loh **skree**-vay
euro (€)	*euro*	ay-**oo**-roh
one / two	*uno / due*	**oo**-noh / **doo**-ay
three / four	*tre / quattro*	tray / **kwah**-troh
five / six	*cinque / sei*	**cheeng**-kway / **seh**ee
seven / eight	*sette / otto*	**seht**-tay / **oh**-toh
nine / ten	*nove / dieci*	**noh**-vay / dee**ay**-chee
20	*venti*	**vayn**-tee
30	*trenta*	**trayn**-tah
40	*quaranta*	kwah-**rahn**-tah
50	*cinquanta*	cheeng-**kwahn**-tah
60	*sessanta*	say-**sahn**-tah
70	*settanta*	say-**tahn**-tah
80	*ottanta*	oh-**tahn**-tah
90	*novanta*	noh-**vahn**-tah

English	Italian	Pronunciation
100	*cento*	**chehn**-toh
I would like...	*Vorrei....*	vor-**reh**ee
We would like...	*Vorremmo...*	vor-**ray**-moh
...this.	*...questo.*	**kweh**-stoh
...more.	*...di più.*	dee pew
...a ticket.	*...un biglietto.*	oon beel-**yay**-toh
...a room.	*...una camera.*	**oo**-nah **kah**-may-rah
...the bill.	*...il conto.*	eel **kohn**-toh
Is it possible?	*È possibile?*	eh poh-**see**-bee-lay
Where is the toilet?	*Dov'è la toilette?*	doh-**veh** lah twah-**leht**-tay
men	*uomini, signori*	**woh**-mee-nee, seen-**yoh**-ree
women	*donne, signore*	**doh**-nay, seen-**yoh**-ray
entrance / exit	*entrata / uscita*	ehn-**trah**-tah / oo-**shee**-tah
no entry	*non entrare, divieto d'accesso*	nohn̲ ehn-**trah**-ray, dee-vee**ay**-toh dahk-**sehs**-soh
open / closed	*aperto / chiuso*	ah-**pehr**-toh / kee**oo**-zoh
When does this open / close?	*A che ora apre / chiude?*	ah kay **oh**-rah **ah**-pray / kee**oo**-day
At what time?	*A che ora?*	ah kay **oh**-rah
Just a moment.	*Un momento.*	oon moh-**mayn**-toh
Now.	*Adesso.*	ah-**dehs**-soh
Soon.	*Presto.*	**prehs**-toh
Later.	*Più tardi.*	pew **tar**-dee
Today.	*Oggi.*	**oh**-jee
Tomorrow.	*Domani.*	doh-**mah**-nee
Monday	*lunedì*	loo-nay-**dee**
Tuesday	*martedì*	mar-tay-**dee**
Wednesday	*mercoledì*	mehr-koh-lay-**dee**
Thursday	*giovedì*	joh-vay-**dee**
Friday	*venerdì*	vay-nehr-**dee**
Saturday	*sabato*	**sah**-bah-toh
Sunday	*domenica*	doh-**may**-nee-kah

German Tear-Out Cheat Sheet

Keep these survival phrases in your pocket, handy to memorize or use if you're caught without your phrase book.

Good day.	*Guten Tag.*	**goo**-tehn tahg
Do you speak English?	*Sprechen Sie Englisch?*	**shprehkh**-ehn zee **ehng**-lish
Yes. / No.	*Ja. / Nein.*	yah / nīn
I don't understand.	*Ich verstehe nicht.*	ikh fehr-**shtay**-heh nikht
Please.	*Bitte.*	**bit**-teh
Thank you.	*Danke.*	**dahng**-keh
You're welcome.	*Bitte.*	**bit**-teh
I'm sorry.	*Es tut mir leid.*	ehs toot meer līt
Excuse me. (to pass or to get attention)	*Entschuldigung.*	ehnt-**shool**-dig-oong
No problem.	*Kein Problem.*	kīn proh-**blaym**
Very good.	*Sehr gut.*	zehr goot
Goodbye.	*Auf Wiedersehen.*	owf **vee**-der-zayn
How much is it?	*Wie viel kostet das?*	vee feel **kohs**-teht dahs
Write it down?	*Aufschreiben?*	**owf**-shrī-behn
euro (€)	*Euro*	**oy**-roh
one / two	*eins / zwei*	īns / tsvī
three / four	*drei / vier*	drī / feer
five / six	*fünf / sechs*	fewnf / zehkhs
seven / eight	*sieben / acht*	**zee**-behn / ahkht
nine / ten	*neun / zehn*	noyn / tsayn
20	*zwanzig*	**tsvahn**-tsig
30	*dreißig*	**drī**-sig
40	*vierzig*	**feer**-tsig
50	*fünfzig*	**fewnf**-tsig
60	*sechzig*	**zehkh**-tsig
70	*siebzig*	**zeeb**-tsig
80	*achtzig*	**ahkht**-tsig
90	*neunzig*	**noyn**-tsig
100	*hundert*	**hoon**-dert
I'd like...	*Ich hätte gern...*	ikh **heh**-teh gehrn
We'd like...	*Wir hätten gern...*	veer **heh**-tehn gehrn

...this.	*...dies.*	deez
...more.	*...mehr.*	mehr
...a ticket.	*...eine Fahrkarte.*	ī-neh **far**-kar-teh
...a room.	*...ein Zimmer.*	īn **tsim**-mer
...the bill.	*...die Rechnung.*	dee **rehkh**-noong
Is it possible?	*Ist es möglich?*	ist ehs **mur**-glikh
Where is the toilet?	*Wo ist die Toilette?*	voh ist dee toh-**leh**-teh
men / women	*Herren / Damen*	**hehr**-ehn / **dah**-mehn
entrance / exit	*Eingang / Ausgang*	**īn**-gahng / **ows**-gahng
no entry	*kein Zugang*	kīn **tsoo**-gahng
open / closed	*geöffnet / geschlossen*	geh-**urf**-neht / geh-**shloh**-sehn
When does this open / close?	*Wann ist hier geöffnet / geschlossen?*	vahn ist heer geh-**urf**-neht / geh-**shlohs**-sehn
Now.	*Jetzt.*	yehtzt
Soon.	*Bald.*	bahlt
Later.	*Später.*	**shpay**-ter
Today.	*Heute.*	hoy-teh
Tomorrow.	*Morgen.*	**mor**-gehn
Monday	*Montag*	**mohn**-tahg
Tuesday	*Dienstag*	**deen**-stahg
Wednesday	*Mittwoch*	**mit**-vohkh
Thursday	*Donnerstag*	**doh**-ner-stahg
Friday	*Freitag*	**frī**-tahg
Saturday	*Samstag*	**zahm**-stahg
Sunday	*Sonntag*	**zohn**-tahg

Making Your Hotel Reservation

Most hotel managers know basic "hotel English." Emailing or faxing are the preferred methods for reserving a room. They're clearer and more foolproof than telephoning. Photocopy and enlarge this form, or find it online at www.ricksteves.com/reservation.

One-Page Fax

To: ______________________ ______________________
hotel *email or fax*

From: ______________________ ______________________
name *email or fax*

Today's date: ____ / ____ / ____
day *month* *year*

Dear Hotel ______________________

Please make this reservation for me:

Name: ______________________

Total # of people: ____ # of rooms: ____ # of nights: ____

Arriving: ____ / ____ / ____ Arrival time: (24-hr clock): ____
day *month* *year* (I will telephone if I will be late)

Departing: ____ / ____ / ____
day *month* *year*

Room(s): Single___ Double___ Twin___ Triple___ Quad___ Quint___

With: Toilet ___ Shower___ Bathtub___ Sink only___

Special needs: View___ Quiet___ Cheapest___ Ground floor___

Please email or fax me confirmation of my reservation, along with the type of room reserved and the price. Please also inform me of your cancellation policy. After I hear from you, I will quickly send my credit-card information as a deposit to hold the room. Thank you.

Name ______________________

Address ______________________

City ____________ State____ Zip Code_____ Country__________

Email address ______________________

NOTES

NOTES

NOTES

NOTES

NOTES

NOTES

NOTES